EDUCATIONAL MALPRACTICE

LIABILITY OF EDUCATORS, SCHOOL ADMINISTRATORS, AND SCHOOL OFFICIALS

JOHN COLLIS

Professor and Director,
Master of Business Administration Programs
St. Ambrose University

THE MICHIE COMPANY
Law Publishers
CHARLOTTESVILLE, VIRGINIA

Dedicated to my wife, Helen, who
has made any obstacle conquerable.

ABOUT THE AUTHOR

DR. JOHN COLLIS is Professor and Director of the M.B.A. Programs at St. Ambrose University. He received his B.S., M.B.A., and J.D. from the University of Kentucky, and his Ph.D. in Educational Administration from the University of Iowa. He has taught more than thirty different courses, at both the graduate and undergraduate levels, including Legal Aspects of School Administration and Legal Aspects of School Personnel. He has served as Associate Dean of the Graduate School of Business Administration at St. Ambrose University, Head of the Department of Business Administration, and Chairman of the Division of Business Administration, Accounting, and Economics at Iowa Wesleyan College. He has held many appointed and elected positions in professional organizations and has served on a number of professional and academic committees. In addition, he is a consultant and conducts numerous seminars in various fields. He has reviewed various books in law, marketing, and management for several publishing companies. His primary research interests are in educational law, business ethics, and organizational behavior.

Dr. Collis has received a number of academic honors, including the Perry Eugene McClenehan Award (1985) for being selected as the outstanding candidate for an advanced degree in educational administration at the University of Iowa and the J. Raymond Chadwick Award for being selected the Outstanding Teacher of the Year at Iowa Wesleyan College.

TABLE OF CONTENTS

PART II. SUMMARY AND ANALYSIS OF EDUCATIONAL MALPRACTICE CASES

4. THE LANDMARK "PURE" EDUCATIONAL MALPRACTICE CASES: EDUCATIONAL COMPETENCY CASES ... 77

TABLE OF CONTENTS

PART III. ANALYSIS OF ARGUMENTS ADVANCED FOR AND
AGAINST RECOGNIZING EDUCATIONAL MALPRACTICE
VIEWED FROM THE EDUCATIONAL, LEGAL AND
PHILOSOPHICAL PERSPECTIVES — EVALUATION
OF FINDINGS — APPLICATION OF VALIDITY
CRITERIA

TABLE OF CONTENTS

PREFACE

Professional malpractice suits are not new. As a matter of fact, in the medical profession such suits had their origin over one hundred years ago. Other professions, such as psychiatry, accounting, and law have experienced a multitude of malpractice suits. Now, educators are being "plagued" with them. Given a litigious society and a climate of heavy criticism of the public schools, it should not come as a surprise that frustrated individuals who believe they have been "academically" damaged by the educational system may turn to the courts for redress. Governor Brandstad of Iowa, Chairman of the National Governor's Association, chose education for the 1990 agenda and stated that it is estimated that high schools are graduating 700,000 functionally illiterate young people each year, and an equal number of students drop out. He further stated that the private sector spends approximately $210 billion a year to upgrade the skills of current employees. Terry Brandstad "Needed: National consensus on education," *U.S.A. Today* (February 26, 1990), p. 8A (Guest columnist). Ann Morrison states, "[e]very year the U.S. system graduates 700,000 young people who cannot read their diplomas. Little wonder that *A Nation at Risk,* the landmark 1983 report on education made the point: 'If an unfriendly foreign power had attempted to impose on America the mediocre educational performance that exists today, we might well have viewed it as an act of war.'" Ann M. Morrison, "Saving Our Schools", *Fortune* (Special Issue) (Spring 1990), p. 8. An elementary principal is quoted as stating that "2.3 million students graduating this year [1990] will be semi-illiterate." Jennifer Waddell, "Educator: 'All kids can learn,'" *Quad-City Times* (May 10, 1990), Section B, p. 1. Studies indicate that approximately ten percent of Americans are illiterate, and many of our students are ranked behind students of other nations, particularly in math and in science. A recent article entitled, "Education report rips U.S. schools" stated, "[d]espite billions of dollars in new spending, the nation's schools are not getting any better, the U.S. Department of Education said. For the fourth year in a row, we find no overall improvement," said Education Secretary Lauro Cavazos. "We have reached a plateau. Moving beyond this point will require radical changes. We are still not seriously committed to improving education for all Americans" he said. "Often I see indifference, complacency and passivity, despite the demonstrated need for immediate and radical school reform." "Education report rips U.S. schools," *Quad-City Times* (May 3, 1990), p. 3.

A new type of suit in education is surfacing — the educational malpractice suit or as otherwise termed, "educational negligence," "academic negligence" or "intellectual damage." The suit is aimed at holding educators and educational systems legally accountable for negligent acts or omissions that cause inadequate education.

The courts have been frustrated with these new educational malpractice suits and are pondering whether to recognize a claim based on educational negligence resulting in "intellectual damage" — in "intellectual injury."

While the author was conducting a nationwide study for a doctoral dissertation in this area, overwhelming interest was displayed by various publics. This enthusiastic interest prompted the writing of this book. The research revealed that no other book existed regarding educational malpractice and that almost all of the articles treating educational malpractice have viewed this subject matter generally from one aspect — the social, the economic, the educational, the philosophical, or the legal. Most articles in this area have been written primarily by legal or educational scholars and tend to reflect either a legal or educational perspective and approach. In order to understand the problems connected with educational malpractice and in order for justice to ensue for all concerned, educational malpractice needs to be examined from all perspectives, and any conclusions reached must encompass and be based upon all of them. A careful approach to this troublesome area can lead to a better understanding of the delicate and complex issues which, in turn, could and should help ease tensions which exist. It is hoped that this has been achieved in this work, by virtue of the author's unique background, having been trained in business, law, and education. This book is intended to serve the needs of various publics, including professional educators — teachers (from grade school to university professors), administrators (from principals to university presidents), school board members, boards of trustees, boards of regents, school attorneys, judges, insurance companies, students of the law, parents, and students.

We live in a nation where children are encouraged to excel — where quality and excellence are sought and rewarded. One of the main factors in achieving that goal is education. The education, of course, is entrusted to our educators. Therefore, our educational system should be as near to perfect as possible — it must be of the highest quality — anything less is unacceptable. Yet, studies have revealed that a number of defects, unfortunately, do exist. Many of them can and must be corrected. The time is nearing, if it is not already here, for those who are dissatisfied with the system to take drastic action, including litigation, to correct that which they perceive as "defective." One may reasonably assume that in a climate of such heavy criticism of the public schools, some of those who are frustrated enough with the system will turn to the courts for redress, perhaps in the form of educational malpractice suits.

Lawsuits sometimes tend to be epidemic and contra-productive. They usually surface as a last resort — when all other more "healthy" measures fail. Consequently, when possible, they should be prevented. Educators should lead in this area — not be led. In the words of Aristotle, "I have gained this by philosophy: that I do without being commanded what others do only from fear of the law." Those involved in the school system must keep abreast of the legal entanglements. After all, even liability insurance cannot protect the educator from being damaged by a law suit, regardless of how frivolous it may be. The best way to win is to avoid litigation — not to be sued.

This treatise is a compilation of various malpractice cases, reported and "unreported," as well as other references regarding this subject matter, including related malpractice cases from other professions, such as medicine, law and psychiatry, into one document which may serve as a source for a better understanding of the complex and sensitive problems relating to educational malpractice. Relevant portions of complaints, answers, briefs, memorandums, court opinions, and articles are included in the text since such documents are not readily assessable and reveal how various judges, scholars, educators, and lawyers reach their conclusions. Furthermore, considerable space has been devoted to an in-depth analysis of the various arguments advanced in favor of, as well as against, recognizing educational malpractice as a new cause of action. Seventy-five principles, truisms, and statements derived from the research have been enumerated.

This text examines the status of educational malpractice in the United States — focusing more specifically on the question, "Should courts entertain educational malpractice suits?" At the heart of this issue is the additional question of whether the public schools and the education profession might be held liable for professional misjudgments that result in the failure of students to succeed academically? In dealing with these questions, particular attention is given to the following:

1. The origin of professional malpractice suits in general, and their implications on educational malpractice.
2. The origin, development, and current status of educational malpractice (academic negligence — intellectual harm) determined through the historical and judicial review of pertinent court decisions.
3. An analysis of the legal, educational, practical, and philosophical arguments (policy considerations and implications) advanced for and against educational malpractice suits. This includes an analysis of the *raison d'etre* of educational malpractice suits in the school system.
4. The legal steps or hurdles that a claimant needs to overcome before he or she may have his or her case heard by a jury.
5. Caveats, principles, and truisms that courts might follow when considering educational malpractice claims that may help to avoid possible pitfalls.

The author wants to clarify, at the outset, one important point — the purpose of the book is not to promote litigation in this area, but rather to avoid it. It is not intended to force anyone to take a particular position on educational malpractice, but rather to inform the reader of the various issues involved in this area. It is better to lead by reason rather than by force. It is believed that once informed and once aware of these issues, the reader can be guided or persuaded in making his or her decision. It is believed that an informed profession is a better profession and that an educator or an administrator who is informed of the various legal entanglements has a better chance to avoid unnecessary litigation. The teacher's presence is needed more in the classroom than in the lawyer's office or in the courtroom. While the idea of suing many professionals is no longer novel, suing a school system for failing to properly educate is novel, but may not be for long. Given the proper facts, a properly drafted complaint for educational malpractice, brought in a proper court, and argued in a proper manner, may very well be sustained.

No book is the work of a single person, and mine is no exception. I would like to express my sincere appreciation to all who assisted me in the development of this treatise. I am indebted to many professional associations and organizations, courts, attorneys, litigants, state and local officials, and school personnel for their cooperation. I am grateful to the staff of The University of Iowa libraries for their valuable help and advice on the research process. I am greatly indebted to the various authors who either wrote or spoke in the area of my research and whose works are reflected herein. I have gained insight for the development of the project from these various people, who were willing to share their experience, ideas, and expertise with me by responding to phone calls and questionnaires. A sincere thanks to all the other many people, colleagues, and friends who helped directly or indirectly in the completion of this research project. Each of them gave of their time freely and willingly. I gratefully acknowledge the permission of publishers and authors to use quotations or excerpts from copyrighted material.

I would like to pay a special tribute to Dr. Willard R. Lane and Dr. Franklin D. Stone whose wisdom, guidance, and friendship have been invaluable. Dr. Stone was very supportive and encouraged me to take on this project as did Dr. Lane who served both as my program advisor and chairperson of the dissertation committee. I wish they were with us to see the final product. Since this book is an outgrowth of my Ph.D dissertation I must also express my appreciation to Dr. George Chambers, Dr. Bradley Loomer, Dr. Russell Ross, and Dr. William Bozeman, who served on my dissertation committee, for their counsel, guidance, and intellectual support. They played a vital role in helping to shape the final product.

I am appreciative to my dean, colleague, and friend, Dr. James O. Jensen, for the advice, encouragement, and interest he expressed in this work. Thanks also to my colleague and friend, Mr. O. Page Wilson, for his support, suggestions, and for just listening as I talked out a difficult area.

Sincere appreciation is extended to Mrs. Jean Gilmer for her careful preparation of both this and the dissertation manuscripts. She was tireless in her efforts to meet deadlines. Her professionalism, good nature, enthusiasm, and positive attitude made this task much more enjoyable.

I also want to thank the many people at the Michie Company who provided a great deal of assistance and support whenever I needed it. They consistently strive to produce quality products. In particular, I want to express my thanks to Frances H. Warren, Ruth Knight, Anna May Cutitta, Debbie Kennedy, and Kathy Brown. They proved to be unfailingly helpful and supportive. Special thanks to my editor, Cyndra H. Van Clief, for her professional expertise, creativity, enthusiasm, and commitment to the book. Her editorial talents have been invaluable. She played a critical role in the development of this treatise. It certainly was a pleasure working with her.

I am greatly indebted and appreciative to my family and to my parents for their love and support and for instilling in me the value and importance of education. I am also indebted to my wife's parents for their trust, faith, and encouragement in my endeavors.

Mostly, I am grateful to my wife, Helen, not only for her valuable contributions (research and "editorial" comments) to this book, but also for her unending support, encouragement, faith, patience, tolerance, love, and devotion that have made any obstacle conquerable.

Finally, this list would be incomplete if I didn't mention Penelope, our cat, who during those long and lonely "wee" hours of the morning consistently and faithfully kept me company and made sure I stayed awake and that the papers on my desk were warm and "properly" scattered!

I extend my thanks to Sandy Carlson and all the staff at the St. Ambrose M.B.A. office for their support and help in completing this work.

PART I

SETTING THE STAGE TO TACKLE THE ISSUE — THE STATUS OF EDUCATIONAL MALPRACTICE — THE PAST, THE PRESENT

Chapter 1

INTRODUCTION: A GENERAL OVERVIEW

> To be denied access to the courts
> is to be denied a very basic con-
> stitutional right.

§ 1.0. The Educational Malpractice Climate.

Recent developments have caused the public to examine and scrutinize the educational system and profession more than ever before. This has led a number of students to question the sufficiency of their education and the professional competency of their educators. As may be expected, when there is a feeling by students that they have been deprived of what they perceive as a "proper" education, some of them or their parents may turn to the courts for redress — to "right" their perceived wrong. An analysis of how the public views the competency of the educational system and their views regarding litigation may help predict the future of educational malpractice. Predicting the future is certainly not an easy task; however, considering the present circumstances, one can reasonably predict that there will be much more "legal" activity in this area. Naturally, such litigation is, and will remain, of great concern to those in the educational profession as well as those in the general public. Consequently, a clearer understanding of the issues involved in this area is needed. If a problem is to be corrected it must first be understood — one must first understand its ramifications.

3

It has been argued that "if researchers and other members of the educational profession do nothing to improve the knowledge base in this area, such external forces as the legislature and the courts, through statutes and judicial decisions, will eventually establish guidelines for educators, and all of society will suffer the resulting inflexibility."[1] Those involved in the school systems must keep abreast of various legal trends in order to avoid legal entanglements. Even liability insurance cannot protect the educator from being damaged by a law suit, regardless of how frivolous it may be. There can still be hours of worry, inconvenience, and damage to his or her professional reputation as a result of a law suit. The best way to win is to avoid litigation.[2] Today the professional educator not only must be aware of the possibility of legal involvement, but must also be able to deal effectively with the litigious environment in which he or she operates. By being aware of what situations have led to a law suit in the past, the educator may be able to avoid litigation by taking appropriate corrective action.

§ 1.1. Legal Pollution.

Access to the courts is a basic legal right which has been honored in American society from its beginning. Believing that there should be a remedy for every wrong, those who believed they were wronged turned to the courts, when other means failed, to have their wrongs "righted." Consequently, almost every important issue ultimately had its

---

1. David G. Carter, Sr., *The Educator and the Liability Law of Professional Malpractice: A Historical Analysis,* pp. 20-21, Paper presented in 1979 AERA Annual Convention, San Francisco, California, April 8-12, 1979.

2. Deborah Elaine Bembry, *An Assessment of Teacher's Knowledge of the Attitude Toward Tort Liability in Selected Iowa School Districts,* (Ph.D. dissertation, The University of Iowa, 1978), p. 5.

day in court. Contemporary America certainly has not seen any slack in litigation. Jethro Lieberman notes that this American tradition of seeking legal redress for every injury, real or imagined, has assumed epidemic proportions, invading previous immune areas and drastically raising the costs and frustrations of most professions and businesses.[3] The National Center for State Courts estimates that more than 15.7 million new civil cases and 11 million new criminal cases were filed in the state trial courts during 1986. These figures represent a 5% increase in the number of civil filings from the figures reported to the National Center for State Courts for 1985. In 1986, more than 208,000 appeals and petitions were filed in state supreme courts and intermediate courts of appeals. This is a 10% increase over the total appellate court caseload reported in 1985.[4] Another source reports that there were 206,193 civil lawsuits filed in federal courts in 1982 — twice the number filed in 1974, and three and a half times the number filed in 1960. Furthermore, federal appeals increased sevenfold between 1960 and 1982. Suits in state courts increased by 22% between 1977 and 1982, while state appeals increased by 32% in the same period.[5] These figures give credence to the suggestion that we are living in an age of "legal pollution": a growing feeling that it is virtually impossible to move "without running into a law

---

3. JETHRO K. LIEBERMAN, THE LITIGIOUS SOCIETY (New York: Basic Books, Inc., 1981).

4. National Center for State Courts, STATE COURT CASELOAD STATISTICS: ANNUAL REPORT 1986 (Williamsburg, Virginia 1988), p. 5. Includes reported filings of general and limited jurisdiction and represent aggregate data. The total civil and criminal figures are incomplete; these case filing statistics represent the most complete portrait available of the activities of state appellate and trial courts.

5. Newton N. Minow, *Accountants' Liability and the Litigation Explosion: CPA's Liability — No Further Than Fair*, JOURNAL OF ACCOUNTANCY (September 1984), p. 70.

or a regulation or a legal problem."[6] Lawsuits are surfacing in all areas — some based on "legal theories that would have been unthinkable only a decade or two ago."[7]

§ 1.2. Suits in Education.

Certainly, the public school system and the educational profession have not escaped the deluge of lawsuits. Lawsuits are not new in education. In fact, the trial of Socrates, who was charged with "corruption of the young," dates back to 399 B.C.[8] There were other trials, such as the famous "Monkey Trial," in which John Scopes was prosecuted for teaching the theories of Darwinian evolution and the less famous trial of a high school teacher who was fired for posing nude for a magazine.[9] Eugene Connors estimates that there are between 1,200 and 3,000 suits for tort liability brought against teachers or administrators every year.[10] While not all trials dealing with the educational

---

6. George A. Steiner, *An Overview of the Changing Business Environment and Its Impact on Business*, (Paper presented at a conference at UCLA, in July, 1979). He stated (p. 13) that Thomas Ehrlich, Dean of the Law School at Stanford University used the phrase, "legal pollution."

7. Minow, *supra* note 5, at 72.

8. RENNARD STRICKLAND, JANET FRASIER PHILLIPS & WILLIAM R. PHILLIPS, AVOIDING TEACHER MALPRACTICE: A PRACTICAL LEGAL HANDBOOK FOR THE TEACHING PROFESSIONAL (New York: Hawthorne Book, Inc., 1976), p. 3.

9. *Id.* at 3-7.

10. EUGENE T. CONNORS, EDUCATIONAL TORT LIABILITY AND MALPRACTICE (Bloomington, Indiana: A publication of Phi Delta Kappa, Inc. 1981), p. IX, © [1981], Phi Delta Kappa, Inc. As to how he arrived at these figures, the author explains:

> There is apparently no published source that provides an accurate accounting of tort liability suits against educators. However, I can make a reasonable guess. The tort cases reported in law books are only those that have been appealed from a trial court. Obviously, this is a small percentage. I estimate that one-third of the suits brought against educators are settled out of court in the U.S., because the teachers were so obviously negligent that the insurance

system have had the publicity of the Scopes trial or the political overtones of the Socrates trial, nevertheless, they have had an impact on the educational system. In the past, suits in education generally centered on such issues as safety, supervision, and discipline of students. Recently, however, frustrated students who believe the schools have failed in their duty to educate all children with equal success, have become increasingly aware of the possibility of a legal remedy for their grievances, and suits have been filed for failure to educate.[11] Consequently, some of these students are alleging that their nonlearning was caused by incompetent academic counseling and instruction.[12] As a result, a new type of suit in education is surfacing — "educational malpractice, or as otherwise termed," "educational negligence," "academic negligence," "intellectual harm," "intellectual damage," or "diminished intellectual development." The theory behind educational malpractice, simply stated, "is to place a duty on the school to provide that standard of education appropriate for the particular stu-

---

companies involved did not want to face juries. I also estimate that approximately one-third of the suits brought against educators are routinely dismissed by trial judges as being trivial, because the teachers were obviously not negligent. That leaves about 33% of the suits resulting in jury trials where the issue of negligence is real. Of that number, about one-half are appealed. There are between 200 and 500 appealed cases reported every year; this means that there are probably between 1,200 and 3,000 suits brought against teachers or administrators every year. Even though I estimate that only one-third of that number are decided by the juries, there is still a greater amount of litigation.

11. Nancy L. Woods, *Educational Malfeasance: A New Cause of Action for Failure to Educate?*, 14 TULSA LAW JOURNAL 383 (1978). Copyright by the University of Tulsa.

12. Destin Shann Tracy, *Educational Negligence: A Student's Cause of Action for Incompetent Academic Instruction*, 58 NORTH CAROLINA LAW REVIEW 561 (March 1980). Reprinted with permission from 58 N.C.L. REV. 561 (1980). Copyright 1980 by the North Carolina Law Review Association.

dent."[13] In addressing this question, the court, in *Donohue v. Copiague Union Free School District*,[14] observed that the troublesome question is whether a person who claims to have been inadequately educated while a student in a public school system may state a cause of action in tort against the public authorities who operate and administer the system. It is aimed to hold educators legally accountable for negligent acts or omissions that cause inadequate education, or "intellectual damage."

The courts have been frustrated with these new educational malpractice suits and are pondering whether to recognize claims based on educational negligence. Even though there have not been any successful *final* judgments in favor of the claimants on "pure"[15] educational malpractice, such suits are being noticed.

New torts, such as educational malpractice, generally develop in response to society's demand that the judicial system aid the claimant who has suffered injury through a defendant's wrongdoing.[16] In order to put educational malpractice litigation in its true perspective we need to examine the forces that initiated and encouraged such claims. Several issues and questions need to be considered, such as: (1) whether the school system and the educational profession failed in any of their duties and whether such failure caused injury. (2) whether adequate forums, procedures,

---

13. M. CHESTER NOLTE, YEARBOOK OF SCHOOL LAW 1980 (New York: Parker Publishing Company, Inc., 1980), p. 243.

14. 47 N.Y.2d 440, 391 N.E.2d 1352 (1979).

15. The word "pure" denotes suits filed against professionals on the theory of educational malpractice (academic negligence) as contrasted with suits filed on related theories such as fraud, misrepresentation, breach of contract, violation of a statute or constitutional provision, or a combination of theories.

16. Cynthia A. Jorgensen, *Donohue v. Copiague Union Free School District: New York Chooses Not to Recognize 'Educational Malpractice,'* 43 ALBANY LAW REVIEW 339, 358 (1979).

and remedies are available to those seeking redress. (3) whether it is necessary or desirous for courts to become involved. (4) whether the school system and the educational profession should be exempt from litigation, or whether they should be held accountable for wrongs committed. (5) whether there should be a remedy for every wrong. Isn't redress a fundamental concern of human beings? Isn't a citizen's right to petition the government for redress guaranteed by the first amendment to the United States Constitution? Do we need to debate the principle that "no man or entity is above the law" or is it an axiomatic principle well ingrained in our legal system? The United States Supreme Court noted that "students do not shed their constitutional rights at the schoolhouse gate."[17] Judge Learned Hand once said: "If we are to keep our democracy, there must be one commandment: Thou shalt not ration justice."

§ 1.3. Importance of Education in Our Society.

Education has held a high place in the hearts and minds of the people in America. During the entire history of the United States, religion and education have been recognized as the foundation pillars of American civilization.[18] It has been said that "education, beyond all other devices of human origin, is the great equalizer of conditions of men — the balance-wheel of the social machinery."[19] In 1786, Thomas Jefferson equated education with democracy. "No other sure foundation," he said, "can be devised for the

---

17. Tinker v. Des Moines Independent Community School District, 393 U.S. 503 (1969).

18. Lee A. Magnuson, *South Dakota's System of Financing Public Education: Is It Constitutional?*, 24 SOUTH DAKOTA LAW REVIEW 365 (Spring 1979).

19. *Id.*

preservation of freedom and happiness." It has been contended that, "no government activity exerts a more pervasive influence on Americans for a longer period of their
lives than the regulation of education."[20] The recognition
by the judicial system of the importance of education is
emphasized by the 1954 landmark case of *Brown v. Board
of Education.*[21] In that case the United States Supreme
Court stated:

> Today, education is perhaps the most important func-
> tion of state and local governments. Compulsory school
> attendance laws and the great expenditures of educa-
> tion both demonstrate our recognition of the impor-
> tance of education to our democratic society.... Today
> it is a principal instrument in awakening the child to
> cultural values, in preparing him for later professional
> training, and in helping him to adjust normally to his
> environment. In these days, it is doubtful that any
> child may reasonably be expected to succeed in life if
> he is denied the opportunity of an education.[22]

However, despite the vital role of education in our society in recent years, public school education has increasingly come under great scrutiny, and there has been an
increase in public dissatisfaction with our educational system and the educational profession. Many believe that our
public schools have failed to provide students "proper" education. Consequently, public education has been "under a
national microscope, as witnessed by a series of reports by
government and private agencies on the quality of teaching, curricula, and schools. The reports are long on alarm,
but short on practical solutions."[23] In 1976, in a well publi-

---

20. *Education and the Law: State Interests and Individual Rights,* 74
Michigan Law Review, 1373 (June 1976).
21. 347 U.S. 483 (1954).
22. *Id.* at 493.
23. Gil Klein, *'Math Is the Great Equalizer': Program Rouses Dead-
End Students,* Winston-Salem Journal (December 28, 1986), p. A-1
(Editor's note).

cized malpractice case, the California Court of Appeals commented:

> Few of our institutions, if any, have aroused the controversies, or incurred the public dissatisfaction, which have attended the operation of the public schools during the last few decades. Rightly or wrongly, but widely, they are charged with outright failure in the achievement of their educational objectives; according to some critics, they bear responsibility for many of the social and moral problems of our society at large. Their public plight in these respects is attested in the daily media, in bitter governing board elections, in wholesale rejections of school bond proposals, and in survey upon survey. To hold them to an actionable "duty of care," in the discharge of their academic functions, would expose them to the tort claims — real or imagined — of disaffected students and parents in countless numbers. They are already beset by social and financial problems which have gone to major litigation, but for which no permanent solution has yet appeared [citations omitted]. The ultimate consequences, in terms of public time and money, would burden them — and society — beyond calculation.[24]

§ 1.4. Illiteracy in America.

Illiteracy has always been an area of concern in our society. However, recently it has become a focus of national concern. Consequently, with increasing recognition of this national problem, spurred by a surge of media attention, it is understandable why questions have surfaced concerning the overall effectiveness of our public educational system. One writer states that "When students attend an individual school system for twelve years or more, subsequently graduating and entering the work force as functional illit-

---

24. Peter W. v. San Francisco Unified School District, 60 Cal. App. 3d 814, 821, 131 Cal. Rptr. 854, 861 (1976).

11

erates, the implications of illiteracy suggest the presence of some serious flaws in the educational system."[25]

Jonathan Kozol, in *Illiterate America*,[26] states "[t]wenty-five million American adults cannot read the poison warnings on a can of pesticide, a letter from their child's teacher, or the front page of a daily paper. An additional 35 million read only at a level which is less than equal to the full survival needs of our society."[27] This represents more than one-third of the entire adult population. Kozol further writes:

> Sixteen percent of white adults, 44 percent of blacks, and 54 percent of Hispanic citizens are functional or marginal illiterates. Figures for the younger generation of black adults are increasing. Forty-seven percent of all black seventeen-year-olds are functionally illiterate. That figure is expected to climb to 50 percent by 1990.
>
> Fifteen percent of recent graduates of urban high schools read at less than sixth grade level. One million teenage children between twelve and seventeen cannot read above the third grade level. Eighty-five percent of juveniles who come before the courts are functionally illiterate. Half of the heads of households classified below the poverty line by federal standards cannot read an eighth grade book. Over one-third of the mothers who receive support from welfare are functionally illiterate. Of 8 million unemployed adults, 4 to 6 million lack the skills to be retrained for hi-tech jobs.
>
> The United States ranks forty-ninth among 158 member nations of the U.N. in the literacy levels.
>
> In Prince George's County, Maryland, 30,000 adults cannot read above a fourth grade level....

----

25. Kimberly A. Wilkins, *Educational Malpractice: A Cause of Action in Need of a Call for Action,* 22 VALPARAISO UNIVERSITY LAW REVIEW, 427 (Winter 1988).

26. JONATHAN KOZOL, ILLITERATE AMERICA (Garden City, New York: Anchor Press/Doubleday, 1985).

27. *Id.* at 4.

> In Boston, Massachusetts, 40 percent of the adult population is illiterate....
>
> In San Antonio, Texas, 152,000 adults have been documented as illiterate....
>
> Fourteen years ago, in his inaugural address as Governor of Georgia, a future President of the United States proclaimed to the crisis of Illiterate America. "Our people are our most precious possession.... Every adult illiterate ... is an indictment of us all.... If Switzerland and Israel and other people can end illiteracy, then so can we. The responsibility is our own and our government's. I will not shirk this responsibility."
>
> Today the number of identified nonreaders is three times greater than the number Jimmy Carter had in mind when he described this challenge and defined it as an obligation that he would not shirk.[28]

Other people, from educators to corporate officials, have spoken out regarding the illiteracy problems that our nation is facing. "America's public schools have 'put this country at a terrible competitive disadvantage' by turning out workers with 'a 50 percent defect rate,' charged the chairman of Xerox Corp. In 'an open letter' to presidential candidates, [he] 'called for a complete restructuring of the schools to improve those results.' Xerox, he said, expects '100 percent defect-free parts from our suppliers.... We're getting 99.9 percent and we're still going after that last one-tenth of a percent. The public schools are the suppliers of our workforce. But they're suppliers with a 50 percent defect rate.'"[29]

In an article in *The Wall Street Journal*, *Julia Amparano Lopez reports:*

> Chicago's Campbell-Mithun-Esty Advertising finds that only one applicant in 10 meets the minimum liter-

---

28. *Id.* at 4-6.
29. *Xerox boss blasts U.S. schools,* QUAD-CITY TIMES (Oct. 27, 1987), p. A-1.

acy standard for mail-clerk jobs. About 80% of all applicants screened nationally by Motorola, Inc. fail an entry-level exam that requires seventh-grade English and fifth-grade math. Last year, New York Telephone Co. received 117,000 applications when several hundred full-time positions opened up. Fewer than half these applicants qualified to take the basic employment exam, and of those, only 2,100 passed.[30]

Furthermore, she reports that "[d]espite five years of educational reform, recent reports indicate that a majority of 17-year-old high school students continue to lack the skills necessary to function productively in today's workplace."[31]

The U.S. Department of Education estimates that the functionally illiterate now account for 30% of unskilled workers, 29% of semi-skilled workers, and 11% of all managers, professionals, and technicians.[32] Robert Goddard quotes Sherman Swenson, chairman of B. Dalton Bookseller, as stating, "In dollar terms alone adult illiteracy is costing the country an estimated $225 billion annually in lost industrial productivity, unrealized tax revenues, welfare, prisons, crime and related social ills."[33] Goddard states:

> According to the Center for Public Resources, 75 percent of the country's largest corporations now offer some kind of basic skills training. A.T.&T., for example, spends $6 million annually on remedial courses for employees. General Motors and IBM spend a total of

---

30. Julie Amparano Lopez, *System failure: businesses say schools are producing graduates unqualified to hold jobs*, THE WALL STREET JOURNAL (March 31, 1989), p. R-12. Reprinted by permission of (THE WALL STREET JOURNAL), Dow Jones & Company, Inc. (1989). All Rights Reserved Worldwide.

31. *Id.* at R-15.

32. Robert W. Goddard, *Combating Illiteracy in the Workplace*, MANAGEMENT WORLD (March/April 1989), p. 8. Reprinted from MANAGEMENT WORLD (March/April 1989), with permission from AMS. Copyright 1989, AMS.

33. *Id.*

$700 million annually on adult education. Ford offers basic reading courses at 25 plants. Pratt & Whitney operates an in-house general education program so employees can get high school equivalency diplomas. United Technologies has employees tutor coworkers on a one-to-one basis. Polaroid targets 500 to 750 employees annually for remedial programs. These include teaching English to immigrants.[34]

Another writer states:

Five years after *A Nation at Risk* warned of a woefully undereducated population, America continues to face a daunting education challenge. There are 23 million functionally illiterate people in America today, fully 10 percent of the population. The dropout rate, which is in effect a second measure of the state of literacy, stands at nearly 30 percent. Meanwhile, jobs are getting more complicated, and the competition is getting stiffer.... As we stand today, 23 million of the nation's workers (20 percent) read at no better than an 8th grade level, according to a study by the Business Council for Effective Literacy. Yet 70 percent of the reading material used for a cross-section of jobs across the country requires a reading level of 9th grade or higher.[35]

An article titled, "Teens Flunk Economic Literacy Test" states:

American high school students have an alarming deficit of economic knowledge, according to a survey in which two-thirds didn't understand profits, and more than half couldn't supply a definition for demand.... The survey, ... found:

- Only 34 percent could correctly define profits as "revenue minus costs."

---

34. *Id.* at 10.

35. Andrew Barbour, *Creating a Nation of Learners: Meeting the Literacy Challenge,* ELECTRONIC LEARNING-SPECIAL SUPPLEMENT (Scholastic, Inc., January-February, 1989), pp. 4-5.

- 39 percent selected the correct definition of Gross National Product....
- Only 45 percent realized that government deficits result when spending exceeds tax revenues.
- Less than half — 47.7 percent — knew that "economic demand" for a product refers to how much "people are willing and able to buy at each price."[36]

The National Center for Education Statistics reported that 82% of colleges and universities offered at least one remedial course in mathematics, reading, or writing in 1983-84, but only 30% of them allowed students to use those courses to fulfill degree requirements. "One-quarter of all college freshmen enrolled in at least one remedial mathematics course, 21 percent took remedial writing, and 16 percent took remedial reading."[37]

The Department of Labor estimates that "three out of four people collecting unemployment lack the basic skills necessary to be retrained for high-tech jobs. And a staggering $6 billion goes each year to welfare programs and unemployment compensation directly traceable to illiteracy."[38]

Furthermore, there is the tremendous impact of illiteracy on the nation's soaring crime. "An enormous amount of crime and drugs could be prevented if more people could read and write," says Mrs. Bush. "Our prisons are filled with functional illiterates. Some 85% of the children who

---

36. Lee Mitgang, *Teens flunk economic literacy test,* DAILY PRESS (December 29, 1988), p. C-1.

37. Jean Evangelauf, *82 Percent of Colleges Said to Offer Remedial Courses,* THE CHRONICLE OF HIGHER EDUCATION (November 1985), p. 20. Copyright 1985, THE CHRONICLE OF HIGHER EDUCATION. Reprinted with permission. *Many College Freshmen Take Remedial Courses,* THE STATISTICAL INFORMATION OFFICE, NATIONAL CENTER FOR EDUCATION STATISTICS (Washington, D.C.).

38. Edward Klein, *Everything Would Be Better If More People Could Read,* PARADE MAGAZINE (May 21, 1989), p. 5.

appear in juvenile courts have some 'learning disabilities' — a phrase that actually covers a multitude of sins ... some people who have so-called learning disabilities really haven't had the attention and the teaching that they need." All that tells us, says Mrs. Bush, is that, "some people can't make a living in the legitimate world and they turn to crime and sometimes even to drugs out of frustration. I'm not making excuses for them, I'm just telling you a fact of life."[39]

It is difficult to discuss illiteracy without broaching emotional arguments about the academics of some athletes. Fueling these arguments are articles such as: "'Functionally illiterate athletes are no rarity;"[40] and, "case for requiring college athletes to be students, not 'gladiators.'"[41] One also reads about athletes who took a lot of "rinky dink" courses to remain eligible, and how pro stars return to get high school or college diplomas.

The well-publicized report of the National Commission on Excellence in Education in 1983 indicated that mediocrity, not excellence, is the norm in American education.[42] It stated that the educational foundations of our society are presently being eroded by a rising tide of mediocrity. It further noted that about 13% of the United States teenagers and approximately 40% of minority adolescents are functionally illiterate.[43] It indicated that according to the

---

39. *Id.*

40. Ron Maly, *'Functionally Illiterate' Athletes Are No Rarity,* THE DES MOINES REGISTER (April 13, 1983), pp. S-1, S-4. Copyright 1989, DES MOINES REGISTER and Tribune Company.

41. Edward Foote II, *Case For Requiring College Athletes To Be Students, Not 'Gladiators',* DES MOINES SUNDAY REGISTER (November 7, 1982), p. C-3.

42. Milton Goldberg and James Harvey, *A Nation at Risk: The Report of the National Commission on Excellence in Education,* PHI DELTA KAPPAN (September 1983), pp. 14-15. © [1983], Phi Delta Kappa, Inc.

43. *Id.*

College Board's Scholastic Aptitude Test, there was almost
an unbroken decline from 1963 to 1980 in verbal skills
scores. Verbal skills scores fell over 50 points and average
mathematics scores fell nearly 40 points. Furthermore,
nearly 40% of 17-year-old Americans cannot draw inferences from written materials; only one-third can solve a
mathematical problem requiring several steps; and only
one-fifth can write a persuasive essay.[44] The report was
thoroughly scrutinized and once again public schools were
in the limelight. But was this report in line with the views
held by the American people?

The 15th Annual Gallup Poll of the Public's Attitudes
Toward the Public Schools indicated that the public's rating of the local public schools in 1983 followed the down-
ward trend reported in the years since 1974 as evidenced
by the response to the following question: "Students are
often given the grades *A, B, C, D*, and *FAIL*, to denote the
quality of their work. Suppose the public schools themselves in the community were graded in the same way,
what grade would you give the public schools here — *A, B,
C, D*, or *FAIL*?" In 1974, 48% gave local public schools a
rating of *A* or *B*. In 1983, the comparable figure was 31%.[45]
The survey also indicated that in 1974, 64% of the parents
gave the public schools in which their children attended an
A or *B* rating, while in 1983 that figure was 42%.[46] Furthermore, the respondents in the survey gave their local
schools higher ratings than they gave public schools nationwide. Nineteen percent of the general public gave the

---

44. A NATION AT RISK: THE IMPERATIVE FOR EDUCATIONAL REFORM,
AMERICAN EDUCATION, June 1983 (Final Report of the National Commission on Excellence in Education), p. 2.

45. George H. Gallup, *The 15th Annual Gallup Poll of the Public's
Attitudes Toward the Public Schools,* PHI DELTA KAPPAN (September
1983), pp. 33, 35. © [1983], Phi Delta Kappa, Inc.

46. *Id.*

schools a rating of *A* or *B* and 22% gave them a rating of *D* or *FAIL*.[47] It is also interesting to note the possible impact or influence that the report of the National Commission on Excellence in Education had on the ratings of the public schools in general. The survey indicated that those respondents who were familiar with the findings of the report were more critical of the U.S. schools than was the public at large. While only 12% of those familiar with the commission report gave the public schools nationally a rating of *A* or *B*, 30% gave them a rating of *D* or *FAIL*.[48]

A similar survey taken in 1986 indicated that 41% of Americans rate the public schools locally (in "this community") as either *A* or *B*. Similarly, 28% of the public gave the public schools, *nationally,* either an *A* or *B*. Teachers received an *A* or *B* from almost half of the public (48%) while administrators were given a grade of *A* or *B* by 42% of the public. Public school parents, again in 1986, graded the public schools in their own community substantially higher than the public schools nationally, and they rated the public schools their own children attended even higher than the local schools. While 28% of the parents gave the public schools, nationally, an *A* or *B*, nearly twice as many (55%) gave the local schools an *A* or *B*, and almost two-thirds (65%) gave the schools their children attended one of the top two grades.[49]

In order to ascertain how the public felt about toughening requirements for grade promotion and for high school graduation, as had been recommended in national education reports, respondents to the 1986 survey were asked a series of questions. The survey revealed that

---

47. *Id.*

48. *Id.* at 36.

49. Alec M. Gallup, *The 18th Annual Gallup Poll of the Public's Attitudes Toward the Public Schools,* PHI DELTA KAPPAN (September 1986), pp. 43, 46. © [1986], Phi Delta Kappa, Inc.

Americans strongly favored stricter requirements for both grade promotion and high school graduation, and by virtually identical margins: 72% to 6% and 70% to 5%. "These findings correspond closely with the public's support for testing to determine both grade promotion and high school graduation, as revealed in earlier surveys...."[50]

Americans tend to mention job- and finance-related reasons first as the reasons why they want their children to get an education. This was evidenced by the following question: "People have different reasons why they want their children to get an education. What are the chief reasons that come to your mind?" Approximately one-third (34%) cited job opportunities, 8% said to get a better-paying job, 4% to obtain specialized training, and 9% to achieve financial security. Relatively few mentioned preparation for life (23%), to acquire knowledge (10%), to become a better citizen (6%), to learn how to get along with others (4%), or to contribute to society (3%).[51]

A similar survey was taken in 1988. When asked to identify the biggest problems with which the local public schools must deal, 32% of those interviewed for the 1988 Gallup education poll said, "use of drugs by students." Lack of discipline was a distant second, mentioned by 19% of the respondents.[52] When asked how much confidence they had in their local public schools to deal with drug abuse, the national totals revealed that 9% had a great deal, 37% a fair amount, 35% not very much, and 12% none at all.

The ratings people gave their local schools were: *A* and *B* ratings, 40%; *C, D*, and *F* ratings, 48%.[53] When asked,

---

50. *Id.* at 52.

51. *Id.* at 49.

52. Alec M. Gallup & Stanley M. Elam, *The 20th Annual Gallup Poll of the Public's Attitudes Toward the Public Schools,* PHI DELTA KAPPAN (September 1988), p. 34. © [1988], Phi Delta Kappa, Inc.

53. *Id.* at 36.

20

"Should all high school students in the U.S. be required to pass a standard nationwide examination in order to get a high school diploma?," 73% approved of such an exam.[54]

Two-thirds of the respondents believe that the schools are the same or better today than they were five years ago, and almost half of the respondents believe that children now get a better education than they themselves got. It should be noted, however, that people in communities of more than one million residents generally believe that their schools are worse today than they were five years ago.[55] When asked, "Would you like to have a child of yours take up teaching in the public schools as a career?," 58% said "yes" while 31% answered "no." To the question, "Would you favor or oppose the idea of establishing a national set of standards for the certification of public school teachers?," 86% are in favor while 9% oppose it.[56] The respondents have overwhelmingly pointed to a good education system as the main source of the nation's future strength (88%).[57] A recent poll conducted for the Quad-City Times by Per Mar Research shows nearly 55 percent of Quad-Citians gave local schools a grade of *A* or *B*. That percentage "compares to 40 percent of Americans who gave their local schools an *A* or *B* in a nationwide Gallup Poll. And Quad-Citians believe their schools are better than schools nationwide. About 25 percent of Quad-Citians gave public schools nationally an *A* or *B*. (That compares to 23 percent in the Gallup Poll)."[58]

The report of the Twentieth Century Fund Task Force of Federal Elementary and Secondary Education Policy con-

---

54. *Id.* at 40.
55. *Id.* at 42.
56. *Id.* at 44.
57. *Id.*
58. Rod Thomson "Q.C. schools get high marks," *Quad-City Times*, (May 20, 1990), p. 1A.

tains similar allegations as the report of the National Commission on Excellence in Education. In substance, it states that the United States schools are in dire straits and do not come close to living up to expectations.[59] The report by the Carnegie Foundation for the Advancement of Teaching, *High School: A Report on Secondary Education in America*,[60] is less critical of the educational system but not very complimentary. An article commenting on the report notes that "each weekday morning, more than 13 million young people stream into America's 16,000 public high schools. One in 10 receives an education as fine as any in the world; twice as many are condemned to schools that mock the name. The majority glide through with the understanding that they won't demand too much from schools, and the schools won't demand too much from them."[61]

A Study of Schooling, a comprehensive study sponsored by an independent research organization, the Institute for the Development of Educational Activities, which took more than eight years and included about 27,000 interviews, found the problems of the American educational system to be "deeply entrenched and virtually chronic." The study said, the schools should undergo "far-reaching restructuring."[62] John Goodlad, former dean of the Graduate School of Education at the University of California, at Los Angeles, and the director of the study, said, "American

---

59. Patricia Albjerg Graham, *The Twentieth Century Fund Task Force Report on Federal Elementary and Secondary Education Policy,* PHI DELTA KAPPAN (September 1983), p. 19. © [1983], Phi Delta Kappa, Inc.

60. Dennia A. Williams, Barbara Burgower, Joe Contreras, Darby Junkin, Patricia King & Dianne H. McDonald, *Rx for High Schools,* NEWSWEEK (September 26, 1983), p. 97.

61. *Id.*

62. *New Study: American schools are in trouble,* THE MT. PLEASANT NEWS (Vol. 105, No. 168, July 19, 1983), p. 1.

schools are in trouble. Large numbers of students are leaving school ill-prepared for jobs and effective citizenship, and even many of those who appear to be 'making it' are short-changed."[63]

There are a number of articles appearing in the media with titles such as "Diplomas with Meaning," which are critical of the educational system. For example, that particular article states, "[t]oo often a high-school diploma is little more than a glorified certificate of attendance, critics of the educational system complain with reason."[64] Education Secretary Lauro Cavazos announced tough new steps to eliminate schools that fail to meet expectations by "taking decisive action against those who cheat our citizens; those who promise to educate but deliver only a debt. We must weed out unethical schools."[65] Another article, "Suits Accuse Business Schools of Fraud" states that the Attorney General filed lawsuits seeking to close five Cook County business schools for deceiving students for financial gain. "This is a particularly cruel and offensive form of fraud," Hortigan said, "It victimizes young people, particularly minorities and the disadvantaged, who want to improve their lives."[66]

Charles Sykes, in his book, *Prof Scam: Professors and the Demise of Higher Education,* is also critical of the educational system. A commentator states:

> The book taps into the same public concerns over the failures of American education that in recent years has [have] fueled works such as Allan Bloom's "The

---

63. *Id.*

64. Editorial appearing in DES MOINES SUNDAY REGISTER (October 7, 1984), p. C-1. Copyright 1989, DES MOINES REGISTER and Tribune Company.

65. *A-P Washington,* QUAD-CITY TIMES (June 2, 1989), p. 1.

66. *Suits Accuse Business Schools of Fraud,* QUAD-CITY TIMES (January 15, 1988), p. 5.

Closing of the American Mind," and E.D. Hirsch's "Cultural Literacy: What Every American Needs to Know." Has America lost a whole generation of young people through the ineptitude of its teachers? asks Sykes. He wonders what is to be done about college students "unable to write a coherent sentence, analyze even simple problems or understand why their elders keep talking about a Second World War (was there a First?)." *Prof Scam* however, is aimed at a broader audience than is Bloom's or Hirsch's books. "I did not write this book as an academic exercise," Sykes says, "I want people to read this book and be outraged about the situation and do something about it."

Prof Scam directs its criticism specifically at the professors who Sykes believes have perverted the institution of the university for their own purposes.[67]

The writer continues her comments about the book by stating: "The question remains whether the academic profession is capable of reforming itself. Sykes is not sanguine about the prospects. Pressure, he believes must come from legislators, parents, and students."[68]

In an article entitled, "Profs are under fire for abandoning the classroom," the author, Dennis Kelly, comments on the book, *Killing the Spirit: Higher Education in America*, which is written by Page Smith, once head of the University of California, Santa Cruz. He states that Mr. Smith charges that "[p]rofessors increasingly fob off teaching duties, viewing the 'student as enemy', in their efforts to do research that will get them published and bring them promotions or tenure."[69] Smith writes that the worst is that it robs students of "the thoughtful and considerate attention

---

67. Helle Bering-Jensen, *Giving Universities a Failing Grade,* INSIGHT (December 19, 1988), p. 58.

68. *Id.* at 59.

69. Dennis Kelley, "Profs are under fire for abandoning the classroom," *U.S.A. Today,* (March 20, 1990), p. 4D.

of a teacher deeply and unequivocally committed to teaching".[70] Mr. Kelly continues his article by stating:

> Higher education was kicked in the rear last year with the publication of *Prof Scam* by journalist Charles J. Sykes. He's more conservative than Smith, but charged across the same turf, saying teachers - fleeing - teaching - for - research stampede has turned U.S. university students into "the orphans of higher education"
>
> ....
>
> Smith says books like his own and Sykes' as well as assaults on curriculum (Allan Bloom's *The Closing of the American Mind*) are all signals "that the long love affair that Americans have had with education (higher education in particular) may be coming to an end."[71]

Another article, "American Teen-Agers Come in Last in Assessment of Mathematics Skills," states:

> American teen-agers ranked last in mathematics skills and far below their peers in other countries in scientific abilities in the first International Assessment of Educational Progress, the Educational Testing Service reported ....
>
> Only 40 percent of American 13-year-olds can use intermediate mathematics skills to solve problems, compared with 78 percent of their South Korean peers, who ranked highest, according to the study. In science, 42 percent of U.S. teenagers can use scientific procedures and analyze scientific data, compared with more than 70 percent of South Korean youths.[72]

---

70. *Id.*

71. *Id.*

72. *American Teen Agers Come in Last in Assessment of Mathematics Skills,* THE CHRONICLE OF HIGHER EDUCATION (February 8, 1989), p. A-30; Copyright 1989, THE CHRONICLE OF HIGHER EDUCATION. Reprinted with permission. *See also A World of Difference* (a 95-page report by the Center for the Assessment of Educational Progress, Educational Testing Service, Princeton, New Jersey).

Commenting on a survey by the National Education Association in the 1960's, which revealed that 150,000
teachers believed they were not qualified for their jobs, one
writer asserts that in most states the tenure laws make it
almost impossible to dismiss incompetent, bigoted, cruel,
or often mentally unbalanced teachers. Conservative estimates by school personnel experts and administrators suggest that between 5% and 10% of those teaching in the
United States are in that category.[73] However, all the
blame should not be placed on the tenure laws. Besides the
tenure laws, there are other laws and factors which contribute towards this problem.

One writer states, "[t]eachers are now in short supply,
particularly in math and sciences .... Among the advanced
nations of the world, only America has teacher short-
ages."[74] He states that professors in other departments often disparage schools of education in front of their students. Economist Thomas Sowell has written that schools
of education are "the intellectual slums" on most
campuses.[75] James D. Koerner, the author of *The
Miseducation of American Teachers,* published in 1963,
said: "the inferior intellectual quality of the education faculty is the limitation of the field."[76] Mary Futrell, president of the National Education Association, proposed that
junior-year college students wanting to become education
majors meet a minimum grade point average requirement.
Her standard: only 2.5 on a 4.0 scale. (Minimum require-

---

73. Jay M. Pabian, *Educational Malpractice and Minimal Competency Testing: Is There a Legal Remedy at Last?,* 15 NEW ENGLAND LAW
REVIEW 101, 112 (1979-1980).

74. Reginald G. Damerell, *Teachers' Colleges Foster an Educational
Underclass,* THE WALL STREET JOURNAL (October 24, 1985), p. 28.

75. *Id.*

76. *Id.*

ments currently vary from school to school, but are usually below the 2.5 standard.)[77]

She further states:

> The teacher shortage is greater than is apparent. A sizeable part is hidden within the public schools, and is called their 'dirty little secret' by Albert Shanker, president of the American Federation of Teachers. An estimated 200,000 teachers nationwide are teaching subjects for which they have little or no preparation. Some are temporary and per-diem teachers who nevertheless teach continuously and regularly for years.[78]

Schools are being studied and debated each year not only by educators — students of education and policy makers — but also by pollsters, politicians, and editorial writers throughout the United States. What are we to conclude from such studies? Are they accurate? Do they represent a true picture of our educational system?[79] Determining whether the previous evaluation of the public school system and the educational profession is or is not an accurate picture of the present status may need much more analysis.

In a climate of such heavy criticism of the public schools, inevitably some of those who are frustrated with the system will turn to the courts for redress. In many instances it is not important whether one's frustration arises from a real or from an imagined problem with the educational system. If the problem is perceived as real, a frustrated individual living in a litigious society, who perceives the educational system as being less than adequate or less than what it should be, may turn to the courts for help. In this era of litigation some parents may not hesitate to seek

---

77. *Id.*

78. *Id.*

79. Stanley M. Elam, *The Gallup Education Surveys: Impressions of a Poll Watcher,* PHI DELTA KAPPAN (September 1983), p. 26. © [1983], Phi Delta Kappa, Inc.

a judicial remedy when they believe their children have been injured, either intellectually or physically, by the school system. It is because of this that educational malpractice must be examined from various perspectives — legal, educational, practical, and philosophical. Obviously, this is an extremely important, yet very sensitive, area. We can no longer ignore it or address it in a courtroom under an adversarial atmosphere. It is believed that approaching it in a careful and logical manner can lead to a better understanding of the complicated and intricate issues that are involved herein.

Chapter 2

PROFESSIONAL MALPRACTICE: A SURVEY OF THE LAW

> If a doctor has treated a Free Man with a metal knife for a severe wound, and has cured the Free Man ... then he shall receive ten shekels of silver.
>
> If a doctor has treated a man with a metal knife for a severe wound, and has caused the man to die ... his hands shall be cut off.
>
> — The Code of Hammurabi[1]

§ 2.0. Introduction.

Educational malpractice (academic negligence — intellectual harm) is a recent concept and courts have been struggling with whether to accept or reject educational malpractice as a cause of action. When confronted with a novel issue, courts generally turn to related cases for guidance in making their judgments. Consequently, when faced

---

1. DONALD J. FLASTER, MD., LLB., MALPRACTICE: A GUIDE TO THE LEGAL RIGHTS OF PATIENTS AND DOCTORS (New York: Charles Scribner's Sons, 1983), p. 28.

29

with educational malpractice cases, courts examine malpractice cases concerning various professions. The applicable law in some of these professions, such as medicine, is fairly well-settled. It would therefore seem logical that in order to fully understand the various aspects of educational malpractice, we should first examine the general law of professional malpractice.

§ 2.1. Malpractice Defined.

When one refers to *Black's Dictionary of Law,* First edition (1891), under the term "malpractice" he or she is referred to "mala praxis," which is defined as "Malpractice; unskillful management or treatment. Particularly applied to the neglect or unskillful management of a *physician, surgeon,* or *apothecary*" [emphasis added].[2] In *Black's* Second edition, (1910), malpractice is defined:

> As applied to physicians and surgeons, this term means, generally, professional misconduct towards a patient which is considered reprehensible either because immoral in itself or because contrary to law or expressly forbidden by law. In a more specific sense it means bad, wrong, or injudicious treatment of a patient, professionally and in respect to the particular disease or injury, resulting in injury, unnecessary suffering, or death to the patient, and proceeding from ignorance, carelessness, want of proper professional skill, disregard of established rules or principles, neglect or a malicious or criminal intent (citation). The term is occasionally applied to *lawyers,* and then means generally any evil practice in a professional capacity, but rather with reference to the court and its practice and process than to the client (citation) [emphasis added].[3]

---

2. HENRY CAMPBELL BLACK, A DICTIONARY OF LAW (St. Paul: West Publishing Co., © 1981), pp. 744, 746.
   3. *Id.* at 751-52.

In *Black's* Fifth edition, (1979), the term "malpractice" is defined:

> Professional misconduct or unreasonable lack of skill. This term is usually applied to such conduct by doctors, lawyers and *accountants*. Failure of one rendering professional services to exercise that degree of skill and learning commonly applied under all the circumstances in the community by the average prudent reputable member of the profession with the result of injury, loss or damage to the recipient of those services or to those entitled to rely upon them. It is any professional misconduct, unreasonable lack of skill or fidelity in professional or fiduciary duties, evil practices, or illegal or immoral conduct (citations) [emphasis added].[4]
>
> *Legal malpractice.* Consists of failure of an attorney to use such skill, prudence, and diligence as lawyers of ordinary skill and capacity commonly possess and exercise in performance of tasks which they undertake, and when such failure proximately causes damage it gives rise to an action in tort (citations).
>
> *Medical malpractice.* In medical malpractice litigation, negligence is the predominant theory of liability. In order to recover for negligent malpractice, the plaintiff must establish the following elements: (1) the existence of the physician's duty to the plaintiff, usually based upon the existence of the physician-patient relationship; (2) the applicable standard of care and its violation; (3) a compensable injury; and, (4) a casual connection between the violation of the standard of care and the harm complained of (citations). See also Captain of ship doctrine; Discovery rule; Maltreatment [emphasis added].[5]

It is evident from the foregoing definitions of malpractice that the courts have both clarified the meaning of malpractice as well as expanded its application to include various professions.

---

4. *Id.* at 864.
5. *Id.*

§ 2.2. Genesis of Malpractice.

§ 2.2(A). Medical Malpractice.

The Code of Hammurabi was the first set of codified laws to deal with social rules and included some specific regulations about the practice of medicine. The Code was assembled and inscribed in stone about four thousand years ago. The Code described the payment due a physician for various services, and the penalty for certain acts that we now term malpractice.[6] It provides as follows:

> If a doctor has treated a Free Man with a metal knife for a severe wound, and has cured the Free Man ... then he shall receive ten shekels of silver.
> If a doctor has treated a man with a metal knife for a severe wound, and has caused the man to die ... his hands shall be cut off.[7]

In 1514 one Fitzherbert is quoted as having said, "it is the duty of every artificer to exercise his art rightly and truly as he ought."[8] Donald Flaster reports that the first recorded malpractice suit in the United States was filed against a Stafford, Connecticut doctor in 1793 for incompetent and cruel amputation of a breast that resulted in the death of a woman. The doctor lost the case and had to pay compensatory damages.[9] Since then the law relating to medical malpractice is more well-settled, although not always easily applied. In 1898, in the landmark medical malpractice case of *Pike v. Honsinger,*[10] the court specified the implied representations and duties of a physician to his patient — the general statement of the standard of care to

---

6. FLASTER, *supra* note 1, at 28.
7. *Id.*
8. WILLIAM O. MORRIS, DENTAL LITIGATION (Charlottesville, Virginia: The Michie Company, 1972), p. 4. PENNSYLVANIA LAW REVIEW 418.
9. FLASTER, *supra* note 1, at 28.
10. 155 N.Y. 201, 49 N.E. 760 (1898).

be applied to physicians in New York malpractice cases. The court stated:

> The law relating to malpractice is simple and well settled, although not always easy of application. A physician and surgeon, by taking charge of a case, impliedly represents that he possesses, and the law placed upon him the duty of possessing, that reasonable degree of learning and skill that is ordinarily possessed by physicians and surgeons in the locality where he practices, and which is ordinarily regarded by those conversant with the employment as necessary to qualify him to engage in the business of practicing medicine and surgery. Upon consenting to treat a patient it becomes his duty to use reasonable care and diligence in the exercise of his skill and the application of his learning to accomplish the purpose for which he was employed. He is under the further obligation to use his best judgment in exercising his skill and applying his knowledge. The law holds him liable for an injury to his patient resulting from want of the requisite knowledge and skill, or the omission to exercise reasonable care, or the failure to use his best judgment. The rule in relation to learning and skill does not require the surgeon to possess that extraordinary learning and skill which belong only to a few men of rare endowments, but such as is possessed by the average member of the medical profession in good standing. Still, he is bound to keep abreast of the times, and a departure from approved methods in general use, if it injures the patient, will render him liable, however good his intentions may have been. The rule of reasonable care and diligence does not require the exercise of the highest possible degree of cure; and to render a physician and surgeon liable, it is not enough that there has been a less degree of care than some other medical man might have bestowed, but there must be a want of ordinary and reasonable care, leading to a bad result. This includes not only the diagnosis and treatment, but also the giving of proper instructions to his patient in relation to conduct, exercise, and the use of an injured

limb. The rule requiring him to use his best judgment does not hold him liable for a mere error of judgment, provided he does what he thinks is best after careful examination. His implied engagement with his patient does not guarantee a good result, but he promises by implication, to use the skill and learning of the average physician, to exercise reasonable care and to exert his best judgment in the effort to bring about a good result.[11]

An analysis of the case reveals that the standard annunciated by the court for medical malpractice has two dual requirements and two prohibitions. The physician must *possess* and *use* with reasonable care and diligence that *medical skill* and *learning* possessed by like physicians. Furthermore, he is liable if he fails (1) to exercise care or (2) to use his best judgment.[12]

It should be noted that this care does not make the doctor a guarantor of his work. Robert Conason contends that the *Pike* case places four limitations upon the obligation of care of physicians to patients.[13] These are:

1. First, the physician is not to be held to the highest possible degree of care.
2. Second, the physician is not to be held to the highest degree of skill and knowledge, or as is sometimes said, he is not required to possess that extraordinary learning and skill which belong to only a few men of rare endowment. In each instance, he has merely to measure up to the standard of the average physician in his like position and circumstances.
3. A third limit on the duty is that the physician is not a guarantor of a good result and cannot be held liable merely because a bad or unexpected

---

11. 155 N.Y. 201, 209, 49 N.E. 760, 762 (1898).
12. ROBERT L. CONASON, MODERN TRENDS IN MEDICAL MALPRACTICE (New York: Practicing Law Institute, 1978), p. 14.
13. *Id.*

result follows his treatment. The strict liability of product liability cases has not yet been applied to malpractice. The case is to be judged by foresight, not hindsight.

4. The fourth limit states that the doctor is not liable for a "mere" error of judgment which results in injury, "provided that he does what he thinks is best after careful examination." This is the counterbalance to the requirement that the physician exercise his best judgment and is consistent with it. The introduction of the concept of "judgment," however, into a determination by the trier of the fact as to whether there has been a deviation from the standard of care has created many unnecessary problems.[14]

Even though the *Pike* case was decided in New York by a state court, it appears that the holding of this case is the law of medical malpractice virtually everywhere. The shift in medical malpractice is from a subjective to objective standard to evaluate professional conduct.[15]

Mr. Lieberman writes that "on the face of it, malpractice litigation ought to be easy to justify. A doctor bungles, the patient suffers, a lawyer brings suit on behalf of the injured patient to compensate for economic losses and trauma." He further asserts that "beyond immediate redress, a larger good is ostensibly served: Risk can be spread through widely held insurance, and bad medical practices can be deterred."[16] He quotes Robert Cartwright, a president of the Association of Trial Lawyers of America, as saying, "successful medical cases have caused hospitals and doctors to utilize such safety techniques and procedures as sponge counts, instrument counts, electrical

---

14. *Id.* at 14-15.
15. *Id.*
16. JETHRO K. LIEBERMAN, THE LITIGIOUS SOCIETY (New York: Basic Books, Inc., 1981), p. 67.

grounding of anesthesia machines, padding of shoulder bars on operating tables, the avoidance of colorless sterilization solutions in spinal anesthesia counts, and colored bandages."[17] Mr. Cartwright stated that "the sole cause of medical malpractice cases is medical malpractice."[18] When a physician accepts a patient for diagnosis and/or treatment both parties acquire legal rights and legal obligations. These rights and obligations affect every aspect of this physician-patient relationship.[19] Flaster observes that "the right of every citizen to seek compensation for wrongful acts or acts of negligence committed on him or her is fundamental to our American way of life. But when dissatisfaction is not the result of negligence, there is no inherent right to compensation, no matter how well-off the doctor may be or how good an insurance policy the doctor may have."[20]

Even though it always has been possible in the United States for patients to sue their doctors for causing them injury while being treated, such suits remained extremely rare into the 1950s, and it wasn't until the mid-1960s that the amount of litigation began to rise sharply; "at that time, increments, in the filing of malpractice claims, which had been hovering between 2% and 5% each year, suddenly rose to 15% per annum, a pace that has been more or less maintained ever since."[21] Guinther reports that in 1972, a federal study of malpractice noted that two-thirds of all Americans had no awareness that a problem of any kind existed. Three years later a Gallup Poll revealed that 90%

---

   17. Id.
   18. Id.
   19. ANGELA RODDEY HOLDER, MEDICAL MALPRACTICE LAW (New York: John Wiley and Sons, 1975).
   20. FLASTER, supra note 1, at 167.
   21. JOHN GUINTHER, THE MALPRACTITIONERS (Garden City: Anchor Press/Doubleday, 1978), p. 3.

of the people sampled were now aware that the nation was facing a "malpractice crisis."[22] Television and newspapers helped publicize multimillion dollar verdicts for injured patients as well as the threats of doctors who were threatening to stop treatment of their patients unless the high increases in their malpractice insurance premiums were rescinded.[23]

In 1976, estimates were that doctors paid approximately 1.5 billion dollars in premiums for malpractice insurance while paying $370 million in 1970 and $60 million in 1960.[24] Another source reports that malpractice insurance premiums paid by the medical industry in 1976 was $1.13 billion, in 1981 was $1.34 billion, and in 1986 was $2.98 billion.[25] Before World War II, medical malpractice premiums amounted to less than $500. In 1986, the premiums for surgical specialists were from $80,000 to $120,000. Suits against physicians were virtually unheard of before World War II and certainly not a concern of those engaged in the every day practice of medicine.[26]

One source estimates the cost of defensive medicine at $15.1 billion per year, a cost ultimately borne, to a large extent, by the consumer.[27] A report states that, "[t]he St. Paul [Insurance] companies with 14.6% of the national medical market, reported 5,870 claims in 1983 — 2,757

---

22. *Id.*

23. *Id.* at 4.

24. FLASTER, *supra* note 1, at 169.

25. Julie Stacey, *A Look at Statistics That Shape Your Finances: Cost of Malpractice Insurance,* USA TODAY (Source: BESTIS INSURANCE MANAGEMENT REPORTS).

26. ALBERT BARNETT FERGUSON, THE LIABILITY CRISIS AND HOW TO SOLVE IT (The Claymore Press, Inc., 1987), p. xi.

27. S.Y. Tan, *The Medical Malpractice Crisis: Will No-Fault Cure The Disease?,* UNIVERSITY OF HAWAII LAW REVIEW, 242 (Summer 1987).

more than in 1979, an increase of 88.6%."[28] Another source commenting on the number of claims and suits states:

There has been a dramatic increase in the number of claims and formal suits filed against physicians. In 1975, the crisis year of the 1970's, 14,074 malpractice claims were filed against physicians. By 1983, an estimated 42,018 claims were filed. This figure represented an increase of 200%, or 25% per year. By 1985, 10 out of every 100 physicians were sued compared to 3.3 per 100 in 1978. In 1985, 75% of the neurosurgeons and 50% of the obstetricians in Florida were sued or had claims filed against them for alleged medical malpractice.[29]

Concerning the size of verdicts/awards, Dr. Schwartz states:

The average size of the verdict/awards increased 363% between 1975 and 1985. Specifically, in 1975, the average verdict award was $220,018. By 1985, the average award had reached $1,017,716.

In 1984, a total of $66.5 billion, or 1.76% of the GNP and 16.8% of the health care costs, was paid for tort claims and lawyer fees. Interestingly, only 30-40% of these awards even reach the plaintiffs or the injured parties. The remainder has gone to cover the costs of litigation, including lawyer fees.

Looking at this issue from the number of million dollar awards made, an even more dramatic increase may be observed. In 1975, there were 25 million dollar awards. By 1984, there were 71 or 3 times as many as in 1975. Similar trends have occurred in the California

---

28. *Id.* at 241. *See also* AMERICAN MEDICAL ASSOCIATION SPECIAL TASK FORCE ON PROFESSIONAL LIABILITY AND INSURANCE, PROFESSIONAL LIABILITY IN THE 80's, REPORTS 1, 2 & 3 (1984-85).

29. M. ROY SCHWARTZ, MEDICAL MALPRACTICE — TORT REFORM (Memphis: The University of Tennessee, 1987), pp. 17-18 (edited by James E. Hamner III and B.R. Jennings); *see also* AMERICAN MEDICAL ASSOCIATION TASK FORCE REPORT I ON "PROFESSIONAL LIABILITY IN THE 80s" (October 1984), pp. 10-16.

Superior Court verdicts where in 1975, the average plaintiff award was $152,970. By 1983, this had increased to $649,210, a 324% increase.

That these increases are especially severe in medical malpractice cases was demonstrated by a Rand Corporation study of 9,000 civil jury cases in Cook County, Illinois, between 1960-1979. The Rand study concluded,

> Jurors seemed even more sympathetic to plaintiffs injured by medical malpractice ... among plaintiffs with the same injury, a malpractice plaintiff received an award *five times* the size of an award to an injury-on-property plaintiff and almost *twice as large* as the award to a work injury or product liability plaintiff.[30]

From 1965 to 1975, the rates for nonsurgeons increased 540% and the surgeons' premiums increased by 950%.[31] In 1985, annual malpractice premiums for neurosurgeons in Florida reached a high of $97,000.[32] Another writer states, "[h]orror stories abound of New York neurosurgeons paying premiums of over $125,000, obstetricians $100,000,

---

30. *Id.* at 18; *see also* REPORT ON THE TORT POLICY WORKING GROUP ON THE CAUSES, EXTENT AND POLICY IMPLICATIONS OF THE CURRENT CRISIS IN INSURANCE AVAILABILITY AND AFFORDABILITY, (Richard K. Willard, Chairman), pp. 35-42, 1986; S. Wermiel, WALL STREET JOURNAL 66: 1, 11, May 16, 1986. Reprinted by permission of THE WALL STREET JOURNAL, Dow Jones & Company, Inc. (1986). All Rights Reserved Worldwide. Quotes from study by Tillinghast, Nelson and Warren; Longley, M., *Generous Juries.* WALL STREET JOURNAL 66: 1, 20, May 29, 1986. Quoting report from Jury Verdicts Research, Inc., Solon, Ohio; AMERICAN MEDICAL ASSOCIATION TASK FORCE REPORT I ON PROFESSIONAL LIABILITY IN THE 80s, pp. 17-21, October, 1984; Chin, A. and Peterson, M., *Deep Pockets, Empty Pockets,* RAND CORPORATION INSTITUTE FOR CIVIL JUSTICE, 54, 1985.

31. Lieberman, *supra* note 16, at 67.

32. Richard K. Willard, MEDICAL MALPRACTICE — TORT REFORM (Memphis: The University of Tennessee, 1987), p. 4 (edited by James E. Hamner III and B.R. Jennings); *see also* U.S. GENERAL ACCOUNTING OFFICE REPORT 6AO/HRO-86-112. *Medical Malpractice: Insurance Costs Increased But Varied Among Physicians and Hospitals,* pp. 2-29, 1986.

and orthopedists $80,000 for a year's coverage."[33] Kirk
Johnson, general counsel of the AMA, was quoted as stating:

> Liability and increasing government regulations are
> discouraging America's most talented young people
> from pursuing medical careers, and that creates con-
> cern for long-term quality of health care.
> Obstetricians and gynecologists possibly are affected
> most severely — seven out of 10 OB/GYNs will be sued
> for malpractice during their careers, and 12 percent of
> them are leaving the field each year.[34]

In a recent article it was reported that the "average
yearly premium for an obstetrician is about $60,000, but
two Quad-City OB/GYNs paid $160,000 in malpractice pre-
miums during their first year of partnership," according to
James Koch, executive director of the Scott and Rock Island County Medical Society.[35]

A New York City hospital, in 1975, had to pay $558,000
for insurance as compared to $40,000 the previous year.[36]
At the same time a major teaching hospital had its insurance premiums increased from $245,000 to $1,500,000.[37]

§ 2.2(B). Malpractice in the Legal Profession.

Likewise, the legal profession has been troubled with
malpractice claims. Hilliker writes, "[a]s long as 100 years
ago the United States Supreme Court observed that a lawyer 'must be understood as promising to employ a reason-

---

33. ARTHUR H. BERNSTEIN, AVOIDING MEDICAL MALPRACTICE (Chicago: Pluribus Press, 1988), p. 5.

34. Carie Dann, *Malpractice Suits Scare Doctors Away*, QUAD-CITY
TIMES (Sept. 7, 1988), p. 3.

35. Carrie Dann, "Who'll deliver our babies?," QUAD-CITY TIMES (May
13, 1990) pp. 1A, 10A.

36. LIEBERMAN, *supra* note 16, at 67.

37. GUINTHER, *supra* note 21, at 18.

able degree of care and skill in the performance of [his or her] duties; and if injury results to the client from a want of such a degree of reasonable care and skill, the attorney may be held to respond in damages ....'"[38] In recent years, however, the legal profession has begun to experience a professional malpractice crisis.[39] The reason for this, according to former Chief Justice Warren Burger, is due to a decline of professionalism. He is quoted as saying that "the legal profession as a whole has a very poor standing .... There are many causes for this, one of them being the incompetence ... and lack of training of a great many lawyers who appear in the courts."[40] Between 1975 and 1980 legal malpractice insurance rates had increased some 300% to 526% or more.[41] Jerome Janzer observes that "[r]epresentatives of the insurance industry and independent observers have indicated that the attorney professional liability claims frequently quadrupled between 1973 and 1976, from about 1.8 claims to about 7.2 claims per 100 insurance policies."[42]

It has been stated that "[a]ttorneys are held to the same standard of care applicable to all professionals: the duty owed a client to exercise the knowledge, skill and ability customary to members of the profession similarly situated. Where the duty is breached, the attorney will be held liable

---

38. Donald B. Hilliker, *Why Lawyer Liability and the Costs of Insurance Are Increasing,* 7 THE BARRISTER 17 (Fall 1980).

39. James K. Meguerian, *The Illinois Legal Malpractice Tort: Basic Tenets and Recent Trends,* 2 UNIVERSITY OF ILLINOIS LAW FORUM 427 (1980). Copyright held by the Board of Trustees of the University of Illinois.

40. *Id.,* citing Burger, *A Sick Profession,* WISCONSIN BAR BULLETIN (Oct. 1969), p. 7.

41. Meguerian, *supra* note 39, at 427.

42. Jerome M. Janzer, *Countersuits to Legal and Medical Malpractice Actions: Any Chance for Success,* 65 MARQUETTE LAW REVIEW, 93 (1981); citing Pfennigstorf, *Types and Causes of Lawyers' Professional Liability Claims: The Search for Facts,* 1980 A.B.F. RES. J. 255, 258.

for any damages sustained by the client which are attributable to his negligence."[43] Four elements are necessary to establish a *prima facie* case under the negligence theory for a malpractice suit: (1) that an attorney-client relationship existed between the plaintiff and defendant; (2) that the attorney deviated from the standard of care owed to the client; (3) that this alleged departure from the applicable standard of care constituted the actual and proximate cause of the plaintiff's injury; and (4) that as a result of this injury, the plaintiff suffered actual damages. In addition, the plaintiff must commence his action within the relevant limitations period.[44] Generally, the standard of care to which a lawyer must adhere is defined specifically with reference to the liability of his practice.[45] As other professionals, attorneys "are being sued for errors and omissions in the performance of their services, and are being attacked for decisions and judgments made in the course of their day-to-day activities."[46]

In a legal malpractice case the plaintiff may rely on principles of either tort or contract law. In some instances the plaintiff may base his claim on both theories. Under the contract theory, "a court would characterize an attorney's negligence as a breach of an express or implied promise to exercise his best efforts on behalf of the client in performing his contractual duties."[47] Under the tort theory, "a court would characterize an attorney's negligence as a tortious breach of his duty to exercise reasonable care in han-

---

43. Thomas W. Wilson, Kenneth J. Balkan and Barry B. LePatner, *Legal Malpractice and Professional Liability Insurance,* NEW YORK STATE BAR JOURNAL 462, 464 (October 1980).

44. Meguerian, *supra* note 39, at 430.

45. Meguerian, *supra* note 39, at 443.

46. Wilson, *supra* note 43, at 462.

47. A.L.B. III, *Malpractice Suits Against Local Counsel or Specialists,* 68 VIRGINIA LAW REVIEW 571, 577 (1982).

dling the client's legal affairs."[48] There are several legal theories that civil liability may be predicated upon: "fraud, breach of either express or implied contract and breach of fiduciary duty,"[49] Meguerian observes that "recently, several courts and commentators also have pressed for recognition of a legal malpractice cause of action based on breach of implied warranty.[50] The courts hold that even though an attorney is not considered an insurer of his work product he or she must exhibit that degree of legal knowledge and skill which is ordinarily possessed by members of the legal profession. Thus, an objective standard defines the duty owed by a lawyer to his client in the handling of the client's business."[51] The plaintiff must first prove that the attorney deviated from the applicable standard of care and secondly the attorney must establish that *but for* the defendant-attorney's conduct, he or she would have suffered no injury or a lesser injury. Generally, the question of causation presents little difficulty unless the factual basis for alleged malpractice is litigation related.[52]

Even if the plaintiff is able to establish the necessary proof of malpractice, the defendant may be able to assert one of the several defenses available in legal malpractice actions. These recognized defenses include expiration of the limitations period, privilege, contributory negligence, assumption of the risk, release, immunity, prematurity, *res judicata,* and estoppel.[53] Traditionally, attorneys were largely immune from nonclient claims short of fraud or collusion. Their liability for negligence ran only to clients

---

48. *Id.*
49. Meguerian, *supra* note 39, at 428.
50. *Id.*
51. *Id.* at 438.
52. *Id.* at 456.
53. *Id.* at 467; citing Sanders, *Defenses to a Legal Malpractice Action,* CASE & COMMENT (July-August 1979), p. 36.

because of the protective barrier of privity of contract.[54] Probert and Hendricks contend that "[a]lthough the courts historically used privity to insulate all manner of activities, the concept has had a special appeal and lasting quality in the area of lawyer malpractice. Understandably, the judiciary has tended to reflect the general professional attitude that a lawyer should be concerned mainly, if not only, with his client's interest .... It now appears that most states will come to reject privity as an absolute requirement."[55]

This brief discussion on legal professional malpractice indicates that professional malpractice in the legal profession is not being curtailed. Rather, the claims against attorneys are increasing in number and complexity. There is no indication that professional malpractice claims against the legal profession will soon be eliminated. What is being recommended is "for the legal profession to educate itself as to the pitfalls of malpractice and the means to limit exposure in the event that a claim becomes a reality."[56]

§ 2.2(C). Malpractice in Psychiatry.

Psychiatrists have not been spared from professional malpractice. Such cases as *Tarasoff v. Regents of the University of California,*[57] firmly established that psychiatrists may be held liable for professional negligence. *Tarasoff* involved an action brought against the university regents,

---

54. W. Probert & R. Hendricks, *Lawyer Malpractice: Duty Relationships Beyond Contract,* 55 THE NOTRE DAME LAWYER 708 (June 1980).
55. *Id.*
56. Thomas W. Wilson, Kenneth J. Balkan & Barry B. LePatner, *Legal Malpractice and Professional Liability Insurance,* NEW YORK STATE BAR JOURNAL 565, 598 (November 1980).
57. 17 Cal. 3d 425, 551 P.2d 334 (1976). *See also* C. Eric Funston, *Made Out of Whole Cloth? A Constitutional Analysis of the Clergy Malpractice Concept,* 19 CALIFORNIA WESTERN LAW REVIEW 507 (1983).

psychotherapists employed by university hospital, and the campus police to recover for the murder of plaintiff's daughter by a psychiatric patient. The complaint alleged that poychothorapioto, to whom pationt oonfidod hio inton tion to kill another, who knew the patient was at large and dangerous, who were unsuccessful in their attempt to confine the patient, and who failed to warn the intended victim or persons likely to apprise her of the danger, breached their duty to exercise reasonable care in protecting the intended victim.[58] The trial court dismissed the complaint, holding that, despite the tragic events, there was no legal basis in the state law for a claim against them.[59]

The case was appealed to the California Court of Appeals. The court of appeals affirmed the trial court's decision.[60] On appeal, the Supreme Court of California stated that once a psychotherapist in fact determines, or under applicable professional standards, reasonably should have determined, that a patient poses a serious danger of violence to others, he bears a duty to exercise reasonable care to protect the foreseeable victim of that danger; while a discharge of such duty of due care will necessarily vary with the facts of each case, in each instance the adequacy of the therapist's conduct must be measured against the traditional negligence standard of reasonable care under the circumstances.[61] The Court further commented that professional inaccuracy in predicting violent behavior by a patient cannot negate a psychotherapist's duty to protect the threatened victim; risk that unnecessary warnings may be given is a reasonable price to pay for the lives of possible

---

58. 17 Cal. 3d 425, 551 P.2d 334 (1976).
59. *Id. See also* Alan A. Stone, M.D., *The Tarasoff Decision: Suing Psychotherapists to Safeguard Society,* 90 HARVARD LAW REVIEW 358 (1976).
60. *Id.*
61. 17 Cal. 3d 425, 427, 551 P.2d 334, 336 (1976).

victims that may be saved.[62] Obviously, this decision poses
a troublesome dilemma for the therapist — "How do you
balance the two?" On the one hand, the therapist has an
obligation to protect the patient's confidence given in therapy, while on the other hand, the therapist's concern for
public safety places him or her in a position of having to
take some kind of action.[63] This poses a serious dilemma for
the therapist. An argument advanced for the resolution of
this problem is "to place on the therapist the duty to protect society in the manner least harmful to the interests of
the patient."[64] It is argued that this duty will vary depending on the case and will in many times take the form of a
duty to warn potential victims. This reasoning is premised
on the belief that the breach of confidentiality required by
a duty to warn the necessary party is far preferable to the
abusive and customary alternative of confining the patient.[65]

Another problem that the *Tarasoff* holding presents is
the problem of establishing a reasonable standard of professional care — preferably an objective rather than a subjective standard. The American Psychiatric Association argued in *Tarasoff* "that a psychiatrist cannot predict dangerousness with sufficient reliability to make reasonable a
duty to protect others from dangerous conduct."[66] The
court's response was that the therapist will be expected to
display only "that reasonable degree of skill, knowledge,
and care ordinarily possessed and exercised by members of
[that professional specialty]."[67] Concerning the court's con-

---

62. *Id.*
63. Alan A. Stone, M.D., *The Tarasoff Decision: Suing Psychotherapists to Safeguard Society,* 90 HARVARD LAW REVIEW 358, 362 (1976).
64. *Id.*
65. *Id.* at 362-63.
66. *Id.* at 363.
67. *Id.* at 363-64.

clusion, Dr. Alan Stone states that the court did not reflect on what sense this test makes when no member of the profession can reliably predict dangerousness. "Nor did it consider whether the kind of breach it endorsed would accord with the legitimate expectations of the patient or what its consequences might be for the nature of the therapist-patient relationship and ultimately for the safety of the public."[68] He concludes his comment of the *Tarasoff* case by noting that the tragedy of *Tarasoff* is the price society pays for restraints on the "coercive power" of psychiatrists. "Their unwillingness," he states, "to recognize that fact leads them to a result that will reduce the ability of the mentally ill in California to obtain effective therapy and consequently will diminish public safety. The decision is counterproductive of the goal of public safety it professes."[69]

Even though there have been cases against psychiatrists for malpractice, as the *Tarasoff* case demonstrates, the psychiatrists have long enjoyed a relative freedom from malpractice litigation. It is suggested that the reason for this is due to "the diversity of acceptable therapeutic techniques, it has been difficult to establish definite guidelines for professional psychiatric judgment in clinical situations."[70] This becomes obvious when one refers to the definition of psychotherapy. It is defined as:

> A method or system of alleviating or curing certain forms of disease, particularly diseases of the nervous system or such as traceable to nervous disorders, by suggestion, persuasion, encouragement, the inspiration of hopes or confidence, the discouragement of mor-

---

68. *Id.* at 364.

69. *Id.* at 377-78.

70. Henry B. Rothblatt & David H. Leroy, *Avoiding Psychiatric Malpractice,* 9 CALIFORNIA WESTERN LAW REVIEW 260 (1973). Reprinted with permission of CALIFORNIA WESTERN LAW REVIEW.

bid memories, associations, or beliefs, and other similar means addressed to the mental state of the patient, without (or sometimes in conjunction with) the administration of drugs or other physical remedies.[71]

Regarding the liability of a psychiatrist for malpractice, one author has stated:

> Psychiatric negligence may consist of either failing to diagnose or cure or causing additional suffering. In order for there to be recovery there must be persuasive proof that the deviation from professional standards caused or contributed to the patient's present condition. The damages recoverable are for personal injuries including the pain and suffering which naturally flow from the negligent act.[72]

Another troublesome area in establishing malpractice is the requirement of proving actual injury. It is difficult to ascertain whether the injuries complained of resulted from tortious conduct or were the natural course of the illness itself. In fact, contends Marjory Harris, "the patient may never even consider suing the psychotherapist because the patient may not associate the treatment (or lack of it) with the injury."[73]

Rothblatt asserts that "proving that a particular act or omission of the physician 'proximately caused' injury to the patient has been a demanding task because of limited knowledge concerning the natural course of mental illness."[74] Furthermore, he notes, "because psychiatric trials often involve complex medical, legal and factual issues, and focus upon conflicting expert testimony, it is difficult

---

71. HENRY CAMPBELL BLACK, BLACK'S LAW DICTIONARY (St. Paul: West Publishing Company, 5th ed., © 1979), p. 1104.

72. Marjory Harris, *Tort Liability of the Psychotherapist*, 8 UNIVERSITY OF SAN FRANCISCO LAW REVIEW 405, 511 (Winter 1973).

73. *Id.* at 412.

74. Rothblatt, *supra* note 70, at 260.

for the complaining patient to sustain the burden of proving his case to a jury of ordinary citizens."[75]

Generally, the cases against psychiatrists for malpractice have been in areas of treatment other than verbal therapies such as psychoanalysis. There have been relatively few cases dealing with the liability of a psychiatrist for negligence in the conduct of therapy under psychoanalysis.[76] Patrick Cassidy states that cases against psychiatrists for malpractice involving treatment have centered generally in such areas as electroshock therapy, suicide, patient causing harm to others, failure to consult or refer, abandonment, failure to commit, premature discharge, improper commitment, cases involving drugs, sexual involvement, breach of confidentiality, fee disputes, unauthorized treatment, and battery by psychiatrists.[77] He concludes an article on the psychiatrist's liability for malpractice by noting that "the present state of the law contains several potential pitfalls in the path of recovery against a psychotherapist. If the law could be clarified in the proper manner, future recipients of negligent psychiatric care would certainly be benefitted."[78] An authority on psychiatric malpractice has set forth a concise formula for avoiding malpractice:

> It becomes essential that the professional man develop those arts and skills necessary to effectively render his professional services as he carries out his professional duties; that he acquire that degree of knowledge necessary to have something to profess; that he profess it with discretion; and that he develop that degree of

---

75. *Id.*

76. Patrick Sean Cassidy, *The Liability of Psychiatrists for Malpractice*, 36 UNIVERSITY OF PITTSBURGH LAW REVIEW 108 (1974). Reprinted with permission of the UNIVERSITY OF PITTSBURGH LAW REVIEW.

77. *Id.; See also* Harris, *supra* note 72, at 412.

78. Cassidy, *supra* note 76, at 137.

moral fibre necessary to profess it with sincerity, integrity, and good conscience (ethics).[79]

§ 2.2(D). Clergy Malpractice.

It is not surprising, given the proliferation of malpractice suits against other professions, that another group of counselors, the clergy, are faced with claims of "clergy malpractice." The first suit in this profession was filed in California in 1980. *Nally v. Grace Community Church of the Valley*[80] was filed by the parents, as heirs, of a seminary student who committed suicide the previous year. It named as defendants a church, its head pastor, and three other pastors. The suit was filed under the California wrongful death statute and asserted three claims: (1) clergy malpractice, (2) negligence, and (3) outrageous conduct.[81]

In a law review article Samuel Ericsson summarizes the three counts of the complaint as follows:

> In the first count, the parents alleged that the pastor and staff had counseled their son to read the Bible, pray, listen to taped sermons, and counsel with church counselors. They alleged that the defendants were aware that their son was depressed and had suicidal tendencies and was in need of professional psychiatric and psychological care. Notwithstanding such knowledge, plaintiffs alleged that the church and its staff discouraged and effectively prevented their son from seeking professional help outside the church.
>
> In the second count, the complaint alleged that the defendants were negligent in the training, selection, and hiring of its "lay spiritual counselors." The court additionally alleged that these counselors were unavailable when Nally requested counseling.

---

79. Harris, *supra* note 72, at 436; citing Bellany, *Malpractice in Psychiatry,* 26 DISEASES OF THE NERVOUS SYSTEM 312, 320 (1965).

80. 157 Cal. App. 3d 912, 204 Cal. Rptr. 303 (Cal. Ct. App. 1984).

81. *Id.*

The third count alleged that the defendants ridiculed, disparaged, and denigrated the Catholic religion, and faith and belief of the decedent's parents, and that this exacerbated Nally's pre-existing feelings of guilt, anxiety, and depression. It was further alleged that defendants effectively required the decedent to spend time in isolation, thereby preventing him from contacting or consulting with persons not affiliated with the church and that this proximately caused the young man to take his own life.[82]

In the first count for clergy malpractice it was further stated that "by virtue of such acts and omissions alleged, the defendant John MacArthur was negligent in failing to exercise the standard of care for a clergyman of his sect and training in the community which proximately resulted in Kenneth Nally committing suicide ...."[83] The *Nally* case has raised the question of whether a court may impose judicial standards and duties on pastoral counselors or whether their church-related activities are protected from the imposition of state control, review, or interference by virtue of the first amendment.[84] This case goes beyond the tort question of causation and the imposition of liability in the case of suicide and raises constitutional issues. Ben Bergman asserts:

Stated broadly, can any suit for clergy malpractice be sustained since it places the court in the position of having to pass judgment on competence, training,

---

82. Samuel E. Ericsson, *Clergyman Malpractice: Ramifications of a New Theory,* 16 VALPARAISO UNIVERSITY LAW REVIEW 163, 164 (1981).
83. Nally v. Grace Community Church, 157 Cal. App. 3d 912, 921, 204 Cal. Rptr. 303 (Cal. App. 1984).
84. Michael J. Fiorillo, *Clergy Malpractice: Should Pennsylvania Recognize a Cause of Action for Improper Counseling by a Clergyman?,* 92 DICKINSON LAW REVIEW 223 (Fall 1987). Reprinted from DICKINSON LAW REVIEW, Vol. 92, No. 1, Fall 1987. Copyright © 1987 by Dickinson School of Law. *See also* Note, 1 ARIZONA STATE LAW JOURNAL 213 (1985).

methods, contents, and other aspects of the clergyman's function? Furthermore, does not a complaint of
malpractice presume a definable duty which the practitioner (in this case, the clergyman) has violated? Can
that duty be defined by a body other than the religious
order which has ordained and/or which the clergyman
serves? In other words, if the court were to determine
the scope of the clergy's duty of care, would that determination not be in violation of the first amendment?
Does the concept of religious liberty require that the
clergy not be regulated at all in their functions or can
one differentiate between the purely ecclesiastical
functions of the clergy and those functions, albeit traditionally within the clergyman's purview, that are
not sacerdotal in character and which might therefore
be legitimately regulated by the court under the police
power of the state to protect the health, safety, morals
and welfare of its citizens? Does the traditional priest-
penitent privilege militate against clergy malpractice
liability?

These and other questions are basic issues which
will have to be dealt with to determine whether a suit
for malpractice may or may not be brought against a
clergyman.[85]

These types of malpractice cases raise some issues that
are not only unique but also difficult and perplexing for the
courts. In "counseling malpractice" cases the issue that
may be facing the courts may be one of choosing between
competing religious dogmas.[86] Ericsson notes five problems
facing the courts in clergy counseling cases.

1. While it is true that courts are confronted with
   and deal with issues that are beyond their own
   expertise, those issues are empirical in nature.
   This is not the case in clergy counseling cases in
   that the issues are not emperical, but religious.

---

85. Ben Zion Bergman, *Is the Cloth Unraveling? A First Look at
Clergy Malpractice,* 9 SAN FERNANDO LAW REVIEW 47, 48 (1981).
86. Ericsson, *supra* note 82, at 169.

"They are not conducive to judicial review because they lack objective standards."[87]

2. There is a problem with identifying the scope and nature of church-related counseling. "As a matter of law, what constitutes spiritual guidance and counseling? Does it include the one time, five-minute emergency telephone call that pastors and counselors may receive in the course of their day from distressed individuals, members as well as non-members of their congregations? Does it include confessions? Or is "spiritual counseling" limited to formal office visits where a pastor or other counselor counsels, notebook in hand, at a scheduled time, on a regular basis, over a long period of time?"[88]

3. Another problem is determining whether the duty owed to a counselee would be any different depending upon the counselor's ecclesiastical office and the authority or function flowing from such office.[89]

4. As in other professional malpractice cases, the courts must review the training and competence of individual counselors. This will present a number of new problems. "Shall the review be limited to the training received in secular institutions on secular subjects, such as psychology, psychiatry and mental health counseling? Would a degree in clinical psychology from an accredited university provide the desired training .... If the professional "jury" is still out on what secular professionals shall know and be able to do in the area of counseling, what standards should the court look to when faced with the issue of the competence and training of church counselors? ... Aside from secular training, a Christian counselor's competence may depend upon many "spiritual" qualifications such as the counselor's spiritual gifts and

---

87. *Id.*
88. *Id.* at 169-70.
89. *Id.* at 170.

his or her spiritual maturity .... Might someone
with a number of key spiritual gifts, such as wisdom, knowledge, or exhortation be held to a
higher standard of care (akin to a specialist) than
other spiritual counselors who may have been endowed with fewer, if any, of these specific gifts? ...
A secular court, however, may decide to apply
purely secular criteria, such as that of clinical
psychology, and dismiss the religious standard as
irrelevant and inapplicable."[90]

5. The fifth problem deals with the content of the
counsel given by the counselor. "As a practical
matter, wholly apart from the constitutional prohibitions, the courts are not equipped to evaluate
the content of the counsel provided by a church to
those individuals who voluntarily embrace the
doctrine stance of the church."[91]

Ericsson concludes his article as follows:

The law of torts has been the battleground for social
theory. Every new theory raises far more questions
than answers and the theory of clergyman malpractice
is no exception. Since clergyman malpractice inevitably deals with doctrinal, ecclesiastical, and spiritual
issues, judicial review will force the courts into dangerous territory. Thus, with the possible exception of
the instance when "actual malice" on the part of the
counselor is alleged to exist, it seems clear that the
first amendment will bar the introduction of this theory into the legal arena.[92]

The trial court concluded that the evidence failed to establish a triable issue of fact with regard to the plaintiffs'
cause of action for wrongful death caused by the alleged
intentional infliction of emotional distress and granted de-

---

90. *Id.* at 171-72.
91. *Id.* at 172.
92. *Id.* at 184.

fendants' motion for summary judgment.[93] The case was then appealed to California Court of Appeals. In reversing the trial court, the Court of Appeals held:

> [T]hat a cause of action for wrongful death arising out of intentional infliction of emotional distress was adequately pled by allegations that individual defendants, as agents of the church, knowing that decedent was depressive and had suicidal tendencies, exacerbated his feeling of guilt, anxiety, and depression with reckless disregard that their conduct would increase the likelihood that decedent would commit suicide, and that, as a result of such conduct, decedent's depression increased, causing him to commit suicide. It further held defendants' motions failed to establish that there was no triable issue of fact with respect to the count containing such allegations. While defendants' religious beliefs were absolutely protected by the U.S. Const., First Amdnd., the free exercise clause of that amendment did not license intentional infliction of emotional distress in the name of religion and could not shield defendants from liability for wrongful death for a suicide caused by such conduct.[94]

Concerning the question of whether a clergyman or church should be immune from liability for intentional infliction of emotional distress caused by the nature or content of counseling simply because the counseling may have a spiritual aspect, the court stated:

> The free exercise clause of the First Amendment to the Constitution "embraces two concepts — freedom to believe and freedom to act. The first is absolute but, in the nature of things, the second cannot be." Counseling falls within the latter category.[95]

---

93. Superior Court of Los Angeles County, No. NOC 18668B (1981).

94. Nally v. Grace Community Church of the Valley, 157 Cal. App. 3d 912 (1984).

95. *Id.* at 918.

The decision by the Court of Appeals in this case was not unanimous. One of the three justices dissented. In his dissent, Justice Hanson argued:

> To hold otherwise, under the facts of this case, could have the deleterious effect of opening a virtual Pandora's box of litigation by subjecting all of the various religious faiths and their clergy (*e.g.,* ministers of the numerous Protestant denominations; priests of the Roman Catholic faith and the various Eastern Orthodox religions; rabbis of the Jewish faith, orthodox, conservative and reform, etc.) to wrongful death actions and expensive full-blown trials simply because they are unsuccessful in their sincere efforts through spiritual counseling to help or dissuade emotionally disturbed members of their congregations, who may be suicide prone, from carrying out such a predisposition.
> I am not saying that a church under any conceivable set of facts could never be liable for the intentional infliction of emotional distress. I am saying that in the case at bench, through the proper and fair application of the statutorialy created summary judgment procedures, there are no triable issues of fact upon which to base liability under any theory alleged, including intentional infliction of emotional distress.[96]

The trial court dismissed the lawsuit by granting the defendants' motion for summary judgment. Such motion, in effect, states that, based on the various papers submitted (pleadings, depositions, affidavits etc.) to date, there is no genuine issue of material fact and the movant is entitled to prevail as a matter of law.[97] The appeal was taken on the ground that the trial court should not have dismissed the suit summarily. The appellate court was requested to reverse the lower court and allow the plaintiffs to prove their case.

---

96. *Id.* at 938.

97. HENRY CAMPBELL BLACK, *Black's Law Dictionary* (St. Paul: West Publishing Co., 5th ed., © 1979), p. 1287.

The California Court of Appeals reversed the trial court on the basis that a cause of action for intentional infliction of emotional distress was adequately pleaded by the plaintiffs; however, the court did not discuss the issue of liability for negligent counseling. It is still unclear what, if any, duty is owed church members by a religious counselor. Furthermore, it is not clear what standard of care should be applied to measure such a duty.[98] Subsequent to the decision by the court of appeals, a second appeal was filed with the California Supreme Court. The court denied a hearing and decertified the lower court's decision. The case was then returned to trial. Following plaintiff's case-in-chief, the defendants' motion for nonsuit was granted. Plaintiffs have again filed an appeal with the Second Appellate District.[99]

On retrial a California Superior Court judge dismissed the *Nally* suit, basing his objections in part on the emphasis the founding fathers placed on freedom of religion and speech. The court found no compelling reason to interfere with the counseling at the church and stated that any "attempt to impart standards of pastoral counseling would open the floodgates of clergy malpractice suits."[100] Throughout the entire procedural history of this case all of the courts have avoided addressing the issue of the duty owed by any of the defendants.[101]

---

98. M. Maureen Anders, *Religious Counseling — Parents Allowed To Pursue Suit Against Church And Clergy For Son's Suicide — Nally v. Grace Community Church,* ARIZONA STATE LAW JOURNAL 213 (1985).

99. Lawrence M. Burek, *Clergy Malpractice: Making Clergy Accountable To A Lower Power,* 14 PEPPERDINE LAW REVIEW 137, 141 (1986); *see also Nally v. Grace Community Church of the Valley,* No. BO15721 (Cal. App., Second App. Dist., 1985).

100. Kimberly Anne Klee, *Clergy Malpractice: Bad News for the Good Samaritan or a Blessing in Disguise?,* 17 TOLEDO LAW REVIEW 209, 248 (1985). Reprinted by permission of the UNIVERSITY OF TOLEDO LAW REVIEW, Volume 17 (1985).

101. Burek, *supra* note 99, at 141.

Considerable debate has surfaced regarding clergy malpractice. One commentator concludes an article on clergy malpractice by stating:

> The tort concept of clergy malpractice imposes a duty on the clergyman to recognize his own counseling limitations and refer those cases beyond the scope of his competence to counseling practitioners with more specialized training. In *Nally v. Grace Community Church,* the California Court of Appeals determined that pastoral counseling, although religiously motivated, is not absolutely immune by virtue of the first amendment. Rather, the clergyman's first amendment protection is subject to being outweighed by the state's duty to protect its citizens ....
>
> As evidenced by the *Nally* case, the concept of clergy malpractice has received mixed reviews. In reality, the duty imposed is no greater than the ethical duty imposed by the clergyman's own conscience. Consequently, the imposition of liability would serve both to provide justice to the victims of incompetence and to secure the clergyman's ongoing relationship with the parishioners of his counsel ....
>
> Only time will reveal whether clergy malpractice will become a widely accepted cause of action. Nevertheless, its emergence provides an important opportunity for clergymen, courts, and legislatures to reevaluate the evolving role of today's pastoral counselor. The proper approach to the theory of clergy malpractice is one of prevention, through education, clinical training, and consultation.[102]

The fear of more litigation in this area brought about malpractice insurance for clergy malpractice. Three major Christian denominations began providing malpractice insurance.[103] Insurance, of course, may seem to be very valu-

---

102. Klee, *supra* note 100, at 253.

103. Fiorillo, *supra* note 84, at 230. The United Presbyterian Church, the Lutheran Church in America, and the United Methodist Church provide malpractice insurance for their clergy.

able in this area. However, it also raises the question of whether it would damage or destroy the value of pastoral counseling. Those who oppose clergy malpractice actions suggest that "the intimacy between the clergyman and parishioner is lost when such techniques are utilized."[104] They reason thusly:

> Recognition of clergy malpractice may pressure clergymen into disclosing the contents of confidential communications to members of the counselee's family or others .... A clergyman who refuses to disclose confidential communications that are vital to defending an action may violate his duty to cooperate with his insurer, thereby releasing the insurer from its duty to defend the suit. Thus, in order to obtain a proper defense, the clergyman will be compelled to violate his counselee's confidence.[105]

The previous discussion clearly points out some of the novel and troublesome questions that the *Nally* case raises. Nevertheless, once the courts are presented with these questions, they should not adopt a hands off policy and leave the questions unanswered. When a legitimate dispute arises that cannot be solved without the courts' intervention, the courts must act. After all, it is the business of the courts to remedy wrongs that deserve it.[106]

§ 2.2(E). Malpractice in Other Professions.

Other professionals, including accountants, architects, engineers, and dentists have experienced the threat of, and

---

104. *Id.;* Comment, *Made Out of Whole Cloth? A Constitutional Analysis of the Clergy Malpractice Concept*, 19 CALIFORNIA WESTERN LAW REVIEW 507 (1983).

105. Fiorillo, *supra* note 84, at 230-31; Ericsson, *Clergyman Malpractice: Ramifications of a New Theory*, 16 VALPARAISO UNIVERSITY LAW REVIEW 163, 174 (1981).

106. *Educational Malpractice,* 124 UNIVERSITY OF PENNSYLVANIA LAW REVIEW 755, 765 (1976).

some have encountered the actual reality of, a malpractice suit. However, the basis for the suits, and the defenses used by those who have been sued, are similar to the other professions we briefly discussed. For example, dentistry is a portion of medicine in the eyes of the courts, especially when the subject is malpractice. "Malpractice cases involving physicians and surgeons antedate those which involve dentists. In dental malpractice cases the courts frequently make reference to cases which involve physicians or surgeons. Because the legal principles are the same ...."[107] One court, in considering the issues raised in a dental malpractice case, said, "[I]t may be pointed out that in the performance of services within their own profession, dentists, as being of a kindred branch of the healing art, are subject to the same rules that govern the duties and liabilities of the general physicians and surgeons."[108] Another court stated that "a dental surgeon cannot be held responsible, any more than a physician or surgeon, for the failure of his patient to respond satisfactorily to treatment or make rapid progress towards recovery, provided he has used the treatment recognized and customary in the profession and employed reasonable skill and diligence."[109]

Given the increasingly litigious nature of our society, the following shouldn't come as a big surprise. A twenty-five-year-old man sued his mother for "parental malpractice," alleging intentional infliction of emotional distress. The suit was thrown out by a judge who ruled that it was wholly without merit, whereupon the mother then sued the son's psychiatrist, contending that the doctor had encour-

---

107. MORRIS, *supra* note 8, at 12.

108. *Id.* at 12-13; Tanner v. Sanders, 247 Ky. 90, 92, 56 S.W.2d 718, 719 (1933).

109. MORRIS, *supra* note 8, at 13; McCartney v. Hyman, 134 Pa. Super. 524, 530, 4 A.2d 581, 584 (1939).

aged the son's suit and thus held her up to nationwide ridicule.[110]

§ 2.3. Summary.

The foregoing analysis demonstrates that suits for professional malpractice are not an imagined threat to professions but a real cause of action which poses a serious concern for many professions. It is a cause of action that is not new, but rather one that has been recognized by the law for many years. In struggling with it, courts have defined, and in some cases redefined, the basic elements of malpractice. Courts have enumerated what is needed to be alleged and proven in professional malpractice cases and have also spoken regarding possible defenses that may be available to the professional who is being sued.

---

110. FLASTER, *supra* note 1, at 193.

Chapter 3

LEGAL THEORIES AVAILABLE TO THOSE SEEKING REDRESS AGAINST PROFESSIONALS; DEFENSES AVAILABLE TO PROFESSIONALS

> It is the business of the law to remedy wrongs that deserve it — for every man that is injured ought to have his recompense.
> — William L. Prosser[1]

§ 3.0. Introduction.

To err is human and professionals are human. Consequently, it shouldn't come as a big surprise to learn that professionals do not always accomplish what they want in their work. Many times when their desired result is not achieved, nothing happens to the professional, even though someone — their client or patient — was harmed; however, occasionally that someone who has been injured, or thinks that he or she has been injured, turns to the courts for help. Unfortunately, according to some critics, what should oc-

---

1. WILLIAM L. PROSSER, LAW OF TORTS (St. Paul: West Publishing Company, © 1983).

63

cur occasionally now happens much too much — especially in the last two decades.

Suing someone is easy — some would say too easy! Winning a suit is much more difficult. Complaints must be properly drafted and brought under a specific legal theory. A number of legal theories have been used to bring suits against professionals, but professionals have not been left defenseless. Professionals may assert a number of recognized defenses to protect themselves. In order to properly set the stage to better understand educational malpractice, we will summarize and briefly discuss the theories and defenses used in various professional malpractice cases. This chapter will specifically focus on the following two questions: (1) If someone has been harmed (injured) by a professional while the professional was exercising his or her "professional duty," what legal theories are available to pursue a claim for injuries? (2) What defenses are available to the professional?

§ 3.1. Theories for Recovery.

There are several theories which may be available to those seeking damages against professionals. The traditional ones are tort, contract, and breach of statutory duty. Other theories that may be applicable under specific circumstances include *res ipsa loquitur,* mandamus, promissory estoppel, breach of fiduciary duty, "assumption of duty," and implied warranty. In this chapter will be discussed the traditional theories that have been used in various suits against professionals. The non-traditional theories will be discussed in a subsequent chapter dealing specifically with educational malpractice.

§ 3.1(A). Tort Theories.

Tort theories generally consist of negligence, intentional tort, and misrepresentation (deceit and negligent misrepresentation).[2]

§ 3.1(A)(1). Negligence.

Prosser states that negligence is simply one kind of conduct.[3] However, a cause of action based upon negligence, from which liability will follow, requires more than conduct. The elements necessary for a cause of action in a negligence suit are:

a. A duty or obligation, recognized by the law, requiring the defendant to conform to a certain standard of conduct, for the protection of others against unreasonable risks.
b. A failure by the defendant to conform to the standard required.
c. A reasonably close causal connection between the conduct and the resulting injury.
d. Actual loss or damage resulting to the interests of another[4] (the plaintiff).

The difficulty in establishing and proving these elements obviously varies from case to case as well as from one profession to another. For example, the second element — a failure by the defendant to conform to the standard required — is hard to establish and prove in a number of cases, i.e., clergy malpractice, previously discussed, and educational malpractice, which will be dealt with in subsequent chapters. This stems from the fact that it is difficult

---

2. *Educational Malpractice,* 124 UNIVERSITY OF PENNSYLVANIA LAW REVIEW 755, 767 (1976). Reprinted with permission of AL. PA. L. REV., from 124 U. PA. L. REV. 755 (1976).

3. PROSSER, *supra* note 1, at 143.

4. *Id.*

to set a specific standard so that the conduct in question can be compared and evaluated. The standard must be objective rather than subjective. The standard must be clear so that the professional understands what is expected of him or her.

§ 3.1(A)(2). Intentional Tort.

Another tort theory that may be used by someone who has been harmed by the professional is the intentional tort theory. Intentional tort is defined as:

> Tort or wrong perpetrated by one who intends to do that which the law has declared wrong as contrasted with negligence in which the tort-feasor fails to exercise that degree of care in doing what is otherwise permissible.[5]

One writer uses the following example to illustrate this theory. A high school English teacher, with preconceptions about the limited educability of his or her ghetto students, decides not to teach literature, but instead distribute comic books or third-grade reading material.[6]

§ 3.1(A)(3). Misrepresentation.

A third tort theory under which a claimant may recover is misrepresentation. Misrepresentation can be either negligent or intentional. Misrepresentation is defined as:

> Any manifestation by words or other conduct by one person to another that, under the circumstances, amounts to an assertion not in accordance with the facts .... That which, if accepted, leads the mind to an apprehension of a condition other and different from that which exists .... In limited sense, an intentional

---

5. HENRY CAMPBELL BLACK, BLACK'S LAW DICTIONARY (St. Paul: West Publishing Co., 5th ed., © 1979), p. 1335.

6. *Educational Malpractice, supra* note 2, at 781.

false statement respecting a matter of fact, made by one of the parties to a contract, which is material to the contract and influential in producing it. A "misrepresentation" which justifies the rescission of a contract is a false statement of a substantive fact, or any conduct which leads to a belief of a substantive fact material to proper understanding of the material in hand, made with intent to deceive or mislead.[7]

The necessary elements of the tort cause of action for misrepresentation are as follows:

1. A false representation made by the defendant. In the ordinary case, this representation must be one of fact.
2. Knowledge or belief on the part of the defendant that the representation is false — or, what is regarded as equivalent, that he has not a sufficient basis of information to make ....
3. An intention to induce the plaintiff to act or to refrain from action in reliance upon the misrepresentation.
4. Justifiable reliance upon the representation on the part of the plaintiff, in taking action or refraining from it.
5. Damage to the plaintiff, resulting from such reliance.[8]

Prosser further notes that a representation made with an honest belief in its truth may still be negligent, due to lack of reasonable care in ascertaining the facts or in the manner of expression, or absence of the skill and competence required by a particular business or profession.[9] It has been generally held that misrepresentations of opinions are not a basis for relief. However, there are several exceptions to this rule. Regarding these exceptions, Prosser states:

7. BLACK, 5th ed., *supra* note 5, at 903.
8. PROSSER, *supra* note 1, at 685-86.
9. *Id.* at 704.

Apparently all of these may be summed up by saying that they involve situations where special circumstances make it very reasonable or probable that the plaintiff should accept the defendant's opinion and act upon it, and so justify a relaxation of the distrust which is considered admirable between bargaining opponents. Thus where the parties stand in a relation of trust and confidence ... it is held that reliance upon an opinion, whether it be as to a fact or a matter of law, is justifiable, and relief is granted.

Further than this, it has been recognized very often that the expression of an opinion may carry with it an implied assertion, not only that the speaker knows no facts which would preclude such an opinion, but that he does know facts which justify it. There is quite general agreement that such an assertion is to be implied where the defendant holds himself out or is understood as having special knowledge of the matter which is not available to the plaintiff, so that his opinion becomes in effect an assertion summarizing his knowledge. [footnotes omitted][10]

§ 3.1(B). Contract Theory.

If a professional agrees to perform a certain task for an individual and the individual is harmed as a result of same, he or she may have a cause of action against the professional under the contract theory — for breach of either an express or implied contract. Since courts have extended liability for misfeasance to virtually every type of contract where defective performance may injure the promisee, a claimant may have the option to sue in tort, contract, or both.[11]

Blackstone defined a contract as "an agreement, upon sufficient consideration, to do or not to do a particular

---

10. *Id.* at 726.
11. *Educational Malpractice, supra* note 2, at 784.

68

thing."[12] The Restatement of Contracts defines a contract as:

> A promise or set of promises for the breach of which the law gives a remedy, or the performance of which the law in some way recognizes as a duty.[13]

The Restatement defines a promise as:

> A manifestation of intention to act or refrain from acting in a specified way, so made as to justify a promisee in understanding that a commitment has been made.[14]

Many statements that might be characterized as predictions or expressions of opinion are clearly unenforceable because they are gratuitous.[15] In *Hawkins v. McGee,* when a surgeon undertook to do a skin-grafting operation on a boy he told his father that the boy would be in the hospital "not over four days; then the boy can go home and it will be just a few days when he will be able to go back to work with a perfect hand." The court stated that these words were mere "expressions of opinion or predictions." The surgeon, however, had gone on to say, "I will guarantee to make the hand a hundred percent perfect hand." The court considered evidence showing that the surgeon "had repeatedly solicited" the opportunity to perform the operation as an "experiment in skin grafting" and held that it was proper to submit the question of his liability based upon the statement to the jury.[16] The question for the jury, under the

---

12. LEN YOUNG SMITH, G. GALE ROBERSON, RICHARD A. MANN & BARRY S. ROBERTS, SMITH AND ROBERSON'S BUSINESS LAW: UNIFORM COMMERCIAL CODE (St. Paul: West Publishing Company, 5th ed., © 1982), p. 125.

13. *Id.*

14. *Id.*

15. E. ALLAN FARNSWORTH, CONTRACTS (Boston: Little, Brown & Company, 1982), p. 115.

16. *Id.,* citing Hawkins v. McGee, 84 N.H. 114, 146 A. 641 (1929).

objective theory, would be "whether the father had reason to believe that the doctor was making a commitment and amounted to a promise."[17]

Furthermore, the Uniform Commercial Code defines an agreement as:

> The bargain of the parties in fact as found in their language or by implication from other circumstances including course of dealing or usage of trade or course of performance as provided in this act. Whether an agreement has legal consequences is determined by the provisions of this act, if applicable; otherwise by the law of contracts.[18]

The requirements for the formation of an informal contract are:

1. Mutual assent.
2. Consideration.
3. Two or more parties having at least limited legal capacity.
4. The agreement must not be one declared void by statute or by rule of the common law.

In addition, for an informal contract to be wholly enforceable, i.e., not voidable at the election of a party thereto, the following additional requirements are necessary.

5. The parties must have complete legal capacity.
6. There must be reality of consent.
7. The agreement must be in the form required by law.
8. The object of the contract must be a lawful one.[19]

At the time of contracting the parties manifest their willingness either by express language or by conduct from which such willingness is implied. A contract in which the

---

17. FARNSWORTH, *supra* note 15, at 115-16.

18. SMITH, *supra* note 12, at 125.

19. LAURENCE P. SIMPSON, CONTRACTS (St. Paul: West Publishing Company, 2d ed., © 1965), p. 7.

parties manifest assent in words is called an express contract; on the other hand, if the contract is formed by conduct it is an implied contract. Both are genuine contracts and equally enforceable.[20] Even though in many instances obtaining recovery from a professional that did not give the claimant what was "bargained" for may be very hard to establish, nevertheless, the contract theories are viable theories under proper circumstances.

§ 3.1(C). Breach of Statutory Duty.

Another negligence theory that may be used to bring suit against a professional is breach of a state or federal statute governing a specific activity, such as the education of the handicapped. Recovery under this theory is much more difficult than it appears. Besides proving that there was a breach, it has to be determined that the act or statute created a private cause of action for damages. When Congress adopted the Education for All Handicapped Children Act of 1975 (EAHCA) there was an initial fear that the law would spawn numerous suits against individual educators and school districts. That fear was quickly dispelled. A number of federal cases have held that the act did not create a private cause of action for damages, but it was intended to provide an administrative procedure for insuring the proper placement and evaluation of handicapped students.[21] Thus, it is important that the intent of the statute be carefully analyzed.

§ 3.1(D). Other Theories.

Besides the traditional theories, there are several other ones which may be used under very limited circumstances.

---

20. Smith, *supra* note 12, at 126.

21. Eugene R. Butler, *Educational Malpractice Update,* 14 Capital University Law Review 609, 624-25 (1985).

For example, the claimant may petition the court for a writ of mandamus.[22] This is a writ that may be issued by a court of competent jurisdiction, commanding an inferior tribunal, board, corporation, or person to perform a purely ministerial duty imposed by law.[23] This might apply if a state statute directs school officials to hire teachers with certain qualifications, and an official hires a teacher without those qualifications. Mandamus might be used to enjoin the official from rehiring that teacher. Furthermore, the writ might be used to stop the practice of graduating students who fail to obtain the minimum level of reading competence required by a state statute for graduation.[24]

Another theory is *res ipsa loquitur.* This theory, which will be developed in a later chapter, is defined:

> The thing speaks for itself. Rebuttable presumption or inference that defendant was negligent, which arises upon proof that instrumentality causing injury was in defendant's exclusive control, and that the accident was one which ordinarily does not happen in absence of negligence. Res ipsa loquitur is rule of evidence whereby negligence of alleged wrongdoer may be inferred from mere fact that accident happened provided character of accident and circumstances attending it lead reasonably to belief that in absence of negligence it would not have occurred and that thing which caused injury is shown to have been under management and control of alleged wrongdoer.[25]

The California Supreme Court, in reversing the trial court in a case where *res ipsa loquitur* was used, commented as follows:

> Where a plaintiff receives unusual injuries while unconscious and in the course of medical treatment, all

---

22. *Educational Malpractice, supra* note 2, at 789.
23. BLACK, 5th ed., *supra* note 5, at 866.
24. *Educational Malpractice, supra* note 2, at 789-90.
25. BLACK, 5th ed., *supra* note 5, at 1173.

those defendants who had any control over his body or
the instrumentalities which might have caused the injuries may properly be called upon to meet the inference of negligence by giving an explanation of their
conduct.[26]

Promissory estoppel, breach of fiduciary duty, assumption of duty, and implied warranty are additional theories
which may be used under certain circumstances, as will be
discussed in subsequent chapters.

§ 3.2. Defenses.

To sue someone is not difficult. Many professions and
professionals have suffered from an influx of malpractice
suits. Some of them have been meritorious, resulting in
favor of the plaintiff, while others, as should be expected,
were dismissed. As it is with any other type of suit, the
professional may avail himself or herself of a number of
defenses, depending upon the prevailing circumstances.
These recognized defenses include: assumption of the risk,
contributory or comparative negligence, unavoidable accident, contractual waiver or release — consent, or possibly
common law sovereign immunity, statutory immunity, expiration of limitations period, prematurity, and *res judicata*. Which defense(s) one may assert, of course, depends
on the particular facts. If the defense is appropriate the
professional may be exonerated from the claim and the law
suit dismissed.

Dismissal of a law suit does not necessarily clear the
individual in the eyes of the public. Unfortunately, one's
reputation may be tarnished. Some defenses, such as contractual waiver or release, may dismiss the law suit

---

26. Ybarra v. Spongard, 25 Cal. 2d 486, 494, 154 P.2d 687, 691 (1944);
Thomas A. Eaton, *Res Ipsa Loquitur and Medical Malpractice in Georgia: A Reassessment,* 17 GEORGIA LAW REVIEW 33, 68 (1982).

against the professional, however, that doesn't mean that
the professional is cleared "professionally." The professional may have to account for his or her action to his
colleagues. The application of these defenses will be discussed in a subsequent chapter.

§ 3.3. Summary.

The foregoing discussion has enumerated several avenues of legal redress that might be available to those who
have been injured by professionals during their course and
scope of employment. These theories must be tested and
balanced against applicable legal defenses available to professionals. Courts have been called to rule on many of these
theories and defenses in a number of professions. Consequently, there are many cases which may be used as persuasive authority by the courts, if and when they are
called, to decide cases dealing with educational malpractice. These professional malpractice cases will serve as a
guide and as a standard to compare and to test the various
arguments advanced for and against the recognition of educational malpractice as a cause of action.

PART II
SUMMARY AND ANALYSIS OF EDU-CATIONAL MALPRACTICE CASES

Chapter 4

THE LANDMARK "PURE" EDUCATIONAL MALPRACTICE CASES: EDUCATIONAL COMPETENCY CASES

> The novel — and troublesome — question on this appeal is whether a person who claims to have been inadequately educated, while a student in a public school system, may state a cause of action in tort against the public authorities who operate and administer the system. We hold that he may not.[1]

---

1. Peter Doe v. San Francisco Unified School District, 60 Cal. App. 3d 814, 817, 131 Cal. Rptr. 854, 855 (1976).

§ 4.0. Introduction.

In previous chapters an attempt was made to summarize some of the legal principles and precedents relating to professional malpractice in general. This was necessary to set the stage in order to fully understand the various aspects of educational malpractice. The next several chapters will focus on the status of educational malpractice. Primarily cases on educational malpractice which have been decided to date will be summarized herein. Generally, locating cases that have been appealed to higher courts is not a difficult task since there are well-established research techniques to locate them; however, locating cases that have been brought in various trial courts and which have not been appealed is a long and arduous task.

In order to conduct a comprehensive study of educational malpractice, the author of this book located as many of these unreported cases as possible in order to gain a better understanding of the attitudes of the various litigants and courts toward this surfacing possible new cause of action. By contacting over 1,000 individuals and/or institutions for assistance in locating the unreported cases that were filed in trial courts throughout the United States, many unreported cases have been located. A summary of these educational malpractice decisions will provide a background for analyses of this novel and controversial cause of action.

§ 4.1. "Pure" Educational Malpractice Cases.

Review and analysis of the "pure" educational malpractice cases filed against elementary and secondary educational school systems reveal the theories upon which claims are based and methods of measuring damages. This chapter, as well as the next chapter, will focus on these cases.

78

§ 4.1(A). Peter Doe (Peter W.) v. San Francisco Unified School District.

Peter Doe v. San Francisco Unified School District[2] is a landmark case, and likely the first "pure" case alleging educational negligence (malpractice) in a public school system. (*See* Appendix 5). The *Peter Doe* case, which was later changed to *Peter W.,* was filed in California in 1972.

§ 4.1(A)(1). Complaint and Amended Complaint.

The complaint and amended complaint alleged that the plaintiff, an 18-year old, received a high school diploma. Plaintiff was subject to the compulsory school attendance laws of the State of California and was enrolled in various elementary and secondary schools operated by the defendant school district for 12 years.[3] Even though he received a high school diploma he was functionally illiterate; plaintiff had a reading ability of approximately fifth grade level at the time of his high school graduation. Furthermore, he had similar deficiencies in other basic academic skills such as writing.[4] Intelligence tests show that plaintiff had an average or slightly above average I.Q. He received average grades, attended school regularly, and had not been a serious discipline problem. It was further alleged that plaintiff's mother and natural guardian made repeated attempts to secure accurate information as to the educational progress of plaintiff. The defendant repeatedly offered assurances that plaintiff was performing at or near grade

---

2. 60 Cal. App. 3d 814, 131 Cal. Rptr. 854 (1976).

3. Peter W. Doe v. San Francisco Unified School District, et al., Complaint numbered 653-312, was filed November 20, 1972, in the Superior Court of the State of California in and for the City and County of San Francisco; the first amended complaint was filed October 31, 1973. For alleged facts see pp. 4-6.

4. *Id.* at 5.

level and that no special, remedial, or compensatory instruction was necessary for plaintiff. Yet, the plaintiff could not read a job application or fill out the required forms in case of an accident. Furthermore, the plaintiff alleged that he "is and has been an educable individual, as demonstrated particularly by the fact that since graduation from public high school with a fifth grade reading ability, plaintiff has been privately tutored by reading specialists and has made significant advancements in his reading abilities since that time."[5]

The plaintiff based his complaint on nine counts or legal theories. In the first cause of action, based on negligence, the plaintiff alleged:

> Defendant School District, its agents and employees, negligently failed to use reasonable care in the discharge of its duties to provide plaintiff with adequate instruction, guidance, counseling and/or supervision in basic academic skills and failed to exercise that degree of professional skill required of an ordinary prudent educator under the same circumstances as exemplified by, but not limited to, the following acts:
>
> 1. Negligently and carelessly failed to take notice of plaintiff's reading disabilities, despite evidence found in plaintiff's reading test scores, class performance, and parental inquiries from which defendants with exercise of reasonable care knew or should have known of the existence of plaintiff's severe reading disabilities, disabilities from which serious injury to plaintiff would follow with near certainty unless adequate and competent reading instruction was promptly provided to him;
> 2. Negligently and carelessly assigned plaintiff to classes where the books and other materials were too difficult for a student of plaintiff's reading ability to read, comprehend or benefit from;

---

5. *Id.*

3. Negligently and carelessly allowed plaintiff to pass and advance from a course or grade level although the defendants knew or with the exercise of reasonable care and skill should have known that plaintiff had not achieved the knowledge, understanding, or skills required for completion of said course or grade level and necessary for him to succeed or benefit from subsequent courses; and

4. Negligently and carelessly assigned plaintiff to class with instructors not qualified or unable to teach the particular subject, and classes not geared towards students with his reading abilities and disabilities; and

5. Negligently and carelessly permitted plaintiff to graduate from high school although he was unable to read above the eighth grade level, as required by Education Code Section 8573, effective on the date of plaintiff's graduation from high school, thereby depriving him of additional instruction in reading and other academic skills.[6]

The plaintiff further contended that as a direct and proximate result of the negligent acts and omissions the plaintiff graduated from high school with a reading ability of only the fifth grade and "suffered a loss of earning capacity by his limited ability to read and write and is unqualified for any employment other than the most demeaning, unskilled, low paid, manual labor which requires little or no ability to read or write."[7]

Besides using negligence as a legal theory for recovery, the plaintiff's complaints contained eight additional counts or legal theories. These were:[8]

---

6. *Id.* at 6-8. Editor's note — paragraphs in complaints have been renumbered.

7. *Id.* at 8.

8. *Id.* Complaint and First Amended Complaint, at 8-15; *see also* David Abel, *Can a Student Sue the Schools for Educational Malpractice?*, HARVARD EDUCATIONAL REVIEW 44:4, pp. 416-36. Copyright ©

1. Misrepresentation — defendants falsely and fraudulently represented to plaintiff's mother and natural guardian that plaintiff was performing at or near grade level in basic academic skills such as reading and writing and was not in need of any special or remedial assistance in such basic skills. However, it was alleged that the true facts were that the plaintiff was seriously and drastically below grade level in the basic skills of reading and writing and in severe need of special or remedial instruction in each of these areas to bring him up to grade or near grade level.

2. Breach of Statutory Duty — defendants violated certain statutory provisions which charged the defendants with the duty of keeping parents accurately advised as to educational progress and achievements of their children. Without such accurate information, plaintiff's mother and natural guardian was rendered unable to take any action to protect her minor son from the harm suffered.

3. Breach of Constitutional and Statutory Duty — defendants violated relevant constitutional and statutory provisions charging defendants with the duty of instructing plaintiff, and other students, in the basic skills of reading and writing.

4. Breach of Statutory Duty — despite mandatory statute requirements, the defendants failed to adopt high school graduation requirements equal to or exceeding those adopted by the State Board of Education, and despite said mandatory duty not to graduate students from high school without demonstration of proficiency in basic skills, defendant failed to discharge said duties and permitted plaintiff to graduate from the 12th grade with a reading ability of fifth grade level and little or no ability in other basic skills.

5. Breach of Statutory Duty — defendants violated certain statutory provisions which required the

school officials to inspect and ascertain the management, needs, and conditions of the public schools operated by said School District and to revise and adjust the curriculum and operation of said schools where necessary to promote the education of the pupils enrolled therein.

6. Breach of Statutory Duty — defendants violated certain applicable statutory provisions requiring school districts to design the course of instruction offered in the public schools to meet the needs of the pupils for which the course of study was prescribed.

7. Breach of Statutory Duty — the defendants failed to properly supervise, control, and regulate the public schools as specified by statute, including promulgating a minimum course of instruction to meet the needs of pupils enrolled in the public schools and failure to promulgate a minimum standard of proficiency for graduation from the 12th grade to the end that every student who graduates from any state-supported educational institution should have sufficient marketable skills for legitimate remunerative employment.

8. Constitutional Duty — as a direct and proximate result of the acts and omissions of defendants, plaintiff has been denied his fundamental right to an education, guaranteed by the United States Constitution, and the laws and Constitution of the State of California.

The plaintiff demanded $500,000 for general damages, $500,000 for punitive damages, and for such sum as proof may be had for the cost of providing plaintiff with tutoring by a reading specialist.

§ 4.1(A)(2). Answer.

The defendants filed general demurrers to all seven counts (in the original complaint there were nine counts).

§ 4.1(A)(3). Decision by the Trial Court.

The trial court sustained the defendant's demurrers with 20 days leave to amend. When plaintiff failed to amend within that period, the court entered a judgment dismissing his action.

§ 4.1(A)(4). Court of Appeals.

The plaintiff then appealed to the Court of Appeals. On appeal the court opined:

> The novel — and troublesome — question on this appeal is whether a person who claims to have been inadequately educated, while a student in a public school system, may state a cause of action in tort against the public authorities who operate and administer the system. We hold that he may not.[9]

The court noted that according to the familiar California formula there are three requisites to a cause of action for negligence. These are "(1) facts showing a duty of care in the defendant, (2) negligence constituting a breach of duty, and (3) injury to the plaintiff as a proximate result."[10] The court further observed that there is no debate with respect to the elements of negligence, proximate cause, and injury; the focus is exclusively upon the issue of "whether it alleges facts sufficient to show that defendant owed him a 'duty of care'."[11]

In his complaint, plaintiff argued that the defendant's duty of care was based on three theories: (1) the assumption of the function of instruction of students imposes the duty to exercise reasonable care in its discharge; (2) there is a special relationship between students and teachers which supports the teachers' duty to exercise reasonable

---

9. 60 Cal. App. 3d 814, 817, 131 Cal. Rptr. 854, 855 (1976).
10. 60 Cal. App. 3d 814, 820, 131 Cal. Rptr. 854, 857 (1976).
11. *Id.*

care; and (3) the duty of teachers to exercise reasonable care in instruction and supervision of students is recognized in California. The court acknowledged that in common parlance every educator owes a duty of care to every student. However, the appellate court stated that this did not satisfy the technical requirements of "duty of care" in tort litigation.[12] The court emphasized that applications of "duty of care" to novel situations to a great extent turn upon questions of public policy, including such considerations as:

> The social utility of the activity out of which the injury arises, compared with the risks involved in its conduct; the kind of person with whom the actor is dealing; the workability of a rule of care, especially in terms of the parties' relative ability to adopt practical means of preventing injury; the relative ability of the parties to bear the financial burden of injury and the availability of means by which the loss may be shifted or spread; the body of statutes and judicial precedents which color the parties' relationship; the prophylactic effect of a rule of liability; in the case of a public agency defendant, the extent of its powers, the rule imposed upon it by law and the limitations imposed upon it by budget.[13]

In support of its refusal to allow a cause of action for educational malfeasance, the court observed:

> On occasions when the Supreme Court has opened or sanctioned new areas of tort liability, it has noted that the wrongs and injuries involved were both comprehensible and accessible within the existing judicial framework [citations omitted]. This is simply not true of wrongful conduct and injuries allegedly involved in

---

12. Edward W. Remsburg, *Liability for Wrongful Identification, Evaluation for Placement — Is There Malpractice?* COUNCIL OF SCHOOL ATTORNEYS (National School Boards Association: 1980).
13. 60 Cal. App. 3d 814, 827, 131 Cal. Rptr. 854, 862 (1976).

educational malfeasance. *Unlike the activity of the highway or the marketplace, classroom methodology affords no readily acceptable standards of care, or cause, or injury. The science of pedagogy itself is frought with different and conflicting theories of how or what a child should be taught, and any layman might — and commonly does — have his own emphatic views on the subject.* The "injury claimed here is plaintiff's inability to read and write. Substantial professional authority attests that the achievement of literacy in the schools, or its failure, are influenced by a host of factors which affect the pupil subjectively, from outside the formal teaching process, and beyond the control of its ministers. They may be physical, neurological, cultural, environmental; they may be present but not perceived, recognized but not identified [emphasis added].[14]

The court continued its rationale for denying the plaintiff recovery by explaining:

We find in this situation no conceivable "workability of a rule of care" against which the defendants' alleged conduct may be measured [citations omitted], no reasonable "degree of certainty that ... plaintiff suffered injury" within the meaning of the law of negligence ... and no such perceptible "connection between the defendant's conduct and the injury suffered," as alleged, which would establish a causal link between them within the same meaning [citations omitted].

These recognized policy considerations alone negate an actionable "duty of care" in persons and agencies who administer the academic phases of the public educational process. Others, which are even more important in practical terms, command the same result. *Few of our institutions, if any, have aroused the controversies, or incurred the public dissatisfaction, which have attended the operation of the public schools during the last few decades. Rightly or wrongly, but widely, they are charged with outright failure in the achievement*

---

14. 60 Cal. App. 3d 814, 824, 131 Cal. Rptr. 854, 860-61 (1976).

of their educational objectives; according to some critics, they bear responsibility for many of the social and moral problems of our society at large. Their public plight in these respects is attested on the daily media, in bitter governing board elections, in wholesale rejections of school bond proposals, and in survey upon survey. To hold them to an actionable "duty of care," in the discharge of their academic functions, would expose them to the tort claims — real or imagined — of disaffected students and parents in countless numbers. They are already beset by social and financial problems which have gone to major litigation, but for which no permanent solution has yet appeared [citation omitted]. The ultimate consequences, in terms of public time and money, would burden them — and society — beyond calculation [emphasis added].[15]

In concluding that the second cause of action was also not actionable, the court reasoned as follows:

For the public policy reasons heretofore stated with respect to plaintiff's first count we hold that this one states no cause of action for *negligence* in the form of the "misrepresentation" alleged. The possibility of its setting a cause of action for *intentional* misrepresentation, to which it expressly refers to the alternative, is assisted by judicial limitations placed upon the scope of the governmental immunity which is granted, as to liability for "misrepresentation" [citations omitted].

The second count nevertheless does not state a cause of action, for intentional misrepresentation, because it alleges no facts showing the requisite elements of *reliance* upon the "misrepresentation" it asserts [citations omitted]. Plaintiff elected to stand upon it without exercising his leave to amend. The trial court's action, in sustaining defendant's general demurrer to it, is therefore to be regarded as conclusive for our purposes.[16]

The court also found against the plaintiff on the remaining counts. The court, after concluding that the theory of

---

15. 60 Cal. App. 3d 814, 825, 131 Cal. Rptr. 854, 861 (1976).
16. 60 Cal. App. 3d 814, 827, 131 Cal. Rptr. 854, 862-63 (1976).

each count was premised on the fact that it stated a cause of action for breach of a "mandatory duty" under the statute, maintained:

> If it be assumed that each of these counts effectively pleads the district's failure to have exercised "reasonable diligence to discharge the duty" respectively alleged, as mentioned in the statute ..., none states a cause of action. This is because the statute imposes liability for failure to discharge only such "mandatory duty" and is "imposed by an enactment that is designed to protect against the risk of a particular kind of injury" .... The various "enactments" cited in these counts ... are not so "designed." We have already seen that the failure of educational achievement may not be characterized as an "injury" within the meaning of the tort law. It further appears that the several "enactments" have been conceived as provisions directed to the attainment of optimum educational results, but not as safeguards against "injury" of any kind: i.e., as administrative but not protective. Their violation accordingly imposes no liability under Government Code section 815.6.[17]

§ 4.1(B). Donohue v. Copiague Union Free School District.

In 1977, approximately one year after the *Peter W.* case was finalized, a similar case was filed in New York. This well-publicized case was *Donohue v. Copiague Union Free School District.*[18] (*See* Appendix 6).

§ 4.1(B)(1). Complaint.

The plaintiff was a student at a high school operated by the defendant. Even though he received failing grades in several subjects and lacked basic reading and writing

---

17. 60 Cal. App. 3d 814, 826, 131 Cal. Rptr. 854, 862 (1976).
18. 95 Misc. 2d 1, 408 N.Y.S.2d 585 (1977).

skills, he was allowed to graduate. He then found it necessary to seek tutoring in order to acquire those basic skills which he had not obtained in high school. The plaintiff's complaint against the defendant for $5,000,000.00 in damages alleged deficiencies in his knowledge. The plaintiff's complaint contained two causes of action. The first cause of action alleged that the defendant was under an obligation and duty to:

> Teach the several and varied subjects to the plaintiff; ascertain his learning capacity and ability; and correctly and properly test him for such capacity in order to evaluate his ability to comprehend the subject matters of the various courses and have sufficient understanding and comprehension of subject matters in said courses as to be able to achieve sufficient passing grades in said subject matters, and therefore, qualify for a Certificate of Graduation.[19]

The complaint further averred that since the plaintiff, following graduation, was unable to read and write simple basic English and did not have an understanding of the other subjects covered in his high school courses, the defendant, by and through its agents, servants, and/or employees, failed to perform its duty to him in that defendant and defendant's agents:

> Gave to the plaintiff passing grades and/or minimal or failing grades in various subjects; failed to evaluate the plaintiff's mental ability and capacity to comprehend the subjects being taught to him at said school; failed to take proper means and precautions that they reasonably should have taken under the circumstances; failed to interview, discuss, evaluate and/or psychologically test the plaintiff in order to ascertain his ability to comprehend and understand such subject

---

19. Complaint, Donohue v. Copiague Union Free School District, was filed on March 22, 1977, in the Supreme Court of the State of New York — Suffolk County — Index number 77-1128; quote from p. 3.

matter; failed to provide adequate school facilities,
teachers, administrators, psychologists, and other personnel trained to take the necessary steps in testing
and evaluation processes insofar as the plaintiff is concerned in order to ascertain the learning capacity, intelligence and intellectual absorption on the part of
the plaintiff; failed to hire proper personnel, experienced in the handling of such matters; failed to teach
the plaintiff in such a manner so that he could reasonably understand what was necessary under the circumstances so that he could cope with the various subjects which they tried to make the plaintiff understand; failed to properly supervise the plaintiff; failed
to advise his parents of the difficulty and necessity to
call in psychiatric help; that the processes practiced
were defective and not commensurate with a student
attending a high school within the county of Suffolk;
failed to adopt the accepted professional standards and
methods to evaluate and cope with plaintiff's problems, which constituted educational malpractice.[20]

He further alleged that he was unaware of his lack of
such learning capacity or ability when the defendant issued a Certificate of Graduation to him. He first became
aware of the acts and conduct of the defendant after graduation when the grades achieved by him were reviewed on
his behalf. As a result of this he has been unable to cope
with his day-to-day affairs.[21]

For his second cause of action the plaintiff stated that he
was the third-party beneficiary of a duty imposed upon the
defendant by section I of article XI of the New York State
Constitution, which provides: "The legislature shall provide for the maintenance and support of a system of free
common schools, wherein all the children of this state may

20. *Id.* at 4.
21. *Id.*

be educated."[22] Furthermore, the plaintiff alleged that pursuant to this duty, the defendant undertook to operate a public school, but that it failed to educate him.

§ 4.1(B)(2). Answer.

The defendant moved to dismiss the complaint, *inter alia,* for failure to state a cause of action.

§ 4.1(B)(3). Decision by the New York State Supreme Court, Special Term.

The New York State Supreme Court granted the motion to dismiss. The court held:

> The first cause of action sounds in negligence and malpractice; the second in breach of a statutory duty. Taking the second cause of action first, the facts alleged fail to state a claim upon which relief can be granted. [Citations omitted]. Turning to the first cause of action, a reading of the complaint reveals that it is parallel if not identical to the complaint in *Peter W. v. San Francisco School District* [citations omitted]. While different statutes are concededly involved the Court finds the reasoning of the California intermediate appellate court persuasive. Concededly no statutory liability is here involved [citations omitted]; based upon the cogent reasoning in the cited case, the court finds no common-law duty in New York upon which the complaint at bar, alleging both negligence and malpractice, can be bottomed. Defendant's motion to dismiss for failure to state facts sufficient to constitute a cause of action is granted.[23]

The court then went on to state:

> The court notes that this is apparently a case of first impression in New York, and that the commencement

---

22. Donohue v. Copiague Union Free School District, 64 A.D.2d 29, 32, 407 N.Y.S.2d 874, 877 (1978).
23. 95 Misc. 2d 1, 2-3, 408 N.Y.S.2d 584, 585 (1977).

91

of this action has received substantial attention both in education circles and in the news media. This factor, combined with the recent adoption of 8 N.Y.C.R.R. Section 3.45 by the Board of Regents (amended July 2, 1976 effective June 1, 1979), and the establishment by the Commissioner of basic competency tests pursuant to such provision, *justifies the Court's suggesting that the grave policy questions posed by the issue at bar should be passed upon by Appellate Courts* [emphasis added].[24]

§ 4.1(B)(4). Appeal to Supreme Court, Appellate Division.

The case then was appealed to the Supreme Court, Appellate Division. (*See* Appendix 7). The Appellate Division, in affirming the Supreme Court's decision, held: (1) educators do not owe a legal duty of care to their students upon which to base a negligence action for "educational malpractice;" (2) the educators' failure to evaluate an "underachiever" student as set forth in a statute did not give rise to action sounding in tort, and (3) because of a multitude of factors affecting the learning process it would be impossible to prove that acts or omissions of educators were proximate causes of student illiteracy.[25]

In justification of its holding, the court commented:

Upon our own examination and analysis of the relevant factors discussed above, which are involved in determining whether to judicially recognize the existence of a legal duty of care running from educators to students, we, like the court in *Peter W.,* hold that no such duty exists. Other jurisdictions have adopted this reasoning as well (see *Beaman v. Des Moines Area Community College,* 5th Judicial District of Iowa, March 23, 1977, Law No. CL 15 8532, *Holliday J.;*

---

24. 95 Misc. 2d 1, 3, 408 N.Y.S.2d 584, 585 (1977).
25. *Id.*

Garrett v. School Board of Broward County, Circuit Court, 17th Judicial Cir., Broward County, Florida, December 5, 1977, Case No. 77-8703). This determination does not mean that educators are not ethically and legally responsible for providing a meaningful public education for the youth of our State. Quite the contrary, all teachers and other officials of our schools bear an important public trust and may be held to answer for the failure to faithfully perform their duties. It does mean, however, that they may not be sued for damages by an individual student for an alleged failure to reach certain educational objectives.

The courts are an inappropriate forum to test the efficacy of educational programs and pedagogical methods. That judicial interference would be the inevitable result of the recognition of a legal duty of care is clear from the fact that in presenting their case, plaintiffs would, of necessity, call upon jurors to decide whether they should have been taught one subject instead of another, or whether one teaching method was more appropriate than another, or whether certain tests should have been administered or tests results interpreted in one way rather than another, and so on, ad infinitum. It simply is not within the judicial function to evaluate conflicting theories of how best to educate. Even if it were possible to determine with exactitude the pedagogical course to follow with respect to particular individuals, yet another problem would arise. Public education involves an inherent stress between taking action to satisfy the educational needs of the individual student and the needs of the student body as a whole. It is not for the courts to determine how best to utilize scarce educational resources to achieve these sometimes conflicting objectives. Simply stated, the recognition of a cause of action sounding in negligence to recover for "educational malpractice" would impermissibly require the courts to oversee the administration of the State's public school system.

On a number of occasions, the Court of Appeals has explicitly stated that educational policies are solely the province of the duly constituted educational authorities in this State. Thus, in *Matter of Vetere v. Allen,* 15 N.Y.2d 259, 267, 258 N.Y.S.2d 77, 80, 206 N.E.2d 174, 176, the Court of Appeals upheld the power of the Commissioner of Education to direct local school boards to take steps to eliminate racial imbalance, noting:

"Disagreement with the sociological, psychological and educational assumptions relied on by the Commissioner cannot be evaluated by this court. Such arguments can only be heard in the Legislature which has endowed the Commissioner with an all but absolute power, or by the Board of Regents, who are elected by the Legislature and make public policy in the field of education" (emphasis added).[26]

Concerning the plaintiff's second cause of action, the court noted:

It is our opinion that these enactments require the creation of a system of free common schools. Their purpose is to confer the benefits of a free education upon what would otherwise be an uneducated public. They were not intended to protect against the "injury" of ignorance for every individual is born lacking knowledge, education and experience. For this reason the failure of educational achievement cannot be characterized as "injury" within the meaning of the tort law.[27]

The court further added:

Finally, *the plaintiff's complaint must be dismissed because of the practical impossibility of demonstrating that a breach of the alleged common law and statutory duties was the proximate cause of his failure to learn. The failure to learn does not bespeak a failure to teach.* It is not alleged that the plaintiff's classmates, who were exposed to the identical classroom instruction, also failed to learn. From this it may reasonably be

---

26. 64 A.D.2d 29, 35-36, 407 N.Y.S.2d 874, 878-79 (1978).
27. 64 A.D.2d 29, 37, 407 N.Y.S.2d 874, 880 (1978).

inferred that the plaintiff's illiteracy resulted from other causes. A school system cannot compel a particular student to study or to be interested in education. Here, the plaintiff is not totally illiterate and his academic record indicates satisfactory achievement in several subjects. In addition to innate intelligence, the extent to which a child learns is influenced by a host of social, emotional, economic and other factors which are not subject to control by a system of public education. In this context, it is virtually impossible to calculate to what extent if any, the defendant's acts or omissions proximately caused the plaintiff's inability to read at his appropriate grade level. [Emphasis added].

Accordingly, we hold that the public policy of this State recognizes no cause of action for educational malpractice. We note that unlike the case of *Peter W.*, *supra*, the complaint here contains no allegation of a cause of action for intentional and fraudulent misrepresentation. We, therefore, do not pass upon the viability of any such cause of action.[28]

There was a dissenting opinion by one of the justices, who argued that the complaint did state a valid cause of action. Justice Suozzi contended:

Initially, it must be emphasized that the policy considerations enunciated in *Peter W.*, *supra* do not mandate a dismissal of the complaint. *Whether the failure of the plaintiff to achieve a basic level of literacy was caused by the negligence of the school system, as the plaintiff alleges, or was the product of forces outside the teaching process, is really a question of proof to be resolved at a trial. The fear of a flood of litigation, perhaps much of it without merit, and the possible difficulty in framing an appropriate measure of damages, are similarly unpersuasive grounds for dismissing the instant cause of action.* Fear of excessive litigation caused by the creation of a new zone of liability was effectively refuted by the abolition of sovereign immunity many years ago, and numerous environ-

---

28. 64 A.D.2d 29, 39, 407 N.Y.S.2d 874, 881 (1978).

mental actions fill our courts where damages are difficult to assess. Under the circumstances, there is no
reason to differentiate between educational malpractice on the one hand, and other forms of negligence and
malpractice litigation which currently congest out [*sic*]
courts.

    ....

    In my view, *the negligence alleged in the case at bar
is not unlike that of a doctor who, although confronted
with a patient with a cancerous condition, fails to pursue medically accepted procedures to (1) diagnose the
specific condition and (2) treat the condition, and instead allows the patient to suffer the inevitable consequences of the disease. Such medical malpractice
would never be tolerated. At the very least, a complaint alleging same would not be dismissed upon motion.* In the case at bar, the plaintiff displayed, through
his failing grades, a serious condition with respect to
his ability to learn. Although mindful of this learning
disability, the school authorities made no attempt as
they were required to do, by appropriate and educationally accepted testing procedures, to diagnose the
nature and extent of his learning problem and thereafter to take or recommend remedial measures to deal
with this problem. Instead, the plaintiff was just
pushed through the educational system without any
attempt made to help him. Under these circumstances,
the cause of action at bar is no different from the analogous cause of action for medical malpractice and, like
the latter, is sufficient to withstand a motion to dismiss[29] [emphasis added].

§ 4.1(B)(5). Appeal to the Court of Appeals of New York.

The case was then appealed to the Court of Appeals of
New York.[30] (*See* Appendix 8). In 1979, the Court of Ap-

---

29. 64 A.D.2d 29, 41-2, 407 N.Y.S.2d 874, 883 (1978).
30. 47 N.Y. 2d 440, 418, N.Y.S.2d 375 (1979). In New York the New
York Court of Appeals is a higher court than the New York Supreme
Court.

peals affirmed the decision by the Supreme Court, Appellate Division. The Court of Appeals held that: (1) although the Constitution places the obligation of maintaining and supporting a system of public schools on the legislature, such general directive was not intended to impose a duty flowing directly from a local school district to individual pupils to insure that each pupil receives the minimum level of education, the breach of which duty will entitle the student to compensatory damages, (2) the cause of action against the school district seeking monetary damages for educational malpractice is not recognizable in the courts as a matter of public policy.[31]

After first disposing of the second cause of action, the court observed:

> Appellant's first action bears closer scrutiny. It may very well be that even within the strictures of a traditional negligence or malpractice action, a complaint sounding in "educational malpractice" may not be formally pleaded. Thus, *the imagination need not be overly taxed to envision allegations of a legal duty of care flowing from educators, if viewed as professionals, to their students. If doctors, lawyers, architects, engineers and other professionals are charged with a duty owing to the public whom they serve, it could be said that nothing in the law precludes similar treatment of professional educators. Nor would creation of a standard with which to judge an educator's performance of that duty necessarily pose an insurmountable obstacle* [citations omitted]. *As for proximate causation, while this element might indeed be difficult, if not impossible, to prove in view of the many collateral factors involved in the learning process, it perhaps assumes too much to conclude that it could never be established.* This would leave only the element of injury and who can in good faith deny that a student who upon graduation from high school cannot comprehend sim-

---

31. 47 N.Y.2d 440, 418 N.Y.S.2d 375-76 (1979).

ple English — a deficiency alleged attributable to the
negligence of his educators — has not in some fashion
been "injured" [emphasis added].

   ... *The fact that a complaint alleging "educational
malpractice" might on the pleadings state a cause of
action within traditional notions of tort law does not,
however, require that it be sustained. The heart of the
matter is whether, assuming that such a cause may be
stated, the courts should, as a matter of public policy,
entertain such claims. We believe they should not* (emphasis added).[32]

The court continued:

To entertain a cause of action for "educational malpractice" would require the courts not merely to make
judgments as to the validity of broad educational policies — a course we have unalteringly eschewed in the
past — but, more importantly, to sit in review of the
day-to-day implementation of these policies. *Recognition in the courts of this cause of action would constitute blatant interference with the responsibility for
the administration of the public school system lodged
by Constitution and statute in administrative agencies*
[citations omitted]. *Of course, "[t]his is not to say that
there may never be gross violations of defined public
policy which the courts would be obliged to recognize
and correct"* [citations omitted].

   Finally, not to be overlooked in today's holding is *the
right of students presently enrolled in public schools,
and their parents, to take advantage of the administrative process provided by statute to enlist the aid of
the Commissioner of Education in insuring that such
students receive a proper education.* The Education
Law (310, subd. 7) permits any person aggrieved by an
"official act or decision of any officer, school authorities, or meetings concerning any other matter under
this chapter, or any other act pertaining to common

---

32. 47 N.Y.2d 440, 443, 418 N.Y.S.2d 375-76 (1979).

schools" to seek review of such act or decision by the commissioner [emphasis added].[33]

Judge Wachtler wrote a separate short concluding opinion in which he stated:

> I agree that complaints of "educational malpractice" are for school administrative agencies, rather than the courts, to resolve.
> *There is, however, another even more fundamental objection to entertaining plaintiff's cause of action alleging educational malpractice. It is a basic principle that the law does not provide a remedy for every injury* [citations omitted]. As the majority notes, the decision of whether a new cause of action should be recognized at law is largely a question of policy. Critical to such a determination is whether the cause of action sought to be pleaded would be reasonably manageable within our legal system. The practical problems raised by a cause of action sounding in educational malpractice are so formidable that I would conclude that such a legal theory should not be cognizable in our courts. These problems, clearly articulated at the Appellate Division, include the practical impossibility of proving that the alleged malpractice of the teacher proximately caused the learning deficiency of the plaintiff student. Factors such as the student's attitude, motivation, temperament, past experience and home environment may all play an essential and immeasurable role in learning. Indeed, as the majority observes, proximate cause might be difficult, if not impossible, to prove [emphasis added].[34]

§ 4.2. Summary.

Because of the impact that the *Peter Doe* and the *Donohue* cases had on other courts called upon to decide similar cases, the progress of these cases from the filing of the

---

33. 47 N.Y.2d 440, 445, 418 N.Y.S.2d 375, 378 (1979).
34. 47 N.Y.2d 440, 445-46, 418 N.Y.S.2d 375, 378-79 (1979).

complaints to their final determination by the appellate courts, has been detailed. As will become obvious in subsequent chapters, other courts relied heavily on these cases when deciding claims brought on the theory of educational malpractice. In later chapters the arguments advanced by the two courts will be analyzed — compared and contrasted — with established principles of law.

Chapter 5

ADDITIONAL "PURE" MALPRACTICE CASES: REPORTED AND UNREPORTED

> I do not agree with my colleagues that adequate internal administrative procedures designed for the achievement of educational goals are available within the educational system. In my view none of the available procedures adequately deal with incompetent teaching or provide adequate relief to an injured student. A cause of action for educational malpractice meets these social and individual needs.[1]

---

1. Statement made by Justice Davidson of the Maryland Court of Appeals, who concurred in part and dissented in part, in Hunter v. Board of Education, 439 A.2d 582, 589 (1982).

§ 5.0. Introduction.

The *Peter W.* and the *Donohue* cases have had significant impact in shaping the law of educational malpractice in the United States. Courts in various jurisdictions have cited them as persuasive authority when deciding similar cases. In addition to these cases, however, there are a number of other cases which may be classified as "pure" educational malpractice that have been filed in a number of jurisdictions. In these cases claimants have presented facts allegedly constituting educational malpractice. Courts have handled educational malpractice cases in several ways. Some have adopted the holdings and rationale of other cases while other courts have either expanded on previous arguments or used new ones to justify their positions.

In subsequent chapters cases will be analyzed to assess the role, if any, that the tort of negligence can play in providing redress to a student who suffers non-physical harm as a result of receiving, in whole or in part, an inadequate, incompetent, and negligent education.[2]

§ 5.1. Additional "Pure" Educational Malpractice Cases in Public Schools.

§ 5.1(A). Hunter v. Board of Education.

The case of *Hunter v. Board of Education*[3] was filed in 1978 in a Maryland Circuit Court. The plaintiff, by and through his parents, filed a six count declaration seeking recovery for "educational malpractice" from the Board of Education of Montgomery County and three of its employees: the principal of plaintiff's grammar school, the

---

2. W.F. Foster, *Educational Malpractice: A Tort for the Untaught?*, University of British Columbia Law Review 161 (1985).
3. 47 Md. App. 709, 425 A.2d 681 (1981).

person, who according to the declaration, "engaged in diagnostic testing," and, his sixth grade teacher. In general, Count I of the complaint alleged "educational malpractice" in the traditional negligence form. Count II realleged the allegations of Count I and, in addition, asserted that the acts were willful and deliberate. Count III alleged that the Board was negligent in evaluating its personnel and programs. Count IV was the same as Count I except that it also alleged a statutory duty. Count V alleged a breach of implied contract. These first five counts constituted the suit of the minor plaintiff and the defendants while Count VI, brought by his parents, incorporated by reference all the allegations of the prior counts.[4] The complaint alleged that the defendants negligently evaluated his learning abilities and caused him to repeat first-grade materials while placing him in the second grade. Specifically, the plaintiff in the complaint in Count I stated:

1. That the individual defendants and others presently unknown to the plaintiffs, but whose names will be supplied if determined by discovery, owed a duty to the minor plaintiff to comport themselves within the standards of their profession, and to exercise that degree of care and skill ordinarily exercised by those similarly situated in the profession;

2. That notwithstanding the above, the defendants breached the duty;

3. That the breach consisted of, but is not limited to, the following acts or omissions:

    (a) requiring the minor plaintiff, after physical placement in the second grade, to repeat completely the first grade materials although he had successfully and satisfactorily completed those first grade materials during his first year in school;

4. 47 Md. App. 709, 710-11, 425 A.2d 681, 682 (1981).

103

(b) subsequently placing him physically in a grade ahead of the material he was actually studying;

(c) without reasonable grounds, furnishing false reports and information to the plaintiffs so that they were unable to uncover or diagnose accurately the nature or extent of the minor plaintiff's learning deficiencies;

(d) without reasonable grounds, preparing inaccurate materials for inclusion in the official files and record of the minor plaintiff so that the plaintiffs and others needing accurate information were deprived of access thereto;

(e) testing the minor plaintiff so incompletely and inadequately so as to result in the total failure of evaluation of the problems in any meaningful or constructive manner;

(f) insulting and demeaning the minor plaintiff in private and public;

(g) changing, altering, removing and falsifying records so as to cover up the result of the above acts.

4. The acts of the defendants were the direct and proximate cause of great injury to the minor child;

5. That the injuries include, but are not limited to:

(a) great embarrassment to the minor plaintiff before his peers;

(b) substantial learning deficiencies;

(c) internal psychological scars which today hinder his ability to learn or to be tested on what he has learned;

(d) severe loss of self-confidence;

(e) depletion of ego strength.[5]

In Count III the plaintiff averred:

---

5. First Amended Declaration, pp. 2-4, Hunter v. Board of Education of Montgomery County, in the Circuit Court for Montgomery Cty., Md. Law No. 48108 (1978).

1. That the defendant, independently of the specific acts previously enumerated, owed a duty to the plaintiffs to establish appropriate procedures to evaluate its programs and personnel, and further to secure to the minor plaintiff an adequate education;
2. That the defendant has failed in its undertaking, and instead has approved, condoned, and/or failed properly to investigate fully the acts of its personnel, including, but not limited to, the individual defendants;
3. That defendant negligently retained personnel with the knowledge of their deficiencies;
4. Had the defendant fulfilled its duty, the injuries described would have been averted.[6]

In Count IV, the plaintiff alleged that the statutory framework required all defendants to provide the minor plaintiff with quality education and equal educational opportunity. He further alleged that certain statutes establish a duty on the defendants and because of the breach of said duty by the defendants the plaintiff was injured as described hereinbefore.[7]

In Count V, the plaintiff, among other things, stated:

1. That there exists an implied contract between the plaintiffs, for the benefit of the minor plaintiff, and the defendants;
2. That the defendants have breached the contract;
3. That as a result the minor plaintiff has been proximately injured.[8]

In the sixth Count, plaintiffs alleged, *inter alia,* as follows:

1. That as a result of the acts of the defendants, and the injuries to the minor plaintiff whose care and treatment is the obligation of plaintiffs, the plain-

---

6. *Id.* at 5.
7. *Id.* at 5-6.
8. *Id.* at 6-7.

tiffs have incurred substantial medical, psychological care, educational testing, and tutoring expenses for the treatment and care of the minor plaintiff during his minority, together with transportation, legal, and other expenses, and will continue to do so in the future;

2. That they have further been deprived of the services of their son.[9]

The Circuit Court stated that public policy barred the action and sustained a demurrer without leave to amend.[10] The plaintiffs appealed to the Court of Special Appeals of Maryland. In 1981, the Court of Special Appeals affirmed the decision of the Circuit Court, stating that public policy bars an action for educational malpractice.[11] The court opined that to decide this case it "must travel a route that is unmapped in this State" since neither of the two appellate tribunals has heretofore faced a suit founded in educational malpractice.[12] The court turned to other jurisdictions that have had occasion to discuss the subject. The Court then reviewed the *Peter W.* case, the *Smith v. Alamedo County Social Services Agency*[13] case, the *Donohue* case, and the *Hoffman* case. The court, in declining to recognize the neoteric tort of educational malpractice, held:

To adopt the position that appellants urge upon us would place all teachers under judicial scrutiny. Courts would sit in judgment not only of educational policies and matters entrusted by the General Assembly to the Department of Education [citations omitted], and to the local school boards [citations omitted], but also of day-to-day implementation of those policies.

It is conceivable that, if allowed, suits for educational malpractice might arise every time a child

9. *Id.* at 7.
10. 47 Md. App. 709, 425 A.2d 681 (1981).
11. *Id.*
12. *Id.* at 682.
13. 90 Cal. App. 3d 929, 153 Cal. Rptr. 712 (1979).

106

failed a grade, subject, or test, with the result that teachers could possibly spend more time in lawyers' offices and courtrooms than in classrooms. That happening could give rise to claims of educational malpractice predicated on the teacher's failure to devote sufficient time to teaching. The opposite side of the matter is that if, to avoid suits arising from a student's failing a grade, subject, or test, the teacher "passed" the child, the teacher would likely find himself or herself defending a malpractice suit because the child was promoted when promotion was not warranted.

We are aware that a serious social problem exists when, as here, a student is "promoted" through the school system, from grade to grade, and yet, he or she has not been taught to read. We are equally cognizant of criticisms of the teaching profession. The situation is even more serious when one recalls to mind the words of Thomas Jefferson, that a nation cannot be ignorant and free, in a state of civilization, at one and the same time. [Footnotes omitted.]

The seriousness of a matter, however, does not mean that a solution may be found, or redress obtained, through the use of the courts. Courts cannot solve every societal problem. The courts, on constitutional grounds, can decide that all schools must afford equal protections of the laws, but courts may not decide the curriculum, nor the degree of proficiency needed to advance from grade to grade through the school system. The field of education is simply too fraught with unanswered questions for the courts to constitute themselves as a proper forum for resolution of those questions.[14]

The case was appealed to the Maryland Court of Appeals. In January 1982, the Maryland Court of Appeals, in a 6 to 1 decision, rejected the plaintiff's claim of educational malpractice.[15] The court commented that this case primarily presented the troubling but nevertheless important ques-

---

14. 47 Md. App. 709, 715-16, 425 A.2d 681, 684-85 (1981).
15. Hunter v. Board of Education, 439 A.2d 582 (1981).

tion, which had not been previously addressed by the court, of whether an action can be successfully asserted against a school board and various individual employees for improperly evaluating, placing, or *teaching* a student. The court agreed with the lower court's determination that an educational negligence action could not be maintained, and affirmed that portion of the judgment, but reversed with respect to petitioners' allegations concerning the commission of an intentional tort by certain individual employees of the board. The court stated:

> We find ourselves in substantial agreement with the reasoning employed by the courts in *Peter W.* and *Donohue,* for an award of money damages, in our view, represents a singularly inappropriate remedy for asserted errors in the educational process. The misgivings expressed in these cases concerning the establishment of legal cause and the inherent immeasurability of damages that is involved in such educational negligence actions against the school systems are indeed well founded. Moreover, to allow petitioners' asserted negligence claims to proceed would in effect position the courts of this state as overseers of both the day-to-day operation of our educational process as well as the formulation of its governing policies. This responsibility we are loathe to impose on our courts. Such matters have been properly entrusted by the General Assembly to the State Department of Education and the local school boards who are invested with authority over them ....
>
> Our conclusion on this point, however, does not imply that parents who feel aggrieved by an action of public educators affecting their child are without recourse. For example: (1) the General Assembly has provided a comprehensive scheme for reviewing a placement decision of a handicapped child including an appeal to the circuit court ...; (2) both parents and child have the right to review educational records and, if appropriate, insist that the documents be amended ...; (3) section 4-205(c)(3) of the Education Article com-

mands that each county superintendent, "without charge to the parties concerned ... shall decide all controversies that involve: (i) [t]he rules and regulations of the county board; and (ii) [t]he proper administration of the county public system" with the decision being appealable to the county board and then to the state board of education, § 4-205(c)(4), and further, if appropriate, to the courts through the administrative procedure act ...; and (4) county boards of education are required to establish "at least one" citizen committee "to advise the board and to facilitate its activities and programs in the public schools," and similar committees may be established for an individual school [citations omitted]. Thus, it is preferable, in the legislative's view, to settle disputes concerning classification and placement of students and the like by resort to these and similar informal measures than through the *post hoc* remedy of a civil action. With this we have no quarrel, for, as aptly noted by the Alaska Supreme Court in this regard, "[p]rompt administrative and judicial review may correct erroneous action in time so that any educational shortcomings suffered by a student may be corrected. Money damages, on the other hand, are a poor, and only tenuously related, substitute for a proper education" ....

Count II represents the parents' somewhat amorphous claim that the respondents intentionally and maliciously acted to injure their child. Research reveals that none of the prior cases discussing educational malpractice have squarely confronted the question of whether public educators may be held responsible for their intentional torts arising in the educational context. In declining to entertain the educational negligence and breach to contract actions, we in no way intend to shield individual educators from liability for their intentional torts. It is our view that where an individual engaged in the educational process is shown to have willfully and maliciously injured a child entrusted to his educational care, such outrageous conduct greatly outweighs any public policy considerations which would otherwise preclude liability so

109

as to authorize recovery. *It may well be true that a claimant will usually face a formidable burden in attempting to produce adequate evidence to establish the intent requirement of the tort, but that factor alone cannot prevent a plaintiff from instituting the action.* Thus, the petitioners are entitled to make such an attempt here [footnotes omitted] [emphasis added].[16]

Mr. Justice Davidson concurred in part and dissented in part. He wrote:

> I agree with the majority that individuals engaged in the educational process who intentionally injure a child entrusted to their educational care should be held liable. Accordingly, I agree with the majority's holding that petitioners are entitled to maintain an action against the individual defendants for the intentional injuries alleged.
> I do not agree with the majority, however, that individuals engaged in the educational process who, through professional malpractice, negligently injure a child entrusted to their educational care should not be held liable. In my view a cause of action against such individuals should exist for such negligent injuries.[17]

Justice Davidson further stated:

> *Thus this Court has consistently recognized, notwithstanding the existence of a myriad of intangibles, a multiplicity of unknown quantities and a variety of other uncertainties attendant in any profession, that a professional owes a duty of care to a person receiving professional services; that a standard of care based upon customary conduct is appropriate;* and that it is possible to maintain a viable tort action against a professional for professional malpractice. Finally, ... this Court has recognized that under certain circumstances there can be recovery for mental or emotional distress resulting from non-intentional negligent acts. The ap-

---

16. *Id.* at 585-87.
17. *Id.* at 587-88.

plication of all of these principles to this case leads me to the conclusion that there should be a viable cause of action on the facts alleged here [emphasis added].[18]

The justice concluded his lengthy dissenting opinion by maintaining:

> In my view, *public educators are professionals.* They have special training and state certification is a prerequisite to their employment. They hold themselves out as possessing certain skills and knowledge not shared by non-educators. As a result, people who utilize their services have a right to expect them to use that skill and knowledge with some minimum degree of competence. In addition, like other professionals, they must often make educated judgments in applying their knowledge to specific individual needs. As professionals, they owe a professional duty of care to children who receive their services and a standard of care based upon customary conduct is appropriate. *There can be no question that negligent conduct on the part of a public educator may damage a child by inflicting psychological damage and emotional distress. Moreover, from the fact that public educators purport to teach it follows that some causal relationship may exist between the conduct of a teacher and the failure of a child to learn. Thus, it should be possible to maintain a viable tort action against such professionals for educational malpractice.*
>
> Here the declaration alleges, in pertinent part, that the individual defendants "owed a duty to the minor plaintiff to comport themselves within the standards of their profession, and to exercise that degree of care and skill ordinarily exercised by those similarly situated in the profession; ..." The declaration further alleges that the defendants breached that duty by, among other things, placing the child in the second grade and requiring him to repeat first grade materials even though he had satisfactorily completed these materials in his first year in school, subsequently placing him in

---

18. *Id.* at 589.

a grade ahead of the material he was actually studying, testing the child so incompletely and inadequately
as to result in total failure of evaluation of the problems, and insulting and demeaning the child in private
and public. Finally, the declaration alleges that the
defendants' acts in breach of their duties were the
proximate cause of injuries to the child which included, among other things, substantial learning deficiencies, psychological damage and emotional stress.
This declaration alleges that the defendants owed a
professional duty to the child to act in conformity with
an appropriate standard of care based upon customary
conduct, that there was a breach of that duty, and that
unforeseeable injuries were proximately caused by
that breach. Manifestly, it states a cause of action that
comports with traditional notions of tort law.

Unlike my colleagues, I believe that public policy
does not prohibit such claims from being entertained.
It is common knowledge, and indeed the majority recognizes, that the failure of schools to achieve educational objectives has reached massive proportions. It is
widely recognized that, as a result, not only are many
persons deprived of the learning that both materially
and spiritually enhances life, but also that society as a
whole is beset by social and moral problems. These
changed circumstances mandate a change in the common law. New and effective remedies must be devised
if the law is to remain vital and viable.

Moreover, I do not agree with my colleagues that
adequate internal administrative procedures designed
for the achievement of educational goals are available
within the educational system. In my view none of the
available procedures adequately deal with incompetent teaching or provide adequate relief to an injured
student. A cause of action for educational malpractice
meets these social and individual needs.

In addition, I do not agree with the majority that
recognition of such a cause of action will result in a
flood of litigation imposing an impossible burden on
the public educational system and the courts. Similar
arguments appearing in cases that recognized the con-

stitutional rights of students have not been validated by subsequent empirical evidence [citations omitted].

Finally, I do not agree with the majority that the recognition of such a cause of action "would in effect position the courts of this State as overseers of both the day-to-day operation of our educational process as well as the formulation of its governing policies," roles that have been "properly entrusted by the General Assembly to the State Department of Education and the local school boards." That the Legislature has delegated authority to administer a particular area to certain administrative agencies should not preclude judicial responsiveness to individuals injured by unqualified administrative functioning. *In recognizing a cause of action for educational malpractice, this Court would do nothing more than what courts have traditionally done from time immemorial — namely provide a remedy to a person harmed by the negligent act of another. Our children deserve nothing less.* [Emphasis added].[19]

§ 5.1(B). Garrett v. School Board.

In 1977 George H. Garrett, Jr. filed a complaint against the School Board of Broward County, Florida.[20] In the complaint it was alleged that as a result of the defendant's failure and refusal to properly test and evaluate the plaintiff, and to provide her with basic skills development in reading, writing, language arts, arithmetic, measurements, and problem solving, the plaintiff has been damaged in that she has been denied the basic skills necessary to seek and retain gainful employment, or otherwise provide for her own support and welfare. More specifically, the result of a test showed that the plaintiff, an 18 years of age

---

19. *Id.* at 589-90.

20. Garrett v. School Board, Circuit Ct. of the Seventeenth Judicial Circuit, in and for Broward County, Florida, Case No. 77-8703 "J" SEAY (1977).

senior, was functioning at approximately the fourth grade level in English, and the second to third grade level in math.[21]

The Circuit Court judge, in dismissing the complaint, briefly stated:

[H]aving heard oral arguments of counsel and having reviewed Florida Statutes 768.28(s) and 768.28(6), and further, having reviewed the case of *Peters vs. San Francisco Unified School District* [sic] ... the amended complaint is hereby dismissed with prejudice.[22]

§ 5.1(C). Torres v. Little Flower Children's Services; Torres v. City of New York.

Frank Torres filed two suits in New York. One was against Little Flower Children's Services,[23] and the other against the City of New York.[24] These suits, which were consolidated, sought damages for graduating and discharging the plaintiff from school without having taught him to read. It was alleged:

In 1964, at the age of 7, the NYC Department of Social Services assumed legal custody of plaintiff and pursuant to a series of contracts with Little Flower Children's Service (hereinafter Little Flower) had day to day responsibility of plaintiff's basic care including education and vocational training.

Plaintiff attended P.S. 181M, a school maintained by the Board of Education on the premises of Little

---

21. Complaint for Negligence, Garrett v. School Board, Circuit Ct. of the Seventeenth Judicial Circuit in and for Broward County, Florida, Case No. 77-8703 "J" SEAY (1977).

22. Order, Garrett v. School Board, Circuit Ct. of the Seventeenth Judicial Circuit in and for Broward County, Florida, Case No. 77-8703 "J" SEAY (1977).

23. Torres v. Little Flower Children's Services, Supreme Ct. of the State of N.Y., City of N.Y., Index No. 07875/77 (1977).

24. Torres v. City of New York, Supreme Ct. of the State of N.Y., City of N.Y. (1978).

Flower. Upon his graduation from school, plaintiff alleges that he is unable to read or write.

Plaintiff contends that 1) Little Flower was negligent in the exercise of its legal and contractual duty to care for, supervise and educate the plaintiff; 2) The Board of Education and The City of New York failed to provide plaintiff with an appropriate education and 3) the Department of Social Services breached their obligation to the plaintiff as a third party beneficiary of the purchase of service agreement between Little Flower and New York City Department of Social Services. Further it is alleged that in failing to provide plaintiff with an appropriate education, the defendants violated plaintiff's rights to constitutional due process and equal protection of law.[25]

The Supreme Court, New York County, Special Term, held that the causes of action against the Board of Education should be dismissed. The Court commented that plaintiff argued that his cause of action is not educational malpractice, but actionable negligence; however, plaintiff's labelling the cause of action does not prevent its dismissal as educational malpractice. Citing the *Hoffman*[26] case, the court stated that a cause of action for educational malpractice does not exist. Furthermore, the court stated that the causes of action alleging breach of contractual duty to care for, supervise, and educate the plaintiff should be dismissed. The court reasoned that the contract entered into with Little Flower required basic care to the plaintiff, defined as "the provision of room, board, clothing, recreation, medical and dental care and treatment and the arrangement as needed for religious educational and vocational

---

25. Torres v. Little Flower Children's Services, Supreme Ct. of the State of N.Y., County of New York, City of N.Y., Special Term: Post I, Index No. 07875/77 (1981).

26. Hoffman v. City of New York, 64 A.D.2d 369, 410 N.Y.S.2d 99 (1978).

training." The contract required for the arrangement for education, and plaintiff admits he was placed in a public school. As such, defendant did not breach its contractual obligation.[27]

§ 5.1(D). Irwin v. School Directors.

Thomas R. Irwin, a minor, brought a suit against the School Directors of McHenry Community Consolidated School District demanding a judgment in the sum of $1,000,000.00.[28] The suit was filed in the Circuit Court of McHenry County, Illinois. The complaint alleged, among other things, the following:

1. That plaintiff attended the aforesaid school for more than two consecutive years next foreceding [following] the filing of this action.
2. That on or about February of 1977, defendant, through its agents, employees, staff, principals, teachers, and administrators became aware that plaintiff possessed an atypically high Intelligence Quotient and verbal ability and was a "Gifted Child" as defined in Article 14A-2 of the Illinois School Code.
3. That the defendant, through the Constitution of the State of Illinois and the Illinois School Code has the duty of providing for the educational development of all persons to the limits of their capabilities.
4. That in willful and wanton breach of its aforesaid duty defendant has been and remains guilty of one or more of the following negligent acts or omissions:

   (a) Defendant has willfully and wantonly failed to promulgate a curriculum designed to meet the special needs of the Gifted Child.

---

27. Torres, *supra* note 25, at 3.
28. Irwin v. School Directors, Circuit Ct. of the Nineteenth Judicial Circuit, McHenry County, Ill., No. 79L49 (1979).

(b) Defendant has willfully and wantonly failed to provide faculty qualified to effectively teach the Gifted Child.

(c) Defendant has willfully and wantonly failed and refused to institute any program whatsoever designed to meet the needs of a Gifted Child so that he or she may be provided with the educational development to the limits of their capabilities.

(d) Defendant has repeatedly refused, and continues to refuse, to find essential supplementary programs within or without the District designed to afford plaintiff with the educational development to the limit of his capabilities.

(e) That the *ONLY* "program" ever allowed by defendant to enhance plaintiff's educational development was the arrangement whereby defendant was allowed to take Spanish language instruction at the East Campus of the McHenry High School and that "program" was willfully and wantonly stopped by the action of defendant only a few weeks after being instituted.

6. That as a direct and proximate result of the aforesaid willful and wanton conduct of defendant, plaintiff has been denied an opportunity to obtain educational development to the limits of his capabilities.

7. By reason of the previous, plaintiff has been caused to suffer great mental pain and anguish, has become bored and indifferent towards school, has been denied adequate mental stimulation and development, has become frustrated and has developed behavioral problems requiring extraordinary care, counseling and attention, has failed to perform to his fullest potential, has been placed in jeopardy of being forever denied a reasonable opportunity for future educational development commensurate with his demonstrated ability and potential, has been required to expend or become

117

liable for immense sums of money for alternative educational and psychological programs in an effort to overcome the mental anguish by the willful and wanton acts and omissions of defendant, has been severely and permanently emotionally injured, and, has been cruelly retarded in his educational, emotional, and intellectual development, all to plaintiff's damage in the sum of $1,000,000.00.[29]

The circuit judge, after considering the arguments and briefs in conjunction with defendant's motion to strike and dismiss plaintiff's first amended complaint, ruled on all issues in favor of the defendant. The court did state, however, that if the plaintiff wished to file an amended complaint, the court would grant him twenty-eight days for that purpose.

§ 5.1(E). Myers v. Medford Lakes Board of Education.

In 1983 a complaint was filed by Glenn Myers against the Medford Lakes Board of Education and Lenape Regional High School District.[30] The alleged facts, as related in plaintiff's amended complaint, are as follows:

1. Plaintiff, having his birth date December 6, 1954, was a student with defendant, Medford Lakes Board of Education School District, throughout first grade and until such time as he entered the School District of Lenape Regional High School.
2. During his academic career within defendant, Medford Lakes Board of Education School District, plaintiff experienced severe difficulties with his

---

29. Complaint at Law, pp. 1-3, Irwin v. School Directors, Circuit Ct. of the Nineteenth Judicial Circuit, McHenry County, Ill., No. 79L49 (1979).

30. Myers v. Medford Lakes Board of Education, Superior Court of New Jersey, Law Division, Burlington County, Docket No. L-56068-81.

plaintiff experienced severe difficulties with his academic studies. On account thereof, plaintiff's parents made numerous inquiries of defendant, Medford Lakes Board of Education with regard to special classes and remedial courses of education for plaintiff.

3. In 1966 plaintiff was evaluated by St. Christopher's Hospital for Children and was found to suffer from mild perceptual-motor inefficiency. It was recommended that plaintiff be placed in a class for brain damaged children or, in the alternative, the school should provide exceptional training and counseling.

4. Defendant Medford Lakes Board of Education was under a duty to provide such remedial course of education and failed to provide same.

5. As a result thereof, plaintiff suffered damages.

6. Defendant Medford Lakes Board of Education held itself out to plaintiff as a school having and exercising that skill and knowledge necessary to competently educate elementary students.

7. Defendant Medford Lakes Board of Education deviated from the standard of care exercised by educators in that said defendant failed to provide plaintiff with a remedial course of education designed to assist plaintiff in overcoming the educational deficiencies he possessed.

8. As a result of defendant Medford Lakes Board of Education's deviation from said standard, plaintiff suffered damages.

9. In or about September 1970, plaintiff enrolled in the Lenape Regional High School District school system at Shawnee High School. Plaintiff graduated from said school district in or about June 1974.

10. During the time within which plaintiff was enrolled within defendant Lenape Regional High School District, plaintiff experienced continuing and severe difficulties in his course of academic study. On account of said difficulties, plaintiff caused to be instituted through his parents inqui-

119

ries regarding special education and courses of remedial study.

11. Defendant Lenape Regional High School District
was under the duty to provide plaintiff a thorough
and efficient education including such remedial
and special education courses of instruction necessary for plaintiff to overcome his educational deficiency.

12. Defendant Lenape Regional High School District
failed to carry out its duty to provide plaintiff a
thorough and efficient education and on account
thereof, plaintiff suffered damages.

13. Defendant Lenape Regional High School District
held itself out to plaintiff as an educational facility
having that skill and knowledge commonly possessed by educational institutions.

14. Defendant Lenape Regional High School District
deviated from the standard of care exercised by
educators in that said defendant failed to provide
plaintiff with a remedial course of education designed to assist plaintiff in overcoming the educational deficiencies he possessed.

15. As a result of defendant Lenape Regional High
School District's deviation from said standard,
plaintiff suffered damages.

16. Defendant Lenape Regional High School District
had the responsibility to advise plaintiff as to further remedial courses of instruction and training
which could be obtained by plaintiff following his
graduation from said high school facility.

17. Defendant Lenape Regional High School District
has failed, in dereliction of its responsibility, to so
inform plaintiff, and on account thereof, plaintiff
suffered damages.[31]

In 1985 the Superior Court of New Jersey, Appellate
Division, affirmed the Superior Court, Law Division and
stated:

Plaintiff appeals from summary judgement dismissing

---

31. *Id.* Amended Complaint (1983).

his complaint, *R.* 4:6-2(e). Against both defendants he alleged educational malpractice in failing to provide him with a special remedial education to assist him to overcome his academic deficiencies. On defendants' motion for dismissal, the allegations of the complaint were accepted as true, including the claim of damages proximately resulting from the alleged educational malpractice [citation omitted].

Although the complaint sounds in tort against two public entities, plaintiff did not follow the notice procedure set down in the Tort Claims Act, *N.J.S.A.* 59:1-1 *et seq.,* or plead the act; defendant did not plead immunity under the act; the trial judge did not apply the act *sua sponte;* and neither party has briefed the act on appeal before us. The trial judge rested his dismissal of the complaint on the conclusion that, as educational malpractice is not a recognized cause of action, he should not innovate by sanctioning it without the imprimatur of a higher court.

Educational malpractice has not been approved as a theory of recovery in this state or elsewhere. *See Hunter v. Board of Ed. of Montgomery County,* 292 Md. 481, 439 A.2d 582 (Ct. App. 1982); *D.S.W. v. Fairbanks No. Star Bor. Sch. Dist.,* 628 P.2d 554 (Alaska Sup. Ct. 1981); *Hoffman v. Board of Ed. of City of N.Y.,* 49 N.Y.2d 121, 400 N.E.2d 317, 424 N.Y.S.2d 376 (Ct. App. 1979); *Peter W. v. San Francisco Unified School District,* 60 Cal. App. 3d 814, 131 Cal. Rptr. 854 (Ct. App. 1976).

....

We affirm but for reasons other than those stated by the trial judge. Whether a cause of action lies for educational malpractice against defendant public entities must be determined pursuant to the Tort Claims Act. The act limits and circumscribes governmental tort liability; apart from the act no tort cause of action lies

121

against a public entity of this state [citations omitted].[32]

The court continued:

Educational malpractice, like other professional or occupational malpractice, would arise, if recognized as a cause of action, out of negligence principles, with liability restricted to breach of the standard of care and responsibility prevailing at the time among professional educators. Under *N.J.S.A.* 59:2-2a any liability of a public entity for educational malpractice would be vicarious under *respondeat superior* and not direct.

Plaintiff joined no individual defendant and charged no individual or individuals with educational malpractice. He failed to allege *respondeat superior* as a theory of recovery against defendants. He charged breach of care and responsibility directly against defendants in their respective capacities as a board of education and a high school district. Without alleging *respondeat superior* liability, plaintiff failed to state a cause of action under *N.J.S.A.* 59:2-2a.

Because of the significance of the issue before us, we point out that immunity under *N.J.S.A.* 59:2-3a would have been a bar, in our view, even if a cause of action under *N.J.S.A.* 59:2-2a had been pleaded. *N.J.S.A.* 59:2-3a grants immunity from governmental liability for exercises of judgment or discretion, such as the evaluation of a course of education for plaintiff. Outside this state *respondeat superior* has been held inapplicable to malpractice claims for breach of professional standards by professional employees in public employment [citations omitted].

Finally, even if plaintiff's cause of action fitted within a specific liability provision of the Tort Claims Act, which we hold that it did not, his complaint would have been subject to dismissal for failure to comply with the notice of claim requirements of the act, *N.J.S.A.* 59:8-3 [citations omitted].

---

32. Myers v. Medford Lakes Board of Education, 199 N.J. Super. 511, 514-15 (1985).

We affirm summary judgment in favor of defendants.[33]

§ 5.1(F). Camer v. Brouillet.

In 1982 the Washington State Court of Appeals heard a case on the issue of educational malpractice. The plaintiff, Dorothy Camer, filed a complaint for herself and as parent and guardian of her minor children against defendants Frank B. and Jane Doe Brouillet and Seattle School District, in the Superior Court of Washington, for King County.[34] The Superior Court sustained defendant's motion for summary judgment. In the complaint, the plaintiff alleged that in June, 1979, Kirk, one of her children, completed the 6th grade and Pepi, her other child, completed the 5th grade at Jefferson School in the Seattle School District. Their report cards indicated satisfactory or better work. However, both children failed to achieve certain student learning "bench marks" for their grade level because of alleged failure by the school district to provide adequate instruction. The court summarized the alleged facts as follows:

> Plaintiff further alleges that the school staff failed to provide a healthy environment conducive to education and to provide a program to meet the individual and collective needs of plaintiff's children and their fellow students. She concludes with the allegation that because the Seattle School District failed to properly implement the Student Learning Objectives law [citations omitted] and the Basic Education Act [citations omitted] plaintiff's children were not provided with a constitutionally guaranteed basic program of education, as required by article 9, section 1 of our state constitution. In support of her complaint, plaintiff sub-

---

33. *Id.* at 515-16.
34. Camer v. Brouillet, Supreme Court No. 47394-3, in the Washington State Court of Appeals, Division 1 (1982).

mits a long record of correspondence as evidence of her attempts to bring alleged instructional deficiencies to the attention of the defendants. Her most specific objections were (1) a disciplinary measure that separated boys and girls at recess, (2) a school practice of not obtaining excuses from parents for absences and tardiness, and (3) failure of her children to meet "bench mark" learning objectives.[35]

In affirming the trial court's decision the Appellate Court wrote:

> The plaintiff's cause of action sounds in *"educational malpractice," an issue of first impression in this state.* The defendants cite cases from other jurisdictions that have considered the issue and have declined to recognize an actionable "duty of care" in persons and agencies who administer the public educational process. See *Peter W. v. San Francisco Unified Sch. Dist.* [citations omitted]; *Donohue v. Copiague U. Free Sch. Dist.* [citations omitted]. We do not find it necessary to decide if such an action exists in the State of Washington until a more appropriate case is presented to us. The plaintiff has failed to *establish a breach of duty on the part of the defendants.* The Seattle School District's duty to educate under the Basic Education Act and to make achievement reports under the Student Learning Objectives statute does not include a duty to insure that every student, including the children of the plaintiff, will be able to achieve every bench mark. The action was properly dismissed by the trial court for failure to state facts giving rise to a cause of action [emphasis added].[36]

§ 5.1(G). Denson v. Ohio Board of Education.

In 1985 Tony Denson filed a complaint in the Common Pleas Court of Jefferson County, Ohio, against the Ohio

---

35. Torres, *supra* note 25, at 3.
36. *Id.* at 5-6.

Board of Education, the Steubenville Board of Education and its Governing Board, as well as its principal and the present and former superintendent.[37] The complaint contained two causes of action. In the first cause of action the plaintiff alleged, *inter alia,* that the "defendants, their agents, and employees, negligently and carelessly failed to provide plaintiff with adequate instruction, guidance, counseling, and/or supervision in basic academic skills, such as reading and writing; although said defendants had the authority, responsibility, and ability to do so."[38]

He further alleged as follows:

1. Defendants, their agents and employees, negligently failed to use reasonable care in the discharge of their duties to provide plaintiff with adequate instruction in basic academic skills, and failed to exercise that degree of professional skill required of an ordinary prudent educator under the same circumstances as exemplified, but not limited to, the following acts:

   (1) Negligently and carelessly failed to apprehend plaintiff's reading disabilities.
   (2) Negligently and carelessly assigned plaintiff to classes in which he could not read the books and other materials.
   (3) Negligently and carelessly allowed plaintiff to pass and advance from a course or grade level, with knowledge that he had not achieved either its completion or the skills necessary for him to succeed or benefit from subsequent courses.
   (4) Negligently and carelessly assigned him to classes in which the instructors were unqualified, or which were not geared to his reading level.

---

37. Complaint, Denson v. Ohio Board of Education, in the Common Pleas Court of Jefferson County, Ohio, Case No. 85-CIV-167 (1985).
38. *Id.* at 3.

(5) Negligently and carelessly permitted him to obtain the twelfth grade level, although plaintiff was unable to read or write above the first grade level; thereby depriving plaintiff of additional instruction in reading and other academic skills.

2. As a direct and proximate result of the negligent acts and omissions by the defendants, their agents and employees, plaintiff obtained the twelfth grade level, and left Steubenville High School with a reading ability of only the first grade.

3. As a further proximate result, plaintiff has been unable to obtain or hold any substantial job, and has become a burden upon himself, society and the welfare system of this state. And as a further direct result, plaintiff has suffered a loss of earning capacity by his limited ability to read and write, and is unqualified for any employment other than menial labor, which requires little or no ability to read or write.

4. As a further direct result, plaintiff's inability to read or write has caused him undue embarrassment and ridicule from his friends and society at large.

5. As a further direct result of the negligent acts of the defendants, due to plaintiff's permanent disability and inability to gain meaningful employment, plaintiff has and will suffer the loss of employment and income for the rest of his natural life, estimated to be in excess of ONE MILLION, TWO HUNDRED THOUSAND AND 00/100 DOLLARS ($1,200,000.00).[39]

6. Plaintiff further states that because of his size and strength, through grade school, junior high school and high school, he was encouraged by the school officials to participate in football, basketball, and track activities.

7. Plaintiff, whose I.Q., as tested in 1966, ranged from seventy-eight (78) to eighty-four (84) percen-

---

39. *Id.* at 3-4.

tile, and whose I.Q., tested in 1970, ranged as high as eighty-two (82) percentile, was never taught to read or write, other than his own name; and to this day does not know how to write or read other than a few recognizable words.

8. As a direct and proximate result of defendants' failure to provide proper training and education, by negligently passing plaintiff from grade to grade, through the twelfth grade of high school, so as to keep plaintiff in sports activities for the benefit of the athletic system in the schools, plaintiff was not encouraged by defendants to learn to read or write as required by their positions in the educational system.

9. Defendants' failure to exercise reasonable diligence and care in discharging their duties to provide instruction, guidance and supervision in the basic academic skills, including reading and writing, while fostering sports activities for the benefit of the school system, has placed plaintiff in a lifelong position where he has become a burden upon himself, his family and society at large.

10. Defendants should have foreseen that by their failure to exercise the proper and requisite duties of care, to provide plaintiff with adequate instruction in basic academic skills, including reading and writing, that plaintiff would be incapable of holding any substantial job or employment other than menial labor, and that their acts and omissions would cause plaintiff to suffer this economic loss described above.[40]

The defendant, the Ohio Board of Education, filed a Motion to Dismiss on the following grounds:

1. The court lacks jurisdiction over defendant.
2. The court lacks jurisdiction over the subject matter.
3. The complaint fails to state a claim upon which relief can be granted.

40. *Id.* at 5-6.

127

4. The complaint is barred by the statute of limitations.
5. The complaint is barred by the doctrine of laches.[41]

The court dismissed the complaint as to the Defendant Ohio State Board of Education.[42] The remaining defendants also filed a motion to dismiss for failure to state a claim upon which relief can be granted.[43] The court sustained the motion dismissing the complaint and stated that the complaint failed to state a claim for which relief could be granted against any defendant and for the further reason that, assuming such a cause of action did exist, the complaint was not filed within the period of the applicable statute of limitations.[44]

The case was then appealed to the Court of Appeals of Ohio.[45] As to the first assignment of errors that the common pleas court erroneously determined that plaintiff's complaint failed to state a claim upon which relief could be granted, the court, after citing several authorities, including the *Peter W.* and *Donohue* cases, stated that those courts recognized the problems inherent in educational malpractice and did not consider it to be a viable concept.

---

41. Motion to Dismiss of Defendant Ohio Board of Education, Denson v. Ohio Board of Education, in the Common Pleas Court of Jefferson County, Ohio, Case No. 85-CIV-167 (1985).

42. Denson v. Ohio Board of Education, in the Court of Common Pleas of Jefferson County, Ohio, Case No. 85-CIV-167 (1985).

43. Motion to Dismiss of Defendant Steubenville Board of Education et al. to dismiss Denson v. Ohio Board of Education, in the Court of Common Pleas of Jefferson County, Ohio, Case No. 85-CIV-167 (1985).

44. Denson v. Ohio Board of Education, in the Court of Common Pleas of Jefferson County, Ohio, Case No. 85-CIV-167 (1985).

45. Denson v. Ohio Board of Education, in the Court of Appeals of Ohio, Seventh District, Jefferson County, Case No. 85-J-31 (1985).

Based upon that reasoning it overruled the first assignment of error.[46]

In overruling the second assignment of error dealing with the statute of limitations, the court stated that since the last possible date on which some alleged cause of action arose was some nine years prior to the time suit was initiated, it would be barred by a state statute providing that except as provided by a certain section of the code, "an action upon a contract not in writing, express or implied, *or upon a liability created by statute* other than a forfeiture or penalty, shall be brought within six years after the cause thereof accrued."[47]

One of the justices, Cox, wrote a separate opinion, concurring in part and dissenting in part. He stated that although he concurred with the result reached by the majority, he would reach this conclusion for different reasons.[48] He stated that he would sustain appellant's first assignment of error that the common pleas court erroneously determined that plaintiff's complaint failed to state a claim upon which relief could be granted.[49] He reasoned as follows:

> It may be a correct statement of the law today to say "the overwhelming line of authority maintains that educational malpractice is not actionable." Still, nationally, few jurisdictions have addressed the issue. The courts' reluctance to recognize educational malpractice is not surprising considering the obvious difficulties in formulating a workable rule of law and in evaluating educational policy from the standpoint of the individual pupil. However, judicial review of such

---

46. Denson v. Ohio Board of Education, in the Court of Appeals of Ohio, Seventh District, Jefferson County, Case No. 85-J-31 (1985), pp. 1-2.

47. *Id.* at 2-3.

48. *Id.* at 1.

49. *Id.* at 1 (second part of Opinion).

claims is not completely unmanageable. In fact, such review is compatible with the remedial policy of tort law and the traditional concept of negligence.

Actionable negligence consists of three essential elements: a duty of care which the defendant owes to the plaintiff, a breach of that duty, and an injury to the plaintiff proximately resulting from the breach. On its face, appellant's complaint asserts these three elements. Even the New York court which ultimately rejected a claim for educational malpractice in *Donohue v. Copiague Union School District* (1979), 418 N.Y.S.2d 375, admitted that the cause of action could at least be stated 'within the strictures of a traditional negligence or malpractice action.' *Donohue, supra,* at 377. That court and others (see *Peter W. v. San Francisco Unified School District* (1976), 60 Cal. App. 3d 814; *Hunter v. Board of Education of Montgomery County* (1982), Md. 439 A.2d 582), found public policy reasons to be dispositive.

I do not agree that, as a matter of public policy, the courts should excuse themselves from addressing alleged failures of our educational system. Judicial review of claims involving decisions made by educators is no more "unmanageable" than review of claims involving decisions made by other professionals, including doctors, lawyers, accountants, or engineers. With the assistance of expert testimony, and other evidence, the judge or jury can determine whether the educator's performance meets the standard of ordinary knowledge and skill in his or her profession. The dilemma of "second guessing" the qualified school teacher does not compel the courts to dismiss on motion the claim of a pupil who was graduated without being taught to read.

Appellant alleges that school officials promoted him from grade one through twelve without teaching him how to read, asserting the teachers nurtured his athletic ability at the expense of his formal education. Assuming this allegation is true, the school officials could be accountable for appellant's injuries resulting from this failure to instruct and their failure to recognize appellant's inability to read. Appellant should at

130

least be given the chance to prove that, as certified professionals, his teachers and school administrators could have but did not even minimally educate him.

Evidentiary problems are not insurmountable in this case. I see no more difficulty in allowing a damage award for failure to educate, for instance, than in measuring "pain and suffering" in a medical malpractice case. The burdens imposed upon the appellant to demonstrate educational malpractice are inherent in all negligence actions.

The first assignment of error should be sustained.

However, I would affirm the trial court based solely on the fact that appellant's complaint is barred by the statute of limitations ... [emphasis added].[50]

Justice O'Neill wrote a separate concurring opinion in which he stated:

I concur in the dismissal of this action in the trial court but only for the reason that the plaintiff's complaint failed to state a claim upon which relief could be granted. Under the law of the State of Ohio compulsory education is not provided. Compulsory attendance at schools provided by the State is the law. The Supreme Court of Ohio has held that: "... One of the most important natural duties of the parent is the obligation to educate his child; and the duty he owes not to the child only, but to the commonwealth. If he neglects to perform it, or willfully refuses to do so, he may be coerced by the law to execute such civil obligation. *Parr v. State* (1927), 117 Ohio St. 23, 26."

Thus, the primary duty of education lies with the parent to vigilantly pursue the education of his or her children. The duty of the State is to provide the means of education. Thus, a child who attends school for 12 years and receives no education must look not to the State but rather to his or her parents for their failure to perform a duty imposed by nature and by law.[51]

---

50. *Id.* at 1-4.
51. *Id.* at 1 (third part of Opinion).

§ 5.2. Educational Malpractice Cases in Private Schools.

The previous cases have arisen in the context of public education. The same rationale for denying a cause of action for educational malpractice has been found to apply when the defendant is a private school.

§ 5.2(A). Helm v. Professional Children's School.

In *Helm v. Professional Children's School,*[52] the New York Supreme Court had an opportunity to decide whether a claim for educational malpractice lies against a private educational institution. The action was commenced by plaintiff's parents alleging, *inter alia,* that the defendant failed to teach verbal and nonverbal skills commensurate with normal first grade education. In affirming the lower court, the Supreme Court, Appellate Term, held that, as a matter of public policy, a private school could not be liable for claimed educational negligence. The court, in citing and adopting the reasoning of the *Donohue* and *Hoffman* cases, stated that it found the considerations to be equally applicable to any attempt to assess the educational experience, whether in the context of public or private education.[53]

§ 5.2(B). De Pietro v. St. Joseph's School.

Vincent De Pietro, as parent and natural guardian of Michael De Pietro, filed a suit in the Supreme Court of the State of New York against St. Joseph's School, a private, parochial school licensed and approved by the Board of

---

52. 431 N.Y.S.2d 246 (1980).
53. *Id.*

Regents of the State of New York.[54] The complaint contained four causes of action.

The first cause alleged that the infant plaintiff attended St. Joseph's School from 1970 to 1978, and that the defendant promised to provide an education to the infant, to teach him, to ascertain his learning capacity and ability and to properly test him, and to evaluate his ability to comprehend the course of studies. On the contrary, defendant failed to: ascertain whether plaintiff, Michael De Pietro, was capable of learning and failed to provide special educational facilities in accordance with Education Law; failed to evaluate the plaintiff's mental ability and capacity to comprehend the subjects being taught to him at said school; failed to take proper means and precautions that they reasonably should have taken under the circumstances; failed to interview, discuss, evaluate, and/or test the plaintiff in order to ascertain his ability to comprehend and understand such subject matter; failed to provide adequate school facilities, teachers, administrators, psychologists, and other personnel trained to take the necessary steps in testing and evaluation processes insofar as the plaintiff is concerned in order to ascertain the learning capacity, intelligence, and intellectual absorption on the part of the plaintiff; failed to hire proper personnel, experienced in the handling of such matters; failed to teach the plaintiff in such a manner so that he could reasonably understand what was necessary under the circumstances so that he could cope with the various subjects which they tried to make the plaintiff understand; failed to properly supervise the plaintiff; failed to advise his parents that the processes practiced were defective and not commensurate with a student attending a school within the County of

---

54. De Pietro v. St. Joseph's School, Supreme Ct. of the State of New York, Cty. of Suffolk, Index No. 79-10023 (1979).

Suffolk; and failed to adopt the accepted professional standards and methods to evaluate and cope with plaintiff's problems. Such constituted educational malpractice. Plaintiff alleged that by reason of defendant's failure to provide proper education, plaintiff was deprived of an opportunity to learn and to reach the full potential of his ability and will be severely handicapped in his social and economic development during his entire lifetime.[55]

Plaintiff alleged that as a result he was damaged in the sum of $3,000,000.00.

The second cause of action alleged that during 1977, and several times during each preceding seven year, the adult plaintiff complained to various persons on the school staff regarding the infant's treatment and progress, but certain representations made to him were false, known to be false, and intended to deceive him, by reason of which he allowed the boy to continue in school.[56]

In the third cause of action plaintiff sought recovery of the tuition paid to defendant in consideration of defendant's alleged promises to provide a quality education. Plaintiff alleged defendant failed to provide said education. In the fourth cause of action plaintiff alleged that teachers and other school personnel held the infant up to ridicule, punched, prodded, and struck him and threatened him with further physical punishment, all of which has resulted in the plaintiff becoming extremely nervous, has made him shy, fearful of adults, and inclined to make strange noises, to his damage in the sum of $50,000.00.[57]

After reviewing the alleged facts, the New York State Supreme Court made the following conclusions regarding the four causes of action:

---

55. Complaint, pp. 1-2, De Pietro v. St. Joseph's School, Supreme Ct. of the State of New York, Cty. of Suffolk, Index No. 79-10023 (1979).
56. *Id.* at 4.
57. *Id.* at 5-6.

As to the first cause of action, the Court of Appeals recently decided, on June 14, 1979 in *Donohue v. Copiague UFSD* [citations omitted], that though a complaint alleging "educational malpractice" might on the pleadings state a cause of action within traditional notions of tort law does not require that such a complaint be sustained and the courts of this state should not, as a matter of public policy, entertain such claims. Though the *Donohue* case involved [a] public school district and not a private or parochial school, the same problems attended the consideration of the claim for "educational malpractice" against the private school as against a public school.... Defendant's motion addressed to the first cause of action must be granted for it does not state a cause of action cognizable in our courts.

As to the second cause of action, in order to prove a prima facie case of fraud, a plaintiff must allege representation of material existing fact, falsity, scienter, deception and injury, and in addition each of these elements must be supported by factual allegations sufficient to satisfy the statutory requirement that circumstances constituting the wrong be stated in detail when a cause of action based upon fraud, misrepresentation or a breach of trust is involved [citations omitted]. Defendant's motion to dismiss the second cause of action is granted, with leave to the plaintiff to serve an amended complaint as to such cause of action.

As to the third cause of action, the court is of the opinion that it also partakes of a claim for 'educational malpractice' for here the plaintiff is seeking to recover his special damages, the tuition allegedly paid to the school, recovery of which is sought by reason of the defendant's wrong.

The Court can perceive of a case where a parent might be entitled to the recovery of tuition paid where an express agreement had been entered into between a parent and a school and in which the school contracted that the student would reach a certain proficiency in a certain subject or subjects after pursuing such studies in their school for a stated time and where it was al-

135

leged that the student at the end of such period had failed to attain such proficiency. This, however, is not the case here and the defendant is entitled to dismissal of the third cause of action.

As to the fourth cause of action, in the opinion of the Court a cause of action is stated. All pleadings must be liberally construed. Draftsmanship is quite secondary. Under the CPLR, of the pleading, a cause of action is stated and no motion lies under CPLR 3211 (a) (7). The pleading can be pathetically drawn; it can reek of miserable draftsmanship. That is not the inquiry. We want only to know whether it states a cause of action — any cause of action. If it does, it is an acceptable CPLR pleading [citations omitted]. The motion is denied as addressed to the fourth cause of action.[58]

§ 5.3. Summary.

It is apparent from the foregoing cases that there is reluctance by some courts to give educational institutions and their staff complete freedom from judicial interference in their dealings with educational matters. Yet, despite that fact, the courts are not yet ready and willing to recognize educational malpractice as a cause of action.

---

58. De Pietro v. St. Joseph's School, Supreme Ct. of the State of New York, Cty. of Suffolk, Index No. 79-10023 (1979).

Chapter 6

EDUCATIONAL MALPRACTICE "HYBRID" CASES

> A school can be viewed as a trustee, charged with the duty to protect, preserve and promote the intellectual development of its students.[1]

§ 6.0. Introduction.

Besides the so-called "pure" educational malpractice cases, there are a number of instances where the school officials allegedly misdiagnosed or failed to diagnose the students' learning disabilities and consequently the students were "intellectually" damaged. Some of these instances resulted in litigation.

---

1. Cynthia A. Jorgensen, *Donohue v. Copiague Free School District: New York Chooses Not to Recognize 'Educational Malpractice,'* 43 ALBANY LAW REVIEW 339, 353 (Winter 1979).

§ 6.1. The Landmark Case: Hoffman v. City of New York.

§ 6.1(A). Facts.

The fact that the California Court dismissed the *Peter W.* case and the New York Court did not recognize a cause of action for educational malpractice in the *Donohue* case did not stop or discourage another New York student, Danny Hoffman, from bringing a suit based on a similar theory. In 1976 the case of *Hoffman v. City of New York*[2] was filed. The alleged facts are as follows: The plaintiff was born in April of 1951. His father died when the plaintiff was 13 months old. Prior to his father's death plaintiff had started talking and walking. He retrogressed after his father's death; for a while he stopped both walking and talking. In February 1956, when he was four years and 10 months old, his mother took him to the National Hospital for Speech Disorders. The hospital's records noted that the plaintiff was "a friendly child with little or no intelligible speech. Produced infantile equivalents for names of some objects — or will vocalize in imitations of inflection.... Appears to be retarded and should have psychological [sic]."[3] The hospital reports also noted: "Mongoloid eyes, otherwise no Mongoloid features." The stated "impression" was "borderline Mongolism." It should be noted that plaintiff, in fact, was not a Mongoloid child. The notation of "Mongoloid eyes" apparently referred to the fact that the angles on each side of his eyes formed by the junction of the upper and lower lids were somewhat greater than is usual among occidental children. He also had unusually large ears, a characteristic he had inherited from his mother.[4]

---

2. No. 71-12593 Sup. Ct. (N.Y., 1976).
3. 64 A.D.2d 369, 371, 410 N.Y.S.2d 99, 101 (1978).
4. *Id.*

One month later, a nonverbal intelligence test known as the Merrill-Palmer Test was administered to the plaintiff by a psychologist employed by the same hospital. Plaintiff scored an I.Q. of 90, with a mental age of four years and five months, as against his actual age of four years and 11 months. This was within the range of normal intelligence. The "interpretation" included the note that "his range — particularly whenever form perception and problem-solving acuity are involved — indicates that he can work well into the average and even brighter range. Pursuant to the follow-up recommendation, plaintiff's mother took him to the New York Speech Institute for weekly therapy for some period of time and, apparently, until after his placement in his first CRMD class.

In September 1956 he entered kindergarten in the New York City school system. Four months later, plaintiff was examined by a certified clinical psychologist who had started his employment with the defendant about a week earlier. He administered the primarily verbal Stanford-Binet Intelligence Test. His report included the following:

> Mongoloid tendencies, severe speech defects, slow in response. *RECOMMENDATION:* Eligible for placement in a CRMD class at P77Q in September 1957.
> ....
> Danny impresses as a shy, cooperative youngster. *Mongoloid features are observable.* There is a marked speech defect which makes Danny hesitant in speaking up. He obviously understands more than he is able to communicate. With careful listening, it is frequently possible to understand what he is driving at.
>
> On the Stanford-Binet, L, he achieves a mental age of 4-3 and an I.Q. of 74, indicating borderline intelligence. The obtained I.Q. may be higher than it ought to be as the Examiner was confronted with the task of having to interpret what Danny was trying to say, Danny being given the benefit of the doubt when it seemed reasonable to do so.

139

Danny is frequently bored in class and needs a specialized individualized teaching program. At this point, a continued, yet varied readiness program should be offered to him. He is not yet able to do formal learning. He needs help with his speech problem in order that he be able to learn to make himself understood. Also *his intelligence should be reevaluated within a two-year period so that a more accurate estimation of his abilities can be made.* (emphasis added).[5]

This same psychologist testified in court that he *recommended CRMD placement because an I.Q. of 75 was the cut-off point pursuant to State law* and because of "the general incapacities that seemed to be there."[6] In discussing his difficulty in understanding plaintiff's speech, he testified:

It was like listening to a radio at a very low level, with a lot of static. You think you know what is being said, but you can't be sure, and I think that comes through here, that I really wasn't sure and that's why we wanted him retested within two years. This was always Bureau procedure. We were always concerned in the B.C.G., not to make mistakes with kids and we were careful to see to it if we had doubts about what we were doing, that *we recommended that he be retested and say it, and that's what happened here* (emphasis added).[7]

The Bureau that he was referring to was the Bureau of Child Guidance (B.C.G.), where he had been previously employed. He further testified that:

It was assumed that there was retardation and there were also contributing factors. How much was a pure retardation and how much was the result of contributing factors couldn't be known, at least by me ....

---

5. 64 A.D.2d 369, 372, 410 N.Y.S.2d 99, 102 (1978).
6. 64 A.D.2d 369, 373, 410 N.Y.S.2d 99, 102 (1978).
7. *Id.*

> *It was my feeling that there was retardation, but I doubted some of the results and therefore I suggested a retesting* [emphasis added].[8]

In relating the facts, the New York Supreme Court, Appellate Division, stated:

> Despite his borderline finding of retardation and that "he doubted some of the results," he made no requests to interview plaintiff's mother, or to learn whether plaintiff had been receiving treatment for his speech condition. Indeed, no attempt was made to obtain his social history and the mother was never told that the diagnosis of retardation was based on her son's falling short of the cut-off score of 75 by only one point or that, upon her request, the school authorities, by their own rules, would be required to retest the child. If they had informed her of her right to have her son retested, they might well have learned that he had achieved an I.Q. rating of 90 on the non-verbal Miller-Palmer Test given only 10 months earlier at the National Hospital for Speech Disorders.[9]

Plaintiff's mother was called to plaintiff's school after the administration of the I.Q. test in January 1957. She then spoke to someone in the principal's office. She testified:

> He told me they had a report from the Bureau of Child Guidance that my son was a Mongoloid child, and I asked him, I said, "Well, what can I do?" and he says, "Well, there are several things you can do. *One, you can put him in an institution.*" And I believe I asked him if that meant keeping him away from home and I told him I could never do that and then he says, "The only thing, they could put him in special classes" [emphasis added].[10]

---

8. *Id.*
9. 64 A.D.2d 369, 373-74, 410 N.Y.S.2d 99, 102-03 (1978).
10. 64 A.D.2d 369, 374, 410 N.Y.S.2d 99, 103 (1978).

141

Because of his CRMD placement, the plaintiff was forced to be transferred a number of times. The facts reveal that:

> He was transferred to P.S. 11 on October 11, 1957 and remained there for two years. Thereafter he was transferred to P.S. 77 and then to P.S. 88; he remained in each school for two years; in September, 1963 he was transferred to P.S. 87, where he remained for one year; in September, 1964 he was transferred to P.S. 93, where he remained until the close of the 1967/1968 academic year. During all of this time, plaintiff resided at the same address. In September, 1968 he was transferred to the Queens Occupational Training Center (OTC). This is a manual and shop training school for retarded youths which provides no academic education. At the start of his second school year there (September, 1969) he was told that since it had been determined that he was not retarded he was not eligible to remain at the OTC.[11]

On May 12, 1969, after the plaintiff "had been closeted with mentally retarded children for more than 12 years," he was administered an I.Q. test by one of the doctors at the Bureau of Child Guidance. At that time, he was one month past his eighteenth birthday, and he was approaching the end of his first year at the Queens Occupational Training Center.[12] The doctor's report explains the reasons for administering that I.Q. test as follows:

> Danny is being re-evaluated as to intellectual status, following an interview with his mother, who came to the school very much disturbed because her son has been rejected by Social Security for continuance of payments after the age of 18, the S.S.A. feeling he was not sufficiently handicapped by his retarded status to pursue gainful employment. On January 9, 1957, the Bureau of Child Guidance found a Binet I.Q. of 74.[13]

---

11. *Id.*
12. 64 A.D.2d 369, 376, 410 N.Y.S.2d 99, 104 (1978).
13. *Id.*

At this time (May 12, 1969), the plaintiff was administered a Wechsler Intelligence Scale for Adults (W.A.I.S.)
test. He scored a verbal I.Q. of 107 resulting in a full-scale
I.Q. of 94. The report of the test includes the following:

> He is a tall, well-built boy, alert-looking and charm-
> ing in manner, who is so incapacitated by a speech
> defect that communication is difficult for him. He re-
> lates very well, displays humor, and appears reality
> oriented.
>
> *On the W.A.I.S., he obtained a Verbal Scale I.Q. 85,
> Performance I.Q. 107, and Full Scale I.Q. 94. This
> places him in the normal range.* However, his superior
> performance on tests of non-verbal intelligence, as
> well as the fact that his extremely poor academic back-
> ground severely depreciated his scores on some verbal
> tests, make it very likely that *his intellectual potential
> is at least Bright Normal.*
>
> *Projective tests and tracings of geometric designs
> confirm the impression of good intelligence and contra-
> indicate organicity.* He is however extremely compul-
> sive, to a degree that sometimes reality testing suffers
> in his distribution of time for a task.
>
> This boy has above average intellectual potential
> and a good personality structure. Due to his being al-
> most immobilized in the speech area, as well as consid-
> ering his extremely defective academic background, he
> would find it difficult, if not impossible, to function in
> a regular high school. Psychomotor coordination is
> good, however. Referral for [Division of Vocational Re-
> habilitation of the State Education Department] is
> suggested for specialized training and alleviation of
> the speech problem (emphasis added).[14]

Neither the plaintiff nor his mother was informed at that
time of the test results. He remained at the Occupational
Training Center until the end of the spring semester.
When he returned to the OTC on September 8, 1969, he
was told to leave because he didn't belong there anymore.

---

14. 64 A.D.2d 369, 377, 410 N.Y.S.2d 99, 104-05 (1978).

One of the school officials told the plaintiff's mother that "from their tests they discovered he was not retarded and they could no longer keep him there because he doesn't qualify."[15]

In January 1979 the plaintiff was referred to another clinical psychologist by a neurologist and psychiatrist who had examined the plaintiff at the request of plaintiff's counsel. He administered several tests, including the Wechsler Adult Intelligence Scale. On the predominantly *verbal* part of that test he attained an I.Q. of 89; on the *performance* subtests he attained an I.Q. of 114. Combining the level of these tests resulted in a full-scale I.Q. of 100. He explained that the plaintiff's lower score on the verbal part of the test was largely influenced by his schooling.[16]

The doctor concluded that:

> *Plaintiff's learning potential had always been above average* and that one of the reasons his intellectual development had been diminished was the assumption of the correctness of the school's diagnosis by his family and others, by reason of which they did not provide the stimulation that would otherwise have been given the child .... Plaintiff felt that he was substantially without an education; that he did not know what he could do to earn a living; and that he did not know "where he fitted in the world, and even where he fitted into his family." All this was a competent producing cause of the condition of depression that he noted in plaintiff (emphasis added).[17]

§ 6.1(B). Complaint.

Regarding the negligence of the defendants, the plaintiff, in his complaint, alleged:

---

15. 64 A.D.2d 369, 377, 410 N.Y.S.2d 99, 105 (1978).
16. 64 A.D.2d 369, 379, 410 N.Y.S.2d 99, 106 (1978).
17. *Id.*

> That the defendants herein were negligent, reckless and careless in failing to provide adequate and/or sufficient procedures for the purpose of true evaluation of this infant's mental intelligence; in hiring incompetent personnel; in failing to properly supervise said personnel; in failing to retest and re-evaluate this infant's condition so as to prevent the contingency which here occurred; in failing to use adequate and/or sufficient testing; in causing and/or permitting this infant to remain for approximately 12 years without an adequate and/or sufficient test of his true capacity; in depriving this infant of speech therapy which he required for the purpose of improvement; in misleading this infant's guardian as to the true nature of this infant's capacities and condition; in lulling said guardian into a false sense of belief that the infant plaintiff was a retarded child when in fact the child was not retarded, and the defendants were in other ways negligent and careless.[18]

The second cause of action referred to damages suffered by the plaintiff's mother, who was also a plaintiff, as a result of the defendant's negligence. In part, the complaint alleged:

> That as a result of the aforementioned, this plaintiff has been caused severe financial loss as the result of the loss of the earning capacity of her infant son, and has further been caused to expend diverse sums of money for the purpose of obtaining transportation to special schools required under the direction of the Board of Education of the City of New York, otherwise unnecessary, and has been in other ways severely damaged without want of contributory negligence on her behalf, and further this plaintiff may be required to expend substantial sums of money for re-training

---

18. Complaint at p. 4, Hoffman v. City of New York, No. 71-12593 Sup. Ct. (N.Y., 1976).

and further treatment required by her infant son as the result of the aforementioned ....[19]

The plaintiffs demanded judgment against the defendants for the first cause of action in the sum of one million five hundred thousand ($1,500,000.00) dollars, and for the second cause of action in the sum of five hundred thousand ($500,000.00) dollars.

§ 6.1(C). Decision by the New York Supreme Court, Trial Term.

The Supreme Court, Trial Term, entered a judgment on a jury verdict in the principal amount of seven hundred and fifty thousand ($750,000.00) dollars.

§ 6.1(D). Appeal to the Supreme Court, Appellate Division.

A timely appeal was taken by the defendant, the Board, to the Supreme Court, Appellate Division. (*See* Appendix 9). The supreme court held that:

(1) board was liable to plaintiff for damage resulting from negligence of board's employees in failing to follow board's school psychologists' recommendation that plaintiff's intelligence be re-evaluated within two years after he was placed in class for children with retarded mental development, on basis of intelligence test indicating he was just below cut-off point for attending classes for normal children, and (2) plaintiff who as result of negligence of board's employees had diminished intellectual development and psychological injury was entitled to recover $500,000 from the board.[20]

The court reversed the judgment and granted a new trial on the issue of damages only, unless plaintiff consented to

---

19. *Id.* at 5.
20. 64 A.D.2d 369, 410 N.Y.S.2d 99 (1978).

a reduction of a verdict of $500,000.00, in which event judgment would be affirmed. The court reasoned as follows:

> Defendant's affirmative act in placing plaintiff in a CRMD class initially (when it should have known that a mistake could have devastating consequences) created a relationship between itself and plaintiff out of which arose a duty to take reasonable steps to ascertain whether (at least, in a borderline case) that placement was proper [citations omitted]. We need not here decide whether such duty would have required "intelligence" retesting (in view of plaintiff's poor showing on achievement tests) had not the direction for such retesting been placed in the very document which asserted that plaintiff was to be placed in a CRMD class. It ill-becomes the Board of Education to argue for the untouchability of its own policy and procedures when the gist of plaintiff's complaint is that the entity which did not follow them was the board itself.
>
> New York State and its municipalities have long since surrendered immunity from suit. Just as well-established is the rule that damages for psychological and emotional injury are recoverable even absent physical injury or contact [citations omitted]. *Had plaintiff been improperly diagnosed or treated by medical or psychological personnel in a municipal hospital, the municipality would be liable for the ensuing injuries. There is no reason for any different rule here because the personnel were employed by a government entity other than a hospital.* Negligence is negligence, even if defendant and Mr. Justice Damiani prefer semantically to call it educational malpractice. Thus, defendant's rhetoric constructs a chamber of horrors by asserting that affirmance in this case would create a new theory of liability known as "educational malpractice" and that before doing so we must consider public policy [citations omitted] and the effects of opening a vast new field which will further impoverish financially hard pressed municipalities. Defendant, in effect, suggests that to avoid such horrors, educational entities must be insulated from the legal responsibili-

147

ties and obligations common to all other governmental entities no matter how seriously a particular student may have been injured and, ironically, even though such injuries were caused by their own affirmative acts in failing to follow their own rules.

I see no reason for such a trade-off, on alleged policy grounds, which would warrant a denial of fair dealing to one who is injured by exempting a governmental agency from its responsibility for its affirmative torts. Such determination would simply amount to the imposition of private value judgments over the legitimate interests and legal rights of those tortiously injured. That does not mean that the parents of the Johnies who cannot read may flock to the courts and automatically obtain redress. Nor does it mean that the parents of all the Johnies whose delicate egos were upset because they did not get the gold stars they deserved will obtain redress. If the door to "educational torts" for nonfeasance is to be opened [citations omitted], it will not be by this case which involves misfeasance in failing to follow the individualized and specific prescription of defendant's own certified psychologist whose very decision it was in the first place, to place plaintiff in a class for retarded children, or in the initial making by him of an ambiguous report, if that be the fact.

As Professor David A. Diamond noted [citations omitted], when discussing this very case after the judgment at Trial Term, and contrasting it with the *Donohue* case, upon which Mr. Justice Damiani lays so much stress "the thrust of the plaintiff's case is not so much a failure to take steps to detect and correct a weakness in a student, that is, a failure to provide a positive program for a student, but rather, affirmative acts of negligence which imposed additional and crippling burdens upon a student" and that "it does not seem unreasonable to hold a school board liable for the type of behavior exhibited in *Hoffman*." I agree.[21]

In concluding the opinion for the majority, Justice Shapiro added:

Therefore, not only reason and justice, but the law as

---

21. 64 A.D.2d 369, 385-86, 410 N.Y.S.2d 99, 109-10 (1978).

well, cry out for an affirmance of plaintiff's right to a recovery. Any other reason would be a reproach to justice. In the words of the ancient Romans: *"Fiat justitia, ruat coelum"* (Let justice be done, though the heavens fall).[22]

Two of the justices, however, dissented and in their separate opinions voted to reverse the judgment and dismiss the complaint. In his dissent, Justice Martuscello mentioned:

> The two theories of liability as pleaded in the complaint were submitted to the jury. The jury returned a general verdict in favor of the plaintiff awarding him damages of $750,000. On this appeal the defendant challenges, *inter alia,* each theory of liability on the ground that the plaintiff failed to sustain his burden of proving his claim as a matter of law and therefore neither theory of liability should have been submitted to the jury.
>
> I find merit in the defendant's position. *It is conceivable that a case of educational malpractice may be pleaded and established against a board of education for an act of misfeasance.* However, the plaintiff in the instant case has failed to establish the negligence of the defendant by its breach of a duty owed to the plaintiff under either theory of liability. Therefore, the plaintiff's complaint should have been dismissed at the close of the entire case [emphasis added].[23]

He further contended:

> The issue of whether the Board of Education had a duty to periodically retest plaintiff's I.Q. should not have been submitted to the jury.... A jury should not be permitted to evaluate the merits of plaintiff's disagreement with the educational assumptions relied upon by a board of education. Questions regarding a

---

22. 64 A.D.2d 369, 387, 410 N.Y.S.2d 99, 111 (1978).
23. 64 A.D.2d 369, 391, 410 N.Y.S.2d 99, 113-14 (1978).

149

board's exercise of judgment and discretion, and its allocation of available resources, are inappropriate for resolution in the courts [citations omitted]. Under the guise of enforcing a vague educational policy, a jury should not be permitted to assume the exercise of an educational policy that is vested by constitution and by statute in school administrative agencies [citations omitted].[24]

Justice Damiani, the other justice who dissented, voted to reverse the case and dismiss plaintiff's complaint. He reasoned that it was the policy of the state that no cause of action existed to recover for so-called educational malpractice. He cited the *Donohue* case as authority. He wrote:

In the *Donohue* case, this court decided that the strong public policy of this state was to avoid judicial interference in educational matters and that the recognition of a cause of action sounding in negligence to recover for so-called "educational malpractice" would impermissibly require the courts to oversee and, with hindsight, to evaluate the professional judgment of those charged with the responsibility for the administration of public education. As was predicted in *Donohue,* this case has involved the courts in an evaluation of judgments and actions of educators. In addition, the jury here was required to decide, among other issues "whether certain tests should have been administered or test results interpreted in one way rather than another" [citations omitted]. The result was a trial transcript of some 2036 pages, wherein the parties explored every facet of the plaintiff's education. Questions as to the propriety of educational judgments and actions are inappropriate for resolution in the judicial arena [citations omitted].[25]

---

24. 64 A.D.2d 369, 397, 410 N.Y.S.2d 99, 117 (1978).
25. 64 A.D.2d 369, 397-98, 410 N.Y.S.2d 99, 117-18 (1978).

§ 6.1(E). Appeal to the Court of Appeals of New York.

The decision was appealed to the Court of Appeals of New York.[26] (*See* Appendix 10). In December 1979 the Court of Appeals reversed the Appellate Division and stated that the cause of action in this case sounded in educational malpractice. Following a review of its holding in the *Donohue* case the court concluded:

> In order to affirm a finding of liability in these circumstances, this court would be required to allow the finder of fact to substitute its judgment for the professional judgment of the board of education as to the type of psychometric devices to be used and the frequency with which such tests are to be given. Such a decision would also allow a court or a jury to second-guess the determinations of each of plaintiff's teachers. To do so would open the door to an examination of the propriety of each of the procedures used in the education of every study in our school system. Clearly, each and every time a student fails to progress academically, it can be argued that he or she would have done better and received a greater benefit if another educational approach or diagnostic tool had been utilized. Similarly, whenever there was a failure to implement a recommendation made by any person in the school system with respect to the evaluation of a pupil or his or her educational program, it could be said, as here, that liability could be predicated on misfeasance. However, the court system is not the proper forum to test the validity of the educational decision to place a particular student in one of the many educational programs offered by the schools of the State. In our view, any dispute concerning the proper placement of a child in a particular educational program can best be resolved by seeking review of such professional edu-

---

26. 49 N.Y.2d 119, 424 N.Y.S.2d 376 (1979).

cational judgment through the administrative processes provided by statute.[27]

Three other justices concurred with the majority opinion written by Justice Josen. There was, however, a dissent by three justices. Thus, this opinion was a 4-3 decision. Justice Meyer, writing the dissent, argued:

> I agree with Mr. Justice Irwin Shapiro, on the analysis spelled out in his well-reasoned decision at the Appellate Division [citations omitted] that this case involves not "educational malpractice" as the majority in this court suggests [citations omitted] but discernible affirmative negligence on the part of the board of education in failing to carry out the recommendation for re-evaluation within a period of two years which was an integral part of the procedure by which plaintiff was placed in a CRMD class, and thus readily identifiable as the proximate cause of plaintiff's damages. I therefore dissent.[28]

§ 6.2. Snow v. State of New York.

In 1976 a claim was brought against the state of New York by Donald Snow, both individually and by his parent and natural guardian, to recover damages emanating from infant claimant's admission and confinement to Willowbrook State School from June 1965 to August 1972 and at a Suffolk State School from August 1972 to December 31, 1974.[29] Subsequent to his birth, plaintiff was hospitalized for 103 days. Following his discharge, he underwent repeated hospitalizations. It became apparent that his development was slower than normal. In December 1964 he was institutionalized at the Brunswick Home for Mental

---

27. 49 N.Y.2d 119, 126-27, 424 N.Y.S.2d 376, 379-80 (1979).
28. 49 N.Y.2d 119, 127, 424 N.Y.S.2d 376, 380 (1979).
29. Snow v. State, 98 A.D.2d 442, 469 N.Y.S.2d 959, 960 (1983).

Defectives, from which he was discharged in May 1965. He was admitted to Willowbrook in June 1965.[30]

In summarizing the facts the court stated as follows:

> As per the notice of claim, Donald Snow had been illegally admitted, detained and confined at Willowbrook and the Suffolk State School and had suffered mentally and physically as a result of incompetent supervision, negligent and incompetent treatment, wanton negligence in the examination, treatment and diagnosis of the infant claimant during his admittance and confinement, and failure to educate or train him. It was further alleged that the State had been wantonly negligent in the retention, supervision and maintenance of the infant claimant, both in medical treatment and in general overall conditions of his confinement. Claimants initially sought damages in the amount of $1,000,000 for each of the following elements: (1) the pain and suffering, both physical and mental, sustained by the infant claimant during his confinement; (2) violation of his civil rights with respect to his admission and incarceration; (3) damages as a result of the retardation and corruption of the normal learning process allegedly resulting from inadequate medical treatment and loss of contact with normal society; and (4) breach of contract. Despite the fact that the claim set forth numerous tortious acts allegedly committed by the State, the case was submitted to the court by claimants' attorneys solely upon the theories of medical malpractice and negligent supervision and care.
>
> The Court of Claims found, notwithstanding allegations to the contrary, that the State's employees had not been negligent in failing to prescribe a hearing aid for the infant claimant at an earlier age, because the record contained conflicting expert testimony as to that issue. However, liability was imposed upon the State for having failed to evaluate the claimant as a deaf child in the first instance and for its inordinate

---

30. *Id.*

delay in re-evaluating his true level of intelligence.
The initial error was compounded by the failure to re-
evaluate claimant intellectually, particularly in view
of the affirmative entries in claimant's records. Notations on the medical records dating back to Donald's
admission at Willowbrook in June, 1965 indicate that
his hearing was questionable. However, a Kuhlmann
intelligence test was administered and a score of 24
recorded on Donald's record. On the basis of such a low
intelligence quotient (I.Q.), a decision was made that
Donald was not suitable for a trainable and educable
program. In May, 1967, however, Donald, then almost
five years of age, was enrolled in a speech class. His
teacher at the time labeled him as a "very bright"
child who would "learn quickly." In August, 1967,
Donald was described as an interested youngster who
was extremely alert but deaf. Despite these observations inconsistent with his recorded I.Q. of 24, the child
was not re-evaluated intellectually until June, 1971.[31]

Based upon these circumstances, the trial court made the
following finding:

Here the original evaluation of Donald was made without the knowledge that he had a hearing impairment.
Accordingly, an improper test was utilized in determining his level of intelligence. Therefore, it is clear
that the case is not one involving an exercise of professional medical judgment. The erroneous evaluation
was compounded by the fact that no further reevaluation was made. This despite the many notes and observations of Donald's teachers and a statute that called
for reevaluation. Under such circumstances, the Court
finds that there was no exercise of medical judgment.[32]

The court went on to state:

Having determined that the initial evaluation of
claimant by the State staff at Willowbrook was im-

31. *Id.* at 960-61.
32. *Id.* at 961.

proper and that proper procedure dictated that Donald should have been more promptly re-evaluated, *the court focused its attention upon whether the State's error constituted medical or educational malpractice.* A key factor in the determination was the court's realization that the failure to have re-evaluated this claimant's intelligence level with a reasonable degree of diligence necessitated his remaining institutionalized with severely retarded patients, bereft of the companionship of normal society at a stage of his development when such contact could have been most advantageous. Based upon a trial record replete with allegations of departures from accepted medical practice, the State was found liable for medical malpractice in its evaluation and treatment of Donald Snow. In the language of the court:

> *It is clear to the Court that the malpractice which was committed was not one of educational malpractice, but rather medical malpractice.* This finding is substantiated by the very nature of the Willowbrook State School. The patients are under continuous treatment. They receive continuous medical, as well as, psychological treatment. Even Willowbrook's records belie the State's assertion that it is merely a school. Without performing a textual exegesis on Claimant's Exhibit '1,' it is clear that it is a hospital or medical and not a school record. Also, the payment for Donald's treatment was made under his father's medical plan. Based upon the above, as well as other testimony and documents submitted in evidence, the Court finds that the malpractice committed by the employees of Willowbrook was medical in nature, and hence governed by the law applicable to medical malpractice (emphasis added).[33]

The court then summarized the state's position thusly:

> The State's position, in essence, is that claimant is improperly seeking in this claim for medical malpractice and negligence to recover upon the nonactionable

---

33. *Id.*

theory of educational malpractice (see *Hoffman v. Board of Educ.*, 49 N.Y.2d 121, 424 N.Y.S.2d 376, 400 N.E.2d 317; *Donohue v. Copiague Union Free School Dist.*, 47 N.Y.2d 440, 418 N.Y.S.2d 375, 391 N.E.2d 1352). As per the State's view of the evidence, expert opinion was divided as to the practicality of more frequent re-evaluation of Donald's I.Q. level inasmuch as earlier independent diagnosis had revealed him to be mentally retarded. Moreover, the State maintains that since Donald scored a mere 57 on the Hiskey-Nebraska I.Q. test administered in 1971, "it defies logic to believe that anything other than a mentally retarded score would have been measured had more testing been done between 1965 and 1971." Thus, the State contends, even if the Willowbrook staff erred in determining the form and extent of treatment best suited to claimant's needs, such error would merely constitute one of professional judgment and hence not be legally cognizable [citations omitted].[34]

The court then opined as follows:

We conclude in this case that the mistaken institutionalization which caused the infant claimant severe and permanent psychological damage and irreparably impaired his ability to speak, communicate and read emanated from the use of an improper I.Q. test to assess the child's intellectual capacity. The allegations in *Donohue v. Copiague Union Free School Dist. (supra)* are pale in comparison to the reality of Donald Snow's situation. The thrust of the plaintiff's allegations in *Donohue (supra)* was that notwithstanding his acquisition of a high school diploma, he lacked the ability to comprehend written English on a level sufficient to enable him to complete applications for employment. The essence of the plaintiff's complaint was that this deficiency was attributable to the failure of the defendant school district to perform its duties to educate him. The court refused to recognize the claim on the ground that jurisdiction over educational affairs

---

34. *Id.* at 962.

is vested in the Board of Regents and the Commissioner of Education rather than the courts.

To entertain a cause of action for educational malpractice would require the courts not merely to make judgments as to the validity of broad educational policies — a course we have unalteringly eschewed in the past — but, more importantly, to sit in review of the day-to-day implementation of these policies. Recognition in the courts of this cause of action would constitute blatant interference with the responsibility for the administration of the public school system lodged by Constitution and statute in school administrative agencies (*James v. Board of Educ.*, 42 N.Y.2d [357], at p. 367 [397 N.Y.S.2d 934, 366 N.E.2d 1291], *supra.*) (*Donohue v. Copiague Union Free School Dist., supra,* 47 N.Y.2d p. 444-445, 418 N.Y.S.2d 375, 391 N.E.2d 1352).

In *Hoffman v. Board of Educ. (supra)* the Court of Appeals again considered the issue of educational malpractice and precluded recovery for claims based upon that theory. That case is readily distinguishable from the instant situation in several important respects.

Initially we note that there was no evidence that the original evaluation of Daniel Hoffman was conducted improperly. Secondly, the failure to have re-evaluated Daniel Hoffman's intelligence constituted a justifiable exercise of judgment in view of his teacher's daily observations regarding his lack of progress. In marked contrast, the recorded observations of Donald Snow's teachers were sufficient to have impugned the accuracy of the original diagnosis. Moreover, upon discovery of Donald's deafness, the State, having based the initial I.Q. classification upon a test designed for persons who could hear, was required to re-assess the results of that test. The failure to so act constituted a discernible act of medical malpractice on the part of the State rather than a mere error in judgment vis-a-vis claimant's educational progress. Consequently, this appeal does not involve a noncognizable claim for educational malpractice, and the *Hoffman (supra)* line of cases is not controlling.

With respect to the matter of damages, we conclude
that while the Court of Claims was correct in its finding of liability, the award of $2,500,000 to claimant for
all his present and future damages was excessive. The
computation of damages in a case of such stunted development is necessarily speculative and fraught with
difficulties. Notwithstanding the fact that the years
lost due to the State's improper diagnosis, treatment
and training of claimant are irretrievable, we are of
the view that the exorbitant dollar amount of the
award is reflective of the court's sympathy for this unfortunate claimant (cf. *Juditta v. Bethlehem Steel
Corp.,* 75 A.D.2d 126, 138, 428 N.Y.S.2d 535). Accordingly, we order that the award on claimant's behalf be
reduced, as an exercise of discretion, to the sum of
$1,500,000. As so modified, the judgment under review
should be affirmed.

Judgment of the Court of Claims, dated January 19,
1982, modified, on the facts and in the exercise of discretion, by reducing the award to claimant Donald
Snow to the principal sum of $1,500,000. As so modi-
fied, judgment affirmed, without costs or disbursements, and matter remitted to the Court of Claims for
entry of an appropriate amended judgment.[35]

The case was then appealed to Court of Appeals of New
York, which in a one sentence memorandum stated: "Order
affirmed, with costs, for reasons stated in the opinion by
Justice Moses M. Weinstein at the Appellate Division (98
A.D.2d 422, 469 N.Y.S.2d 959).[36]

---

35. *Id.* at 963-64.
36. 64 N.Y.2d 745, 475 N.E.2d 454 (1984).

§ 6.3. Morse et al. v. Henniker School District.

A front page newspaper article, "Illiterate Honor Graduate Sues School For $17,000,"[37] related the plight of a high school graduate. The article began as follows:

> Karen Morse was voted president of her senior class and student council president and was elected to the National Honor Society. She captained the soccer team and won letters in two other sports.
> But for nine years, neither her teachers nor her friends knew she couldn't read.[38]

Karen, who says she was labeled "learning disabled" in the ninth grade sued her high school "to cover bills at a special school where she caught up on learning."[39] She alleged that after school authorities discovered her reading problem they did very little for her. The article quotes Karen as saying, "I was hiding my not being able to read more from my peers than from my teachers because the judgment of your friends is more important."[40]

She did not accept her diploma or formally graduate so that her high school would pay her tuition at the school she was attending which specialized in helping those with dyslexia. The complaint was filed in the United States District Court for the District of New Hampshire and stated, in part, as follows:

> 1. This is an action brought by Karen Ann Morse, an educationally handicapped student enrolled at the Landmark School, Pride's Crossing, Massachusetts ("Landmark"), and by her parents, Wallace Morse and Barbara Morse. This action seeks:

---

37. *Illiterate Honor Graduate Sues School For $17,000*, REGISTER, October 27, 1986, Des Moines, Iowa, p. 1.
38. *Id.*
39. *Id.*
40. *Id.*

(a) A temporary restraining order against the defendants ordering them to provide Karen Ann
Morse with the federal and state statutorily
mandated due process hearing to appeal the dis-
continuation of her special education funds, ordering the Henniker School District (the "School
District") to continue the funding of Karen Ann
Morse at Landmark pending the outcome of that
appeal, and ordering the defendants to comply
with all other obligations imposed by federal and
state law in this matter;

(b) A preliminary and permanent injunction continuing the provisions of the temporary restraining
order; and

(c) An award of attorneys' fees pursuant to 42
U.S.C. § 1988.[41]

The background of the lawsuit is contained in a letter
(made part of the complaint) that was sent by the attorney
for the plaintiffs to the Commissioner of Education. It
stated, in part:

This office represents Karen Ann Morse and her parents, Mr. and Mrs. Wallace Morse, all of Henniker,
New Hampshire. On their behalf, I am filing this Complaint against the Henniker School District
("Henniker") pursuant to § 1127.01 of the Rules of New
Hampshire State Board of Education, the New Hampshire Standards for the Education of Handicapped Students (the "Regulations"), for violations of State and
Federal requirements regarding the education of an
educationally handicapped student.

Karen Morse, date of birth May 14, 1966, is an educationally handicapped student. Her handicap consists
of an inability to read, which was not positively identified until she was in the 11th grade. She has been in
the Henniker School system for her entire educational
career.

---

41. Complaint; Morse v. Burnelle, United States District Court for
the District of New Hampshire, Civil Action File No. C 85 608L.

Karen completed the prescribed curriculum of Henniker High School in June of 1984. Recognizing that she was nevertheless unable to read, Henniker withheld her diploma and approved an Individualized Education Plan ("IEP") for the 1984-85 school year. Under the IEP, Karen attended the Landmark School, Pride's Crossing, Massachusetts ("Landmark"), a private facility with approved programs for the benefit of educationally handicapped students. Her program at Landmark was fully funded by Henniker for the school year 1984-85.

Karen's IEP for the 1985-86 school year was given an Annual Review by the Special Education Evaluation/Placement Team on May 28, 1985, and continuation in the Landmark program was recommended. However, by letter dated June 6, 1985 from Dr. Cynthia E. Mowles, acting Superintendent of Schools, the Morses were informed that the Henniker School Board had decided that public education funds should not be expected on a second year at Landmark for Karen. Shortly thereafter, Karen's Henniker High School diploma was mailed to her.

A bill from Landmark for the 1985-86 school year was subsequently tendered to and rejected by Henniker. However, Landmark is presently holding a place for Karen to continue in its special education program.

Based upon the foregoing facts, the Morses hereby make the following substantive complaints against the Henniker School District, all of which we request you to review, investigate, report upon and otherwise address according to the Complaint Procedures contained in your Regulations:

(a) Henniker arbitrarily, capriciously and without due process abridged Karen Morse's right to continue in the approved program at Landmark, and thereby (1) deprived her of her right to a Free, Appropriate Public Education, and at the same time (2) failed in its responsibility to meet the special educational needs of Karen Morse, an educationally handicapped student.

161

(b) Henniker unlawfully attempted to circumvent its statutory responsibilities to the Morses under RSA 186-C by the simple administrative action of delivering a high school diploma to Karen Morse. Henniker had previously acknowledged its responsibilities to the Morses and had undertaken a program to satisfy said responsibilities, which program it now refuses to complete. The delivery of Karen Morse's diploma should therefore be rescinded and declared null and void for all purposes under RSA 186-C.

(c) Henniker unreasonably, arbitrarily, capriciously and without due process determined that Karen Morse no longer requires special education in accordance with the provisions of RSA 186-C, and thereby unlawfully deprived Karen Morse of her statutory right under RSA 186-C:9 to attend an approved program of special education which can implement her IEP.

(d) Henniker failed to give the Morses the fundamental procedural safeguards required by § 125.01 of the Regulations, in that (1) the Morses were not notified in writing before Henniker proposed to terminate Karen's placement at Landmark; (2) they were not given a written description of the proposed action, an explanation of why Henniker proposed to take such action, a description of the information on which the action was based, or a statement informing them of all rights and procedures available under the Regulations; and (3) no written consent was ever obtained from or even presented to the Morses with respect to terminating Karen Morse's placement at Landmark.

(e) Henniker failed to initiate the Due Process Hearing Procedures when it did not obtain the Morses' consent to the termination of Karen Morse's placement at Landmark. The Regulations, § 1125.01(b)(3)b, provide that lack of parental response shall be interpreted as *disagreement* with the decision or proposed action con-

162

cerning placement, and throws the burden upon the Local Education Agency, i.e., Henniker, to initiate the Due Process Procedures.

Your assistance in processing this Complaint is sincerely appreciated. Please contact this office if you need any further information or documentation concerning this matter, and also send us any reports or hearing notices.[42]

The plaintiffs had moved the Court to grant a temporary restraining order pursuant to Counts I and II of the Complaint.[43] The Court overruled same.[44] In the Memorandum of Law in Support of Defendant's Motion to Dismiss and Objection to Plaintiff's Request for Temporary Restraining Order, it was stated:

Plaintiff Karen Morse is a 19-year-old resident of Henniker, New Hampshire. Plaintiffs Wallace and Barbara Morse are her parents. Karen Morse was identified as an educationally handicapped student during the 1981-82 school year at Henniker High School. While a student at Henniker High School, Karen received special education pursuant to an approved education program which implemented her Individual Education Plan. In June of 1984, Karen Morse successfully completed all requirements for graduation from Henniker High School. Her transcript reflects that her grades were in the 80's and 90's. In 1982, the PSAT's were administered to Karen. Karen scored a 46 in the verbal and a 45 in the math. These scores placed her in the 84 percentile for verbal

---

42. Letter dated August 30, 1985 from Michael G. Gfroerer, attorney for the plaintiffs, in the *Morse* case sent to Robert L. Brunelle, Commissioner of Education; letter was attached to the *Morse* Complaint as "Exhibit F."

43. Plaintiffs' Motion for a Temporary Restraining Order, Morse *supra* note 41, dated November 13, 1985.

44. *See* Post-Hearing Memorandum, Morse, *supra* note 41, dated January 24, 1986.

nationally and the 73 percentile in math nationally. The PSAT's were taken by Karen through standard administration. In 1984 Karen took the SAT's. She scored a 43 in the verbal and a 48 on the math. The SAT's were administered to Karen through nonstandard administration, that is audiocassette tapes were utilized because of Karen's diagnosed learning disability. Although Karen Morse had successfully completed all requirements for graduation in June of 1984, the Henniker School District agreed to provide Karen with one (1) additional year of education at the Landmark School in Massachusetts. An agreement was made that the Henniker School District would provide Karen with one additional year of education at the Landmark School and that upon completion of one year at the Landmark School, Karen's diploma would be delivered to her. To provide for this year-long placement, an Individual Education Plan was developed by the school in conjunction with and approved by Karen's parents. Said I.E.P. was to terminate in June, 1985. In June of 1985, Karen Morse completed a year at the Landmark School and acquired her high school diploma. Since Karen's diploma was awarded to her in June of 1985, the Henniker School District did not convene an I.E.P. or Pupil Placement Team meeting at the conclusion of the 1985 school year. They awarded Karen her diploma. The standard procedure for any educationally handicapped student is that if they have successfully completed all requirements for graduation and will acquire a diploma, a Pupil Placement Team is not convened at that time. Neither Karen nor her parents sought any appeal of the award of her diploma until August 30, 1985, over 60 days after her high school diploma was delivered to her. At that time they appealed to the State Department of Education. A prehearing conference was held on September 25, 1985. The purpose of the hearing was to clarify the issues and to determine whether a due process hearing was necessary. The threshold issue was determined to be whether the delivery of a diploma took a student out of the requirements of RSA 186-C, Section 8 or constituted a change of placement, keeping the student in RSA 186-C:8. The hearings officer found that the earning of a diploma completed the School District's responsibility for the education of a handicapped child. Neither Karen nor her parents appealed the determination of the hearings officer. They subsequently, on or about November 13, 1985, filed the present action in this Court.

It is not contested that Karen Morse satisfied all requirements for graduation in June of 1984. It is also not contested that the Henniker School District funded the 1984-85 program for Karen at Landmark School, and that an I.E.P. existed for Karen for that year. The parties also do not contest that a diploma was acquired by Karen Morse in June of 1985.

In his order the U.S. District Judge summarized the case as follows:

Plaintiffs bring this action against Robert Brunelle, Commissioner of the New Hampshire Department of Education and the Henniker School Department. Plaintiffs seek enforcement of their rights under the Education for All Handicapped Children Act, 20 U.S.C. § 1415 (1982) (EAHCA). Specifically, plaintiffs seek a preliminary and permanent injunction ordering defendants to provide Karen Morse with a due process hearing; ordering defendants to continue Karen Morse's funding at Landmark School, pending appeal; and ordering defendants to comply with all other obligations under federal and state law, specifically the notice and hearing requirements as set forth in paragraph 18 of plaintiffs' complaint. Plaintiffs also bring this action under 42 U.S.C. § 1983 and seek attorneys fees under 42 U.S.C. § 1988.

The facts of this case are as follows:

Karen Morse is an educationally handicapped 19 year old student, currently attending the Landmark School in Pride's Crossing, Massachusetts. In the 1981-82 school year, while she was attending Henniker High School, Karen was identified as education-

165

ally handicapped. The Individualized Education Program (I.E.P.) designed for that school year, lists
Karen's primary disability as "speech/language" and
secondary disability as "mild learning disability."
Plaintiffs' Exhibit 1.

It was not until 1983 that the extent of Karen's disability was discovered. In September, 1983 she was
evaluated at Children's Hospital Medical Center, Boston, Massachusetts at the request of her special education teachers. The diagnostic report (Plaintiff's Exhibit 9) states the reason for referral.

> Karen is virtually a non-reader who has coped
> very well ... Karen's special education teachers are
> concerned that the problem has been overlooked
> until recently due to Karen's excellent coping mech-
> anisms and they request an evaluation to determine
> the etiology of her disability and recommendations
> for an educational program to remedy the situation.
> Plaintiffs' Exhibit 9, at 7.

The evaluation was as follows:

> Quite amazingly, Karen has remained a non-
> reader in her educational career. At this testing, it
> became evident that she has only the very basic and
> rudimentary skills that disallow her from reading at
> the first grade level. Further investigation indicated
> that she is familiar with approximately eight to ten
> letters with some level of mastery. She is able to
> write from a system that she has created herself in
> which she used several letters, yet not all of the
> alphabet sequence. Her coding is very difficult to
> read, even for herself. Karen has trained herself so
> that she uses auditory memory quite well.
>
> The results of this testing indicate that Karen has
> poor visual memory, poor sound-symbol association
> and possible weaknesses in several other areas, in-
> cluding difficulty with blending, difficulty with size
> discrimination, discrimination of directionality in-
> cluding vertical versus horizontal and left versus
> right, and difficulty with sound discrimination.
> These weaknesses, although present, are not

thought to be of the magnitude that would prevent her from learning how to read. Plaintiffs' Exhibit 9, at 17-18.

After the evaluation at Children's Hospital, the Henniker Pupil Placement Team discussed out-of-district placement for Karen. Although the team felt that such a placement was indicated for Karen, it was determined that Karen would complete her senior year at Henniker High School and then be placed in a special school; Landmark School was mentioned as a possibility. See Letter of December 19, 1983, Plaintiffs' Exhibit 6. Exhibit 6 also contains a letter whereby the Henniker School District informed Landmark School that Henniker would be responsible for payment of tuition costs for Karen if she were accepted and if the pupil placement team approved the placement. The placement was approved and made part of Karen's I.E.P. for the 1984-85 school year. Plaintiffs' Exhibit 4. Mr. Thomas Watman, Superintendent of Henniker Schools, testified that Karen had educational needs that required further special education assistance, even though she had completed her twelfth grade at Henniker High School.

Defendants claim that there was an agreement that the school district would fund only one year at Landmark School. There is no support for defendants' contention that the funding would be limited to that one year. Mr. Watman testified that commitments were for a year at a time. He stated that there was no decision that the funding would be limited. Defendants' witness, Mr. Donald Jones, who was Principal of Henniker High School during the 1983-84 school year and now is Assistant Superintendent, admitted that there were no limitations placed on the funding and, in fact, no limitations were even discussed. Further, the I.E.P. is developed on a year to year basis. See 20 U.S.C. § 1401(19).

Karen was enrolled at Landmark School during the summer of 1984 and for the school year 1984-85. On May 28, 1985, a meeting was held at Landmark School where a proposed I.E.P. for Karen was reviewed by

Landmark staff, Henniker School District representatives and the Morses. The Landmark plan for the 1985-86 school year was based on Karen staying at Landmark School. Dr. Cynthia Mowles, Superintendent of Henniker School District, testified that the I.E.P. meeting held at Landmark School was not binding on Henniker since it was the local school district that was responsible for developing the I.E.P. Dr. Mowles testified that she told the group at the meeting that Henniker School District would not fund another year at Landmark School for Karen Morse.

On June 6, 1985 Mr. and Mrs. Morse were informed by letter from the office of Dr. Cynthia Mowles[45] that "the Henniker School Board has confirmed the earlier decision stating that public education funds should not be expended on a second year at Landmark School for Karen." Plaintiffs' Exhibit 6. The Morses had no notice of this decision, other than the remark made the previous week by Dr. Mowles. Shortly thereafter Karen was sent her diploma.

On August 30, 1985 plaintiffs, through counsel, requested in writing an "impartial due process hearing" to appeal the decision of the Henniker School District to discontinue funding and to award Karen her diploma. The request was sent simultaneously to both Henniker School District and Robert Brunelle Commission of Education.

Apparently a hearing was scheduled through the Department of Education Due Process Coordinator, for October 1, 1985. Prior to that hearing a pre-hearing conference was held on September 25, 1985 before a hearing officer who decided that the awarding of Karen's diploma ended the school district's responsibility to provide special education to Karen. No hearing was ever conducted at the administrative level. Plain-

---

45. Memorandum of Law in Support of Defendant Cynthia E. Mowles' Motion to Dismiss and Objection to Plaintiffs' Request for Temporary Restraining Order, Morse, *supra* note 41, dated December 20, 1985.

tiffs sought judicial review from this court by filing the present action on November 12, 1985.[46]

The court went on to state:

Consequently, the decision of the hearing officer was erroneous and must be reversed.

The defendant Brunelle in his capacity as Commissioner of the Department of Education is hereby ordered to conduct an impartial due process hearing in the present case, pursuant to 20 U.S.C. § 1415(b)(2). The defendant is further ordered to comply with the mandate of 20 U.S.C. § 1415(d) as follows:

'Enumeration of rights accorded parties to hearings. Any party to any hearing conducted pursuant to subsections (b) and (c) shall be accorded (1) the right to be accompanied and advised by counsel and by individuals with special knowledge or training with respect to the problems of handicapped children, (2) the right to present evidence and confront, cross-examine, and compel the attendance of witnesses, (3) the right to a written or electronic verbatim record of such hearings and (4) the right to written findings of fact and decisions ....'

Finally, defendants are ordered to comply with all other obligations under federal and state law as it relates to the present case and others within the ambit of the EAHCA.

Specifically, defendants are ordered to comply with the notice and opportunity for hearing requirements of 20 U.S.C. § 1415 and state law and regulations promulgated thereunder.[47]

Following the hearing, it was decided that the plaintiff should recover for a second year tuition at Landmark School. No further appeal was taken.

---

46. Morse, *supra* note 41, Order pp. 1-5.
47. *Id.* at 22-23.

§ 6.4. Summary.

In order to set the stage to delve into the effects of misdiagnosed or failure to diagnose students' learning disabilities and to understand how courts have treated such actions, substantial portions of three cases have been reported herein. The following chapter will briefly summarize additional cases. After reading these cases, the questions that need to be answered are: (1) Do the facts of these cases warrant a recovery for intellectual damage under the theory of educational malpractice? (2) Do they warrant recovery under any other theory?

Chapter 7

ADDITIONAL "HYBRID" EDUCATIONAL MALPRACTICE CASES

> The basis of the plaintiff's complaint was a mistesting and misclassification resulting in the minor plaintiff being placed in an improper special educational program for a number of years to his detriment. We hold that even if these allegations are correct there is no cause of action stated.[1]

---

1. Tubell v. Dade County Public Schools, 419 So. 2d 388 (Fla. 1982).

§ 7.0. Introduction.

This chapter will briefly summarize the alleged facts, as well as the various courts' rationales, for the decisions reached in other "hybrid" educational malpractice cases. These cases are classified as "hybrid" since many of them arose out of situations where the student's alleged misclassification resulted in the "intellectual" harm of the student. This harm precipitated the bringing of a lawsuit, in some instances, under several theories, including the theory of educational malpractice.

§ 7.1. Additional "Hybrid" Educational Malpractice Cases.

§ 7.1(A). McNeil v. Board of Education.

In 1975 a suit was brought by Thomas McNeil in a Superior Court of New Jersey against officials in the South Orange-Maplewood school system.[2] This appears to be the first such educational malpractice case in New Jersey.[3] In the complaint and amended complaint the plaintiff alleged generally that the defendants failed to diagnose and treat him for a visual disorder and that he was awarded a high school diploma though he could read only at a second-grade level. More specifically, the plaintiff alleged in the complaint:

> He was deprived of an education consistent with his full potential, never learned to read beyond a second grade level, was denied the opportunity to benefit from therapy and other programs of education which the defendants knew or should have known would have

---

2. McNeil v. Board of Education, No. L-17297-74 Super. Ct. Law Div. (N.H., 1975).

3. Thorough search for reported and unreported cases had been made; *see also* Joy McIntyre, Expert: *McNeil Could Be Steered Into College*, DAILY NEWS (N.J.) April 25, 1978, p. JL 7.

corrected his handicap. Plaintiff was "socially promoted" and allowed to graduate from the aforementioned schools, was deprived the opportunity to develop and utilize his skills and talents, suffered emotional disturbance, will have to incur expenses in an effort to cure himself, and otherwise suffered injuries, some of which are permanent.[4]

The suit alleged that school officials, the superintendent, principals at the schools the youth attended, school psychologists, social workers, and members of a child-study team "negligently and in violation of statutory duties failed to properly identify, classify, examine, diagnose, consult, treat and educate the plaintiff, ..."[5] Generally, they had failed to diagnose that he was suffering from dyslexia, a condition that causes a person to reverse letters and read words backwards, and promoted him from grade to grade until he graduated.

The defendant's answer contained 12 defenses, one of which states as follows:

> Plaintiff seeks to recover for educational malpractice on the theory that the educational practices and duties here involved can be a basis for tort liability. His action in so doing violates public policy in that teaching processes are not yet understood adequately and there is no model of competent educational practice comparable to that which exists in medicine or law. Also, the allowance of a malpractice action on the basis of the educational practices and duties here involved would lead to an excess of caution and the adoption of less progressive practices. In addition, it would lead to a diversion of large sums of money from the school system.[6]

---

4. Complaint at p. 4, McNeil v. Board of Education, No. L 17297-74 Super. Ct. Law Div. (N.H., 1975).

5. *Id.*

6. Answer at p. 5, McNeil v. Board of Education, No. L 17297-74 Super. Ct. Law Div. (N.H., 1975).

The trial court didn't dismiss the complaint by granting a summary judgment as was the case in the *Peter W.* and *Donohue* cases. Instead, the New Jersey court submitted the case to the jury, as did the New York court in the *Hoffman* case. The case came to trial in 1978. The trial, which lasted for over eight weeks, received considerable publicity. The plaintiff sought no specified amount of damages. The Judge who presided over the trial ruled out damages for loss of income. He noted that New Jersey law bars the plaintiff from collecting damages for emotional suffering if there is no physical damage. He added that if the jury finds for the plaintiff, he could only receive the amount it would cost for lessons and therapy to improve his reading. According to the testimony in the case, that would have been approximately $40,000.00.[7] The jury of four women and two men, who had heard a number of educators and medical doctors testify for and against contentions that plaintiff's visual and perceptual problems had been improperly diagnosed and treated and that plaintiff failed to receive proper attention in school, leaving him to flounder from the seventh grade on, found against the plaintiff. The jury who deliberated for only one hour and a half found that none of the defendants negligently failed to meet professional standards of care and conduct.[8]

§ 7.1(B). Pierce v. Board of Education.

In the case of *Pierce v. Board of Education*[9] , the Illinois Supreme Court decided an apparent educational malprac-

---

7. *See* Joy McIntyre, *School Exonerated in McNeil Case,* DAILY NEWS (N.J.) June 1, 1978. © 1978 New York News, Inc. Reprinted with permission.

8. *See* Donald Warshaw, *McNeil Jury Returns "No Cause for Action,"* STAR LEDGER (N.J.) pp. 1 and 16, June, 1978.

9. 69 Ill. 2d 89, 370 N.E.2d 535 (1977).

tice case without specifically recognizing it as such.[10] The complaint alleged that the student was suffering from a specific learning disability, that the school board was advised of that fact, that the school board refused to transfer the student into special education classes, that the student remained in normal classes where he competed with students not suffering from his learning disability, and that as a result of the school board's refusal to place the student in the special education class, he suffered severe and permanent emotional injury requiring hospitalization and medical treatment. It was further alleged that despite the recommendation of the doctors that the plaintiff be transferred from regular classes, the defendant failed to transfer the plaintiff or to undertake its own testing and evaluation of him.[11]

The circuit court granted the Board's motion to dismiss. On review, the appellate court found that the complaint stated a cause of action, and reversed the circuit court.[12] In reversing the judgment of the appellate court and affirming the judgment of the circuit court, the Illinois Supreme Court commented that the plaintiff based his complaint on the allegations that the Board breached a duty to place him in a special education facility. The issue at hand, said the court, is not whether the Board has fulfilled its mandate to establish and maintain special education facilities for handicapped children, but rather, the precise question concerns the determination of eligibility for such classes and the role of the Board in making that ultimate decision.

The court went on to state:

---

10. Edward W. Remsburg, *Liability for Wrongful Identification, Evaluation for Placement — Is There Malpractice?* COUNSEL OF SCHOOL ATTORNEYS (National School Boards Association, 1980).

11. 69 Ill. 2d 89, 91-92, 370 N.E.2d 535-36 (1977).

12. 69 Ill. 2d 89, 91, 370 N.E.2d 535 (1977).

In support of his arguments that there exists such a duty on behalf of the Board, plaintiff relies on the language of article X, section 1, of the Illinois Constitution, stating as a "fundamental goal of the People of the State ... the educational development of all persons" and section 14-4.01 of the School Code [citations omitted], which directs school boards to establish and maintain "special educational facilities as may be needed ... for handicapped children" ... we find the plaintiff's arguments unpersuasive.

Article X, section 1, of the Illinois Constitution does not impose a duty on boards of education to place students in special education classes. The article is not self-executing. Its pronouncement of the laudable goal of "the educational development of all persons to the limits of their capacities" is a statement of general philosophy, rather than a mandate that certain means be provided in any specific form.

....

Under the rules and regulations, detailed procedures are prescribed for determining the eligibility of children and for placing them in special education. The regulations place primary responsibility upon the local school district for initiating and determining the appropriateness of the referrals of students. However, if the local district fails to act or if it refuses to act after a referral or request by a parent, the rules provide a detailed procedure for review of the board's conduct by administrative officials and for an ultimate determination by the State Superintendent of Education ....

Thus, the ultimate responsibility for determining whether a pupil is eligible for special education rests with the State Board of Education and not the board of education at the local district. Also, the complaint does not allege compliance with the administrative procedures established for a review of the defendant's failure or refusal to admit the plaintiff to special education classes. Plaintiff has therefore not exhausted the administrative remedies [citations omitted]. The complaint, for these reasons, fails to state a cause of action against the defendant.[13]

§ 7.1(C). Doe v. Board of Education.

In the case of *Doe v. Board of Education,*[14] a student complained that as a result of the school's misdiagnosis, he is virtually illiterate. A Circuit Court in Maryland granted defendant's summary judgment. The court wrote:

> [I]t is well-settled in Maryland that before any plaintiff can recover in a negligence action, they must show a breach of either a common law duty or statutory duty of care resulting in an injury to the plaintiff, and there is always a question whether in any particular set of circumstances one party owes a duty to another, and that is a question of law to be decided by the court.
>
> Now, *the courts of first resort, the trial courts, are free to find new causes of action, and they are not bound by those that have been found in the past where, in fact, there is a new duty arising to some person through new law or even social change,* but the question of whether or not there is a duty arising here so that an individual student can bring a suit for damages to correct an inadequacy or something that is wrong in the school system is one that I think is better dealt with procedurally in the case of *Peter W. v. San Francisco School District.* [citations omitted].
>
> Now, those cases both held decisively that no such duty existed toward the student, and they did not hold that the schools did not have to be run properly, and it did not mean that educators are not ethically and legally responsible for providing a meaningful education for the youth of the state, and, of course, this might be done by other types of suits. It did mean, however, that they ruled that there was not a suit available for damages by an individual student for al-

---

13. 69 Ill. 2d 89, 92-93, 370 N.E.2d 535, 536-37 (1977).

14. No. 48277, Circuit Ct. Montgomery County Maryland (July 6, 1979).

leged failure to reach certain educational objectives, and *I think that would be a very sad state of affairs if juries were able to decide whether or not the school system had functioned properly, in any case, and dole out the taxpayers' money with the idea that in some way this might correct the situation.* I do not believe that that is the type of cause of action that is in the public interest to adopt in this state.

....

... I don't believe that the act of creating insurance and protecting themselves from what may be this type of suit necessarily gives rise to any cause of action; and the court holds specifically that there is no doubt existing on the part of the School Board, Montgomery County or the Montgomery County Department of Health which will inure individually to benefit any student to the extent that he may bring an action at law for damages on the basis that he did not receive a proper education as required by law [emphasis added].[15]

§ 7.1(D). Smith v. Alameda County Social Services.

In the same year (1979), the California Court of Appeals, First District, decided the case of *Smith v. Alameda County Social Services.*[16] The plaintiff, a 17-year-old boy, brought suit, alleging, *inter alia,* that the school district had negligently placed him in remedial classes for the mentally retarded when, in fact, he was not retarded. The plaintiff asserted that by so doing, the school district breached its duty of providing appropriate educational training. The superior court dismissed the suit. On appeal, the appellate court applied the rules as set out in *Peter W.* and held that no valid claim for the recovery of damages had been stated.

---

15. *Id.* Opinion, at 3-6.
16. 90 Cal. App. 3d 929, 153 Cal. Rptr. 712 (1979).

§ 7.1(E). Goldberg v. Cronin.

A complaint for injunctive relief and damages was filed by Michael Goldberg and Donald Goldberg, individually and as next friend, for Michael Goldberg, in the United States District Court for the Northern District of Illinois, Eastern Division.[17] It was filed against Joseph Cronin, Wesley Gibbs, Gary Hahn, Vernon F. Frazee, Niles Township District 219, School District 68, and State Board of Education. The plaintiffs alleged:

> That beginning in third grade and continuing throughout the balance of the time spent in DISTRICT 68 elementary schools, Plaintiff Michael Goldberg was continually diagnosed as a learning disabled child and, in particular, a dyslexic child. That continual testing programs were conducted and Michael was continually identified as a child in need of special learning programs and special learning environments. That it was apparent to all concerned that Michael was not succeeding or adapting well to normal classroom environments. Plaintiff Donald Goldberg had several psychologists and doctors conduct diagnostic tests and made the same available to DISTRICT 68 and Defendant Vernon F. Frazee while Michael was in attendance in the fifth, sixth, and seventh grades.
>
> That despite the recommendations of Michael's doctor that he be specially placed and Michael's apparent inability to adjust to the normal classroom situation, Defendant Vernon Frazee and Defendant DISTRICT 68 totally failed and refused to place Michael Goldberg in the proper educational setting. Defendant Frazee, without any justification, and in derogation of his duties as Executive Director of the Niles Department of Special Education, stated that he was aware of the recommendations but would not implement them.

---

17. Complaint for Injunctive Relief and Damages, Goldberg v. Cronin, No. 79C5039, U.S. District Ct. for the Northern District of Ill., Eastern Div. (1979).

....
That disregarding their duty and with full knowledge of all attendant facts and circumstances, Defendants Frazee and DISTRICT 68 wholly failed and refused to properly place Plaintiff Michael Goldberg in appropriate classrooms and educational programs. As a direct and proximate result of Defendant Frazee's and School District 68's failure and refusal as aforesaid, Plaintiff, Michael Goldberg, was not properly educated, was emotionally damaged by improper placement and was denied his potential for achieving social and economic self-sufficiency and well-being.[18]

Michael was then transferred for secondary placement. Even though all of the aforementioned psychological and diagnostic materials were made available to personnel in his new educational domain, they failed and refused to properly place him in appropriate classrooms and educational programs, and in fact placed him in programs damaging to his emotional and educational well-being. The plaintiff further stated that he was deprived of an education, that he was denied his potential for achieving social and economic self-sufficiency and well-being, that he was, and still is, deprived of special education services, that he was denied his rights under the Education For All Handicapped Children Act of 1975, that he was deprived of life, liberty, and property without the due process of law, that he was deprived of exercising his rights and privileges as a citizen of the United States of America and the State of Illinois, that he was deprived of equal protection of the laws, and that his family has been financially and emotionally harmed.[19]

---

18. *Id.* at 4-5.

19. Answer to Defendants' Motions to Dismiss and Memorandum of Law, at pp. 14-15, Michael Goldberg v. Cronin, No. 79C5039, U.S. District of Ill., Eastern Division (1979).

Plaintiffs averred in the complaint that the defendants were guilty of negligence and educational malpractice, causing irreparable harm, and this will continue each day that appropriate placement is not made. Therefore, the plaintiffs demanded an order for mandatory injunction and demanded that the defendants provide the plaintiff, Michael, with a free and appropriate placement in a suitable educational institution. Furthermore, the plaintiffs demanded the sum of $1,000,000.00 for compensatory damages.[20]

There was no adjudication of the issues in the U.S. District Court. The case was dismissed for lack of federal jurisdiction. The case was refiled in the State Circuit Court. It was scheduled for hearing in November 1989. The case was dismissed for want of prosecution.[21]

§ 7.1(F). Loughran v. Flanders.

In 1979, the case of *Loughran v. Flanders*[22] was decided by the United States District Court for the District of Connecticut. The facts, as related by the court, are as follows:

> The plaintiff, Kenneth Loughran, is a fifteen-year-old minor who resides with his parents in the Town of Windsor Locks. A lifelong resident of the town, he has been enrolled in the Windsor Locks school system since 1970. The complaint alleges that since 1971, the year he entered first grade, it has been apparent that Kenneth has suffered from educational disabilities, which greatly impair his reading and writing skills.
>
> The plaintiff's difficulties were first formally recognized by the defendants in October of 1974 when an educational re-evaluation disclosed that Kenneth was

---

20. Complaint for Injunctive Relief and Damages, p. 12, Goldberg v. Cronin, No. 79C5039, U.S. District of Ill., Eastern Division (1979).

21. Goldberg v. Board of Education, Cook County Circuit Court Law Division Case No. 83 L 7892 (Illinois).

22. 470 F. Supp. 110 (1979).

in fact learning disabled. It is the assertion of the plaintiff that this re-evaluation was deficient in that it failed to fully identify the extent of the problem. The complaint also alleges that the education which Kenneth has subsequently received has been inadequate due to a lack of educational resources within the Windsor school system.

The essence of Kenneth's claim is that through their negligence, the defendants have breached a duty under both state and federal law to provide him with a free and appropriate public education. This breach of duty allegedly arises from the defendants' failure to properly diagnose and take effective steps toward remedying his learning disabilities.

Apart from affirmative educational relief, the complaint also seeks one million dollars in damages to compensate both Kenneth and his parents for the emotional trauma suffered by them as a result of the defendants' conduct. The complaint alleges that the defendants' negligence has made it virtually impossible for Kenneth to function at his full intellectual capacity and to thus reap those personal, social and financial rewards which are commensurate with his intelligence.[23]

The defendants moved to dismiss the complaint, *inter alia,* on grounds that plaintiff:

(1) is impermissibly attempting to formulate a private cause of action out of the Aid to All Handicapped Children Act of 1975, (2) has failed to exhaust his available state remedies, (3) is asserting claims predating either in whole or in part the effective date of the federal legislation, and (4) is barred from seeking money damages by the Eleventh Amendment and/or common law immunity.[24]

The federal district court held that there is no implied cause of action arising out of violation of the Act. The court reasoned that:

---

23. *Id.* at 112.
24. *Id.*

[T]here is a common theme contained within the legislative history of these acts for which the plaintiff traces his alleged cause of action. Each demonstrates a congressional *attempt to improve the educational opportunities* afforded the estimated four million handicapped students who, due to the limited financial and educational resources of the states, were not receiving an adequate education. The acts sought to mitigate this problem by providing funds to expand and improve the educational resources of the several states.

The legislative histories of these acts share a second common trait; *each is devoid of even the slightest suggestion that Congress intended for it to serve as a vehicle for which to initiate a private cause of action for damages* [emphasis added].[25]

In granting defendant's motion to dismiss, the court stated that the thrust of the plaintiff's action for damages is the assertion that the defendants' negligence, in failing to both diagnose and remedy his learning disabilities, deprived him of a federal statutory right to special education. The court added:

A final factor to be considered is whether the purported cause of action is one traditionally relegated to state law, in an area basically the concern of the states [citations omitted]. The plaintiff is essentially alleging that he is the victim of educational malpractice. The few reported cases on this type of claim have all arisen in a state forum. [Citing the *Donohue, Peter W.,* and *Hoffman* cases] ....

The plaintiff has not cited nor can this court find any federal case which has recognized this type of action. The claim for damages necessarily hinges upon questions of methodology and educational priorities, issues not appropriate for resolution by this Court, since they present a "... myriad of intractable economic, social, and even philosophical problems" [emphasis added].[26]

---

25. *Id.* at 114.
26. *Id.* at 115.

§ 7.1(G). Lindsay v. Thomas.

The Commonwealth Court of Pennsylvania, in the case of *Lindsay v. Thomas*,[27] stated that the statutory and regulatory scheme for the education of exceptional children in Pennsylvania is consistent with the federal scheme of educating handicapped students as required by the Education For All Handicapped Children Act of 1975 (Act), 20 U.S.C. §§ 1401—1461.[28] The Court summarized the alleged facts:

> The appellants seek damages in trespass from the appellees and allege that the School District violated the special education provisions found in Sections 1371 and 1372 of the Public School Code of 1949, Act of March 10, 1949, P.L. 30, as *amended,* 24 P.S. §§ 13-1371—13-1372. They assert that the appellant, Frederick Lindsay, suffers from a "specific learning disability" and that during his attendance at a Philadelphia public school, the appellees failed to identify him as a student requiring special education classes and failed to educate him properly. The only claim which is now before this Court is the appellants' claim for money damages, which, they contend, is owed to them as a result of the alleged mental and emotional suffering and loss of earnings which they have experienced by virtue of the appellees' failure to follow the statutory mandates of the Public School Code.[29]

The court stated:

> It is undisputed that the appellees have a statutory duty to identify exceptional children and a duty to provide them with a proper education. These duties are clearly spelled out in Sections 1371 and 1372 of the Public School Code. There is, however, no statutory provision whatever for a monetary remedy arising out of a breach of these statutory duties. *Of course, the*

---

27. 465 A.2d 122 (Pa. Cmwlth. 1983).
28. *Id.* at 123.
29. *Id.*

> *appellants here had other remedies to compel compli-*
> *ance with the statutory duties, and, indeed, did avail*
> *themselves successfully of two such remedies ...* [2] [em-
> phasis added].[30]

The court, in dismissing the complaint, cited with approval the *Flanders* case.

§ 7.1(H). Clareen F. v. Western Placer Unified School District.

In 1981, the California Court of Appeals decided the case
of *Clareen F. v. Western Placer Unified School District*,[31]
and affirmed the judgment of dismissal entered after the
defendants' demurrer to plaintiff's complaint was sustained without leave to amend. The complaint undertook to
state six causes of action for damages based primarily on
the asserted duty of a public school district to provide a free
and appropriate education for a student afflicted with mental, educational, and learning disabilities.[32]

The court summarized the facts as follows:

> As alleged in the first two causes of action sounding in
> negligence, plaintiffs Clareen and Ray F. are husband
> and wife and are the parents of plaintiff Bobby F.,
> fifteen years of age. Bobby possesses "special mental,
> educational and learning disabilities" and was edu-
> cated from kindergarten through the eighth grade
> within the educational system of defendant Western

---

30. *Id.*; the court's citation states: "Frederick Lindsay brought a civil
rights action on behalf of himself and 'all children attending public
school within the City of Philadelphia who have specific learning disabilities and who are deprived of education appropriate to their special
needs.' In that case, the court ordered the appellees to identify learning
disabled children and to provide them with an appropriate education.
Injunctive relief was ordered. Frederick L. v. Thomas, 419 F. Supp. 960
(E.D. Pa. 1976) *aff'd,* 557, F.2d 373 (3d Cir. 1977).

31. Super. Ct. No. 53919, Ct. of App. Third Appellate Dist. (Calif.,
1981).

32. *Id.*

Placer Unified School District. The District has the
duty to provide a "free, appropriate public education"
to children with "special mental, educational or learning disabilities." Such duty includes the responsibility
to (1) identify, by generally recognized and accepted
educational and psychological testing, those students
who possess such disabilities; (2) to segregate them
from regular educational classes, and (3) to provide
them with individual educational programs appropriate to their particular needs. The District and individually named defendants who are employees of the District breached this duty by "negligently and carelessly" (1) failing to test for Bobby's special disabilities; (2) failing to design an individualized educational
program for him; (3) assigning him to "regular" education classes; (4) promoting him when defendants knew
or should have known that he was not meeting the
minimum requirements, and (5) allowing him to graduate when defendants knew or should have known
that he did not meet minimal education requirements
for graduation. As a proximate result of defendants'
failure to provide Bobby with an education commensurate with his disabilities Bobby suffered a diminution
in educational and learning skills and irreparable loss
of earning capacity as well as irreversible aggravation
of his disabilities.

In the second count, plaintiffs specifically alleged
that defendants' negligence in failing to provide an
individualized education program for Bobby violated
the equal protection and privileges and immunities
provisions of the California Constitution.[33]

The plaintiffs, after incorporating the allegations of the
first cause of action in their third count for intentional or
negligent representation, further alleged:

The District and its employees continuously administered certain psychological and educational tests to
Bobby, that the results of these tests repeatedly confirmed that Bobby had disabilities requiring an indi-

---

33. *Id.* at 2-3.

vidualized educational program, but that defendant ... (the principal of the school) knowingly concealed these test results and intentionally or negligently misrepresented to plaintiffs that Bobby's academic deficiencies were the result of his "lack of industry rather than any mental, educational, or learning disabilities." [The principal] allegedly made such representation with the intent to induce plaintiffs to maintain Bobby in the regular educational program and unaware of the falsity of the principal's representation, Clareen and Ray F. acted in reliance thereon by retaining Bobby in the District's educational system.[34]

The court maintained that according to the California Tort Claims Act, a public entity is liable for injury proximately caused by an act or omission of an employee within the scope of his employment except as otherwise provided by statute. The court, after assuming that defendants are not otherwise immune from liability under the Tort Claims Act, observed that the issue confronting it was:

> Whether under the common law a legal duty exists to provide a student with learning disabilities an individualized education program appropriate to his or her needs, the breach of which entitles that student to recover damages for deficiencies in knowledge proximately caused thereby.[35]

After an analysis of the various arguments advanced, the court of appeals, in affirming the lower court's decision, noted that as in the *Peter W.* case, plaintiffs' "educational malpractice" claims are precluded by considerations of public policy and that plaintiffs' related claims for damages are deficient as well.[36]

An injury flowing from a failure specially to educate is "too remote, uncertain and speculative to form the basis for

---

34. *Id.* at 11-12.
35. *Id.* at 3-4.
36. *Id.* at 1.

187

recovery." Moreover, the social consequences in terms of public time and money, particularly in the wake of budget cuts resulting from the Jarvis-Gann Initiative, would be burdensome beyond calculation.[37]

§ 7.1(I). D.S.W. v. Fairbanks North Star Borough School District.

The same year, the Supreme Court of the State of Alaska rendered an opinion in two companion cases; *D.S.W. v. Fairbanks North Star Borough School District*[38] and *L.A.H. v. Fairbanks North Star Borough School District.*[39]

These cases also presented the question of whether an action for damages may be maintained against a school district for the negligent classification, placement, or teaching of a student. In summarizing the allegations of the complaints, which the court took as true since this was an appeal from orders granting motions to dismiss, the court stated:

> L.A.H. is seventeen years old and suffers from a learning disability commonly known as dyslexia. L.A.H. attended Borough School District schools from kindergarten through the sixth grade during which time the District negligently failed to ascertain that he was suffering from dyslexia. On the last day of L.A.H.'s second year in the sixth grade the District determined that he was dyslexic. Thereafter, for a time, the District gave him special education courses to assist in overcoming the effect of this disability. These courses were then negligently terminated, despite the District's awareness that L.A.H. had not overcome his dyslexia, and were never resumed. The complaint alleges that L.A.H. has suffered damage caused by the negligent acts and omissions of the District including loss of edu-

---

37. *Id.* at 8.
38. File No. 4938 Super. Ct. of the State of Alaska.
39. File No. 4959 Super. Ct. of the State of Alaska.

cation, loss of opportunity for employment, loss of opportunity to attend college or post-high school studies, past and future mental anguish and loss of income and income earning ability.

D.S.W.'s claim is similar. He too is dyslexic. The School District discovered this condition in the first grade but did not assist him in overcoming it until the fifth grade. The School District gave D.S.W. a special education program during the fifth and sixth grade but negligently discontinued it in the seventh grade knowing that he had not been adequately trained to compensate for dyslexia at that point. Beginning with the seventh grade and continuing to the present, the defendant has failed to provide proper education to assist D.S.W. in overcoming his dyslexia. D.S.W. claims money damages against the School District for the same injuries claimed by L.A.H.[40]

In affirming the superior court's dismissal of the claims, the Supreme Court of the State of Alaska stated that although these claims are claims of first impression in Alaska, two other jurisdictions have considered the question of whether a claim may be maintained against a school for failing to discover learning disabilities or failing to provide an appropriate educational program once learning disabilities are discovered. In neither of these jurisdictions has a claim for damages been permitted. The court then went on to discuss and quote language from the *Peter W., Donohue, Hoffman,* and *Smith v. Alameda County Social Services Agency* cases.[41] The court proceeded to state:

> We agree with the results reached in these cases and with the reasoning employed by the California Court of Appeals in *Peter W.* and *Smith.* In particular we think that the remedy of money damages is inappro-

---

40. The two cases were consolidated and a single opinion, No. 2352, by the Supreme Court of the State of Alaska was rendered (1981), pp. 2-3.

41. 153 Cal. Rptr. 712 (Cal. App. 1979).

priate as a remedy for one who has been a victim of errors made during his or her education. The level of success which might have been achieved had the mis- . takes not been made will, we believe, be necessarily incapable of assessment, rendering legal cause an imponderable which is beyond the ability of courts to deal with in a reasoned way.

No different result is mandated under the Alaska statutes to which Appellants have referred us [citations omitted] the so-called Education for Exceptional Children Act. Nothing in the Act either expressly or impliedly authorizes a damage claim. The same considerations which preclude a damage claim at common law for educational malpractice precludes inferring one from the Act. Similar statutory claims were presented, and rejected, in *Peter W. v. San Francisco Unified School District* [citations omitted], and *Donohue v. Copiague Union Free School District* [citations omitted].[42]

The court also commented concerning the rights of parents who believed their children were wrongfully classified or placed. The court noted:

Our conclusion does not mean that parents who believe that their children have been inappropriately classified or placed are without recourse, as 14.30.191(c) provides that any parent believing classification or placement to be in error may request an independent examination and evaluation of the child and for [sic] a hearing before a hearing officer in the event of a substantial discrepancy. Further, that section provides that the proceedings so conducted are subject to the Administrative Procedure Act, which in turn expressly provides for judicial review [citations omitted].

In our view it is preferable to resolve disputes concerning classification and placement decisions by using these or similar (see U.S.C. 1415), procedures

---

42. D.S.W. v. Fairbanks North Star Borough School District, Supreme Court of the State of Alaska, No. 2352 (1981), pp. 7-8.

than through the mechanism of tort action for damages. Prompt administrative and judicial review may correct erroneous action in time so that any educational shortcomings suffered by a student may be corrected. Money damages, on the other hand, are a poor, and only tenuously related, substitute for a proper education. We recognize, of course, that there may be cases when a student in need of special placement is negligently not given it by the school district, and the student's parents, having no reason to know of the need, do not initiate an administrative review proceeding. In such cases there are authorities suggesting that corrective tutorial programs may be appropriately mandated [citations omitted]. However, we need not reach that question here.[43]

§ 7.1(J). Tobias v. New Jersey Department of Education.

Frank Tobias, Jr. filed a complaint in the Superior Court of New Jersey against the State of New Jersey, Department of Education, et al.[44] The suit, which contained two counts, alleged in Count I that one or more of the defendants were lawfully responsible for special education services in the state's public schools and were lawfully obliged to evaluate and care for handicapped persons. It was further alleged that the defendant, New Jersey School for the Deaf, is a state-sponsored institution lawfully obliged to provide care for handicapped persons. Furthermore, it was alleged that the defendants, jointly and severally, misclassified, mistreated, and failed to properly train and educate the plaintiff thereby depriving him of his rights and privileges accorded to him under law. As a result of the careless-

---

43. *Id.* at 8-10.
44. Complaint, Tobias v. New Jersey Department of Education, Docket No. L-63615-79 Super. Ct. of New Jersey, Law. Div., for Somerset Cty. (1980).

ness and negligence of each of the defendants, and as a further result of their failure to conform to standards and breach of duty under law, the plaintiff sustained severe, diverse, and permanent personal injuries and damages.[45]

In Count II it was alleged that each of the defendants had failed and refused to provide competent and adequate care and treatment for the plaintiff in violation of existing law. Wherefore, the plaintiff demanded an order directing each of the defendants to immediately provide extensive rehabilitation and vocational training as required by statute and law of the State of New Jersey, together with damages.[46]

The defendants filed a Motion to Dismiss and Motion for a More Definite Statement. The motion to dismiss the first count was based on the ground that plaintiff had failed to comply with the requirements of the New Jersey Tort Claims Act. Specifically, it stated, "plaintiff has failed to file a notice of claim which is a precondition for maintaining a cause of action alleging tortious conduct on the part of a State entity ...."[47]

The court ordered that the first count of plaintiff's complaint be dismissed without prejudice.[48] Furthermore, the court, in response to defendants' request for an order requiring plaintiff to state specifically which statutes and law of the State of New Jersey are at issue for the second

---

45. *Id.* at 2-3.

46. *Id.* at 3.

47. Motion to Dismiss and Motion for a More Definite Statement, at pp. 1-2, Tobias v. State of New Jersey Department of Education, Docket No. L 63615-79 Super. Ct. of New Jersey, Law. Division, Somerset Cty. (1980).

48. Order, at p. 2, Tobias v. State of New Jersey Department of Education, Docket No. L-63615-79 Super. Ct. of New Jersey, Law. Division, Somerset Cty. (1980).

count, granted the motion and ordered that a more definite statement must be filed within 20 days.[49]

In response to the court's order for more definitive statement, the plaintiff stated:

> In May 1958 when the plaintiff was 4 years of age the Manville Elementary School Supervisor recommended to the Superintendent of Manville Schools that tutoring be afforded to the plaintiff during the period of time that he was being considered for placement in the New Jersey School for the Deaf in Trenton. In April of 1958 the Somerset County Guidance Center, (Dr. Boutelle), recommended to the Manville Elementary School Supervisor that the plaintiff be given immediate special speech training.
>
> In May 1959 the Manville Supervisor recommended to the Superintendent of Schools that the Bruce Street School in Newark could ready the plaintiff for the Trenton School for the Deaf. At that time the Supervisor acknowledged Manville's obligation to provide education for the plaintiff, but at the same time recognized that no facilities were available in the Manville area. In June, the plaintiff was accepted in the Newark Program of Special Education (Bruce Street School). In January of 1960, the Manville school nurse wrote to the New Jersey School for the Deaf in Trenton recommending the plaintiff's entrance into that institution.
>
> From February 11, 1960 through 1966 the New Jersey School for the Deaf located in Trenton continued to find reasons not to accept the plaintiff into its school program, but continued from year to year to leave the door open for continued application. In March of 1966 the New Jersey School for the Deaf in Trenton recognized the Plaintiff's plight as a "sad case."
>
> From May 1958 and for approximately the next 9 succeeding years, despite recommendations by various consultants, and institutions such as the Bruce Street School in Newark, Somerset County Guidance Center, the Woodbridge Township Board of Education Special

---

49. *Id.* at 1-2.

Class for the Deaf, the Johnstone Training Center, and Pine Grove School in Saugerties, New York, the New Jersey School for the Deaf refused to admit plaintiff to its institution.

From approximately September 1969, through November 30, 1973, the plaintiff received sporadic vocational and technical training primarily at the Raritan Valley Workshop. This training was terminated approximately November 30, 1973 and plaintiff was placed in "competitive employment."

Although through consultations and evaluations over the years from 1959 the defendants were well aware of the plaintiff's deafness as well as physical handicap, the plaintiff was caused to accept "hit and run schooling" totally inadequate for his needs. Despite earlier recommendations and reports indicating that his IQ level was potentially greater than test results, the defendants negligently failed to properly schedule the appropriate schooling and training so as to enable him to read lips, use sign language, or articulate adequately.[50]

The court, in 1982, dismissed the case on the basis that the plaintiff did not comply with the New Jersey Torts Claims Act in that he failed to file proper notice.

§ 7.1(K). Debra P. v. Turlington.

In the case of *Debra P. v. Turlington*,[51] the plaintiffs brought a class action challenging the constitutional and statutory validity of the Florida State Student Assessment Test, a functional literacy examination. Plaintiffs' contented the test perpetuates and reemphasizes the effects of past purposeful discrimination. The plaintiffs further contended:

---

50. More Definite Statement Augmenting the Allegations Contained in the Complaint, at pp. 1-3, Tobias v. New Jersey Department of Education, Docket No. L-63615-79 Super. Ct. of New Jersey, Law. Division, Somerset Cty. (1980).

51. 474 F. Supp. 244 (1979).

1. that the test is unreliable, invalid and not correlated to the public school curriculum,
2. that the test instrument is racially biased, and finally
3. that passage of the test was not required for graduation in Florida private schools.

Plaintiffs further contend that the higher percentage of black twelfth grade failures was the probable and foreseeable consequence of enactment and implementation of the statutory scheme by the Defendants.[52]

The United States District Court (M.D. Florida) held that: (1) In view of the history of segregation in Florida public schools, the test unlawfully discriminated against black children in violation of the equal protection clause; (2) The test had adequate content and construct validity and bore a rational relation to a valid state interest; (3) Plaintiffs failed to establish that the test was racially or ethically biased; (4) The failure to apply the test to private schools was not unconstitutional; (5) The inadequacy of notice provided prior to the indication of diploma sanction, objectives, and test was a violation of due process clause; (6) The use of the test to classify students for remediation was constitutionally permissible, and (7) The state would be enjoined from requiring passage of the test as a requirement for graduation for period of four years.[53]

The court concluded by stating:

In the school term 1982-1983, the state will be permitted to utilize the SSAT II as a requirement for graduation. In the interim the SSAT II can be administered as directed by the State DOE to assist in the identification and remediation of the SSAT II skill objectives. The state Defendants will be permitted to retain the SSAT II scores in a fashion consistent with the manner

52. *Id.* at 250-51.
53. 474 F. Supp. 244 (1979).

in which the state retains other achievement test scores.

The Court is of the opinion that the present remediation program is not constitutionally or statutorily invalid. The progress of students out of the program and the limited duration of the daily instruction comports with applicable standards.[54]

§ 7.1(L). Jack M. v. School Board of Santa Rosa County.

In 1980, the parents of Kenneth M., a learning disabled and emotionally handicapped child, filed suit against the School Board of Santa Rosa County, et al.[55] The suit, filed in the United States District Court for the Northern District of Florida, alleged that since 1970, Kenneth has been excluded from school and denied educational services by the Santa Rosa County School District and that the Department of Education was duly notified but failed to act. Plaintiffs asked for compensatory and punitive damages and declaratory and injunctive relief. The complaint was brought under § 8504 of the Rehabilitation Act of 1973 and the Education for All Handicapped Children Act of 1975. It also alleged fourteenth amendment violations.

The defendants contended there is no private right of action under either the Rehabilitation Act or the E.H.A., that no claim for relief has been stated sufficient to invoke 42 U.S.C. § 1983, and that no fourteenth amendment violation was shown. Insofar as damages were concerned, contentions were also presented respecting qualified and elev-

---

54. *Id.* at 269.
55. Jack M. v. School Board of Santa Rosa County, in the U.S. Distrist Ct. for the Northern District of Florida, Pensacola Division, No. PCA 79-0050 (1980).

enth amendment immunities and whether any damages may be claimed.[56]

In dismissing the case the court stated that the complaint was insufficient to state any claim for relief against these defendants under the Education for All Handicapped Children Act or the fourteenth amendment. There was no due process violation, a deprivation of fundamental rights, or a denial of equal protection. In discussing whether this is a matter traditionally relegated to state law the court opined:

> This suit is based in reality not upon misapplication of federal funds but upon what might be termed *"educational malpractice"* in that defendants have failed to properly provide an appropriate public education under their duty to educate all children. Under that theory this is indeed a concern of the state and is an appropriate vehicle to infer a cause of action based solely on federal law [emphasis added].[57]

§ 7.1(M). Tubell v. Dade County Public Schools.

In 1982, the District Court of Appeals of Florida decided the case of *Tubell v. Dade County Public Schools.*[58] The plaintiff's complaint alleged, in separate counts, causes of action for negligence, false imprisonment, violation of civil rights and equal protection, violation of state constitutional rights to enjoy and defend life and liberty, to pursue happiness, and be rewarded in industry, and denial of due process. The underlying facts pleaded to support each count were, as noted by the court, those that would support a

---

56. Order, pp. 1-2, Jack M. v. School Board of Santa Rosa County, in the U.S. District Ct. for the Northern District of Florida, Pensacola Division, No. PCA 79-0550 (1980).

57. *Id.* at 7.

58. 419 So. 2d 388 (Florida, 1982).

claim for "educational malpractice," regardless of the no-
menclature.[59] The court, in a short opinion, stated:

> Should a cause of action for "educational malpractice"
> be recognized in the State of Florida? The trial court
> answered this in the negative by entering a final sum-
> mary judgment adverse to the plaintiff-appellants
> herein. We agree and affirm.
>
> The basis of the plaintiff's complaint was a
> mistesting and misclassification resulting in the minor
> plaintiff being placed in an improper special educa-
> tional program for a number of years to his detriment.
> We hold that even if these allegations are correct there
> is no cause of action stated. *D.S.W. v. Fairbanks North
> Star Borough School District,* 628 P.2d 554 (Alaska
> 1981); *Smith v. Alameda County Social Services,* 90
> Cal. App. 3d 929, 153 Cal. Rptr. 712 (1979); *Peter W. v.
> San Francisco Unified School District,* 60 Cal. App. 3d
> 814, 131 Cal. Rptr. 854 (1976); *Hunter v. Board of
> Education of the City of New York,* 49 N.Y.2d 121, 424
> N.Y.S. 376, 400 N.E.2d 317 (1979); *Helm v. Profes-
> sional Childrens' School,* 103 Misc. 2d 1053, 431 N.Y.S.
> 246 (1980); *Donohue v. Copiague Union Free School
> District,* 47 N.Y.2d 440, 418 N.Y.S.2d 375, 391 N.E.2d
> 1352 (1979).[60]

§ 7.1(N). Morris v. McKay.

In 1982, the Superior Court of Washington for Yakema
County rendered its findings of fact and conclusions of law
in *Morris v. Jack McKay.*[61] The trial concerning the plaintiff, Vickie Morris, who had a specific learning disability,
lasted several days. The evidence revealed that, pursuant
to appropriate sections of the Washington Administrative

---

59. *Id.* at 389.

60. *Id.*

61. Findings of Fact and Conclusions of Law at pp. 1-8, Morris v. Jack
McKay, No. 80-2-02559-6, Super. Ct., State of Washington for Yakima
County (1982).

Code, the plaintiffs initiated an evidentiary hearing in which they questioned the appropriateness of Vickie's educational program. The hearing took place in February, 1980. The evidence further revealed that:

> At the time of this administrative hearing, Vickie Morris was a seventeen year old who was reading six to seven years below grade level and who was classified as having a specific learning disability.
>
> At the evidentiary hearing the parents sought an order requiring the district to: (1) provide Vickie independent tutoring until such time as the district made a tutor available. The hearing examiner ruled against the parents on March 3, 1980 and the parents appealed to the Superintendent of Public Instruction.
>
> ... The Administrative Review Officer ordered: (1) tutoring at least one hour per day; (2) psychological counseling for her previously identified but untreated emotional maladjustment; (3) compensatory individualized instruction during the summer of 1981; and (4) denied costs and attorneys fees.[62]

The order of the Administrative Review Officer was then appealed to the superior court, which found that the petitioner was not provided an appropriate educational program. Furthermore, the court determined:

> Prior to entering Selah High School, Vickie had made little or no growth in general information or in her particular areas of weaknesses, *i.e.* visual and auditory memory. Upon completion of the eighth year (1976-1977) her parents employed a tutor for the summer of 1977, and a second tutor during the summer of 1979. Following graduation in June, 1981, the first tutor has worked with her extensively. Both tutors testified that Vickie made progress under their tutorage. Carol Rothe, a certified teacher and language therapist, testified that Vickie's progress was excellent.

---

62. *Id.* at 2-3.

The court further finds that Doctor Von Pein's and Joyce Jones' opinions were supported by a preponderance of the evidence. Significant defects in her school program included: (1) the reliance upon high school student aides instead of individualized instruction by a qualified teacher; (2) failure to provide emotional counseling when identified. Vickie's own testimony clearly demonstrated her frustration and lack of progress resulting from a lack of individualized instruction by a qualified teacher ....

The Morrises were required to expend $2300 from their own funds for the education of their child by the time of trial. Carol Rothe testified that a reasonable and probable future tutorial expense, computed at a very modest hourly rate, is another $3700.00 for a total of $6000.00 for past and future tutoring. The court finds this testimony credible, and the figures reasonable.

Vickie Morris was the victim of discrimination. Other children were permitted to be withdrawn from school, some for educational tutoring. It was the policy of the school to allow a child to leave [to] study piano, but not to learn to read. She was not treated the same as others similarly situated. The school district was fully aware of her disability, yet she was not afforded an appropriate education, although hundreds of other students were. This discrimination was based upon her handicap.

The court finds that an attorney fee of $4616.50 is reasonable and should be included in the judgment.
....

Vickie Morris met the standards for graduation set by the defendant school district. Vickie was graduated during the pendency of this course in Superior Court, in June, 1981. She participated in the graduation ceremony and was given a diploma. This fact should not prevent the relief herein provided.[63]

The court concluded:

---

63. *Id.* at 4-5.

Vickie Morris' entitlement to an educational opportunity should be extended until she is 21 years of age plus 15 months, representing the elapsed time between Hearing Officer Ralph Steven's opinion dated November 19, 1980 and the date of judgment, herein. This conclusion is implemented by the award of damages for tutorial costs, and does not require further educational participation by the defendants.[64]

The court then entered a judgment which, *inter alia,* provided:

That the plaintiffs are hereby awarded judgment jointly and severally against the defendants: Jack McKay, Superintendent of Selah School District #119; Selah School District #119; Frank B. Brouillet, Superintendent of Public Instruction of the State of Washington, and the State of Washington, in the amount of $1730.50 for costs incurred in furtherance of this litigation.

That the plaintiffs are hereby awarded judgment jointly and severally against the defendants Jack McKay, Superintendent of Selah School District #119; Selah School District #119; Frank B. Brouillet, Superintendent of Public Instruction of the State of Washington, and the State of Washington in the amount of $4616.50 for attorneys fees incurred in furtherance of this litigation.[65]

It was noted that dyslexia is a generic trait afflicting people such as Nelson Rockefeller, Winston Churchill and Lewis Carroll, author of *Alice in Wonderland.*[66] Plaintiff's counsel charged the district "didn't pay sufficient attention to this child until they had to — until some lawyer himself from downtown was on his way (to the school) two years

---

64. *Id.* at 6-7.

65. Judgment, at pp. 1-2, Morris v. McKay, No. 80-2-02559-6, Super. Ct., State of Washington for Yakima Cty. (1982).

66. *See* Lyn Watts, *Graduate Sues For Education: Suit Contends Student Was Denied Needed Instruction,* YAKIMA HERALD-REPUBLIC, January 8, 1982, at p. 3A.

201

ago. If they would have put one-tenth the effort into helping her that they put into fighting her, they could have
helped a lot of kids."[67]

The defendants appealed this landmark case[68] to the Supreme Court of the State of Wisconsin. Before the case
could be decided by the Supreme Court a Stipulation for
Dismissal of Appeal and Satisfaction of Judgment was filed
and approved by the Supreme Court.[69] The Stipulation provided as follows:

1. The Appeal pending before the Supreme Court in
   the State of Washington shall be dismissed without prejudice.
2. A Satisfaction of Judgment shall be entered herein;
3. *An Order shall be entered directing the parties
   hereto not to disclose the terms of the settlement
   between the parties* [emphasis added].[70]

§ 7.1(O). Board of Education v. Rowley.

While the *Morris* case was on appeal, the Supreme Court
of the United States decided the case of *Board of Education
v. Rowley.*[71] It is likely this case had some impact upon the
dismissal of the appeal of the *Morris* case.

In summarizing some of the provisions of the Education
for All Handicapped Children Act of 1975, the U.S. Supreme Court noted:

67. *See* Lyn Watts, *Selah Graduate Was Denied Proper Help, Yakima
Judge Rules,* YAKIMA HERALD-REPUBLIC, January 9, 1982, at p. 1 and
11A.

68. *Id.* at 1.

69. Stipulation for Dismissal of Appeal and Satisfaction of Judgment,
at pp. 1-2, Morris v. McKay, No. 80-2-02559-6 Super. Ct. State of Washington for Yakima Cty. (1982). *See also* Mandate, Morris v. McKay,
Supreme Ct. of the State of Washington, No. 48706-5 (1982).

70. *Id.*

71. 102 S. Ct. 3034 (1982).

The Education of the Handicapped Act (Act), 84 Stat. 175, as amended, 20 U.S.C. § 1401 *et seq.* (1976 ed. and Supp. IV), provides federal money to assist state and local agencies in educating handicapped children, and conditions such funding upon a State's compliance with extensive goals and procedures. The Act represents an ambitious federal effort to promote the education of handicapped children, and was passed in response to Congress' perception that a majority of handicapped children in the United States "were either totally excluded from schools or [were] sitting idly in regular classrooms awaiting the time when they were old enough to 'drop out.'" H.R. Rep.No. 94-332, p. 2 (1975) (H.R.Rep.). The Act's evolution and major provisions shed light on the question of statutory interpretation which is at the heart of this case.

Congress first addressed the problem of educating the handicapped in 1966 when it amended the Elementary and Secondary Education Act of 1965 to establish a grant program "for the purpose of assisting the States in the initiation, expansion, and improvement of programs and projects ... for the education of handicapped children." Pub.L. 89-750, § 161, 80 Stat. 1204. That program was repealed in 1970 by the Education of the Handicapped Act, Pub.L. 91-230, 84 Stat. 175, Part B of which established a grant program similar in purpose to the repealed legislation. Neither the 1966 nor the 1970 legislation contained specific guidelines for state use of the grant money; both were aimed primarily at stimulating the States to develop educational resources and to train personnel for educating the handicapped.[72]

Following is a brief statement of the case — its history and holding:

This case arose in connection with the education of Amy Rowley, a deaf student at the Furnace Woods School in the Hendrick Hudson Central School District, Peekskill, N.Y. Amy has minimal residual hear-

---

72. *Id.* at 3037.

ing and is an excellent lipreader. During the year before she began attending Furnace Woods, a meeting between her parents and school administrators resulted in a decision to place her in a regular kindergarten class in order to determine what supplemental services would be necessary to her education. Several members of the school administration prepared for Amy's arrival by attending a course in sign-language interpretation, and a teletype machine was installed in the principal's office to facilitate communication with her parents who are also deaf. At the end of the trial period it was determined that Amy should remain in the kindergarten class, but that she should be provided with an FM hearing aid which would amplify words spoken into a wireless receiver by the teacher or fellow students during certain classroom activities. Amy successfully completed her kindergarten year.

As required by the Act, an IEP was prepared for Amy during the fall of her first-grade year. The IEP provided that Amy should be educated in a regular classroom at Furnace Woods, should continue to use the FM hearing aid, and should receive instruction from a tutor for the deaf for one hour each day and from a speech therapist for three hours each week. The Rowleys agreed with parts of the IEP, but insisted that Amy also be provided a qualified sign-language interpreter in all her academic classes in lieu of the assistance proposed in other parts of the IEP. Such an interpreter had been placed in Amy's kindergarten class for a 2-week experimental period, but the interpreter had reported that Amy did not need his services at that time. The school administrators likewise concluded that Amy did not need such an interpreter in her first-grade classroom. They reached this conclusion after consulting the school district's Committee on the Handicapped, which had received expert evidence from Amy's parents on the importance of a sign-language interpreter, received testimony from Amy's teacher and other persons familiar with her academic and social progress, and visited a class for the deaf.

When their request for an interpreter was denied, the Rowleys demanded and received a hearing before an independent examiner. After receiving evidence from both sides, the examiner agreed with the administrators' determination that an interpreter was not necessary because "Amy was achieving educationally, academically, and socially" without such assistance. App. to Pet. for Cert. F-22. The examiner's decision was affirmed on appeal by the New York Commissioner of Education on the basis of substantial evidence in the record. *Id.,* at E-4. Pursuant to the Act's provision for judicial review, the Rowleys then brought an action in the United States District Court for the Southern District of New York, claiming that the administrators' denial of the sign-language interpreter constituted a denial of the "free appropriate public education" guaranteed by the Act.

The District Court found that Amy "is a remarkably well-adjusted child" who interacts and communicates well with her classmates and has "developed an extraordinary rapport" with her teachers. 483 F.Supp. 528, 531 (1980). It also found that "she performs better than the average child in her class and is advancing easily from grade to grade," *id.,* at 534, but "that she understands considerably less of what goes on in class than she could if she were not deaf" and thus "is not learning as much, or performing as well academically as she would without her handicap," *id.,* at 532. This disparity between Amy's achievement, and her potential led the court to decide that she was not receiving a "free appropriate public education," which the court defined as "an opportunity to achieve [her] full potential commensurate with the opportunity provided to other children." *Id.,* at 534. According to the District Court, such a standard "requires that the potential of the handicapped child be measured and compared to his or her performance, and that the resulting differential or 'shortfall' be compared to the shortfall experienced by nonhandicapped children." *Ibid.* The District Court's definition arose from its assumption that the responsibility for "giv[ing] content to the requirement

205

of an 'appropriate education'" had "been left entirely
to the [federal] courts and the hearing officers." *Id.,* at
533.[8]

A divided panel of the United States Court of Appeals for the Second Circuit affirmed. The Court of
Appeals "agree[d] with the [D]istrict [C]ourt's conclusions of law," and held that its "findings of fact [were]
not clearly erroneous." 632 F.2d 945, 947 (1980).[73]

In reversing the court of appeals, the Supreme Court, in
an opinion written for the majority by Justice Rehnquist
held:

> That the Act imposes no clear obligation upon recipi-
> ent States beyond the requirement that handicapped
> children receive some form of specialized education is
> perhaps best demonstrated by the fact that Congress,
> in explaining the need for the Act, equated an "appro-
> priate education" to the receipt of some specialized ed-
> ucational services. The Senate Report states: "[T]he
> most recent statistics provided by the Bureau of Edu-
> cation for the Handicapped estimate that of the more
> than 8 million children ... with handicapping condi-
> tions requiring special education and related services,
> only 3.9 million such children are receiving an appro-
> priate education." S.Rep., at 8, U.S.Code Cong. &
> Admin.News 1975, p. 1432.[19] This statement, which
> reveals Congress' view that 3.9 million handicapped
> children were "receiving an appropriate education" in
> 1975, is followed immediately in the Senate Report by
> a table showing that 3.9 million handicapped children
> were "served" in 1975 and a slightly larger number
> were "unserved." A similar statement and table ap-
> pear in the House Report. H.R.Rep., at 11-12....
> Respondents contend that "the goal of the Act is to
> provide each handicapped child with an equal educa-
> tional opportunity." Brief for Respondents 35. We
> think, however, that the requirement that a State pro-
> vide specialized educational services to handicapped
> children generates no additional requirement that the

---

73. *Id.* at 3037, 3038.

services so provided be sufficient to maximize each child's potential "commensurate with the opportunity provided other children." Respondents and the United States correctly note that Congress sought "to provide assistance to the States in carrying out their responsibilities under ... the Constitution of the United States to provide equal protection of the laws." S.Rep., at 13, U.S. Code Cong. & Admin.News 1975, p. 1437.[22] But we do not think that such statements imply a congressional intent to achieve strick equality of opportunity or services....

When the language of the Act and its legislative history are considered together, the requirements imposed by Congress become tolerably clear. Insofar as a State is required to provide a handicapped child with a "free appropriate public education," we hold that it satisfies this requirement by providing personalized instruction with sufficient support services to permit the child to benefit educationally from that instruction. Such instruction and services must be provided at public expense, must meet the State's educational standards, must approximate the grade levels used in the State's regular education, and must comport with the child's IEP. In addition, the IEP, and therefore the personalized instruction, should be formulated in accordance with the requirements of the Act and, if the child is being educated in the regular classrooms of the public education system, should be reasonably calculated to enable the child to achieve passing marks and avance from grade to grade.[74]

§ 7.1(P). B.M. v. State.

Despite the trend of other courts, the Montana Supreme Court recognized a tort action for negligent administration of a special education program in the case of *B.M. v. State*.[75] The court summarized the facts as follows:

---

74. *Id.* at 3045-047, 3049.
75. 649 P.2d 425 (Mont. 1982).

The child's complaint alleged that the State was negligent in placing her in such a program and that the alleged misplacement violated her constitutional rights of due process and equal protection. After extensive discovery, all parties moved for summary judgment. On November 18, 1980, the District Court granted summary judgment for all respondents, "the State," ruling that they were immune from liability for claims arising from the states' "discretionary acts." The trial court also ruled that the State owes no legal duty of care to students negligently placed in special education programs. The trial court also held that such misplacement does not violate the constitutional rights of the student to due process and equal protection of the law.

The child's foster mother contends here that the trial court erred in ruling that the State was immune from negligence actions arising from the administration of special education programs in public schools. She further argues that the trial court erred in holding that the State owes no legal duty of care toward students who are negligently misplaced in special education programs. We reverse the trial court and hold that the State is not protected by immunity and that the State has a duty to use due care in placing students in special education programs. The question of whether the State breached that duty of care and whether the breach was the cause of any injury raise material questions of fact for which a trial is necessary. We further hold, however, that the trial court properly dismissed the claims that the child's due process and equal protection rights were violated. No facts were alleged sufficient to allege a constitutional violation.

The child was born in 1967 and at nine months of age was placed in the foster home of Fred and Leona Burger. While in kindergarten in Nashua, Montana, she displayed learning difficulties, apparently the result of a speech problem. In January 1973, upon the recommendations of Superintendent of Schools Sam Gramlich, and with the consent of her foster father, the child was tested by psychologist William Jones of the Eastern Montana Regional Mental Health Center.

As a result of this testing, Jones recommended that the child either repeat her year in kindergarten or receive special educational help. The school officials decided that state funds would be sought for a special education program for first graders, including the child.

An application and plan were submitted to the office of the Superintendent of Public Instruction outlining the needs of the children for special help. On the application, the child was classified as "educable mentally retarded (EMR)." To be eligible under State policy for EMR status, absent sufficient written justification, a student must have an individual learning aptitude score of 50 to 75. (*Special Education Handbook; Program Procedures and Guidelines for Children and Youth With Learning Handicaps*, § III, B, February 1973 (Handbook).) The child's overall IQ was determined to be 76.

The state superintendent approved the application and the program was started in September 1973. The program intended for this "primary educable class" was a "team-teaching situation." The four children in the program were to attend the regular first grade classroom, but their special education teacher was also to give them the special help and support needed "without segregating and labeling them." Of the four children in this program, only the child involved here was not mentally retarded.

The program involved two teachers. The regular first grade teacher and a special education teacher would both work with the students classified as EMR. This work would take place in the same classroom as the other students. But after five weeks, the child and the other three EMR students in the special program were found to be easily distracted and were moved to the "resource room" for their morning classes. This constituted approximately 40 percent of their daily classroom time, the rest of the day being spent as before. While in the resource room, the newly hired teacher taught the children with the same materials, but at a slower pace. The foster parents were not told of this change in the program.

The foster mother learned that the child was in the segregated classroom only after the child had been attending classes there for nine weeks. The foster mother immediately removed the child from the program and the school officials then abruptly terminated the program. It was during this nine week period that the foster mother claims she witnessed a dramatic worsening in the child's behavior. For example, the child refused to dress herself and refused to eat properly. The foster mother then filed suit as a result of this alleged misplacement of the child in the segregated classroom for the mentally retarded.[76]

The trial court ruled that the State's acts were not subject to judicial review because they were discretionary.[77] The supreme court stated:

The Montana Constitution (Art. II, § 18), abolishes sovereign immunity except in situations where the legislature, by a two-thirds vote, enacts contrary legislation. Section 2-9-102, MCA, enacted to give meaning to this constitutional provision, provides:

"Every governmental entity is subject to liability for its torts and those of its employees acting within the scope of their employment or duties whether arising out of a governmental or propriety function except as specifically provided by the legislature...."

The legislature has not enacted legislation to limit the liability of the school boards in the administration of special education programs. It is, furthermore, our duty to strictly construe any attempted governmental immunity — that is, every act expanding statutory immunity, must be clearly expressed. See *Orser v. State* (1978), 178 Mont. 126, 582 P.2d 1227; *Noll v. City of Bozeman* (1975), 166 Mont. 504; 534 P.2d 880.

---

76. *Id.* at 425-27.
77. *Id.* at 427.

210

Despite these clear constitutional and statutory provisions, and the failure of the legislature to enact laws expanding immunity to the situation involved here, the State argues that public policy prohibits a holding that the State can be held liable for negligent administration of a special education program. Not only do we not see any public policy requirements in support of such an argument, in the absence of a clear statutory declaration granting immunity, it is our duty to permit rather than to deny an action for negligence.

We have no difficulty in finding a duty of care owed to special education students. The general tenor of education for all citizens in Montana is stated in Art. X, § 1, 1972 Mont. Const.:

"It is the goal of the people to establish a system of education which will develop the full educational potential of each person. Equality of educational opportunity is guaranteed to each person of the state."

To implement this policy, section 20-5-102, MCA, makes attendance at State approved schools mandatory. Other statutes specifically govern the administration of special education programs.

For example, section 20-7-402, MCA, provides that school districts "shall comply" with policies recommended by the State Superintendent of Public Instruction in administering special education programs. The Superintendent's office, under this statutory mandate has published a "Special Education Handbook" which outlines for individual school districts, the procedures and guidelines to be followed in administering special education programs.

In addition, section 20-7-401, MCA, sets up a special class of students for which special education programs are provided. The child clearly falls within this class. The complaint here is that the school district failed to follow the statutory and regulatory policies governing the placement of students in the special education program.

The school authorities owed the child a duty of reasonable care in testing her and placing her in an appropriate special education program. Whether that

211

duty was breached here, and assuming a breach, whether the child was injured by the breach of duty, are questions not before this Court. Nor were those issues placed before the trial court in the motion for summary judgment. We therefore reverse the trial court's order and remand for further proceedings.

Without specifying how the child's due process rights were violated, a right guaranteed by statute (section 20-7-402(1)(b), MCA), and more explicitly set forth in the Special Education Handbook, the complaint alleges a constitutional denial of due process. But the complaint alleges no constitutional claim which goes beyond the protection provided by the statute and the regulations. It was proper, therefore, for the trial court to dismiss the due process claim based on a violation of the United States and Montana Constitutions.

The equal protection claim is also without merit. The sole basis for the equal protection violation is that William Jones, in evaluating the child's needs, considered the child's ethnic background (Indian) in relation to the child's learning difficulty. Jones stated that children who lived in non-English speaking homes may suffer what is known as bilingual language interference which is caused by the child's sudden exposure to an English-speaking environment. Jones also considered several other possible causes of the child's learning problems. This cannot be classified as invidious racial classification, nor can it be said that Jones had the purpose to discriminate on the basis of the child's race. A psychological evaluation which considers the cultural factors cannot be avoided if it is to have any validity. The evaluation cannot take place in a vacuum. The equal protection claim, therefore, raises no material question of fact, and the trial court's dismissal was proper.

The order of the district court is reversed in part, affirmed in part, and we remand for further proceedings.[78]

---

78. *Id.* at 427-28.

Chief Justice Haswell wrote a separate concurring opinion. He stated, in essence, that he concurred in the result. In his view there were genuine issues of material fact precluding summary judgment. He continued by saying:

> This is not a case of educational malpractice of the genre of *Peter W. v. San Francisco Unified School Dist.* (1976), 60 Cal. App. 3d 814, 131 Cal. Rptr. 854, or *Donohue v. Copiague Union Free School Dist.* (1979), 47 N.Y.2d 440, 418 N.Y.S.2d 375, 391 N.E.2d 1342, 1 A.L.R. 4th 1133, involving negligent failure to adequately educate a child in basic academic skills. No action lies for this type of claim for public policy reasons, and Annot., *Tort Liability of Public Schools and Institutions of Higher Learning for Educational Malpractice,* 1 A.L.R. 4th 1133 (1980). Here the claim involves violation of mandatory statutes alleged to constitute negligence and denial of procedural due process.
>
> I agree with the majority's remarks regarding sovereign immunity. However, the statutes make it clear that the governmental employer will ultimately bear the burden of liability for torts committed by its employees in the scope of their employment.[79]

There were also two dissents. The first, written by Justice Sheehy and concurred in by Justice Harrison, stated:

> We are faced here with a difficult public policy determination, whether courts should entertain claims based on these or similar facts. The District Court concluded that they should not, and I agree. The underlying public policy considerations are best evidenced by a review of two recent New York cases, *Donohue v. Copiague Union Free School Dist.* (1979), 391 N.E.2d 1352, 418 N.Y.S.2d 375, 47 N.Y.2d 440; and *Hoffman v. Board of Ed. of City of N.Y.* (1979), 400 N.E.2d 317, 424 N.Y.S.2d 376, 49 N.Y.2d 121.
>
> ....

---

79. *Id.* at 428.

The most recent case our research has discovered is *D.S.W. v. Fairbanks No. Star Bar. Sch. Dist.* (Alaska 1981), 628 P.2d 554, wherein an action was brought to recover against a school district for negligent classification, placement, or teaching of students suffering from dyslexia. Citing *Peter W., Donohue, Hoffman,* and *Smith* with approval, the Alaska Supreme Court went on to state the following, and I agree:

> In particular we think that the remedy of money damages is inappropriate as a remedy for one who has been a victim of errors made during his or her education. The level of success which might have been achieved had the mistakes not been made will, we believe, be necessarily incapable of assessment, rendering legal cause an imponderable which is beyond the ability of courts to deal with in a reasoned way. 628 P.2d at 556.

> Further, several United States Supreme Court cases have vitiated lower court decisions which found the unintended stigmatization from inaccurate assessment or placement to be an actionable constitution violation. A plaintiff seeking to allege deprivation of his liberty interest without due process of law on account of a special placement program should be required to plead and prove an untrue, derogatory publication which seriously stigmatized him in the community, coupled with an expulsion or exclusion comparable to a discharge of an employee. See *Codd v. Velger* (1977), 429 U.S. 624, 97 S.Ct. 882, 51 L.Ed.2d 92; *Bishop v. Wood* (1976), 426 U.S. 341, 96 S.Ct. 2074, 48 L.Ed.2d 684; *Paul v. Davis* (1976), 424 U.S. 693, 96 S.Ct. 1155, 47 L.Ed.2d 405; also 45 Missouri Law Review 667, 696 (1980).[80]

Justice Weber, in his brief dissent, stated:

> I concur in the foregoing dissent of Justice Sheehy. In view of the difference of opinion expressed by the members of this Court, and because of the potential for claims by disaffected students and parents in countless

---

80. *Id.* at 429-30.

numbers, I suggest that the legislature properly may consider whether it desires to impose an appropriate limit in this type of litigation.[81]

§ 7.1(Q). DeRosa v. City of New York.

In the case of *DeRosa v. City of New York*[82] it was alleged that:

> During the school year 1973 the infant plaintiff (hereinafter "infant") Clara DeRosa was a kindergarten student at PS 226 in Brooklyn, New York. At that time she was tested and found to have an IQ of 56. Based upon that score the infant was classified as retarded and placed in pre-primary class for mentally deficient children. Subsequently, in April 1975 the infant was rediagnosed as "deaf" with moderate to severe sensorineural hearing loss and appropriately placed. Plaintiffs complain that the placement of the infant, a misdiagnosed deaf child, in a class for retarded children had and continues to have a severe emotional impact and a psychological scarring all to her detriment and damage.[83]

The court stated that the complaint primarily pleads an action for educational malpractice but there is also a suggestion of a cause of action in ordinary negligence.[84] In analyzing the case the court reasoned:

> The law is well settled that educational malpractice is not recognized in New York. The courts in this state have consistently disallowed any claim for educational malpractice, thus the Court of Appeals in a recent case (*Torres v. Little Flower Children's Service,* 64 N.Y.2d 119) reaffirmed its previous earlier determination in rejecting judicial intervention in educational decision-making, refusing to place its imprimatur of legal ac-

---

81. *Id.* at 430-31.
82. 1985-86 EHLR DEC. 557:279.
83. *Id.*
84. *Id.*

ceptability to the doctrine. The court in *Torres* rejected a claim which in essence alleged educational malpractice, and, quoting from its previous decision in *Donohue v. Copiague Union Free School District* (47 N.Y.2d 440, 445) stated, "... As a result of public policy ... courts should not entertain such claims because to do so would require the courts not merely to make judgment as to the validity of broad educational policies — a course we have unalteringly eschewed in the past — but, more importantly to sit in review of the day-to-day implementation of these policies" (see also *Hoffman v. Board of Education,* 49 N.Y.2d 121).

The argument against judicial intervention in educational decision-making because of its disruptive effect was given its fullest exposition in Justice Powell's dissenting opinion in *Goss v. Lopez* (419 U.S. 565). The Supreme Court in *Goss* held that as a matter of due process of law before a public school student may be suspended he at least has the right to notice of the charge against him and, if he denies the charges, a right to have an explanation of the evidence against him and an opportunity to present his side of the story. It was against this background that Justice Powell expressed his concern with judicial intervention. He argued in dissent that the majority misapprehended the realities of the normal teacher-pupil relationship in which the teacher, as part of an ongoing relationship with his students, acts as educator, advisor, friend and at times parent-substitute and only rarely in an adversary relationship, viz., when he takes on the mantle of discipline of disruptive and insubordinate pupils. He stated that this "warmly-remembered" vision of the student-pupil relationship is sufficient protection for the student since it is predicated upon a teacher's responsibility for and commitment to, his pupils, absent in due process settings. Justice Powell concluded that "....One can only speculate as to the extent to which public education will be disrupted by giving every school child the power to contest *in court* any decision made by his teacher which arguably infringes the state-conferred right to education" (emphasis supplied).

The Supreme Court subsequently found an opportunity to tacitly approve Justice Powell's condemnation in a subsequent case, *Board of Curators of the University of Missouri v. Horowitz* (435 U.S. 78, 90) in which the court found a hearing not constitutionally required before a public medical school could dismiss a student for deficiencies in her clinical performance "....We decline," the court said, "to further enlarge the judicial presence in the academic community and thereby risk deterioration of many beneficial aspects of the faculty-student relationship."

However, this is not to say that academic and administrative decisions of educational institutions are beyond all judicial review. Thus, a claim involving a matter of contractual right, may, of course, be vindicated in an action at law (see *Matter of Golomb v. Board of Ed.*, 92 A.D.2d 256). Judgments of professional educators are likewise subject to judicial scrutiny to the extent that appropriate inquiry may be made to determine whether they abided by their own rules, and whether they have acted in good faith or their action was arbitrary or irrational (*Tedeschi v. Wagner College*, 49 N.Y.2d 652, 58).

It is likewise patently obvious that to prevent the law of torts from drowning in the reasonableness standard of negligence the courts have taken a posture of judicial abstinence. However, to justify this approach will require more than the broadside statement that declares that courts ought to leave the area alone — finely honed policy arguments tied specifically to the facts of each case will be required.

In the case at bar, the challenge is not only to the failure of the educational function but plaintiffs also plead an action in negligence.

At this juncture it should be emphasized that the matter is only at the pleading stage and the inquiry as to the viability of plaintiffs' action must be considered in that context.

217

The court recognizes that educational malpractice is a noncognizable tort insufficient to support a cause of action but the court is also mindful of the necessity of striking a balance between the concern of the courts not to interfere in the educational process and the need to redress wrongs committed by educators in the name of education.

Plaintiffs' attempt to spell out negligence claiming defendants' failure to advise the infant's parents of administrative review procedures before a child may be designated handicapped and placed in a special class is without merit. It is not too clear whether the present statute, Education Law section 4402(b)(43)(c), requires such consent as distinguished from a requirement of notice of hearing regarding the placement of a child. In any event, any such direction may not retroactively bind the defendants: the event having taken place in 1973 prior to the enactment of the present statute in 1976.

To repeat: the court is satisfied that educational malpractice is a nonrecognized cause of action in this state and finds no statutory duty sufficient to support an action in negligence. The issue is thus narrowed to whether plaintiffs may maintain an action in common law negligence. Thus, the court will turn to the common law to fulfill its traditional ameliorative social role of redressing wrongfully inflicted personal injuries and of deterring socially harmful conduct. In a most exhaustive and brilliant analysis of the problems presented at bar, Professor John Elson of the Northwestern University School of Law in an article entitled *"A Common Law Remedy for the Educational Harms Caused by Incompetence of Careless Teaching,"* Professor Elson quotes from Edward Levy, *"An Introduction to Legal Reasoning,"* 5-6, [1948] as follows:

"The development of the common law is a process of reasoning by analogy in which the rule of law discerned from precedent is applied to subsequent cases on the basis of both the prior and instant cases' factual similarities and the relevant new social reality. When the realities of modern urban education are introduced into this process of legal reasoning, the recognition of an independent judicial remedy for serious educational harms would seem to be a logical development. The high degree of dissatisfaction, often desperation, that many parents and students feel towards their schools and towards the professionals who staff them, the recognition of the crucial societal, as well as individual, loss from having students improperly educated, and the broad movement among educators, legislators and laymen toward bringing about a greater accountability in public education, are such realities which as a part of a generally shared social consensus will have increasing impact on the courts. If courts can be convinced that the societal and personal consequences of miseducation are both critically imported [important] and judicially remediable, then the logic of legal reasoning should dictate that the same common law principles which established the legal duty of care owed to a patient by his physician, to a student gymnast by his gym teacher, or to a minor by his legal guardian, must also be applied to establish the legal duty of care owed to a student by his ... teacher."

Negligence by its intrinsic nature presents some problems in reading an action in negligence under the facts herein.

The three basic elements of actionable negligence including [include] a duty owing to the person complaining, a breach of that duty and injury resulting therefrom. Thus, negligence as it is legally understood refers to a failure to perform, or to the improper performance of a legal duty which results in injury to another (*Holodook v. Spencer*, 43 A.D.2d 129, aff'd 36 N.Y.2d 35); "... It is the absence of care according to the circumstances ..." and is not actionable "... unless it involves the invasion of a legally protected interest" (*Palsgraf v. Long Island Railroad*, 248 N.Y. 339).

But, in order to sustain a cause of action in negligence, plaintiff must prove that a legal duty was owed him, that this duty was not performed or was improperly performed and that injury resulted therefrom (*Holodook v. Spencer, supra*). The ideas of negligence

219

and duty are correlative and as Judge Cardoza stated in the landmark case of *Palsgraf v. Long Island Railroad, supra,* "… The risk reasonably to be perceived defines the duty to be obeyed, and risk imports relation." Moreover, as was stated very succinctly by the Court of Appeals in *Williams v. State* (308 N.Y. 548), "… Without duty there can be no breach of duty and without breach of duty there can be no liability."

The degree of care required of an actor is determined by the "reasonable man" test under a particular set of circumstances, that is, what a reasonable, prudent and careful person would have done under the circumstances in the discharge of his duty to the injured party. This reasonable man of ordinary prudence, although mythical and of an abstract and hypothetical character, is the bedrock of the law of negligence serving as it does as the measuring rod of a uniform standard of behavior (Prosser, Law of Torts, 3d Ed. p. 153) or as further defined by Prosser, "A personification of community ideal of reasonable behavior, determined by jury's social judgment" (Prosser, Law of Torts, 4th Ed., p. 151).

The court is convinced under all of the circumstances and the principles of law as enunciated that the issue presented is not the viability of the testing program in all its educational ramifications but whether defendants, under all of the facts, were diligent in preventing the placement of the infant in a retarded program. The court finds that the situation such as presented at bar is distinguishable from malpractice and accordingly amenable to a negligence treatment; defendants are not being held to a malpractice standard but that of a "reasonable man" test, what a reasonable and prudent man could or should have done to prevent the serious wrong that was perpetrated upon plaintiffs.

Whereas in a malpractice action a professional is held to the duty of using care and diligence in the exercise of his skill and the application of his learning to accomplish the purpose for which he is employed. The professional owes a duty to possess the requisite

220

knowledge and skill such as possessed by the average member of his profession, and a duty to exercise ordinary and reasonable care in the application of such professional knowledge and skill and the duty to use his best judgment in the application of that knowledge and skill (see *Hale v. State* [53 A.D.2d 1025]), where the aforementioned rules are described in a medical malpractice context equally applicable to all malpractice actions.

This fine distinction between educational negligence and educational malpractice was recognized by Judge Shapiro in his brilliant and well-reasoned opinion in *Hoffman v. Board of Ed.* (64 A.D.2d 369) sustaining a complaint in negligence. However, the difficulty with his position was that the case was couched, pleaded and submitted under the concept of educational malpractice (a theory previously dismissed as not being the law in New York by the Court of Appeals in *Donohue v. Copiague Union Free School District* (47 N.Y.2d 440) and therefore reversed by the Court of Appeals (*Hoffman v. Board of Ed.*, 49 N.Y.2d 121). *The case at bar is distinguishable, plaintiffs having pleaded a separate action in negligence in addition to their pleas in educational malpractice.*

At this juncture, the court would like to pose an interesting theory of negligence supportive of the holding herein as set forth by Professor Elson in his article in the Northwestern Law Review cited above. It should be clear indeed that this article under discussion is broad in its sweep covering not only educational negligence but also brings within its scope the problems of educational malpractice.

Professor Elson points out the weaknesses in the ordinary negligence concepts in educational negligence law, particularly in using the "reasonable man" test to measure defendants' duty. Thus, he states:

"Even if judges and jurors were more familiar with the realities of the educational process, it would still be questionable whether the reasonable man standard of care would satisfy the requirements of justiciability for a legal standard that can be applied with a fair degree

221

of accuracy and consistency. Under the moralistic or 'gestalt' approach toward reasonable care, in which lay jurors measure the challenged conduct against their own moral and social concepts of the community ideal of reasonable behavior, decision-making would tend towards arbitrariness and inconsistency. With the exception of some basic principles of human decency, the common culture does not share any broad understanding as to what is fundamentally acceptable or unacceptable teaching behavior. Although each individual may have a personal predilection for a particular teaching style (e.g., the strict disciplinarian, the easygoing friend, the motherly helper, or the socratic discussion leader), such preferences do not form the basis for approximating a social consensus as to the nature of blameworthy or non-blameworthy teaching conduct."

Accordingly, Professor Elson suggests in place of and instead of the ordinary "reasonable man" test, the Professional's Duty to Exercise Due Care. This duty to exercise reasonable due care is the same duty required of laymen under the "reasonable man" standard of care, however, to the extent that the professional's expertise alerts him to the need for special precautions, he must act accordingly to this special knowledge. Professor Elson further points out that this standard of care required of a professional is conceptually distinguished from the professional skill and judgment standard, required in an educational malpractice case. The negligence standard does not question the professional's possession of the requisite level of skill and judgment, but requires that he exercise that customary skill and judgment with reasonable attentiveness and caution (infra, p. 10). Under this standard of care, Professor Elson points out "... The lay trier of facts' independent determination of the professional's exercise of carefulness or attentiveness in his method of reaching his judgments is more practicable than would be such trier of facts' determination either of the reasonableness of the professional's judgments themselves, or of the competence of the professional's per-

222

formance under the reasonable man ordinary negligence standard of care. The trier of fact, in making the latter two types of determinations, has no clearly ascertainable clear standards for reviewing the substantive educational practices of the educator. He can therefore only speculate as to what is reasonable educational behavior.... However, the determination of the professional's exercise of due care in the manner in which he makes his judgments requires the trier of fact to draw upon his understanding of the commonly experienced and appreciate human attributes of diligence, carefulness, and attentiveness to one's duties, whatever those duties may be."

Interestingly enough, Professor Elson points out the mandate of Education for All Handicapped Children Act (20 U.S.C. §§ 1401-1461) which in placing, and teaching the handicapped sets forth the criteria which could also be considered in determining the duty or like approach of the defendants. Thus, the act generally provides for the systematic identification and evaluation of the children with educational handicaps and for the development and annual review of written individualized educational plans for meeting each handicapped child's special educational needs. The Act directs that such plans must include statements of the child's personal level of educational performance, short and long term goals for the child's performance, the specific educational service to be provided the child and specific criteria to be used to measure the child's progress.

However valid and exciting the views of Professor Elson may be, the court recognizes that such a drastic change in this area of the law would be better left to legislative fiat. However, the concepts elaborated by Professor Elson may be considered in deciding the ordinary negligence case.

Having distinguished between "reasonable man" test and professional practice, the court concludes that a teacher or Board of Education may be held liable in common law negligence. Thus, there are certain duties placed upon educators that do not fall within pedagogi-

223

cal methodology and therefore are actionable. The allegations of negligence pleaded in the complaint herein are not based on the failure to teach but a failure to
observe that it was a hearing defect, not retardation,
which was the primary cause of the infant plaintiff's
difficulties. Defendants are not charged with failure to
exercise the proper professional judgment, but rather
the school system is charged with a breach of its public
trust to properly perform its duties.

A guarantee of intellectual capability is not at issue
in this case, but a failure to recognize the cause of the
infant's low IQ score based on performance and observation. In this setting, the teacher or school system is
held to a degree of care commensurate with a duty
owed created by a public trust. Consequently, the
teaching professional is held to a standard of care
above that of the reasonable man, yet not equal to the
standard accepted practice in the community as generally held for professional malpractice. The failure to
inquire as to the plaintiff's learning deficiency is a
breach of duty not resting on an error of pedagogical
judgment but fits into the category of a negligent failure to foresee the likely consequences of inactivity.
Although plaintiffs' proof may be difficult, to dismiss
the negligence claim at this juncture would be clearly
inappropriate.

Thus, liability may be found to perceive the basis of
the learning difficulty (hearing loss, etc.), which could
be remedied with specific testing, such as a request for
a physical examination, including a hearing test.
Thus, the teacher is in reality held to a standard of
care higher than that of a reasonable man to the extent that he or she has the daily opportunity to observe
the student and is duty bound to make at least an
attempt to discover the reason for a student's below
average performance. This does not rest upon an error
of judgment, but bespeaks of a duty to inquire before
placing a child in a class for mentally retarded children.

Accordingly, the motion to dismiss the complaint for
failure to state a cause of action is granted with re-

spect to those causes of action pleading educational and medical malpractice; denied as to the cause of action regarding educational negligence. The alternative motion for summary judgment is denied; there are some serious issues of fact which can only be resolved at a trial. [Emphasis added].[85]

§ 7.2. Educational Malpractice ("Hybrid") Cases in Private Schools.

§ 7.2(A). Paladino v. Adelphi University.

In 1982, the New York Supreme Court, Appellate Division, decided the case of *Paladino v. Adelphi University*.[86] The court summarized the facts:

> Michael Paladino was enrolled at the nursery grade level at the Waldorf School in 1972 and continued at the school through the fifth grade. His teachers during this period sent evaluation reports to Michael's parents that assessed his performance in each area of his curriculum. In 1979, while he was attending fifth grade, Michael evidenced certain learning problems and his parents sent him to a private testing institution for independent evaluation. The results showed that Michael was not equipped with sufficient skills for fifth grade and was several grades below fifth grade level in arithmetic, reading and writing. Thereafter, the school refused to promote Michael to the sixth grade and his parents enrolled him in public school where he repeated the fifth grade.
>
> Michael's father alleged in his complaint that the Waldorf School breached its agreement by failing to provide quality education, qualified and expert teachers, necessary tutorial and supportive skills, accurate and factual progress reports; and that it furnished false and misleading progress reports which reflected that Michael was making satisfactory progress

---

85. *Id.* at 279-83.
86. 89 A.D.2d 85, 454 N.Y.S.2d 868 (1982).

in his studies and promoted him each year to the next grade. A second cause of action was asserted on behalf of Michael as a third-party beneficiary of the agreement with the school and the father pleaded a third cause of action sounding in deceit based on the allegedly inaccurate progress reports and misrepresentations concerning the quality of the education. A fourth cause of action for deceit was also pleaded on behalf of Michael.[87]

The supreme court, special term, denied the school's motion for summary judgment, holding that the established policy of our courts in refusing to entertain lawsuits for educational malpractice did not bar an action in contract nor one based upon fraudulent misrepresentation.[88] The New York Supreme Court, Appellate Division stated:

At issue is whether recovery may be had against a private elementary school for breach of contract based upon its alleged failure to provide a quality education to a student enrolled in a school. We hold that such action does not lie. Further, we conclude that, under the facts here present, related claims predicated upon fraudulent misrepresentation and deceit must similarly be dismissed.[89]

The court further stated, in their view, "the soundness of this policy of noninterference is equally applicable when the action is brought against a private educational institution and is formulated in contract."[90] The court went on to state:

Professional educators — not judges — are charged with the responsibility for determining the method of learning that should be pursued for their students. When the intended results are not obtained, it is the

---

87. *Id.* at 870.
88. 110 Misc. 2d 314, 442 N.Y.S.2d 38 (1981).
89. 89 A.D.2d 85, 454 N.Y.S.2d 868, 870 (1982).
90. *Id.* at 871-72.

educational community — and not the judiciary — that must resolve the problem. For, in reality, the soundness of educational methodology is always subject to question and a court ought not in hindsight, substitute its notions as to what would have been a better course of instruction to follow for a particular pupil. These are determinations that are to be made by educators and, though they are capable of error, their integrity ought not be subject to judicial inquiry. In this regard, we cannot perceive how the professional judgment of educators concerning the course of teaching a particular student in a private school, as opposed to a public school, becomes more amenable to attack in the courts. Public policy should similarly prevent a court from interfering with private schools when the controversy requires the examination of the efficacy of the course of instruction.

If in a case such as this, a private school were simply to accept a student's tuition and thereafter provide no educational services, an action for breach of contract might lie. Similarly, if the contract with the school were to provide for certain specified services, such as for example, a designated number of hours of instruction, and the school failed to meet its obligation, then a contract action with appropriate consequential damages might be viable. However, here the essence of the contract cause of action pleaded is that the Waldorf School failed to educate Michael. The asserted breach is predicated upon the quality and adequacy of the course of instruction. The claim requires the factfinder to enter the classroom and determine whether or not the judgments and conduct of professional educators were deficient. The specific allegations in support of the claimed breach are that the school failed to provide a "quality education ... qualified and expert teachers ... necessary tutorial and support services ... in the area of the basic academic skills [and] accurate and factual progress reports" and "furnished ... false and misleading progress reports which reflected that ... [Michael] was making satisfactory progress in his studies and promoted ... [Michael] each year to the

227

next class grade." It is readily apparent that the claims entail an analysis of the educational function. The sufficiency of tutorial services, academic assessments as to Michael's performance and determinations relative to graduation are not matters that should be subject to judicial review (see *Hoffman v. Board of Educ.*, 49 N.Y.2d 121, 126, 424 N.Y.S.2d 376, 400 N.E.2d 317; *supra; Hunter v. Board of Educ. of Montgomery County*, 47 Md.App. 709, 425 A.2d 681, 684, mod. 292 Md. 481, 439 A.2d 582, *supra*). The quality of the education and qualifications of the teachers employed by the private school are concerns not for the courts, but rather for the State Education Department and its commissioner (Education Law, § 5003).

Accordingly, the first two causes of action sounding in contract must be dismissed.[91]

Concerning the other causes of action, the court stated:

Finally, the plaintiffs have failed to support the allegation that the school misrepresented that it would provide necessary tutorial services. The record indicates that additional educational help was provided to Michael during the third and fourth grades and that he was tutored in reading in the third grade. Where the misrepresentation is a promise to perform a service in the future, an action for deceit is not available and plaintiff is relegated to contractual remedies unless it can be shown that the promisor had no intention of performing the future act at the time the promise was made (*Rudman v. Cowles Communications*, 30 N.Y.2d 1, 9, 330 N.Y.S.2d 33, 280 N.E.2d 867; *Adams v. Clark*, 239 N.Y. 403, 410, 146 N.E. 642; *Brown v. Lockwood*, 76 A.D.2d 721, 731-733, 432 N.Y.S.2d 186). Since special attention was given to Michael and tutoring was in fact provided, the statement of future intention was kept and may not provide a basis for recovery.

Thus, the third and fourth causes of action must similarly be dismissed.[92]

---

91. *Id.* at 873.
92. *Id.* at 875.

§ 7.2(B). Village Community School v. Adler.

A private school brought an action to recover tuition monies from the mother of a student. The mother counterclaimed for breach of contract, fraudulent/negligent misrepresentation, and negligent infliction of emotional distress. The school moved to dismiss the mother's counterclaim for failure to state a cause of action.[93] The Civil Court, City of New York, held that:

> (1) mother's breach of contract claim alleging that school agreed to detect student's learning deficiencies and to provide necessary tutorial and guidance services but failed to do so was permissible; (2) mother could make claim for fraudulent misrepresentation if she could show scienter of school, but could not maintain action based on negligent misrepresentation; and (3) mother could not maintain action for mental distress caused by school's alleged negligence in educational practices.[94]

The court stated:

> Ms. Adler's first counterclaim alleges that plaintiff's agents represented to her that they possessed a specialized faculty that could identify and individually treat children with learning disabilities. She claims that those representations were fraudulently and/or negligently made, and that to her detriment, she relied on the representations in entering into her agreement with plaintiff. Defendant also claims that the School did not provide the aforementioned services, and therefore breached their contract. Defendant's third counterclaim is for negligent infliction of emotional distress. She alleges that psychiatric intervention was necessary because her son received services which proved to be inappropriate and harmful when plaintiff

---

93. Village Community School v. Adler, 124 Misc. 2d 817.
94. 478 N.Y.S.2d 546 (1984).

failed to diagnose or misdiagnosed his learning disability.

The issue at bar is whether claims for breach of contract, fraudulent/negligent misrepresentation and negligent infliction of emotional distress in the educational context may be entertained by this court.

The courts have uniformly refused to determine negligence claims that are predicated upon educational malpractice. *Donohue v. Copiague Union Free School District,* 47 N.Y.2d 440, 418 N.Y.S.2d 375, 391 N.E.2d 1352 (1979); *Washington v. City of New York,* 83 A.D.2d 866, 442 N.Y.S.2d 20 (2d Dept. 1981); *Helm v. Professional Children's School,* 103 Misc. 2d 1053, 43 N.Y.S.2d 246 (App. Term, 1st Dept.). The leading case in this area is *Donohue v. Copiague Union Free School District.* It involved a recent high school graduate who lacked the basic ability to comprehend English on a level sufficient to complete employment applications. Although the court declined to impose liability on the school district for failure to provide a quality education, the court acknowledged that a complaint could be successfully pleaded.

"If doctors ... and other professionals are charged with a duty owing to the public whom they serve, it could be said that nothing in the law precludes similar treatment of ... educators. Nor would creation of a standard ... necessarily pose an insurmountable obstacle... As for proximate causation ... it perhaps assumes too much to conclude that it could never be established." 47 N.Y.2d at 443, 418 N.Y.S.2d at 377, 391 N.E.2d at 1353. *Donohue* concluded, however, that such claims should not be entertained as a matter of public policy. 47 N.Y.2d at 444, 418 N.Y.S.2d at 377, 391 N.E.2d at 1354.

In *Hoffman v. Bd. of Educ.,* 49 N.Y.2d 121, 424 N.Y.S.2d 376, 400 N.E.2d 317 (1979), the plaintiff was examined by a kindergarten school psychologist who recommended placement in a class for Children with Retarded Mental Development (CRMD). Although a reevaluation in two years was also recommended, the defendant did not retest until the plaintiff was 18. At

230

that time, they determined that he was not retarded. The Plaintiff there sued for damages sustained from his diminished capacity for employment, but the court refused to allow the action. The *Hoffman* court followed *Donohue* and declined to recognize negligence claims for failure to provide a quality education.

The case at bar is different from the aforementioned ones in that it is based upon a breach of contract entered into with a private institution. The facts of *Paladino v. Adelphi University,* 89 A.D.2d 85, 454 N.Y.S.2d 868 (2d Dept. 1982), more closely resemble the facts of the case before this court. That action was for breach of contract against a private school for failure to provide an effective education. The court declined to evaluate the soundness of the teaching methods because a breach of contract for quality instruction would force them to become overseers of the learning process. 89 A.D.2d at 90-91, 454 N.Y.S.2d at 872. However, that made an exception for one situation where liability could be imposed.

"If the contract with the school were to provide for certain specified services ... and the school failed to meet its obligation ... a contract action with appropriate consequential damages may be viable." 89 A.D.2d at 92, 454 N.Y.S.2d at 873. This is the situation with which this court is now presented.

Ms. Adler alleges that the School agreed to detect learning deficiencies and to provide the necessary tutorial and guidance services, but failed to do so. When defendants promised to detect learning disabilities, they effectively waived the implementation of competency testing and other educational tools as a discretionary measure and made it a requirement for full contract performance. In deciding whether to allow this action, this court is not required to review any discretionary actions taken as a result of plaintiff's professional judgment. The claim is therefore permissible. *Donohue,* 47 N.Y.2d at 444, 418 N.Y.S.2d at 378, 391 N.E.2d at 1354.

Also at issue is whether an action for fraudulent or negligent misrepresentation can be maintained. If the

231

duty that is claimed to be violated through negligence is one owed to the general public, the act or decision is immune from review. *Poysa v. State,* 102 Misc. 2d 269, 423 N.Y.S.2d 617. Therefore, a cause of action based on negligent misrepresentation in the educational context is precluded. *See Donohue,* 47 N.Y.2d 440, 418 N.Y.S.2d 375, 391 N.E.2d 1352; *Hoffman,* 49 N.Y.2d 121, 424 N.Y.S.2d 376, 400 N.E.2d 317.

Fraudulent misrepresentations of a material fact made without any attempt to perform is a sufficient basis for an action in deceit. Prosser, *Law of Torts,* Section 104, 3d Edition. Because of the problems of proof, however, the various remedies for deceit are not available for misstatements of opinion and quality, only for misstatements of fact. As the court in *Paladino v. Adelphi University* enunciated:

"An action for fraudulent misrepresentation in the educational context bespeaks an abuse of the trust imparted to our educators and should be entertained by the courts. Deception has no place in the educational process. While negligent misrepresentation and judgmental errors ought not be actionable ... misrepresentations coupled with the element of *scienter* should result in the imposition of liability." 89 A.D.2d at 94, 454 N.Y.S.2d at 874. In that case, alleged misrepresentations as to educational quality were not found to be capable of proof.

Unlike the plaintiff in *Paladino,* Ms. Adler does not claim that this plaintiff misrepresented the quality of the education that her children would receive. She alleges that the School told her that they would detect and treat any learning disability that her children may have, and that she justifiably relied on this information. Defendant states a viable cause of action because her claim for deceit requires the element of *scienter.* She can establish a prima facie case if she shows that plaintiff had no intention to fulfill its promise, that its resources were not adequate at the time of the contract or that it never performed such a service before.

232

Defendant's third counterclaim is based on the theory of negligent infliction of mental distress. In New York, it is well established that physical contact or injury is no longer necessary for such a claim. *See Battalla v. State,* 10 N.Y.2d 237, 219 N.Y.S.2d 34, 176 N.E.2d 729 (1961). Thus, there may be recovery for emotional distress resulting from a negligent act. However, the courts have unanimously held that monetary damages for educational malpractice based on a negligent theory are not recoverable. *Donohue v. Copiague Union Free School District,* 47 N.Y.2d at 440, 418 N.Y.S.2d at 375, 391 N.E.2d at 1352; *Hoffman v. Board of Ed.,* 49 N.Y.2d at 121, 424 N.Y.S.2d at 376, 400 N.E.2d at 317; *Helm v. Professional Children's School,* 103 Misc. 2d at 1053, 431 N.Y.S.2d at 246; *Washington v. City of New York,* 83 A.D.2d 866, 442 N.Y.S.2d 20. Defendant therefore, may not sue for the mental distress caused by negligence in educational practices.

For the foregoing reasons, plaintiff's motion to dismiss the defendant's counterclaims for breach of contract and fraudulent misrepresentation is denied and its motion to dismiss defendant's claim for negligent infliction of emotional distress is granted.[95]

---

95. *Id.* at 547-49.

Chapter 8

EDUCATIONAL MALPRACTICE IN HIGHER EDUCATION

> While the university-student relationship is indeed unique, it does not vest a university with unlimited power to do or not to

do as it pleases without facing
the consequences.[1]

§ 8.0. Introduction.

Suits by students against educational institutions have
not been limited to elementary and secondary schools but
have also been brought against trade schools, junior and
four year colleges, universities, and professional schools.
This chapter will briefly discuss some of these suits and the
theories under which they were brought.

§ 8.1. Educational Malpractice in Higher Education.

§ 8.1(A). Trustees of Columbia University v. Jacobsen.

One of the first cases dealing with educational malpractice in the United States was filed in 1957. The case of
Trustees of Columbia University v. Jacobsen[2] was initiated
in the district court by Columbia University against the
defendant (a student) and his parents for the balance of
tuition. The student filed a counterclaim, demanding
money damages in the sum of $7,016.00 and other relief.
The counterclaim was in 50 counts and alleged that the
plaintiff had represented that "it would teach defendant
wisdom, truth, character, enlightenment, understanding,
justice, liberty, honesty, courage, beauty and similar vir-
tues and qualities; that it would develop the whole man,
maturity, well-roundedness, objective thinking, and the
like; and that because it had failed to do so it was guilty of
misrepresentation, to defendant's pecuniary damage."[3] The
student based his allegations on quotations from the col-

---

1. Lowenthol v. Vanderbilt University, Chancery Court for Davidson
County, Part Three, Nashville, Tenn., No. A-8525 (1976).
2. 53 N.J. Super. 574, 148 A.2d 63 (1959).
3. 53 N.J. Super. 574, 576, 148 A.2d 63, 64 (1959).

lege catalogue and brochures, including inscriptions over university buildings and addresses by university officers. The University admitted many of these quotations, however, it denied that it had failed to carry out its promises and committed fraud. The question before the court was whether these statements constituted actionable misrepresentations. The court concluded:

> The attempt of the counterclaim, inartistically drawn as it is, was to state a cause of action in deceit. The necessary elements of that action are by now hornbook law; a false representation, knowledge or belief on the part of the person making the representation that it is false, an intention that the other party act thereon, reasonable reliance by such party in so doing, and resultant damage to him. [Citations omitted].
>
> We are in complete agreement with the trial court that the counterclaim fails to establish the very first element, false representation, basic to any action in deceit. Plaintiff stands by every quotation relied on by the defendant. Only by reading into them the imagined meanings he attributes to them can one conclude — and the conclusion would be a most tenuous, insubstantial one — that Columbia University represented it could teach wisdom, truth, justice, beauty, spirituality and all the other qualities set out in the 50 counts of the counterclaim.[4]

In its opinion the court quoted a statement made by the defendant, wherein he stated:

> I have really only one charge against Columbia: that it does not teach wisdom as it claims to do. From this charge ensues an endless number of charges, of which I have selected fifty at random. I am prepared to show that each of these fifty claims in turn is false, though the central issue is that of Columbia's pretense of teaching wisdom.[5]

---

4. 53 N.J. Super. 574, 577-78, 148 A.2d 63, 65 (1959).
5. 53 N.J. Super. 574, 579-80, 148 A.2d 63, 66 (1959).

The court then went on to comment on the statement by noting:

> We agree with the trial judge that wisdom is not a subject which can be taught and that no rational person would accept such a claim made by any man or institution. We find nothing in the record to establish that Columbia represented, expressly or even by way of impression, that it could or would teach wisdom or the several qualities which defendant insists are "synonyms for or aspects of the same Quality." The matter is perhaps summed up in the supporting affidavit of the Dean of Columbia College, where he said that "All that any college can do through its teachers, libraries, laboratories and other facilities is to endeavor to teach the student the known facts, acquaint him with the nature of those matters which are unknown, and thereby assist him in developing mentally, morally and physically. Wisdom is a hoped-for end product of education, experiencing and ability which many seek and many fail to attain."[6]

The appellate court affirmed the trial court's order granting the University a summary judgment.

§ 8.1(B). Asher v. Harrington.

In the early 1970's the courts were faced with the issue of whether the courts should entertain a cause of action against educators if students alleged that they did not receive the education which they were promised.[7] In 1970 the United States District Court decided the case of *Asher v. Harrington*.[8] An action was brought by university students

---

6. *Id.*
7. Patricia Claire Karman, "Beyond Educational Malpractice: Breach of Contract Actions Against Institutions of Higher Learning." Paper presented at Midwest Business Administration Association Conference, Chicago, Illinois.
8. 318 F. Supp. 82 (1970).

against university officials, including the President of the University, the chancellors of the Madison and Milwaukee campus, and also the regents of the University of Wisconsin. It was alleged in the complaint that officials had failed to reasonably maintain the University in operation for the benefit of the majority of students during periods of campus demonstrations following reports of American military activities in Cambodia in April 1970. More specifically, in their first cause of action the plaintiffs claimed a denial of rights and privileges under the first and fourteenth amendments of the Constitution and a violation of 42 U.S.C. § 1983. It was further alleged that the plaintiffs had paid their tuition as students for the spring semester of 1970 and that:

> [They] were therefore granted certain individual rights and privileges including but not limited to the following: to pursue an education at the University; the unencumbered use and enjoyment of the facilities and grounds of the University while pursuing their education at said University; to attend classes and study courses conducted under the tutelage and supervision of qualified faculty and administrator [administrative] personnel, said classes leading to the award of graduation credits prerequisite to a degree from the University.[9]

The third cause of action alleged that the University "expressly or impliedly offered the following [academic services] to plaintiffs in return for their payment of tuition and fees;" the defendants and their agents breached their agreement and failed to provide the plaintiffs with an opportunity to pursue their continued education.[10]

In granting a motion to dismiss, the court concluded that the first two causes of action failed to state a civil rights

---

9. *Id.* at 83.
10. *Id.* at 84.

claim and there was no jurisdiction for the court to entertain the third cause of action. More specifically, the court held:

> Paragraphs 9 and 11 of the complaint contain the assertion that the defendants' actions "discriminatorily deprived plaintiffs of their rights of free speech, free inquiry, free thought and free assembly" but such charge is a mere conclusion. There is no logical nexus between the conclusion and the statement of facts set forth in the first course of action. Similarly in the second cause of action, the plaintiffs conclude in paragraph 14 that they were denied equal protection of the laws by the defendants. There is a gap, too, between this conclusory assertion and the facts asserted in the second cause of action.
>
> ....
>
> ... Whether an education is a privilege or a right, the plaintiffs contend that the denial of the right to *continue* in the educational process is a denial of a constitutional right. However, I find that there is a major hiatus between the rights claimed in paragraph 9 (e.g., "to pursue an education"), and the conclusion that the plaintiffs were deprived of "free speech, free inquiry, free thought, and free assembly."[11]

The court opined that the third cause of action cannot stand by itself in the absence of either the first or second cause of action. The court commented that:

> There is an obvious lack of diversity of citizenship in the case at bar, and it is also likely that the amount in controversy is less than $10,000 as to any individual plaintiff [citations omitted]. There is no jurisdiction in this court over the third cause of action under 28 U.S.C. § 1343 since it alleges a breach of contract [citations omitted]. The third cause of action belongs in a state court.[12]

---

11. *Id.* at 84-85.
12. *Id.* at 85.

The case was then appealed to the United States Court of Appeals, which affirmed the U.S. District Court's decision, in 1972. The court reasoned:

> In *Keyishion v. Board of Regents of the Univ. of N.Y.*, [citations omitted], for example, the Court found New York's teacher loyalty laws unconstitutional on the grounds that the first amendment "does not tolerate laws that cast a pall of orthodoxy over the classroom" [citations omitted]. But in holding that the classroom was entitled protection as the "marketplace of ideas" the Court was not suggesting that the classroom was the only setting that would so qualify. Indeed, to call upon courts to delineate the specific form in which academic inquiry must occur would itself place an impermissible burden on academic freedom. Respect for the autonomy of educational institutions has resulted in focusing judicial protection of first amendment rights primarily on extra-curricular speech and assembly. Courts have generally hesitated to review purely academic matters, as in cases involving administrative decisions about curriculum, where the danger of impinging upon the authority of the institution to determine educational programs was greatest [citations omitted].
>
> These considerations are especially compelling in the instant case. We are at a loss to ascertain the standards by which federal courts are to judge the rights to continue normal educational activities. We find no guidance in the first amendment itself or in the cases construing it. Clearly, the plaintiffs are not suggesting that we have the power — quite apart from the competence — to evaluate which aspects of a university's functions we consider to be "normal." Rather plaintiffs are suggesting that we take statements of university officials in catalogues and other publications at face value as defining what constitutes education for that institution. As such, *they are asking that we elevate to constitutional status what is in essence only a contract claim.* We are convinced that nothing in the first

241

amendment requires this construction (emphasis added).[13]

Judge Campbell dissented. In his dissenting opinion he noted:

> When the complaint is viewed in what I consider to be its proper light, I can only conclude that it states a proper federal claim under Section 1983 of the Civil Rights Act, 42 U.S.C. § 1983. There can be no dispute that the constitutional assurances of speech and assembly are intertwined with and involved in the educational process [citations omitted]. It therefore follows that the arbitrary denial of the opportunity to exercise such constitutional guarantees suffices to state a claim for relief under Section 1983. If a dissident student has a constitutionally protected right to wear, in nondisruptive circumstances, a black armband into a classroom as a peaceful expression of his anti-war views, then students who wish merely to pursue their customary educational opportunities also possess a constitutional right to enter the classroom and express their ideas of normal educational pursuit, free from arbitrary interference by school officials [citations omitted].
>
> *It seems to me unfair, to say the least, that the Federal Courts which seem to welcome — almost solicit — every possible type of student rights case, from hair styles to the destruction of school property, for approval as proper forms of student protest should here close their doors to a group of students who seek merely their civil and contractual rights to pursue peacefully their studies without the violent interference of a well organized disruptive mob allegedly, supported by the University* [emphasis added].[14]

---

13. 461 F.2d 890, 894 (1972).
14. *Id.* at 896-97.

§ 8.1(C). Paynter v. New York University.

The case of *Paynter v. New York University*,[15] dealt with an action brought by a father against the university for refund of tuition paid for his son's attendance. The Civil Court of the City of New York held that the university, which cancelled classes for balance of the semester because of riots, disorders, and acts of vandalism occurring on its campuses, was liable to the tuition payer for breach of contract, notwithstanding that the university bulletin stated that programs and requirements were subject to change without notice at any time at the discretion of the administration.[16]

The claim was for $277.40 of the tuition paid for the 19 days of cancelled instruction. The defendant pointed out that, under the statute applicable to private education institutions, the Board of Trustees is empowered to "use its property as they shall deem for the best interests of the institution ...;" and further to make all "rules necessary and proper for the purposes of the institution and not inconsistent with law or any rule of the university ...."[17]

The University offered in evidence a bulletin which is delivered to all students at the time of their enrollment wherein it is stated "that programs and requirements are subject to change without notice at any time at the discretion of the administration." Concerning this, the court commented:

> To argue that this rule contemplated, envisioned, and/or in any way intended the closing of classes scheduled, to attend which students had already paid tuition, and the suspension of the balance of the semester is too specious to merit any consideration.

---

15. 64 Misc. 2d 266, 314 N.Y.S.2d 676 (1970).
16. *Id.*
17. *Id.* at 676-77.

> *Moreover, assuming that the defendant's Senate took the aforesaid action before the semester had begun, or during the early part of the semester instead of the last month, could it thereby have successfully contended that because of the invoked rule the students would not be entitled to a return of their tuition?*
>
> The principle of law is the same. The defendant breached its contract during its lifetime. It matters not in what point in its duration. The courts find neither form nor substance in defendant's denial of liability in its breach of contract suit [emphasis added].[18]

The case was then appealed to the New York Supreme Court, Appellate Division, which reversed the judgment and dismissed the complaint. In reversing the case the court concluded:

> Private colleges and universities are governed on the principle of self-regulation, free to a large degree, from judicial restraints (Education Law, § 226, subd. 10), and they have inherent authority to maintain order on their campuses. In light of the events on the defendant's campus and in college communities throughout the country on May 4th to 5th, 1970, the court erred in substituting its judgment for that of the university administrators and in concluding that the university was unjustified in suspending classes for the time remaining in the school year prior to the examination period. Moreover, while in a strict sense, a student contracts with a college or university for a number of courses to be given during the academic year, the services rendered by the university cannot be measured by the time spent in a classroom. The circumstances of the relationship permit the implication that the professor or the college may make minor changes in this regard. The insubstantial change made in the schedule of classes does not permit a recovery of tuition. We conclude that substantial justice was not done between

---

18. *Id.* at 680.

the parties "according to the rules and principles of substantive law" [citations omitted].[19]

§ 8.1(D). Harte v. Adelphi University.

An action was brought by five students at Adelphi University for an order directing the University to reopen the University and permit continuation of studies.[20] The court summarized the facts as follows:

> Following the entry of the United States forces into Cambodia and the Kent State University tragedy the University took certain action. On May 5, 1970, a resolution was adopted by the full-time faculty of Adelphi University urging the University's administrative officials to "cancel all classes till such time as in the judgment of this faculty the appropriate administration for growth and learning is reestablished."
>
> Following the adoption of such faculty resolution by a vote of 146 to 52 consultations were had among the senior University officials, the Deans of the several colleges and schools and the Dean of Students to make a determination with respect to action on the aforesaid resolution.
>
> On May 6, 1970 the President of the University, "... giving high priority to consideration for the continuance of the personal safety of faculty and students on this campus and for the protection of the physical plant ...", issued an announcement cancelling all classes until further notice. A similar notice dated the same day was issued by the Vice-President for Academic Affairs.
>
> On May 9, 1970 the University's Board of Trustees held a special meeting and agreed that while an open campus would be maintained classes would only be resumed when the President, Chairman of the Board of Trustees and Chairman of the Faculty-Student Sen-

---

19. 319 N.Y.S.2d 893, 894 (1971).

20. Harte v. Adelphi University, 63 Misc. 2d 228, 311 N.Y.S.2d 66 (1970).

ate determined that appropriate conditions were established for safeguarding the persons of the faculty and students, as well as the physical plant.

On Monday, May 11, 1970 the University Faculty held a meeting and adopted resolutions providing for the resumption of classes and the grading of students under the special circumstances. On said date the President ordered and announced the resumption of classes effective beginning with the evening classes of May 11, 1970.

On May 7, 1970 the plaintiffs in their own behalf secured the subject order to show cause returnable May 8, 1970 before this Court for a mandatory injunction addressed to the University and its President seeking a full reopening of classes based upon their alleged contractual rights as paying students. Nothing less than a full resumption of University activity is demanded.

It should be noted that the plaintiffs sue in their own names. It does not appear, nor does this Court question at this time for the purposes of this decision, the rights of the plaintiffs, who may be infants, to bring this proceeding. Assuming that the plaintiffs are at least 21 years old and assuming that they have, although this Court has grave doubts, properly pleaded a class action as well as one in their individual capacity, (CPLR 1005(a); cf. Gaynor v. Rockefeller, 15 N.Y.2d 120, 256 N.Y.S.2d 584, 204 N.E.2d 627), this Court finds that the plaintiffs are not entitled to the drastic temporary relief sought by this application.

Under the statute applicable to private education institutions, such as Adelphi University, (Education Law § 226, subs. 6), the Board of Trustees is empowered to "... use its property as they shall deem for the best interests of the institution ..."; and further (Subd. 10), to "... make all by-laws and rules necessary and proper for the purposes of the institution and not inconsistent with law or any rule of the university ...".[21]

The court then went on to state:

---

21. *Id.* at 67-68.

This Court takes judicial notice of the prevailing atmosphere of unrest, and even violence in some instances, which pervades the patterns of College and University life in these times. This Court also finds plausible and reasonable the statement of the University's President that the cessation of classes, for even the short time involved was solely to maintain the safety of all persons on the campus and for the safeguard of the University property.

Indeed, the standard of care in the exercise of their duties and prerogatives as is given to the Trustees of a public institution in respect to danger to the safety and welfare of their charges, both human and property, is equally applicable to the defendants [citations omitted].

This Court does not equate the precautionary measures taken by the defendants with arbitrary or capricious conduct so as to invoke the drastic remedy sought here.

A mandatory injunction of the type petitioned for here is rarely granted, (12 Carmody-Wait 2d, Injunctions, § 78:24, and cases therein cited). It is the general rule that the relief requested on this application must be based upon an indisputable clear showing of a factual pattern that to deny it would be captious or unconscionable, circumstances which are totally deficient on the papers before this Court.

It appears to this Court that under the unique and trying circumstances that the defendants acted in good faith with their judgment being directed by a primary concern for preservation of life and property, which was not only their right by their duty. The burden to show that their acts were capricious and illegal has not been met by the plaintiffs.

Application denied.[22]

---

22. *Id.* at 8.

§ 8.1(E). DeVito v. McMurray.

The *DeVito*[23] case was decided in New York in 1970. The court stated:

> It appears that because of certain demands and/or disruptions by a portion of the student body on the campus of Queens College, that institution was closed on May 6 and 7, 1970. Apparently there was some serious question as to when the regular classes of instruction would continue in the City University and Queens College, in particular. By a resolution of the Board of Higher Education dated May 10, 1970 that body determined:
>
> > That the Board of Higher Education states that it is the duty of the City University to remain open in order to continue to offer instruction to the students enrolled in the University;
> >
> > That faculties have the responsibility to meet with and teach their students in order to pursue the academic mission of their colleges. Colleges may adjust their programs of courses, attendance, examinations and grading as in their judgment may seem necessary and appropriate.
> >
> > That letter grades will be given to students who request them and that no student may be granted a passing grade for a course unless in the judgment of the instructor he has met the standards of that course.
>
> By two letters dated May 11, 1970, the president of Queens College indicated that in addition to the regular course of studies seminars would be offered dealing with subjects of current political interest on the campus. He further indicated that there would be a modification in the grading system, although students were still given the right to elect letter grades.
>
> By a letter dated May 12, 1970, the dean of the faculty of Queens College restated the administration's position with regard to the procedure on grades and

---

23. DeVito v. McMurray, 311 N.Y.S.2d 617 (Supreme Court, Special Term, Queens County, Part 1, N.Y., 1970).

generally stated that, by reason of the Board of Higher Education's resolution, faculty members had the responsibility to meet with and teach their students.

Plaintiffs contend that in many instances the faculty discontinued the course of study and either suggested that the students attend the several seminars or it conducted such seminars in place of the regular curriculum.

The defendants, in reply, contend that students have the right to bring such grievances before the respective departmental chairmen and also the Committee on Scholastic Standards, referring particularly to the provisions of the letter of May 12, 1970.

The Court notes in that regard that the provision in said letter specifically deals with grade complaints and does not indicate that this course should also be followed where an instructor might terminate the course of study. Assuming, without deciding, that either procedure is an administrative remedy which the students would otherwise be required to pursue before bringing this proceeding, the Court notes that, pursuant to the Queens College catalogue, regular classes are to terminate on May 23, 1970, and the scholastic year would end June 6, 1970.[24]

The court reasoned as follows:

Inasmuch as the evidence is unclear as to the time such administrative procedures would entail, and since the dean of the faculty testified that it could take as long as three weeks, it appears to the Court that such administrative remedies, because of the time factor, would be futile and, under the circumstances, should not be a bar to the present court proceeding.

It appears to the Court that the principal question is whether or not the defendants have complied with the directive of the Board of Higher Education dated May 10, 1970. Clearly Education Law, paragraphs 6201 and 6202, give the Board of Higher Education the sole and exclusive power for the running and maintenance

---

24. *Id.* at 618-19.

of the university. Under such power, the board issued
its May 10th resolution.

It is the function of the president of any branch of
the university, as the executive agent of the board, to
enforce and carry out its by-laws and resolutions. (By-
laws of the Board of Higher Education of the City of
New York, paragraph 7.4.) Apparently the president of
Queens College interpreted the portion of the resolution providing that the college may adjust its program
of courses to mean that the college might introduce
new courses in the place and stead of existing curriculum.

The Court notes at this time that generally it will
not interfere with the exercise of administrative discretion vested with the administrators in charge of the
educational institution. However, where there is no
scope for the use of that discretion, the Court may find
that the administrator has exceeded his authority.
(Matter of Lesser v. Board of Education of City of New
York, 18 A.D.2d 388, 390, 239 N.Y.S.2d 776, 779.)

The Court finds here that there was no discretion in
the administration of Queens College as to whether or
not to continue the regular course of study. The resolution of the board is clear that the City University must
remain open in order to offer instruction to its students
and that the faculty had the responsibility to meet
with and teach these students.

The Court does not believe that this directive is sus-
ceptible of any interpretation other than that the university will offer to these students a continuation of
the courses and curriculum which they started in the
beginning of the semester. While the discretion
granted to the president might allow him to introduce
other courses or even workshops to fulfill the need that
he finds present in the demands of the students, under
no circumstances is that discretion so broad as to allow
those other courses or workshops to interfere with the
completion of the courses begun in the beginning of the
semester.

The Court finds as a fact that the administration did
not comply with the aforementioned directive in that it

permitted seminars in many instances to be conducted at the same time and in the same place as regularly scheduled classes.

Further, upon a review of the description of the regular classes, as set forth in the catalogue of Queens College, and from the testimony of the administrators who appeared as witnesses, the Court finds that the subject matter of these seminars or workshops could in no way be found to be an integral part of or related to the courses of study originally scheduled at those times and in those rooms.

Further, the Court finds that in the instances where the plaintiffs sought to meet with faculty members or departmental chairmen, oftentimes they were unable to locate either.

Further, the Court finds that there has been no major disturbance on the campus since May 10, 1970, so as to justify the discontinuance of the regular classes scheduled.

Inasmuch as the evidence is inconclusive as to whether this situation existed with regard to all or a substantial part of the course curriculum offered at Queens College, the Court does not believe that its decision can go beyond the courses in which the present plaintiffs are involved. Under the circumstances, the defendants are directed to offer to plaintiffs the completion of the course of studies in the following list of classes in which the evidence has indicated the defendants have failed to meet their obligations under the resolution of May 10, 1970.

As to Plaintiff DeVito, the Court finds these courses: Physics 2, Square Dancing, Physical Education (restricted course).

As to Plaintiff Zurl: Square Dancing.

As to Plaintiff Kleim: English 3, Anthropology, French 1 and Art 7.

Further, the Court directs that the defendants, pursuant to the directions of the board, permit plaintiffs to elect whether they will receive letter grades in these courses or, in the alternative, to elect any other grading system offered to the student body in general. Such election should be made upon the completion of the regular course of study.

The Court finds that the rulings of the administration with regard to attendance, final examinations and grades are generally in conformity with the resolution and the prior practices at Queens College and, accordingly, makes no disposition in that regard.[25]

§ 8.1(F). Zumbrun v. University of Southern California.

Two years later, the California Court of Appeals decided the case of *Zumbrun v. University of Southern California.*[26] This was an action by a student against the University and other defendants seeking damages for, among other things, failure of defendant professor to give all lectures in the course and to give the final examination due to his joining a faculty strike protesting United States foreign policy. The superior court dismissed the complaint, which was entitled, "Complaint for Breach of Fiduciary Duties, Unjust Enrichment, Punitive Damages and Other Relief." The court of appeals, in affirming in part and in reversing and remanding with directions in part, held, *inter alia,* that whether the partial failure of consideration was minimal, so as to render application the maximum "de minimum non curat lex," or whether it justified a refund of a portion of the tuition and fees allocable to the course, was a matter of proof, under the present state of the pleadings, at a trial in an appropriate forum.[27]

Plaintiff's grievance arose out of the following alleged facts:

Plaintiff, who was 63 years old, enrolled in the University of Southern California (USC) for the purpose of

---

25. *Id.* at 619-21.
26. 25 Cal. App. 3d 1, 101 Cal. Rptr. 499 (1972).
27. *Id.*

concluding her college education and "becoming fully qualified in the field of Gerontology and Sociology." On November 7, 1969, she was admitted as a full-time student in the College of Letters, Arts, and Sciences of USC as a "junior." "[T]ime was of the essence due to plaintiff's age, ... the employment situation in the field of Gerontology and in the Southern California area, and due to other related factors." She paid her required tuition and other fees amounting to $518 on January 28, 1970. (It is not stated whether the $518 was the total amount paid or just the portion allocable to the course "Sociology 200.")

"Sociology 200" was required of sociology majors and was a prerequisite to other advanced courses in sociology and gerontology. On February 3, 1970, she commenced attending the spring classes, including "Sociology 200" taught by defendant Jon P. Miller, an assistant professor in the Department of Sociology and Anthropology.

[D]efendants, and each of them, represented, agreed, promised, and warranted to plaintiff that said Sociology 200 course would be a full and complete course with a final examination, that said class would be conducted on Tuesdays and Thursdays at 11:00 a.m. until 12:50 p.m. beginning February 3, 1970, and ending with a final examination on or before June 2, 1970, and that defendants would exercise good faith and judgment concerning said course ....

Defendant Miller refused to teach the class commencing on May 1, 1970, and refused to conduct a final examination despite plaintiff's written demand (dated May 18, 1970) that he complete "Sociology 200" as originally planned. (Exhibit A, attached to complaint.) In said demand, she stated, *inter alia,* "at age sixty three it is essential that I ... become qualified to commence my intended profession of Gerontology prior to reaching age sixty five. Your course was to be the foundation for my education in this field. The mere

253

receipt of a grade in this course does not add a thing to my actual qualifications."[28]

In summing the facts, the court further stated that from admissions in plaintiff's opening brief we learn:

Professor Miller's conduct was a part of a faculty strike to register disapproval of United States policies being pursued in Cambodia and that plaintiff did receive a grade of "B" for the course. In response to this court's inquiry as to what prevented her enrollment in any advanced courses, her counsel replied that it was due to too many students signing up for those she wanted to take.

Plaintiff avers as to compensatory damages that she "has been deprived of her education, has suffered mental and financial strain and distress, has wasted $518.00 for tuition and other fees, has wasted other sums for books and other necessities, has suffered a potential loss of future income estimated to be $60,000, and other damage, the exact amount of which is unknown at the present time.

The complaint also included a second count which attempts to plead a cause of action in the form of a common count. In her first count, which is the one in which she pleads specific matters, there are allegations indicative of an attempt to plead (as claimed in her opening brief) theories of breach of fiduciary duties, fraud, constructive fraud, breach of warranty, misrepresentation, negligence, breach of trust, and conspiracy. To minimize repetition, we shall refer to such averments more specifically where pertinent to the discussion below.[29]

In its decision the court stated that the basic legal relation between a student and a private university or college is contractual in nature. The catalogues, bulletins, circulars, and regulations of the institution made available to

---

28. 25 Cal. App. 3d 1, 6-7, 101 Cal. Rptr. 499, 501-02 (1972).
29. 25 Cal. App. 3d, 1, 7, 101 Cal. Rptr. 499, 502 (1972).

the matriculant become a part of the contract.[30] The court went on to examine the various grounds for her complaint. Concerning the *breach of contract* the court concluded:

> The allegations heretofore summarized spell out a contract obligating defendant USC to give the course "Sociology 200" consisting of a given number of lectures and a final examination in consideration of the tuition and fees for the course paid by plaintiff. The stated number of lectures and the normal type of final examination were not given. The reason for this deviation from the announced schedule is alleged to have been a faculty strike protesting the United States foreign policy in Cambodia. It is obvious that plaintiff did not receive all that she bargained for when she enrolled in "Sociology 200." She was credited with a "B" for the course. To the average undergraduate this would be received with delight as full satisfaction for taking the course. It was enough to enable plaintiff to academically qualify for advanced courses for which it was a prerequisite. It has been held that a minimal departure from a projected course of study does not entitle the student (or his parent who paid for it) to recover the tuition paid or any part of it [citations omitted]. However, whether the partial failure of consideration was minimal so as to render applicable the maxim "de minimis non curat lex" or whether it justifies refund of a portion of the tuition and fee allocable to the course is a matter of proof, under the present state of the pleadings, at trial in an appropriate forum .... We do not believe separate treatment of an alleged breach of warranty is necessary at this time.[31]

The court then briefly commented regarding the *third party beneficiary* claim. The court observed:

> Plaintiff alleges that defendant Miller did not decline acceptance of his salary and other compensation exceeding $7,000 despite his refusal to teach "Sociology

---

30. 25 Cal. App. 3d 1, 10, 101 Cal. Rptr. 499, 504 (1972).
31. 25 Cal. App. 3d 1, 10-11, 101 Cal. Rptr. 499, 504-05 (1972).

200" and other courses assigned to him. This is insufficient on its face to spell out a contract in which plaintiff is a third party beneficiary.[32]

The court further examined *fraud, negligence, and conspiracy* as grounds for recovery and rejected all three. The court reasoned:

> We omit a detailed statement of the allegations pointing to an attempt to aver a right to recovery sounding in fraud, negligence, and conspiracy since the vulnerability of the complaint on these theories goes to the allegations pertaining to damages. As previously set forth, plaintiff alleges that the failure of defendant Miller to complete "Sociology 200" as originally announced deprived her of her education and caused her mental and financial strain and distress resulting in the waste of $518 for tuition and other fees, present income of $5,000 and potential loss of an estimated $60,000 .... There is no allegation which informs defendants of the causal connection between the averred delicts of the defendants and these damages claimed. Allegations of damages without allegations of fact to support them are but conclusions of law, which are not admitted by demurrer [citations omitted]. In fraud, the pleading must show a cause and effect relationship between the fraud and damages sought; otherwise no cause of action is stated .... A similar requirement applies to negligence. "It has ... been held, in order that a complaint shall sufficiently allege a cause of action based upon negligence, that it should appear in what respect the defendant was negligent and that such negligence had a causal connection with plaintiff's injury ...."
>
> It is also familiar law that the gist of an action charging civil conspiracy is not the conspiracy, but the damages suffered. No cause of action exists for conspiracy itself; the pleaded facts must show something

---

32. 25 Cal. App. 3d 1, 11, 101 Cal. Rptr. 499, 505 (1972).

which, without the conspiracy, would give rise to a cause of action.[33]

The court also addressed plaintiff's argument that there was liability for breach of fiduciary duty and reasoned:

> We do not believe that the allegations of the complaint plead sufficient facts to impose a liability for a breach of a fiduciary duty which caused plaintiff to suffer an economic damage, other than possibly the unearned amount of tuition and costs allocable to "Sociology 200." The initial difficulty with this breach of fiduciary duty theory is that facts giving rise to a confidential relationship have not been pleaded. As explained previously, the normal relationship between a student and the university and its agents is contractual. A bare allegation that defendants assumed a fiduciary relationship or that they entered into an educational joint venture with plaintiff are conclusions. "[I]t is the general rule that an allegation that one is a trustee is but a conclusion of law ... " [citations omitted]. An "allegation that defendant holds the property as Trust is a naked conclusion of the pleader" [citations omitted]. "[T]here is not a fiduciary relation between the promisor or promisee and the beneficiary of a contract" [citations omitted]. No facts have been alleged setting forth a project, educational in nature, with a common purpose of mutual interest to all parties and one in which there was a mutual right to control the management and operation [citations omitted]. The mere placing of a trust in another person does not create a fiduciary relationship [citations omitted]. Finally, an agreement to communicate one's knowledge, exercising his special knowledge and skill in the area of learning concerned, does not create a trust but only a contractual obligation [citations omitted].[34]

---

33. 25 Cal. App. 3d 1, 11-12, 101 Cal. Rptr. 499, 505-06 (1972).
34. 25 Cal. App. 3d 1, 13, 101 Cal. Rptr. 499, 506 (1972).

§ 8.1(G). Peretti v. State of Montana.

In 1979, the United States District Court for the District of Montana decided the case of *Peretti v. State of Montana.*[35] The plaintiffs brought an action for damages, alleging that the aviation technology course, for which they had enrolled and in which they had completed three out of six quarters, was unlawfully terminated to their damage. The students' course of study in the aviation technology program offered by Montana State Vocational Education Center was interrupted due to a legislative cut in appropriations. The district court held that there was a contract between the plaintiffs and defendants whereby plaintiffs, who were enrolled in defendant's aviation course, would be permitted an opportunity to complete the course and earn a diploma. "A right arising out of an implied contract is within the 14th amendments protection of life and property.[36]

In deciding whether plaintiffs are entitled to relief, it is necessary to examine the relationship between a public post-secondary educational institution and the student. The court stated that there seems to be almost no dissent from the proposition that the relationship is contractual in nature.[37] In summarizing this contractual relationship, the court quoted from the *Notre Dame Law Journal,* which stated:

> This contract is conceived of as one by which the student agrees to pay all required fees, maintain the prescribed level of academic achievement, and observe the school's disciplinary regulations, in return for which the school agrees to allow the student to pursue his course of studies and be granted a diploma upon the successful completion thereof. Since a formal contract

---

35. 464 F. Supp. 784 (1979).
36. *Id.* at 787.
37. *Id.* at 786.

is rarely prepared, the general nature and terms of the agreement are usually implied, with specific terms to be found in the university bulletin and other publications; custom and usages can also become specific terms by implication. This contract has been upheld against attacks based upon lack of consideration, the statute of frauds, and lack of mutuality of obligation.[38]

The court concluded its opinion by holding that: "The State of Montana is liable to each of the plaintiffs in such amounts as they may show they have been damaged."[39]

§ 8.1(H). Stad v. Grace Downs Model and Air Career School.

The case of *Stad v. Grace Downs Model and Air Career School*[40] was an action to recover the sum paid for tuition to the defendant for an air career course; the defendant having agreed to place plaintiff in the airline industry. Before analyzing the facts in this case the court stated:

> In this day of belated and overdue sensitivity to consumer problems, the instant case offers a classic example of consumer vulnerability. As a prefatory statement, this Court asserts that just as the courts and our legal system are designed as bulwarks to protect individual rights as against the arrayed might of the State in criminal actions, so must they be bulwarks in civil actions for the individual to prevent his rights as a consumer from being overwhelmed by the mighty array of businessmen competitively and alluringly advertising their wares and services. After all, what protective devices does the consumer have as against modern merchandising techniques? These techniques are an onslaught upon the senses, a brainwashing of advertising brandishments puffing the products to be

---

38. *Id.*
39. *Id.* at 788.
40. Stad v. Grace Downs Model and Air Career School, 319 N.Y.S.2d 918 (Civil Court, City of New York, Queens County, New York, 1971).

sold and to which the consumer eventually succumbs, since he has been overstimulated to buy. He often becomes a compulsive purchaser lulled into a sense of euphoria by the repetition of half-truth slogans and luring come-ons which produce the desired conditioned reflex leading to a signature on the "dotted line" proffered by the seller.[41]

The court then went on to state:

Let us consider the instant case in this light: Plaintiff, a young lady, saw the advertisement of the Defendant in the "Yellow Pages" of the New York Telephone Directory and in Glamour Magazine. The advertisements contained such key phrases as: "Head Start for High School Grads. Combine vacation with learning on beautiful 16 acre estate in Glen Cove, L.I., where school and magnificent mansion (your home while attending) are located — with swimming pool, tennis courts, etc. Equivalent 2 years training covered in 42 weeks. Executive Secretarial '3 in 1' course includes all secretarial skills — stewardess * ticketing * reservations * sales * travel agent * plus model course for spare time modeling and airline publicity. *Free Placement Service all Divisions* (Emphasis supplied)." Further, another ad says: "The World is yours with a Jet Age Career! Airline stewardess * airline secretaries trained and placed by Grace Downs *(Graduates in Demand)* (Emphasis supplied) Air Career School. Free Brochure — state age, telephone number and graduation date."

So much for the Defendant's opening gambit. Next step: The Plaintiff wrote away for Defendant's brochure and she got one along with an application blank. The brochure attractively designed has imprinted on its cover: "Prepare for an exciting future at Grace Downs Air Career School. Training and *Free Placement of Women stewardesses, ground hostesses, reservation agents, ticket agents, bus hostesses. (Emphasis supplied).* New York's first and only Air Career School

---

41. *Id.* at 918-19.

Licensed by the New York State Department of Education." The second page shows the "campus" at Glen Cove which is labeled "Glamor Manor". On that page is also printed: "Grace Downs Sky Stars ... *enjoy playing first fiddle because of their Grace Downs Training. They rate high in the books of personnel directors everywhere. During the past decade, Grace Downs School placed 97% of its graduates with major airlines. FREE PLACEMENT SERVICE established 1927"* *(emphasis supplied).*

Further, on page 3 of the brochure it says, "A staff of experts in personality development guide your every step to perfection during the training period. Grace Downs teaches her students personally in 'Employment Preparation — Employment Interviews'. More than 3 decades directing her success school *she surely knows how to make you get that assignment, hold it and advance to executive posts." [Emphasis supplied].*

On the 4th page of the brochure are pictured five pretty girls and facsimiles of newspaper clippings announcing their engagements to be married and all are identified as Grace Downs Air Career School graduates. The legend below the news clips states: *"the girls depicted here bespeak their contentment resulting from rich opportunities awarded them as Grace Downs graduates. It would take a 'mile long' folder to feature the thousands upon thousands of these typical news reports clipped and sent to us from newspapers all over the world" (Emphasis supplied).* Pretty heady stuff that! And pretty difficult for the young, impressionable, and unsophisticated reading audience to whom this advertising is directed — "High School Grads."

Now for the coup de grace comes the second gambit: Accompanying this brochure mailed to the plaintiff is a covering letter on the letterhead of the Grace Downs Air Career School which bears the legend *"Free Placement to Graduates" (Emphasis supplied).* The letter says in part:

"We are pleased to provide you with the information you requested regarding our Air Career Course. This course covers various positions with the Airlines such as ticketing, reservations, ground hostess, and of course, air hostess or stewardess. These positions are inter-related so that in order to be proficient in any one phase, you must know the duties involved in each. A brochure describing this unique course is enclosed....

Placement opportunities as a graduate of Grace Downs are great. We do not send our graduates 'hither and yon' to battle through their own employment interviews but airline personnel executives come directly to the school to interview and hire our trained people.

We will call you within a few days in order to arrange an interview appointment for you. The interview will enable us to assess your qualifications and also answer any questions you may have. It will not obligate you to attend, nor the Grace Downs School to accept you, *but if you are accepted you may rest easy about your future in the fascinating airlines field. ...(Emphasis supplied).*

Cordially yours,
Grace Downs Air Career School
Donald M. Myrick
Director of Admissions.

Following this broadside, the Plaintiff signed the enrollment agreement and paid to the Grace Downs School the sum of $502.50, for her air career course. And the official receipt she received stated "Our Alumnae bear Brilliant Testimony of the Effectiveness of our Methods." After having satisfactorily completed the Air Career Course of 200 hours, a card certificate of graduation was given to the Plaintiff in April 1969.

Since her graduation, Plaintiff testified that although she had asked the defendant to place her in an airlines position, the defendant has not placed her in an airline job. As a result, plaintiff brings this action to recover the $502.50 paid for her tuition to the defendant for "Breach of agreement as to placement" which is the nature and substance of her complaint.[42]

The issues, said the court, that are to be decided by the court as the trier of the fact and the law are:

> Did the defendant misrepresent its intentions as to placement to the plaintiff? Did the misrepresentation mislead the plaintiff and induce her into enrolling in the Defendant's Air Career Course where otherwise she might not have so enrolled? Did the misrepresentation work a hardship and cause damage to the plaintiff? Was there a breach of agreement to make free placement of the plaintiff?[43]

The court then proceeded to state:

> On one side of the coin, the cases hold that the representation made, in order to sustain rescission or an action for damages for deceit, must be one of "fact as distinguished from a mere promise or prophecy or expression of opinion." (Jacob Goodman & Company v. Pratt, Sup., 138 N.Y.S.2d 89, 92). While on the obverse, there are cases generally holding that "every misrepresentation of a material fact, made with the intention to induce another to enter into an agreement and without which that individual would not have done so, justifies a court in invalidating the agreement." (See 24 N.Y. Jur., Sec. 157, Pages 224-225.)
>
> I find that the blandishments in this case held out to the plaintiff in the quoted advertising materials were strong and heady stuff, difficult for a young girl, yearning for a glamour career and the possibility of marrying Prince Charming, to resist. The advertising, fortified by the brochure, and then "hard hit" home by the Director of Admissions' letter, all acted to create an atmosphere of guaranty of placement which became an integral part of the enrollment contract under the entire climate and atmosphere of the situation. It is

42. *Id.* at 919-21.
43. *Id.* at 921.

difficult for the Court to hold that the placement service of the School only held out to a prospective enrollee a mere good probability of success in obtaining
placement with an Airline, for it was hardly an expression of opinion or a prophecy that the plaintiff merely
would have a good chance to get an airline job with
defendants course "under her belt." I am of the opinion
that all of the written and puffing statements of the
defendant, topped by the statement: *"If you are accepted you may rest easy about your future in the fascinating airlines field,"* when taken into the cumulative consideration of an enrollee would entitle that enrollee to conclude that an out-and-out guaranty by the
defendant has been made which entitles enrollee to
free placement for employment. The defendant had its
chance to assess plaintiff's qualifications before accepting her for the course. If it found her to be wanting
in any way or suspected that she was not employable,
then defendant never should have accepted her tuition
and the plaintiff for actual schooling in light of its
"rest easy" representation. Whenever anyone says
"rest easy," it means *"have no concern"* and here, to
paraphrase in effect, defendant told plaintiff "your
worries are over once you come to our school...we'll
get you a job!" Indeed, the defendant never qualified
its assurance of employment by an airline in the pre-
school interview with the plaintiff or during her 200
hours of schooling. On the contrary, all of defendant's
dealings with plaintiff appeared to have the aura of
reassuring her of employment upon completion of her
course.

On all the proof, this Court feels that the representation herein conveyed a general false impression even
though not specifically false since there was some attempt by defendant to find employment for the plaintiff, which failed. However, I find that the general false
impression, created by the defendant in its ever-enthu-
siastic advertising and letter communication, was relied upon by this plaintiff who has sustained her burden of proof in this action. The defendant herein led
the plaintiff down an illusory and glamorous

"primrose path" and then left her out-in-the-cold at the end of that path, without the sweet smell of primroses to comfort her, and with only a laminated 3-1/2 by 2-1/2 inch card diploma of graduation for security. Further, defendant's advertising had the effect of raising plaintiff to a level of "great expectations" regarding future airlines placement which were frustrated by defendant's desultory and unsuccessful attempt to place her after graduation. See Volume 24, N.Y. Jur., Sec. 135; and see Downey v. Finucane, 205 N.Y. 251, at 264, 98 N.E. 391, at 395, which holds: "If by a number of statements you intentionally give a false impression and induce a person to act upon it, it is not the less false, although, if one takes each statement by itself, there may be a difficulty in showing that any specific statement is untrue."

In actuality, the defendant here breached its implied contract with plaintiff — that part of the contract which spelled out a guarantee of placement; and I base my decision on that theory, as well as the theory involving misrepresentation.

Inasmuch as the plaintiff did complete an Air Career Course of 200 hours, she cannot claim that she did not benefit in part from this schooling. In view of the fact that she did get some benefit from this schooling, I award to the plaintiff the sum of $250 as and for damages sustained by her by virtue of the breach of contract herein, plus interest thereon from May 1, 1969.[44]

§ 8.1(I). Ianniello v. University of Bridgeport.

In this case, a student, Ilene Ianniello, filed a complaint against the University of Bridgeport seeking damages in the amount of $2,500.00.[45] In her two-count complaint the plaintiff alleged that the University did not provide the course described in the catalogue and that she did not learn

---

44. *Id.,* at 921-22.
45. Ianniello v. University of Bridgeport, Court of Common Pleas, G.A. 2, County of Fairfield at Bridgeport, No. 100009 (1975).

anything in the course. The only requirement in the course, "Method and Materials in Teaching Basic Business Subjects," she stated, was to hand in one book report. All 14 students in the required course received As.[46] More specifically, she stated that the University had not performed its agreement with the plaintiff in the following respects:

    (a) The course content failed to substantially comply with the course description.....

    (b) There were no tests given or grading of any work done.

    (c) There was little or no class discussion by the course instructor or any critique of the plaintiff's work or other student's work from which the plaintiff could benefit.

    (d) The plaintiff was not taught any substantial part of the course as delineated by the Academic bulletin.

    (e) The plaintiff received little or no benefit from attending and enrolling in said course of instruction.

    (f) The defendant failed to supervise the teaching of said course, or the course content.

That by reason of such breach of contract, the plaintiff has sustained damages in that she failed to receive the instruction and education she had paid for; in that she expended money for traveling to attend said course; in that she lost wages by reason of her absence from her employment; in that she paid a registration fee; in that she was inconvenienced by attending said class and not receiving the benefit of the education contracted for; in that she had incurred reasonable attorney's fees in attempting to obtain restitution for her losses; all of the above at a monetary loss to herself.[47]

---

46. *Mrs. Ianniello Complains in Court: That Education Methods Course Was Worthless,* PHI DELTA KAPPAN, (April, 1975), p. 577; *see also Suing for Not Learning,* TIME, (March 3, 1975), p. 73.

47. Substitute Complaint, pp. 2-3, Ianniello v. University of Bridgeport, Court of Common Pleas, G.A. 2, County of Fairfield at Bridgeport, No. 100009 (1975).

Plaintiff alleged in the second count:

The defendant in said Academic Bulletin and Catalogue represented to the enrolling students and the plaintiff that the contents of said course would consist of the following:

"Education 380 — *Methods and Materials in Teaching the Major Fields.* Assists students in the development of objectives, learning activities, teaching procedures, organization and presentation of materials in the following subject areas to be taught in the secondary schools .... Education 380F — Basic Business Subjects and Bookkeeping."

The defendant, its counselors, professional staff and prescribed course of study informed the plaintiff that the enrollment in said course 380F was a necessary prerequisite for her to obtain a major in the field of education.

Relying upon the representation of the defendant as set forth ... the plaintiff paid said tuition fee of $155.00, purchased books for $15.00 and attended the class of instruction, completing same.

The representations of the defendant as set forth ... were false in that said course of instruction was not given as represented, and although the plaintiff notified the defendant of same the defendant failed to correct the failure to give a meaningful and beneficial course of instruction as represented.[48]

The defendant asserted seven defenses to plaintiff's complaint, among them the following:

1. So long as not acting in an arbitrary, discriminatory or unreasonable manner, the Defendant and its faculty must have academic freedom, without interference, to fully conduct the affairs of the University, both administrative and educational.
2. The Defendant has not acted in such an arbitrary, discriminatory or unreasonable manner with respect to the Plaintiff.

---

48. *Id.* at 3-4.

267

3. The description of the said course known as Education 380F, as contained in the University catalog, is, as a matter of custom and common understanding, intended to serve only as a general description of the anticipated course content, and same is subject to modification and change in emphasis by the instructor teaching said course in order to satisfy the current needs, developments during the course and/or desires of the students enrolled in such course.

4. A modification of the content of said course would be permitted, in any case, pursuant to the language of Page ii of the University catalog, as follows:

The University reserves the right to make changes in the regulations and courses announced in this catalog as circumstances may require.[49]

The court did not dismiss the complaint without a hearing, but allowed the testimony to be presented in trial; however, at the conclusion of the testimony the court directed a verdict in favor of the University.

§ 8.1(J). Lowenthol v. Vanderbilt University.

Eight former doctoral students at Vanderbilt's Graduate School of Management brought an action against Vanderbilt University.[50] The issues were (1) whether a contract existed between the doctoral students and the University, (2) whether the University breached the contract, and (3) whether there were damages. The Chancery Court for Davidson County at Nashville, Tennessee, held that contracts did exist and that Vanderbilt breached them. The court stated:

---

49. Answer, pp. 2-3, Ianniello v. University of Bridgeport, Court of Common Pleas, G.A. 2, County of Fairfield at Bridgeport, No. 100009 (1975).

50. Lowenthol v. Vanderbilt University, Chancery Court for Davidson County, Part Three, Nashville, Tenn., No. A-8525 (1976).

Vanderbilt University enjoys a tradition and reputation for excellence and quality in higher education. In a sharp departure from that tradition, Vanderbilt hastily embarked upon a vague and ill-defined doctoral studies program when it knew or should have known that it did not have the resources to operate the program. Vanderbilt received something of value from these plaintiffs and gave little or nothing in return. The University must bear the responsibility for its conduct.

Vanderbilt has argued that a finding that it breached its contract with the students will have dire consequences for it and higher education generally. To the contrary, should this court ignore the obvious failure of Vanderbilt to live up to its contractual obligations to these students, it would be a signal to Vanderbilt and other institutions that they are immune from the same legal principles which govern other relationships in our society. *While the university-student relationship is indeed unique, it does not vest a university with unlimited power to do or not to do as it pleases without facing the consequences* [emphasis added].[51]

The court then proceeded to award damages to the various defendants ranging from $10 for nominal damages to $11,740.[52] In arriving at its conclusion, the court stated that there was an important distinction between complaints which seek judicial review of university determinations of academic qualifications and suits which charge that the university has breached its contract with the students. The distinction is crucial to the outcome of this case.[53] The court explained:

There has been a growing trend towards judicial cognizance of disputes arising out of higher education. This

---

51. Memorandum opinion, pp. 39-40, Lowenthol v. Vanderbilt University, Chancery Court for Davidson County, Part Three, Nashville, Tenn., No. A-8525 (1976).

52. *Id.* at 40-41.

53. *Id.* at 13.

trend has resulted in needed changes in the procedures and attitudes of universities and a realization that universities, as other citizens and entities, are not above the law. However, there are limits to the extension of such judicial cognizance. A court must abstain from substituting its judgment for that of the university faculty on such matters as degree requirements and academic dismissals of students. As has been repeatedly held, these are matters for determination by the university and courts must not interfere absent a clear showing that decisions are arbitrary, capricious, and made in bad faith.

....

Unquestionably, the relationship between a student and a university is contractual in nature. Courts have repeatedly held that a contract exists which imposes rights and duties on each of the parties [citations omitted].

Determining the precise terms of the contract is difficult. Its content is derived from the written and oral representations made by each party and from other somewhat amorphous implied terms. The school's catalog, the guidelines for doctoral study, and oral representations made by the faculty each helped to define Vanderbilt's duty to the GSM doctoral students, but by no means limited it.

But, as stated by Dean Campbell, it is neither possible nor desirable to attempt to define the student-university contract in explicit, fixed, contract terms. Graduate education must be undertaken in a flexible and adaptable environment where most of the vital decisions affecting the students are often quite subjective. The rigid application of commercial contract law to the doctoral student-university relationship would no doubt impair the quality of any graduate program and not be in the best interests of the students or the university. While affirming the existence of the university-student contract, the Tenth Circuit Court of Appeals correctly stated that "The student-university relationship is unique and should not and cannot be stuffed into one doctrinal category" [citations omitted].

270

The uniqueness of the relationship was ably described by Peter D. Vaill, Dean of the School of Government and Business Administration at George Washington University, a witness for the plaintiffs; *the student-university relationship is "fundamentally a major power imbalance; the university and the faculty have an enormous power," it is "one of the most imbalanced situations" left in society* [citations omitted].

The power in the hands of a university places an enormous responsibility and corresponding duty on it to exercise the power fairly, consistently, and without arbitrariness and prejudice. Once it has made the promise to do so, the university has a duty to provide a high quality of academic training leading to an academically respectable doctoral degree which may be earned by the satisfaction of reasonable and consistent standards and procedures. The university must provide the resources necessary to accomplish this end. This was Vanderbilt's contractual obligation to the doctoral students at the GSM.

In the case of the GSM doctoral program, the university did not discharge its duty reasonably and consistently. It did not provide a high quality of academic training, and consistent standards and procedures were not employed. The necessary faculty and financial resources were lacking. Even the written documents which helped compose the contract were not followed by the GSM faculty. In short, the GSM doctoral program ceased to function at all [emphasis added].[54]

§ 8.1(K). Beaman v. Des Moines Area Community College.

A number of students brought suit in the District Court of Iowa against Des Moines Area Community College.[55] The plaintiffs, after alleging that they were students en-

---

54. *Id.* at 14-17.
55. Beaman v. Des Moines Area Community College, Law No. CL 15-8532, in the District Court of Iowa for Polk County (1978).

rolled in the Basic Telecommunications Program, pleaded certain standards and guidelines regarding instructor qualifications and the supplying of classroom equipment. Plaintiffs then alleged that the defendant failed to comply with these standards and guidelines and concluded therefrom that defendant was negligent because of its failure to comply with such standards and guidelines.[56]

The court, in sustaining defendant's motion to dismiss, reasoned:

> Plaintiffs' claim raises a novel question in this jurisdiction: Do students who claim that they have failed to have received the requisite education in a particular course or program have a cause of action against the public institution offering and administering such course or program of which such course is a part? This case is not unlike the recent case of *Doe v. San Francisco Unified School District* .... Here, as the California Court did there, this court refuses to expand the concept of negligence to include complaints arising from the area of academic education. Judicial recognition of such a duty in the Defendant with the consequential liability for its negligent breach is initially to be dictated or precluded by considerations of public policy .... The court necessarily finds itself confronted with these "delicate policy judgments" and, therefore, must consider matters of public policy which can be affected by the decision reached. Here, as there, any departure from these fundamental principles involves the balancing of a number of considerations ....
>
> Accordingly, the Court adheres to the conclusion reached by public policy up to this point in time and concludes that there exists no legally recognized duty of care owing from the Defendant to the Plaintiffs, such as may establish liability for negligence. Without the existence of such duty Plaintiffs would of necessity have to fail in their efforts to establish an essential

---

56. *Id.* Order and Decree, at 1.

element of any cause of action based on negligence [citations omitted].[57]

§ 8.1(L). Dizick v. Umpqua Community College.

The Court of Appeals of the State of Oregon decided the case of *Dizick v. Umpqua Community College.*[58] The plaintiff had brought this action under the Oregon Tort Claims Act, alleging fraud by the defendant community college. The trial court had entered a judgment for defendant notwithstanding a jury verdict of $12,500.00 on the ground that the defendant was immune from tort liability for the alleged misrepresentation.[59] Plaintiff's complaint alleged:

> On or about the month of February or March, 1974, plaintiff enrolled as a student in the welding technology program of defendant, Umpqua Community College ....
> Plaintiff's said enrollment was in reliance upon representations made in the 1973-74 catalog of defendant, and upon personal representations by agents and employees of defendant. Particularly, said representations by defendant through its catalog, its agents, and its employees, were that certain specific welding courses, namely, Course No. 4.164 entitled "Advanced Welding Processes" and Course No. 4.182 entitled "Machine Processes" would be available to plaintiff, that certain welding machines and related materials, namely, a milling machine, metal inert gas welder, tungsten inert gas welder, welding rods and other supplies would be available to plaintiff, and that upon satisfactory completion of the one-year welding technology program offered by defendant, plaintiff would be prepared for employment in the welding market in the State of Oregon. Said representations were false in that said courses, as offered, were not made available

---

57. *Id.* at 2-4.
58. 33 Or. App. 559, 577 P.2d 534 (1978).
59. 33 Or. App. 559, 561, 577 P.2d 534 (1978).

to plaintiff, said machines and materials were not
made available to plaintiff, and the one-year welding
technology program was and is insufficient to adequately prepare students, more particularly plaintiff,
for employment in the welding market in the State of
Oregon.[60]

Furthermore, the plaintiff made allegations that the representations were false, were either intentionally or recklessly made to induce him to enroll in defendant's one-year
welding technology program, that the plaintiff did enroll in
reliance on such representations, and as a result forwent
gainful employment, causing damages in the amount of
$25,000.00.[61]

In affirming the decision of the circuit court, the court of
appeals concluded:

The method of instruction and course content obviously involve complex judgmental decisions by college
officials. A jury verdict here is tantamount to a direction to the college to provide practical use training as
part of the curriculum for the courses offered in the
catalog. *The legislature intended that such decisions
be made by college officials, not by judges and juries in
tort actions* [emphasis added].[62]

The court quoted approvingly a portion of the language
in the case of *Smith v. Cooper*[63] where that court commented:

The most decisive factor but one most difficult to articulate is that it is essential for efficient government
that certain decisions of the executive or legislative
branches of the government should not be reviewed by
a court or jury. The reason behind such factor is that
the bases for the legislative or executive decision can

---

60. 33 Or. App. 559, 561, 577 P.2d 534, 535 (1978).
61. 33 Or. App. 559, 562, 577 P.2d 534, 535 (1978).
62. 33 Or. App. 559, 566, 577 P.2d 534, 537 (1978).
63. *Id.; see also* 566 Or. 485, 475 P.2d 78 (1970).

cover the whole spectrum of the ingredients for governmental decisions such as the availability of funds, public acceptance, order of priority, etc.[64]

The court went on to add:

Arguably, a different result might occur if college officials had specifically represented that the welding courses included the practical training that plaintiff contends he should have had. We do not reach that question because there is no allegation or evidence of specific representations of this nature ever being made. The catalog merely states that students "will learn" and will be "introduced to" certain subjects and other subjects will be "emphasized" and "stressed." There is no statement that students will use equipment or as to how the courses will be taught.

The oral representations made by the dean of the college that "[w]e have the M.I.G. and T.I.G. and a milling machine on order ... we have everything you need ... [w]e'll be able to train you" is not necessarily a promise that plaintiff will be able to actually use the equipment as a part of the training offered by the college. The fact that a jury might reasonably draw such inference in a fraud action between private parties is insufficient. [Citations omitted]. Reasonable persons could draw a variety of different inferences from such representations. *The purpose of immunizing governmental agents is to prevent litigious interference with important governmental functions. That purpose is defeated if courts or juries are permitted to draw specific inferences from general statements. By plaintiff's own testimony, the statements were made by the dean in counseling plaintiff concerning his educational program. ORS 341.290 charges community colleges with performing the counseling function as an important part of the educational program .... Effective counseling depends upon free and open communication between the counselor and the counselee. Such communication would be chilled if the college counselor faced*

---

64. 33 Or. App. 559, 567-69, 577 P.2d 534, 538-39 (1978).

potential liability for every statement from which an
adverse inference might be drawn.

Immunity does not disappear because plaintiff alleged or introduced evidence of culpable fraud as distinguished from negligence. The controlling consideration is not the degree of culpability, but rather
whether the act or function is of the nature that it is
essential for efficient government that it not be subject
to judicial interference arising out of tort liability [ci-
tation omitted]. The purpose of the immunity would be
defeated if, as suggested by plaintiff, it were restricted
only to actions for negligence. The present case is illustrative. The evidence of culpability is wholly circumstantial and largely undisputed. The jury reasonably
could have inferred that defendant intentionally or
recklessly misrepresented. The jury also could have
reasonably inferred there was neither intent nor recklessness because there was no misrepresentation.

Alternatively, it could have reasonably concluded
that defendant's agents were only guilty of negligence
and not fraud. The jury also could have given greater
weight to other evidence in the record, evidence that
was also undisputed, and concluded that defendant's
failure to achieve proficiency in welding was not due to
any lack of availability of equipment, but was the result of his own doing.

We conclude that the allegations and evidence of
representations by community college officials presented here constitute acts for which the defendants'
agents, and thereby defendants, are immune from tort
liability [emphasis added].[65]

In a concurring opinion, the Chief Judge stated that he
was in agreement with the majority's statement of the general principles governing tort liability of public bodies and
agreed with the result reached, but did not agree that immunity can be determined by the specificity of the representations made by the college officials to the plaintiff. He
added:

---

65. 33 Or. App. 559, 568-69, 577 P.2d 534, 538-39 (1978).

The recruiting and counseling of students is an activity which either is immune or is not. Unlike the distinction between highway maintenance and highway design, it is not practically possible to divide recruiting and counseling into separate components, some of which are immune and others are not [citations omitted]. Assuming, *arguendo,* that there is evidence of fraudulent statements that fall within the scope of the pleadings, I would hold the Umpqua Community College immune on the ground that recruiting and counseling of students is a government activity not to be reviewed by court or jury.[66]

Judge Roberts, in dissenting, contended that he could not accept the reasoning of the majority as to the applicability of governmental immunity to this case. He further reasoned:

While I agree that an action based on the failure of the college to include certain courses in the curriculum or teach certain techniques in the courses would be barred by governmental immunity, I see no relevance to that position in this case. The plaintiff sued on account of statements made to him in order to induce his enrollment. The statements were specific and factual and concerned not the level of proficiency plaintiff would reach, but rather what machines were to be available for training plaintiff.

....
... [A] suit based on the college's failure to offer certain courses or offer a certain type of instruction in the courses would be barred by immunity. Curriculum planning is an activity peculiarly within the purview of another branch of government and should not be made the basis of liability. The suit before us seeks damages for fraud committed by college officials in soliciting plaintiff's enrollment in the college. Such solicitation does not involve policy-based political decisions affecting or concerning the people as a whole. It

---

66. 33 Or. App. 559, 569-70, 577 P.2d 534, 539 (1978).

is my opinion that there is no governmental immunity for the acts involved in this case.

I would remand this case for a new trial on account of two errors below. First, the complaint which went to the jury allowed it to find fraud on the basis of statements made in defendant's catalog. I would hold that in this case fraud could not be predicted on statements made in college catalogs since there are no specific factual representations contained in that catalog. [Citation omitted]. *Statements in the catalog can properly be classified as "puffing" and thus not actionable as fraud, and arguably, fall in the category of a policy-based political decision.*

The second reason I would remand this case is the trial judge's failure to instruct the jury on "recklessness." No definition was given to the jury, although it was a central issue in the case. Although I would not agree that defendant's requested instruction on recklessness correctly states the law I would hold that the trial judge has the obligation to instruct the jury on all relevant matters. [Emphasis added].[67]

§ 8.1(M). Spier v. American University of the Caribbean.

Two students filed suit against the American University of the Caribbean and Paul S. Tien, its president.[68] The complaint, which was in three counts, alleged, *inter alia,* as follows:

1. Defendant The American University of the Caribbean (hereafter "A.U.C.") is a non-profit institution created under the laws of the Colony of Montserrat, British West Indies.
2. Defendant Paul S. Tien is and at all times relevant hereto was a resident of the State of Ohio, and is the organizer and administrator of defendant A.U.C.

---

67. 33 Or. App. 559, 570-73, 577 P.2d 534, 539-41 (1978).

68. Spier v. American University of the Caribbean, Court of Common Pleas, Hamilton County, Ohio, Case No. A7900947 (1979).

3. Throughout the Winter and Spring months of 1978, defendant Paul S. Tien personally and on behalf of defendant A.U.C. falsely and fraudulently represented that the school was being formed by a "group" of American educators

4. Throughout the Winter and Spring months of 1978, defendant Paul S. Tien personally and on behalf of defendant A.U.C. falsely and fraudulently represented that the school was of a "high-quality."

5. Throughout the Winter and Spring months of 1978, defendant Paul S. Tien personally and on behalf of defendant A.U.C. falsely and fraudulently represented that the school incorporated the most advanced medical technology available.

6. Throughout the winter and spring months of 1978, defendant Paul S. Tien personally and on behalf of defendant A.U.C. falsely and fraudulently represented that the school was "recognized" by the World Health Organization.

7. Throughout the Winter and Spring months of 1978, defendant Paul S. Tien personally and on behalf of defendant A.U.C. falsely and fraudulently represented that the main campus of the school existed on the island of Montserrat, British West Indies.

8. Throughout the Winter and Spring months of 1978, defendant Paul S. Tien personally and on behalf of defendant A.U.C. falsely and fraudulently represented that the school offered teaching techniques and an instructional approach equivalent to U.S. medical schools.

9. Throughout the Winter and Spring months of 1978, defendant Paul S. Tien personally and on behalf of defendant A.U.C. falsely and fraudulently represented that the school offered clinical training in U.S. hospitals.

10. Throughout the Winter and Spring months of 1978, defendant Paul S. Tien personally and on behalf of defendant A.U.C. falsely and fraudulently represented that graduation from a foreign medical school and passing the required United States Medical Board examinations entitled the

graduate to practice medicine in the United States.

11. Throughout the Winter and Spring months of 1978, defendant Paul S. Tien personally and on behalf of defendant A.U.C. falsely and fraudulently represented that the school was part of a larger University.

12. Each of the above representations were untrue, and the failure to provide a medical education as represented constituted a breach of contract by defendants.

13. Upon learning that the above representations were false, plaintiff Mark Spier withdrew as a student of A.U.C. and demanded return of his application fee of $500 and his first semester tuition of $2,500.

14. Upon learning that the above representations were false, plaintiff Raymond Filipponi withdrew as a student of A.U.C. and demanded the return of his application fee of $500 and his first semester tuition of $2,500.

15. Defendants refused, and continue to refuse to return the above payments despite demand.

16. As a direct and proximate result of defendants' breach of contract, plaintiff Mark Spier has suffered consequential damages of $1,073 in out-of-pocket expenses and $1,250 in lost wages.

17. As a direct and proximate result of defendants' breach of contract, plaintiff Raymond Filipponi has suffered consequential damages of $1,316 in out-of-pocket expenses and $1,250 in lost wages.

18. Each of the above representations made by defendants were false and fraudulent, were known by defendants to be false, and were made by defendants with the intent to defraud and deceive plaintiffs and to induce them to enroll as students at A.U.C.

19. Plaintiffs enrolled as students at A.U.C. in reliance on the above representations, believing them to be true.

20. As a direct and proximate result of the fraud and misrepresentations by defendants, plaintiff Mark Spier has suffered damage of $3,000 for tuition and application fee, $1,073 for out-of-pocket expenses and $1,250 in lost wages.
21. As a direct and proximate result of the fraud and misrepresentations of defendants, plaintiff Raymond Filipponi has suffered damage of $3,000 for tuition and application fee, $1,316 in out-of-pocket expenses, and $1,250 in lost wages.
22. As a direct and proximate result of the fraud and misrepresentations by defendants, plaintiffs have expended $400 for attorneys fees and will expend $5,000 in the future.

WHEREFORE, plaintiffs demand judgment against defendants, jointly and severally for the following:

1. For plaintiff Mark Spier, rescission of his contract of enrollment and damages of $5,323;
2. For plaintiff Ray Filipponi, rescission of his contract of enrollment and damages of $5,566;
3. Punitive damages of $100,000;
4. Reasonable attorney fees of $5,000;
5. For the class of all students, former students, and future students A.U.C., a permanent injunction prohibiting defendants from soliciting students and promoting A.U.C. in a false and fraudulent manner, and compensatory damages of $1,500,000; and
6. Interests, costs of this action, and whatever other relief to which they are at law and in equity entitled.[69]

The court ruled in favor of the plaintiffs.[70]

§ 8.1(N). Maas v. Corporation of Gonzaga University.

In a related issue, the Court of Appeals of Washington affirmed the superior court's order dismissing a claim by a

---

69. *Id.* Complaint, at 1-4.
70. *Id.*

law student that the law school negligently failed to warn
her of probable failure in law school.[71] The facts of this
case, *Maas v. Corporation of Gonzaga University*,[72] as summarized by Judge Munson, are as follows:

> Maas left her tenured teaching position in Alaska to
> attend Gonzaga University School of Law in 1974.
> Maas' law school admission test (LSAT) score of 438,
> with a writing ability index of 45. Her undergraduate
> GPA at Brooklyn College, achieved in the late 1940's
> was 1.84. In graduate school during the 10 years prior
> to her application to law school, however, she had
> maintained a grade point average of 3.1. In applying to
> Gonzaga, Maas also enclosed several persuasive letters
> of recommendations. She was accepted, and attended
> Gonzaga ....
> Gonzaga requires its students to maintain a cumula-
> tive 2.2 grade point average. She had failed to main-
> tain this grade point at the end of the first year and
> was dismissed. However, she successfully petitioned
> for readmission prior to her second year of law school.
> Again she failed to maintain a 2.2 cumulative average
> and was again dismissed from the law school. After
> attending summer courses in Ghana, Africa, under the
> auspices of Temple University Law School, she again
> appealed and, with the support of a professor from
> Temple and the Gonzaga Women's Law Caucus, was
> reinstated. This reinstatement was on the condition
> she would attain a cumulative 2.2 grade point average
> at the end of that semester. When she again was un-
> able to meet the condition, she was dropped from the
> university without the option to further petition for
> readmission.
> Maas then completed additional credits at the Uni-
> versity of Washington giving her sufficient credits to

---

71. Maas v. Corporation of Gonzaga University, 27 Wash. App. 397,
618 P.2d 106 (1980).
  72. *Id.*

graduate; Gonzaga has refused those credits and has refused to award her a law degree.[73]

On motion by the defendant, the trial court dismissed the plaintiff's claim. Plaintiff argued that the defendant had the duty to warn her that she was unlikely to successfully complete law school, and the University's negligence in failing to so warn resulted in the loss of her tenured teaching job in Alaska, with resulting damages. Furthermore, plaintiff argued that a confidential or fiduciary relationship arises between the university and a student since the university is in a better position to know of the student's probable success than is the student. *De facto* confidential relationships may arise whenever one party reposes confidence in another who in turn exercises dominion and influence over the first.

The court, in rejecting those arguments, contended:

> The relationship of students and universities is generally contractual rather than confidential or fiduciary. [Citations omitted]. The possibility of academic failure is implicit in the nature of the educational contract between a student and a university. A graduate student seeking admission to a university knows a certain level of performance is necessary to obtain a degree. It is unreasonable to require the university to warn applicants of the obvious [citations omitted].
>
> The university cannot be burdened with the duty of advising her of prospective failure, based solely upon the fact her LSAT and undergraduate grade point averages were below the statistical norms for acceptance into the university.[74]

The superior court said that it lacked authority to order a private institution to award a degree where its refusal to do so is based upon academic performance. The court of

---

73. *Id.* at 107-08.
74. *Id.* at 108-09.

appeals agreed, as a general rule, that courts will not interfere with purely academic decisions of a university. The
court further stated:

> Professors in the position of making academic deci-
> sions will not be second-guessed by the courts. Where a
> university acts in an arbitrary and capricious fashion
> or in bad faith, then the courts generally have accepted
> review of these decisions [citations omitted].
> The decision to award or not award a degree, and
> based upon what criteria, is one uniquely within the
> academic sphere. The courts should abstain from inter-
> ference in this process unless arbitrary and capricious
> decision making or bad faith is present ... [75]

§ 8.1(O). John Doe I v. Maharishi Mahesh Yogi.

In 1985, a suit was filed in the United States District
Court for the District of Columbia for $9 million against
Maharishi Mahesh Yogi, World Plan Executive Council —
United States and Maharishi International University.[76]
The suit, filed by a former student, was in six counts.
Count One alleged fraud and fraud in the inducement. It
was alleged, *inter alia,* as follows:

1. The defendants, by and through their agents and
   employees, promote and sell a meditation technique
   called Transcendental Meditation (hereinafter,
   "T.M."). Any person who wishes to learn this technique must pay a fee and undergo an induction ceremony performed by a T.M. teacher, an employee
   and agent of defendants.
2. Defendants induced plaintiff and other members of
   the public to pay money to learn T.M. by means of
   defendants' advertising and other oral and written
   representations that the practice of this technique

---

75. *Id.* at 109-10.
76. John Doe I v. Maharishi Mahesh Yogi, Civil Action No. 85-2848,
United States District Court for the District of Columbia (1985).

had numerous physical, mental and psychological benefits. These representations were made to plaintiff during standardized introductory lectures which plaintiff attended prior to being taught the practice of T.M.

Defendants represented that the practice of T.M.:

a) reduced stress;
b) improved memory;
c) reversed the aging process;
d) permitted one to achieve one's full potential;
e) conferred perfect health;
f) reduced depression, anxiety and other emotional disturbances;
g) purified the nervous system;
h) promoted better social relations;
i) increased academic ability;
j) expanded awareness;
k) led to the attainment of personal enlightenment;
l) conferred the ability to promote world peace and improve society; and
m) prevented the occurrence of personal misfortune or difficulties.

3. In order to further induce plaintiff and other members of the public to learn T.M., defendants represented that the T.M. technique came from ancient Indian tradition and that it was the only method by which plaintiff could achieve the benefits set forth above. However, defendants also represented that T.M. was not a religion but a scientifically tested procedure whose beneficial results had been confirmed by numerous scientific studies. Defendants distributed copies of these alleged scientific studies to plaintiff and other members of the public.

4. In order to induce plaintiff and other members of the public to learn T.M., defendants also represented that defendants were fully knowledgeable concerning the mental, physical, emotional and psychological effects of the T.M. techniques and other techniques taught by defendants' employees and

285

agents and that defendants and their agents and employees were able to guide and direct plaintiffs in their use.

5. All of the foregoing representations were made both by Mahesh Yogi and by the employees and agents of all defendants acting within the scope of their employment and in accordance with the policies of Mahesh Yogi and were made in the full knowledge and awareness that such representations were untrue. Said representations were made with the express intention of inducing plaintiff to purchase defendants' goods and services.

6. In reliance upon the above representations, plaintiff purchased instruction in T.M.

7. Once plaintiff had been introduced into the practice of T.M., the employees and agents of defendants attempted to persuade plaintiff to take additional courses developed by defendants. Defendants represented that these courses were a means by which plaintiff might speed his progress toward the physical, mental and social goals defendants had represented could be achieved.

8. In reliance on these representations, plaintiff paid money for additional courses including SCI, or the Science of Creative Intelligence, residence courses, preparatory courses and Teacher Training courses. All of these courses involved the practice "rounding," that is, increasing the number of meditation periods per day, which was mentally and emotionally harmful to plaintiff.

9. In 1976, Mahesh Yogi introduced a course called the "Sidhis." Defendants falsely represented to plaintiff that the knowledge given in this course would enable him to rapidly develop certain desirable characteristics such as friendliness, happiness and compassion and attain certain extraordinary powers such as clairvoyance or the ability to fly. Defendants represented that plaintiff would ultimately become a "Master of Creation" with the ability to manipulate the physical world and the laws of nature. The practice of the Sidhis also was repre-

sented as greatly speeding plaintiff's progress toward personal enlightenment.

10. During the Sidhis course plaintiff was instructed in a technique which defendants represented would allow him to levitate or fly. "Flying" in fact constituted hopping with the legs folded in the lotus position.

11. Defendants also induced plaintiff and other members of the public to purchase the Sidhis and T.M. instruction courses by means of representations that individual and group performance of these techniques would have a beneficial effect on society. When any improvement occurred in any aspect of society in any country, defendants represented that the improvement resulted from the practice of T.M. and the Sidhis. Defendants distributed to plaintiff and other members of the public studies which allegedly scientifically demonstrated the beneficial effects of group meditation on society.

12. All of the foregoing representations were made both by Mahesh Yogi and by the employees and agents of all defendants acting within the scope of their employment and in accordance with the policies of Mahesh Yogi and were made in the full knowledge and awareness that such representations were untrue. Said representations were made with the express intention of inducing plaintiff to purchase defendants' goods and services.

13. In reliance on the defendants' representations, plaintiff purchased the SCI course, preparatory courses and the Sidhis course and regularly practiced T.M. and the Sidhis practice of "flying."

14. Contrary to defendants' express representations that the practice of T.M. and the Sidhis would reduce stress, anxiety and depression, such practice caused plaintiff to experience negative emotional and psychological effects such as depression, anxiety, irritability, rage, guilt and mental confusion, reduced plaintiff's mental stability and mental

287

health and caused plaintiff to have severe difficulty in coping with the real world.

15. Contrary to defendants' express representations
that the practice of T.M. and the Sidhis would increase intellectual ability and memory, such practice caused plaintiff to suffer decreased intellectual power resulting from disorientation, inability
to concentrate or focus, and loss of memory.

16. Contrary to defendants' express representations
that the practice of T.M. and the Sidhis would result in perfect health, such practice caused plaintiff to suffer ill health, including severe headaches,
fatigue and other physical discomfort. Because of
the stress exerted on the body as a result of the so-
called practice of flying, plaintiff suffers severe
and continuing pain in his joints.

17. Contrary to defendants' express representations
that mental, physical and societal benefits of T.M.
were scientifically proven and documented, the alleged scientific studies which defendants represented as demonstrating these benefits were
fraudulent, inaccurate and unscientific, contain-
ing manipulated conclusions and manipulated
data.

18. Contrary to defendants' express representations
that the effects of the practice of T.M. and the
Sidhis were beneficial, and that they could properly guide and direct plaintiff in their safe and
beneficial use, defendants knew or in the exercise
of reasonable care should have known of numerous
instances of emotional and psychological injury
arising from such practice. Further, defendants
did not know the full extent of the potential negative effects of the practice and used plaintiff as an
experimental subject to determine such effects.

19. In order to induce plaintiff and other members of
the public to continue to purchase courses and instruction from defendants, defendants represented
to plaintiff that the negative effects experienced
by plaintiff were simply the result of "unstress-
ing," the process by which the nervous system rid

itself of the stress of past experience in the process of purification.

20. At no time did defendants suggest or direct that plaintiff cease the practice of T.M.

21. In order to induce plaintiff and other members of the public to continue to purchase courses and instruction from defendants, defendants represented to plaintiff that it was his own weaknesses rather than the practice of the technique that created the negative effects experienced by plaintiff. Defendants also represented that bad things would happen to plaintiff or that he would fail to achieve personal enlightenment, if he reduced or discontinued his practice.

22. By means of circulating rumors and publicizing to plaintiff and other practitioners of T.M. instances of physical or mental intimidation and harassment of persons who sought to leave the T.M. movement or whom defendants believed to be injurious to the defendants, defendants frightened and intimidated plaintiff so that he believed it was not possible to leave the movement.

23. Because of the emotional and psychological dependency defendants created in plaintiff, plaintiff was prevented from realizing that the negative emotional, psychological and physical effects he was experiencing were the result of the practice of T.M. and the Sidhis rather than a result of his own weakness or inadequacy.

24. Because of the mental confusion, disorientation and inability to think clearly caused by the practice of T.M. and the Sidhis, plaintiff was unable to realize that the negative emotional, psychological and physical effects he was experiencing were the result of the practice of T.M. and the Sidhis.

25. By means of social pressure and the threat of being refused admission to further courses or expelled from the organization, defendants enforced a policy which prohibited plaintiff and other practitioners of T.M. from raising or discussing or asking questions about any negative aspect of his per-

289

sonal experience with the practice of T.M. and the Sidhis.

26. In the fall of 1983, plaintiff began to realize that the negative effects he was experiencing were the result of the practice of T.M. and the Sidhis.

27. At the same time, plaintiff also came to recognize that, although he had been practicing the prescribed length of time to attain the benefits promised by defendants, these had not been forthcoming. Shortly thereafter, plaintiff ceased the practice of T.M. and the Sidhis.

28. Within the months thereafter, plaintiff began to consider a lawsuit to redress the fraud that had been perpetrated on him but because he feared retaliation on the part of the organization, plaintiff did not take immediate action.

29. As a direct and proximate result of defendants' fraudulent misrepresentations, plaintiff was induced to spend eleven years of his life practicing T.M. and performing services for defendants' organization.

30. As a direct and proximate result of defendants' fraudulent misrepresentations, plaintiff was induced to take and make payment for the following courses offered by defendants:
    T.M. initiation — $35
    SCI — $125
    Advanced Techniques — $700
    Advanced Teacher Training — $1,500
    Sidhis — $4,000
    In addition to course fees, plaintiff was induced to make monetary contributions to the support of the T.M. movement.

31. As a direct and proximate result of defendant's fraudulent misrepresentations, plaintiff was induced to work for the organization for a period of four years. He worked ten hours a day, six days a week, fifty-two weeks a year. During two of these years, plaintiff was paid nothing for his work. During the two remaining years, he was paid $25 per month.

32. As a direct and proximate result of defendants' fraudulent misrepresentations, whereby plaintiff was induced to practice T.M. and the Sidhis, plaintiff has suffered and will continue to suffer the severe mental anguish, trauma and humiliation of realizing that he had devoted a substantial portion of his youth to serving and supporting defendants' organization which had perpetrated a massive fraud on him and other members of the public.

33. As a direct and proximate result of defendants' fraudulent misrepresentations, whereby plaintiff was induced to practice T.M. and the Sidhis and subject himself to the practice of rounding, plaintiff was caused to become psychologically ill and undergo psychological trauma to the extent that he feared he would suffer total mental and physical collapse. Plaintiff continues and will continue to suffer psychological injury as a result thereof.

34. As a direct and proximate result of defendants' fraudulent misrepresentations, whereby plaintiff was induced to participate in the T.M. movement, plaintiff has lost a crucial period of his life during which he would otherwise have been developing a career and establishing family relationships, a loss which will continue to affect plaintiff for the rest of his life.

35. As a direct and proximate result of defendants' fraudulent misrepresentations, whereby plaintiff was induced to participate in the T.M. movement, plaintiff was arrested and retarded in the normal process of maturation and development, an injury which will continue to affect plaintiff for the rest of his life.

36. As a direct and proximate result of defendants' fraudulent misrepresentations, whereby plaintiff was induced to participate in the T.M. movement, plaintiff lost and will continue to lose the earnings he would have gained had he pursued the career he had been pursuing and would have pursued but for his involvement in the T.M. movement.

37. As a direct and proximate result of defendants' fraudulent misrepresentations, plaintiff has suffered and continues to suffer inability to concentrate on and complete tasks, and loss of memory and the ability to concentrate on and complete tasks.

38. As a direct and proximate result of defendants' fraudulent misrepresentations, whereby plaintiff was induced to practice T.M. and the Sidhis, plaintiff has suffered and will continue to suffer the humiliation and mental anguish of being fired from a job.

39. As a direct and proximate result of defendants' fraudulent misrepresentations, whereby plaintiff was induced to practice T.M. and the Sidhis, plaintiff has suffered and will continue to suffer frequent pain, throbbing and stiffness in his knees, hips and ankles which creates difficulty in the performance of his daily activities.[77]

In Count II, plaintiff alleged negligence. More specifically, he stated:

40. All damages sustained by plaintiffs were directly and proximately caused by defendants' negligence and reckless disregard of plaintiffs' mental, emotional and physical health as follows:

a) Defendants negligently and recklessly failed to adequately prepare plaintiff for the practice of T.M.

b) Defendants negligently and recklessly failed to inform themselves fully of the effects of the practice of T.M. and the Sidhis, although defendants knew or should have known of numerous adverse reactions thereto.

c) Defendants negligently and recklessly failed to screen plaintiff and other prospective participants for the practice of T.M. and the Sidhis in order to eliminate those to whom mental, emotional or psychological harm would likely occur.

---

77. *Id.* Complaint, at 4-15.

d) Defendants negligently and recklessly failed to hire qualified personnel or to train its personnel to guide and direct plaintiff in the practice of T.M. and the Sidhis.

e) Defendants negligently and recklessly failed to warn plaintiff of the reasonably foreseeable possibility of psychological and/or physical harm resulting from the practice of T.M. and the Sidhis, although defendants knew or should have known of numerous instances of such harm resulting from such practice.

f) Defendants negligently and recklessly subjected plaintiff to the practice of "rounding," which defendants knew or should have known was mentally and psychologically harmful to plaintiff.

g) Defendants negligently and recklessly instructed and encouraged plaintiff in the practice of "flying," which defendants knew or should have known was physically and psychologically harmful to plaintiff.

h) Defendants negligently and recklessly failed to provide plaintiff with an individualized program for the use of T.M. and the Sidhis.

i) Defendants negligently and recklessly failed to assist plaintiff when he experienced the negative effects of the practice of T.M. and the Sidhis or to provide on a routine basis follow-up services directed toward assessing possible damaging effects of its techniques, and the need for further services, but to the contrary, abandoned plaintiff after the initiation of a mentally, physically, and psychologically disruptive and debilitating practice.

j) Defendants negligently and recklessly caused plaintiff to suppress questions or discussion concerning the negative effects he was experiencing as a result of the practice of T.M. and the Sidhis.

k) Defendants negligently and recklessly failed to conduct valid scientific research studies that would accurately evaluate methods, processes, and results of defendants' courses and the prac-

293

  tice of T.M., the Sidhis and rounding and ascertain potential safety problems and thereby identify necessary precautionary safeguards.

 l) Defendants negligently and recklessly induced in plaintiff a dependency on defendants and a state of mind such that plaintiff was incapable of functioning adequately in the real world.

 m) Defendants were otherwise negligent and reckless under the circumstances.[78]

Count III alleges a breach of express warranty.[79] Count IV alleges breach of implied warranty "since the practice of T.M. and the Sidhis was not reasonably fit for the particular purposes for which they were offered to the public."[80]

In Count V, the plaintiff alleges that the previously stated facts state a cause of action for intentional infliction of emotional distress causing plaintiff severe psychological damages.[81] Count VI alleged that the defendants acted in reckless disregard of the health, safety, and welfare of plaintiff, and accordingly, the plaintiff is entitled to punitive damages.[82]

The jury in the month-long trial awarded the plaintiff $137,890 but refused to grant the punitive damages he had sought in the $9 million lawsuit. Concerning the verdict, a counsel for MIU was quoted as saying:

> It's not obvious what the jury awarded for what .... It might include $12,000 he spent over 11 years for T.M. courses. There also were different charges of fraud, and we don't know what the jury settled on. It only

---

78. *Id.* at 15-18.
79. *Id.* at 18.
80. *Id.* at 18-19.
81. *Id.* at 19-20.
82. *Id.* at 20.

took one. The negligence finding would be because it was thought we didn't take care of him.[83]

According to an article, seven other former T.M. followers have filed similar lawsuits against the groups and the lawsuits are pending in federal court in Washington.[84] The article goes on to state:

> Coincidentally, a $16 million lawsuit charging Lifespring, Inc., another self-improvement group, with inflicting emotional damage on five people was filed Tuesday in federal court.
> The lawsuit was brought by a Maryland couple who obtained a court order to allow themselves and their three children to remain anonymous pending further court proceedings in this case.
> It charged that despite claims Lifespring offered opportunities for personal growth, the training was simply "for the purpose of subjecting the trainees to a 'thought reform' process in which trainees' personalities are disrupted and ultimately displaced and supplanted with a 'reformed' personality which is emotionally and ideologically committed to recruiting additional trainees," according to court papers.[85]

The case was appealed and as of this writing (May 18, 1990) no final judgment has been reached on appeal.

§ 8.1(P). Scott v. Rutledge College.

Christine Scott, a former student at Rutledge College, filed suit in the Court of Common Pleas in South Carolina, against Rutledge College, claiming that it fraudulently en-

---

83. Marni Mellen, *Plaintiff Says TM Testimony Is "Only Beginning."* THE FAIRFIELD LEDGER, No. 11, January 14, 1987, p. 1. Reprinted with permission, Fairfield Ledges, Inc.

84. *Nearly $138,000 Awarded by jury to former TM followers,* THE MOUNT PLEASANT NEWS (Mt. Pleasant, Iowa) January 14, 1987, p. 5.

85. *Id.*

ticed her into a "medical administrative assistant" training program.[86] The complaint alleged, *inter alia,* as follows:

1. That on or about March, 1985, the Plaintiff enrolled
   as a student at Rutledge College and that the Plaintiff has paid certain fees, tuitions, and charges
   made by Rutledge College.
2. That the Defendant has and does hold itself out to
   the public as an educational institution offering
   various courses of study and said Defendant accepts
   tuition and fees for the educational courses that it
   offers.
3. That Rutledge College offers among its courses of
   study training for a career as a "Medical Administrative Assistant."
4. That the Plaintiff has enrolled in the course of
   study known as "Medical Administrative Assistant."
5. That the Defendant herein represented by and
   through its employees and agents that upon completion of said course the Plaintiff would be eligible
   for certification by a South Carolina State Board or
   other appropriate licensing body and become
   employable as a medical administrative assistant.
6. That the Defendant herein represented to the
   Plaintiff that upon completion of said course by the
   Plaintiff, that Rutledge College, the Defendant
   herein, would arrange job placement for graduates
   as licensed "Medical Administrative Assistant."
7. That the representations made by the Defendant to
   the Plaintiff as set out herein were false, and that
   the Defendant knew of the falsity of the representations or through diligence should have known of the
   falsity of these statements and made with reckless
   disregard of its truth or falsity, and that the Plaintiff believed the representations of the Defendant to
   be true and the Plaintiff relied upon the representation and had a right to so rely, and that the Plaintiff

---

86. Scott v. Rutledge College, In the Court of Common Pleas, State of
South Carolina, County of Greenville, No. 86-CP-23-3164 (S.C., 1986).

enrolled as a student at Rutledge College in the Medical Administrative Assistant" program based upon the aforementioned representations.

8. That the representations made by the Defendant, as set out herein, were fraudulent and that the Plaintiff has been damaged by said fraud in the following particulars:
   1. loss of tuition, fees, cost of books and other related charges made by Rutledge College for their course as Medical Administrative Assistant;
   2. loss of future income based upon the representation made by the Defendant that the Plaintiff would be certified as "Medical Administrative Assistant", and that the Plaintiff would be placed in a career position by the Defendant after graduation;
   3. loss of income for the period of time spent attending Rutledge College pursuing the course as represented;
   4. punitive damages;
   5. allowable legal fees and court costs.[87]

Nine other former students filed similar suits against Rutledge College. The cases did not go to trial, but were dismissed settled.[88]

§ 8.1(Q). Lyons v. Salve Regina College.

The alleged facts of the *Lyons*[89] case, as related by the court are as follows:

> In this action, plaintiff Sheila Lyons, a former nursing student at defendant Salve Regina College, seeks specific relief and damages for an alleged breach of contract. According to plaintiff, the defendant breached

---

87. *Id.* Complaint, at 1-3.

88. *Wilson v. Rutledge College of Greenville, Inc.,* in Court of Common Pleas, State of South Carolina, County of Greenville, C.A. No. 86-CP-23-3165 (July 15, 1987).

89. Lyons v. Salve Regina College, 422 F. Supp. 1354 (1976).

its contract by taking actions unauthorized by, and
contrary to, the rules of the College. The parties are
agreed that these rules, promulgated by the College
and accepted for consideration by the plaintiff, constituted a contract. As a result of this alleged breach,
plaintiff claims that she was improperly forced out of
the Nursing Department, graduating with a psychology degree instead.[90]

The court further stated:

Defendants, at the time this case was heard, moved the
Court to dismiss the complaint for lack of subject matter jurisdiction, contending that plaintiff was in fact a
Rhode Island resident and that the amount in controversy did not exceed $10,000, exclusive of interest and
costs. The Court reserved judgment on this motion,
pending the hearing, at which the parties offered evidence on both the jurisdictional questions and the
merits. The Court is now prepared to rule on defendants' motion to dismiss and the same is hereby denied
for the reasons that follow.[91]

In arriving at its decision the court reasoned:

It follows that defendants' action in refusing to abide
by the decision of the Appeals Committee constituted a
breach of contract. In making this finding, the Court is
not, as defendants contend, arbitrarily imposing the
legal technicalities of a commercial transaction upon
what is essentially an academic dispute. Rather, the
Court is simply holding that the College, as any other
promissor, must abide by procedures to which it has
bound itself and its students, until such times as it
sees fit to change those procedures.
....
The Court is prepared to order the award of the grade
of "Incomplete" at this time. Furthermore, reinstatement is the appropriate remedy in this type of case;

90. *Id.* at 1356.
91. *Id.*

damages cannot make plaintiff whole. *See Slaughter v. Brigham Young University,* 514 F.2d 622, 627 (10th Cir. 1975); *Anthony v. Syracuse University,* 130 Misc. 249, 223 N.Y.S. 796, 806 (Sup. Ct. 1927). Although this case is unusual because plaintiff has already received a degree from the College, reinstatement would nevertheless seem to be proper. The purpose of reinstatement, like any other contract remedy, is to put plaintiff in the same position she was in before the breach of contract occurred, insofar as a court can do this. In the present case, if the College had kept its bargain, Lyons would have had the opportunity to take such additional courses as would have permitted her to graduate with a major in nursing.

That is what Lyons bargained for when she enrolled in Salve Regina College; she did not bargain for a degree in psychology, nor is there any evidence that she accepted such a degree for any reason besides mitigation of damages. Therefore, it would appear that the College will not have fulfilled its contractual obligation to Lyons until it gives her the opportunity to meet its requirements for a nursing major. *Cf. Slaughter v. Brigham Young University, supra* at 627.[92]

§ 8.1(R). Tanner v. Board of Trustees of the University of Illinois.

The alleged facts, summarized by the court, in the case of *Tanner v. Board of Trustees of the University of Illinois*[93] are as follows:

The plaintiff, Gerard E. Tanner, was a Ph.D. candidate in the Department of Business Administration at the Champaign-Urbana campus of the University of Illinois. Plaintiff's major concentration was in the area of Management Science, an area in which he had completed the required course work and in which he had

---

92. *Id.* at 1363-64.
93. Tanner v. Board of Trustees of the University of Illinois, 363 N.E.2d 208 (1977).

submitted an original doctoral dissertation titled, "Performance Modeling with Time-shared Computers." Plaintiff was also employed by the University as a graduate assistant to the assistant professor in the Department of Business Administration.

For the purposes of this appeal, we deem the following well-pleaded facts to be correct. A thesis committee composed of five professors from the Department was formed to evaluate plaintiff's dissertation and to conduct comprehensive oral and written examinations of the plaintiff. In December, 1972, plaintiff completed the written examinations submitted by two members of the committee and, in March, 1973, he completed a written examination submitted by a third member of the committee. Although plaintiff completed his oral examinations and submitted his dissertation to a committee member in August, 1973, he was informed in December, 1973, that he would have to be re-evaluated in a single, written examination. Plaintiff alleges that he agreed to take the single examination, but that the University thereafter informed him that the examination would be in two parts, both oral and written.

In June, 1975, plaintiff was informed by George Russell, Vice Chancellor and Dean of the Graduate College, that the thesis committee, the examinations and dissertation submitted by plaintiff were all unacceptable because the committee was never formally recognized by the Graduate College, and that he would have to be re-evaluated.

Thereafter, on July 25, 1975, plaintiff commenced this action in the Circuit Court of Cook County seeking a writ of mandamus compelling the University to issue him a Ph.D. degree in Business Administration, or alternatively, $100,000 damages for breach of an implied contract to issue the degree. The University was granted a venue transfer to the Circuit Court for the Sixth Judicial Circuit, Champaign County, on September 29, 1975, and on February 13, 1976, that court dismissed the complaint, finding that no set of facts could be proved to support plaintiff's stated theories of mandamus and contract.[94]

The court based its opinion on the following rationale:

Mandamus is an extraordinary remedy and should not issue unless the plaintiff demonstrates a clear right to the writ and a clear obligation on the defendant to perform the act sought to be performed [citations omitted]. Although we recognize that the University is under a discretionary and not a mandatory duty to issue degrees to persons participating in its curricula (section 10 of the Act providing for the University of Illinois (Ill. Rev. Stat. 1975, ch. 144, par. 31)), the University may not act maliciously or in bad faith by arbitrarily and capriciously refusing to award a degree to a student who fulfills its degree requirements. *Connelly v. University of Vermont* (D.C. Vt. 1965), 244 F. Supp. 156, 159.

In *Connelly,* the plaintiff was a dismissed medical student seeking readmission to the University after being dismissed for failing 25 percent or more of his third year major courses. The plaintiff alleged that he was ill for approximately one month during which time he missed parts of a course in pediatrics-obstetrics. Upon his recovery and return to class, the pediatrics-obstetrics teacher allegedly refused to give plaintiff a passing grade regardless of the quality of his work. In denying a motion to dismiss for failure to state a claim upon which relief can be granted, the court stated:

Where a medical student has been dismissed for a failure to attain a proper standard of scholarship, two questions may be involved; the first is, was the student in fact delinquent in his studies or unfit for the practice of medicine? The second question is, were the school authorities motivated by malice or bad faith in dismissing the student, or did they act arbitrarily or capriciously? In general, the first question is not a matter for judicial review. How-

---

94. *Id.* at 209.

ever, a student dismissal motivated by bad faith, arbitrariness or capriciousness may be actionable." 244 F. Supp. 156, 159.

In this case, the trial court expressly found that "... no set of facts stated on amendment of Plaintiff's Complaint would state a cause of action under the theory of Mandamus." In view of *Connelly,* we disagree with the trial court's conclusion and we remand the cause to the trial court for repleading on plaintiff's mandamus theory.[95]

§ 8.1(S). Kantor v. Schmidt.

A student brought an action to compel the president of the State University of New York at Stony Brook to grant, produce, and deliver to her a Bachelor of Arts degree.[96] The Supreme Court, Kings County, granted the petition and directed the appellant to approve, authorize, and confer upon the petitioner the degree of Bachelor of Arts *nunc pro tunc* as of May, 1979.[97] In affirming the judgment, the Supreme Court, Appellate Division held:

> Petitioner is entitled to relief solely on the ground that the appellant failed to comply with a regulation of the Commissioner of Education. The University was required to make adequate provisions "to record student progress toward the achievement of requirements, and to inform students periodically of their progress and remaining obligations" (see 8 NYCRR 52.2 [b][4]). Since this regulation was not complied with in petitioner's case and she completed 120 credits, she was entitled to receive her degree.[98]

---

95. *Id.* at 209-10.
96. In the Matter of Kantor v. Schmidt, 73 A.D.2d 670, 423 N.Y. Supp. 2d 208 (1979).
97. *Id.* at 209.
98. *Id.*

§ 8.1(T). Regents of University of Michigan v. Ewing.

In the case of *Regents of University of Michigan v. Ewing*[99] a university student was enrolled in a 6 year program of study at the University of Michigan known as the "Inteflex." The program was designed in such a way that upon successful completion of it a student was awarded both an undergraduate degree and a medical degree. In order to qualify for the final two years of the program the student had to pass an examination known as "NBME Part I." In the case at bar the University dismissed the student when he failed this examination with the lowest score recorded in the history of the Inteflex program. Upon being refused readmission to the program and to retake the examination he filed suit in federal court, alleging a right to retake the examination on the ground, *inter alia,* that he had a property interest in the program and that his dismissal was arbitrary and capricious in violation of his "substantive due process rights" guaranteed by the fourteenth amendment. The district court found no violation. The court of appeals reversed the decision.[100] The case was appealed to the United States Supreme Court, which held:

> It is important to remember that this is not a case in which the procedures used by the University were unfair in any respect; quite the contrary is true. Nor can the Regents be accused of concealing nonacademic or constitutionally impermissible reasons for expelling Ewing; the District Court found that the Regents acted in good faith.
>
> Ewing's claim, therefore, must be that the University misjudged his fitness to remain a student in the Inteflex program. The record unmistakably demon-

---

99. Regents of the University of Maryland v. Ewing, 106 S. Ct. 507 (1985).
100. *Id.*

strates, however, that the faculty's decision was made
conscientiously and with careful deliberation, based on
an evaluation of the entirety of Ewing's academic career. When judges are asked to review the substance of
a genuinely academic decision, such as this one, they
should show great respect for the faculty's professional
judgment. Plainly, they may not override it unless it is
such a substantial departure from accepted academic
norms as to demonstrate that the person or committee
responsible did not actually exercise professional judgment. Cf. *Youngberg v. Romeo,* 457 U.S. 307, 323, 102
S. Ct. 2452, 2462, 73 L. Ed. 2d 28 (1982).

Considerations of profound importance counsel re-
strained judicial review of the substance of academic
decisions. As Justice WHITE has explained:

> Although the Court regularly proceeds on the as-
> sumption that the Due Process Clause has more
> than a procedural dimension, we must always bear
> in mind that the substantive content of the Clause is
> suggested   neither   by   its   language   nor   by
> preconstitutional history; that content is nothing
> more than the accumulated product of judicial inter-
> pretation of the Fifth and Fourteenth Amendments.
> This is ... only to underline Mr. Justice Black's con-
> stant reminder to his colleagues that the Court has
> no license to invalidate legislation which it thinks
> merely arbitrary or unreasonable (citations omit-
> ted).

> Added to our concern for lack of standards is a reluc-
> tance to trench on the prerogatives of state and local
> educational institutions and our responsibility to safe-
> guard their academic freedom, "a special concern of
> the First Amendment." *Keyishian v. Board of Regents,*
> 385 U.S. 589, 603, 87 S. Ct. 675, 683, 17 L. Ed. 2d 629
> (1967). If a "federal court is not the appropriate forum
> in which to review the multitude of personnel deci-
> sions that are made daily by public agencies," *Bishop
> v. Wood,* 426 U.S., at 349, 96 S.Ct., at 2079, far less is
> it suited to evaluate the substance of the multitude of
> academic decisions that are made daily by faculty

members of public educational institutions — decisions that require "an expert evaluation of cumulative information and [are] not readily adapted to the procedural tools of judicial or administrative decision-making." *Board of Curators, Univ. of Missouri v. Horowitz,* 435 U.S., at 89-90, 98 S.Ct., at 954-955.

This narrow avenue for judicial review precludes any conclusion that the decision to dismiss Ewing from the Inteflex program was such a substantial departure from accepted academic norms as to demonstrate that the faculty did not exercise professional judgment. Certainly his expulsion cannot be considered aberrant when viewed in isolation. The District Court found as a fact that the Regents "had good reason to dismiss Ewing from the program." 559 F.Supp., at 800. Before failing the NBME Part I, Ewing accumulated an unenviable academic record characterized by low grades, seven incompletes, and several terms during which he was on an irregular or reduced course load. Ewing's failure of his medical boards, in the words of one of his professors, "merely culminate[d] a series of deficiencies .... In many ways, it's the straw that broke the camel's back." App. 79. Accord, *id.,* at 7, 54-55, 72-73. Moreover, the fact that Ewing was "qualified" in the sense that he was eligible to take the examination the first time does not weaken this conclusion, for after Ewing took the NBME Part I it was entirely reasonable for the faculty to reexamine his entire record in the light of the unfortunate results of that examination. Admittedly, it may well have been unwise to deny Ewing a second chance. Permission to retake the test might have saved the University the expense of this litigation and conceivably might have demonstrated that the members of the Promotion and Review Board misjudged Ewing's fitness for the medical profession. But it nevertheless remains true that his dismissal from the Inteflex program rested on an academic judgment that is not beyond the pale of reasoned academic decision-making when viewed against the background of his entire career at the University of

Michigan, including his singularly low score on the NBME Part I examination.

The judgment of the Court of Appeals is reversed and the case is remanded for proceedings consistent with this opinion.[101]

Justice Powell concluded his concurring opinion by stating:

> I agree fully with the Court's emphasis on the respect and deference that courts should accord academic decisions made by the appropriate university authorities. In view of Ewing's academic record that the Court charitably characterizes as "unfortunate," this is a case that never should have been litigated. After a four-day trial in a District Court, the case was reviewed by the Court of Appeals for the Sixth Circuit, and now is the subject of a decision of the United States Supreme Court. Judicial review of academic decisions, including those with respect to the admission or dismissal of students, is rarely appropriate, particularly where orderly administrative procedures are followed — as in this case [citations omitted].[102]

§ 8.1(U). Roth v. University of Central Florida.

Nora Roth, a student who failed an economics test twice but who had made good class grades, sued the University of Central Florida to either receive a master's degree in business administration or get her $5,000 tuition back.[103] She was quoted as saying, "[a]fter paying my dues and having a good average, I just feel abused. I really don't want their money. I just want what I earned, which is a master's degree."[104] Before the case could be tried the University with-

---

101. *Id.* at 513-15.

102. *Id.* at 516.

103. *Student Fails Test, Sues University,* QUAD-CITY TIMES, October 5, 1988, p. 5.

104. *Id.*

drew its test requirement, and the plaintiff received her degree.

§ 8.1(V). Wai-Chung NG v. West Virginia Board of Regents.

In 1982, a college student filed suit in the Circuit Court of Kanawha County, West Virginia, alleging that the college he attended failed to adequately prepare him for a teaching career.[105] The suit was filed by Peter Wai-Chung NG against West Virginia Board of Regents, West Virginia State College, Board of Education of the County of Kanawha, a corporation, Dr. Corrine Davis, Professor, West Virginia State College, *et al.* The complaint contained three counts.

In Count I, the plaintiff alleged that from 1972 through 1977 he was a student pursuing a program of instruction in the Department of Education at West Virginia State College, leading to a baccalaureate degree in Education. One of the requirements for completing such a program and obtaining certification to teach in the public schools of West Virginia was the completion of a course in "Student Teaching."[106] The plaintiff enrolled in the student teaching course and was given an assignment to teach two months at a high school, with the first month teaching the Spanish language and the second month teaching English. The plaintiff alleged that at the completion of the first month of his student teaching in the Spanish language he received compliments for his work and was told his grade was between the grades of "B" and "C." Then, without being given any reason, he was transferred to another school to com-

---

105. Complaint, Wai-Chung NG v. West Virginia Board of Regents, Civil Action No. CA-82-404, Circuit Ct. of Kanawha County W. Va. (1982).

106. *Id.* at 3.

plete his student teaching. He further alleged that after completing his student teaching he was advised by his supervising teacher that his grade would be a "C" but was admonished by the supervisor that it would not be good for him, as a Chinese, to teach the English language in American schools.[107]

Plaintiff further alleged that despite these previous assurances given to him that he would receive a creditable and passing grade for student teaching, he received a grade of "D", which grade, according to the college's policy, prohibits the plaintiff from obtaining certification to teach in the public schools of West Virginia. When he inquired as to why he received a grade of "D" he was told that they did not think he should teach the English language in American schools.[108]

Furthermore, it was alleged:

> That at no time was plaintiff ever counseled during his student teaching by the defendants herein or by any of the representatives of the defendants herein, their agents, employees, and/or representatives that his performance was inferior or unsatisfactory, but at all times was led to believe by the defendants herein, their agents, representatives and/or employees that he was performing satisfactorily and creditably in order to attain at least a "C" grade in his Student Teaching course, which would assure teacher certification through the defendant, State College, and with the defendant, Department of Education, nor at any time was plaintiff ever counseled that improvement was necessary in order to obtain his certification, but at all times, he was told by representatives, employees, and/or agents of the defendants, Board of Regents, State College, and Board of Education, that his performance was satisfactory, but that he was told by the defendants, C. Davis and Securro, that he was being

107. *Id.* at 4.
108. *Id.* at 4-5.

treated in this discriminatory, arbitrary, and capricious manner and received the unsatisfactory grade which he did because he was Chinese and told by the defendant, Jarvis, that it would be good for him if he were not to teach in American schools.[109]

The complaint also stated that plaintiff requested to view his records and student evaluation but was denied access to such and therefore could not ascertain the validity of, and underlying basis for, his unsatisfactory grade. In December, 1977, plaintiff graduated with a B.S. degree in Education, but without the required teacher certification to teach in the public schools of West Virginia. Because of this the plaintiff was denied the right to participate in his chosen profession of school teaching, all of which was and has been to plaintiff's detriment and injury.[110]

The plaintiff further contended in his complaint as follows:

> That in February of 1981, plaintiff undertook to appeal or protest the "D" grade he received in the aforesaid student teaching course, and the defendant Bickley, undertook to form a faculty committee at State College in order to investigate the grade received by plaintiff in his student teaching course, but after a number of meetings, such efforts were halted and discontinued and no further action was taken upon plaintiff's grade appeal, an action which has been upheld by the defendants, State College and Board of Regents so that no further action in this regard will be undertaken.
>
> That in undertaking said action on plaintiff's grade appeal through the aforesaid meetings, the plaintiff herein was not accorded his due process rights of notice to hearing, his right to be present at said hearings, his right to have an attorney present at said hearings, his right to be confronted by those witnesses against him, his opportunity to present evidence, his right to an

---

109. *Id.* at 5-6.
110. *Id.* at 6.

unbiased hearing tribunal, and his right to an adequate record of the proceedings, all of which has been,
and will be, to his injury and detriment, both past and
future.

That in failing to accord plaintiff the aforesaid
rights and in terminating the hearings as they did, the
defendants, ... have violated plaintiff's due process
rights and have substantially hurt his reputation since
plaintiff cannot now obtain certification to teach in
any state.[111]

In Count II of the complaint plaintiff alleged the formation and breach of contract and averred:

That plaintiff herein entered into a contract with defendants herein by virtue of his enrollment at West
Virginia State College, that if the said plaintiff successfully completed certain requirements, including
teacher certification, the student teaching course, and
completion of certain course requirements leading to
the baccalaureate degree in Education (B.S.), he would
be entitled to teach in the public schools of the State of
West Virginia, as well as in any other State which said
certification would have an effect.

That all times herein, plaintiff has complied with
and successfully fulfilled all of the terms and conditions of the aforesaid contract with defendants herein,
but the defendants herein, either in concert or individually, by virtue of their aforesaid wrongful, arbitrary
and capricious acts, either express or implied, in
awarding plaintiff an unfair and unjust grade of "D" in
the student teaching course and insubsequently
upholding the award of said grade on appeal in violation of plaintiff's due process rights aforesaid, have
wrongfully, arbitrarily and capriciously failed to
award to plaintiff his aforesaid significant liberty and
property interest to participate in the teaching voca-
tion after his successful completion of all the requirements, and in so doing, the defendants herein have
breached the aforesaid contract with plaintiff, all to

111. *Id.* at 6-7.

the plaintiff's detriment and economic loss, both past and future.[112]

In Count III it is stated:

That in wrongfully, arbitrarily and capriciously denying to plaintiff his significant liberty and property interest to which he was entitled in the form of his teaching certification and his right to participate in his chosen teaching profession by virtue of his successful completion of the course of study in the Education Department at State College, the defendants herein, either in
concert or individually, acted in bad faith, maliciously,
arbitrarily, capriciously, oppressively and discrimina-
torily to the interests of plaintiff, and as such, is conduct of which an example should be made and is conduct which should be punished.[113]

For the wrongful conduct alleged the plaintiff demanded damages for violation of his due process rights, damages for destruction of his reputation, punitive damages, and actual damages due to breach of the alleged contract. In the alter- native he asked that the defendants be ordered to change plaintiff's grade in his student teaching course from a "D" to a satisfactory passing grade.[114]

The case was dismissed, not on its merits, but due to the statute of limitations.

§ 8.1(W). Pierre-Marie Luc Robitaille v. Schwartz.

In this case, the plaintiff, Pierre-Marie Luc Robitaille, was working toward a graduate degree at the University of Northern Iowa. He had what may best be described as a clash of ego with a professor. The dispute, triggered by a disagreement over a computer-coding project that the plaintiff did for Schwartz' class, ended in Robitaille receiv-

---

112. *Id.* at 9-10.
113. *Id.* at 12.
114. *Id.* at 11, 13.

311

ing an "F" and his ultimately leaving the University.[115] It was further stated that Schwartz declared plaintiff's project "junk" and also told him he was "stupid." Finally, he ordered the plaintiff to quit his course and took steps to have him thrown out of the graduate school. After the plaintiff dropped the class, an "F" went on his record, even though the evidence showed he had not been failing. He sought relief through the university grievance process, but the Department denied his request to withdraw from the class without a grade report, a student-appeals board refused to hear an appeal, saying it did not have jurisdiction, and a second appeal was rejected as being untimely.[116]

The court awarded the plaintiff $56,000 plus interest for loss of income, expenses, and compensatory damages, and the University was directed to remove the "F" from plaintiff's records.[117] He also received attorney's fees.

An editorial commenting on this case states:

> There would be cause for concern if judges meddled in every little disagreement between students and professors. But academics are not immune to lawsuits when they breach the implied agreement of good faith between the university and students.
> It is a good thing the courts were available to Robitaille because in this case the academic community failed to render justice.[118]

---

115. Pierre-Marie Luc Robitaille v. Schwartz, District Court of Blackhawk County Civil Action No. 64830 (Iowa, 1983). *See also Justice In Academe* (The Register's Editorials), THE DES MOINES REGISTER, November 11, 1987, p. 8A. Copyright 1989, DES MOINES REGISTER and Tribune Company.

116. *Id.*

117. *Id.*

118. *Justice In Academe* (The Register's Editorials) THE DES MOINES REGISTER, November 11, 1987, p. 8A. Copyright 1989, DES MOINES REGISTER and Tribune Company.

§ 8.1(X). Ross v. Creighton University.

In July 1989, Kevin Ross, a former University of Creighton basketball player, filed suit in Chicago seeking an unspecified amount of damages. The suit contends, *inter alia,* that when Creighton University recruited him for basketball it knew or should have known that he was "ill-equipped and unable to successfully participate in the university's academic program" and failed to adequately teach him.[119] He claimed that he suffered from depression because of the way Creighton treated him. Plaintiff, now 30, gained national attention in 1982 when he left Creighton University after four years on a basketball scholarship. He was unable to compete academically with eighth-grade students and enrolled in a private school. Ross stayed at Creighton for four years despite a lack of success either as a student or an athlete, keeping his eligibility by taking such courses as the theory of basketball. The year that he should have graduated, Ross was more than 30 academic hours short of a degree. His teacher at Westside Preparatory School said he displayed the reading ability of a second-grader.[120]

Steve Kline, Creighton director of media relations, is quoted as telling *The World Herald:*

> Characterizing what happened here as an abuse is bunk. We feel there are no grounds for such a lawsuit. We honored all of our commitments to Kevin and more.
>
> Creighton made an "administrative exception" to admit Ross in spite of his scoring 9 out of a possible 36

---

119. Michael Kelly, *CU Official: Abuse of Ross Unfair Charge,* OMAHA WORLD HERALD, July 26, 1989, p. 41.

120. *Id.; see also* Editorial Page, *Creighton Takes a Late Hit,* OMAHA WORLD HERALD, July 29, 1989, p. 16; Bill Norton, *The Education of Kevin Ross,* KANSAS CITY STAR MAGAZINE, September 13, 1987.

on his ACT college entrance exam. Does the university regret doing so?

"The university long ago admitted that in this specific case it was a mistake," Kline said. "But regret is not the right word.

"If you see a student who has been graduated from high school and yet had a disadvantaged background, and you offer that student an opportunity and assistance, and at the end of four years that student walks out of here with a degree and a chance to go out into the world and make something of himself, you've accomplished a lot. We had a good record in making that kind of opportunity available to students with backgrounds very similar to Kevin's."

Kline said that Tom Apke and Dan Offenburger, at the time the basketball coach and athletic director, respectively, urged Ross early in his time at Creighton to transfer to another school "that might be less competitive academically and athletically."

"At that time," Kline said, "Kevin tearfully begged to be given another chance. He promised that he would work hard and apply himself both in the classroom and athletics. He was given another chance. We did keep him here when, in all likelihood, had he been at another institution he may have been bounced out the door."

Partly as a result of the Ross case, Creighton decided not to recruit athletes who don't meet the Proposition 48 guidelines of the National Collegiate Athletic Association, including a "C" average in high school "core" courses and a 15 on the ACT test (or 700 on SAT.)[121]

The defendant filed a motion to dismiss the case on June 14, 1990. The court sustained the defendant's motion and dismissed the case.

§ 8.1(Y). Jackson v. Drake University.

In May 1990, a former basketball player filed suit in Iowa District Court against Drake University alleging, *in-*

---

121. Kelly, *supra* note 119, at 41, 45.

ter alia, fraud in that the defendant failed in its commitment to educate him.[122] More specifically the complaint alleges as follows:

1. Defendant, through its agent, recruited Mr. Jackson from inner-city Chicago to play basketball for Drake University.

2. In return, Defendant was to receive a college education.

3. In reliance thereon, Plaintiff moved from Chicago, Illinois to Des Moines, Iowa, forfeiting other athletic opportunities.

4. Mr. Jackson, before coming to Drake University, was on the Academic All-Conference list and was majoring in psychology.

5. Once Mr. Jackson moved to Des Moines, he found the circumstances under which he was to play basketball and obtain his education were drastically different from which were originally represented to him.

6. The coaching staff mandated that time committed to basketball practice, games and meetings was to take precedence over academics.

7. Players were only expected to perform at minimum academic levels to ensure adequate basketball practice time.

8. To further relieve the "burden" of academics from the players, the coaching staff provided term papers which players were expected to turn in as their own work.

9. In some instances these staff prepared term papers which had been plagiarized from other work.

10. In at least two incidents, players who turned in these plagiarized term papers were reprimanded and academically punished by their respective professors.

---

122. Jackson v. Drake University, Iowa District Court for Polk County, Law No. CL 84-49942 (1990).

11. At the request of the coaching staff, Mr. Jackson was instructed to turn in one of these plagiarized term papers. Mr. Jackson refused and instead chose to write his own. The coaching staff was appalled and aggravated by this action and Mr. Jackson was reprimanded.

12. Defendant provided no independent academic counseling for student athletes. All counseling was placed under the control of the athletic department.

13. The coaching staff also advised players of which classes they must register for that would least interfere with the time constraints of the basketball program and would be easy to pass. Emphasis was placed on remaining academically eligible to play basketball, not on obtaining an education.

14. In its academic counseling capacity, Defendant was solely looking out for its own interest and was in complete disregard for the academic achievement of the players. Progress toward a college degree was not an objective of Defendant.

15. Because of these practices and procedures, Defendant intentionally deprived Plaintiff of the educational opportunity promised to him. Further, these practices and procedures are in direct conflict with Defendant's public image for academic excellence.

16. Additionally, Defendant took advantage of the fact that Plaintiff was a disadvantaged black youth from inner city Chicago.

17. Defendant, through its agent, subjected Plaintiff to physical, verbal and mental abuse.

18. Defendant, through its agent, threatened to revoke Plaintiff's scholarship.

19. These threats continued because Defendant knew that Mr. Jackson was in no position to question authority due to his disadvantaged background and limited financial means.

20. In January of 1990, Plaintiff had no alternative but to quit the Drake University Men's Basketball team.

COUNT I

BREACH OF CONTRACT

21. Defendant recruited Plaintiff to play basketball for Drake University. Plaintiff was offered and accepted an athletic scholarship which provided, among other things, that he was eligible to enroll as a full-time student at Drake University.

22. In consideration for these services, Defendant agreed to provide Plaintiff with a college education and support system so he could take full advantage of his educational opportunity.

23. Plaintiff accepted Defendant's offer and moved from Chicago, Illinois, to Des Moines, Iowa.

24. The offer and acceptance of basketball services for an education gave rise to a contract between Plaintiff and Defendant.

25. Plaintiff performed in accordance with the contract by attending practice sessions and regularly playing in basketball games.

26. Plaintiff has not been able to take advantage of his educational opportunity because of the practices and procedures of Defendant which are an impediment to a student athlete's academic gain.

27. Plaintiff has not received the benefit of the bargain because Defendant has breached the contract by:

a) Failing to provide independent and adequate academic counseling and tutoring;

b) Failing to provide adequate study time;

c) Requiring Plaintiff to turn in plagiarized term papers, not of player's own work;

317

d) Completely disregarding Plaintiff's progress toward an undergraduate degree; and

e) Requiring or strongly urging Plaintiff to register for classes that detracted from, and conflicted least with, the basketball schedule and which also provided high grades essential to maintaining academic eligibility, regardless of their academic merit.

28. Defendant's breach of contract is a proximate cause of Plaintiff's injury.

29. Defendant's breach has resulted in damage to Plaintiff.

30. Defendant has acted wilfully, wantonly and fraudulently in breaching the contract and Plaintiff should be awarded punitive damages.

COUNT II

NEGLIGENCE

31. Defendant, by recruiting Plaintiff and relocating him from Chicago to Des Moines, promising him an education, and offering him a full scholarship in return for his basketball talents, undertook a duty to educate Plaintiff. At the very least Defendant undertook the duty to provide a complete and genuine opportunity for Plaintiff to gain an education.

32. Defendant breached this duty to educate or provide reasonable opportunity for education by:

a) Failing to provide independent and adequate academic counseling and tutoring;

b) Failing to provide adequate study time;

c) Requiring Plaintiff to turn in plagiarized term papers, not of player's own work;

d) Completely disregarding Plaintiff's adequate progress toward an undergraduate degree;

318

e) Requiring or strongly urging Plaintiff to register for classes that detracted from, and conflicted least with, the basketball schedule and would provide high grades essential to maintaining academic eligibility regardless of their academic worth.

33. This breach of duty was a proximate cause of Plaintiff's injury.

34. Defendant's breach has resulted in damage to the Plaintiff.

COUNT III

NEGLIGENT MISREPRESENTATION

35. Defendant made false and misleading representations and/or omitted to state facts to Plaintiff regarding the academic integrity of the athletic program.

36. Such misrepresentations were made knowing that Plaintiff was completely relying and did completely rely on such information in determining his actions.

37. By inducing Plaintiff to move from Chicago to Des Moines and play basketball for Drake University, Defendant had a duty to exercise reasonable care in obtaining and communicating to Plaintiff such information regarding academics, and the athletic program.

38. Defendant failed to exercise reasonable care because statements made to Plaintiff were false and/or misleading. Such statements include:

a) Defendant had adequate academic counseling for athletes;

b) Student-athletes have adequate study time;

c) Competent tutors would be provided to student athletes; and

d) Drake University, in and of itself, was committed to academic excellence.

319

e) Drake University's commitment to academic excellence carried over to the athletic department.

39. Plaintiff relied on these misrepresentations to his detriment.

40. Defendant's negligent misrepresentations were a proximate cause of Plaintiff's injury.

41. Defendant's negligent misrepresentation has resulted in damage to Plaintiff.

COUNT IV

FRAUD

42. Defendant intentionally induced Plaintiff to move from Chicago to Des Moines by promising a college education and full support services to Plaintiff could fully utilize his educational opportunity while playing basketball.

43. When Plaintiff moved to Des Moines and joined the basketball program, he found that academics were not emphasized and the atmosphere was not conducive to academic achievement.

44. Defendant intentionally and fraudulently deprived Plaintiff of his educational opportunity by:

a) Failing to provide independent and adequate academic counseling and tutoring;

b) Failing to provide adequate study time;

c) Requiring Plaintiff to turn in plagiarized term papers, not of players own work;

d) Completely disregarding Plaintiff's academic progress toward an undergraduate degree; and

e) Requiring or strongly urging Plaintiff to register for classes that detracted from, and conflicted least with, the basketball schedule and would provide high grades essential to maintaining academic eligibility, regardless of their academic worth.

45. All of the above were promised to Plaintiff and used to lure Plaintiff to Drake University when in fact Defendant had no intention of bestowing such academic services or opportunity on Plaintiff.

46. Defendant's fraudulent conduct was a proximate cause of Plaintiff's injury.

47. Defendant's fraudulent conduct has resulted in damage to the Plaintiff.

48. Defendant has acted wilfully, wantonly and fraudulently and Plaintiff should be awarded punitive damages.

COUNT V

NEGLIGENT HIRING

49. Defendant, through its agent, totally disregarded NCAA regulations regarding practices, academics and recruiting as well as disregarding Drake University's rules and regulations governing student athletes.

50. Defendant, through its agent, also physically, mentally and verbally abused his players and coaching staff.

51. Defendant had a duty to Plaintiff and other team members to hire a coach that could not only follow NCAA and Drake University rules and regulations, but would also emphasize academics to the level commensurate with the level of academic excellence which Drake University portrays to its athletes, students and the public.

52. Defendant breached this duty by hiring a head coach who had a reputation for underhandedness, academic impropriety and player abuse.

53. Defendant failed to sufficiently investigate, or chose to ignore, the background of the coach.

54. The Defendant's breach of its duty to hire an academically qualified coach is a proximate cause of Plaintiff's injury.

55. Defendant's negligent hiring has resulted in damage to Plaintiff.

56. Defendant has acted wilfully, wantonly and fraudulently and Plaintiff should be awarded punitive damages.

COUNT VI

CIVIL RIGHTS

(41 U.S.C. § 1981)

57. Plaintiff, Terrell Jackson, is a young, black man from inner-city Chicago.

58. Defendant knew Plaintiff was a disadvantaged black youth that had few opportunities open to him.

59. Defendant, through its agent, intentionally and wilfully took advantage of Plaintiff's race and disadvantaged financial position.

60. Defendant, through its agent, intentionally threatened to revoke Plaintiff's scholarship, physically, mentally and verbally abused him, humiliated him and deemphasized his education knowing that Plaintiff was in no position to complain because his future depended on his basketball scholarship.

61. Because of Defendant's unlawful conduct, Plaintiff has not enjoyed the full and equal benefit of the laws or security of his person or property and has been subject to punishment and pains because of his race and disadvantaged background, in violation of 42 U.S.C. § 1981.

62. Defendant's intentional actions are a proximate cause of Plaintiff's injury.

63. Defendant's illegal actions have resulted in damage to Plaintiff.

64. Defendant has acted wilfully and wantonly, and Plaintiff should be awarded punitive damages.[123]

§8.2. Summary.

It is obvious from the foregoing that the student-university relationship is not always what it ought to be. Whether the relationship is, as Dean Vaill maintains — "one of the most imbalanced situations" left in society[124] — may well be a topic for debate. The fact is, however, that occasionally the perception is that students have been unfairly treated. Consequently, in order to get what they feel they deserve, students turn to courts for help with their grievances. A number of theories have been used as the basis for their claims. In addition to constitutional rights, students often have contractual rights. Students pay tuition to the university and in turn expect educational services — a "proper" education. Where from here remains to be seen. The one thing that seems certain, however, is that the matter is not closed. There will be additional activity and more litigation.

---

123. Id. at 1-13.
124. Memorandum opinion, pp. 14-17, Lowenthol v. Vanderbilt University, Chancery Court for Davidson Cty., Part Three, Nashville, Tenn., No. A-8525 (1976).

Chapter 9

EDUCATIONAL MALPRACTICE — PERIPHERAL CASES

> To allow a physician to file suit for educational malpractice against his school and residence program each time he is sued for malpractice would call for a malpractice trial within a malpractice case.[1]

§ 9.0. Introduction.

As we have seen in previous chapters, the issue of whether to create a tort for educational malpractice generally has arisen in a limited number of factual contexts. The plaintiff has been either a high school student who had not acquired basic academic skills, *Peter W., supra, Donohue, supra,* or a grade school student who was improperly placed in a special education program. *Hoffman, supra, DSW, supra.* These cases surfaced in the context of public education. The same rationale for precluding a cause of action for educational malpractice has also been found to apply when the defendant is a private school, *Helm, supra.*

---

1. Swidryk v. Saint Michael's Medical Center, *et al.,* 201 N.J. Super. 601, 493 A.2d 641 (N.J. Super. L. 1985).

In this chapter the issue of whether or not to establish a cause of action for educational malpractice arises in a different context from those already mentioned.[2]

§ 9.1. Educational Malpractice — Peripheral Cases.

§ 9.1(A). Swidryk v. St. Michael's Medical Center.

Swidryk involved an educational malpractice claim brought by a physician against a hospital's director of medical education. This educational malpractice action was prompted by a separate suit brought against the physician, which arose out of his delivery of a child during the physician's first year of residency at the hospital. On the director's motion for summary judgment the court held that the physician could not maintain an educational malpractice claim under either the tort or contract theory.[3] The court stated:

> This summary judgment motion raises the novel issue of whether a physician may maintain a cause of action for educational malpractice against a director of medical education for an incident alleged to have occurred during the physician's residency at the medical center.
>
> The underlying claim of malpractice is attributed to negligence in the delivery of a child in July 1973. At that time plaintiff, Dr. John P. Swidryk, had just begun his first year of residency in obstetrics and gynecology at St. Michael's and was in the third week of the program. Dr. Swidryk has been named as a defendant in a malpractice suit for his alleged participation in the delivery of a child later determined to have severe brain damage.
>
> Dr. Swidryk has brought this declaratory judgment suit against, among others, Dr. Leon Smith, the Director of Medical Education at St. Michael's. It is alleged that Dr. Smith was negligent in failing to supervise

---

2. *Id.* at 643.
3. *Id.* at 641.

adequately the intern and resident program and as a proximate result of Dr. Smith's negligence, Dr. Swidryk has been sued for malpractice. Further, Dr. Swidryk claims Dr. Smith breached a contractual duty to him by failing to provide a suitable environment for a medical educational experience in that Dr. Smith failed to supervise adequately the intern and resident program.

Dr. Smith has moved for summary judgment on a number of grounds; however, this motion will only address the argument that the amended complaint fails to state a cognizable tort or breach of contract. It is mere characterization to label this cause of action a breach of contract. The dominant trend in pleading is to dispose of the technical distinctions between similar causes of action and to achieve substantial justice. *M v. F,* 95 *N.J. Super.* 165, 170, 230 A.2d 192 (Cty. Ct. 1967); *see Jersey City v. Hague,* 18 *N.J.* 584, 115 A.2d 8 (1955). The public policy considerations which bar the tort claim also act to bar the contract claim. *Hunter v. Board of Education of Montgomery County,* 292 *Md.* 481, 439 A.2d 582, 586 n. 5 (1982); *Smith v. Alameda Cty. Soc. Serv. Agency,* 90 Cal. App. 3d 929, 943, 153 Cal. Rptr. 712, 719 (1979). For the reasons previously stated at oral argument and elaborated on in this opinion, the court concludes that there is no cause of action for educational malpractice either on a tort or contract theory.

The foundation of Dr. Swidryk's claim is that Dr. Smith's conduct was negligent in that his actions as director of medical education fell below the standard of care essential to protect others from an unreasonable risk of harm. The vast majority of courts to consider this issue have refused to recognize a cause of action for educational malpractice.[4]

After reviewing the various educational malpractice cases, the court went on to state:

---

4. *Id.* at 642.

Here, the issue of whether or not to establish a cause of action for educational malpractice arises in a different context from those already mentioned. Dr. Swidryk is a physician, not a high school student or a grade school student with a learning disability. He was not required by law to attend medical school. St. Michael's is not a school board, but a graduate medical residence program. However, the same public policy considerations control the issue of whether to recognize the tort of educational malpractice in New Jersey in the factual context presented.

In order to find a defendant liable for negligence a legal duty must be found to exist and there must have been a breach of that duty. *Fortugno Realty Co. v. Schiavone-Bonomo Corp.,* 39 *N.J.* 382, 393, 189 A.2d 7 (1963), *McIntosh v. Milano,* 168 *N.J. Super.* 466, 403 A.2d 800 (Law Div. 1979). Whether or not a duty exists is ultimately a question of fairness and the inquiry involves a consideration of the relationship of the parties, the nature of the risk and the public interest in the proposed solution. *Essex v. New Jersey Bell Telephone Company,* 166 *N.J. Super.* 124, 399 A.2d 300 (App. Div. 1979). Public policy considerations must play a major role in the determination of whether a legal duty exists. *See Wytupek v. Camden,* 25 *N.J.* 450, 462, 136 A.2d 887 (1957).

As a general rule courts will not interfere with purely academic decisions of a university. *See, e.g., Maas v. Corporation of Gonzaga University,* 27 Wash. App. 397, 618 P.2d 106, 109 (1980). The New Jersey courts should not be required to sit in day to day review of the academic decisions of a graduate medical education program. This function is best left to the state board of medical examiners, the board of higher education and the Advisory Graduate Medical Education Council of New Jersey.

New Jersey has enacted many regulations and statutes to insure that proper medical education is provided within the State. *N.J.S.A.* 18A:68-12 empowers the state board of medical examiners to issue licenses to schools or colleges which seek to qualify students to practice medicine. The school must provide a detailed explanation of its program of medical studies before the board of medical examiners will issue a license. *N.J.S.A.* 18A:68-13. The state board of medical examiners further requires that all who wish to practice medicine in New Jersey obtain a license to do so. *N.J.S.A.* 45:9-6. The license is generally granted only after successful completion of an examination. In order for an individual to qualify to take the examination he must establish he has satisfactorily completed high school, college, medical school and a one year internship program. *N.J.S.A.* 45:9-6 through -8.1.

New Jersey's regulation of medical education does not end after the issuance of a license. *N.J.S.A.* 18A:64H-2 establishes the Advisory Graduate Medical Education Council of New Jersey. The council makes recommendations for the development and implementation of graduate medical education programs. *N.J.S.A.* 18A:64H-2. The board of higher education, along with the advice of the council and concurrence of the commissioner of health set the standards which graduate medical education programs must meet in order to participate in a program which provides state and federal funding of graduate medical programs. *N.J.S.A.* 18A:64H-1; 64H-5b. The specific requirements for participation in the program are detailed in the New Jersey Administrative Code, *N.J.A.C.* 9:15 *et seq.* The council also has the power to review the qualifications of the director of medical education of each program to insure he is of the highest quality. *N.J.S.A.* 18A:64H-6(e).

The Legislature has vested the board of medical examiners, the board of higher education and the advisory graduate medical education council with the authority to insure that a proper medical education is delivered within New Jersey. It would be against public policy for the court to usurp these functions and inquire into the day to day operation of a graduate medical education program. From the standpoint of court administration, it is also unwise to recognize a claim for educational malpractice where an individual

329

physician is attempting to defend against a malpractice claim. To allow a physician to file suit for educational malpractice against his school and residence program each time he is sued for malpractice would call for a malpractice trial within a malpractice case. Creation of the tort of educational malpractice in this context would substantially increase the amount of time which a medical malpractice case takes to try now as well as have the potential to confuse the jury in its consideration of the underlying issues. The litigation explosion has limits and this is one area in which those limits should be definitely marked. Therefore, for reasons of public policy, there is no legal duty which will support a tort for educational malpractice in this class of case.

For the foregoing reasons and those expressed at the time the motion was initially heard, Dr. Smith's motion for summary judgment to dismiss Dr. Swidryk's complaint against him is granted. [Footnotes omitted][5]

§ 9.1(B). Moore v. Vanderloo.

In 1986, the Iowa Supreme Court decided a case brought by an oral contraceptive user who suffered a stroke after undergoing chiropractic manipulation of her neck.[6] She had sued the chiropractor, the college of chiropractice, and the contraceptive manufacturer. Claims against the chiropractor were settled before the trial. The district court rendered summary judgment for the school and entered judgment on a jury verdict for the manufacturer, and appeal was taken. The supreme court, in affirming the district court, held:

(1) the school could not be held liable on express-warranty theory based on granting of a diploma and advertising material provided by it; (2) school could not be held liable on theory of educational malpractice; (3)

---

5. *Id.* at 643-45.
6. Moore v. Vanderloo, 386 N.W.2d 108 (Iowa 1986).

in view of medical literature at time of injury the contraceptive manufacturer had no duty to warn chiropractors of risks of a patient taking birth control pill and then receiving chiropractic manipulations; and (4) one juror's reading newspaper article stating that chiropractor had settled for undisclosed sum did not require new trial.[7]

The court summarized the facts as follows:

> Plaintiff Linda Moore suffered a stroke after undergoing a chiropractic manipulation of her neck. She and her children later filed this suit against the chiropractor, Lance Vanderloo; the chiropractic college which Vanderloo had attended, Palmer College of Chiropractic (Palmer); and the manufacturer of Moore's oral contraceptive, Ortho Pharmaceutical Corp. and Ortho Pharmaceuticals, Inc. (Ortho). The claims against Vanderloo were settled before trial. Plaintiffs have appealed from a summary judgment which was granted in favor of Palmer and from the judgment entered upon the favorable jury verdict for Ortho. Upon consideration of the issues presented for our review, we affirm the district court's rulings as to both defendants.

> In November 1978, plaintiff Linda Moore began receiving chiropractic treatments from Dr. Lance Vanderloo. Dr. Vanderloo had graduated and received a diploma four years previously from defendant Palmer College of Chiropractic. At this time, Moore was thirty-five years old and was taking an oral contraceptive manufactured by defendant Ortho. She had been taking oral contraceptives since 1963 and had been on some type of a birth control pill manufactured by Ortho since 1968. Moore regularly smoked one to one and one-half packs of cigarettes per day.

> On November 20, 1978, Moore went to Vanderloo's office for a chiropractic treatment. After undergoing a cervical manipulation by Vanderloo, Moore experienced a sudden onset of a variety of symptoms. She was transported to the hospital, when her condition

---

7. *Id.*

worsened, where it was determined that she was suffering a cerebral stroke. As a result of the stroke, plaintiff has permanent bodily and emotional impairment.

Moore and her sons subsequently brought actions for personal injuries and loss of consortium against Vanderloo, alleging breach of informed consent and negligence; against Palmer for breach of warranty and negligence for failing to properly research and teach Vanderloo the risk of stroke from chiropractic manipulation of the neck; and against Ortho in a strict liability in tort products action. These actions were consolidated, Iowa Rule of Civil Procedure 185, and the claims against Vanderloo were settled prior to trial.[8]

Concerning the claims against defendant Palmer, the court stated:

We conclude that the dismissal of plaintiff's petition was proper as to defendant Palmer and that judgment was properly entered in favor of defendant Ortho on the favorable jury verdict.

I. *Claims against defendant Palmer.* Plaintiff's action against defendant Palmer specifically raised the issues of whether certain express and implied warranties arose to the public from the granting of Palmer's diploma to Vanderloo, and from Palmer's dissemination of chiropractic advertising to the public. This part of the appeal also presents the question, which has not been previously addressed by this court, of whether an action can be successfully asserted by a third party against an educational institution for improperly teaching a student. The district court dismissed plaintiffs' petition as not stating a claim on which relief could be granted.

A. *Express warranty claims.* Plaintiffs claim that the diploma given to Dr. Vanderloo upon his graduation from Palmer constitutes an express warranty of his competence by Palmer to the public. They also argue that advertising material provided by Palmer

_____

8. *Id.* at 111.

332

expressly warranted the safety of the chiropractic method. In support of this theory, plaintiffs rely on provisions of the Uniform Commercial Code, Iowa Code chapter 554, and a general warranty argument. We believe this reliance is misplaced.

First, the Uniform Commercial Code does not apply to services; Article Two expressly governs transactions involving goods. *See Semler v. Knowling,* 325 N.W.2d 395, 398-99 (Iowa 1982) (contract predominantly for services not within the scope of Article Two of the U.C.C.). Even assuming that the Uniform Commercial Code may be applied here by analogy, Iowa Code section 554.2313(1)(a) (1977) provides that an express warranty is created by "[a]ny affirmation of fact or promise *made by the seller to the buyer* which relates to the goods and *becomes part of the basis of the bargain*" (emphasis added). It would distort the privity concept articulated in section 554.2313(1)(a) to deem Palmer a "seller" and Moore a "buyer" of chiropractic services under our factual context.

Further, section 554.2313(1)(a) states that the express warranty must serve as part of the "basis of the bargain." There is no evidence under this record that Moore read or relied on any of Palmer's informational material. She testified she did not read any chiropractic literature at Dr. Vanderloo's office. Thus, such literature could not have caused her to seek chiropractic treatment from Dr. Vanderloo. As to Vanderloo's diploma, Moore did not know where he obtained his diploma, or that he even had one, and, thus, it did not serve as the basis of her decision to utilize Vanderloo's services. In fact, plaintiff testified in a deposition that she sought treatment from Dr. Vanderloo on the basis of a recommendation made to her by a previous chiropractor's nurse.

Second, if we assume *arguendo* that a general contractual warranty theory is applicable here, apart from the requirements of section 554.2313, serious problems regarding lack of consideration, privity and the nature of the contractual relationship arise. Moore testified by deposition that she did not read any chiro-

333

practic literature in Dr. Vanderloo's office nor did she know he attended Palmer. To create an express warranty in favor of a person who acted without reliance on representations would distort the express warranty theory. If we held there was a warranty created by a school upon issuance of a diploma or advertisements, absent reliance or privity, we would be opening the door to unlimited liability for all educational institutions, and any one of those that issues general informational literature to the public.

Finally, we note that a graduate of Palmer or any chiropractic school may not practice chiropractic in Iowa without a license. Iowa Code § 147.2. *An applicant for a license must pass an examination in order to receive one, Iowa Code section 147.14(8), and a license may be revoked for incompetency. Iowa Code § 147.55. Therefore, if any type of an express warranty is made regarding the competency of a chiropractor, it is given by the state, not Palmer.*

For these reasons, we reject plaintiffs' theories against defendant Palmer regarding an express warranty [Emphasis added].

B. *Implied warranty claims.* Plaintiffs also contend that Vanderloo's diploma and the advertising by Palmer created an implied warranty to the public. Although the previous discussion in subdivision I-A also would seem to apply to an implied warranty theory, we do not consider this claim made by plaintiffs. There was no argument made, nor authority cited, in plaintiffs' briefs regarding this issue; therefore, it is considered to be waived under our rules of appellate procedure. Iowa R. App. P. 14(a)(3).

C. *Educational malpractice claim.* Plaintiffs also assert that defendant Palmer should be held liable under a negligence theory for failure to teach Dr. Vanderloo, its student for four years previously, certain risks created by manipulation techniques.

Both parties recognize this is a case of first impression in Iowa. Plaintiffs contend that educational malpractice is a viable and necessary theory. Defendant Palmer, on the other hand, offers strong policy reasons for refusing to recognize such an action. In connection with those policy reasons, we consider the cases in other jurisdictions which have faced this issue.

The courts in other jurisdictions have considered questions relating to the quality of education, and, in particular, whether tort liability exists on the part of a public school district for failure to adequately educate a student. These cases have arisen in a limited number of factual contexts and seem to fall into three general categories.

In one type of educational malpractice action, the plaintiffs, a student singly or with his or her parent(s), have argued that, in failing to adequately teach a student basic academic skills, the public school district breached a duty owed to the student under common law, constitutional or statutory provisions, or that the public school district was liable for negligently or intentionally representing that a student was performing at or near grade level in basic academic skills. *See Peter W. v. San Francisco Unified School District,* 60 Cal. App. 3d 814, 131 Cal. Rptr. 854 (1976); *Hunter v. Board of Education,* 292 Md. 481, 439 A.2d 582 (1982); *Donohue v. Copiague Union Free School District,* 47 N.Y.2d 440, 418 N.Y.S.2d 375, 391 N.E.2d 1352 (1979).

A second class of educational malpractice cases has arisen out of claims by a student who was either improperly placed in, or removed from, or negligently failed to be placed in, a special education program. *See Loughran v. Flanders,* 470 F. Supp. 110 (D. Conn. 1979); *D.S.W. v. Fairbanks North Star Borough School District,* 628 P.2d 554 (Alaska 1981); *Smith v. Alameda County Social Services Agency,* 90 Cal. App. 3d 929, 153 Cal. Rptr. 712 (1979); *Tubell v. Dade County Public Schools,* 419 So. 2d 388 (Fla. Dist. Ct. App. 1982); *Doe v. Board of Education,* 295 Md. 67, 453 A.2d 814 (1982); *B.M. v. State,* 649 P.2d 425 (Mont. 1982); *Myers v. Medford Lakes Board of Education,* 199 N.J. Super. 511, 489 A.2d 1240 (1985); *Hoffman v. Board of Education,* 49 N.Y.2d 121, 424 N.Y.S.2d 376, 400 N.E.2d 317 (1979); *Helm v. Professional Children's*

335

School, 103 Misc. 2d 1053, 431 N.Y.S.2d 246 (N.Y. Sup. Ct. 1980).

A final category of educational malpractice was raised in *Swidryk v. Saint Michael's Medical Center,* 201 N.J. Super. 601, 493 A.2d 641 (N.J. Super. Ct. Law Div. 1985). There plaintiff, in his first year of medical residency in obstetrics and gynecology, was named as a defendant in a malpractice action for his participation in the delivery of a child. The resident brought an action against the director of medical education at the hospital alleging that he was inadequately supervised and as a proximate result of this negligence, plaintiff was sued for malpractice.

With the exception of one case, *B.M. v. State,* 649 P.2d 425 (Mont. 1982), the courts in each of these three types of actions have unanimously failed to recognize a cause of action for educational malpractice. These decisions generally hold that such a cause of action seeking damages for acts of negligence in the educational process is precluded by considerations of public policy, among them being the absence of a workable standard of care against which the defendant educational institution's conduct may be measured, the inherent uncertainty in determining the cause and nature of any damages and the extra burden which would be imposed on the schools as well as the judiciary. *Hunter,* 292 Md. at 484-86, 439 A.2d at 584.

Although the factual context in the present case varies slightly from those educational malpractice cases previously cited, the public policy considerations raised in them also apply here and control our resolution of the issue of whether to recognize the tort of educational malpractice in Iowa as to a third party patient of a former student.

The first justification for not recognizing an educational malpractice cause of action is the lack of a satisfactory standard of care by which to measure an educator's conduct. As the California court in *Peter W.* stated:

Unlike the activity of the highway or the marketplace, classroom methodology affords no readily ac-

336

ceptable standards of care, or cause, or injury. The science of pedagogy itself is fraught with different and conflicting theories of how or what a child should be taught, and any layman might — and commonly does — have his own emphatic views on the subject. 60 Cal. App. 3d at 824, 131 Cal. Rptr. at 860-61.

We find this reasoning persuasive. What Palmer should have taught its students is a matter open to debate. Plaintiffs contend that the dangers of a certain manipulation should have been taught to Vanderloo. Whether plaintiffs are arguing that a reasonable chiropractic institution would have taught a student of the dangers or whether a special burden is to be placed on Palmer because of its pioneering efforts in the field of chiropractic is unclear. However, we are not prepared to determine what Palmer or any reasonable chiropractic institution should or would have taught to its students.

The second reason for refusing to recognize a claim of educational malpractice is the inherent uncertainty in determining the cause and nature of any damages. *Hunter,* 292 Md. at 487-88, 439 A.2d at 585. This reason is particularly persuasive in the present case involving a third party claim against an institution for what it allegedly did *not* teach a student, four years after that student graduated. We agree with the New York Court of Appeals' observation that although it may assume too much to conclude that proximate causation could *never* be established, that "this element might indeed be difficult, if not impossible to prove." *Donohue,* 47 N.Y.2d at 443, 418 N.Y.S.2d at 377, 391 N.E.2d at 1353-54.

A third jurisdiction [justification] offered for failure to recognize an educational malpractice cause of action is the resulting burden that would be placed on schools in what reasonably may be predicted to be an ensuing flood of litigation. *Hunter,* 292 Md. at 485-86, 439 A.2d at 584. This is a compelling policy reason in defendant Palmer's favor. As Palmer correctly notes, if a cause of action for educational malpractice is recognized in

Iowa, any malpractice case would have a malpractice action within it. For example a doctor or attorney sued for malpractice by a patient or client might have an action over against his or her educational institution for failure to teach the doctor or attorney how to treat or handle the patient or client's problem. This would deplete a great amount of resources, both in terms of time and money spent by an institution, on litigation. Further, if an educational malpractice claim is allowed against a professional school, could we logically refuse to recognize such a cause of action against an institution offering training courses for certain trades? For example, would a homeowner damaged by faulty wiring have a cause of action against the electrician's trade school?

A fourth reason related by the courts in denying educational malpractice claims that is applicable here is that recognizing such a cause of action would force the courts blatantly to interfere with the internal operations and daily workings of an educational institution. *Donohue,* 47 N.Y.2d at 445, 418 N.Y.S.2d at 378, 391 N.E.2d at 1354. This concern is particularly appropriate in the area of higher education. As the Supreme Court stated in *Regents of the University of Michigan v. Ewing,* 474 U.S. 214, —, 106 S. Ct. 507, 513 (1985):

> When judges are asked to review the substance of a genuinely academic decision ... they should show great respect for the faculty's professional judgment. (Footnote omitted.)

It has been recognized that academic freedom thrives on the autonomous decision-making by the academy itself. *See Regents of the University of California v. Bakke,* 438 U.S. 265, 312, 98 S. Ct. 2733, 2759-60, 57 L. Ed. 2d 750, 785 (1978). In essence, plaintiffs are asking this court to pass judgment on the curriculum of Palmer. We decline to do so.

Finally, we refuse to interfere with legislatively defined standards of competency. *See Swidryk,* 493 A.2d at 644-45. As we noted in division I-A above, the legislature requires a license in order to engage in the practice of chiropractic in Iowa. Iowa Code § 147.2. The examining board of chiropractic, Iowa Code section 147.14(8), administers examinations which must be passed in order for an applicant to receive a license. Licenses may be revoked for incompetency. Iowa Code § 147.55. Thus, the issue of competency is closely related to the licensing scheme contained in Iowa Chapter code 147 and controlled by the State of Iowa.

For these reasons, we conclude the district court correctly dismissed plaintiffs' petition against defendant Palmer.[9]

§9.1(C). Louisiana Pacific v. State.

Another case which tests the theory of educational malpractice in a different dimension is *Louisiana Pacific v. State*.[10] This case was filed in Alaska in 1986 and is summarized as follows:

> ... [P]laintiff is a large lumber company which was forced to pay Worker's Compensation in the form of temporary total disability, and then permanent total disability to an injured worker under Alaska's Workers' Compensation law. The company also paid for the worker to relocate from Ketchikan to Juneau so that he could participate in a vocational rehabilitation program provided by the state Department of Education, Division of Vocational Rehabilitation (DVR).
>
> The rehabilitation plan was at first to train the worker to become a fish hatchery manager. He worked as an assistant manager under the guidance of a hatchery manager in Metlakatla, an Indian tribal reservation. Tribal officials soon asked the manager, the injured worker's mentor, to leave his hatchery position. Thus, the worker was left without a program. State vocational rehabilitation officials then approved

---

9. *Id.* at 112-15.

10. Louisiana Pacific Corp. v. Board of Education, No. 1 JU-86-317 Civil, in the Superior Court for the State of Alaska, First Judicial District at Juneau (1986).

his enrollment in a fisheries program at the University of Alaska-Juneau in an attempt to train him as a fish culturist. By the time he finished the program, however, the market for fish culturists had eroded, partially because the same law firm which represents plaintiff brought a successful lawsuit challenging the tax which supported the fish hatcheries. There is also a question as to whether the worker was physically capable of doing the work. At any rate, the worker found it difficult to get a job as a fish culturist, and the Workers' Compensation Board declared him to be totally and permanently disabled. Plaintiff seeks damages from DVR, alleging that the division of vocational rehabilitation decision to train the worker was made negligently. Plaintiff asserts that if DVR counseling had not been negligent, the person would have been trained for and successful at some other occupation.

The state brought a motion to dismiss on the ground that the Alaska Supreme Court had declined to recognize a cause of action for educational malpractice in *D.S.W. v. Fairbanks North Star Borough School District*, 628 P.2d 554 (Alaska, 1981). The court denied the motion and the case is now in the discovery stage.[11]

More specifically, the complaint alleges:

1. Defendant Ira Rosnel was a vocational rehabilitation counselor in the offices for Vocational Rehabilitation in Ketchikan, a division of the state under the Board of Education, State of Alaska.
2. The defendant State of Alaska, Board of Education, pursuant to AS 23.15.010-.210, has implemented a program operating through the Division of Vocational Rehabilitation (DVR) to offer vocational retraining and counseling services to certain disabled (handicapped) persons who meet their qualifications. DVR should conduct those services in a pro-

_____

11. Excerpt from a letter from Thomas E. Wagner, Assistant Attorney General, State of Alaska, written to the author and dated November 13, 1986 in response to author's request for cases filed in the State of Alaska.

fessional manner with the same level of competence as is displayed by and required of all others engaged in performing those services.

3. On or about September 24, 1980, DVR, through Ira Rosnel, began working with Charles Maccagno, an impaired worker who had suffered a back injury at the Annette Hemlock Mill, Metlakatla, Alaska.

4. DVR and Ira Rosnel failed to perform the services and counseling for Maccagno in a competent, professional, and complete manner to the standards established by vocational counselors in Alaska and in the Pacific Northwest states.

5. Maccagno was placed by the defendants in an educational program to become a fish culturist. The defendants advised plaintiff that this was an appropriate vocational rehabilitation plan. The plaintiff, relying upon the advice of the defendants, relying upon the defendants' plan because they held themselves out as professional vocational rehabilitation counselors and claimed to be skilled in such services, paid Charles Maccagno temporary total disability benefits under the Alaska Workers' Compensation Act throughout the period of his educational program. The plaintiff also advanced funds in the amount of Five Thousand Dollars ($5,000.00) to facilitate Mr. Maccagno's move from Metlakatla, Alaska to Juneau, Alaska in order to continue with the fish culturist program at UAJ as that program was designed, arranged, implemented, and supervised by the defendants.

6. Upon completion of the fish culturist program, it was found that Charles Maccagno did not have the physical capacities to engage in that occupation and that even if he had those physical capacities, the training he had taken would not realistically, within the scope of those seeking jobs as fish culturists, have provided him with employment.

7. Since he could not work as a fish culturist and could not return to his former employment, Charles Maccagno requested additional benefits through the Alaska Workers' Compensation Board. The

341

Alaska Workers' Compensation Board determined that Charles Maccagno was not required by law to continue with additional vocational rehabilitation training, that he could not perform work in his prior employment fields or as a fish culturist, and that he was permanently and totally disabled.

8. On account of the defendants' negligence in following appropriate procedures to determine an appropriate retraining program for Charles Maccagno, the plaintiff has had to pay additional periods of temporary total disability which it would otherwise not have had to pay and it will have to continue to pay Charles Maccagno permanent total disability because he has not and will not be able to be retrained to return to employment.

9. The plaintiff has been damaged to the extent of the payments made on account of the negligence of the defendants and by the additional costs of vocational counselors, for attorneys and the litigation costs it has incurred on account of that negligence.[12]

The defendants filed motions to dismiss for failure to state a claim upon which relief can be granted. In the memorandum accompanying the motion filed by the defendant, State of Alaska, Board of Education, Division of Vocational Rehabilitation, the defendant urged the court to dismiss the case by reasoning:

The determination of whether an individual can eventually return to the work force is a difficult and complex decision, even when his or her medical condition is stable [citation omitted]. If an employer could state a cause of action for damages whenever the agency provided services to an injured person whose reintegration into the work force is not a foregone conclusion, and that reintegration is not eventually achieved, the agency would be deterred from providing services to any but the most minimally handicapped. Surely our society cannot afford such a stingy public policy to-

---

12. Complaint, Louisiana Pac. Corp., *supra* note 10, at 1-3.

wards the handicapped. If errors occur, and errors are bound to occur in any human venture, the agency should not be placed in a position of liability if it errs on the side of attempting to help a severely injured individual return to the work force when, it turns out later, that the effort was to no avail.

The Alaska Supreme Court has declined to recognize a cause of action against a school district for negligent classification, placement, or teaching of its students in *D.S.W. v. Fairbanks North Star Borough School District*, 628 P.2d 554 (Alaska 1981), involving claims by dyslexic students that the school district had failed to provide adequate remedial education. The *D.S.W.* court relied on *Peter W. v. San Francisco Unified School District*, 131 Cal. Rptr. 854 (Cal. App. 1976), in which the court defined the problem as whether an actionable duty of care existed, which is essentially a public policy question involving the following considerations:

> The foreseeability of harm to the plaintiff, the degree of certainty that the plaintiff suffered injury, the closeness of the connection between the defendant's conduct and the injury suffered, the moral blame attached to the defendant's conduct, the policy of preventing future harm, the extent of the burden to the defendant and consequences to the community of imposing a duty to exercise care with resulting liability for breach, and the availability, cost and prevalence of insurance for the risk involved.

628 P.2d at 555, quoting *Peter W.,* 131 Cal. Rptr. at 859-60. In a footnote, the Alaska court indicated it applied a similar list of factors in determining whether a cause of action for negligent misrepresentation should exist in *Howarth v. Pfeifer*, 443 P.2d 39, 42 (Alaska 1968). 628 P.2d at 555 n.1.[13]

The defendant further argued:

---

13. Memorandum in Support of State's Motion to Dismiss, Louisiana Pac. Corp., *supra* note 10, at 4-5.

The *D.S.W.* court also relied on *Donohue v. Copiague Union Free School District,* 391 N.W.2d 1352 (N.Y. 1979); *Hoffman v. Board of Education of the City of New York,* 400 N.E.2d 317 (N.Y. 1979); and *Smith v. Alameda County Social Services Agency,* 153 Cal. Rptr. 712 (Cal. App. 1979), which reached similar conclusions. *Hoffman* and *Smith* involved claims of misfeasance rather than nonfeasance, that students with normal learning abilities had negligently been placed in classes for the mentally retarded. The Alaska court expressly adopted the reasoning of *Peter W.* and *Smith,* thus itself rejecting any distinction between misfeasance and nonfeasance. 628 P.2d at 556. *Accord, Hunter v. Board of Ed. of Montgomery County,* 439 A.2d 582 (Md. App. 1982).

The policy reasons for rejecting educational malpractice claims in the public schools apply with equal force in the context at issue here, and apply with even more force when the claimant is not a student who alleges damages as the result of an inadequate educational program, but a third party such as the injured worker's employer.

The assessment of whether and to what extent an injured worker is physically and academically capable of being retrained to return to the workforce is subject to different and conflicting theories of how or what the person should be taught, and his or her progress is subject to the same factors, physical, neurological, emotional, cultural, and environmental, outside the control of the vocational rehabilitation counselors, which precluded the *Peter W.* court from finding any workable "rule of care against which defendant's conduct may be measured," any "degree of certainty that plaintiff suffered injury" within the meaning of the law, and any perceptible "connection between the defendant's conduct and the injury suffered" as alleged which would establish a causal link between them. Moreover, the "foreseeability of harm to the plaintiff" is much more problematic in this context, where there is the possibility that the third party employer will benefit, by way of reduced liability for worker's com-

344

pensation payments, if vocational rehabilitation services are provided and are successful.

For the above reasons, this court should reject any cause of action based upon defendant's decision to provide vocational rehabilitation services to plaintiff's former employee.[14]

The state concluded its memorandum by stating:

> In *D.S.W.*, the Alaska court noted that its refusal to recognize a cause of action for damages did not leave without recourse parents who believed their children had been inappropriately classified or placed in education programs. It cited the provisions for administrative appeal and judicial review of educational placement decisions in the state and federal statutes. 628 P.2d at 557, n. 2-3.
>
> Similar provisions for administrative and judicial review exist here. The handicapped individual who is dissatisfied with agency decisions has appeal rights under the state plan for vocational rehabilitation services. *See* 34 C.F.R. Part 361.48. An employer dissatisfied with decisions made by the Workers' Compensation Board as to how much compensation it must pay has appeal rights under AS 23.30.125 and 23.30.170. Defendant understands that plaintiff is presently exercising such appeal rights in this case. *See Louisiana Pacific Corp., Annette Hemlock Mill Division v. Maccagno,* Nos. 1JU-85-97 Civ. and 1JU-85-1500 Civ., in the Superior Court for the State of Alaska, First Judicial District at Juneau. Thus, as in *D.S.W.* rejection by this court of a cause of action for damages will not leave persons dissatisfied with vocational rehabilitation decisionmaking without recourse to correct erroneous decisions.[15]

The defendant, Rosnel, in a memorandum filed in support of his Motion to Dismiss, stated that in addition to the arguments advanced by the State:

---

14. *Id.* at 7-8.
15. *Id.* at 10.

.... [U]nder the doctrine of *Earth Movers of Fair-banks v. State,* 691 P.2d 281 (Alaska 1984), a state official is immune from personal liability for damages caused by a mistake in judgment or discretion, so long as the official acts pursuant to his or her official duties, or so long as the official made a determination that the acts complained of were within the scope of his or her official duties.

In this case, educational malpractice is alleged on the part of Mr. Rosnel, a vocational rehabilitation counselor. The allegation is either that Rosnel was negligent in determining that plaintiff's former employee was eligible for vocational rehabilitation services, or that the program provided him was inappropriate. In either case, the determinations allegedly made by Mr. Rosnel were clearly within the scope of his official duties.[16]

In his Memorandum in Opposition to Motion to Dismiss Defendant Rosnel, the plaintiff argues:

The public policy decision of *D.S.W. v. Fairbanks Northstar Borough School District,* 628 P.2d 554 (Alaska 1981) which precludes cases of "educational malpractice," refers principally to the claims that the school "failed to teach Johnny to read." Even educational malpractice becomes a viable claim in many jurisdictions if the relief requested is not damages for an individual student/parents, but a mandate to spend funds for certain programs or facilities. Ratner, "A New Legal Duty for Urban Schools: Effective Education in Basic Skills," Tex. L. Rev. Vol. 63, No. 5, pp. 777-864 (Feb. 1985). At pages 851-858 of this article, Mr. Ratner specifically demonstrates how the elements of a tort claim can be found in a claim of educational malpractice.

However, unlike a school, DVR, as alleged in the complaint, did not teach or attempt to educate, or present classes to Maccagno. It is clear from the com-

---

16. Memorandum in Support of Defendant Rosnel's Motion to Dismiss, Louisiana Pacific Corp., *supra* note 10, at 1.

plaint that this is not a claim that DVR failed to teach Maccagno properly, for rather DVR set out a plan and placed Maccagno at UAJ for education as a fish culturist. No claim is being made against UAJ for failure to teach Maccagno to be a *good* fish culturist.

Since the court has no intrinsic knowledge that malpractice by a DVR counselor would be more like "educational malpractice" than malpractice by numerous other professions including doctors, dentists, nurses, emergency medical technicians, lawyers, accountants, pharmacists, architects, engineers, title abstractors, funeral directors, insurance agents and brokers, police officers, and every type of artisan and craftsman who does not do a job to the level of skill required for that trade, how does the State expect this court to deny this case on the basis of a Civil Rule 12(b)(6) motion. It should be clear already that if, as alleged in the complaint, there is a routine standard practice followed by vocational rehabilitation counselors to learn the physical and mental capabilities of clients and to thereby devise an appropriate plan for that person to reenter the job market, and that in the Maccagno case DVR counselor failed to follow these procedures causing damage to Maccagno and LP, then we have on its face a situation more like that of a physician or accountant and so on, than that of a question of competing educational theories.

In order for this court to decide that there was no duty under any conceivable set of circumstances for a DVR counselor to provide a plan in a competent manner, at least this court would have to analyze the standards set out for public policy considerations as enumerated in *D.S.W. vs. Fairbanks Northstar Borough School District,* 628 P.2d 554 (Alaska 1981). But that would have to be done under a motion for summary judgment where the court could consider the facts which might be applicable to a question of duty.

In the case of *Linck v. Barokos & Martin,* 667 P.2d 171 (Alaska 1983) our court has confirmed that a claim for professional malpractice has the same elements as a tort of negligence. In the case of *City of Kotzebue v*

347

McLean, 702 P.2d 1309, 1313-15 (Alaska 1985) the court, using the analytical factors of *D.S.W., supra* decided that a City police officer has a duty to promptly respond to a life threatening phone call under the particular facts there presented. At page 1313, the court said:

> The basic question is whether the defendant has undertaken a responsibility. If it has, and it has failed adequately to discharge that responsibility, it may be liable to people who have been injured ....
> ... We decline to follow a doctrine which automatically insulates government from liability for failure to exercise reasonable care in the delivery of their services.

The case above weighs heavily in favor of denying State DVR's requested dismissal and supports a summary judgment determination in LP's favor on the issue of duty.[17]

The plaintiff continued his argument:

> The "continental divide" case in New York, which for public policy reasons disallowed "educational malpractice" claims, recognized that under traditional tort concepts a claim had been stated:

> > Appellant's first cause of action bears closer scrutiny. It may very well be that even within the strictures of a traditional negligence or malpractice action, a complaint sounding in "educational malpractice" may be formally pleaded. Thus, the imagination need not be overly taxed to envision allegations of a legal duty of care flowing from educators, if viewed as professionals, to their students. If doctors, lawyers, architects, engineers, and other professionals are charged with a duty owing to the public whom they serve, it could be said that nothing in the law precludes similar treatment of professional educators. Nor would creation of a standard with which to judge an educator's performance of that duty nec-

---

17. Opposition to Motion to Dismiss Defendant Rosnel, Louisiana Pac. Corp., *supra* note 10, at 3-5.

essarily pose an insurmountable obstacle. (*See generally* Elson, *A Common Law Remedy for the Educational Harms Caused by Incompetent or Careless Teaching,* 73 N.W.L.Rev. 641, 693-744.) As for proximate causation, while this element might indeed be difficult, if not impossible, to prove in view of the many collateral factors involved in the learning process, it perhaps assumes too much to conclude that it could never be established. This would leave only the element of injury and who can in good faith deny that a student who upon graduation from high school cannot comprehend simple English — a deficiency allegedly attributable to the negligence of his educators — has not in some fashion been "injured."

The public policy considerations enunciated in *D.S.W., supra,* and alluded to in *Donohue, supra* need to be discussed as they apply to State DVR. The foreseeability of harm to the client is readily apparent. The fact that the client will be unable to find employment in that field, makes the degree of certainty that the client suffered injury rather strong. There is a rather close connection between the DVR counselor's failure to perform a routine task, and the injury suffered. If LP is able to prove that at the initiation of the fish culturalist program in 1981 after Maccagno's second back surgery, no physical capacities evaluation or physician's approval of an on-site job analysis of fish culturalist were performed and that if they had been performed, the physicians would have ruled out fish culturalist as an occupation, cause can hardly be doubted.

Other public policy considerations stated in *D.S.W.* are whether moral blame should be attached to the defendant's conduct. This should not be analyzed in the sense of being criminal or wrong, but rather whether one would place blame on a professional person in not having followed regular procedures in order to do a correct analysis and thereby hopefully make a more appropriate decision. The policy of preventing future harm is certainly enhanced by allowing the

349

claim. Following suit, it is more unlikely that State DVR will allow shoddy practices and plans to continue.

Another policy consideration is the extent of the burden to the defendant State DVR. In the educational malpractice situation, the burden could be extremely broad based for a public school provides general public education aimed at no specific goal, occupation, earning capacity, or level of achievement. Free public schools present all children (rather uniquely in the world) the opportunity to achieve. However, vocational rehabilitation counselors have one client at a time for whom they are developing one plan for reemployment at a time. A finding of negligence in this instance does not make the entire Division, all DVR counselors, or all their plans suspect or problematic. An adjacent consideration is the consequences to the community of imposing a duty to exercise care with the resulting liability for breach. That is important in an educational malpractice situation with the multitude of students in general public education, but not a concern in the individual case of a client and a specific DVR counselor or vocational rehabilitation agency. The final consideration enunciated in *D.S.W., supra* is the availability, cost and prevalence of insurance for the risk involved. The State, of course, is self-insured to a large extent, and it would take discovery to determine whether individuals such as DVR counselors have insurance beyond a certain limit provided by the State. It is suspected, however, that they do so in a broad general coverage for all officers, agents, and State officials.[18]

He concludes:

If this court decides to treat this only as a Civil Rule 12(b)(6) motion, a denial of the motion is the only appropriate result since the State has provided no factual basis from which the court could determine that there should be no duty from a professional rehabilitation counselor to the client to perform the job in a compe-

_____

18. *Id.* at 10-12.

tent manner to the standards of professionalism of all vocational rehabilitation counselors in the region. If this court in its discretion decides to treat this as a Civil Rule 56 summary judgment motion, it should determine that this is not a case asserting a claim because "Johnny wasn't taught to read," but rather a case of professional malpractice much like that against a physician, lawyer, dentist, nurse, accountant, engineer, and so on. The vocational rehabilitation counselor simply failed to follow standard procedures (analogous to taking an X-ray or checking the statute of limitations), and that failure resulted in Mr. Maccagno's being trained for a job he could not have performed, and not being trained for a job he could have performed. Finally, the Court should find that LP is entitled to bring this claim in spite of the fact that a portion of any recovery might belong to Maccagno under AS 23.30.015.[19]

The court, in denying the motions to dismiss, stated:

Defendants' motions to dismiss for failure to state a cause of action are denied. As noted by the plaintiff, such motions are disfavored and must be denied "unless it appears beyond doubt that the plaintiff can prove no set of facts in support of his claim which would entitle him to relief," *Shooshanian v. Wagner,* 672 P.2d 455, 460-61 (Alaska 1983), quoting *Conley v. Gibson,* 355 U.S. 41, 45-46, 2 L. Ed. 2d 80, 84 (1957). While the case law appears scant, at best, concerning the liability of vocational rehabilitation counselors, this court is unwilling to say at this stage that under no circumstances could a cause of action sounding in malpractice be made out against such a person. In effect, that is what the state asks the court to do by filing a Civ. R. 12(b)(6) motion.

As to the separate argument that the claim against defendant Rosnel should be dismissed because he was performing an act within his official duties, the motion is denied. On the basis of the record to date, this court

---

19. *Id.* at 14.

cannot say whether this defendant's acts (assuming they involved any negligence at all), were "mistaken 'discretionary judgment-policy decisions'", *Earth Movers of Fairbanks, Inc. v. State,* 691 P.2d 281, 285 (Alaska 1984) (Rabinowitz, J., concurring), quoting from *State v. Stanley,* 506 P.2d 1284, 1292 (Alaska 1973), which would be immune, or were merely negligently performed acts not involving such discretionary judgment-policy decisions, which would not be immune. *Id.* Under these circumstances, the alternative motion to dismiss as to defendant Rosnel must be denied.[20]

The case was set for trial. When the trial began it was determined, due to technical reasons, that the case could not be completed within the allocated time. Consequently, the case was reset for trial in May 1990. Subsequently, the case was settled by a stipulation to dismiss plaintiffs' claims, each side to bear its own costs and attorneys fees.

§ 9.1(D). Hampton v. Tennessee Board of Law Examiners.

Another case involving a school being sued indirectly is *Hampton v. Tennessee Board of Law Examiners.*[21]

The complaint alleged violation of plaintiffs' due process and equal protection rights because defendants denied them the right to practice law and admission to the Tennessee bar. Essentially, the plaintiffs contended that because of a conspiracy or conspiracies between or among certain of the named defendants (allegedly in furtherance of an unspecified "quota" system), their admission to the Tennessee bar was denied. Plaintiffs contended that the

---

20. Order Denying Motions to Dismiss, Louisiana Pac. Corp., *supra* note 10, at 1-2.

21. Hampton v. Tennessee Board of Law Examiners. In the United States District Court for the Western District, Civil Action No. 86-2476-GB.

conspiracy was undertaken, and the decision made to exclude them, before they ever took the bar examination. The plaintiffs do not describe the "quota" they suspect exists, nor do they suggest the motive, or the exact nature, of the alleged conspiracy.[22]

The complaint further alleged in the alternative that:

> ... [D]efendant Cecil C. Humphreys faculty and staff, have committed fraud and intentionally [intentional] misrepresentation in that plaintiffs were awarded juris doctorate degrees certifying at least average competence upon successful completion of what was purported to be an academically proficient course of study when graduates are not capable of successfully passing minimum competence tests in order to obtain certification for a license, even upon supplementing their law school studies with two months of intensive study in review of their law school subjects.[23]

The defendants' motion to dismiss the action was granted and affirmed by the United States Court of Appeals for the Sixth Circuit.

§ 9.1(E). Washington v. City of New York.

In this action a suspended student brought an educational malpractice action seeking monetary damages arising out of a suspension. The Supreme Court, Queens County, dismissed the complaint.[24] The case was appealed to the supreme court, appellate division. The alleged facts were:

> Lamont Washington was suspended from his school on March 1, 1977 for assaulting a teacher and possess-

----

22. Memorandum in Support of Defendants' Motion to Dismiss, Hampton, *supra* note 21, at 1-2.

23. Complaint, Hampton, *supra* note 21, at 9.

24. Washington v. City of New York, 83 A.D.2d 866, 442 N.Y.S.2d 20 (1981).

ing a knife. Following the subsequent suspension hearing held pursuant to section 3214 (subd. 3, par. c) of the Education Law, these facts were confirmed and Lamont was indefinitely suspended for cause. It was recommended that he be examined by the school board's Evaluation and Placement Unit to determine his best interests and the matter was also referred to the Family Court (Education Law, § 3214, subd. 3, par. e). The record reveals that Leonard Washington, Lamont's father, did not co-operate with school officials either in evaluating Lamont or in placing him in a special education facility following a determination by the local Committee on the Handicapped that this would be appropriate.

Lamont did not attend school for a period of about 14 months; the suspension terminated when Leonard Washington notified defendant Julius Zeidman, Supervisor of Guidance of Community School District Number 29, that Lamont was being enrolled in a school in Niagara Falls, New York.[25]

In affirming the case, the court stated:

This action, seeking monetary damages, *claims educational malpractice,* denial of due process rights, breach of an implied contractual duty to educate, improper suspension without cause, and conspiracy to deprive Lamont of his education. Special Term properly dismissed the complaint.

On appeal, plaintiffs' attempt to assert that Lamont's (subsequently determined) status as an "emotionally handicapped" child entitles him to certain procedural safeguards under relevant Federal and State statutes. We need not nor do we address this contention as it was neither raised at Special Term nor alleged in the complaint. There is no factual basis, upon our review of the record, to support any of plaintiffs' contentions. Monetary damages for educational malpractice are not recoverable. (*Donohue v. Copiague Union School Dist.,* 47 N.Y.2d 440, 418 N.Y.S.2d 375,

25. *Id.* at 21.

391 N.E.2d 1352; *Hoffman v. Board of Educ.*, 49 N.Y.2d 121, 424 N.Y.S.2d 376, 400 N.E.2d 317.) We note Leonard Washington's apparent obstructive actions throughout the course of events leading to the present litigation. The indefinite suspension pending Lamont's evaluation was proper and Leonard Washington affirmatively thwarted efforts to place Lamont once his status as "handicapped" had been determined. Plaintiffs were accorded their constitutional rights during these proceedings and may not now be heard to object when they neither took full advantage of these rights nor exhausted the administrative remedies available to them (Education Law, § 310, subd. 7) (emphasis added).[26]

§ 9.1(F). Cavello   v.   Sherburne-Earlville   Cent. School.

The facts, as related by the courts, are as follows:

Plaintiffs [are the parents of two infant children, who are also named as plaintiffs.] The allegations of the complaint, which are assumed to be true for purposes of the motion to dismiss for failure to state a cause of action which is the subject of this appeal (*Cohn v. Lionel Corp.*, 21 N.Y.2d 559, 562, 289 N.Y.S.2d 404, 236 N.E.2d 634), assert the following: that in January of 1983, the Cavello family moved to Chenango County where Tina and AJ thereupon enrolled as high school students in defendant, Sherburne-Earlville Central School District; soon after starting classes, Tina was ceaselessly badgered by another female student named Bobby Jo; verbal abuse, foul language, death threats and the brandishing of a knife characterized the ongoing harassment which Tina claims to have suffered for nearly a year; Tina's brother AJ was subjected to considerably less, but like, harassment.

It is further alleged that plaintiffs repeatedly advised defendant's guidance counselors, dean of students and superintendent of schools of the intimidat-

---

26. *Id.*

ing conditions created by Bobby Jo, and thereafter, by the latter's sister and friends, and that to protect Tina, defendant's officials first segregated her from other students by having her study in the guidance offices and later arranged for tutoring at home. As a specific example of reckless disregard for the safety of Tina, plaintiffs point to an instance when a school guidance counselor "placed Tina and Bobby Jo in a room, telling Bobby Jo to lock the door from the inside and 'settle your differences'." Plaintiffs further state that school officials informed the parents in February 1984 that "it was too dangerous for their children Tina and Anthony, Jr. to come to school and stated that the District would provide the children a correspondence course."

The complaint concludes that negligent handling of the problem by defendant's officials deprived the Cavello children of education and training and subjected them to the continuous emotional distress, for all of which the children seek compensatory damages. In addition to damages for emotional distress, the parents also seek to recover those sums they maintain they will be obliged to expend in the future to secure an appropriate education for their children.

Special Term embraced defendant's suggestion that plaintiffs' complaint sounded only in educational malpractice, a cause of action not recognized in New York (*Hoffman v. Board of Educ. of City of N.Y.*, 49 N.Y.2d 121, 424 N.Y.S.2d 376, 400 N.E.2d 317; *Donohue v. Copiague Union Free School Dist.*, 47 N.Y.2d 440, 418 N.Y.S.2d 375, 391 N.E.2d 1352), and dismissed the complaint in its entirety. Plaintiffs contend that their complaint merely charges defendant with common-law negligence, that of failing to provide adequate supervision over students under its control.[27]

The court, in reaching its conclusion, reasoned as follows:

The *Donohue* and *Hoffman* decisions undeniably

---

27. Cavello v. Sherburne-Earlville Central Sch. Dist., 110 A.D.2d 253, 494 N.Y.S.2d 466, 467 (A.D.3 Dept. 1985).

preclude students from suing school officials for an alleged failure to reach educational objectives. Accordingly, to the extent that the complaint seeks recovery on behalf of the infant plaintiffs for lost education and training due to the school's alleged negligence, no cause of action lies. Nor do the parents enjoy a cause of action for the cost of providing Tina and AJ with alternative education; any such claim necessarily falls within the ambit of foreclosed claims, since it too implicates the quality of education defendant provided.

That parents have, as they now concede, no cause of action for emotional distress is also clear (*Bovsun v. Sanperi*, 61 N.Y.2d 219, 473 N.Y.S.2d 357, 461 N.E.2d 843). However, unlike the parents' claims in this regard, which have no legally cognizable underpinning, those of Tina and AJ for emotional suffering due to defendant's negligent supervision of other students are predicated on well-recognized principles: first, that if there is a duty owed by a defendant to a plaintiff, a breach of that duty resulting directly in emotional harm is compensable even though physical harm is lacking (*Kennedy v. McKesson Co.*, 48 N.Y.2d 500, 504, 462 N.Y.S.2d 421, 448 N.E.2d 1332), and second, that a school district is obliged to adequately supervise the activities of students within its charge. (Citations omitted). And while a school is not an insurer of student safety, it will be held liable in damages for a foreseeable injury proximately related to the absence of supervision (*Lauricella v. Board of Educ. of City of Buffalo*, 52 A.D.2d 710, 711, 381 N.Y.S.2d 566, *supra*). In *Hoose v. Drumm*, 281 N.Y. 54, 22 N.E.2d 233 for example, evidence that teachers were aware that pupils tore off goldenrod stalks and threw them at other students, thereby causing serious injury to the eye of one of the students, suggested that the teachers were at fault; significantly, the court noted that "[t]he effective cause of the plaintiff's injuries was a failure [by the teachers] to protect the boys against themselves" (*id* at 58, 22 N.E.2d 233).

357

The complaint herein, on behalf of the infants, alleges that the parents again and again notified the school about the harassment of Tina and AJ by other students; it particularizes the response by school officials to the infant plaintiffs' plight and concludes that defendant's handling of the situation was negligent and caused the children emotional distress. In our view, the infant plaintiffs' complaint is legally sufficient for it presents a question of fact concerning whether defendant reasonably discharged its duty to supervise the students.[28]

§ 9.1(G). Aubrey v. School District of Philadelphia.

A student and her parents filed suit to recover damages for severe emotional distress and mental anguish, damage to reputation, damage to employment qualifications, and loss of time and wages, from school district after student failed required health education class which covered sexual material. The Court of Common Pleas of Philadelphia County dismissed the complaint in trespass against the School District of Philadelphia and plaintiffs appealed to the commonwealth court.[29] More specifically, the alleged facts were:

> During her senior year of high school, the district required Aubrey to attend a health education class which included coverage of sexual material, and to take an examination on that material. As a result of her grade on the exam, Aubrey failed the health course, and was not permitted to participate in graduation exercises with her class. After successfully completing a summer health course, Aubrey received a high school diploma.
>
> Aubrey and her parents filed a complaint seeking money damages for severe emotional distress and

---

28. *Id.* at 467-68.

29. Aubrey, et al. v. School Dist. of Philadelphia, Pa. Commw., 437 A.2d 1306 (1981).

mental anguish, damage to reputation, damage to employment qualifications, and loss of time and wages. They alleged that the district's program: (1) expressly violated Section 1512 of the Public Code of 1919, because it was not adapted to the age, development, and needs of the pupils; (2) violated the Aubreys' parental rights to make a reasonable selection of the subjects to be studied by their child; (3) breached, without notice, the district's past course of conduct whereby students who failed the health class had participated in graduation ceremonies; (4) was arbitrarily conducted through the "grossly misleading and capriciously graded" examination; (5) deprived Aubrey of liberty and property interests without a hearing; and (6) invaded Aubrey's "right of privacy" under the 9th and 14th Amendments of the Constitution.

The district responded with preliminary objections in the nature of a general demurrer, asserting that the complaint failed to state a claim upon which relief could be granted. Judge Wilson agreed, stating:

> Because of the public policy that money damage actions should not lie against a school district for its exercise of educational policy, because no action for money damages lies for educational malpractice, and because of the long line of cases that keeps the courts out of educational policy, this Court is compelled, and has dismissed plaintiffs' Complaint for failure to state a cause of action.

The Aubreys contend that the court's reliance on the educational malpractice doctrine is misplaced; claiming that those cases are limited to allegations of negligence, the Aubreys insist that the district's action amounted to a gross violation of a defined public policy, to be properly remedied through the award of money damages.[30]

In affirming, the court stated:

Of the cases cited by Judge Wilson, *Donohue v.*

---

30. *Id.* at 1306-07.

Copiague Union Free School, 47 N.Y.2d 440, 418
N.Y.S.2d 375, 391 N.E.2d 1352 (1979) is most clarify-
ing. In disposing of a student's claim for money damages based on the district's alleged failure to teach him
English skills, the court distinguished between the
two causes of action present in the case — one alleging
a negligent breach of the constitutional duty to educate, and the other sounding in "educational malpractice."

Although the court explored the feasibility of "a legal duty of care flowing from educators, if viewed as
professionals, to their students," it also recognized the
public policy considerations of those actions, stating:

> To entertain a cause of action for 'educational mal-
> practice' would require the courts not merely to
> make judgments as to the validity of broad educa-
> tional policies — a course we have unalteringly es-
> chewed in the past — but, more importantly, to sit in
> review of the day-to-day implementation of these
> policies. Recognition in the courts of this cause of
> action would constitute blatant interferences with a
> responsibility for the administration of the public
> school system lodged by Constitution and statute in
> school administrative agencies. *Donohue* at 445, 418
> N.Y.S.2d at 378, 391 N.E.2d 1352.

Our Supreme Court voiced the same concern in
Regan v. Stoddard, 361 Pa. 469, 65 A.2d 240 (1949),
when Philadelphia taxpayers sought injunctions to
change courses of study and methods of promoting pupils. Affirming the dismissal of the complaint, the
court held that "the discretion of school authorities
will be interfered with only when there is a clear abuse
of it, and the burden of showing such an abuse is a
heavy one." *Regan* at 473, 65 A.2d at 242, citing *Hibbs
v. Arensberg,* 276 Pa. 24, 119 A. 727 (1923).

The present case is clearly outside the realm of
"manifestly illegal action ... violating the express
words of statutes defining [the school board's] powers,
or ... bad faith in violation of their public duty," which

might justify judicial interference. *Regan* 361 Pa. at 473, 65 A.2d at 242. The district's graduation and curriculum requirements are in accordance with state law and regulations, which mandate the successful completion of a health education class [footnotes omitted].

The courtroom is not the proper forum for resolution of personal conflicts arising from the State Board of Education's 1969 decision to include sex education in the public school curriculum, the district's program to comply with that decision, nor the pupil's failing grade on a test of that subject matter.[31]

§9.2. Summary.

In the last several chapters, an attempt has been made to bring together, as well as to summarize, the cases relating to academic negligence. Some of the cases relating to academic negligence were brought on the theory of educational malpractice while others were filed under other theories that "sounded like" or had some element(s) of academic or educational malpractice. An analysis of many cases is important in order that those interested can see what kinds of cases end up in court and perhaps determine "the why." These cases differ from the traditional school litigation involving educators' liability for care, safety, and supervision of students, in that these cases address actual instruction. Educators generally agree that proper instruction is their most important duty.[32] As we have seen, courts have used many arguments in deciding these cases. It is obvious, however, that some of the courts are troubled with these cases and are trying to reach solutions that embrace all the parties concerned. The next several chapters will examine these arguments and will test their validity and

---

31. *Id.* at 1307-08.

32. Carter, Sr., "The Educator and the Liability Law of Professional Malpractice: A Historical Analysis." Paper presented at the 1979 AERA Annual Convention, San Francisco, California (April 8-12, 1979), p. 3.

consistency with legal, educational, and philosophical principles.

PART III

ANALYSIS OF ARGUMENTS
ADVANCED FOR AND AGAINST
RECOGNIZING EDUCATIONAL
MALPRACTICE VIEWED
FROM THE EDUCATIONAL,
LEGAL AND PHILOSOPHICAL
PERSPECTIVES — EVALUATION
OF FINDINGS — APPLICATION
OF VALIDITY CRITERIA

363

Chapter 10

EDUCATIONAL MALPRACTICE—THE NOVEL ISSUE ARGUMENT

§ 10.0.   Introduction.
§ 10.1.   Judicial Intervention in the Educational System.
§ 10.2.   Educational Malpractice Contrasted With Malpractice in Other Professions.
§ 10.3.   Educational Malpractice — The Novel Issue Argument.
§ 10.4.   Summary.

> The common law ... does expand with reason. The common law is not a compendium of mechanical rules written in fixed and indelible characters, but a living organism which grows and moves in response to the larger and fuller development of the nation.[1]

§ 10.0. Introduction.

Some of the arguments for and against creating a new cause of action — academic negligence — or as more commonly referred to, "educational malpractice," will be presented and analyzed in the next several chapters. The arguments will be examined from several perspectives, i.e., educational, legal, ethical, and philosophical. An argument may be sound from the legal perspective, but when it is viewed from the practical point of view or from the educational perspective, it may have the opposite effect. The previous chapters presented substantial portions of the texts of opinions of various courts as their justification for deny-

---

1. David Abel, *Can a Student Sue the Schools for Educational Malpractice?*, 44:4 HARVARD EDUCATION REVIEW 416, 425 (November 1974). Copyright © 1974 by the President and Fellows of Harvard College. All rights reserved.

ing recovery to the plaintiffs' claims for educational malpractice. Included in these chapters are also arguments, advanced mainly by dissenting judges, in favor of recognizing educational malpractice as a "new" cause of action. These arguments, as well as arguments advanced by a number of legal and educational writers, will be analyzed.

§ 10.1. Judicial Intervention in the Educational System.

John Elson writes:

> It would seem a common sense conclusion that a student suffers harm when a teacher knowingly or negligently teaches him false information, destroys his confidence through insult or ridicule, teaches in an incomprehensible manner, or does not teach at all. Yet, even in the comparatively rare instances when such not uncommon practices are discovered by higher authorities and an offending teacher is consequently disciplined or dismissed, the teacher's students still have no generally recognized independent legal remedy for the harms suffered from such intolerable teaching practices. The anomaly in this legal posture becomes clear when the denial of a common law remedy to a student whose education is severely impaired by incompetent, careless educators is contrasted with the remedies which the common law now provides to students who are physically injured by the negligence of their teachers, to minors whose guardians do not act in their best interests and to anyone who is injured by the substandard performance of skilled tradesmen or professionals [footnotes omitted].[2]

---

2. John Elson, A Common Law Remedy for the Educational Harm Caused by Incompetent or Careless Teaching, 73 NORTHWESTERN UNIVERSITY LAW REVIEW 641, 644 (1978). Reprinted by special permission of Northwestern University, School of Law #73 (1978), NORTHWESTERN UNIVERSITY LAW REVIEW 641, 644.

There is really no question as to whether the courts have, or can, invade the school system — they have — on many occasions. Historically, school litigation involving educators has centered on issues related to the care, safety, and supervision of students.[3] Courts have not hesitated in deciding how schools should be financed,[4] or whether the school system invoked the correct procedure in suspending[5] or expelling[6] children. Nor have courts refused to decide issues of students' dress,[7] hair grooming,[8] expression,[9] or what school associations[10] they can belong to. Furthermore, courts have not avoided discrimination cases[11] or cases involving charges of teacher incompetency,[12] teacher wrongdoings,[13] and teacher dismissals.[14]

Even though there may have been some initial concern and hesitancy in accepting and deciding each type of case, slowly but surely the courts have made, and will continue to make, an impact on the educational system. Yet, when called upon to examine the conduct of the teachers and/or the school system concerning actual instruction, courts responded by refusing to get involved in that controversy and

---

3. David G. Carter, Sr., *The Educator and the Liability Law of Professional Malpractice: Historical Analysis.* A paper for the 1979 AERA Annual Convention, San Francisco, California (April 8-12, 1979), pp. 2-3.

4. San Antonio Independent School District v. Rodriquez, 411 U.S. 1, 93 S. Ct. 1278, *rehearing denied* 411 U.S. 959, 93 S. Ct. 1919 (1973).

5. C. Goss v. Lopez, 419 U.S. 565 (1975).

6. Wood v. Strickland, 420 U.S. 308 (1975).

7. Westley v. Rossi, 305 F. Supp. 706 (D. Minn. 1969).

8. Jackson v. Dorrier, 424 F.2d 213 (6th Cir. 1970).

9. Tinker v. Des Moines School District, 393 U.S. 503 (1969).

10. Passel v. Fort Worth Independent School District, 429 S.W.2d 917 (1968); 440 S.W.2d 61 (1969); 453 S.W.2d 888 (1970).

11. Brown v. Topeka, 374 U.S. 483 (1954).

12. Scheelhaase v. Woodbury School District, 488 F.2d 237 (1973).

13. Keefe v. Geanakos, 418 F.2d 359 (1st Cir. 1969).

14. Pickering v. Board of Education, 391 U.S. 563, 88 S. Ct. 1731 (1968).

have advanced a number of reasons as justification for their refusal. The issue that needs to be examined then is "why this policy of non-involvement?" Why are courts so loath to become involved by recognizing a cause of action for educational malpractice? Whether the reasonings of the courts are sound and consistent with previous decisions in the field of education, as well as in other professions such as medicine, psychiatry, law, accountancy, and engineering, is subject to dispute. After all, aren't the courts actually ruling on the performance by the professionals of the various mentioned professions when deciding malpractice cases. Is that any different than actual instruction by teachers? If courts were to apply good and sound legal reasoning, what would be the result? Whose interests need to be protected? Is the present law equitable?

§ 10.2. Educational Malpractice Contrasted With Malpractice in Other Professions.

Some have argued that there are circumstances that differentiate educational malpractice from other forms of professional malpractice. One author, for example, makes the following observation:

1. Medical illness can usually be defined with some precision; consensus can be achieved regarding what constitutes a broken arm or a cancerous tumor. This is not the case, however, when educators are asked to define functional illiteracy.
2. Medical malpractice suits hold doctors accountable to "accepted practice." Generally, there are established practices for remedying particular conditions. But in education, few such practices or procedures are rigorously standardized.
3. In medicine the treatment is usually administered by a single individual within a fixed, usually short, period. In education, many persons with varying degrees of authority participate in a fragmented

368

process, and are responsible in varying degrees for the success or failure of a child's education.

4. The patient is usually passive in medical treatment, and the doctor generally bears sole responsibility for the results. Education, on the other hand, is an interactive process—the child is expected to participate and indicate when he is experiencing difficulties, and the parents are expected to participate too.

5. Unlike a patient, students up to a certain age are compelled to attend schools and participate in prescribed courses.[15]

Generally, in other malpractice cases the parties involved are the professional and the party who employed the professional, while in educational malpractice cases there are generally three interested parties involved: (1) the aggrieved student seeking redress for his alleged loss of education; (2) the school system or educator whose competence or judgment is being challenged; and (3) the general public.[16]

It has been stated that education, beyond all other devices of human origin, is the great equalizer of the conditions of humankind — the balance-wheel of social machinery.[17] Consequently, it has been asserted that "to a very significant degree, educational institutions 'select persons to fulfill the hierarchy of social, political and economic roles of society.'"[18]

---

15. David G. Carter, Sr., *supra* note 3, at 6.

16. *Id.* at 4.

17. Robert E. Godwin, *Equality and The Schools: Education as a Fundamental Interest,* 21 no. 4 AMERICAN UNIVERSITY LAW REVIEW 716 (September 1972); Original article published in THE AMERICAN UNIVERSITY LAW REVIEW. citing H. Mann, *The Republic and the School* 87 (L. Cremin ed., 1957).

18. Robert E. Godwin, *Equality and The Schools: Education as a Fundamental Interest,* 21 no. 4 AMERICAN UNIVERSITY LAW REVIEW, 716 (September 1972). Original article published in THE AMERICAN UNIVERSITY LAW REVIEW.

The law is well-settled that "no State shall ... deny to any person within its jurisdiction the equal protection of the laws."[19] Yet courts are refusing to hear lawsuits that are filed which "address the responsibility of a school system to provide equal educational opportunity and to ensure that the rights of students are not violated in the process."[20] Query: If the courts refuse to hear these cases, where can the claimants turn for redress? Should they be denied the opportunity of having their claims determined by their peers? This raises the concern of availability of redress for the student who has suffered harm because a school fails to educate him or her.[21]

It may be too much to ask our public school system to educate its students; and it may be unwise to impose an actionable duty of care on the system[22] where it would be difficult to prove that even with the best instruction available the students in question could not be educated. However, if the proof is easy and there is a showing of "negligence," or "gross negligence" or even "intentional neglect" on the part of school employees, then it is not equitable for the students' claim to go unnoticed and be dismissed. Shouldn't the courts at least require as much honesty and fair dealing between school authorities and parents as between ordinary parties to a contract?[23]

Most claims alleging educational malpractice have been disposed of by the court by merely sustaining the defendants' motion to dismiss the action. In effect, the motion is similar to a demurrer which simply contends that even if all the facts presented by the plaintiff's complaint are true,

---

19. *Id.;* citing U.S. Constitution amendment XIV, § 1.
20. David G. Carter, Sr., *supra* note 3, at 3.
21. Joan Blackburn, *Educational Malpractice: When Can Johnny Sue?,* 7 FORDHAM URBAN LAW JOURNAL 117 (1978).
22. *Id.* at 143.
23. *Id.*

they do not constitute sufficient ground(s) for the court to rule in favor of the plaintiff. Once a motion to dismiss or a summary judgment is granted, the case cannot proceed any further, unless an appeal is taken. The courts, by refusing to recognize educational malpractice as a cause of action, are saying, regardless of the magnitude or seriousness of the alleged violations, regardless of how negligent the teacher might have been, and regardless of what amount of damages were incurred by the plaintiff-student, his or her complaint will not be heard in our court system.

Justice Frankfurter has said: "[t]he law touches every interest of man. Nothing that is human is alien to it." Over time, the tort system has evolved to accommodate the needs and capacities of our society. Factors such as the availability of insurance, environmental concerns, the economy, and public sentiment all influence the recognition and availability of causes of action. Sometimes the judiciary declares that a certain cause of action should not exist, and at times the legislature makes such a determination.[24] Even though the courts have generally refused to recognize educational malpractice as a cause of action, their opinion has not been shared by all. One writer suggests:

> Refusal to recognize the cause of action is incompatible with accepted tort principles, and that a cogent theory supporting nonrecognition cannot be articulated within the confines of the accepted principles and the general policies upon which those principles are based. If special policies justifying nonrecognition exist, then that result should be legislatively prescribed, rather than judicially pronounced in a manner that is antithetical to the recognized, traditional tort principles.[25]

24. Robert H. Jerry II, *Recovery in Tort for Educational Malpractice: Problems of Theory and Policy,* 29 KANSAS LAW REVIEW 195, 196 (1981).
25. *Id.*

It has been argued that many people view education in the same light as any other commodity which is purchased in the United States. If the buyer is not satisfied with the product then he or she can "return it to [the] place of purchase for a complete refund, no questions asked."[26] However, since education is not yet a "returnable commodity," it is believed that the only recourse is to sue for damages suffered as a result of the failure of the product.[27] Education, says one attorney, "should be treated like any other consumer item. People pay and they expect supervision of what happens in the classroom. Academic freedom does not mean leaving teachers alone."[28]

The debate concerning this issue continues. One teacher, commenting on the idea of educational malpractice suits, said, "it is rather like somebody trying to sue a clergyman because a member of the family didn't go to heaven, even though he went to church, listened to the sermons and put money in the collection plate."[29] Can the two really be compared? Obviously there are differences. Furthermore, there is the issue of allocation of burden of proof.

Writing about educational malpractice, one commentator states:

> While malpractice suits attempt to make the teacher and the education system solely responsible for a child's education, the fact is that numerous things in society determine a student's attitude toward education — not simply what the teacher says in front of the class. Yet, what the teacher says in the classroom, like what the minister says to his congregation, has an

---

26. R.C. Newell, *Teacher Malpractice: A New Threat to Education?* 1 Vol. V. no. 2 AMERICAN EDUCATOR (Summer 1977), pp. 2, 4.

27. *Id.*

28. *Id.*

29. R.C. Newell, *Teacher Malpractice: A New Threat to Education?*, SCHOOL LEADER (July 1978), pp. 11, 12.

impact. We can only hope that in neither case will substance give way to form.[30]

The fact that a number of factors, besides the teacher, affect the student's education does not eliminate the damage that can be caused by an incompetent teacher. These other "factors" may be used as a defense in a lawsuit. This, certainly, is not something new in our legal system. Many facts have to be unraveled in cases to determine what really caused the alleged damage. Yet, courts do not shy away from them — they delve ahead and through the assistance of juries try to reach an equitable solution.

Delbert Clear argues:

> A student who fulfills his or her part of the bargain by passing all courses and other experiences and is recommended for [teacher] certification should plausibly expect to have the institution fulfill its part of the bargain in return — teaching sufficient content and skills for entry-level job performance. This expectation, it should be noted, is directed at the institution and its teacher education program rather than at any particular instructor in it. This leads directly away from a plaintiff ultimately asking a court to rule on the validity of a particular professor's decisions (which courts are very reluctant to do) and into the more justifiable realm of asking a court to determine whether a particular program of studies met all known standards for completeness, recency, and scientific validity.[31]

"To state that a teacher is solely responsible because a student is moved from grade to grade without learning to read or write totally ignores a number of things which are beyond the control of the individual teacher."[32]

---

30. *Id.*

31. Delbert Clear, *Malpractice in Teacher Education: The Improbable Becomes Increasingly Possible,* Vol. 34 No. 2 JOURNAL OF TEACHER EDUCATION (March-April 1983), pp. 19, 20.

32. R.C. Newell, *supra* note 29, at 2, 6.

Newell notes:

> As is often the case, it is reasonable to assume that
> parents, by themselves, did not conjure up the legal
> argument that teachers and/or school systems were
> engaged in "malpractice" when they failed to "effec-
> tively educate" the students involved. A reasonable
> assumption is that in the hands of some zealous legal
> eagles, the age-old maxims — that you can lead a
> horse to water but you cannot make him drink — has
> been distorted into a legal concept of malpractice. The
> premise that all children will learn equally by dint of
> court intervention into the educational process is
> patent nonsense.[33]

The author continues the argument against educational
malpractice by stating:

> While it is true that the courts have entered the educa-
> tional process in an effort to ensure equal educational
> opportunity, it is spurious to assume that the courts
> can litigate equality of learning on the part of all stu-
> dents.[34]

The question that needs to be answered is not whether
the courts can litigate equality of learning on the part of all
students but rather: Can sufficient facts be alleged to give
rise to a justifiable educational malpractice case?

It has been noted that one basic assumption of the American educational system has been that, as an institution, it
is a positive means for providing equal opportunities for
persons drawn from heterogeneous backgrounds.[35] According to this view, "free public schooling should assure that
the individual competes on an equal basis, regardless of the
social class into which he or she is born."[36] The theory is

---

33. *Id.*
34. *Id.*
35. Godwin, *supra* note 18, at 717.
36. *Id.*

premised on the notion that the system of public education will create equal educational opportunity.[37] Justice Frankfurter termed the public school "the most powerful agency for promoting cohesion among a heterogeneous democratic people ... at once the symbol of our democracy and the most persuasive means for promoting our common destiny."[38] Justice Brennan said, "Americans regard the public schools as a most vital civic institution for the preservation of a democratic system of government."[39] Underscoring the importance of education is the often-quoted statement by Chief Justice Warren in *Brown v. Board of Education*:[40]

> Today, education is perhaps the most important function of state and local governments .... In these days, it is doubtful that any child may reasonably be expected to succeed in life if he is denied the opportunity of an education. Such an opportunity where the state has undertaken to provide it, is a right which must be made available to all on equal terms.[41]

The contention, therefore, is that contemporary American society assumes that its citizens will have the ability to read and write. The task of teaching these skills should fall primarily on the public schools.[42] When students complete the programs available to them and are still functionally illiterate, the ramifications not only affect the individual students, but society as well.[43] Consequently, regardless of the causes of illiteracy, in all probability these individuals

---

37. *Id.*
38. *Id.* at 728.
39. *Id.* at 729.
40. *Id.*
41. *Id.;* Brown v. Board of Education, 347 U.S. 483, 493 (1954).
42. Alice J. Klein, *Educational Malpractice: Can the Judiciary Remedy The Growing Problem of Functional Illiteracy?* 13 SUFFOLK UNIVERSITY LAW REVIEW 27 (Winter 1979).
43. *Id.*

will have a diminished earning capacity and society will face reduced revenues and increased outlays for public services.[44] It is in this vein that inadequately educated students are seeking to impose liability on educators who fail to exercise reasonable care in the discharge of their official duties. There are plaintiffs with skill deficiencies due to negligent instruction who are seeking to expand that liability to cover their injuries.[45] These are students "who have made bona fide efforts to meet the demands of coursework and the expectations of school officials, who have been led by annual promotions and graduation to believe that they have, in fact, performed in a satisfactory manner, and who have then discovered that they are grossly undereducated according to the demands of contemporary society."[46]

It is against this background that the arguments advanced by the courts in denying the plaintiffs' claims for educational malpractice must be examined.

§ 10.3. Educational Malpractice — The Novel Issue Argument.

The courts, in a hands-off policy, have called educational malpractice, "a novel and troublesome question,"[47] but have not answered the question. Are the courts performing their duty when they make wide-sweeping and general statements that such lawsuits are against "public policy" and ignore the equities involved? Should the mere fact that the claim is novel, in itself, operate as a bar to a claimant's recovery? In their brief to the Court of Appeals the respondents in the *Peter W.* case noted:

---

44. *Id.*
45. *Id.*
46. *Id.*
47. Peter W. v. San Francisco Unified School District, 60 Cal. App. 3d 814, 815, 121 Cal. Rptr. 854, 855 (1976).

376

This theory has never been advanced in tort litigation. Not only has a public official or agency never been held liable for non-personal or property damages resulting from a failure to provide a uniquely public service but also no tort remedy has ever been recognized for the type of interest allegedly involved in the instant case. The precedent sought in this case is of pervasive implication. Not only applying to reading or to skills acquired in school, the rule of law governing this case can be extended to a limitless variety of important, necessary public services not otherwise available to citizens.[48]

Should the test to determine whether a court should hear a case be whether the cause is a new one, or rather, whether the claim has merit? If new causes of action would not be entertained by courts merely on the ground that they raise "new" and "novel" issues, then, are not the courts static and incapable of evolving to adopt to the changing needs and circumstances of modern society? It has been argued that "by recognizing a new tort called 'educational malpractice,' courts would be demonstrating the 'flexibility and capacity for growth ...' [that] is the peculiar boast and excellence of the common law."[49]

Dean Prosser writes:

> The progress of the common law is marked by many cases of first impression, in which the court has struck out boldly to create a new cause of action, where none had been recognized before .... The law of torts is anything but static, and the limits of its development are never set. When it becomes clear that the plaintiff's interests are entitled to legal protection against the

---

48. Respondents' Brief at pp. 2-3, Peter W. v. San Francisco Unified School District, Civil No. 36,851 Ct. of App. (1st App. Dist., Div. 2, Col., 1975).

49. Judith H. Berliner Cohen, *The ABC's of Duty: Educational Malpractice and the Functionally Illiterate Student,* 8 GOLDEN GATE UNIVERSITY LAW REVIEW 293, 304 (1978).

conduct of the defendant, the mere fact that the claim is novel will not of itself operate as a bar to recovery.[50]

New torts, such as educational malpractice, generally develop in response to society's demand that a court aid a plaintiff who has suffered injury through a defendant's wrongdoing. There is evolution of tort law to meet the needs of a changing society. The courts do not, and should not, operate in a vacuum, and public demand for change is one of the factors influencing judicial decisions to recognize new causes of action.[51] Absence of precedent for recognizing a legal duty should not be fatal to a claimant's claim. Judge Crane wrote that the common law "does expand with reason. The common law is not a compendium of mechanical rules written in fixed and indelible characters, but a living organism which grows and moves in response to the larger and fuller development of the nation."[52] It thus follows that courts must examine judicial and legislative trends to discern if public policy compels them to recognize the new theory.[53] "Law is not merely a body of static rules to be obeyed by all citizens who are subject to its sanctions. It is a dynamic process by which rules are constantly being adopted and changed to the complex situations of a developing society."[54] Lawrence M. Friedman writes:

> People commonly believe that history and tradition are very strong in American law. There is some basis for this belief. Some parts of the law can be traced back

---

50. *Educational Malpractice,* 124 UNIVERSITY OF PENNSYLVANIA LAW REVIEW 755, 805 (1976); Delbert Clear, *Malpractice in Teacher Education: The Improbable Becomes Increasingly Possible,* 34 JOURNAL OF TEACHER EDUCATION (March-April 1983), pp. 19, 24.

51. Tracy, *supra* Chapter 1, note 12, at 593.

52. David Abel, *supra* note 1, at 425.

53. *Id.*

54. HAROLD J. GRILLIOT, INTRODUCTION TO LAW AND THE LEGAL SYSTEM (Boston: Houghton Mifflin Company, Third Edition, 1983), p. 1.

very far — the jury system, the mortgage, the trust, some aspects of land law. *But other parts of the law are newborn babies* .... History of law is not — or should not be — a search for fossils, but a study of social dovolopmonts, unfolding through time (emphasis added).[55]

Justice Oliver Wendell Holmes wrote: "The life of the law has not been logic; it has been experience." Another scholar's version concerning the life of the law is:

The life of the law has been logic; it has been experience. The felt necessities of the time, the prevalent moral and political theories, intuitions of public policy, avowed or unconscious, even the prejudices which judges share with their fellow men, have had a good deal more to do than syllogism in determining the rules by which men should be governed.[56]

It becomes evident when one examines the law that courts are not precluded, nor have they abstained, from creating a new cause of action where none has previously existed. For example, courts have allowed claims previously unrecognized in tort law, such as claims for loss of consortium resulting from physical injuries to the plaintiff's husband,[57] intentional infliction and [of] mental distress resulting from extreme and outrageous conduct,[58] prenatal injuries,[59] unwanted childbirth,[60] negligent infliction

---

55. LAWRENCE M. FRIEDMAN, A HISTORY OF AMERICAN LAW (New York: Simon and Schuster, 1973), pp. 13-15; quoted in Charles R. McGuire, THE LEGAL ENVIRONMENT OF BUSINESS — COMMERCE AND PUBLIC POLICY (Columbus: Charles E. Merrill Publishing Company, a Bell & Howell Company, 1986), pp. 11-12.

56. David G. Carter, Sr., *supra* note 3, at 1.

57. Cohen, *supra* note 49, at 303-04; citing, Rodriquez v. Bethlehem Steel Corp., 12 Cal. 3d 382, 525, 115 Cal. Rptr. 765 (1974).

58. Cohen, *supra* note 49, at 303-04; citing Savage v. Boies, 77 Ariz. 355, 272 P.2d 349 (1954).

59. Cohen, *supra* note 49, at 303; citing 38 WASH. L. REV., 390 (1963).

60. Cohen, *supra* note 49, at 303; citing Custodio v. Bauer, 251 Cal. App. 2d 303, 59 Cal. Rptr. 463 (1967).

of emotional distress,[61] invasion of privacy,[62] injuries caused by defective products,[63] and other injuries which do not fit into traditional tort categories.[64]

Furthermore, by recognizing an action for educational malpractice, a court would not be entering an entirely new area. Judicial review has already been extended in the field of education to include such matters as the right of students to symbolize protest in the classroom, personnel practices, liability of school board members for expelling students from school, curriculum, financing policies of school systems, school desegregation, and education of retarded, physically handicapped, and delinquent children.[65] In view of this judicial trend, if courts were to recognize educational malpractice as a cause of action, they would be expanding somewhat the existing trend. Courts, however, would have to proceed cautiously. Prosser notes:

> It does not lie within the power of any judicial system to remedy all human wrongs. The obvious limitations upon the time of the courts, the difficulty in many cases of ascertaining the real facts or of providing any effective remedy, have meant that there must be some selection of those more serious injuries which have the prior claim to redress and are dealt with most easily. Trivialities must be left to other means of settlement, and many wrongs which in themselves are flagrant — ingratitude, avarice, broken faith, brutal words, and heartless disregard of the feelings of others — are be-

---

61. Cohen, *supra* note 49, at 304; citing Dillon v. Legg, 68 Cal. 2d 898, 5 Cal. Rptr. 28 (1960).

62. Cohen, *supra* note 49, at 304; citing Pavesich v. New England Life Ins. Co., 122 Ga. 190, 50 S.E. 68 (1905).

63. *Educational Malpractice,* 124 UNIVERSITY OF PENNSYLVANIA LAW REVIEW 755, 761 (1976).

64. *Id.*

65. Klein, *supra* note 42, at 38.

yond any effective legal remedy, and any practical administration of the law.[66]

However, Prosser further points out that "it is the business of the law to remedy wrongs that deserve it — for every man that is injured ought to have his recompense."[67]

§ 10.4. Summary.

It would appear that the arguments advanced, herein, demonstrate that to deny a cause of action for educational malpractice on the basis that the concept of educational malpractice is new or *novel* is very weak at best. Precedent, in other areas, as well as logic as evidenced by the answers to the following questions dictate otherwise: (1) What if the student alleges sufficient facts which, if proven to be true, will demonstrate that the school which the student attended failed miserably in its primary objective — that of educating him or her?[68] (2) Suppose that if a student is pushed through school and is allowed to graduate, though deficient in all basic skills, even though school authorities were cognizant of the student's learning disabilities and made no attempt to test or diagnose his or her problems or to provide remedial help, would it be proper for the courts to summarily dismiss such a claim?[69] (3) Are the courts saying or are they prepared to say that under *no* circumstances may a student "properly" sue educational malpractice? (4) Can sufficient facts be alleged to give rise to a justifiable educational malpractice course of action? (5)

---

66. WILLIAM L. PROSSER, LAW OF TORTS (St. Paul: West Publishing Company, 1983), © p. 19.

67. *Id.* at 51; see also Brief and Appendix for Plaintiff-Respondent, at p. 60. Hoffman v. The City of New York and the Board of Education of the City of New York, Ct. of App. (N.Y. 1978).

68. Joan Blackburn, *Educational Malpractice: When Can Johnny Sue?,* 7 FORDHAM URBAN LAW JOURNAL 117 (1978).

69. *Id.*

Are all interests being protected — should they, legally and morally? If courts are to continue their refusal to recognize educational malpractice as a new course of action they must base their decision on some other legal and logical ground — not on the basis that it is new or novel.

Chapter 11

THE FLOOD OF LITIGATION AND FINANCIAL BURDEN ARGUMENTS

> It is the business of the law to remedy wrongs that deserve it, even at the expense of a "flood of litigation," and it is a pitiful confession of incompetence on the part of any court of justice to deny relief on such grounds.[1]

§ 11.0. Introduction.

In addition to the "novel" issue argument, a number of other arguments have been advanced by courts and various commentators for refusing to recognize educational malpractice as a new cause of action. This chapter will focus on two of them: (1) the flood of litigation; and (2) the financial burden.

§ 11.1. Flood of Litigation.

It has been argued that "once the door opens, an avalanche of [educational malpractice] litigation will probably ensue, with founded as well as unfounded actions. If every pupil who fails to master all of the survival skills of society should bring suit against his school district and its teachers for educational malpractice, the country's court-

---

1. WILLIAM L. PROSSER, LAW OF TORTS (St. Paul: West Publishing Company), © 1983.

383

rooms would be immediately overwhelmed."[2] Even if it can be assumed, at least at the outset, that this would happen, should the courts deny a claimant who has a "founded" action his or her day in court because of fear that those with "unfounded" claims will rush to the courts. It would appear justice dictates otherwise. Afterall, the system has built-in penalties for those "unfounded" claims. If the penalties are inadequate more should be imposed. It would be more equitable and proper to consider more built-in penalties for the "unmeritorious" claims than to deny the meritorious ones. Should a court deny a meritorious claim because it does not know how to handle it or because the meritorious claim may open the door to other meritorious claims? Would such a denial be consistent with our legal system?

Professor Prosser writes:

> It is the business of the law to remedy wrongs that deserve it, even at the expense of a "flood of litigation," and it is a pitiful confession of incompetence on the part of any court of justice to deny relief on such grounds. "And it is no objection to say, that it will occasion multiplicity of actions; for if men will multiply injuries, actions must be multiplied; for every man that is injured ought to have his recompense." So far as distinguishing true claims from false ones is concerned, what is required is rather a careful scrutiny of the evidence supporting the claim; and the elimination of trivialities calls for nothing more than the same common sense which has distinguished serious from trifling injuries in other fields of the law [citations omitted].[3]

---

2. Eugene T. Connors, *Educational Tort Liability and Malpractice*, Bloomington, IN: A Publication of *Phi Delta Kappa* (1981), p. 149. © [1981], Phi Delta Kappa, Inc.

3. PROSSER, *supra* note 1, at 51. See also Plaintiff's Memorandum in Response to Defendants' Demurrer, at 6, Peter W. v. San Francisco

The plaintiff in the *Peter W.* case argued that "there is a pragmatic response to the floodgates theory. The plaintiff has a heavy burden to establish the negligent conduct of the defendants and it is highly speculative to assume that a flood of similarly situated litigants will emerge and attempt to establish similar culpability."[4] Moreover, a flood of litigation is not likely due to the time and expense of the litigation.[5]

Despite these dire predictions of endless litigation and fraudulent claims, the California Supreme Court refused to be swayed and stated:

> In sanctioning recovery for injury caused by intentional infliction of mental distress, this Court did not differ to the argument that liability should not be imposed because of the possible future difficulty in delimiting the area of liability. Defendants urged that if recovery were to be allowed for intentional infliction of emotional distress, actions would soon be forthcoming based upon every minor personal insult or indignity. We said: "That administrative difficulties do not justify the denial of relief for serious invasions of mental and emotional tranquility is demonstrated by the cases recognizing the right of privacy" [citation omitted]. We rejected the contention that "to allow recovery in the absence of physical injury will open the door to unfounded claims and a flood of litigation and that the requirement that there be physical injury is necessary to insure that serious mental suffering actually occurred" [citation omitted].

Unified School District, Civil No. 653-312, Superior Ct. (Calif., County of San Francisco, 1974).

4. Plaintiff's Memorandum in Response to Defendants' Demurrer, at 6, Peter W. v. San Francisco Unified School District, Civil No. 653-312, Superior Ct. (Calif., County of San Francisco, 1974).

5. Kevin M. McArdle, *Creating an Implied Educational Malpractice Action for the Handicapped in New York*, 46 ALBANY LAW REVIEW 520, 540 (1982).

Indeed, the argument that "there is no point at which such actions would stop" is no more plausible today than when it was advanced ... (in 1842).[6]

Another scholar states:

For several reasons it is unlikely that a flood of litigation will occur: (1) the time and expense of litigation, (2) the fact that students, as minors, are unable to file suit in their own behalf, and (3) the institution of minimal competency tests. Moreover, even if there is a high potential for litigation, an administrative court system could be developed to handle all disputes with the civil courts available if an appeal is taken. This type of procedure has been working successfully in the income tax area, where a large number of cases are filtered through special tax courts. Consequently, the argument of the courts that a flood of litigation would occur is not viable. Rather, it seems a convenient way for the courts to avoid becoming involved in educational matters.[7]

Viewing this from a practical perspective, Professor Foster states:

At a more practical level, there are several factors which militate against the realization of the fears expressed by the courts and others. To begin with, there is the requirement of "victim initiative." Before litigation will arise the student must recognize "that he has been injured and, ... that the injury is the result of negligence, not just a negative outcome of competent services" [citation omitted]. Only rarely will this identification and evaluation be able to be made without the assistance of experts in the field of education, who,

---

6. Appellant's Reply Brief, at 18, Peter W. v. San Francisco Unified School District, Civil No. 36861, Court of Appeals (1st Appellate Dist. Div. 2, 1975).

7. Jay M. Pabian, *Educational Malpractice and Minimal Competency Testing: Is There a Legal Remedy at Last?*, 15 NEW ENGLAND LAW REVIEW 101, 108 (1979-80).

of course, belong to the same professional group as the potential defendant. Such expert assistance may be difficult to obtain. If educators react in the same manner as members of other professional groups who are requested to testify against one of their own, the student may be confronted by the "conspiracy of silence." When these factors are coupled with the not negligible protection afforded educational institutions and educators who come within the compass of public authorities protection legislation, [citation omitted] it is unlikely that the fear of a flood of litigation, emanating from at least the public educational system, will be realized.

It must also be remembered that a large number of students are minors who cannot initiate civil actions in their own names. They must have the active support of a guardian *ad litem* or next friend who is prepared to commence an educational malpractice suit on their behalf. To this extent it will be ensured that it is not "student's immature impulses," which constitute "the sole motivating force behind the lawsuit" [citation omitted].[8]

Furthermore, Professor Foster states an educational malpractice suit is likely to be expensive, requiring the payment of court costs, expert witness fees, and attorney fees, as well as other associated expenses. This will tend to discourage frivolous and fraudulent claims. Professor Foster continues his analysis:

Finally, while it must be accepted that mental trauma can be more easily stimulated than physical injury, it has been suggested that, with respect to intellectual injury caused by educational malpractice, there exist both protection against false claims and standards for assessing the degree of harm which are unavailable in other claims for pure mental and emotional suffering for which the law provides remedies. Thus, for exam-

---

8. W.F. Foster, *Educational Malpractice: A Tort for the Untaught?* 19:2 U.B.C. LAW REVIEW 161, 192-93 (1985). See also notations indicated in the aforementioned article.

ple, where the injury sought to be attributed to the
negligence of educators is: (1) the failure to acquire
knowledge of subject matter or basic skills, comparative methods of proof through the use of standardized
achievement tests are available to assess the degree of
harm; (2) the acquisition of various behavioural disorders, a variety of commonly used diagnostic tools are
available to identify the type of harm; or (3) the failure
to learn because of the omission to discover and deal
with one of the many learning disabilities which may
trouble students, again diagnostic tools are available
to identify and evaluate the extent of the harm [cita-
tion omitted].

In view of the foregoing, it is improbable that the
fears of excessive litigation and baseless claims would
be realized if the courts do recognize educators as being under a legal duty of care to their students. But,
even if these fears prove correct, one cannot overlook
the courts' duty to provide a remedy in meritorious
cases, a "duty [that] should not be abrogated for reasons of administrative convenience" [citation omit-
ted].[9] In *Williams vs. Baker,*[10] the District of Columbia
Court of Appeals, stated: While courts undoubtedly
may well be faced with some dishonest claims, "the
question of proof in individual situations should not be
the arbitrary basis upon which to bar all actions."
Battala vs. State, 10 N.Y. 2d 237, 242, 176 N.E. 2d
729, 731, 219 N.Y.S. 2d 34, 38 (1961). Neither should
fear of opening the gates to a flood of litigation be
determinative of whether the interest in question
should be legally protected. Even if that were a factor
to be considered, we think it doubtful that any significant amount of additional litigation will ensue from
our ruling in this case, given especially our prerequi-
sites for recovery. Any increase should be no greater
than that already shouldered by most jurisdictions. In
any event, if some increase in the litigation should

---

9. *Id.* at 194.

10. *Williams vs Baker* District of Columbia Court of Appeals, No.
84-1508 (1990).

materialize, "the courts must willingly cope with the task." *Robb vs. Pennsylvania R.R.*, 58 Del. 454, 463, 210 A. 2d 709, 714 (1965).

Under our judicial system one can sue just about anybody for anything if he or she is willing to pay the resulting consequences. The fact that our judicial system permits litigants easy access to the courts does not mean that the system permits unjust recoveries. The system should not deny recovery to litigants that are entitled to recovery, because wherever there is a legal wrong, there must be an adequate legal remedy.[11] In fact, it is somewhat shocking and perhaps a foreboding indictment of the school system's educational quality or success rate when a court denies recovery to a claimant out of fear of "flood" of litigation.[12] The courts must be ready and willing to accept, and even welcome, a claimant to present his or her claim in the "halls of justice." Neither the fear of the courts' inability to handle the amount of new litigation nor the possibility of feigned claims should stand in the way.[13] Justice cannot and should not be rationed. If more courts are needed to handle the cases that are filed, then the answer is not to limit the various causes of action, but rather, to provide sufficient courts to handle the cases brought before the judicial system. A system that would shy away of a "just" and "proper" claim because of the possibility of feigned claims has to be questioned. We must stop and examine where such logic will lead our legal system.

---

11. Memorandum of Behalf of Plaintiff, at 74, Edward Donohue v. Copiague Union Free School District, Index No. 77-1128, Sup. Ct. (Suffolk County, N.Y., 1977).

12. Arlene H. Patterson, *Professional Malpractice: Small Cloud, but Growing Bigger,* PHI DELTA KAPPAN (November 1980), pp. 193, 195.

13. Joan Blackburn, *Educational Malpractice: When Can Johnny Sue?,* FORDHAM URBAN LAW JOURNAL 117, 141 (1978); Robert H. Jerry II, *Recovery in Tort for Educational Malpractice: Problems of Theory and Policy,* 29 KANSAS LAW REVIEW 195, 205 (1981).

When the Supreme Court of Pennsylvania was confronted with the "flood of litigation" problem in the case of *Neiderman v. Brodsky*[14] it concluded that the "inherent humanitarianism of our judicial process and its responsiveness to the current needs of justice" mandated that in the absence of actual impact, plaintiffs still should be given the opportunity to present their claims.[15] Difficulty in proving a casual connection did not, in the court's view, "represent sufficient reason to deny [plaintiff] an *opportunity* to prove his case to the jury. The court held that the possibilities of fraudulent claims and increased litigation were minimal and well within the judiciary's ability to manage."[16] Judicial expertise in sorting the valid from the invalid claims should dispel concerns of rewarding undeserving claimants.[17] It should be remembered, however, as was observed by the New York Court,[18] that there must be "in fact, as well as in theory, a remedy for all wrongs."[19]

We should not fall into a trap of over-reacting to our detriment. In his book, *The Litigious Society,* Jethro Lieberman gives an example of possible over-reaction.[20] The example deals with the Good Samaritan Act, which in more than forty states immunizes from liability any doctor who provides emergency roadside medical service. He states:

---

14. 436 Pa. 195, 205, 401, 261 A.2d 84 (1970).

15. Jerry II, *supra* note 13, at 205.

16. *Id.*

17. Alice J. Klein, *Educational Malpractice: Can the Judiciary Remedy The Growing Problem of Functional Illiteracy?* 13 SUFFOLK UNIVERSITY LAW REVIEW 27 (Winter 1979), pp. 29-30.

18. Brief and Appendix for Plaintiff-Respondent, p. 48, Hoffman v. The City of New York, Court of Appeals (N.Y., 1978); *citing* Shuster v. City of New York, 5 N.Y.2d 75, 82-83 (1958).

19. *Id.*

20. JETHRO K. LIEBERMAN, THE LITIGIOUS SOCIETY (New York: Basic Books, Inc., Publishers) (1981).

State legislatures responded to physicians' fear that the potential for suit was too high given the need to act quickly under harrowing circumstances. The legislators responded also to threats that, without protection, doctors would cease to offer emergency care altogether. But the basis for this legislation is chimerical. "There is not one single reported case, in any state, in the entire history of the country, in which a doctor has been held liable because the treatment he provided at a roadside accident or on the street was below professional standards" [citation omitted]. The legislative response is thus not only unnecessary but dangerously overbroad, because it immunizes grossly careless conduct that even in an emergency ought not to be tolerated as well as the kind of reasonable mistake that someone might make under pressure. Nor have even these laws penetrated the medical community: An American Medical Association survey reported that "even after enactment of these laws, only half of the doctors studied said they would stop to help at a roadside accident" [citation omitted].[21]

§ 11.2. Financial Burden.

Another argument given by courts in opposition of recognizing educational malpractice claims is that schools are already beset by social and financial problems which have gone to major litigation and to hold them to an actionable "duty of care," in the discharge of their academic functions, would expose them to the tort claims — real or imagined — of disaffected students and parents in countless numbers.[22] Could physicians and hospitals make the same argument? Is such an argument proper and consistent with our legal system and what interests are served if the argument is followed?

---

21. *Id.*

22. Joseph Beckham, *Educational Malpractice: Breach of Statutory Duty and Affirmative Acts of Negligence By a School District*, 4 JOURNAL OF EDUCATION FINANCE (Winter 1979), pp. 377, 379.

In *Peter W.* the California Court of Appeals, in reviewing the "complex" factors it had to consider in deciding whether to allow a claim of educational malpractice, stated:

> Inherent to this (decision to impose a duty of due care) are various and sometimes delicate policy judgments; ... the relative ability of the parties to bear the financial burden of injury and the availability of means by which the loss may be shifted or spread; ... are the factors which play a role in the determination of duty.[23]

The judges expressed their worries about the financial problems that educational malpractice suits could create for communities. Since any money recovered from a school district by a claimant would be paid from taxes, school systems could collapse under the weight of damages if every student who failed to learn sued and won.[24] One must ask: Is our legal system so weak that it would allow all those who sue to win, regardless of the merits of their claims? A careful study of our system would indicate otherwise. Certainly, every patient that does not get well from an injury or illness is not awarded monetary damages against his or her doctor. Nor does every client that loses a case recover from his or her lawyer.

Furthermore, the flood of litigation argument appears to be weak in view of the fact that an adequate insurance package "will make unlikely any sizeable diversion of educational dollars from public school coffers to individual plaintiffs."[25] Indeed, it has been pointed out that "the

---

23. Blackburn, *supra* note 13, at 120.

24. Dorothy Levenson & Robert R. Spillane, *Malpractice Insurance: Who Needs It?*, Teacher (September 1977), pp. 95, 98.

25. David Abel, *Can a Student Sue the Schools for Educational Malpractice*, 44 Harvard Educational Review 416, 427 (November 1974)

availability of a system by which the defendant in a damage suit can obtain relief from all liability upon payment of a relatively small premium has led courts to abrogate traditional immunities from liability."[26] This does not mean that imposition of liability should be a function of the availability of insurance,[27] although, if a number of claims are sustained the insurance premiums may rise.[28] This, however, should not be the determining factor of whether courts should recognize educational malpractice as a cause of action. The determining factor should be whether a wrong has been committed, resulting in an injury. Is there a legitimate claim?

Commenting on this issue, the Pennsylvania Supreme Court stated:

> Throughout the entire history of the law, legal Jeremiahs have moaned that if financial responsibility were imposed in the accomplishment of certain enterprises, the ensuing litigation would be great, chaos would reign and civilization would stand still. It was argued that if railroads had to be responsible for their acts of negligence, no company could possibly run trains; if turnpike companies had to pay for harm done through negligence, no roads would be built; if municipalities were to be financially liable for damage done by their motor vehicles, their treasuries would be depleted. Nevertheless, liability has been imposed in accordance with elementary rules of justice and the moral code, and civilization in consequence, has not been bankrupted, nor have the courts been inundated with confusion.[29]

---

26. *Id.*

27. Klein, *supra* note 17, at 61-62.

28. Levenson & Spillane, *supra* note 24, at 95.

29. Doyle v. South Pittsburgh Water Co., 414 Pa. 199, 218-19, 199 A.2d 875, 884 (1964); *See also Educational Malpractice,* 124 UNIVERSITY

In response to defendants' demurrer, the plaintiff in *Peter W.* cites several cases addressing this issue. The California Supreme Court has stated:

> Unless the legislature has clearly provided for immunity, the important societal goal of compensating injured parties for damages caused by willful or negligent acts (of government employees) must prevail.[30]

The court further stated:

> It would be unjust in some circumstances to require an individual injured by official wrongdoing to bear the burden of his loss rather than distribute it throughout the community.[31]

Furthermore, in the case of *Johnson v. State*, [32] the court observed:

> Since the entire populace of California benefits from the activity of the (public agency), it should also share equally the burden of injuries negligently inflicted upon individual citizens; suits against the state provide a fair and efficient means to distribute these losses [emphasis added].[33]

In *Millington v. Southeastern Elevator Co.*,[34] the New York court, in rejecting the defendant's claim that the establishment of a "new cause" of action should be the prerogative of the legislature, stated that it is "the policy of modern tort law to expand tort liability 'in the just effort to

---

OF PENNSYLVANIA LAW REVIEW 755, 765 (1976). Reprinted with permission of U. OF PA. L. REV.

30. Plaintiff's Memorandum in Response to Defendants' Demurrer, Peter W., *supra* note 4, at 6; *citing* Johnson v. State, 73 Cal. Rptr. 252, 69 Cal. 2d 782 (1968).

31. *Id.*

32. 73 Cal. Rptr. 252, 69 Cal. 2d 782 (1968).

33. Plaintiff's Memorandum in Response to Defendants' Demurrer, Peter W., *supra* note 4, at 6.

34. 22 N.Y.2d 498 (1968).

afford decent compensatory measure to those injured by the wrongful conduct of others.'"[35]

The plaintiff-respondent, in his brief to the New York Court of Appeals, in the *Hoffman* case wrote:

> Since the entire population of the City of New York benefits from defendant's activities, they should also share equally the burden of injuries, psychological as well as physical, negligently inflicted upon individual children. It would be unjust to require such a child to bear the burden of his loss alone rather than distributing it throughout the community.[36]

A contrary position was taken by the respondents in the *Peter W.* case. They contended as follows:

> The law of torts as it developed involves a balancing of interests. Courts have, for example, frequently been reluctant to saddle an industry with the entire burden of harm it may cause for fear that the burden may ruin the industry. This is particularly true where the liability may extend to an unlimited number of persons and can be neither estimated nor insured against in advance [citations omitted].
>
> The problem of governmental bankruptcy, especially at the municipal level, is more than an abstract question today. Ultimately, the question turns on whether the public interest can best be served by awarding an individual student compensatory damages for the injury he has suffered at the public expense. The budget at the Board of Education is based on how much the members of the Board conclude should be spent on public education and how that money should be allocated. Thus, if Peter Doe recovers a certain sum as compensation for his failure to learn, then some other school program, for example, remedial reading, may be curtailed or eliminated.

---

35. Brief and Appendix for Plaintiff-Respondent, Hoffman, *supra* note 18, at 59.

36. *Id.* at 60.

These arguments have increased cogence now that we have had time to contemplate the lessons of Watergate. That the judiciary may overstep its bounds by imposing a liability such as the one sought in this case, may not be gainsaid.

When the insolvency of local government becomes more than an abstract hypothesis, the judiciary should be extremely cautious about recognizing new rights in tort which could impose excessive burdens on the nearly empty public coffers.

It is submitted that the public interest is best served by making students who fail to learn, due to negligent teaching and/or administration, bear the burden of the loss rather than placing the loss on the public treasury.[37]

Can the same logic be used regarding product liability cases? Should the courts refuse to recognize product liability cases and let the injured claimant suffer and have no redress against the company — regardless of the fault of the company? Should the law be — let the injured claimant suffer rather than the company? After all, one may argue, the company may be forced into bankruptcy. Should society allow the company to go unpunished, regardless of how bad its conduct might have been? If courts are concerned about municipalities going bankrupt, is it too much to ask that they should also be concerned about the future of the "injured" students? Who really is in a better position to "bounce back?" Who caused the damage? If school systems cannot be sued for academic negligence — incompetency — would that tend to make them less competent in the future? — Would it tend to make the schools weaker?

Should the issues of who is better able to bear the loss and who caused the damage, be factors in this matter? The school system can obtain insurance for such damages but how can the students insure themselves from possible

---

37. Respondents' Brief, Peter W., *supra* note 4, at 24.

harm to their educational growth? Where do they turn for relief?

It has been pointed out that "this claimed burden should be evaluated against the children and parents of this state, where untold hundreds of millions of dollars are collected as taxes and disbursed for educational purposes to the end that a child will receive a proper and 'meaningful' education."[38] Even if some money has to be paid by the school district to an injured claimant it does not follow that the quality of education would be diminished. The school district can protect itself through various means, including obtaining insurance.

Furthermore, this argument has not prevented courts from holding school districts liable for physical injuries caused by teacher negligence.[39] Assuming "intellectual harm" can be evaluated and determined — is that damage less harmful than physical damage? Can not municipalities also go bankrupt for allowing damages for physical injuries? Are courts trying to rationalize their decisions in denying educational malpractice or are the arguments they have been advancing good, sound, logical, and legally consistent, or are courts deciding the cases first and then searching for arguments to support their conclusions, or do their conclusions flow logically from the arguments? Is justice for the individual child subordinate to the benefits of society? Should it be? It is further argued that "if the costs of liability would not make public education economically infeasible (a factual question) there is no logical reason why the importance of public education should imply immunity."[40]

---

38. Brief in Behalf of Plaintiff-Appellant, Donohue v. Copiague Union Free School District, p. 11, Court of Appeals (N.Y., 1977).
39. *Educational Malpractice, supra* note 29.
40. *Id.*

§ 11.3. Summary.

Courts have argued that recognizing educational malpractice as a cause of action will spur an enormous amount of litigation and/or that it will cost too much. Consequently, many may suffer a wrong that will not be "righted." Some people find such an argument too superficial, too vague and inconsistent with good sound legal and logical principles. Our legal system and our moral code demand more than that as a justification for not recognizing educational malpractice as a cause of action. If we were to accept those arguments as a justification, are we prepared to apply them to other professions — i.e. medicine? Is not medical malpractice a financial burden on the medical profession? It is true that more medical malpractice suits raise medical insurance for the physicians and for the hospitals, and, consequently, doctors and hospitals may raise their fees — to the detriment of the patients. If that is not acceptable, what is the alternative? The question that will finally have to be answered is: How can the interests of all parties best be balanced?

Chapter 12

COURT EXPERTS IN VARIOUS PROFESSIONS—BUT NOT IN EDUCATION!

§ 12.0. Introduction.
§ 12.1. Judicial Intervention in the Educational Process.

> There is one recurrent theme: the court as a policy matter, even apart from principles of subject matter jurisdiction will abstain from venturing into areas if it is ill-equipped to undertake the responsibility and other branches of government are far more suited to the task ....[1]

§ 12.0. Introduction.

Another argument which has been used in educational malpractice cases is that the courts are not "qualified" or "competent" to deal with the educational matters raised in a claim of educational malpractice. Courts reason that they are an inappropriate forum to deal with public education. Furthermore, they argue that it would be an inappropriate intrusion by the judiciary in the educational decision-making process.

§ 12.1. Judicial Intervention in the Educational Process.

Courts are reluctant to become involved in the actual daily operation of schools unless a gross violation is in-

---

1. Jones v. Beame, 45 N.Y.2d 402 (1978).

volved.[2] This "judicial tradition of abstaining from review of educational decisions is based on the belief that educational policy is too vague and complex to lend itself to judicial review."[3] So, "traditionally the courts have refrained from intruding into classroom teaching matters. Instead, they chose to defer to local school boards on matters of education policy and practice. They wanted to uphold the doctrine of academic freedom. However, there is ample evidence that such restraint is becoming the exception, not the rule. Once the courts interpreted schoolhouse events in terms of personal rights and interests, the door was open to examine the legal nature of school-teacher-student-parent relationships."[4]

There are many questions that need to be posed, addressed, and resolved in connection with this issue. (1) Are lawsuits the proper method to resolve educational grievances? (2) Is there something unique about an educational dispute, involving intellectual harm, that is not present in other professions? (3) Would the courts' involvement in educational malpractice cases disrupt the educational process? (4) Where can one go to resolve claims of academic negligence and intellectual harm? (5) What are the available remedies? (6) Should the educators serve as the judges, jurors, and "executioners" in educational matters? (7) If yes, shouldn't or couldn't doctors, lawyers, engineers, accountants, and other professionals take the same position — should they? (8) Is it better for society if they do — would justice better ensue? (9) Are judges, jurors, and the judicial system less qualified and competent to deal with

---

2. Kevin M. McArdle, *Creating an Implied Educational Malpractice Action for the Handicapped in New York,* 46 ALBANY LAW REVIEW 520, 539 (1982).

3. *Id.*

4. William R. Hazard, *A Tort is Not a Piece of Cake: Teachers' Legal Responsibilities,* MUSIC EDUCATORS' JOURNAL (April 1979), pp. 26, 32.

the sensitive issues of educational malpractice than they are to deal with the delicate issues of medical malpractice or clergy malpractice? (10) Is the concern about the legitimacy of court involvement in educational policy-making the underlying reason for judicial reluctance to recognize a cause of action for educational malpractice?[5]

Alice Klein, an education scholar, writes:

> Although some critics suggest that a lack of expertise in the field justifies restraint, [citation omitted], a look at the wide scope of judicial decisions encompassing medicine, psychiatry and industry, for example, refutes that contention. By appointing masters in complex situations, courts are able to offer relief to injured plaintiffs. Since the *Brown v. Board of Education* decision, [citation omitted], the courts have expended judicial review in the field of education to include such matters as the right of students to symbolic protest in the classroom, [citation omitted], the liability of school board members for expelling students from school, [citation omitted], the financing policies of school systems, [citation omitted] and the education of retarded, physically handicapped and delinquent children [citation omitted].[6]

Another academic, Destin Tracy, explains:

> Several reasons have been offered for judicial restraint. Some courts hesitate to become involved because of their perception of a long-standing historical pattern of judicial noninterference [citation omitted]. Despite a history of decisions favoring judicial noninterference, courts have at times become involved in educational issues, [citation omitted], especially when a constitutional right is allegedly infringed [citation omitted]. There is admittedly little direct precedent,

---

5. Alice J. Klein, *Educational Malpractice: Can the Judiciary Remedy the Growing Problem of Functional Illiteracy?* 13 SUFFOLK UNIVERSITY LAW REVIEW 27 (Winter 1979), p. 37.
6. *Id.*

however, for the kind of detailed involvement required when a student complains about the quality of academic instruction he has received [citation omitted]. Thus the historical record does appear to favor judicial noninterference, and courts relying on this justification have firm support.

A further justification often offered for judicial noninterference is the court's lack of expertise in the educational field, [citation omitted], though judicial expertise in educational policies is probably equal to that in accepted areas of litigation such as medical malpractice [citation omitted]. Although educational issues are complicated by the frequent absence of reliable data or acceptable theory upon which to base a judicial determination [citation omitted], courts may draw on the understandings of educational experts to assist them in formulating decisions [citations omitted].

Judicial noninterference also has been supported on the ground that the social importance of educational issues is better served by political solutions [citation omitted]. Those areas of policymaking involving the identification of the ultimate values and goals of society, however, as opposed to methods of effective implementation of those values and goals, are suitable areas for decision making [citation omitted]. Thus, the courts should not automatically defer to political action when the student alleges negligent educational conduct in direct conflict with ultimate social values.

A final rationale offered for judicial noninterference is the constitutional and statutory delegation of educational matters to state and local administrative bodies [citation omitted]. That the legislature may delegate authority to administer a particular area should not, however, preclude judicial response to individuals injured by incompetent administrative functioning. The courts clearly have an important role to fulfill as a check on administrative malfunctions and abuses [citation omitted].

On balance, judicial reasoning supporting noninterference in educational policymaking does not logically *demand* unqualified restraint, and a complaining student should argue that the nature of his injury justifies the limited degree of interference necessary to adjudicate his claim. If a court is unwilling to interfere in educational policies to any degree, it could refrain from policy interference by hearing only those cases in which it is not called upon to make policy judgments — for example, by recognizing a cause of action only when defendants have allegedly failed to comply with self-imposed policies [citation omitted].[7]

Concerning an alternate procedure for dealing with negligent instruction, Tracy observes:

It has been asserted that existing, intrasystem methods for dealing with incompetent educators are sufficient, therefore obviating the need for judicial intervention. Although each of the internal procedures generally available — for example, the school board's power to dismiss incompetent teachers, [citation omitted], certification procedures that impose minimum qualification, [citation omitted], the use of supervisors who exercise direct control over teaching behaviors [citation omitted] and the presence of a system of professional review for educators analogous to that established by doctors and lawyers [citation omitted], — works to eliminate incompetence from the system, none of them offers relief to the student who is actually injured by incompetence.

Internal grievance procedures may also be available to parents who question the instruction their children are receiving [citation omitted]. If a parent becomes aware of his child's problem while the child is still enrolled and is informed of the availability of the grievance procedure, a resolution may be obtained in time to correct or *ameliorate* any injury already inflicted, or to preclude further injury. If, however, no satisfactory resolution can be achieved through the grievance procedure, or if the injury is not discovered

7. Destin Shann Tracy, *Educational Negligence: A Student's Cause of Action for Incompetent Academic Instruction,* 58 NORTH CAROLINA LAW REVIEW 566, 589-91 (1980).

until after removal from the system, a court action might be the only appropriate method for securing adequate relief.

Whether a court is willing to step in when alternative procedures fail to remedy an individual injury will depend in large part on whether the individual's need for relief is great enough to justify going beyond alternative procedures designed to maintain quality instruction for all students. It has been suggested that recognizing the individual causes of action will pressure educators into developing more effective alternatives or more effectively enforcing existing ones [citations omitted]. If this is correct, it would make recognition of the action more acceptable by spreading the benefit among a large number of students.[8]

The author concludes the article on educational malpractice by commenting:

It is said that procedures within the educational system adequately deal with incompetent teaching and obviate the need for judicial relief. Most internal procedures, however, provide no relief to the individual student who is injured, and those that do may be inadequate or unavailable. The courts should step in on behalf of injured students in genuine need of relief when internal procedures fail to provide a just remedy. An inevitable conflict has emerged between the increasing public demand for educational competency and the potentially harmful social effects of unlimited recognition of an educational negligence cause of action. An appropriate balance of these conflicting factors could be achieved by judicial recognition of a cause of action for educational negligence that is carefully limited in scope for the protection of both educators and society.[9]

In his reply brief to the court of appeals, the appellant in the *Peter W.* case argued:

---

8. *Id.* at 591-92.
9. *Id.* at 597.

Respondents repeatedly suggest that the remedy for appellant's injuries should be political, not judicial. In so doing, respondents ignore the fundamental role of the judiciary in the resolution of conflict in our society. As the United States Supreme Court observed, "American society, of course, buttons its systematic definition of individual rights and duties, as well as its machinery for dispute settlement not on custom or the will of strategically placed individuals, but on the common-law model. It is to the courts or other quasi-judicial official bodies, that we ultimately look for the implementation of a regularized orderly process of dispute settlement."[10]

In concluding his reply brief, the appellant asserts:

Finally, the argument made by the respondents that courts should refuse to hear this case because of the difficulties in evaluating the educational process and determining standards of care was firmly rejected by the Supreme Court in a similar case involving the liability of psychotherapists for negligence, *Tarasoff v. Regents,* [citations omitted]. In refusing to provide blanket immunity for a profession which advanced a similar claim of grave difficulty in establishing common standards of care, the Supreme Court observed, *"But whatever difficulties the courts may encounter in evaluating the expert judgments of other professions, those difficulties cannot justify total exoneration from liability"* [emphasis added].[11]

On the other hand, the defendant, in his memorandum to the New York Supreme Court in the *Donohue* case, contends:

Public education faces ever mounting pressures from a critical society. To some extent our schools have re-

---

10. Appellant's Reply Brief, Peter W. v. San Francisco Unified School District, Civil No. 36851 Ct. of App. (First Dist., Div. 2, Calif. (1975)), pp. 17-18.
11. *Id.* at 18-19.

sponded but education cuts wide lines across every fabric of our democratic institutions and the answers are increasingly complex since the issues are social, political and economic in origin. It thus hardly seems appropriate for the Court to enter an arena in regard to a subject which continues to receive widespread legislative and other public attention.[12]

He further argues:

When the State undertakes public education, it is not contemplating a tort duty which would make the State or individual teachers or administrators liable to students for money damages whenever the students fail to learn because of the alleged careless administration of the schools or negligent teaching in the classroom. The pedagogical process of transferring knowledge and cognitive skills is so complex and as yet inadequately understood, as not properly to be the subject of the imposition of a tort duty.

It is submitted that in light of the complexity of the problems, a court of law is not in a position to decide what is or is not reasonable conduct and furthermore to decide whether there has been established an adequate evidentiary basis to connect the alleged tort with the claimed injury.

When the insolvency of local government becomes more than an abstract hypothesis, the judiciary should be extremely cautious about recognizing new rights which could impose excessive burdens on nearly empty public coffers. A duty such as the one asserted in the complaint would render public education economically unfeasible.[13]

In *Peter W.* the court remarked that a major determinant of "public policy" is whether or not the particular

---

12. Memorandum on Behalf of Defendant, Donohue v. Copiague Union Free School District, Index No. 1128, Supreme Ct. of N.Y. (County of Suffolk), p. 91.
13. *Id.* at 92-93.

wrongs and injuries in question are comprehensible and assessable within the existing judicial framework.[14]

The respondent in *Donohue,* attempts to shift the burden of deciding these matters to the Commissioner of Education.[15] He cites *In the Matter of Vetere v. Allen,*[16] where the court of appeals discusses the nature and functions of the Office of the Commissioner of Education as follows:

> The purpose of the grant of quasi-judicial powers under section 310 of the Education Law is "to make all matters pertaining to the general school system of the state within the authority and control of the department of education and to remove the same as far as practical and possible from controversies in courts" [citation omitted]. "By our state system of education protected by the constitution and developed by much study and experience, the commissioner of education is made the practical administrative head of the system, and in his exercise of sound wisdom, as we believe, the legislature deemed it best to make him the final authority in passing on many questions bound to arise in the administration of the school system, and has provided an expeditious and simple method by which a disposition of such questions could be reached through appeal to him" [citation omitted]. "In appraising the judicial nature of the act of the Commissioner of Education, it must be remembered that he combines both judicial and administrative functions. When he decides appeals where he has occasion to construe statutes, he undoubtedly acts in a judicial capacity. But in passing upon property of educational policy by a particular school board or school district, he acts in a broader capacity than the courts, by reviewing at times administrative acts of discretion of which a court would refuse to take cognizance" [citations omitted].[17]

---

14. *Id.*
15. Respondent's Brief, Donohue, *supra* note 12, at 32-33.
16. *Id.,* 15 N.Y.2d 259 (1965).
17. *Id.* at 33-34.

The court concluded by stating:

> Disagreement with the sociological, psychological and educational assumptions relied on by the Commissioner cannot be evaluated by this court. Such arguments can only be heard in the Legislature which has endowed the Commissioner, or by the Board of Regents, who are elected by the Legislature and make public policy in the field of education.[18]

The court, in *James v. Board of Education,*[19] cited by the respondent in the *Donohue* case, stated:

> In this case, petitioners raise "questions of judgment, discretion, allocation of resources and priorities inappropriate for resolution in the judicial arena" [citation omitted]. The responsibility for resolving these questions is vested in a network of officials and boards, on both the local and state level. To permit this injunction to stand, and this proceeding to be continued, "would in effect attempt displacement, or at least overview by the courts and plaintiffs in litigations, of the lawful acts of appointive and elective officials charged with the management of" the New York City public school system [citation omitted]. With these officials, the matter rests [citation omitted].[20]

In *Jones v. Beame,*[21] the New York court had an occasion to comment on the problem of judicially unmanageable questions. The court explained:

> There is one recurrent theme: the court as a policy matter, even apart from principles of subject matter jurisdiction, will abstain from venturing into areas if it is ill-equipped to undertake the responsibility and other branches of government are far more suited to the task. As put by the then Chief Judge Wyzanski,

---

18. *Id.* at 34.
19. *Id.;* 42 N.Y.2d 357 (1977).
20. *Id.* at 34-35.
21. *Id.* at 34; 45 N.Y.2d 402 (1978).

speaking with respect to a political question, abstention was a "recognition that the tools with which a court can work, the data which it can firmly appraise, [and] the conclusions which it can reach as a basis for entering judgments have limits" [citation omitted].
... The proper forums are the Legislature and the elected officials of State and local government. It is there that the accommodations can be made in determining priorities and allocating resources.[22]

In the *Donohue* case the New York Court, Appellate Division, observed:

The courts are an inappropriate forum to test the efficacy of educational programs and pedagogical methods. That judicial interference would be the inevitable result of the recognition of a legal duty of care is clear from the fact that in presenting their case, plaintiffs would, of necessity, call upon jurors to decide whether they should have been taught one subject instead of another, or whether one teaching method was more appropriate than another, or whether certain tests should have been administered or test results interpreted in one way rather than another, and so on, ad infinitum. It simply is not within the judicial function to evaluate conflicting theories of how best to educate. Even if it were possible to determine with exactitude the pedagogical course to follow with respect to particular individuals, yet another problem would arise. Public education involves an inherent stress between taking action to satisfy the educational needs of the individual student and the needs of the student body as a whole. It is not for the courts to determine how best to utilize scarce educational resources to achieve these sometimes conflicting objectives. Simply stated, the recognition of a cause of action sounding in negligence to recover for "educational malpractice" could impermissibly require the courts to oversee the administration of the State's public school system.[23]

---

22. *Id.*
23. Respondent's Brief, Donohue, *supra* note 12, at 37.

In arguing that the courts should not enter into this area, the defendants in the *Donohue* case maintained in their brief: "It thus hardly seems appropriate for the court to enter an arena in regard to a subject vested in the Legislature and delegated to the Board of Regents and the Commissioner of Education."[24]

Furthermore, the defendants in *Peter W.* contended:

> It is not the function of tort litigation to analyze the sociology of education or to propose solutions to the perplexing problems in this field. The respondents acknowledge that problems exist and they submit that they have, in good faith and in a responsive and responsible manner, sought to deal with these problems. *If the appellant is dissatisfied, his remedy must be political* [emphasis added].[25]

In *Millington v. Southeastern Elevator Co.*[26] the court, in rejecting the defendant's claim that the establishment of a "new cause" of action should be the prerogative of the legislature, said "it is 'the policy of modern tort law' to expand tort liability in the just effort to afford decent compensatory measure to those injured by the wrongful conduct of others."[27] One commentator stated that since 1954, "courts have increasingly scrutinized decisions once made solely by school administrators and boards of education."[28]

When these arguments are closely analyzed it becomes apparent that the courts' hesitation to recognize a cause of action for educational malpractice because of the complexities it may present is somewhat superficial, vague, and

---

24. *Id.*
25. Respondent's Brief, Peter W., *supra* note 10, at 15.
26. Brief and Appendix for Plaintiff-Respondent, Hoffman v. City of New York, 22 N.Y.2d 498 (1968).
27. *Id.*
28. Brief and Appendix for Plaintiff-Respondent, Hoffman, *supra* note 26, at 61.

indefensible. They have willingly or unwillingly shouldered themselves with the task of sitting in judgment in cases involving complex and controversial psychiatric treatment that may have resulted in injuries to individuals. They have also sat in judgment in cases dealing with intricate and delicate operations to the brain resulting in "questionable" successes. Yet, in the area of educational malpractice the courts seem to feel incompetent. When people believe that they have been damaged, through the wrongful conduct of others, they must be able to turn to an "independent" body or tribunal to have their grievance heard and resolved. They have to be able to turn to a "forum" which they perceive as being fair, impartial, and objective. The courts traditionally have been thought of as being such tribunals. There is no claim that school boards or other educational tribunals will be unfair if a hearing is held before them, but the possible conflict of interest is real, or at least can be logically imagined. Consequently, educational tribunals may very well be "perceived" as biased. Such interpretation may lead claimants to be suspicious and mistrustful of the education system. Courts can and should help in this matter — it is their obligation to dispel such appearances. They must not shirk their responsibilities.

Therefore, even though some suggest that a lack of expertise in the field of academics justifies restraint, when one views the wide scope of judicial decisions encompassing medicine, psychiatry, and other fields, such contention is refuted. By appointing masters in especially complex situations, courts can offer relief to injured claimants.[29] Furthermore, "an over-involvement argument hardly seems appropriate when viewed in the light of the activist role courts

---

29. Klein, *supra* note 5, at 38.

have played in defining the responsibilities of education."[30]
Tracy observes:

> Courts stress the importance of avoiding unnecessary
> judicial interference in educational policymaking.
> Precedent may tend to disfavor interference on behalf
> of academically injured students, but it does not de-
> mand judicial non-interference. In any case, it is possi-
> ble to recognize a limited form of educational negli-
> gence resulting in only negligible interference with
> educational policies.
>   ... it is said that procedures within the educational
> system adequately deal with incompetent teaching
> and obviate the need for judicial relief. Most internal
> procedures, however, provide no relief to the individ-
> ual student who is injured, and those that do may be
> inadequate or unavailable. The courts should step in
> on behalf of injured students in genuine need of relief
> when internal procedures fail to provide a just remedy.
>   An inevitable conflict has emerged between the in-
> creasing public demand for educational competency
> and the potentially harmful social effects of unlimited
> recognition of an educational negligence cause of ac-
> tion. An appropriate balance of these conflicting fac-
> tors could be achieved by judicial recognition of a cause
> of action for educational negligence that is carefully
> limited in scope for the protection of both educators
> and society.[31]

Another writer states:

> The facts of each case must be weighed alone to deter-
> mine the viability of a cause of action, and fear of
> similar suits should not be considered by the court as a
> legitimate factor in refusing to hear the action. A pri-
> mary responsibility of the courts is to award damages

---

30. Nancy L. Woods, *Educational Malfeasance: A New Cause of Action for Failure to Educate?,* 14 TULSA LAW JOURNAL 383, 394-95 (1978),
copyright by the University of Tulsa.

31. Tracy, *supra* note 7, at 597.

for sound claims, and this duty should not be abrogated for reasons of administrative convenience.[32]

Patterson, commenting on this matter, writes:

Educational suits seek to redress students who have not received full educational benefits when teachers negligently or intentionally "failed to conform to minimum standards of professional competence ...." The harm suffered is the student's failure to attain the educational level that would probably have been attained had the teacher performed at the required level. Currently, this means that many students who have failed to learn constitute a class of victims without remedy, presenting a dilemma for both the courts and educators.[33]

The question becomes, who — professional educators or the legal system — will provide the remedy? Woods suggests:

The time is right for judicial intervention in upgrading educational standards. Malpractice by school districts cannot be allowed to continue. The courts are proper arbiters, and dismissal of such actions only perpetuates the status quo. If schools are to continue to be responsible for the general education of children, they must be held to this duty and must be liable for its breach.[34]

As professor Foster notes, another policy reason given for the court's reluctance to provide redress for educational malpractice is "that it would constitute illegitimate intrusion by the judiciary in the educational decision-making

---

32. Woods, *supra* note 30, at 394-95.

33. Arlene H. Patterson, *Professional Malpractice: Small Cloud, but Growing Bigger,* PHI DELTA KAPPAN (November 1980), p. 194.

34. Woods, *supra* note 30, at 409.

413

process at all levels."[35] Would it constitute an illegitimate intrusion?

If, as is the case in some states, local school boards make the final decisions regarding school matters, such as "intellectual" harm, what happens if the school board arbitrarily and capriciously decides the case in favor of the teacher and/or the school system? What if the board is biased in its decision and the courts take the position that judicial intervention in the educational process is bad — it should not be allowed — what then? Are society, the child and his or her parents served well? Shouldn't school boards have some accountability for their actions? It is true, that one may argue that school boards do have accountability to the public — to the electorate — but can the public fully correct an injustice, incurred by a student, without court intervention? Should school boards be the final arbitrators on such matters as complaints of students of failure to learn due to incompetency of their teachers? When viewed from all perspectives, isn't the argument that courts should not intervene really vague, illogical and judicially inconsistent? As has been previously pointed out, herein, courts have intervened in other similar matters, including what should or should not be taught and whether the teacher and/or the school should be liable to a student for physical damages resulting from injuries incurred in the school yard, in the gym or on the football field?

Are there adequate internal administrative procedures designed for the achievement of educational goals available within the educational system? Justice Davidson, in his concurring opinion in *Hunter*,[36] stated:

> In my view none of the available procedures adequately deal with incompetent teaching or provide ad-

---

35. W.F. Foster, *Educational Malpractice: A Tort for the Untaught?* 19:2 B.C. LAW REVIEW 161, 200 (1985).
36. Hunter v. Board of Education, 439 A.2d 582 (1981).

414

equate relief to an injured student. A cause of action for educational malpractice meets these social and individual needs.[37]

He concludes his opinion by stating:

Finally, I do not agree with the majority that the recognition of such a cause of action "would in effect position the courts of this state as over-seers of both the day-to-day operation of our educational process as well as the formulation of its governing policies," roles that have been "properly entrusted by the General Assembly to the State Department of Education and the local school boards. That the Legislature has delegated authority to administer a particular area to certain administrative agencies should not preclude judicial responsiveness to individuals injured by unqualified administrative functioning.

In recognizing a cause of action for educational malpractice, this Court would do nothing more than what courts have traditionally done from time immemorial — namely provide a remedy to a person harmed by the negligent act of another. Our children deserve nothing less.[38]

---

37. *Id.* at 589-90.
38. *Id.*

Chapter 13

THE MATTER OF PROOF — LACK OF
RECOGNIZABLE DUTY — NO
STANDARD OF CARE

> The "right to an education today means more than access to a classroom."[1]

§ 13.0. Introduction.

Another major and troublesome concern that surfaces when educational malpractice is debated is the issue of whether the teacher, the administrator, and/or the school district owe the plaintiff, be he or she a student or a parent, a duty of care — a duty to educate, recognized and/or imposed by common law, by statute, or by constitution. If there is no legal duty there can be no actionable negligence. If, however, there is a recognized duty, it must be performed with due care. If there is a recognizable duty, what is it and what must the educator do to meet that duty — to conform to the standard of care? Furthermore, if such a duty is recognized, then the question is, "Did the teacher and/or school district breach same? If there was a breach

---

1. Plaintiff's Memorandum in Response to Defendants' Demurrer, Peter W. v. San Francisco Unified School District, Civil No. 653-312, Superior Ct. (Calif. Cty. of San Francisco, 1974), p. 38.

417

then the next question that needs to be resolved is whether there was a causal relationship between the defendant's acts or omissions and the plaintiff's harm. Even if the plaintiff can establish that the defendant owed a duty to the plaintiff and that the breach of that duty caused the plaintiff's injury, the plaintiff will still have to establish the nature and extent of his or her injuries.[2] Of course, even if the injured claimant can establish a prima facie case, the defendant teacher, administrator, or school district may still have a number of defenses available. These defenses can range from immunity — either common law sovereign immunity or statutory immunity — to the more usual affirmative defenses, to the possible introduction of a different standard of care.[3] This chapter will deal primarily with the first two essential elements of negligence — the duty of care and the breach of such duty.

§ 13.1. Duty of Care.

The law is well-established that before a defendant is held liable for negligence it must be shown, *inter alia,* that the defendant owed a duty to the plaintiff.[4] In the absence of a duty, there is no breach and without a breach there is no liability for negligence. This requirement is expressed in the often quoted remark: "Negligence in the air, so to speak, will not do."[5] The question of duty is best expressed as "whether the plaintiff's interests are entitled to legal

---

2. Cynthia A. Jorgensen, *Donohue v. Copiague Free School District: New York Chooses Not to Recognize "Educational Malpractice,"* 43 ALBANY LAW REVIEW 339, 354 (Winter 1979).

3. NOLPE, YEARBOOK OF SCHOOL LAW, 1980, p. 245.

4. Respondent's Brief, Donohue v. Copiague Union Free School District, Suffolk County Clerk's Index No. 77/1128, Court of Appeals, State of New York, p. 7; *See also* Palsgraf v. Long Island R.R., 248 N.Y. 339, 342, 162 N.E. 99, 102 (1928).

5. *Id.*

protection against the defendant's conduct."[6] It thus follows that there must be a legal duty owed by the defendant, its teachers, and administrators, to the plaintiff before the plaintiff can sustain a cause of action for educational malpractice.

To date there exists no simple or concrete answer, and certainly no unanimous agreement, concerning the issue of duty of care pertaining to educational malpractice. Focusing on the defendant's "duty of care" toward the plaintiff, the appellate court in *Peter W.* labeled as a "truism" the idea that public schools, which are duty bound to educate, are also bound to do it with care. The court declared:

> For want of relevant authority in each instance, plaintiff's allegations of his enrollment and attendance at defendants' schools do not plead the requisite "duty of care," relative to his academic instruction, upon any of the three theories he invokes. *Of course, no reasonable observer would be heard to say that these facts did not impose upon defendants a "duty of care" within any common meaning of the term; given the commanding importance of public education in society, we state a truism in remarking that the public authorities who are duty-bound to educate are also bound to do it with "care." But the truism does not answer the present inquiry, in which "duty of care" is not a term of common parlance; it is instead a legalistic concept of "duty" which will sustain liability for negligence in its breach, and it must be analyzed in that light [emphasis added].*[7]

The court then noted:

> Despite such changes in the concept, several constants are apparent from its evolution. One is that the concept itself is still an essential factor in any assessment of liability for negligence [citations omitted]. An-

---

6. *Id.*
7. *Id.* at 9-10.

other is that "whether a defendant owes the requisite 'duty of care,' in a given factual situation, presents a question of law which is to be determined by the courts alone" [citations omitted]. A third, and the one most important in the present case, is that judicial recognition of such duty in the defendant, with the consequence of his liability in negligence for its breach, is initially to be dictated or precluded by considerations of public policy. From among an array of judicial statements to this effect, the following language by the *Raymond* court is particularly pertinent here:

An affirmative declaration of duty (of care) simply amounts to a statement that two parties stand in such relationship that the law will impose on one a responsibility for the exercise of care toward the other. Inherent in this simple description are various and sometimes delicate *policy judgments.* The social utility of the activity out of which the injury arises, compared with the risks involved in its conduct; the kind of person with whom the actor is dealing; the workability of a rule of care, especially in terms of the parties' relative ability to adopt practical means of preventing injury; the relative ability of the parties to bear the financial burden of injury and the availability of means by which the loss may be shifted or spread; the body of statutes and judicial precedents which color the parties' relationship; the prophylactic effect of a rule of liability; in the case of a public agency defendant, the extent of its powers, the role imposed upon it by law and the limitations imposed upon it by budget; and finally, the moral imperatives which judges share with their fellow citizens — such are the factors which play a role in the determination of duty [citations omitted]. Occasions for judicial determination of a duty of care are infrequent, because in "run of the mill" accident cases the existence of a duty may be — and usually is — safely assumed. Here the problem is squarely presented [citations omitted].[8]

---

8. *Id.* at 10-11.

The court stated that one of the major determinants of "public policy," is whether or not the particular wrongs and injuries in question are comprehensive and assessable within the existing judicial framework. The court remarked:

> This is simply not true of wrongful conduct and injuries allegedly involved in educational malfeasance. Unlike the activity of the highway or the marketplace, classroom methodology affords no readily acceptable standards of care, or cause, or injury. The science of pedagogy itself is fraught with different and conflicting theories of how or what a child should be taught and any layman might — and commonly does — have his own emphatic views of the subject. The "injury" claimed here is plaintiff's inability to read and write. Substantial professional authority attests that the achievement of literacy in the schools or its failure, are influenced by a host of facts which affect the pupil subjectively, from outside the formal teaching process, and beyond the control of its ministers. They may be physical, neurological, emotional, cultural, environmental; they may be present but not perceived, recognized but not identified.[9]

Thus, the court concluded that there was no workable "duty of care" and no degree of certainty that the plaintiff suffered injury within the meaning of the tort law of negligence. Furthermore, the court noted other public "policy considerations" for not imposing liability against school districts in this type of lawsuit.[10] The court observed: "To hold them to an actionable 'duty of care,' in the discharge of their academic functions, would expose them to the tort claims — real or imagined — of disaffected students and parents in countless numbers."[11] Stating that there is no

---

9. *Id.* at 12.
10. *Id.* at 13.
11. *Id.*

readily acceptable standard of care does not mean that a standard of care cannot be established for educators. It may be difficult to do but it can be accomplished.

In *Donohue,* the court detailed some of the factors that should be considered in determining the existence of a duty of care. The court stated:

> Judicial recognition of the existence of a duty of care is dependent upon principles of sound public policy and involves the consideration of numerous relevant factors which include, *inter alia: moral* considerations arising from the view of society towards the relationship of the parties, the degree to which the courts should be involved in the regulation of that relationship and the social utility of the activity out of which the alleged injury arises; preventative considerations, which involve the ability of the defendant to adopt practical means of preventing injury, the possibility that reasonable men can agree as to the proper course to be followed to prevent injury, the degree of certainty that the alleged injuries were proximately caused by the defendant and the foreseeability of harm to the *plaintiff; economic* considerations, which include the ability of the defendant to respond in damages; and *administrative* considerations, which concern the ability of the courts to cope with a flood of new litigation, the probability of feigned claims and the difficulties inherent in providing the plaintiff's case [citations omitted].[12]

The New York court also stated:

> Upon our own examination and analysis of the relevant factors discussed above, which are involved in determining whether to judicially recognize the existence of a legal duty of care running from educators to students, we, like the court in *Peter W.,* hold that no such duty exists. Other jurisdictions have adopted this reasoning as well (see *Beaman v. Des Moines Area*

---

12. *Id.* at 14-15.

Community Coll., 5th Judicial Dist. of Iowa, March 23, 1977, Law No. CL 15 8532, HOLLIDAY, J.; *Garrett v. School Bd. of Broward Co.,* Circuit Ct., 17th Judicial Cir., Broward Co., Fla., Dec. 5, 1977, Case No. 77-8703). *This determination does not mean that educators are not ethically and legally responsible for providing a meaningful public education for the youth of our State. Quite the contrary, all teachers and other officials of our schools bear an important public trust and may be held to answer for the failure to faithfully perform their duties. It does mean, however, that they may not be sued for damages by an individual student for an alleged failure to reach certain educational objectives* [emphasis added].[13]

The *Donohue* court, in effect, is saying, *yes,* teachers and school officials may be held to answer for the failure to faithfully perform their duties but *no,* they cannot be sued for damages by an individual student for an alleged failure to reach certain educational objectives. Questions that need to be explored and answered are: "What are those duties that they have to faithfully perform? Are they identifiable? Are they measurable against a standard? To whom are teachers accountable for the breach of same? Does society want to give educators protection from prosecution by students for intellectual harm? Query: If those in a position to remove a teacher for failure to properly perform his or her duty refuse to do so and the teacher continues to teach, what happens to the students who are "forced" to study under that teacher? If they are intellectually harmed, where do they turn for recompense? If the courts are unavailable, is there really a realistic forum?

In *Peter W.* the plaintiff argued:

At the heart of this action is the question of what function do our public schools serve. *Defendants claim*

---

13. *Id.*

that the public schools exist for the general good and have no obligations to any individual student. Such contention is not only legally unsupportable but makes a mockery of the very concept of public education. If our public schools do not exist to teach individual students such as the plaintiff the basic skills of reading and writing, they do not exist to teach any students such skills or to serve the public by providing an educated citizenry, and we had best spend our tax dollars in more meaningful ways.

If, on the other hand, our public school system is designed to provide an education for the children of this state, then it is clear that having undertaken to provide an educational system, that system must exercise reasonable care in discharging its duties to its captive clientele and comply with the statutory standards set forth in the Education Code in the operation of the schools.

Perhaps, however, one statement needs to be made clear: plaintiff does not claim that the defendants are liable simply because they failed to teach him, or any other student, how to read. Quite to the contrary, plaintiff's claim is based upon the fact that the defendants, their agents and employees failed to teach him how to read because they failed to exercise reasonable care in the discharge of their professional duties, because they failed to exercise that degree of professional skill required of the ordinary prudent educator under similar circumstances, because they made negligent or intentional misrepresentations of fact regarding plaintiff's educational progress and violated mandatory duties imposed upon them in the operation of the public schools under the California Education Code and the administrative regulations promulgated thereto. Plaintiff does not seek to impose upon the public schools of this State an absolute duty to teach every student enrolled therein every subject, but to exercise competence and reasonable care in instructional matters in accordance with professional and statutory standards. That burden is no more than the burden placed upon other state agencies and other professions.

> *... Standards of care for educators, like doctors, engineers, or other professionals, are established in judicial proceedings through the use of expert witness and testimony.* One commentator, in discussing a similar apprehension against judicial determination of adequacy of treatment in mental hospitals observed, ... courts are routinely called upon to evaluate conflicting expert opinions and to resolve technical controversies in areas outside judicial expertise (emphasis added).[14]

The plaintiff in *Peter W.* noted that the argument generally made by defendants that the public schools do not exist for the benefit of individual students but for the benefit of the public in general is not only unsupported by any legal authority, but is totally untenable.[15] As stated in another context:

> The public schools were not created, nor are they supported, for the benefit of the teachers herein ... *but for the benefit of the pupils* and the *remitting* benefit to their parents and the community at large.[16]

The plaintiff further maintained that the argument advanced by the defendants that there is no duty to teach a student any particular subject ignores one of the most fundamental rules of tort law: "where an individual — or a public entity — undertakes to perform an act, *even one voluntarily or gratuitously assumed,* it is under a duty to exercise reasonable care and not perform the act in a negligent manner [emphasis added]."[17] Can legal and logical principles support the argument that this fundamental principle of tort law can be ignored or violated by the educational system? Can one justify permitting teachers to

---

14. Plaintiff's Memorandum in Response to Defendants' Demurrer, Peter W., *supra* note 1, at 2-4.

15. *Id.* at 7.

16. *Id.*

17. *Id.* at 14.

425

teach negligently? Does the school system have any obligation to its students? Do teachers have any obligation to the students? Based on legal and logical principles, can one support the argument that there is no obligation by the school system or teachers? There is no obligation? If one concludes that there is an obligation, then the question that needs to be addressed is: "What is that obligation and corresponding duty? If there is a recognized duty, is the judicial system capable of determining whether the duty was exercised with reasonable care? If the judicial system is not capable of determining how the duty was exercised, what then? If it can be determined that there is a recognized duty, are we prepared to state — to conclude — that our judicial system is not capable of deciding whether that duty was performed negligently or perhaps not at all? The obligation of a teacher to his students to exercise reasonable care in instruction and supervision has been recognized in many states. In a California case holding a teacher liable for monetary damages for failure to exercise reasonable care in the instruction of students, a physical education teacher was found negligent in instructing a student in a physical education class.[18] The court stated:

> The question is whether school officials used the same care as persons of ordinary prudence charged with the duty of carrying on the public school system would use under the same circumstances. The legislature has made school districts responsible for the injury of any pupil resulting from the failure of other officers or employees to use ordinary care. What is ordinary care depends upon the circumstances of each particular case and is to be determined as a fact with reference to the situation and knowledge of the parties.[19]

18. *Id.*
19. *Id.* at 15.

426

Can't the same argument used for physical injuries be used for intellectual harm? Furthermore, the plaintiff states that there is a special relationship between a teacher and a student, and between the school district and the student, upon which to base tort liability. Plaintiff notes the special relationship between students and teachers established both by the existence of the compulsory school attendance laws and the common law relationship of students and teachers — the duty to exercise reasonable care in the instruction and supervision of students.[20] Concerning the argument of compulsory school attendance, the plaintiff stated:

> First of all, it must be recognized that students do not attend public schools as a voluntary matter. Under California's compulsory school attendance laws, minors between the ages of six and sixteen are required, under criminal penalty, to attend public schools.... A student is thus required to surrender a certain measure of his personal liberty for a substantial period of time in order to comply with the provisions of compulsory school attendance laws. Forced to attend school, it is not unreasonable to suggest that the school has some minimal obligation to provide educational services. Indeed, one might fairly challenge the legality of the compulsory school attendance law if defendant's contention that the schools owe individual students no obligation was in fact true [citation omitted].
>
> .... Finally, the long-standing doctrine of *in loco parentis* establishes a special relationship between the student and the teacher. Although recent cases have substantially undercut the absolute control exerted by school officials over students in the past years [citation omitted], school officials have long relied upon the doctrine to exert extraordinary power over student activities and behavior, e.g., ... corporal punishment ... locker searches. The assumption of the broad parental

---

20. *Id.* at 16.

powers under the *in loco parentis* doctrine by the school district necessarily entails the assumption of the correlative obligation to act in the best interests of the child.

Both the cases holding school districts liable for negligence of their employees in instructing and supervising students placed in their custody, and the legal presumptions underlying the compulsory school attendance laws and the common law doctrine of *in loco parentis* make it clear that the school district and its employees have at least the minimal obligation to exercise reasonable care in instructing students. Where the professional standards of care applicable to the teaching profession have been breached, liability attaches as in any other field.[21]

In his memorandum, the plaintiff in *Peter W.* notes that the California Supreme Court has consistently interpreted the provisions of the state constitution relating to education as vesting a legal, enforceable, right in California children to receive a free public education,[22] and in one of the earliest education cases stated:

The opportunity of instruction at public schools is afforded the youth of the state by the statutes of the state, enacted in obedience to the special command of the Constitution of the State .... The advantage or benefit thereby vouchsafe to each child, of attending public school is therefore ... *a right — a legal right — as distinctively so as the vested right in property owned is a legal right and as such it is protected and entitled to be protected by all the guarantees by which the other rights are protected and secured to the possessor.*[23]

---

21. *Id.* at 16-18.
22. *Id.* at 37.
23. *Id.* at 38.

The "right to an education today means more than access to a classroom."[24] Therefore, it has been suggested that the arguments made that the right to an education secured by the California State Constitution means nothing more than the right to a chair in a classroom and the obligation to protect students from physical hazards makes a mockery of our school system.[25] Moreover, the plaintiff's argument that education in the State of California shall consist of more than the mere baby-sitting function is also reiterated throughout the California Education Code.[26] Section 7504 of the Code provides:

> The Legislature hereby recognizes that it is the policy of the people of the State of California to provide an educational opportunity to every individual to the end that every student leaving school should be prepared to enter the world of work; that every student who graduates from any state-supported educational institution should have sufficient marketable skills for legitimate remunerative employment and that every qualified and eligible adult citizen should be afforded an educational opportunity to become suitably employed in some remunerative field of employment.[27]

The plaintiff in *Peter W.* states that the issue presented is whether the public school system owes individual students the "duty" to teach the subject matter in a given course.

> Appellant has never claimed school officials owed him a duty to teach him how to read; the duty asserted by appellant and breached by the respondents is the *duty to exercise reasonable care in teaching him how to read.* Appellant has never even remotely suggested that respondents have an absolute duty to teach him or

24. *Id.*
25. *Id.* at 39.
26. *Id.*
27. *Id.*

429

any other student the subject matter in any given course. What he does claim is that they have an obligation to refrain from negligent conduct in the operation of public schools which results in damage to individual students. That duty is a minimal obligation to impose upon a public school system. Neither does the appellant seek to impose liability for every mistake or error made by school employees. The duty claimed is that of using "the same care as persons of ordinary prudence charged with the duty of carrying on the public school system, would use under the same circumstances" [citation omitted].[28]

In his brief, the plaintiff-appellant in *Donohue* maintained:

If plaintiff's contention and position are correct and tenable, the facts alleged in the complaint, and provable at a trial, will establish that defendant breached this duty and obligation. When defendant accepted plaintiff into its school, it became obligated to educate plaintiff in an adequate and meaningful manner, have its teachers and other trained personnel use their learning, skills and experience in a competent, adequate manner and recognize an obvious condition of a student who is unable to read or comprehend simple written English.

The plaintiff charges that defendant's teachers and personnel were either indifferent or negligently did not observe and recognize this open and obvious condition of the plaintiff. There is, therefore, pleaded every factually legal allegation necessary and sufficient to charge this defendant's employees with negligence in the performance of their duties and obligations because:

    (1) The defendant owed the plaintiff a cognizable duty of care;

---

28. Appellant's Reply Brief, Peter W. v. San Francisco Unified School District, Civil No. 36851, Ct. of App. (First Dist. Dir. 2, Calif., 1975), pp. 17-18.

(2) The defendant failed to discharge that duty; and

(3) The plaintiff suffered damage as a proximate result of such neglectful conduct of defendant's personnel.

Some arguments may be made, and, in fact, the affirming opinion of the Court below argues that *all* students receive the same educational procedures and that many of the students managed to learn and progress. In *Peter W. v. San Francisco, etc., supra,* the court claimed that inability to read and write "... are influenced by a host of factors which affect the pupil subjectively, from outside the formal teaching process and beyond the control of its ministers."

That bland statement is true of *all* human conduct and does not answer the claim of this plaintiff that he went through four years of high school, could not read or write simple English, this deficiency became manifest and obvious at an early stage of his educational process in defendant's school and that it was the indifference and/or neglect of defendant's personnel which "pushed" plaintiff through school, with failing grades, doing absolutely nothing to help or assist plaintiff in an effort to correct his deficiency.

What plaintiff says here is that defendant is obliged to do more than collect state funds, build schools and supply teachers for its students. It is also obliged to see to it that its students obtain a proper and meaningful education. This the defendant did not do. Its attempt at "social promotion" in the face of a large percentage of student illiteracy is wrong. It is the correct time and place for the Court to put a stop to this.

The affirming opinion below argued that plaintiff's report cards "... gave notice to his parents and himself that he had failed in two or more subjects" and imposed upon plaintiff the obligation of demanding special testing. This contention is not supported by the complaint which alleges that neither plaintiff nor his parents were aware of plaintiff's failures until several months after graduation. Furthermore, plaintiff should not be saddled with any alleged neglect on the

431

part of his parents, which the parents are prepared to show is not the fact.

Any determination of the nature, and to what extent, defendant's acts or omissions proximately caused plaintiff's inability to read or write simple English should await a full trial of the issues and proof offered in support of the claim.

It should be pointed out that there is no relation here between the parents' economic level and the illiteracy found in depressed areas. Plaintiff's parents are middle class, productive and enjoy a fair degree of financial security.

It is respectfully submitted that the complaint fully and fairly alleges sufficient facts to establish that defendant breached its duty and obligation to furnish plaintiff with a proper and meaningful education.[29]

The plaintiff argued:

These neglectful acts of defendant's employees were the proximate cause of the harm and damage inflicted on the plaintiff when he was "pushed" through school, given failing grades and was graduated without the basic ability to read or comprehend simple written English.

Further, the failures by the plaintiff appear to have violated the regulation of the State Commissioner, in effect during the period at bar, which provided (8 NYCRR 103.2):

103.2 High school diplomas. In order to secure a State diploma of any type, the following requirements must be met: (1) The satisfactory completion of an approved four-year course of study in a registered four-year or six-year secondary school, including English, social studies including American history, health, physical education and such other special requirements as are required by statute and (re-

---

29. Brief in Behalf of Plaintiff-Appellant, Donohue v. Copiague Union Free School District, Suffolk County Clerk's Index No. 77/1128, Court of Appeals, State of New York, pp. 13-16.

gent's regulations) established by the Commissioner of Education.

As the dissenting Justice below observed:

Anyone reading the plaintiff's high school transcript would be hard pressed to describe his work as a "satisfactory completion" of a course of study.

When defendant, with knowledge of plaintiff's failing grades, promoted the plaintiff in a perfunctory manner, it violated the intent and spirit of former Section 4404 of the Education Law, cited hereinabove.

It is, therefore, respectfully submitted that plaintiff's claim is actionable because the complaint sets forth more than sufficient facts to establish that defendant is liable to plaintiff because it breached a duty and obligation imposed upon it as a matter of law.[30]

On the other side is the argument advanced by the defendant in the *Donohue* case:

When the State undertakes public education, it is not contemplating a tort duty which would make the State or individual teachers or administrators liable to students for money damages whenever the student fails to learn because of the alleged careless administration of the schools or negligent teaching in the classroom. The pedagogical process of transferring knowledge and cognitive skills is so complex and as yet inadequately understood, as not properly to be the subject of the imposition of a tort duty.

It is submitted that in light of the complexity of the problems, a court of law is not in a position to decide what is or is not reasonable conduct and furthermore to decide whether there has been established an adequate evidentiary basis to connect the alleged tort with the claimed injury.

When the insolvency of local government becomes more than an abstract hypothesis, the judiciary should be extremely cautious about recognizing new rights which could impose excessive burdens on nearly empty

---

30. *Id.* at 16-19.

public coffers. A duty such as the one asserted in the complaint would render public education economically unfeasible.[31]

Who should bear the loss resulting from academic negligence — the student who did nothing wrong or the negligent school district? After all, students can't ordinarily insure themselves from negligent instructors — instructors who caused them academic harm. The school districts, on the other hand, may be able to obtain adequate insurance.

It has been argued that the standard of a reasonable educator is difficult to establish because of the vague and undefined principles that characterize the field; the absence of standards, in fact, has militated against the imposition of liability.[32] However, it has been noted:

> This lack of standards need not, however, preclude the judiciary from assessing liability. The field of psychiatry is similarly replete with vague standards. Although psychiatry is a medical specialty, the practitioner has a much wider scope of discretion than the physician because of the limited use of diagnostic tools. The scope of discretion makes the determination of a standard of care difficult and has contributed to a scarcity of successful psychiatric malpractice actions. By eliminating the need for a precise definition of a standard of care, flagrant violations of the doctor-patient relationship have justified the imposition of liability. Where the breach is obvious to any onlooker, the judiciary has recognized it as a breach of an implicit psychiatric standard. By analogy, recognition of a cause of action for educational malpractice should at least be possible where defendant's actions constitute a blatant

---

31. Memorandum on Behalf of Defendant, Donohue v. Copiague Union Free School District, Suffolk County Clerk's Index No. 17/1128, Court of Appeals, State of New York, pp. 92-93.

32. Alice J. Klein, *Educational Malpractice: Can the Judiciary Remedy the Growing Problem of Functional Illiteracy?*, SUFFOLK UNIVERSITY LAW REVIEW 27 (Winter 1979), p. 38.

violation of the legally mandated student-educator relationship, as, for example, in the case of social promotion [footnotes omitted].[33]

Beckman, another education scholar, notes:

Among the numerous public policy considerations which influence judicial notions of a cognizable duty of care, two have received attention in recent litigation involving allegations of educational malpractice. Duty of care has been asserted based on an obligation to teach non-negligently implied by statutory provisions on education. In addition, a school district's acts have been characterized as so "egregious" as to warrant judicial recognition of liability in order to deter future negligent conduct. Taken together, these two policy considerations suggest an analogy to the tortious conduct of a rescuer who abandons a drowning man, only to find that the law will hold the rescuer liable for the resulting injury. Where a school district undertakes to educate a student under statutory [statutorily] mandated educational guidelines, then commits acts so grossly negligent as to deny the student the educational benefits of the statutory mandate, recovery for injuries resulting from that denial are [is] conceivable. A cause of action for educational malpractice may well receive initial judicial recognition through successfully harmonizing allegations of breach of a statutory duty of care and acts of negligence of a type and magnitude that would distinguish a student-plaintiff's injuries from others for whose benefit the statutory duty was created.[34]

It has been held that a teacher is negligent if he fails to carry out a duty owed a student, and that specific omission or unreasonable act is established as the proximate cause

---

33. *Id.*
34. Joseph Beckham, *Educational Malpractice: Breach of Statutory Duty and Affirmative Acts of Negligence by a School District*, 4 JOURNAL OF EDUCATIONAL FINANCE (Winter 1979), pp. 377, 383-84.

of an injury suffered by that student.[35] Over the years, primarily through litigation, the duties of a teacher have been summarized in the following three categories: (1) proper instruction, (2) proper supervision, and (3) proper maintenance and upkeep of all equipment and supplies used by students. All three duties have been and still are fertile grounds for negligence suits against teachers.[36]

Another writer explains:

> Allied to a school's duty to protect students from physical harm while on school grounds is the similar duty of a teacher to exercise reasonable care in the instruction of students to prevent physical injury arising out of the course of instruction. Injury in the chemistry laboratory would be treated by the courts no differently than injury in the sandbox.[37]

The United States Supreme Court imposed on the states the obligation to utilize effective teaching methods to provide particular groups of students with a meaningful education. In *Lau v. Nichols*,[38] the Court found that teaching methods which were incomprehensible to non-English speaking students "make a mockery of public education," and violate the Civil Rights Act of 1964. The Act bans discrimination on the basis of race, color, or national origin in any federally funded program. Bilingual education was thus mandated so that exposure to learning in the classroom did not remain a "hollow privilege."[39] Cohen further states:

---

35. Richard S. Vacca, *Teacher Malpractice*, 8 UNIVERSITY OF RICHMOND LAW REVIEW 447, 451 (1974).

36. *Id.* at 452.

37. Judith H. Berliner Cohen, *The ABC's of Duty: Educational Malpractice and the Functionally Illiterate Student*, 8 GOLDEN GATE UNIVERSITY LAW REVIEW 293, 300 (1978).

38. 414 U.S. 563 (1974).

39. Cohen, *supra* note 37, at 309.

By mandating that non-English speaking students be provided with instruction appropriate to their education needs, has the Court treated education as a fundamental right? The Court did not reach an equal protection argument because it could base its decision on statutory grounds. The language of the majority opinion in *Lau,* however, is language of constitutional import.

There is no equality of treatment merely by providing students with the same facilities, textbooks, teachers, and curriculum .... Basic English skills are at the very core of what these public schools teach. Imposition of a requirement that before a child can effectively participate in the educational program, he must already have acquired those basic skills is to make a mockery of public education.

The concurring opinion by Justice Stewart argued that, in view of changing social and linguistic patterns, a laissez faire attitude by school administrators was no longer acceptable. And, in his separate concurring opinion, Justice Blackmun stressed the large number of children affected by the school district's failure to provide special programs to develop basic skills. He emphasized that the Court's decision was not to be considered conclusive for all special groups if only a very few children were involved.

It was a short step from *Lau* to The Education for All Handicapped Children Act of 1975, which provides that free, appropriate public education in the least restrictive environment possible be available for all handicapped children.[40]

In response to an inquiry concerning the status of educational malpractice, an administrator of the California Professional Standards Commission on Teacher Credentialing states:

While we have no identifiable educational malpractice which sounds in tort as your letter seems to sug-

---

40. *Id.* at 310.

gest, California appellate courts have upheld dismissals of teachers for incompetence in their educational
practice. The next step, which has not yet been taken,
would be to hold the incompetent practitioner personally liable for the damage or injury caused by his/her
incompetence.

I am enclosing copies of two significant California
decisions: *Board of Education v. Mochson, et al.* 127
Cal. App. 3d 522 (1982), which sets forth in considerable detail specific acts/omissions which constitute incompetence; and *Perez v. C.P.C. et al.* (1983) 149 Cal.
App. 3d 1167 which establishes "incompetence" as a
standard if supported by evidence. *The court in the
Perez case has done what California educators have
failed to do, that is, declare a standard for assessing
teacher/educator professional performance* (emphasis
added).[41]

Concerning the *Mochson,*[42] case, the court stated:

This is an appeal by a school teacher and a cross appeal by a school district. The Commission on Professional Competence is a nominal party in the proceedings and has taken the same position as the school
teacher. Because of the three parties and the two appeals, the use of the terms "appellant" and "respondent" would be confusing, and the actual names of the
parties will be used throughout this opinion.

[Ms. Mochson] is a permanent certificated employee
of the Los Angeles Unified School District (hereinafter
School District). During a period from the summer of
1976 until early 1979, her teaching competency and
professional conduct were questioned and became a
matter of concern to the School District. Four separate

---

41. Walter W. Taylor, Administrator, Professional Standards, Commission on Teacher Credentialing, State of California; letter dated October 22, 1986, addressed to the author in response to inquiry concerning
activity in educational malpractice in the state of California.

42. Board of Education v. Commission on Professional Competence,
Mochson, Civ. No. 62857 Second Dist. Div. Two (Jan. 7, 1982), 127 Cal.
App. 3d 522; 179 Cal. Rptr. 605 (1982).

notices of unsatisfactory service were issued to her by
the School District, relating to various specified periods of time. According to the School District, she did
not show any improvement and a final notice of unsatisfactory service was issued on January 24, 1979
Thereafter the School District voted unanimously to
dismiss Ms. Mochson and in March 1979 she was
served by the School District with an accusation and
statement of charges which was the subject of a hearing by a Commission on Professional Competence
(hereinafter the Commission). Said hearing was convened and conducted pursuant to the provisions of Education Code section 44944.

The Commission conducted hearings, took evidence
and issued its decision. Of the 72 individual charges of
incompetency or unprofessional conduct, the Commission found that 14 had been proven. The Commission
also set forth in its decision three excusing justifications for Ms. Mochson's conduct. It declined to order
her dismissal.

The School District filed a petition for writ of mandamus in the superior court to review the decision of
the Commission pursuant to Education Code section
44945. Pursuant to this section, the court, on review,
"shall exercise its independent judgment on the evidence." (Ed. Code, § 44945.)

After appropriate proceedings the trial court rendered its decision. It found that 58 of the 72 charges
against Ms. Mochson had been proved. It further found
no support for the three excusing justifications and
ordered them stricken.

The School District had also asked the trial court to
order the dismissal of Ms. Mochson. The trial court
refused to order dismissal and instead set aside the
decision of the Commission and directed it to recon-
sider its action in the light of the court's decision and
to take any "further action specially enjoined upon it
by law." Following the announcement of its intended
decision, and a contested hearing concerning findings
of fact and conclusions of law, the trial court entered
findings of fact, conclusions of law and judgment.

Ms. Mochson appeals from the portion of the judgment setting aside the Commission decision. The School District appeals from the portion of the judgment returning the matter to the Commission for further action.[43]

The court went on to state:

(1) The scope of appellate review is set forth in *Pasadena Unified Sch. Dist. v. Commission on Professional Competence* (1977) 20 Cal. 3d 309, at pages 313-14 [142 Cal. Rptr. 439, 572 P.2d 53] as follows:

The decision of a Commission on Professional Competence may be challenged in superior court by means of a petition for a writ of mandate.... In reviewing a commission's decision, the superior court 'shall exercise its independent judgment on the evidence.' ... Where a superior court is required to make such an independent judgment upon the record of an administrative proceeding, the scope of review on appeal is limited. An appellate court must sustain the superior court's findings if substantial evidence supports them [citations]. In reviewing the evidence, an appellate court must resolve all conflicts in favor of the party prevailing in the superior court and must give the party the benefit of every reasonable inference in support of the judgment. When more than one inference can be reasonably deduced from the facts, the appellate court cannot substitute its deductions for those of the superior court.

....

(2) In view of our conclusion that the finding as true of the 58 charges by the trial court is supported by substantial evidence, we must consider the contention of the School District that the dismissal of Ms. Mochson should be ordered.

---

43. *Id.* at 524-25.

Under Education Code section 44944, subdivision (c) the Commission has no power to dispose of the charge by imposing probation, suspension of a dismissal or other alternative sanctions. The alternatives are that the employee be dismissed or not dismissed.

The question therefore is whether or not the sustaining of the 58 charges by the trial court requires, as a matter of law, the dismissal of Ms. Mochson. Put another way: If the matter was returned to the Commission with the findings of fact entered by the trial court, would it be an abuse of power or discretion for the Commission to determine that the employee should not be dismissed?

It should be noted that in the present posture of this case there is no further fact finding to be done. Some legal entity must make a decision as to whether or not Ms. Mochson should be dismissed *based solely on the facts* as found *in the 58 charges against her* established *by the trial court.* Those 58 charges are set forth in an appendix because it would be inappropriate to summarize them.

As stated in *Oakland Unified Sch. Dist. v. Olicker* (1972) 25 Cal. App. 3d 1098, 1109 [102 Cal. Rptr. 421]:

Adverting to the facts of the instant case we first observe that they are undisputed. Accordingly, the ultimate conclusion to be drawn from such facts is a question of law. (*Morrison v. State Board of Education, supra* 1 Cal.3d 214, 238; *Yakov v. Board of Medical Examiners, supra,* 68 Cal.2d 67, 74, fn. 7 [64 Cal. Rptr. 785, 435 P.2d 553].) The determination, therefore, of whether or not defendant's conduct demonstrates 'evident unfitness for service' is a question of law in the sense that it should be decided by an appellate court ....

We are not unmindful of the phrase from *Morrison v. State Board of Education* (1969) Cal.3d 214, 233 [82 Cal. Rptr. 175, 461 P.2d 375], to the effect that "Teachers, particularly in the light of their professional expertise, will normally be able to determine what kind of conduct indicates unfitness to teach." We

441

are cautious in substituting our judgment for that of the Commission. However, the Commission in this case is composed of two third grade teachers and an administrative law judge. They would be bound by the same 58 charges established as fact by the trial court. The law permits them, and this court, to consider only two alternatives.

It is significant to note here that the charges against Ms. Mochson do not involve a morals charge as in *Morrison v. State Board of Education, supra,* nor a false bomb threat as in *Board of Education v. Commission on Professional Competence* (1980) 102 Cal. App. 3d 555 [162 Cal. Rptr. 590], nor an alleged homosexual solicitation by a teacher in a public restroom as in *Board of Education v. Jack M., supra,* 19 Cal. 3d 691, nor letters critical of the education process written by a teacher to a local newspaper, as in *Board of Trustees v. Owens* (1962) 206 Cal. App. 2d 147 [23 Cal. Rptr. 710], nor the involvement of a junior college teacher with a student off campus as in *Board of Trustees v. Stubblefield* (1971) 16 Cal. App. 3d 820 [94 Cal. Rptr. 318]. In all of the foregoing cases the evidence against the teacher did not go to fitness to teach nor to professional competence.

In stark comparison we have in this case significant evidence of incompetency, professional unfitness and persistent violation of appropriate educational standards. The charges indicate Ms. Mochson's failure, over a two and one-half-year period, to supervise students assigned to her, a failure to organize and implement a balanced program of instruction and a failure to maintain classroom control. They further establish a continuing failure to follow appropriate administrative directives and to plan instruction.

The Los Angeles Unified School District is the second largest school district in the United States. Students represent a broad spectrum of economic status, cultural heritage, intellectual ability and motivation. They are entitled to an adequate and meaningful educational opportunity. The School District must do its best to provide this opportunity. Ms. Mochson was as-

signed to teach seven- and eight-year-old children. The
established charges disclose a pattern of failure to perform her professional responsibilities, and an inability
or refusal to give her pupils legitimate and responsible
instruction. Admittedly, each charge by itself is not
significant. None are heinous crimes nor immoral acts.
The School District describes this as a "waterwheel
case of an accumulation of multiple instances of care-
lessness, inattention and neglect." Ms. Mochson re-
sponds by characterizing the charges as "cumulative,
duplicative and redundant ...." Both characterizations
are correct, but the very characterization of these
charges by Ms. Mochson as "cumulative, duplicative
and redundant," when it is recalled that the charges
are established as proven, serves to emphasize and
support the position of the School District. At some
point the School District should be able to require
more of its teachers and we believe that point has been
reached in this case.

We hold as a matter of law that the 58 charges established against Ms. Mochson justify and require that
she be dismissed. If we were to agree with the remand
to the Commission ordered by the trial court, the result would most certainly be further delay in carrying
out the School District's decision, and the great likelihood of a further delaying proceeding in the trial court
and an appeal to this court. We should avoid an "unnecessary, inappropriate and ... palpable waste of judicial resources." (Cf. *People v. Davis* (1981), 29 Cal. 3d
814, 831, 835 [176 Cal. Rptr. 521, 633, P.2d 186].)

....

For the reasons discussed above, we are compelled to
the conclusion that the judgment of the trial court
should be modified to direct dismissal of Ms. Mochson
based on the 58 charges found against her. However,
the frivolous nature of *her* appeal and the inappropriate manner in which it has been argued in this court is
another reason why this litigation should be put to rest
without further delay if legally possible.

Accordingly, we affirm the judgment of the trial
court insofar as it found that the 58 charges against
Ms. Mochson were true. We modify the portion of the
judgment remanding the proceedings to the Commission, and in lieu thereof we order that the judgment be
entered confirming the dismissal of Ms. Mochson.[44]

---

44. *Id.* at 525-32; The following is a sample of the charges taken from
the Appendix, pp. 534-35.

44. On or about January 30, 1978, Mr. Sharpe visited Ms.
Mochson's classroom at her request at approximately 9:05 a.m.
When Mr. Sharpe entered the room, Ms. Mochson told the pupils
that Mr. Sharpe did not think the pupils knew what to do in the
classroom, and that the classroom was unorganized. Ms. Mochson
directed the pupils to get settled and then told Mr. Sharpe to go
around and ask the children if they knew what they were doing. She
repeated this several times in a loud voice. Ms. Mochson demonstrated poor judgment and a lack of restraint in the manner in
which she repeatedly urged the principal to check the children's
work.
45. On or about February 9, 1978, Mr. Sharpe visited Ms.
Mochson's classroom at the request of Ms. Gay Okuyama Mori, a
room partner. Ms. Mochson was on a break. Ms. [Mr.] Sharpe observed that Ms. Mochson had failed to provide an activity for the
pupils. There were checkerboards but no checkers. Crayons were
not provided, as they were locked up.
46. On or about February 10, 1978, Ms. Marian K. Kubota,
Braddock Drive ECE Coordinator, asked Ms. Mochson to permit her
to review Ms. Mochson's plan book in order to provide assistance
and guidance in implementing plans. Ms. Mochson stated she would
submit the plans on Tuesday, February 14. Ms. Mochson failed to
submit any plans on Tuesday, February 14, 1978, or on any date
thereafter.
47. On or about March 2, 1978, Ms. Arlene J. Morris, Administrative Area D (now Administrative Area 4) ECE Coordinator, observed Ms. Mochson's classroom on a routine visit to the school. Ms.
Morris reported, in writing, that the door was locked, the learning
centers untouched, and that the language work was below grade
level. In additions, Ms. Morris stated that Ms. Mochson interrupted
the lesson to excuse the children to go elsewhere when she (Ms.
Morris) arrived.
48. On or about March 6, 1978, Mr. Sharpe observed Ms.
Mochson's class at approximately 9:45 a.m. Mr. Sharpe observed a
lack of classroom organization and control. Pupils were inattentive.
49. On or about March 6, 1978, Mr. Sharpe observed Ms.
Mochson's class on the playground at approximately 10:05 a.m. Mr.
Sharpe observed a lack of organization in the games. Some of the

In *Perez v. Commission on Professional Competence*,[45] a California court, in effect, established "competence" as a standard. The alleged facts, as related by the court, are as follows:

> Perez, a permanent certificated employee of the San Diego Unified School District (District), taught Spanish at Mira Mesa High School from 1976 until November 2, 1981, when he was dismissed for unprofessional conduct, incompetence and failure to follow District rules. His petition for a writ of mandate setting the dismissal aside was denied. He appeals, contending improper notice of the charges, due process defects in application of standards of competency and the evidence does not support the findings of the court.
>
> In early 1980, Perez began to lose control of his classroom and his students. Tardiness, inattention, siestas, talking in class, disdain for discipline, reading unrelated paperback books, general goofing off — all characterized his students and the classroom environment. In April, two students set a rug afire. Perez did nothing about it. A student asked him for a pass and reported the fire to the vice principal.
>
> On May 7, 1980, Perez received a summary evaluation report from the District rating him unsatisfactory in all categories — achievement of stated objectives, maintenance of proper control, preservation of suitable environment and performance of other duties and re-

boys were out of their designated area and the girls were assigned to jump rope in an area reserved for first-grade students.

50. On or about March 6, 1978, Ms. Mochson referred a student to the office. Mr. Sharpe counseled the student and took him back to class. When Mr. Sharpe and the student entered the classroom, Ms. Mochson berated the child in a loud voice in front of the class. Mr. Sharpe remained in the classroom to observe a mathematics lesson. All the students in the class were given a ditto sheet to work on. Mr. Sharpe observed that the assignment was different from the stated lesson plan.

45. Perez v. Commission on Professional Competence, Civ. No. 26994, Fourth Dist. Div. One, Dec. 20, 1983, 149 Cal. App. 3d 1167; 197 Cal. Rptr. 390 (Dec. 1983).

sponsibilities. The report noted Perez' failings: poor classroom control, disrespect shown to him by students, inadequate instruction, parental complaints students were not learning the "basics." The evaluators commented Perez denied the complaints were valid and refused any assistance to deal with his problem.

The "hang-loose" classroom environment did not change; the students decorated the walls and desks with graffiti and came and went at their pleasure. Perez continued to conduct his classes interchangeably in English and Spanish contrary to District requirements, and the Spanish instruction was marred by incorrect grammar, spelling, faulty translations and lessons below grade level of the students.

On January 9, 1981, another report rated Perez unsatisfactory in three areas, noted need for improvement in maintenance of classroom control and recommended a notice of incompetency and unprofessional conduct. On January 27, 1981, that notice issued to Perez advising he failed to achieve performance objectives, to maintain classroom control, to supervise, to maintain a suitable learning environment and appropriate relationship with students and parents.

Perez did not react to these reports. The students continued in control. On April 28, 1981, Perez again was evaluated and graded unsatisfactory on all counts. On May 12, the District superintendent filed charges against Perez seeking his dismissal, and an accusation to that effect was filed with the Board of Education May 23. The District's Commission on Professional Competence (Commission) heard the matter, and Perez was dismissed November 2, 1981.[46]

In deciding the case, the court reasoned:

Perez conceded the District "paid lip service" to notice requirements, but contends he was not given opportunity to ascertain the charges or to correct his faults. Education Code section 44938 [All statutory

---

46. *Id.* at 1170-171.

references are to the Education Code unless otherwise specified] at times relevant here required Perez be given during the school term at least 90 days written notice of unprofessional conduct or incompetency with specific instances of behavior sufficient to enable him to correct his faults and overcome the grounds of the charged misconduct. On January 27, 1981, Perez was served with such written notice and with the evaluation reports.

Commencing in May 1980, the evaluations told Perez his work was unsatisfactory and described in detail his unsatisfactory performance. Specific recommendations were made for improvement. Counseling and assistance were offered. Perez failed to correct his faults or to improve his performance. The final written notice on January 27, 1981, was timely given and told Perez again in detail his work was unsatisfactory and suggested curative action. Again, he failed to take corrective action within the 90-day period. The charges were filed May 12 and the accusation May 23, both outside the 90-day period. Nothing more by way of the section 44938 notice was required. (*California Teachers Assn. v. Governing Board* (1983) 144 Cal. App. 3d 27 [192 Cal. Rptr. 358]).

Perez claims the District failed to establish standards against which his teaching performance must be evaluated and as to which his deficiencies were to be assessed. Without objection, the Commission received the foreign language section of the District's course of study for high schools setting out the basis for instruction in foreign languages. That document provides teaching guidelines and was available to Perez. Commencing in 1980, Perez received periodic evaluation reports with unsatisfactory ratings supported by specific instances and including recommendations for improvement. These periodic reports fulfilled the District's requirement to establish a system of evaluation and assessment of Perez' performance under section 44660 which in turn are necessary to fulfillment of notice requirements under section 44938. (*California Teachers Assn. v. Governing Board, supra,* 144 Cal.

App. 3d 27). Perez was thus informed as to the standards expected of him, his failure to attain them and corrective action to be taken by him.

We examine the basis for dismissal for unprofessional conduct and incompetency. Section 44932, subdivision (a) permits dismissal of permanent employees for "immoral or unprofessional conduct." Section 44933 permits dismissal "on grounds of unprofessional conduct consisting of acts of omission other than those specified in Section 44932, but any such charge shall specify instances of behavior deemed to constitute unprofessional conduct." Section 44932, subdivision (d) permits dismissal for "incompetency."

Here, the Commission found cause for Perez' dismissal for unprofessional conduct under both subdivisions (a) and (d) of section 44932 and for incompetency under section 44933. The Commission used the same facts and findings to support Perez' dismissal as to the two counts of unprofessional conduct and the single count of incompetency for consistent failure in each of the following respects:

1. To achieve performance objectives in teaching Spanish;

2. To maintain proper control of assigned students in that they talked during class, moved around the room and paid no attention to Perez;

3. To maintain a suitable learning environment characterized by inadequate progress of students in advanced classes, their inability to speak Spanish, inaccurate instruction, failure to plan class activities and to implement counseling and recommendations;

4. To perform other duties and responsibilities such as submitting lesson plans and failing to use teacher sign-in sheets. (3) The Commission finding of cause to dismiss for unprofessional conduct under section 44933 was based on the *same acts or omissions* specified for dismissal under section 44932, subdivision (a). As a section 44933 dismissal is supportable only on acts or omissions *other* than a section 44932, subdivision (a) dismissal, the Commission's findings and conclusions

cannot support dismissal for unprofessional conduct under section 44933.

We turn, then, to section 44932, subdivision (a) permitting dismissal for "immoral or unprofessional conduct." The phrase is not defined in the Education Code. While, as we have seen, the District promulgated a system of evaluation and assessment constituting standards for performance of Perez' teaching duties, the system did not set out in so many words the kind of conduct that would be considered by the District as comprising grounds for dismissal for "unprofessional conduct." That phrase appears for the first time in the January 9, 1981, evaluation report recommending issuance of a "Notice of Incompetency and Unprofessional Conduct" which was sent to Perez on January 21, 1981, triggering the 90-day period under section 44938.

Morrison v. State Board of Education (1969) 1 Cal. 3d 214 [82 Cal. Rptr. 175, 461 P.2d 375], considered revocation of teaching credentials for "immoral or unprofessional conduct" and acts involving moral turpitude under former sections 13202 and 13219 (now §§ 44421 and 44437). The teacher involved had engaged in homosexual activities for a period of one week, resigned his teaching position a year later and his credentials were revoked five years after his resignation. The court held the term "immoral or unprofessional conduct" authorizes disciplinary action only for conduct indicating unfitness to teach.

We therefore conclude that the Board of Education cannot abstractly characterize the conduct in this case as 'immoral,' 'unprofessional,' or 'involving moral turpitude' within the meaning of section 13202 of the Education Code unless that conduct indicates that the petitioner is unfit to teach. In determining whether the teacher's conduct thus indicates unfitness to teach the board may consider such matters as the likelihood that the conduct may have adversely affected students or fellow teachers, the degree of such adversity anticipated, the proximity or remoteness in time of the conduct, the type of

449

teaching certificate held by the party involved, the extenuating or aggravating circumstances, if any, surrounding the conduct, the praiseworthiness or blameworthiness of the motives resulting in the conduct, the likelihood of the recurrence of the questioned conduct, and the extent to which disciplinary action may inflict an adverse impact or chilling effect upon the constitutional rights of the teacher involved or other teachers. These factors are relevant to the extent that they assist the board in determining whether the teacher's fitness to teach, i.e., in determining whether the teacher's future classroom performance and overall impact on his students are likely to meet the board's standards [footnotes omitted]. (*Id.*, at pp. 229-230.)

Board of Education v. Jack M. (1977) 19 Cal. 3d 691 [139 Cal. Rptr. 700, 566 P.2d 602] construed the phrase "immoral or unprofessional conduct" in former section 13403, subdivision (a) (now § 44932, subd. (a)) as constituting "fitness to teach." There, the court affirmed a trial court determination [that] a single instance of lewd conduct by a teacher whose career had been exemplary did not demonstrate unfitness to teach and noted decisions following *Morrison* have construed "immoral or unprofessional conduct" as used in then section 13403, subdivision (a) (now § 44932, subd. (a)) to mean only such conduct as indicates unfitness to teach.

The decisions requiring unfitness to teach as the measure of unprofessional conduct involved incidents of extracurricular sexual or criminal activity or use of sexually explicit teaching materials [footnote omitted].

Here, the Commission found continuing unsatisfactory teacher performance in the classroom coupled with an inability or unwillingness to conform to required standards. *Morrison* holds civil as well as criminal statutes must be sufficiently clear as to give a fair warning of the conduct prohibited and to provide a standard or guide against which conduct can be uniformly judged by courts and administrative agencies. The fitness to teach standard as a measure of unprofessional conduct makes specific the kind of conduct required of teachers in this regard. So construed, the term "unprofessional conduct" is not vague, and a teacher's dismissal for that reason is not a denial of due process. (*Morrison v. State Board of Education, supra,* 1 Cal. 3d 214, 230-231.)

We conclude unsatisfactory teacher performance said to be unprofessional conduct should be measured by the standard of fitness to teach. Absent this objective measure of performance, the livelihood of the teacher is dependent upon an abstract characterization of conduct which will shift and change from board to board, district to district and year by year. Such discretion is required to be bridled by the restraints of the standard of fitness to teach.

We hold the phrase "unprofessional conduct" as used in section 44932, subdivision (a) is conduct such as to indicate unfitness to teach. The record on appeal does not include any findings by the Commission or the court to the effect Perez is unfit to teach and the transcript of the Commission hearings does not include evidence of the factors enumerated in *Morrison.* Thus, dismissal under section 44932, subdivision (a) is not supported by the evidence.

Having concluded dismissal for unprofessional conduct cannot stand, we turn to the remaining charge of dismissal for incompetence.

A particular act or omission on the part of a teacher may constitute more than one of the causes for his removal under section 44932. (*Tarquin v. Commission on Professional Competence* (1978) 84 Cal. App. 3d 251 [148 Cal. Rptr. 522].) It follows the same acts or omissions may constitute grounds for removal for incompetence or unprofessional conduct.

While causes for dismissal such as moral turpitude, unprofessional conduct and evident unfitness to teach are to be construed against the *Morrison* standard of fitness to teach, incompetency supported by specific acts is a basis for dismissal. *California Teachers Assn. v. Governing Board, supra,* 144 Cal. App. 3d 27, 36 affirmed a judgment denying a writ to set aside the dismissal of a teacher for incompetency under section 44932, subdivision (d). There, classroom discipline problems included students fighting, playing soccer in the classroom, yelling over the school intercom and the back door, throwing pencils, using vulgar language, disregard of instructions, requests for transfer and general disorder. Noting the lack of adopted guidelines for assessing teacher incompetency, the court held *Morrison* factors were not relevant in an incompetency dismissal.

. . . .

Incompetency as a basis for dismissal does not invoke the vagueness and uncertainty of the phrases — moral turpitude, immorality or unprofessional conduct. It is a plain word and means not competent. (The American Heritage Dict. of the English Language (1981) p. 666.) Competent, in turn, means properly or well-qualified; capable — adequate for the purpose, suitable; sufficient. (*Id.* at p. 271.) Incompetency does not invoke subjective analysis of standards of morality or professionalism which vary from individual to individual dependent on time, circumstances or custom. While empirical standards to measure teacher competence are not in the record before us, we have little doubt the teacher members of the Commission have the professional experience and skill meaningfully to assess teacher competence. (*California Teachers Assn. v. Governing Board, supra,* 144 Cal. App. 3d 27, 34.) Importantly, the concept of incompetency is not so arcane as to suggest a court is incapable of reviewing the record of administrative proceedings to determine if substantial evidence supports the agency conclusion. We hold incompetency to be its own standard and consider Perez' last contention, his dismissal for incompetence, is not supported by the record.

On review of Commission action, the trial court exercises its independent judgment on the evidence presented to the Commission. (*Pasadena Unified Sch. Dist. v. Commission on Professional Competence*

452

(1977) 20 Cal. 3d 309, 314 [142 Cal. Rptr. 439, 572 P.2d 53]). The trial court's judgment must be upheld on appeal if supported by substantial evidence. All conflicts are resolved in favor of the prevailing party who is entitled to the benefit of every reasonable inference to support the judgment. (*San Dieguito Unified High School Dist. v. Commission on Professional Competence* (1982) 135 Cal. App. 3d 378, 283 [185 Cal. Rptr. 203]). Where the trial court's findings are challenged, based on insufficiency of the evidence, Perez bears the heavy burden of showing that there is no substantial evidence to support those findings. (*Division of Labor Law Enforcement v. Transpacific Transportation Co.* (1979) 88 Cal. App. 3d 823, 829 [152 Cal. Rptr. 98]). We start with the presumption that the record contains evidence to sustain every finding of fact. (*Foreman & Clark Corp. v. Fallon* (1971) 3 Cal. 3d 875, 881 (92 Cal. Rptr. 162, 479 P.2d 362)). Our inquiry begins and ends with the determination as to whether there is any substantial evidence, contradicted or uncontradicted, which will support the finding of fact. (*Ibid.*)

Applying these rules to the record before us, we conclude sufficient evidence supports the judgment denying the writ and we affirm Perez' dismissal for incompetency.[47]

It can be argued that once a standard for "incompetence" has been established, then that standard could be used in educational malpractice cases. If there is no standard of care and no duty of care owed to the students, does this mean the teachers and the educational system could perform their work negligently and students would not have any recourse? Can a civilized society accept such conduct? Professor Foster,[48] in discussing this issue, quotes a pas-

---

47. *Id.* at 1171-72.
48. W.F. Foster, *Educational Malpractice: A Tort for the Untaught?*, 19:2 B.C. LAW REVIEW 161, 172-73 (1985).

sage by Lord Wilberforce in *Anns v. Merton London Borough Council:*[49]

> Through the trilogy of cases in this House — *Donohue v. Stevenson, Hedley Byrne & Co. Ltd. v. Heller & Partners Ltd.* and *Dorset Yacht Co. Ltd. v. Home Office,* [citations omitted] the position has now been reached that in order to establish that a duty of care arises in a particular situation, it is not necessary to bring the facts of that situation within those of previous situations in which a duty of care has been held to exist. Rather, the question has to be approached in two stages. First, one has to ask whether, as between the alleged wrongdoer and the person who has suffered damage, there is a sufficient relationship of proximity or neighbourhood such that, in the reasonable contemplation of the former, carelessness on his part may be likely to cause damage to the latter — in which case a prima facie duty of care arises. Secondly, if the first question is answered affirmatively, it is necessary to consider whether there are any considerations which ought to negative, or to reduce or limit the scope of the duty or the class of persons to whom it is owed or the damage to which a breach of it may give rise.... [50]

Furthermore, that there is a duty arising from contractual obligation has been based on the theory that accepting a student's enrollment establishes a school's contractual duty to teach. It has been noted that this theory of a contractual relationship between student and school is not new and has received a limited blessing by the courts. In fact, the application of contract theory to post secondary education is well established. As early as 1928, signed registration cards were held to be a formalization of an implied contract between the university and the students.[51]

In discussing this theory, Cohen writes:

---

49. *Id.* at 173; [1977] 2 W.L.R. 1024 (H.L.).
50. Anns v. Merton London Borough Council, at 1032.
51. Cohen, *supra* note 37, at 312.

However, the contract theory has been advanced successfully only when a student has challenged dismissal from the university. Furthermore, the courts have clearly limited the terms of the "agreement" between student and university: a student who has enrolled and who complies with reasonable university regulations, such as scholastic standing, attendance, deportment, and the payment of tuition, is entitled to pursue a course of study at the university. No court has gone so far as to extend a university's contractual obligation to effective teaching in the classroom.[52]

The author concludes by stating "no plaintiff to date has been able to convince a court that a school owes him or her any more than 'a chair in a classroom.'"[53]

Another basis for establishing a school's duty may lie in the state's voluntary assumption of the job of educating children. Once an individual or the state has taken on a responsibility, it must act with care in carrying out that responsibility. Cohen explains:

The policy behind holding a defendant responsible for his or her affirmative acts is to protect a plaintiff from conduct which aggravates an existing condition or leaves him or her worse off than he or she was. Can Peter W., or any similar plaintiff, convincingly argue that he is worse off having been inside a schoolroom? Or that anyone has been injured by receiving a diploma?

The computer-argument is that these students have been misled by an implied promise that the school would teach them to read. Relying on this promise — and it is one often expressed by well-intentioned teachers and school counselors — students do not seek additional tutoring. Or they choose to remain in the public school system rather than transferring to private schools. Insofar as they have been "deluded" into believing that it is not necessary to find alternate

52. *Id.*
53. *Id.*

means of education, the students are arguably worse off than they otherwise would have been. But the argument is speculative for all, and moot for many, since often those students with poor reading skills are from families that could not afford the expense of tutors or private schooling.[54]

Goodwin comments:

> Recent Supreme Court cases dealing with the franchise are based on a rationale that may be used to support the notion of an affirmative duty to provide equal educational opportunities. In the reapportionment cases the principle was established that accidents of geography and the arbitrary boundary lines of local government can afford no basis for discrimination among citizens of a state with respect to the impact of their ballots: the right to vote means more than simply pulling a lever: it signifies the right to an equal vote. Similarly, it may be said that "the right to an education today means more than access to classrooms." It should mean the right to the same quality education afforded every other student within the state. Presumably the rationale behind the one-man vote rule is that voting is a fundamental right which is preservative of other basic civil and political rights and thus it must be afforded to all on an equal basis. Yet, it has been observed, education seems the equal of voting in sheer importance to a democratic society [footnotes omitted].[55]

In response to a request for information regarding educational malpractice an attorney wrote:

> [With regard to allegations of academic negligence, there is] the problem with establishing a standard of

---

54. *Id.* at 313-14.

55. Robert E. Goodwin, *Equality and the Schools: Education as a Fundamental Interest,* 21 AMERICAN UNIVERSITY LAW REVIEW 716, 734 (September 1972). Original article published in the AMERICAN UNIVERSITY LAW REVIEW.

conduct. Most professions have some sort of "objective" standards of conduct. I am not sure that I have ever found such standards in regard to academic performance or capabilities. You can well appreciate my concern as an attorney that we have no benchmark against which to measure performance which is generally acceptable. I find that other malpractice actions generally refer to at least community standards (*e.g.,* medical) in order to provide a benchmark against which the performance of the professional being sued can be measured. Until such time as we can establish such standards, or clearly define the vague ones which may already be in existence, I believe there will be a significant problem with maintaining, much less winning, an educational malpractice suit for academic negligence. I can certainly see where "educational malpractice" in regard to ancillary services (psychological, medical, etc.) should be a viable legal cause of action because, in my opinion, it does not matter where you malpractice psychology, medicine, etc., it matters only whether or not you are guilty of malpractice.[56]

§ 13.2. The Compulsory Education Argument — A Mandate to Use Reasonable Care?

It has been pointed out that "school officials are solely responsible for student placement and should be responsible for the effects of misplacement — economic loss and emotional injury."[57] Furthermore, the compulsory attendance requirements mandate that educators use reasonable care in determining the proper grade level; otherwise, public education would offer little more than custodial care.[58]

---

56. David A. Hamilton, General Counsel, for the Superintendent of Education of the State of Louisiana; letter dated August 19, 1986, addressed to the author in response to inquiry concerning activity in educational malpractice in the State of Louisiana.

57. Klein, *supra* note 32, at 28-29.

58. *Id.*

Additionally, states Cohen:

> The special relationship between school and student
> derives from present-day compulsory attendance laws.
> "Requiring parents to see that their children attend
> school under pain of criminal penalties presupposes
> that an educational opportunity will be made avail-
> able to the children." The legality of compelling atten-
> dance might be questioned if the school district were
> not under a corresponding duty to exercise profes-
> sional care in operating its schools and educational
> programs. "The law has long recognized in many ways
> that children are entitled to special protection. This is
> particularly true during the process and period of their
> compulsory education." That this care extends beyond
> mere [merely] protecting the student from physical
> harm was established over three hundred years ago in
> the early Massachusetts laws ... which defined a
> school's function only in terms of educating children to
> read and write. The *raison d'être* for a school was to
> provide a literate citizenry who could function produc-
> tively for the benefit of the community. To argue that
> the school's duty is no longer to create a literate citi-
> zenry but is merely to protect children from injuries to
> their bodies is a gross distortion of the historical role of
> the public school system. Peter W. asserted: "The argu-
> ment advanced by the school district here that its obli-
> gation ... consists of nothing more than the right of a
> student to a chair in a classroom and protection from
> physical hazards makes a mockery of public education
> . . ." [footnotes omitted].[59]

Another writer commenting on this states:

> The argument for the recognition of a legal duty in the
> educational malpractice field is strengthened by com-
> pulsory education statutes requiring students to at-
> tend school is inherently illogical, if not illegal, where
> evidence indicates that the school fails to educate and
> where the school has no duty to educate. The compul-

---

59. Cohen, *supra* note 37, at 307.

sory education system was not created merely to baby-sit. Educational malpractice cases confront the system as being only half-functional: the schools keep children off the streets only to put them back onto the streets as young adults unable to obtain decent jobs.

The justification for compulsory education laws lies in the recognition of the parents' duty to educate his child for the child's sake, and the parent's duty to have the child educated for the benefit of the state ....

The dual duties of a parent both to his children and to the state are the theoretical bases for our compulsory education laws. If a parent can show that sending his child to public school will not fulfill these duties, then compulsory attendance becomes paradoxical. This anomalous situation in turn calls into question the constitutionality of our compulsory education laws: the due process prohibition against arbitrary confinement focuses on whether the educational program justifies compelling the student to attend school.

The due process argument has been successfully asserted in right-to-treatment cases which defend the rights of those involuntarily committed to state institutions in civil proceedings. The gravamen of the complaint in these cases is as follows: where an institution fails to treat those whose liberty has been taken away for the express purpose of rehabilitation, no justification for their confinement exists. "To deprive any citizen of his or her liberty upon the altruistic theory that the confinement is for humane therapeutic reasons and then fail to provide adequate treatment violates the very fundamentals of due process."

....

Proponents maintain the promise of a quality education is implicit in the compulsory education laws [footnotes omitted].[60]

---

60. Joan Blackburn, *Educational Malpractice: When Can Johnny Sue?*, 7 FORDHAM URBAN LAW JOURNAL 117, 120-21 (1978).

It has been observed that:

> The duty to educate and the requirements of compulsory attendance are not strange bedfellows. A foundation has been laid in the California Constitution and by the California courts which, bolstered by federal divisions, could establish yet another basis for requiring the schools to teach their students how to read.[61]

In view of compulsory education, issues are raised as to whether children who are forced to attend school have rights which are protected by due process of law, and whether such rights include freedom from intellectual damage.

§ 13.3. Duty of Care — Is There One Provided by Statute?

McArdle points out that if a plaintiff seeks to imply a cause of action from a statute which does not provide for such an action, he or she will face a difficult task.[62] The author makes the point that courts are reluctant to recognize implied causes of action, reasoning that if such actions were desired, the legislature would have provided them. Recently, however, courts have shown a greater willingness to imply causes of action in order to protect significant interests. Succeeding is not easy, and one who seeks to recover under that theory must meet a vigorous test.[63]

At common law, parents were solely responsible for their child's education. A duty to educate was owed to the child as well as the state. The rationale for the state's interest in its children was, as it is today, the goal of developing good

---

61. Cohen, *supra* note 37, at 312.

62. Kevin M. McArdle, *Creating an Implied Educational Malpractice Action for the Handicapped in New York,* 46 ALBANY LAW REVIEW 520, 536 (1982).

63. *Id.*

460

citizens and a body politic capable of solving new social problems in an intelligent and democratic way. The state derived its jurisdiction over children's education from two sources — the state police power and its power as *parens patriae*.[64]

Tracy maintains:

> If a common-law, non-professional tort duty is alleged, plaintiff must plead a reasonable person standard of care that brings dangers of arbitrary jury verdicts. A professional standard of care will offer more protection to the educator, but may be difficult to formulate due to conflicting theories of education. The best sources for a professional standard are statutes defining generally competent teaching behaviors and those requiring specific teaching responses to identifiable student problems. An allegation of a statutory duty implies its own standard of care defined by the requirements of the statute on which the alleged duty is based and provides protection against arbitrariness to the extent of its specificity.[65]

Jorgensen notes:

> The historical development of New York's regulation of education, including the state's constitutional amendment, its comprehensive statutory and regulatory framework, and its investigations into the problems existing in the educational system, undoubtedly indicates the state's substantial interest in providing each child with a meaningful education. It is reasonable to conclude that New York (i.e., the school districts) has obligated itself to educate properly the children required to attend its schools. Consequently, fail-

---

64. Jorgensen, *supra* note 2, at 343.

65. Destin Shann Tracy, *Educational Negligence: A Student's Cause of Action for Incompetent Academic Instruction,* 58 NORTH CAROLINA LAW REVIEW 566, 596 (1980).

ure to discharge this duty properly should give rise to a cause of action.[66]

Wilkins states that because of the uniform rejection of educational malpractice by the courts, and the unfortunate victims of negligence in the schools, there is an immediate need for a call to action in this area.[67] She argues:

> Because of the almost uniform rejection of educational malpractice claims by the courts, the most plausible solution appears to lie in the individual state legislatures. Although many state officials fear the creation of new forms of state liability, the role of the legislature is to represent the will of the people. Moreover, many states have abolished sovereign immunity for certain tortious conduct. This abolition represents the will of the people to hold the sovereign responsible for negligent acts or omissions. Therefore, legislative recognition of a cause of action for educational malpractice is a viable remedy for victims of negligent instruction.[68]

She suggests the following model statute may provide such legislative recognition.

> Notwithstanding any inconsistent provision of law, every school district shall be liable for, and shall assume the liability, for damages sustained by any student within the school district by reason of the professional negligence of any teacher, counselor, or official employed by the school district. For purposes of this section, "professional negligence" means any negligent act or omission to act by an education provider in the rendering of professional services, as determined in light of the educators' profession and the knowledge, skill, and care ordinarily employed by members of the

---

66. Jorgensen, *supra* note 2, at 347.

67. Kimberly A. Wilkins, *Educational Malpractice: A Cause of Action in Need of a Call for Action,* 22 (No. 2), VALPARAISO UNIVERSITY LAW REVIEW 427, 460 (Winter 1988).

68. *Id.* at 458.

profession in good standing in this state, which act is the proximate cause of substantial injury.[69]

The writer explains:

> This model statute will provide a workable standard of care for the courts to use in assessing educational malpractice complaints. By employing that standard of care applicable in professional negligence actions, the standard encompasses that which is reasonable for the members of the profession in good standing, in light of their special education, training, knowledge, skill, and experience. Additionally, in utilizing a professional negligence standard, the statute focuses more on the failure to invoke minimally acceptable methods of education rather than the failure to provide a minimally adequate education. By comparing the educator's claimed tortious conduct to the methods of education accepted and used by members of the education profession in good standing, the courts may avoid the broad inquiry required to assess the adequacy of a child's education in general.
>
> The statute intends to provide a standard of care that is both appropriate and workable. In setting forth a basis of liability, the courts will no longer be able to refuse to find a legal duty of care in the educators. The professional negligence standard of care is appropriate to determine whether this duty has been breached.
>
> Moreover, the statute is workable because it remains flexible. Instead of specifically stating the scope of the standard of care, the statute provides a general framework for the courts to apply as different situations arise. Therefore, the statute may withstand the test of time as the profession changes with the times. In addition, despite the courts' reluctance to become involved in the daily implementation of educational policies, the courts should feel comfortable with the

---

69. *Id.* at 458-59. She explains that the statute utilizes the commonly accepted definition of professional negligence.

principles underlying professional negligence. [Foot-
notes omitted][70]

§ 13.4. Additional Theories.

Another attempt to deal with the matter of a standard of
care is by distinguishing between "nonfeasance" and "misfeasance." One of the dissenters in the *Hoffman*[71] case
noted:

> The majority seeks to distinguish the *Donohue* case
> upon the ground that it involved "nonfeasance"
> whereas this case involves "misfeasance." Quite apart
> from the fact that the complaints in both cases allege
> acts both of omission and commission, the main thrust
> of the plaintiff's case at bar was that the defendant
> failed to retest plaintiff within two years after his
> placement in a CRMD class as recommended by its
> own psychologist. This act of omission is one of nonfea-
> sance, which is defined as the failure to perform an act
> which a person should perform. In *Donohue,* the gist of
> the plaintiff's cause of action was that although the
> defendant had given him instruction in reading, it had
> not done so properly or effectively and therefore he
> could not read upon graduation. This was an act of
> commission or misfeasance, which is defined as the
> improper performance of a lawful act.[72]

Jorgensen, commenting on this case, states:

> The *Donohue* court had not addressed this misfea-
> sance/nonfeasance distinction. If it had done so, it
> could have found the school district guilty of misfea-
> sance. State regulations required a student to com-
> plete satisfactorily a precise set of courses in order to
> receive a diploma. The plaintiff had failed numerous
> courses and anyone reading the plaintiff's high school
> transcript would be hard pressed to describe his work

70. *Id.* at 459-60.
71. 49 N.Y. 2d 119, 424 N.Y.S. 2d 376 (1979).
72. Jorgensen, *supra* note 2, at 352.

as a "satisfactory completion" of a course of study. By awarding a diploma to the plaintiff, who had not completed satisfactorily the prescribed coursework, the school district breached its duty.

Additionally, the school district in *Donohue* was guilty of nonfeasance. New York law requires the board of education, as the school district's agent, to examine the causes, whether physical, social, or mental, of a pupil's continuous failure in his studies. A student such as Donohue is usually classified as an "underachiever." However, the school district made no examination of the causes contributing to Donohue's underachievement nor any determination as to whether Donohue might benefit from special educational facilities or services. Thus, the school district failed to carry out its statutory duty to investigate the causes of the plaintiff's underachievement, again breaching its duty to the plaintiff.

Nor should the plaintiff only be limited to a cause of action where he can set forth the breach of a specific statute or regulation. A school can be viewed as a trustee, charged with the duty to protect, preserve and promote the intellectual development of its students. Although a school has discretion as to how to discharge adequately its responsibilities, a plaintiff could challenge a school district's actions by showing an abuse of such discretion. Of course, the difficulty in demonstrating an abuse of discretion would place a heavy burden upon the plaintiff. This, in turn, might deter many injured parties from commencing an action. Nevertheless, implicit within the school's duty, as outlined by statutes and regulations, is the notion that a school district must provide a "qualitative" level of education.[73]

In *Donohue*, the plaintiff had also alleged in his complaint a violation of Article XI § 1 of the New York State Constitution, which provided:

§ 1. [Common schools]

---

73. *Id.* at 353.

The legislature shall provide for the maintenance and support of a system of free common schools, wherein all the children of this state may be educated.[74]

Responding to that allegation, the defendant stated:

It is to be noted that the mandate of the constitution affords no basis for a claim on the part of a particular individual. Such enactment does not impart an intention to protect the interests of any individual except as it secures to all of the members of the community that to which they are entitled only as members of the public.

Additionally, it should be observed that education is not such a "fundamental right" as to be entitled to special constitutional protection (*San Antonio School Dist. v. Rodriquez,* 411 U.S. 1, 16).[75]

The New York Court, Appellate Division, rejected the theory of a constitutional duty, holding:

The plaintiff's second cause of action sounds in negligence and alleges the breach of a duty found in the State Constitution (art XI, § 1) and enabling legislation (Education Law, art. 65). It is our opinion that these enactments merely require the creation of a system of free common schools. Their purpose is to confer the benefits of a free education upon what would otherwise be an uneducated public. They were not intended to protect against the "injury" of ignorance, for every individual is born lacking knowledge, education and experience. For this reason the failure of educational achievement cannot be characterized as an "injury" without the meaning of tort law (*Peter W. v. San Francisco Unified School Dist.,* 60 Cal. App. 3d 814, 826, *supra*). It is a well-established principle of torts that statutes which are not intended to protect against injury, but rather are designed to confer a benefit upon the general public, do not give rise to a cause of action

---

74. Respondent's Brief, Donohue, *supra* note 4, at 23.
75. *Id.*

by an individual to recover damages for their breach [citations omitted].[76]

The court then observed:

The dissent seeks to sustain the second cause of action asserted in the plaintiff's complaint by concluding that the plaintiff has adequately alleged a substantive violation of former section 4404 of the Education Law. That section required, *inter alia,* that each pupil who continuously failed or who was listed as an "underachiever" be evaluated to ascertain the physical, mental and social causes of the underachievement and to further determine if the pupil might benefit from special educational programs. Although the plaintiff was a member of the class of pupils denominated as "underachievers" the defendant's alleged failure to take the actions required thereby did not give rise to an action sounding in tort. For the reasons stated above, this statute was not intended to protect the plaintiff from injury, rather, it merely reflected a legislative direction that greater educational resources be allocated toward satisfying the learning needs of so-called "underachievers." The grades on the plaintiff's periodic report cards gave notice both to his parents and himself that he had failed in two or more subjects, thus meeting the definition of an "underachiever" provided in the regulations of the Commissioner of Education (8 NYCRR 203.1 [2]). Having this knowledge, the plaintiff could properly have demanded the special testing and evaluation directed by the statute. Upon the defendant's failure to do so, the plaintiff's remedy would then have been an appeal to the State Commission of Education [citations omitted].[77]

Masner, an educational malpractice scholar, writes:

An allegation by a parent or student of a denial of substantive due process requires the court to determine whether the education offered by the state justi-

---

76. *Id.* at 24.
77. *Id.* at 25.

fies compelling the student to attend. The question which the court must answer is whether the state's action is "arbitrary and unreasonable." If the court decides the state has not acted arbitrarily or unreasonably, then the court has decided the education offered is adequate to offset any denial of liberty held by the parent or child. This raises the same issue of duty which is present in educational malpractice cases. The extent to which the court is willing to examine the school's educational program is determined by the degree of duty toward the plaintiff which the court is willing to place upon the defendant school.

"The essential question (is) whether the plaintiff's interests are entitled to legal protection against the defendant's conduct." Therefore, at the very least an alternative allegation of denial of substantive due process in an educational malpractice suit would raise the plaintiff's interests to a constitutional level.[78]

Jorgensen states:

For a plaintiff seeking redress against a school system for his illiteracy, a negligence cause of action seems to offer the greatest likelihood of success. However, other legal theories are worthy of consideration. Commentators have suggested two federal constitutional arguments for allowing "educational malpractice" claims — equal protection and due process. An injured student could argue that he was denied equal protection under the laws regulating education if he failed to receive the minimum or basic skills while a student in a public school system. One obvious difficulty with this argument is proving that schools are statutorily responsible for guaranteeing such "equal minimal outcomes." The state also could assert that by giving the student both the equal opportunity to an education and equal access to the schools, it had fulfilled its obligation. The situation would be different if some stu-

---

78. Charles M. Masner, *Educational Malpractice and a Right to Education: Should Compulsory Education Laws Require a Quid Pro Quo?,* 21 WASHBURN LAW JOURNAL 555, 576 (1982).

dents were permitted to participate in remedial programs while others were denied such opportunity.
Those students not allowed to participate could have a
valid claim that they were denied equal protection.

An interesting alternate constitutional theory that
has been suggested is a claim based on substantive due
process. To establish a violation of substantive due
process, one must prove that he was deprived of a right
by arbitrary state action. A student would have to establish that his attendance at school is "in the nature
of a confinement" and, thus, a denial of his constitutional right to "liberty." He would then argue that
forced attendance without education is a denial of due
process. A similar approach was successful in *Wyatt v.
Stickney,* where a patient sought recovery against a
state mental institution when he was involuntarily
committed and failed to receive treatment. The federal
district court held that the institution's involuntary
confinement of the patient, followed by its failure to
treat him, violated the patient's constitutional rights.

However, this approach is not without problems. Establishing a violation of the student's liberty would be
difficult; although subject to compulsory attendance
laws, students are present in school only a fraction of
the day. Additionally, in *Wyatt* the patients received
no treatment at all, whereas even in the most inadequate school district, students receive some form of
education. Finally, it is difficult to set standards by
which to judge the quality of education provided;
whereas in the treatment cases, custodial care can be
distinguished easily from treatment. This problem,
however, might be overcome by using statutes, regulations and expert testimony to establish a minimal educational standard.

Three other possible approaches also should be
noted. First, a plaintiff might argue that a school has
breached its implied contract to teach the student.
Generally, an implied contract is an obligation imposed by law to do justice, even though it is clear that
no promise was ever made or intended. The principal
function of this type of contract is to prevent unjust

enrichment. Herein lies the difficulty with alleging implied contract — courts probably will be extremely reluctant to imply this type of contract between the school district and its students because the former is not unjustly enriched in any manner when a student graduates without basic skills.

Second, a plaintiff could argue that through local property taxes and pursuant to the state constitution there exists a contractual relationship between the taxpayers and the state under which the student is a third party beneficiary. Even assuming that such a contractual relationship could be found to exist, a plaintiff would have the burden of establishing that he was a third party for whose primary benefit the contract was made. Additionally, he would have to show that the state intended to be answerable to its students on the third party contract.

A final approach, and possibly the most promising, is a cause of action alleging intentional and fraudulent misrepresentation. A plaintiff would have to establish the school's misrepresentation, his reliance on that misrepresentation, and the causal relationship between his reliance and resulting injury. Misrepresentation of student progress on report cards, in interviews with parents, or in the award of a diploma would evidence the school's wrongdoing. It should be noted that at least one court has intimated that an action for misrepresentation, if properly pleaded, would not be dismissed [footnotes omitted].[79]

§ 13.5. Standards of Competent Professional Performance.

To argue that there is no standard of care for educators or that educators and/or the educational system does not owe a duty of care to students, one should be prepared to argue that no standard of competence for performance can be imposed upon the educators and/or the educational sys-

---

79. Jorgensen, *supra* note 2, at 356-58.

tem. If it is not possible to establish standards to determine the duty of care of educators to their students, then it is implied that it is not possible to set up standards of competent performance for educators. Conversely, if meaningful and specific standards of competent performance for teachers can be written, then meaningful and specific standards of care, owed by educators to their students, also can be established. Several states have developed standards of professional competence for educators. Excerpts of these standards for Nebraska, Utah, Iowa, and Oregon are reprinted in Appendices 1-4.

The standards for competent performance evidence that there are several states that do have standards with which educators must comply. Failure to comply can lead to the termination of the educator's job. These standards can be, and some have been, codified and courts have determined whether these standards are equitably and legally applied.

Is it too much to ask the courts to determine whether or not students have been intellectually harmed as a result of the teacher's failure to properly adhere to the specified standard — the standard to properly educate? Arguably, the standards used to measure the teacher's performance also can be employed in claims that the teacher failed to properly educate students. Thus, can a standard of care be imposed upon the educational system? If yes, can it be a workable one? If no, should the approach be, let the student beware — a "caveat emptor" mentality? Wouldn't that be inconsistent with our legal system and a basic violation of the principle of accountability? It would appear that it is logically, morally, and legally right that when a student falls victim to negligent instruction and is intellectually harmed, that the student should be able to have an impartial hearing before an impartial tribunal. Our legal system does not, and should not, permit anything less.

471

§ 13.6. Summary.

A commentator has stated that "the amorphous nature of the educative process and educational accountability could not be translated into standards sufficiently ascertainable, breach of which would result in legal accountability."[80] Yet, when a hypothetical case of educational malpractice was proposed, of all the possible defenses suggested by the legal minds, none had suggested a defense of lack of duty, even though they did feel that a workable standard of care might be elusive.[81]

One author states, "if scholars identify dependable correlates of teaching behaviors and student achievement, is it not thereby incumbent upon teacher educators to teach students to do them?"[82] The fact that it may be somewhat difficult to devise a standard of care for educators — a duty of care recognized by law — should not be interpreted that one cannot be formulated or that one has not already been formulated. In this chapter a number of arguments have been presented that would give credence to the statement — a standard of care can and should be established. It is difficult to justify a conclusion that educators have no duty to educate their students in a proper way. Even arguments regarding public policy are subject to attack. Should public policy factors support a departure from the fundamental principle that all persons have a duty to use ordinary care in their conduct to prevent others from being injured?[83] A strong argument can be made that if educational malprac-

---

80. Cohen, *supra* note 37, at 297.

81. *Id.* at 296.

82. Delbert Clear, *Malpractice in Teacher Education: The Improbable Becomes Increasingly Possible,* JOURNAL OF TEACHER EDUCATION XXXIV:2 (March-April 1983), pp. 19, 22.

83. Nancy L. Woods, *Educational Malfeasance: A New Cause of Action for Failure to Educate,* 14 TULSA LAW JOURNAL 383, 388 (1978). Copyright by the University of Tulsa.

tice fails to be recognized as a new cause of action it certainly should not be on the basis that educators do not have a duty of care to the students and that a standard of care for educators cannot be drawn in meaningful and workable terms. Professionals can and must set "standards" for their professions. Teaching is a profession and teachers are professionals. Those who argue that teaching is not a profession and teachers are not professionals need to answer the question: Is it not time for teachers to become professionals?

Chapter 14

PROXIMATE CAUSE: PROVING EDUCATIONAL MALPRACTICE CAUSED INJURY — WHAT INJURY?

§ 14.0.   Introduction.
§ 14.1.   The Proximate Cause Issue — Causation.
§ 14.2.   Determining Resulting Injury — Measuring Damages.
§ 14.3.   Who Should Pay the Damages?

> When a student graduates from high school with a fourth grade reading ability and is unable to complete a simple job application, it would appear that an "injury" has occurred.

§ 14.0. Introduction.

Theodore Sizer, in *Horace's Compromise, The Dilemma of the High School,* states:

> Of all the stages of life, adolescence is the most volatile — full of promise, energy, and because of newly achieved freedom and potency, substantial peril. In its freshness, adolescence is attractive. In its enthusiasm, it can be, to older folk at least, exhausting. For most people, it is pivotal: it is the time of life when we find out who we are becoming, what we are good at, what and who we like. What happens in these years profoundly affects what follows.[1]

Even if the courts recognize educational malpractice as a new cause of action, proving that educational malpractice

---

1. THEODORE R. SIZER, HORACE'S COMPROMISE, THE DILEMMA OF THE AMERICAN HIGH SCHOOL (Boston: Houghton Mifflin Company), 1984, p. 1.

occurred in a particular situation poses great difficulties because of the many variables which need to be considered. Any one of these variables, i.e, intelligence, motivation, environment, or student's attentiveness, can affect student achievement. Measuring the impact of various factors on the student's learning is difficult. Proving what caused Johnny to be a poor writer, a poor reader, a poor thinker, a poor student, or an overall poor achiever is not an easy task. But, proving malpractice, in any profession, is not an easy task, for many factors unique to that profession need to be considered. The impact that each factor may have had on the specific incident needs to be carefully and painstakingly analyzed. Anything less is not acceptable — nor should it be! Perhaps, there is no such thing as being too careful in this area. Besides other damages, the professional's reputation is at stake — once tarnished it is not easy to rebuild. The fact that it will be difficult to prove should not be an added reason for not recognizing educational malpractice — that merely addresses the question.

The issue is whether: Given the right circumstances, can it be proven that certain negligent conduct (assuming a duty and a standard of care has been established), that certain act(s) by a teacher, a school administrator, and/or the school system contributed to or caused a student to incur "intellectual" damage.

If the answer is negative then there is no causation — no proximate cause. Consequently, there cannot be recovery on the theory of negligence — educational malpractice. If, on the other hand, the answer is affirmative, then the third element, proximate cause, necessary to prove negligence, is met. In the first part of this chapter will be explored the issue of proximate cause, which has been labeled as, "clearly the most problematic element of negligence, par-

476

ticularly in an action for 'educational malpractice'" will be explored.[2]

§ 14.1. The Proximate Cause Issue — Causation.

In order to win a negligence action the plaintiff must prove not only that he or she was injured and that the defendant breached a duty owed to the plaintiff, but also that the defendant's conduct (negligence) was the actual cause of injury. A widely used test in this area is the *but for* rule. For example, *B*'s negligence is the cause of the injury (harm) if the injury would not have occurred *but for B*'s negligent conduct. Conversely, an act or omission to act is not a cause of injury if that injury would have occurred regardless of the defendant's act or omission.[3]

Speaking to the issue, Professor Foster states:

> It must first be determined whether the defendant's conduct can be considered a cause in fact of the plaintiff's injury; that is, can it be said in the circumstances of the case that the defendant's conduct produced the injury? Then, assuming an affirmative answer to this inquiry, it must be determined whether the defendant's conduct should be viewed as the legal or proximate cause of the plaintiff's injury; that is, can it be said that there is a sufficiently close connection between the harm threatened by the defendant's conduct and the harm in fact occasioned to the plaintiff to warrant the imposition of liability? For an educational malpractice suit to be successful, the plaintiff must establish cause in both senses of the term.[4]

---

2. Theresa E. Loscalzo, *Liability for Malpractice in Education,* 14 No. 4 JOURNAL OF LAW AND EDUCATION 595 (October 1985).

3. LEN YOUNG SMITH, G. GADE ROBENSON, RICHARD A. MANN & BARRY S. ROBERTS, BUSINESS LAW p. 152, 7th ed. (St. Paul: West Publishing Company, 1988).

4. W.F. Foster, *Educational Malpractice: A Tort for the Untaught?,* 19:2 U.B.C. LAW REVIEW 161, 234 (1985).

In *Donohue*,[5] the court stated:

> Thus, the imagination need not be overly taxed to en-
> vision allegations of a legal duty of care flowing from
> educators, if viewed as professionals, to the students. If
> doctors, lawyers, architects, engineers and other pro-
> fessionals are charged with a duty owing to the public
> whom they serve, it could be said that nothing in the
> law precludes similar treatment of professional educa-
> tors. Nor would creation of a standard with which to
> judge an educator's performance of that duty necessar-
> ily pose an insurmountable obstacle [citations omit-
> ted]. *As far as proximate causation, while this element
> might indeed be difficult, if not impossible, to prove in
> view of the many collateral factors involved in the
> learning process, it perhaps assumes too much to con-
> clude that it could never be established* [emphasis
> added].[6]

The court also observes that: "[t]he failure to learn does
not bespeak a failure to teach."[7]

One author notes that anyone seeking to prove "educational malpractice" faces several major obstacles.

> The first is that education is by no means an exact
> science. Mary Anne Raywid, a professor of education
> at Hofstra University, wrote that malpractice made
> sense in a field like medicine because "the same treat-
> ments typically yield the same results when applied to
> different patients." In teaching though, no such simple
> laws of cause and effect seem to be operating.
>   Recent educational research and development such
> as alternative schools, she argued, belie the existence
> of any method that, however sound, will work with all

---

5. Donohue v. Copiague Union Free School Dist., 47 N.Y.2d 440, 391
N.E.2d 1352, 418 N.Y.S.2d 375 (1979).

6. *Id.* at 377.

7. Donohue v. Copiague Union Free School Dist., 64 App. Div. 2d 29,
407 N.Y.S.2d 874, 888 (1978), aff'd, N.Y.2d 440, 391 N.E.2d 1352, 418
N.Y.S.2d 375 (1979).

children. It is thus difficult to define standards for malpractice.

There is, however, a growing conviction that while teaching methods may be an elusive standard for judging professional competence, acceptability can be measured through student performance. Nearly two dozen states, including New York, have recently enacted "minimum competency" requirements in reading and mathematics that students must meet before receiving a high school diploma. Under the new New York law, which first applies to the class of 1979, a student such as Edward Donohue describes himself would not be able to receive a diploma.

The second obstacle is the difficulty of saying what produces learning. A number of major studies in recent years have pointed up the influence of the home and other forces outside schools on how much students learn. The California court used this as a reason for overturning the conviction in the Peter Doe case.

"Substantial professional authority attests that the achievement of literacy in the schools, or its failure, are influenced by a host of factors which affected pupils subjectively, from outside the formal teaching process, and beyond the control of its ministers," the court declared. "They may be physical, neurological, emotional, cultural, environmental; they may be present but not perceived, recognized but not identified."[8]

Fields and Harris make the following arguments:

In an effort to draw an analogy between medical malpractice and educational malpractice, educators must make several points clear to the legislatures and courts concerning the differences involved. First, while a medical illness can be defined with precision, the concept of functional illiteracy cannot. Second, medical malpractice is designed to hold doctors accountable for "accepted practices." In education no such generally-

---

8. Edward B. Fiske, *Schools, Like Doctors, Being Charged With Malpractice,* THE NEW YORK TIMES (March 9, 1977). Copyright © 1977 by The New York Times Company. Reprinted by permission.

agreed-upon standards exist. Third, in medicine, treatment is usually by a single individual over a short period of time. In education, the treatment received by students usually takes place over differing periods of time and from people with varying degrees of authority over the learning process. Fourth, medical patients are usually passive during the period of their treatment. Education, on the other hand, is an inter-active process in which the child participates and is expected to indicate difficulty when he is experiencing it. Parents are also expected to be active participants. How could the parents of Donohue or Doe possibly fail to notice that their offspring could not read?

Will the public's new accountability movement be the key to forcing the schools to do a better job? It's doubtful. Tradition dictates that school personnel "blame the victim" for their shortcomings. The trend toward certifying those who have learned, rather than accepting responsibility for those who have failed, can only be reinforced by the trend toward "minimal competency tests" for students before they graduate. Progress can be made only by accepting a commitment to solve the problems of students early in order to prevent failures, rather than following the English example of over 100 years ago and teaching only to the minimum level of achievement [footnotes omitted].[9]

With the greater role of the courts in educational matters, there has been an increase in the role of social scientists and social science data and techniques in the legal process.[10] These are needed to provide expert testimony on a number of issues, such as school desegregation and school

9. Richard E. Fields & J. John Harris III, *Educational Malpractice and The Public Demand for Teacher Accountability,* 9 PLANNING AND CHANGING (Spring 1978), pp., 3, 13-14.

10. Ray C. Rist and Ronald J. Anson, *Social Science and the Judicial Process in Education Cases: An Introduction: Dimensions and Implications of the Increasing Role of the Courts in the Formulation of Educational Policy,* 6 JOURNAL OF LAW AND EDUCATION 1 (January 1977).

financing.[11] This, it has been argued, is needed for analysis of broad social and cultural trends since such analyses are needed and used in every stage of the judicial process from describing the fact situation accurately, to proving injury, to creation of adequate remedies.[12] Such evidence would be needed in an educational malpractice case. That being the case, Rist and Anson assert:

> The use of social science evidence in courts raises many corollary issues. What is the usefulness of such information to the court when the evidence in question is not agreed to by the scientific community as a whole? This is clearly a question of proof for the judge or jury to decide, but what are the implications when social scientists testify, with equal conviction, to opposing conclusions about the same fact situation. Should social scientists be involved in educational litigation at all and is the adversary process the proper forum for the airing of controversial and contradictory social science issues? Not only is there a question as to the appropriateness of the forum for the presentation of differences between social scientists, but the very real danger exists that lawyers and judges will not understand the critical differences in interpretation which lead to differing conclusions. There is, indeed, a great burden upon lawyers and judges to sift through the conflicting social science dates [data] to find the heart of the matter, a task often extremely difficult even for those in a particular discipline. Failure to properly educate all the actors in the judicial process leads to improper use of social science evidence or simple rejection of the evidence. Perhaps the view of many legally trained observers (judges and lawyers) is best summed up by U.S. Court of Appeals Judge J. Skelly Wright in *Hobson v. Hansen*:
>
> > [T]he unfortunate if inevitable tendency has been to lose sight of the disadvantaged young students on

---

11. *Id.*
12. *Id.*

whose behalf this suit was brought in an overgrown garden of numbers and charts and jargon like "Standard deviation of the variable," "statistical significance," and "Pearson product moment correlations."

The reports by the experts — one noted economist plus assistants for each side — are less helpful than they might have been for the simple reason that they do not begin from a common data base, they disagree over crucial statistical assumptions, and they reach different conclusions. Having hired their respective experts, the lawyers in this case have a basic responsibility, which they have not completely met, to put the hard core statistical demonstrations into language which serious and concerned laymen could, with effort, understand. Moreover, the studies by both sets of experts are tainted by a vice well known in the statistical trade — data shopping and scanning to reach a preconceived result, and the court had to reject parts of both reports as unreliable because they were biased.

The court has been forced back to its own common sense approach to a problem which, though admittedly complex, has certainly been made more obscure than was necessary. The conclusion I reach is based upon burden of proof, and upon straightforward moral and constitutional arithmetic.
Given the reality of the incursion of the courts into policy making in education and the obvious need for information about some very complex questions, the failure of social science to effectively communicate what is known, as well as to inform when something is not known, will result in a dilution of the effectiveness of judicial decisions in this area. But the inability of actors in education, social science and the judicial process to understand the needs and limitations of the others will just as surely diminish the effectiveness of their concerted action. [footnote omitted].[13]

---

13. *Id.* at 1-2.

Kimberly Wilkins, writing in the *Valparaiso University Law Review*,[14] states:

> In cases like *Hoffman* and *B.M.* [citations omitted], a causal connection is easily established. A specific action either negligently classified a child or failed to follow a specific recommendation at a specific date and time. However, in cases like *Peter W.* and *Donohue,* [citations omitted], establishing a causal connection presents a more difficult problem. Clearly the act of one particular teacher in the school system cannot cause a student to graduate from high school as a functional illiterate. Rather, the causal connection must be established as a chain of events, acts, misrepresentations, and omissions over a period of time. Although such a chain of causation may be difficult to prove, it is possible. The lack of sufficient contact between various teachers and the parents, test scores, homework grades, teacher qualification requirements, past teacher performance, and ultimately the high school diploma will aid the plaintiff in establishing the causal connection.[15]

The court in *Peter W.*[16] contended:

> We find in this situation no conceivable "workability of a rule of care" against which defendants' alleged conduct may be measured, no reasonable "degree of certainty that ... plaintiff suffered injury" within the meaning of the law of negligence, and no such perceptible "connection between the defendant's conduct and the injury suffered" as alleged which would establish a causal link between them within the same meaning [citations and footnotes omitted].[17]

---

14. Kimberly A. Wilkins, *Educational Malpractice: A Cause of Action in Need of a Call for Action,* 22 No. 2 VALPARAISO UNIVERSITY LAW REVIEW 427 (1988).

15. *Id.* at 456-57.

16. Peter W. v. San Francisco Unified School District, 131 Cal. Rptr. 854 (Cal. App. 1976).

17. *Id.* at 860-61.

One may find many good arguments to support the statement that classroom methodology affords no readily acceptable standards of care, or cause, or injury. Having said that, however, are we prepared to dismiss seemingly meritorious claims, without even a hearing, simply because there is "no readily acceptable standards of care, or cause, or injury?" The courts also need to consider various factors in deciding medical and psychiatric malpractice cases, but have not shied away from them.

Addressing this issue, Professor Foster contends:

> Although one can readily agree with the observation that a "failure to learn does not bespeak a failure to teach" [citation omitted], it would be perverse to conclude that a failure to teach or other unreasonable educational behaviour should never be an actionable cause of intellectual or other non-physical harm solely because the learning process can be influenced, in some perhaps inexplicable way, by a number of other factors. After all, many events have numerous and often complex causes. Nevertheless, when confronted with a malpractice claim against a lawyer or doctor, the courts will not dismiss the claim merely because there is a possibility that, even in the absence of negligence on the part of the professional, the client may still have lost his case or the patient may still have lost life or limb. It is not the law that proof of causation is contingent on the plaintiff establishing that no other factors contributed to the harm of which he is complaining [citation omitted].[18]

The author cites Fleming, who observes:

> Fortunately, in legal inquiries it does not matter if we are unable to identify all, or even most, of the individual elements which constitute the complex set of conditions jointly sufficient to produce a given consequence.

---

18. Foster, *supra* note 4, at 237. *See also* R. Jerry II, *Recovery in Tort for Educational Malpractice: Problems of Theory and Policy* (1981) 29 KANSAS LAW REVIEW 195 at 204.

> The reason is that we are usually interested only to investigate whether one, two or perhaps three specific conditions ... were causally relevant.[19]

It has been argued that while good teaching is difficult to define there are certain functions that have long been considered a responsibility of the teacher, i.e., grading.[20] Grading, of course, is important not only to students but to their parents who monitor their progress. Consequently, misleading parents about their children's performance could have serious consequences. Having been erroneously assured of their children's good performance, they may be deprived of an opportunity to seek other professional help for them. Therefore, when teachers keep passing Johnny on from one grade to another and Johnny graduates from high school with a fourth grade reading ability, unable to complete a simple job application, it would appear that an "injury" has occurred. If Johnny's parents, relying on the teachers' judgment in giving grades, were not informed of Johnny's real school achievement, should they have a legal cause of action against the school system? If the teachers that gave Johnny his passing grades believed in the philosophy of "out of sight, out of mind" — out of my classroom and into someone else's classroom, should Johnny and/or his parents have a right to complain? If not, then the question that needs to be asked is: "What is the responsibility of an educator — of a teacher or of an administrator who is given supervision of the student?" Is it none? We need to be mindful of the fact that many parents look at educators as the "pillars of the community" — the guardians of educa-

---

19. *Id.* at 237-38. *See also* J. FLEMING, THE LAW OF TORTS (6th ed. 1983), at 171.

20. V. Pauline Hodges & William H. Johnson, *"Legal Responsibility for Curriculum in the Basic Skills: Whose Job Is It?"* Paper presented at the Annual Meeting of the Regional Conference of the Colorado Language Arts Society (Colorado Springs, CO), March 13-15, 1981, p. 11.

tion — the hope for their children's educational growth and welfare. Many of these parents have little formal education. Many of these parents, even some with substantial education, would not think of questioning, or at least would not question, the judgment of their children's teachers. Consequently, the children's education primarily becomes the responsibility of the teachers. If the teachers do not handle it with care, what then?

§ 14.2. Determining Resulting Injury — Measuring Damages.

Wilkins writes:

> The final element necessary for a negligence action includes the actual loss or damage resulting to the plaintiff. This element can be easily established by the true victims of educational malpractice. Harm resulting from a reduced ability to seek gainful employment certainly is not a novel concept for the courts. Although in most cases the student receives some degree of affirmative education, the student still suffers considerable injury by not seeking an adequate education elsewhere in time to enter the job market.
> The chances of success under a negligent theory of recovery clearly appear to be favorable for the true victims of educational malpractice. Unfortunately, these chances of success themselves fall victim to the semantic game played by the courts. By simply attaching the label "educational malpractice," the courts quickly and unnecessarily deny the plaintiffs an opportunity to recover.[21]

Couldn't a court, given the proper circumstances, reasonably determine that a student who graduated from high school with a fourth grade reading ability and who is un-

---

21. Wilkins, *supra* note 14, at 458.

able to complete a simple job application, suffered an injury? The court in *Donohue*[22] said:

> This would leave only the element of injury and who in good faith can deny that a student who upon graduation from high school cannot comprehend simple English — a deficiency allegedly attributable to the negligence of his educators — has not in some fashion been "injured."[23]

Concerning injuries sustained and damages resulting from said injury, one commentator states:

> Having established that the defendant owed a duty to the plaintiff and that the breach of that duty caused the plaintiff's injury, a successful plaintiff must finally establish the nature and extent of his injuries. Clearly, the presence of this element will depend on the facts of each case. For instance, in *Donohue,* the plaintiff's injury was obvious — he was unable to read or understand simple written English.
>
> Even the majority opinion does not dispute the existence of his injury. Of course, this element might have received more consideration had the court recognized the plaintiff's cause of action and the presence of duty to educate. If an educational malpractice cause of action is recognized in the future, adequate proof of injury to the plaintiff will undoubtedly be required.
>
> Once the requisite elements of a negligence cause of action are established, a plaintiff is entitled to relief. The purpose of such relief is generally to compensate the plaintiff for his injury and to place him in the same position as if the injury had not occurred. A court could award money damages on an educational malpractice claim, compensating the plaintiff for his disability and the effect it will have on his future earning potential. However, money damages would be difficult to calculate, subject to speculation, and a drain on school districts' resources. As an alternative, the courts could

---

22. Donohue, *supra* note 5.
23. *Id.* at 443.

fashion some type of equitable remedy. An injunction ordering the school district to provide remedial measures for the injured party is one possibility. The cost should be less to the school district than an award of money damages and the injured party would receive what he had been deprived of while a student within the system. Moreover, such a remedy would deter the insincere plaintiff who only is seeking a windfall through an award to money damages. Of course, in addition to equitable relief, a court could award an injured party the lost wages or reduction in earnings suffered during a remedial period.[24]

It is true that money damages may be difficult to calculate and subject to speculation, but, the task is not unconquerable. Courts have handled similar issues regarding damages in the past. In *Battalla v. State*,[25] the infant plaintiff's claim was that she was placed in a chair lift by an employee of the state who failed to secure and properly lock the belt intended to protect the occupant and that as a result, the plaintiff became frightened and hysterical upon descent, and suffered consequential injuries. The court, in holding that a cause of action did exist, observed:

> We presently feel that even the public policy argument is subject to challenge. Although fraud, extra litigation and a measure of speculation are, of course, possibilities, it is no reason for a court to eschew a measure of its jurisdiction. "The argument from mere expediency cannot commend itself to a Court of justice, resulting in the denial of a logical legal right and remedy in *all* cases because in *some* a fictitious injury may be urged as a real one" [citations omitted].
>   In any event, it seems that fraudulent accidents and injuries are just as easily feigned in the slight-impact

---

24. Nancy L. Woods, *Educational Malfeasance: A New Cause of Action for Failure to Educate*, 14 TULSA LAW JOURNAL 383, 388 (1978). Copyright by The University of Tulsa.

25. Battalla v. State of New York, 176 N.E.2d 729 (Court of Appeals of New York, 1969).

cases and other exceptions wherein New York permits a recovery, as in the no-impact cases which it has heretofore shunned. As noted by the Law Revision Commission: "The exceptions to the rule cannot be said to insure recovery to any substantial number of meritorious claimants and there is good ground for believing that they breed dishonest attempts to mold the facts so as to fit them within the grooves leading to recovery" [citations and footnotes omitted].

The honest claimant is penalized for his reluctance to fashion the facts within the framework of the exceptions.

Not only, therefore, are claimants in this situation encouraged by the Mitchell disqualification to perjure themselves, but the constant attempts to either come within an old exception, or establish a new one, lead to excess appellate litigation [citations omitted]. In any event, even if a flood of litigation were realized by abolition of the exception, it is the duty of the courts to willingly accept the opportunity to settle these disputes.

The only substantial policy argument of Mitchell is that the damages or injuries are somewhat speculative and difficult to prove. However, the question of proof in individual situations should not be the arbitrary basis upon which to bar all actions, and "it is beside the point ... in determining sufficiency of a pleading" [citations omitted]. In many instances, just as in impact cases, there will be no doubt as to the presence and extent of the damage and the fact that it was proximately caused by defendant's negligence. In the difficult cases, we must look to the quality and genuineness of proof, and rely to an extent on the contemporary sophistication of the medical profession and the ability of the court and jury to weed out the dishonest claims. Claimant should, therefore, be given an opportunity to prove that her injuries were proximately caused by defendant's negligence [footnote omitted].[26]

---

26. *Id.* at 730-33.

In another case, a California court made the observation that the possibility that some fraud will escape detection should not justify abdication of judicial responsibility to award damages for sound claims.[27] The court reasoned:

> The possibility that some fraud will escape detection does not justify an abdication of the judicial responsibility to award damages for sound claims: if it is "to be conceded that our procedural system for the ascertainment of truth is inadequate to defeat fraudulent claims ... the result is a virtual acknowledgment that the courts are unable to render justice in respect to them" [citations omitted].
>
> Indubitably juries and trial courts, constantly called upon to distinguish the frivolous from the substantial and the fraudulent from the meritorious, reach some erroneous results. But such fallibility inherent in the judicial process, offers no reason for substituting for the case-by-case resolution of causes an artificial and indefensible barrier. Courts not only compromise their basic responsibility to decide the merit of each case individually but destroy the public's confidence in them by using the broad broom of "administrative convenience" to sweep away a class of claims a number of which are admittedly meritorious. The mere assertion that fraud is possible, "a possibility [that] exists to some degree in all cases" [citations omitted], does not prove a present necessity to abandon the neutral principles of foreseeability, proximate cause and consequential injury that generally govern tort law.
>
> Indeed, we doubt that the problem of the fraudulent claim is substantially more pronounced in the case of a mother claiming physical injury resulting from seeing her child killed than in other areas of tort law in which the right to recover damages is well established in California. For example, a plaintiff claiming that fear for his own safety resulted in physical injury makes out a well recognized case for recovery [citations and footnote omitted]. Moreover, damages are allowed for

---

27. Dillon v. Legg, 69 Cal. Rptr. 72, 441 P.2d 912 (1968).

"mental suffering," a type of injury, on the whole, less amenable to objective proof than the physical injury involved here; the mental injury can be in aggravation of, or "parisitic to," an established tort [citations omitted]. In fact, fear for another, even in the absence of resulting physical injury, can be a part of these parisitic damages [citations omitted]. And emotional distress, if inflicted intentionally, constitutes an independent tort [citations omitted]. The danger of plaintiff's fraudulent collection of damages for nonexistent injury is at least as great in these examples as in the instant case.

In sum, the application of tort law can never be a matter of mathematical precision. In terms of characterizing conduct as tortious and matching a money award to the injury suffered as well as in fixing the extent of injury, the process cannot be perfect. Undoubtedly, ever since the ancient case of the tavern-keeper's wife who successfully avoided the hatchet cast by an irate customer (I de S et ux v. W de S, Y.B. 22 Edw. iii, f. 99, pl. 60 (1348)), defendants have argued that plaintiffs' claims of injury from emotional trauma might well be fraudulent. Yet we cannot let the difficulties of adjudication frustrate the principle that there be a remedy for every substantial wrong.[28]

§ 14.3. Who Should Pay the Damages?

If damages are to be awarded to a student who has been intellectually harmed, the issue of who should pay is raised. Suppose, as previously hypothesized, a student graduated from high school with a fourth grade reading ability and is unable to complete a simple job application and the jury determines that the student was injured. Who should pay damages to the victim student? After all, the student did attend several schools and had a number of teachers. Therefore, the problems of proof of proximate causation and joint tort-feasors are raised. The problems

---

28. *Id.*

posed are not new to the court. Their magnitude is neither insurmountable nor inconquerable.

How courts sometimes respond to difficult proximate cause and joint tort-feasor situations where a wrong has been committed but there is difficulty in determining exactly who caused it, is exemplified by the case of *Sindell v. Abbott Laboratories.*[29] In that case, the plaintiff filed a class action against a number of drug companies for injuries sustained as a result of having the drug diethylstilbestrol (DES) prescribed for use by her mother to prevent miscarriages. DES, however, proved to have toxic effects on some daughters born to mothers who had taken DES. Some of the daughters developed adenocarcenoma. A large number developed adenosis. The plaintiff was unable to identify which company manufactured the precise drug that caused her injury. The drugs, which were sold generically, were manufactured by more than 200 pharmaceutical companies. Consequently, even if records were available from over 20 years earlier, it was almost impossible to determine who made the particular drug that was taken. The plaintiff based her complaint upon various theories, including negligence and strict liability. The trial court dismissed the complaint but the Supreme Court of California reversed and said, in effect, that it would be unfair to bar her suit just because she could not identify the particular manufacturer. The court stated:

> In our contemporary complex industrialized society, advances in science and technology create fungible goods which may harm consumers and which cannot be traced to any specific producer. The response of the courts can be either to adhere rigidly to prior doctrine, denying recovery to those injured by such products, or to fashion remedies to meet these changing needs. Just

---

29. Sindell v. Abbott Laboratories, 163 Cal. Rptr. 132, 607 P.2d 924 (1980).

as Justice Traynor in his landmark concurring opinion in *Escola v. Coca Cola Bottling Company* (1944) 24 Cal. 2d 453, 467-468, 150 P.2d 436, recognized that in an era of mass production and complex marketing methods the traditional standard of negligence was insufficient to govern the obligations of manufacturer to consumer, so should we acknowledge that some adaptation of the rules of causation and liability may be appropriate in these recurring circumstances.

....

From a broader policy standpoint, defendants are better able to bear the cost of injury resulting from the manufacturer of a defective product. As was said by Justice Traynor in *Escola,* "[t]he cost of an injury and the loss of time or health may be an overwhelming misfortune to the person injured, a needless one, for the risk of injury can be insured by the manufacturer and distributed among the public as a cost of doing business" [citations omitted]. The manufacturer is in the best position to discover and guard against defects in its products and to warn of harmful effects; thus, holding it liable for defects and failure to warn of harmful effects will provide an incentive to product safety [citations omitted]. These considerations are particularly significant where medication is involved, for the consumer is virtually helpless to protect himself from serious, sometimes permanent, sometimes fatal, injuries caused by deleterious drugs.

Where, as here, all defendants produced a drug from an identical formula and the manufacturer of the DES which caused plaintiff's injuries cannot be identified through no fault of plaintiff, a modification of the rule of *Summers* is warranted. As we have seen, an undiluted *Summers* rationale is inappropriate to shift the burden of proof of causation to defendants because if we measure the chance that any particular manufacturer supplied the injury-causing product by the number of producers of DES, there is a possibility that none of the five defendants in this case produced the offending substance and that the responsible manufacturer, not named in the action, will escape liability.

But we approach the issue of causation from a different perspective: we hold it to be reasonable in the present context to measure the likelihood that any of the defendants supplied the product which allegedly injured plaintiff by the percentage which the DES sold by each of them for the purpose of preventing miscarriage bears to the entire production of the drug sold by all for that purpose ....

If plaintiff joins in the action the manufacturers of a substantial share of the DES which her mother might have taken, the injustice of shifting the burden of proof to defendants to demonstrate that they could not have made the substance which injured plaintiff is significantly diminished ....

The presence in the action of a substantial share of the appropriate market also provides a ready means to apportion damages among the defendants. Each defendant will be held liable for the proportion of the judgment represented by its share of that market unless it demonstrates that it could not have made the product which caused plaintiff's injuries. In the present case, as we have seen, one DES manufacturer was dismissed from the action upon filing a declaration that it had not manufactured DES until after plaintiff was born. Once plaintiff has met her burden of joining the required defendants, they in turn may cross-complain against other DES manufacturers, not joined in the action, which they can allege might have supplied the injury-causing product.

....

We are not unmindful of the practical problems involved in defining the market and determining market share, but these are largely matters of proof which properly cannot be determined at the pleading stage of these proceedings. Defendants urge that it would be both unfair and contrary to public policy to hold them liable for plaintiff's injuries in the absence of proof that one of them supplied the drug responsible for the damage. Most of their arguments, however, are based upon the assumption that one manufacturer would be held responsible for the products of another or for those of all other manufacturers if plaintiff ultimately prevails. But under the rule we adopt, each manufacturer's liability for an injury would be approximately equivalent to the damages caused by the DES it manufactured [footnotes omitted].[30]

The "rightness" or "wrongness" of this decision can be debated. One thing seemed certain to the corporate community — this case was a departure from previous cases and from established law. This case illustrates how courts can sometimes render a somewhat "revolutionary" ruling in order to remedy what they perceive to be wrong, even at the risk of involving the entire industry. We also have seen how courts, to right wrongs, had to come up with other theories such as *res ipsa loquitur*. Whether the principles annunciated in *Sindell* and other cases and whether an extension of these principles will be implemented in educational malpractice cases will be debated.

It is likely that if society wants students who have been wronged by the educational community to be compensated, then courts will develop theories to accomplish the task.

---

30. *Id.*

PART IV
MEASURES TAKEN TO MONITOR
THE PROFESSION

Chapter 15

WHO MONITORS THE EDUCATORS?

> A profession is better off if it can govern itself than if it has to be governed by others.

§ 15.0. Introduction.

In a perfect world all the teachers would be perfect teachers, all the school administrators would be perfect administrators, and all the students would be perfect students. Our system is not perfect. Some would argue, as evidenced herein, that it is far from perfect. There are some students in our school system that are far from being "model" students. There are some administrators that perform their jobs haphazardly. If we were to grade them on job performance some would get "*D*s" and "*F*s" on their report cards. So would a number of teachers. When it comes to job performance, the grades of some teachers would put them in the failing range. A number of teachers believe that they are not qualified for their jobs. Some people feel that the tenure laws make it almost impossible, in

499

most states, to dismiss incompetent, bigoted, cruel, or mentally unbalanced teachers.[1]

Who monitors the actions of the educators? This chapter will briefly discuss some of the internal measures taken by educators in monitoring their profession. Primarily, the focus will be on dismissal of teachers and the role of the Teachers' Professional Practices Commissions.

§ 15.1. Dismissal of Teachers.

If a teacher's performance is not satisfactory, can he or she be dismissed? What obstacles confront those who attempt to dismiss teachers?

Dismissing a tenured teacher is not, and should not be, an easy task. Generally, a teacher who achieves tenure status has the right to continued employment subject only to dismissal "for cause." In most states a teacher can be dismissed for a number of reasons including incompetence, neglect of duty, inefficiency, incapacity, and good or sufficient cause. The meaning of these causes varies from state to state and the procedure followed in attempting to dismiss a teacher is not identical in all states. Generally, the problem is not that a certain state doesn't have a statute specifying the grounds for dismissal, but rather defining these grounds. What, for example, constitutes "incompetence" or *exactly* what constitutes "good or sufficient cause?" Even where an "exact" definition seems to exist there is the further problem of proving the allegations that would constitute the specific cause. Two authors commenting on incompetency state:

> Incompetency has been given broad interpretation by the courts. Incompetency is defined as "want of physi-

---

1. Jay M. Pabian, *Educational Malpractice and Minimal Competency Testing: Is There a Legal Remedy at Last?*, 15 NEW ENGLAND LAW REVIEW 101, 112 (1979-1980).

cal, intellectual, or moral ability; insufficiency; inadequacy; specific want of legal qualifications or fitness;" .... It generally concerns a fitness to teach which contains a broad range of factors. The courts have included in incompetency, lack of knowledge of subject matter, lack of discipline, unreasonable discipline, unprofessional conduct, and willful neglect of duty.

A teacher who has been certified by the state is assumed to be competent and it is the responsibility of the school board to prove incompetency. As long as school boards are not arbitrary or capricious, the courts will generally not interfere. The fifth Circuit Court of Appeals stated that "[f]or sound policy reasons, courts are loathe to intrude upon the internal affairs of local school authorities in such matters as teacher competency" ....

The manner of offering evidence in incompetency cases is generally through testimony. Both the quantity and quality of evidence is important. The courts have liberally allowed opinions of principals, curricular supervisors, and other supervisory personnel to stand as expert testimony. Other testimony by students and parents may be important, but the actual observations, by supervisors, of what transpired in the classroom, are very significant. One court said, "This court, in absence of proof of an abuse of discretion, cannot substitute its opinion for the decision of the school board and of the district court where both of these tribunals were presented with substantial evidence upon which to base their decision" [citations omitted].[2]

In many cases, good and just cause or sufficient cause is difficult to define. This term is sometimes used by the school board as a catchall clause to cover dismissals that are not covered by any other provisions. Sometimes the school boards are empowered to decide what causes may be

---

2. KERN ALEXANDER & M. DAVID ALEXANDER, THE LAW OF SCHOOLS, STUDENTS, AND TEACHERS IN A NUTSHELL. pp. 314-315 (St. Paul, MN: West Publishing Company, 1984).

good and just — having only the qualified restriction that a good cause must be equal in degree to other causes. The causes for dismissals must be substantial and not easily remediable. There should be a showing that this "good cause" is directly related to the teacher's efficiency in the classroom. It must be done in a way that the teacher receives due process of law — "fair play," the essence of due process.[3] Dismissing a teacher does not only deprive the teacher of the present employment but of possible future opportunity — for the stigma attached to the dismissed teacher is not easily overcome.

It would be difficult to argue and justify the dismissal of a teacher by the board without giving the teacher due process of law. Anything short of due process would be unacceptable. Yet, while due process guarantees the teacher "fair play" — "substantial justice" — and hopefully, a fair disposition of the controversy, it may help increase the student's academic injury. While the school system is going through the various steps necessary to comply with due process of law in order to remove a teacher for incompetency, time elapses and the student continues to study under that teacher, perhaps resulting in further intellectual harm. This being the case, the student's rights need to be considered. What about the students' due process? Do they park their rights at the school house gate? The point is not that students have more rights than teachers or other citizens, but that they too have rights. Students should be provided an adequate forum in which to air grievances concerning the quality of their education. Students have a right to complain if they are wronged, and if their complaint is substantiated then an appropriate remedy must be found — a remedy that would compensate for the wrong

---

3. LOUIS FISCHER & DAVID SCHIMMEL, THE RIGHTS OF STUDENTS AND TEACHERS p. 299 (New York: Harper and Row Publishers, 1982).

that was committed. Anything short of that would seem to defy our legal system.

Teachers have been dismissed and some of them have been dismissed for incompetency. Some probably should not have been hired at all — they were not qualified for the job. Were those who hired the "alleged" or "proven" incompetent teachers negligent in their operation of duty? If yes, should the negligence be "swept under the rug" and those that have been damaged as a result of the negligence be denied a remedy? If A, through his negligence, injures C without any fault on C's part, should C be denied an opportunity to present and prove her claim? Even if those that hired the "incompetent" teacher were not negligent, should the teacher be liable for any proven damage that he or she has caused a student? Is there a legal basis for the application of the product liability theory? Furthermore, if a teacher is dismissed for incompetency, wouldn't that be a rebuttable presumption that the teacher has caused damage to his or her students?

A similar situation is where an employer, in private industry, hires a negligent or incompetent employee who causes harm to someone, while the employee is engaged in the scope and course of his employment. If a doctor hires an incompetent or "negligent" nurse who injures a patient during the course and scope of employment, due to negligence or because of incompetency, shouldn't the doctor be liable? Mr. Elson states:

> If courts can be convinced that the societal and personal consequences of miseducation are both critically important and judicially remedial, then the logic of legal reasoning should dictate that the same common law principles which establish the legal duty of care owed to a patient by a physician, to a student gymnast by his gym teacher, or to a minor by his legal guardian must also be applied to establish the legal duty of care

503

owed to a student by his reading, mathematics, or science teacher.[4]

The foregoing discussion demonstrates that removing an incompetent teacher is not only difficult, but also, in many cases, is not a solution to a student's claim for educational malpractice. Except for the fact that the teacher is removed from his or her job, nothing else really happens. The student receives no recompense — no damages — for his or her injury. The student often has no real voice — no real choice — as to where he or she will attend school and what school room he or she will be assigned to, or who the teacher will be in that classroom. Therefore, if we are to recognize the fact that some students are intellectually harmed, we need to provide them with an additional remedy besides removing the teacher. What productive avenues, short of going to court, are available to students. True, there are administrative remedies provided by state law. For example, students could complain to the principal, the superintendent, and even to the school board, but all of them could side with the teacher and/or the school. Furthermore, there is a tendency in these types of situations to view any decision by the principal or the superintendent or the school board as somewhat biased. Such a perception of bias, whether in fact true, creates dissatisfaction for the aggrieved, for he or she does not believe that there has been an opportunity for justice to be rendered. Also, the jurisdiction and power of those holding administrative hearings are limited. Generally, for example, a remedy for money damages for the aggrieved is not an available rem-

---

4. John Elson, *A Common Law Remedy for the Educational Harms Caused by Incompetent or Careless Teaching,* 73:4 NORTHWESTERN UNIVERSITY LAW REVIEW 641, 645 (November 1978). Reprinted by special permission of Northwestern University School of Law #73 (1978), NORTHWESTERN UNIVERSITY LAW REVIEW.

edy regardless of whether the student is entitled to monetary damages.

§ 15.2. Teachers' Professional Practices Commissions — Their Impact in Curtailing Educational Malpractice.

As criticism of the educational system progresses, the validity of arguments that have been advanced are being debated. Educators, legislatures, and the general public have demonstrated concern. Some states have taken measures to improve both the quality and perception of education and educators, such as establishing a Teachers' Professional Practices Commission. (*See* Appendices 1-4). An argument can be made that these commissions can and do serve as an alternative to settling alleged complaints, and therefore, courts are not needed to try malpractice cases. While on the surface this argument may have some merit, it is weakened when the commission's make-up, purpose, authority, and powers are examined. In order to understand how these commissions operate and what they can accomplish, several of these commissions will be briefly analyzed. All states do not have such commissions and some of the ones in existence are not very active.

§ 15.2(A). State of Georgia Professional Practices Commission.

One of the most active commissions in the United States is the State of Georgia Professional Practices Commission. Its executive director states:

> The State of Georgia Professional Practices Commission has jurisdiction over any professional educator in this state who holds a valid Georgia teaching certificate. The general mandate of the Commission is that it protects the educator from arbitrary, capricious and otherwise unwarranted accusation, attack or harass-

505

ment on the part of fellow educators, employers, or the general public and to protect, at the same time, the public and the teaching profession from incompetent, unethical and otherwise unworthy educators.

Within this general mandate the Professional Practices Commission is authorized to investigate and, if appropriate, to adjudicate:

(1) Alleged violations by an educator of any law of this state pertaining to educators or the profession of education;

(2) Alleged violations by an educator of the code of ethics of the Commission;

(3) Alleged violations by an educator of rules, regulations, or policies of the State Board, the Commission or a local board; or

(4) Complaints alleging a failure by an educator to meet or comply with standards of performance of the Commission, the State Board or a local board.

In the discharge of this mandate, the Professional Practices Commission handles annually over 2,000 formal and informal cases, ranging from murder to manslaughter, to rape, assault and battery, child molestation, other sexual misconduct, drug trafficking or possession, to matters of insubordination, willful neglect of duty, incompetency, and other unprofessional conduct warranting administrative action adverse to the educator, to other questions and disputes arising out of the employment relationship.[5]

The executive director further stated:

While employment matters are generally of local concern and are disposed of on the local level, severe infractions on the part of the educator usually become matters for the state to decide. They address the question of whether or not a teaching certificate should be revoked, suspended or denied. Local entities, therefore, have no jurisdiction over these matters. In one way or

---

5. Letter by Hans J. Schacht, Executive Director of State of Georgia Professional Practices Commission, written in response to information requested (November 7, 1989).

another, the cases mentioned above often fall within the general realm of educational malpractice.

According to the Georgia Quality Basic Education Act, every educator has to be formally evaluated on an annual basis. If teaching or administrative deficiencies are found, the local system is held to design and implement an individualized improvement plan for the sole purpose to insure that the deficiencies found are eliminated. If they cannot be eliminated to the extent that the educator's performance ceases to be a liability to the students or the system, charges of professional incompetency may be instituted against the educator.

Local systems may also avail themselves of the opportunity to request that the Professional Practices Commission provide a professional review of the services of the educator to obtain an outside expert opinion with regard to the questioned performance of the individual. The Professional Practices Commission has trained a core of experts to assist individuals and local school systems in this endeavor. Upon request, this trained expert will observe the educator's performance for at least three consecutive days, evaluate that educator's performance, write a detailed report on the observation and attach to the report a detailed plan of improvement. We found that such professional assistance either yields positive results or, at times, brings about a resignation if the educator finds that the improvement expectations cannot be fulfilled by the educator. In any event, this peer review, as it is called, has proven to be most effective and, legally as well as ethically, defensible.

... [T]he degree of incompetency might be so substantial or severe that the state would be authorized to seek the revocation of that educator's certificate ....

While matters of investigation and adjudication consume considerable time on the part of the Commission and the staff, the greater amount of time is spent on preventing adverse situations to arise; [sic] and it is for that reason that this endeavor of the Commission is contributing substantially to stabilizing employment conditions within the state. In that respect, the consul-

507

tative work of the Commission is of paramount importance.

Finally, in the 16-year history of the Commission's work in this state, it has never received a formal complaint against a teacher, administrator or system charging educational malpractice in that a student has claimed that the reason for his illiteracy is found in the incompetent instruction of his teachers.[6]

§ 15.2(B). Texas Teachers' Professional Commission.

The Texas Teachers' Professional Commission was created in 1969 by the legislature as part of the Texas Education Code. It states its purpose as:

> [It] seeks to promote high standards of ethical conduct for the membership of the education profession through the establishment of the Code of Ethics and Standard Practices for Texas Educators. It provides a means for the profession to discipline members who allegedly violate standards of the Code of Ethics, and it serves as an advisory board to the Commissioner and State Board of Education on matters related to the code.[7]

Its responsibilities are:

1. Develop and adopt, based upon a referendum vote of the profession, a code of ethics and standard practices.
2. Develop and adopt, based upon a referendum vote of the profession, revisions or amendments to the code of ethics and standard practices.
3. Establish operating and hearing procedures.
4. Conduct hearings of jurisdictional complaints filed by one active certified member of the profession

---

6. *Id.* at 2-3.

7. "Code of Ethics and Standard Practices for Texas Educators and Teacher's Professional Practices Commission of Texas." Brochure published by the State of Texas.

against another active certified member of the profession for alleged violations of a standard or standards of the Code of Ethics and Standard Practices for Texas Educators.
5. Advise the Commissioner of Education of its recommendations for the disposition of complaints.
6. Advise the Commissioner of Education, the State Board of Education, and the profession on matters of professional ethics and standard practices.[8]

Since its inception, the Professional Practices Commission has received hundreds of complaints alleging various violations of the code.[9]

§ 15.2(C). California Commission for Teachers' Preparation and Licensing.

The California Commission for Teachers' Preparation and Licensing sought in fiscal year 1981-82 to raise its standards for "tomorrow's" teachers. Its purpose was to assure the public that teachers and other professional educators will continue to be prepared, as well as possible, for their critically important and demanding work. Many Californians had expressed increased concern for educational standards, which are critically important to the state's cultural vitality and economic prosperity. As a public service agency of California government, the Commission responded by striving to raise its standards for future teachers. Higher standards of teacher preparation and licensing will mean that public school personnel throughout the state will satisfy rigorous requirements for entering the profession, and for remaining in it.[10]

---

8. *Id.*
9. Robert McCorkle, "PPC — Watchdog or Paper Tiger? Code of Ethics: Out of Sight, Out of Mind," *ATPE News* (December 1981), p. 8.
10. State of California Commission for Teacher Preparation and Licensing, *Standards for Tomorrow's Teachers,* ELEVENTH ANNUAL REPORT, 1981-82, p. i.

The Executive Secretary for the Commission for Teachers' Preparation and Licensing, commenting in the Eleventh Annual Report, stated:

> Education and educators have been treated very badly in recent years. Financing for schools is rapidly becoming a national disgrace. Teacher morale has fallen to record lows. School boards and administrators are paralyzed in their efforts to design educational goals and curriculums for the future. Extracurricular activities, which help to develop the whole person, are being dropped. And most frustrating, we may be condemning the best and the brightest of our children to lives of diminished intellectual curiosity, achievement and fulfillment. In a world that grows more complex exponentially, what has been happening to our profession is deeply appalling.
> ....
>
> Fundamentally, the most critical question concerns the value that Californians place on education. Our commitment to schooling is the key to the future of our state. If we value eduction [education]; we simply must provide the means for teachers to serve and create, for children to challenge and be challenged, for administrators to become creative leaders, and for parents to help us shape and direct the future.[11]

§ 15.2(D). Nebraska Professional Practices Commission. (*See* Appendix 1).

The Nebraska Professional Practices Commission was established to assist the Nebraska State Board of Education in enforcing standards of ethical and competent professional performance. It receives complaints against certifi-

---

11. *Id.* at 2.

cated educators in the public schools of Nebraska for any violation of those standards.[12]

The Executive Director of the Nebraska Professional Practices Commission, commenting on the increase of complaints of teacher incompetence, stated in a letter:

> As you review the nature of the inquiries received by the Nebraska Commission, you will note that the number of cases regarding complaints of teacher incompetence is increasing. I'm not sure whether that speaks to the question of more incompetent teachers or whether the public is better informed and willing to pursue the removal of incompetent teachers from the classroom.[13]

The following analysis was contained in one of the Commission's Biennial Reports:

> The past two years have shown continual growth in the number of new inquiries and formal complaints received by the Commission. The 1980-81 school year did show a slight drop in this upward trend; however, in the 1981-82 school year there was a 20 percent increase in the number of inquiries over the previous highest year and the greatest number of formal complaints received in any one year. The statistics reflect a change in the type of complaint received. Contract abrogations previously constituted the greatest number of complaints. That number has dropped substantially with increased efforts to inform educators and boards of education of the proper procedure to follow in requesting a release from an employment contract.
>
> Many of the new inquiries and complaints involve the inappropriate use of physical force by an educator. Many of these complaints are from parents in school

---

12. Nebraska Professional Practices Commission, pamphlet describing the *Complaint Procedure* of the Commission.

13. Letter by Robert Wagner, Executive Director of Nebraska Professional Practices Commission, written in response to requested information (November 1, 1982).

511

districts in which no corporal punishment policy has been developed either by the school administrator or the board of education.

The Commission has also seen a significant increase in complaints involving special education students and complaints questioning the competency of both teachers and administrators. A record 17 peer reviews were conducted during the 1981-82 school year alone. Twelve of these reviews were conducted as a result of complaints against educators alleging incompetency ....[14]

§ 15.2(E). Louisiana Teaching Professional Practices Commission.

In 1980, the Louisiana Legislature passed the "Teaching Professions Practices Act," declaring *teaching* and all professional, administrative, and supervisory services rendered by persons holding certificates, licenses, or permits issued by the BESE, be recognized as a *profession*.[15] The Louisiana Teaching Professions Practices Commission is described as:

An autonomous state body consisting of 15 members including five public elementary teachers, four public secondary teachers, one elementary and one secondary public principal, one member from the post-secondary vocational-technical schools, one member of the State Department of Education, and two members appointed at-large. All members must be certified by the State Board of Elementary and Secondary Education to teach in Louisiana. The Commission will employ a professional staff.[16]

---

14. Nebraska Professional Practices Commission, *Biennial Report* (July 1, 1980 to June 30, 1982), pp. 7-8.

15. Louisiana Teaching Professions Practices Commission, *An Introduction to the Teaching Professions Practice Commission*, pamphlet (Baton Rouge, Louisiana).

16. *Id.*

As to the functions of the Commission, it is stated that the Commission may do the following:

May make recommendations to the state superintendent, the BESE, or any local board on improvement of the teaching profession.

Conducts inquiry at any appropriate site within the state to carry out the responsibilities of the commission.

Conducts inquiry into any reasonable alleged grievance or the violation of any law of this state pertaining to educators, the alleged violation of any policy, rule, or minimum accepted standard adopted by the BESE or any local school board.

Make recommendations such as remedial programs for educators.

Holds hearings. The Commission conducts hearings for the purpose of investigations and for determining whether probable cause exists that mandates formal adjudicatory action.

Makes recommendations to the BESE in cases which may result in the suspension, or revocation of certification.

Conducts professional reviews. In cases where an educator's professional performance is in question, the Teaching Professions Practices Commission will conduct upon request a professional review of the services of the educator. Professional reviewers are carefully selected master teachers and administrators who have undergone an extensive training program to obtain particular assessment and evaluation skills. These expert reviewers spend at least three days with the educator in question observing his or her performance in the classroom or the administrative office and write a report of their observations. They make recommendations specifically designed to help remediate any performance deficiencies that might have been observed so that, with the help of an established assistance program, the educator should be able to improve his or her skills to an acceptable level. Case histories and results from other states have shown that, in most cases where professional reviews have been conducted, the educator's performance has improved, thereby often averting an administrative decision adverse to that educator.[17]

It is further stated that the following individuals may request assistance:

a) The parents of the child attending school.
b) Any educators; teachers, principals, superintendents, and superintendents.
c) Boards of Education.
d) A concerned citizen of the age of majority who is related by blood or marriage to or is legally responsible for the child who is a student.[18]

The Governor appoints all Commission members with the consent of the Senate. The qualifications necessary to become a member and the nominating procedure are as follows:

To be qualified for appointment to the Commission, a person must (1) be certified to teach in Louisiana, (2) be a citizen of the United States and a resident of Louisiana, (3) be employed in the public schools of Louisiana under the jurisdiction of the BESE, and (4) have been employed as an educator in the public schools for five years prior to appointment. The two at-large members and the SDE members are exempt from 3 and 4 above.

Commission members are nominated by recognized statewide or local professional public education organizations that represent educators who are under the jurisdiction of the BESE. The state superintendent of education nominates the individual representing the state departments of education and the governor directly appoints the two at-large members.[19]

---

17. *Id.*
18. *Id.*
19. *Id.*

In 1980, the Louisiana Legislature passed the "Teaching Professions Practices Act" declaring *teaching* and all professional administrative, and supervisory services rendered by persons holding certificates, licenses or permits issued by the BESE to be recognized as a *profession.* This somewhat determined the issue of whether teaching is a profession in Louisiana.[20] At least *legally* in Louisiana teaching is, as it should be, recognized as a profession.

§ 15.2(F). Iowa Professional Teaching Practices Commission. (*See* Appendix 3).

The Iowa Professional Practices Commission was created in 1967 and given the responsibility "of developing criteria of professional practices including such areas as contractual obligations, competent performance of all members of the teaching profession, and ethical practice toward other members of the profession, parents, students and the community."[21]

For the purpose of the Act, the "profession of teaching" or "teaching profession" shall mean persons engaged in teaching or providing related administrative, supervisory, or other services requiring certification from the State Board of Public Instruction.[22] As to who may initiate a complaint, the rules of the Commission allow the following:

a) Certified personnel or their recognized local or state professional organization.
b) Local boards of education.
c) Administrators, supervisors and other members of the teaching profession employed by a school district or other educational entity outside of Iowa.

---

20. *Id.*
21. Iowa Professional Teaching Practices Commission, pamphlet dated June, 1978, describing the set-up and operation of the Commission, p. 1.
22. *Id.* at 1-2.

d) Parents or guardians of students involved in the alleged complaint.[23]

It is interesting to note that in an Act of the Iowa House of Representatives to establish an autonomous Board to perform the duties of the Board of Educational Examiners and Professional Practices Commission, the definition of "teacher" is:

"Teacher" means a licensed member of a school's instructional staff who diagnoses, prescribes, evaluates, and directs student learning in a manner which is consistent with professional practice and school objectives, shares responsibility for the development of an instructional program and any coordinating activities, evaluates or assesses student progress before and after instructor, and who uses the student evaluation or assessment information to promote additional learning.[24]

This definition places some direct responsibilities on the teachers and obviously weakens the argument that teachers owe no duty to students — or that there is no established standard of care for teachers. It may be a broad standard, but so are standards in other professions.

§ 15.2(G). Other Professional Teaching Practices Commissions.

Another Professional Teaching Practices Commission is the Oregon Teacher Standards and Practices Commission. (*See* Appendix 4). An Executive Secretary of that Commission notes:

Our greatest concern, as may be the situation with most states, is over [our] inability to promulgate appropriate criteria (standards) for defining improper

---

23. *Id.* at 13-14.
24. Iowa House of Representatives, House File 794, Seventy-Third General Assembly (1989), p. 3.

conduct. Presently we are attempting to improve our definition of "gross unfitness," "gross neglect of duty," "good moral character" and "fitness to serve." Courts have been telling agencies similar to us that they must define these terms, as the Legislatures left that an unfinished task.[25]

Other commissions include the Florida Education Practices Commission, the Oregon Teacher Standards and Practices Commission and the Utah Professional Practices Advisory Commission. (*See* Appendix 2).

Information regarding various commissions and the way these commissions are organized has been presented to illustrate, among other things, how some state legislatures and the educational systems in those states have responded to the mounting concerns about educators and the educational system. Furthermore, an analysis of this information shows the limitations that are placed on these commissions. While their existence aids in the prevention and correction of some of the problems in the educational system, their scope and their present limited authority prevent them from remedying students who are "academically" harmed. For example, dismissing an incompetent teacher may very well prevent future problems in that classroom but does not really cure or remedy the "intellectual" damage that that teacher inflicted upon the student(s), prior to the teacher's dismissal. As the commissions are organized, they are not a substitute or alternative to the courts in resolving a complaint of "educational malpractice." Other professions such as the medical, legal and accounting professions have similar commissions which discipline members of their profession, but these commissions do not decide all aspects of all matters regarding injuries resulting

---

25. Letter by Richard S. Jones, Executive Director of Teacher Standards and Practices Commission, written in response to requested information (July 28, 1982).

from alleged malpractice. Courts are available to deal with complaints by the injured.

PART V
GENERAL VIEWS ON EDUCATIONAL MALPRACTICE AND SUMMATION

Chapter 16

GENERAL VIEWS CONCERNING EDUCATIONAL MALPRACTICE

§ 16.0. Introduction.
§ 16.1. Accountability in Education.
§ 16.2. Various Views on Educational Malpractice.
§ 16.3. Principles, Truisms and Statements.

> It is hard to argue against
> accountability.

§ 16.0. Introduction.

As stated previously, the purpose of the study which resulted in this book was to examine the status of educational malpractice — focusing more specifically on the issue of whether courts should entertain educational malpractice suits. At the heart of this issue is the additional
issue of whether the public schools and the educational
profession could or should be held liable for professional
judgments that result in the failure of students to succeed
academically. The resolution of these issues involve complex and sensitive topics. Thus, it was necessary that these
issues and the questions they pose be analyzed from the
educational, social, legal, economic, administrative, ethical, and philosophical perspectives. Furthermore, they
needed to be viewed from the perspective of all concerned,
including students, teachers, administrators, parents,
school systems, local communities, and the public at large.
The various arguments advanced by judges, justices, attorneys, educators, legislators, students, administrators, parents, commentators, and others were gathered and analyzed. This compilation will produce decision-makers able
to analyze the complex issues and reach informed conclusions.

There is a concern that "if researchers and other members of the educational profession do nothing to improve the knowledge base in this area, such external forces as the legislature and the courts, through statutes and judicial decisions, will eventually establish guidelines for educators and all society will suffer the resulting inflexibility."[1] This chapter will summarize various views on educational malpractice which have been expressed by various writers. It will also list a number of Principles, Truisms, and Statements regarding educational malpractice.

§ 16.1. Accountability in Education.

Woods, an educational malpractice scholar, maintains that "there is little doubt that educational malpractice will continue as a subject for judicial consideration. A frustrated public continues to seek the ultimate solution to the problem of declining effectiveness of schools, and the courtroom provides an avenue for redress to dissatisfied parents and students."[2] "Nearly every state requires children to attend schools for eight to ten years. Many states provide, either through the state constitution or legislative enactment, that the education provided be 'adequate' or 'effective' and recently all 50 states have considered some form of legislation to hold schools accountable for providing such an education."[3] Concerning accountability in education, one writer states:

---

1. David G. Carter, Jr., *The Educator and the Liability Law of Professional Malpractice: A Historical Analysis,* pp. 20-21. Paper presented in 1979 AERA Annual Convention, San Francisco, California, April 8-12, 1979.

2. Nancy L. Woods, *Educational Malfeasance: A New Cause of Action for Failure to Educate?,* 14 TULSA LAW JOURNAL 383, 409 (1978). Copyright by the University of Tulsa.

3. Arlene H. Patterson, *Professional Malpractice: Small Cloud, but Growing Bigger,* PHI DELTA KAPPAN (November 1980), p. 193.

In 1970, President Nixon announced to the nation that "school administrators and school teachers are responsible for their performance and it is in their interests, as well as in the interests of their pupils, that they be held accountable." This doctrine of accountability seems to have been generated out of a theory developed by Dr. Leon Lessinger, Assistant Commissioner of Education, who stated that Americans were becoming "fed up" with public education. Dr. Lessinger felt that public education is "too costly, too nebulous, too many children have failed, and nobody's accountable." Lessinger also said that "today about one out of every four American children drops out of school. Hundreds of thousands of parents have decided that their children are not stupid and that either some educators are incompetent or that methods they are using are inadequate" [footnote omitted].[4]

As noted previously, when a doctor accepts a patient for diagnosis and treatment, both parties acquire legal rights and legal obligations. These rights and obligations affect every aspect of the physician-patient relationship.[5] It would seem that when a school system accepts a student, both parties should acquire legal rights and legal obligations arising out of the student-teacher relationship. It would seem a common sense conclusion, states one writer, "that a student suffers harm when a teacher knowingly or negligently teaches him false information, destroys his confidence through insult or ridicule, teaches in an incomprehensible manner, or does not teach at all."[6] Yet, states

4. Richard E. Fields & J. John Harris III, *Educational Malpractice and the Public Demands for Teacher Accountability,* 9 PLANNING & CHANGING (Spring 1978), p. 3. Reprinted with permission of Editor, PLANNING & CHANGING.

5. Angela Roddy Holder, MEDICAL MALPRACTICE LAW (New York: John Wiley and Sons, 1975).

6. John Elson, *A Common Law Remedy for the Educational Harms Caused by Incompetent or Careless Teaching,* 73 NORTHWESTERN UNIVERSITY LAW REVIEW 641, 644 (November 1978).

the author, "even in the comparatively rare instances
when such not uncommon practices are discovered by
higher authorities and an offending teacher is consequently disciplined or dismissed, the teacher's students
still have no generally recognized independent legal remedy for the harms suffered from such intolerable teaching
practices."[7] Should any group or any individual be immune
from his or her negligent or "gross" negligent conduct?
Should anyone be above the law? Generally, teachers do
not have to act under emergency conditions as perhaps a
doctor must act. Normally, the negligence of a teacher that
results in a student's "academic or intellectual" injury is
not a single negligent act, but a number of negligent acts;
thus, the negligent act becomes somewhat chronic. That
being the case, query: Is it fair and equitable to hold a
physician, psychiatrist, or attorney, acting under "press-
ing" conditions, liable for a single negligent act, yet not
even entertain the complaint of a student who claims academic injury, by not one, but by a continuous number of
negligent or "gross" negligent acts committed by a teacher
or an employee of the educational system? Generally, proponents for recognition of educational malpractice do not
argue that students should recover automatically from a
teacher if there is negligence on the part of the teacher, but
rather, that if a student properly files a claim "alleging"
negligence, the courts have a responsibility to hear the
complaint instead of automatically dismissing same. A
hearing or a trial does not necessarily result in the plaintiff
receiving an award for the alleged wrongdoing. Not only
must the claimant prove the allegations and show their
sufficiency for establishing a claim, but also must show
that all defenses against the claim are not valid. Furthermore, proximate cause and damages must be proven. Obvi-

---

7. *Id.*

ously, this is not an easy task for the claimant, nor should it be. Likewise, argue the proponents of educational malpractice, the granting of a motion to dismiss without giving the claimant an opportunity to have his or her cause *heard,* irregardless of how "severe" and "gross" the alleged negligent acts are, is certainly not equitable. Moreover, they maintain, lack of accountability may help promote inefficiency and negligent conduct. Klein suggests:

> Holding educators legally accountable for negligent acts or omissions that cause inadequate education hopefully will result in an improvement of the educational process. Opening the process to public scrutiny may bring the weight of popular opinion to bear on improving it. Justification for providing external stimulants arises from the compulsory nature of public schooling. School systems and education are virtually assured of their place in society as long as there are children of school age. As a result, there is limited incentive for self-regulation. The standard of care a court would probably adopt is that of a reasonable educator under similar circumstances, so reasoned judgment reflecting skill and knowledge will suffice. Setting the standard of care at a level that does not imply an absolute duty to educate may also result in realistic expectations of the potential of the school system to solve the problems of the society.

> A successful malpractice action, however, may have negative effects on educational policy. Teaching in the face of liability may mischannel resources just as defensive medicine does. The practices of defensive medicine, such as administering unnecessary tests, do not reduce the total amount of available health care but rather misallocate the current resources. In a comparable way, teachers may, for example, focus on basic

skills to the exclusion of other important areas such as music and art. Another possibility is that test-taking skills will become the instructional emphasis; as a result, scores may improve without a corresponding improvement in the students' educational level. In addition to restricting the goals of education, malpractice actions may also stifle classroom experimentation. The level of acceptance of new methods and materials in educational circles may determine whether it is reasonable to employ innovative methods.[8]

Klein further reasons:

> One of the difficulties inherent in making a qualitative assessment of educational programs is the lack of established standards in the field. Practitioners and theorists dispute whether the primary goal of education is to develop creative thinking, to stress basic skills, or to socialize the students. There is no consensus about how best to teach or to measure what has been taught. Educational malpractice actions rest on the assumption that there is some degree of skill chargeable to an educator in the exercise of his official functions.
>
> The standard of a reasonable educator is difficult to establish because of the vague and undefined principles that characterize the field; the absence of standards, in fact, has militated against the imposition of liability.
>
> This lack of standards need not, however, preclude the judiciary from assessing liability. The field of psychiatry is similarly replete with vague standards. Although psychiatry is a medical specialty, the practitioner has a much wider scope of discretion than the physician because of the limited use of diagnostic tools

8. Alice J. Klein, *Educational Malpractice: Can the Judiciary Remedy the Growing Problem of Functional Illiteracy?*, 13 SUFFOLK UNIVERSITY LAW REVIEW 27, 59-60 (Winter 1979).

....

By analogy, recognition of a cause of action for educational malpractice should at least be possible where defendant's actions constitute a blatant violation of the legally mandated student-educator relationship ....[9]

There are dilemmas that must be carefully weighed and analyzed concerning this matter. Robin Farquhar comments:

In education, our confusion is reflected in many dilemmas we currently confront. On the one hand, we are asked to "return to the basics" but on the other hand, we are urged to adopt more innovations. There is support for teachers developing their own courses of study to meet local community needs, but there is pressure to return to a more standardized curriculum and examination procedure. School staffs are supposed to listen more to what the pupils have to say in shaping learning experiences, but at the same time to give more positive direction to the work of students. Educational systems are expected to become more open and flexible, less rigid and bureaucratic; yet it is required that they exercise greater control and accountability in monitoring their performance.[10]

Even though these problems are in some cases real and in some cases imagined, it does not mean that educators and courts should push them aside. Out of sight may be out of mind, but generally not the answer to a reoccurring problem. This is heightened by a climate of heavy criticism of public schools for their failure to solve the social problems of our times and their inability to educate all children

---

9. *Id.* at 38-39.

10. Robin H. Farquhar, *Our Schools Need Help: Toward an Open Sector Adjunct in Public Education,* EDUCATION CANADA (Summer 1978), p. 8.

with equal success.[11] Appropriate answers to reoccurring problems must be found which consider all publics and are viewed from all dimensions and are equitable. Thus, the perception that the decision-maker is independent from bias certainly will have an impact on the acceptability of the decision. This is not to say that in order for a decision to be fair it must be accepted — for there are those who may not accept any decision that goes contrary to their own selfish interests. The objective is to correct a wrong that has been committed by not only compensating those that were "wronged" or "injured," but by helping prevent a possible reoccurrence and compensate for wrongs, rather than compensate those that are dissatisfied. Commenting on the subject of medical malpractice, regarding this issue, Flaster notes:

> The right of every citizen to seek compensation for wrongful acts as acts of negligence committed on him or her is fundamental to our American way of life. But when dissatisfaction is not the result of negligence, there is no inherent right to compensation, no matter how well off the doctor may be or how good an insurance policy the doctor may have.[12]

The same argument can be made concerning educators. Claims must be carefully analyzed and only valid meritorious claims should prevail. Determination of the merits of a claim should be based on previously determined standards — standards established after careful analysis and set in a non-adversary atmosphere under proper conditions. The goal of these standards should be to maximize learning. "Preventive" medicine is certainly preferred to "corrective"

11. R.C. Newell, *Teacher Malpractice: A New Threat to Education,* AMERICAN EDUCATOR (Summer 1977), p. 2.

12. DONALD J. FLASTER, MALPRACTICE: A GUIDE TO THE LEGAL RIGHTS OF PATIENTS AND DOCTORS (New York: Charles Scribner's Sons, 1983), p. 167.

medicine. Preventing negligence is preferred over remedying a negligent act or compensating one for a negligent act.

Education is best served when parents, students, teachers, and school administrators work cooperatively. A court's examination of a complaint brought by a student and/or parent will not necessarily result in a determination by the court that the defendant was negligent or committed a particular wrong. The claimant bears the burden of proof. The court is merely providing a forum where a dispute can be equitably examined and resolved and the court's intervention should not be viewed as judicial interferences in the public education system. Courts should not force themselves on the educational system nor should they turn their backs and close their doors to those who legitimately question the educational system. This, of course, does not mean that the courts should open their doors at the outset of a dispute, but at an appropriate stage in the administrative process — when all the appropriate administrative remedies have been exhausted. This gives the parties ample opportunity to define the issues and settle their differences. It is only after all the various attempts to correct or remedy any wrongs committed have failed, that the courts should open their doors to the educational system. The mere possibility of court intervention, even though at a later stage, may serve not only as a deterrent to unacceptable educational practices, but also serve as a stimulus to correcting or remedying a wrong that has been committed.

Generally, all parties concerned will try to avoid litigation — for litigation is generally not a preferable remedy — not only because of the costs and time involved in processing a claim through courts, but also due to the resulting effects that such an adversary hearing will have on the parties. But, litigation may provide a forum in which to "air" a grievance when no other remedy is available or practical, or where other remedies are ineffective. There is, of course, the fear that someone may improperly use the courts, in effect, to "blackmail" the other party into doing something, merely to avoid litigation and not because it was the proper thing to do. However, that fear is ever present in practically all dealings. For example, doctors are subject to the same tactics. That fear should not deter the establishment of a legal remedy to correct a wrongdoing. Legislatures and the court systems can build in safeguards to prevent misuse of the courts.

§ 16.2. Various Views on Educational Malpractice.

As noted, the fact that the courts are accessible to those who may seek to have their claims heard does not mean that the courts will decide in their favor. All that is demanded is that the courts should and must provide a proper resolution to the claims presented to them. Patterson explains:

> Educational malpractice suits seek to redress students who have not received full educational benefits when teachers negligently or intentionally "failed to conform to minimum standards of professional competence ...." The harm suffered is the student's failure to attain the educational level that would probably have been attained had the teacher performed at the required level. Currently, this means that many students who have failed to learn constitute a class of victims without remedy, presenting a dilemma for both the courts and education. The question becomes, Who — professional educators or the legal system — will provide the remedy?[13]

It is the responsibility of the courts to dismiss unmeritorious claims and sustain those that are meritorious. The New York Court of Appeals stated:

---

13. Patterson, *supra* note 3, at 194.

We presently feel that even the public policy argument is subject to challenge. Although fraud, extra litigation and a measure of speculation are, of course, possibilities, it is no reason for a court to eschew a measure of its jurisdiction. The argument from [for] mere expediency cannot commend itself to a Court of justice, resulting in the denial of a right and remedy in all cases because in some a fictitious injury may be urged as a real one.[14]

Blackburn maintains:

The school system will assert that the remedies for educational malpractice are in the hands of the legislature or the executive body created by statute to run the school system. However, these extra-legal processes have so far failed to remedy the situation. Ideally, the court system, through the educational malpractice suit, will make school systems more responsive to students' learning problems and will constrain the schools to improve the education they impart [footnote omitted].[15]

Commenting on the *Peter W.* case, David Abel reasons:

The *Doe* court would, by way of precedent, establish a procedure for educational negligence actions that would serve to deter all but the most meritorious suits. Tests and other instruments of educational achievement are not precise, nor is their validity universally accepted; even so, very low performance on tests (or other measures) probably indicates the presence of educational deficiencies. It seems reasonable that such crude evidence be required in any complaint that asks damages for educational negligence. In this way speculative suits, such as those that ask damages simply because jobs are unavailable, would be eliminated un-

---

14. Battalla v. State, 10 N.Y.2d 237, 240-42, 219 N.Y.S.2d 34, 37 (1961). *See also* Joan Blackburn, *Educational Malpractice: When Can Johnny Sue?*, 7 FORDHAM URBAN LAW JOURNAL 117, 142 (1978).

15. Joan Blackburn, *Educational Malpractice: When Can Johnny Sue?*, 7 FORDHAM URBAN LAW JOURNAL 117, 142 (1978).

less specific educational injury was documented. Similarly, by requiring that evidence of probable deficiency be presented, the court could concentrate on violations of minimal standards rather than on the broader range of student and parent dissatisfaction with schools. Thus, failure to gain admission to medical school, for example, would probably not constitute grounds for tort action.[16]

Faye Coultas notes that the large number of statutory requirements and regulations in the area of special education suggests that this is a fertile area for future litigation.[17] She further adds:

When the number of potential plaintiffs is considered in conjunction with these requirements, the number of possible lawsuits increases exponentially. For example, the definition of a learning disabled child in the EAHCA states that such children have a disorder in one or more of the basic psychological processes involved in understanding or in using language, spoken or written, which disorder may manifest itself in imperfect ability to listen, think, speak, read, write, spell, or do mathematical calculations. If imperfect ability in an area denotes below-average performance, then half of all school children could claim at least the right to an evaluation, since theoretically half the population would score below the fiftieth percentile.

Reflection on these numerous possibilities suggests why the law of torts has been described as a battleground of social theory. Allowing the public schools to become ungoverned participants in this battleground will evoke responses detrimental to society which may well outweigh in importance the individual wrongs for

---

16. David Abel, *Can a Student Sue the Schools for Educational Malpractice?*, 44 Howard Educational Review 416, 428 (November 1974). Copyright © 1974 by the President and Fellows of Harvard College. All rights reserved.

17. Faye M. Coultas, *Educational Malpractice and Special Education Law,* 55 Chicago-Kent Law Review 685, 709 (1979).

which redress is sought in specific lawsuits. The accountability involved in the possibility of legal liability could work to improve, to a degree, the negative results of excessive bureaucracy in school situations. However, this would apply chiefly to suits against school districts. Suits against individuals employed by those school districts, on the other hand, could interfere with effective educational programs. Members of the educational profession can hardly be expected to function optimally under the Damoclean sword of the ungoverned threat of litigation. It is the students who suffer most when their teachers function less than optimally. Further, as its extreme, if the threat is frequent and strong, older members may be prompted to leave the profession while fewer young people may be attracted to it, since it is unlikely that salaries in public school settings could be increased to a sufficiently attractive level to compensate for the threat. Should these tendencies bring about a shortage of personnel, universities could be forced to lower admissions criteria and standards for teacher training programs in order to induce more individuals to enter the field. The result would be a poorer caliber of education professionals. Such a result would impact on the school children, who would receive poorer instruction and academic training, as well as on society, for those children would enter society less well prepared to assume the responsibilities of citizenship. Also, as the number of claims increases, the cost of professional liability insurance increases. Where school districts are required to indemnify their employees, the increase in insurance premiums would necessitate increased financial support for schools or a reduction in monies devoted to direct student services. Again, the same detrimental effects on children and society would ensue. The whole of society therefore suffers if the balance between societal needs and those of individual members is disturbed through litigation or judicial interference.

On the other hand, a student's individual rights are too precious to be derogated by granting no remedy for deprivation of those rights. A tax supported social in-

stitution such as the public school system should not
be allowed to operate in a totally unfettered fashion,
free to devote its resources in the most financially ex-
pedient manner, with little regard for its responsibilities. Allowing the assertion of meritorious claims will
prompt educational personnel to function more effectively and will operate as a balance between the competing interests of the school system and those of the
children it serves.

The judiciary will have to observe scrupulous care in
opening the way to educational malpractice claims, in
order to allow valid claims while preventing the public
waste and negative societal effects which attend
groundless or frivolous litigation. It is suggested that
special education malpractice claims should be permitted where the following minimum criteria have been
met:

(1) Available administrative remedies have been
exhausted. Although this should not preclude the possibility of a negligence action, it will ensure that
proper placement has been effected so that damages do
not continue to accrue.

(2) The duty of care is readily apparent and clearly
defined. While a lucid statutory requirement would
satisfy this standard, professional expectations would
seldom do so, since these are vague and for the most
part undefined, unless the violation appears to be particularly flagrant or wanton.

(3) The alleged breach is a definite act or failure to
act. Nonfeasance with regard to a mandatory duty
would satisfy this standard better than an allegation
of misfeasance in performing a professional responsibility. For example, failure to complete an evaluation
of a child within sixty school days is easily established,
whereas demonstrating that a spelling program was
poorly planned is unlikely to be successful.

(4) The damages resulting from the alleged breach
are clearly demonstrated and carefully documented.
Where this documentation is questionable, the action
for damages should be dismissed.

534

Finally, where a case has advanced to trial and a decision in favor of the plaintiff has been reached, financial awards should be carefully scrutinized. The plaintiff should be reimbursed for clearly documented damages, but it must be borne in mind that awards levied against a school district affect public funds derived from taxpayers either directly or indirectly, such as through increased liability insurance premiums. In either case, the overall financial resources remaining available for educating all the students in the system will be reduced [footnotes omitted].[18]

Coultas concludes the article by stating:

Handicapped children have been granted not only access to education equal to that of their nonhandicapped peers, but also safeguards which go beyond those for children attending the standard program. These safeguards, when violated or poorly observed, may provide the basis for a personal damage action, an educational malpractice suit, by a handicapped child or his parents. The availability of such lawsuits can serve as a check on the impersonal, unbridled bureaucracy of school systems. Nonetheless, the unconditional use of such lawsuits could provoke an imbalance between the individual and the system which would be detrimental to other school children and the community at large.

Therefore, safeguards to control the litigation of educational malpractice suits must be imposed. Observation of such safeguards should facilitate the orderly conduct of the educational process, so that the individual's need for protection is balanced by the overall good of society. The result will be to improve education for all children, not only the handicapped, and thereby enhance society as a whole.[19]

Lee Magnuson advances the argument that where modern industrial technology requires that a person acquire certain language and computational skills in order to effec-

---

18. *Id.* at 709-10.
19. *Id.* at 711-12.

tively function in society, education must provide such skills or it is constitutionally defective.[20] The author further writes:

> This emphasis on educational results seems to be a very realistic way of evaluating equal educational opportunities. It would effectively implement an idea inspired by Horace Mann, who wrote:
>
>> I believe in the existence of a great, immortal, immutable principle of natural law, or natural ethics, — a principle antecedent to all human institutions, and incapable of being abrogated by any ordinance of man ... which proves the *absolute right* to an education of every human being that comes into the world, and which of course, proves the correlative duty of every government to see that the means of that education are provided for all.
>
> Equal education has to be given concreteness and specificity as educational policy. Thus, where educational policy concludes that equal education requires certain specific practices, the courts should make those practices a part of the constitutional dimensions of the equal education guarantee. The courts must ask the question: "What are the essential ingredients needed for equality of educational opportunity?" When this question is answered, the mandate of the equal protection clause will be clear [footnote omitted].[21]

Destin Tracy lists the following suggested parameters of an educational negligence cause of action:

> The courts should give limited recognition to a cause of action in educational negligence, and this tort duty to act with due care while engaging in academic instruction could be created under either of two theories. First, when educators hold themselves out as possess-

---

20. Lee A. Magnuson, *Equality and the Schools: Education as a Fundamental Interest,* 21 AMERICAN UNIVERSITY LAW REVIEW 717, 735-36 (September 1972).

21. *Id.*

ing special skills and knowledge, the student has a right to expect them to use their special skills and knowledge non-negligently. This reasonable expectation demands the creation of a professional educator's duty to the extent that special skills are claimed. Second, a statutory duty of care can properly be recognized on the basis of detailed statutes and regulations that speak to particular students' problems and that do not call for the discretionary exercise of judgment. By limiting a public educator's tort duty of competent academic instruction to these two situations, the courts will avoid significant interference in educational policymaking. A professional duty only requires educators to act with care while performing functions for which they themselves claim expertise; it does not involve the courts in determination of the functions in which educators *should* have expertise. Similarly, a statutory duty is derived from a legislative expression of public policy that has already been imposed on the educational system from without; the role of the judiciary in applying such a statutory duty is not to determine policy but merely to enforce a policy already in effect. Regulations promulgated pursuant to a statute are frequently formulated by educators themselves. When these are the source of a statutory duty, the court is merely demanding that educators act in conformity with their own expressed policies.

Moreover, it is possible to formulate a workable standard of care corresponding to each suggested source of duty. A professional standard of care may be drawn from customary behaviors of the profession generally, when widespread conformity exists, or from conduct common to the defendant's local educational system. Alternatively, a professional standard may be derived from definitive statutory expressions of desirable teaching behaviors and from regulations developed by educators to achieve these desired goals. When a statutory duty is created, a statutory standard of care is embodied in the requirements and prohibitions of the statute on which the duty is based.

Both the professional and statutory standards of care outlined above avoid the need for judicial interference in educational policymaking. The proposed standards measure breach either by the educators' own determination of proper behavior, self-imposed through custom or regulations, or by public policy judgments of appropriate behavior implicit in statutory requirements to which educators have already been subjected.

The complaining student should be free to plead any injury for which a cause-in-fact relationship with the alleged incompetent teaching can be proved. The use of proximate cause to limit the types of injuries for which the plaintiff may recover is not desirable because the same result may be effected by explicitly invoking the vital policy concerns that would otherwise be obscured by the rhetoric of proximate cause. The courts must preserve the flexibility to provide the kind and degree of relief necessitated by the nature and extent of the student's particular injuries. In determining the appropriate remedy, the courts must balance the needs of the individual plaintiff against the potential effect on the ability of the educational system to serve the needs of students collectively. Toward this end, remedies with potentially far-reaching detrimental effects, such as substantial compensatory or punitive monetary awards, should be rejected in favor of alternative remedies with the potential for benefiting more students, such as remedial education for the plaintiff or dismissal of incompetent teachers. By careful [carefully] limiting remedies pursuant to this balancing process, the courts will support the policy favoring nonjudicial solutions to the maximum extent possible consistent with satisfying a genuine need for individual relief.

The combined effect of these suggested limitations on an educational negligence cause of action would be to greatly reduce the number of cases that could be successfully litigated, thereby reducing the feared flood of excessive litigation.[22]

In concluding an article on this subject, Blackburn states:

> The strong public policy considerations of excessive liability and scarcity of funds are reasons successfully presented to quash educational malpractice suits. The problems of proof inherent in establishing causality for the plaintiff's poor learning create further difficulties. Negligent teaching is a concept of flux, not yet determined by expert testimony. The great number of educational theories in the field obfuscate any single standard. The success of a plaintiff's case will depend on stressing the wrong done to an individual in light of the importance of the duty vested in the school system. The action for negligent misrepresentation is the best of those surveyed for proving liability, although this theory must still overcome the obstacles of public policy erected by all the courts considering the matter to date.[23]

In summarizing the implications of recognizing a cause of action for educational malpractice, Alice Klein suggests:

> The most clear-cut and predictable impact of a decision to recognize an educational malpractice cause of action and to grant relief will be on the individual plaintiff. A successful suit will result in compensation in the form of limited money damages and remedial instruction. Unsuccessful litigants, on the other hand, will continue to bear the burden of inadequate education alone. The implications for educational policy decisions and for educational personnel are broader and less certain than they are for plaintiffs.

---

22. Destin Shann Tracy, *Educational Negligence: A Student's Cause of Action for Incompetent Academic Instruction,* 58 NORTH CAROLINA LAW REVIEW 561, 594-95 (March 1980).

23. Blackburn, *supra* note 15, at 144.

There are also conflicting potential consequences for the education profession generally. Seen as a demand for a higher quality of education, a damage award may stimulate professional self-evaluation and raise the standards for hiring and evaluating personnel. Potential liability may encourage educators to improve teacher training programs and expand continuing education. These efforts will reduce the numbers of incompetent personnel and improve the public image of educators. Nevertheless, a find of educational malpractice may carry with it unwarranted connotations; the public might infer widespread incompetence, for example. The possibility of facing courtroom proceedings and liability may discourage qualified individuals from becoming educators.

The financial impact on educational services depends largely on insurance. The imposition of liability, in fact, may be a function of the availability of liability insurance. The cost of the premiums is not the sole financial consideration; malpractice actions also involve investigative and defense expenditures. If it is necessary to divert funds from the school budget for these expenses, educational services would decrease. Successful plaintiffs might, therefore, benefit at the expense of the rest of the school population.

The potential repercussions of recognizing a cause of action cover a broad spectrum. The precise impact depends on the responses of educators to the judicial determination. Educators would prefer accountability to be an internal affair. Beginning in the late 1960s members of the profession were active in an accountability movement; however, they have not yet developed a system of self-regulation. The absence of self-regulation in the face of large numbers of inadequately educated students should convince the courts of the propriety of imposing liability in an attempt to stimulate professional review and educational improvement [footnotes omitted].[24]

---

24. Klein, *supra* note 8, at 58-61.

In concluding her article on educational malpractice, Klein writes:

> The present judicial approach to the problem of inadequate education insulates the educational establishment from accountability to the public. Compulsory attendance requirements, billion dollar educational expenditures, the importance of education, and the failure of the profession to institute internal review mechanisms shed doubt on the validity of this abstentionist attitude.
>
> The ambiguous nature of the educational process has discouraged judicial involvement. Nevertheless, courts have rendered judgments pertaining to special education students. This body of law, which entails similar determinations about educational decision making, provides the foundation for assessing conduct affecting the majority of the public school population — children of normal intelligence. By establishing educational goals, the statutory developments in the area of minimum competency standards may alleviate some of the problems of judicial review.
>
> Plaintiffs seek to improve educational techniques and outcomes, as well as to recover for failings that could have been prevented by the exercise of due care. They want to establish a standard of care relative to factors within the control of educators and to the norms of the educational community. Experts have isolated responsibilities chargeable to personnel involved in the educational process. Evaluation of the performance of these tasks must reflect the uncontrollable variables such as the pupil's capabilities, home environment and the subjective interaction between student and teachers.
>
> Inherent in educational malpractice decisions are competing policy considerations and a wide range of potential consequences.. Nevertheless, the judiciary should recognize a cause of action not only to compensate injured plaintiffs but also to open the educational

541

process to public scrutiny in an attempt to stimulate improvement and foster professional review.[25]

Arlene Patterson, writing on professional malpractice, argues:

> Educating our youth is an integral part of American society, involving enormous resources and costing billions of dollars each year. Yet occasionally something goes wrong. A law is passed that is unfair to a particular group of students, a school district fails to enforce its own rules, an incompetent teacher is employed, or an otherwise competent teacher violates his or her professional obligations. For whatever reason a student may be injured academically because of a negligent action on the part of the public school educators who have been entrusted with providing an effective and adequate education.
>
> If that same student suffered harm as the result of the negligent action on the part of the motorist, a lawyer, or a physician, he or she could expect to be compensated through a court of law for injury suffered. If that student suffered a physical injury caused by an over-zealous wack or by a teacher's failure to provide ordinary care, the student could expect compensation through the courts. However, if a student's learning problems should be misdiagnosed as the result of a violation of a school's own rule, causing the student to suffer a loss of achievement given — if the injury tended to be academic rather than physical — under current law the student could not expect remedy even if the actions of the school district were deemed to be "egregious."[26]

Another author commenting on educational malpractice states:

> At the present time, the problems involved in bringing a suit for failure to learn because of teacher negligence

---

25. *Id.* at 61-62.
26. Patterson, *supra* note 3, at 193.

or incompetence may seem insurmountable. Traditional legal principles, however, provide ample guidance for fashioning a viable cause of action.

First, failure to learn is not a harm beyond the law's remedial capabilities. The replacement of incompetent teachers, the provision of, or payment for, remedial instruction, and monetary compensation for diminished future income could "make whole" public school students who have suffered a loss of educational benefits.

Second, tort law, contract law, and mandamus provide legal theories on which a suit for failure to learn might be based. A negligence suit stands the most chance of success; various statutory, common law, and scholarly authorities support the contention that school districts and teachers should be held liable for the failure of students to learn because of the negligence of the teachers. The standard of acceptable instruction should be comparative, that is, the level of skill and learning of the minimally acceptable teacher in the same or similar communities. In limited circumstances, causes of action based on intentional tort or misrepresentation may also be available. Contract law may supply the public school student with a cause of action if the factfinder can be persuaded of the existence of implied contracts between the student and the teacher or between the student and the school district, with an implied promise of non-negligent instruction. Although in many cases the contract theory may be less plausible than the tort theory, the contract approach has several advantages: Governmental immunity, which may bar recovery in tort, might not preclude a successful contract action; courts may be more willing to allow recovery for loss of an expectancy or benefit in contract than in tort; defenses such as contributory negligence or assumption of risk may bar recovery in tort but not in contract; and statutes of limitations are generally longer for contract actions. A contract theory would, of course, be of more use to a private school student than to a public school student.

543

Finally, in narrowly defined circumstances, mandamus may provide minimal relief.

Third, there are several methods of proving teacher
negligence and causation of harm. The latter can be
established if the plaintiff proves that a class of which
he was a member performed significantly worse than
did classes identical in all essential respects except
that they were not taught by the defendant teacher.
Negligence can be established if the plaintiff proves
that the teacher's performance fell significantly below
the average worst performance of teachers in classes
identical to the plaintiff's in all essential respects.
Lack of certification, a supervisor's poor evaluations,
failure to conform to statutory educational requirements, and failure to use recognized teaching methods
might provide other evidence of negligence.

The legal framework for a cause of action for failure
to learn is supported by strong policy considerations,
including the importance of education, the ability of
teachers and school districts to bear or spread the costs
of students' failure to learn, and the desirability of
deterring negligent teaching and the hiring of incompetent teachers.

The novelty of the theories advanced in this Comment does not condemn educational malpractice suits
to an eternity of sustained demurrers and motions to
dismiss for failure to state a cause of action. Dean
Prosser's tribute to the flexibility of tort law is an ac-
knowledgment of the dynamism of the common law
generally:

> [T]he progress of the common law is marked by
> many cases of first impression, in which the court
> has struck out boldly to create a new cause of ac-
> tion, where none had been recognized before ....
> The law of torts is anything but static, and the
> limits of its development are never set. When it
> becomes clear that the plaintiff's interests are en-
> titled to legal protection against the conduct of the
> defendant, the mere fact that the claim is novel

> will not of itself operate as a bar to recovery [footnote omitted].[27]

Klein maintains:

> An educational malpractice claim is intended to redress the injuries suffered by serious students — those who have made bona fide efforts to meet the demands of coursework and the expectations of school officials, who have been led by annual promotions and graduation to believe that they have, in fact, performed in a satisfactory manner, and who have then discovered that they are grossly undereducated according to the demands of contemporary society. Critics may argue that claims for educational malpractice should not go forward because they may benefit lazy, unmotivated students who seek only a large demand award. Judicial expertise in sorting the valid from the invalid claims, however, should dispel concerns of rewarding undeserving plaintiffs. Furthermore, fear of fraudulent claims should not bar redress of legitimate ones.
>
> Named defendants are usually the governmental bodies responsible for education and their officials, rather than individual instructors. The issue is the cumulative effect of the conduct of educators who fail to assess the needs of students and who promote students regardless of performance; it appears unlikely, therefore, that the negligent conduct of an individual instructor would result in such debilitating skill deficiencies. A comparable action in the field of medical malpractice names the hospital as a defendant, basing the suit for physical injuries caused by the negligence of the physician either on the imprudent or careless hiring of staff members or on the doctrine of respondent superior [footnotes omitted].[28]

Robert Jerry, II states:

---

27. *Educational Malpractice,* 124 UNIVERSITY OF PENNSYLVANIA LAW REVIEW 755, 803-05 (1976). Reprinted with permission of U. PA. L. REV., from 124 U. PA. L. REV. 755, 803-05 (1976).

28. Klein, *supra* note 8, at 28-29.

The theoretical inconsistencies inherent in the principle that no cause of action exists for educational malpractice do not prove that the special policy objectives of the principle are not meritorious. In other words, questioning the logic of the courts' analyses is not equivalent to questioning the view that our educational system is more viable if the cause of action is not recognized. Yet the inability of courts to reconcile nonrecognition of the cause of action with well-recognized tort principles suggests that legislatures — and not courts — should make the ultimate policy determination. A legislature, believing for public policy reasons that the cause of action should not be recognized, could mandate this result by reviving a measure of sovereign immunity or by prescribing exclusive administrative remedies [footnote omitted].[29]

Fields and Harris note that students' dissatisfaction with some teachers is not new. They write:

Friedrich Herr's writing about university life in 13th century Bologna gives us this account of the days when medieval law professors were paid directly by the students. The students, who had the whip [in] hand, kept their professors to a punctual observance of the lecture timetable under threat of financial penalties and revenged themselves on unpopular teachers by boycotts.[30]

It is difficult to argue against accountability, however, the duty to get involved in accountability is upon not only the school administrators and teachers, but on the students and parents as well. The schools cannot expect to make themselves responsible for the total learning process.[31] It is argued that students who have attempted to bring educa-

---

29. Robert H. Jerry, II, *Recovery in Tort for Educational Malpractice: Problems of Theory and Policy,* 29 KANSAS LAW REVIEW 195, 211-12 (1981).
30. Fields and Harris, III, *supra* note 4, at 3.
31. *Id.*

tional malpractice lawsuits have often misrepresented their role in the educational process by assuming no responsibility to learn at all.[32] In an attempt to explain the true role of the student in the learning process, it has been stated: "Success in teaching is a function of the recipient as well as the communicator: a good deal of failure of it there must always and in every system of education, necessarily be."[33]

Concerning teacher accountability, Fields and Harris report:

> The first actions involved attempts to reform educational management and curriculum implementation methods. This was to be accomplished through the application of business techniques to the field of education. In this method, the accountability movement falls under the theory of Management By Objectives (MBO). This theory indicates that you decide exactly what you want to do, then move your resources and personnel in the most effective patterns necessary to achieve the stated objective. Among the varied attempts to put the theory into action were the Voucher System, Alternative Schools, Performance Contracting, Performance-Based Teacher Certification (PBTC), and Competency-Based Teacher Certification.
>
> The Voucher Plan was designed to give parents a "credit" equal to the amount of money normally spent on their children's education. The parents were then free to use the credit at a school of their own choosing. Two problems were immediately apparent with this plan. (1) Parental pressure to improve schools or to actively seek improved funding of public schools was effectively removed. If a parent was dissatisfied with the school that he had chosen, he could not receive any

32. J. John Harris, III, "Educational Malpractice and Intentional Student Misrepresentation." Paper presented at the Annual Meeting of the American Educational Research Association (AERA), held at San Francisco, California, April 8-12, 1979, p. 17.

33. *Id.*

547

extra money to improve the school. He could only go
elsewhere and find another school which he liked. And
(2) there was the possibility of large national chains of
schools in the corporate society pattern resulting from
this plan such as monolithic and monopolistic systems
controlled by the profit motive.

The second great movement, and the one which
gained the most national attention at the beginning of
this decade, was performance contracting. Here private business firms were asked to bid on specific school
programs; and, on award of the bid, payment was to be
based on the achievement of agreed upon objectives.
The students are perceived as clients who have an "indisputable right" to learn. If the learning failed to occur in the classroom, it was the administrators and
teacher, the educational caretakers, not the students,
who had failed. This concept of accountability shifted
the learning responsibility from student "input" to
professional "output." Emphasis was placed upon the
"concrete elements of the curriculum and less was
heard of the humane components." Activities such as
music and art, being extremely difficult for measure-
ment experts to evaluate, were passed over in favor of
reading and math skills which were more easily evaluated [footnotes omitted].[34]

Fields and Harris conclude their article by stating:

The key to success ultimately rests in the hands of
those in charge, those individuals that administer the
educational process. Administrators must make positive efforts to reform their schools and make them accountable to the public. They must learn to budget
their time more efficiently so that more of it may be
devoted to supervision and the improvement of the
quality of the educational program. Curriculum development and improvement must be a continuing process, no longer just a "one-shot chore" to be forgotten
amid the volumes of paperwork until just before the
school's next periodic evaluation for certification. Ad-

---

34. Fields and Harris, III, *supra* note 4, at 2-3.

ministrators will have to reacquaint themselves with their own teachers through classroom visitations and experience firsthand, new teaching methods and curriculae, rather than meeting them secondhand through journal articles. An active partnership between administrators and teachers is a necessary prerequisite to any active defense of a school's philosophy and goals in the public's eye. The public has already begun storming the gates of the educational citadel demanding its rights. It's time that educational administrators either decide to stand up and fight for the system as they want to see it, or resolve themselves to be swept away by the winds of public opinion.[35]

Concerning the possible defenses that could be asserted by the defendants in an educational malpractice case, Klein suggests:

Theoretically, a potentially viable affirmative defense against an educational malpractice charge is contributory negligence, which would bar recovery in jurisdictions that do not recognize comparative negligence. Defendants could offer evidence of a poor attendance record or a generally negative attitude toward school, for example, to support the allegation that the behavior of plaintiff was below the standard of care he owed himself and, together with defendant's negligence, was a proximate cause of plaintiff's inadequate education. The standard of care the law imposes on a child for his own protection varies with the age, maturity, knowledge, and experience of the individual. This relative standard of care reduces the possibility of assigning fault to a child for conduct which allegedly demonstrates a lack of responsibility for his own education. Because courts are hesitant to attribute contributory negligence to a child the jury would have to consider the particular ability of plaintiff to understand the risks of his conduct. Tactical considerations, as well as the modified standard of care, diminish the validity of the defenses. Asserting the defense of contributory

---

35. *Id.*

negligence may, for example, cause a jury to draw negative inferences concerning the nature of the conduct of defendant, attributing to him an admission of negligence. Nevertheless, the existence of contributory negligence as an affirmative defense can curb the appetite of litigious individuals and thereby protect school systems [from] extreme claims. Thus contributory negligence represents a viable response to the floodgate argument advanced by critics of educational malpractice.

The law does not permit the imputation of the contributory negligence of a parent to his child. Home environment and parental involvement can affect the attitude and achievement of a student and may predominate over defendant's conduct, which will not therefore constitute a substantial causal factor. Although parental negligence cannot be imputed to a child; imputation of negligence can operate in the reverse situation; the negligence of a child may bar a separate parental claim for recovery.

Comparative negligence statutes generally reduce the harshness of the contributory negligence defense, providing for the apportionment of damages according to the relative fault of the parties. Comparative negligence may be of little value to defendant educators, however, who still face the mitigating effect of the age of the child in the determination of plaintiff's obligation to exercise due care. The impact of comparative negligence statutes on the issue of imputation of negligence remains unsettled.

The mitigating effect of the age of the child restricts the viability of defendant's affirmative defense. Nevertheless, recognition of a cause of action for educational malpractice would not be tantamount to imposing strict liability because defendant can prove the absence of any one of the requisite elements of negligence and thereby avoid liability [footnotes omitted].[36]

Bernstein, writing about social workers sued for malpractice, asserts:

---

36. Klein, *supra* note 8, at 52-55.

The best defense to a malpractice suit is for the social worker to show that his client's treatment was appropriate, necessary, and supported by professional colleagues and by the literature. An expert, who is paid, must testify. He must believe in the treatment in question and share his expertise with the judge and jury, and often with the media as well. The social worker must involve colleagues in his case. All of this is embarrassing as well as costly.[37]

Commenting on damages resulting from malpractice cases against social workers, Bernstein observes:

Monetary damages are not the only danger in cases of malpractice. If they were, malpractice insurance would be all that is necessary. There are damages to the social worker that often far exceed the money which a client might recover in a successful suit. One of these is the damage to the professional's reputation. Every method of treatment must have the support of a majority or of a respected minority. Whether the outcome is successful or not, every case places the reputation of the social worker on the line. If the treatment or handling of a given client is not professionally applicable to a situation, the social worker's reputation will suffer, both in the eyes of past and future clients as well as professional colleagues.

Whether or not a social worker is ultimately found liable, the time spent in preparation of pleadings, depositions, interrogatories, briefs, and courtroom testimony can be both financially and emotionally taxing. And, of course, even if the social worker is victorious, the time lost can never be regained.[38]

Concluding an article on educational malpractice, Kimberly Wilkins asserts:

Educational malpractice has not yet been recognized as a legally remediable cause of action. The courts

---

37. Barton E. Bernstein, *Malpractice: An Ogre on the Horizon,* SOCIAL WORK (March 1978), p. 110.

38. *Id.*

have refused to recognize educational malpractice because of the general fear of developing and assessing a workable standard of care by which to measure the educator's conduct. However, a profession that plays such a vital role in contemporary society should not be allowed to operate outside the realm of the justice system simply because the profession involves delicate, day-to-day policy implementation.

The uniform rejection of educational malpractice by the courts, and the unfortunate victims of negligence in the schools, illustrate the immediate need for a call of action in this area. However, the courts are unwilling to alter their paths, despite repeated attempts to persuasion. Therefore, legislative recognition of educational malpractice will prove to be the most efficient means for redressing the injuries suffered from educational malpractice. The standard of care generally applicable to professional negligence actions can be successfully used in the education profession as well. More importantly, however, recognition of this cause of action may be one approach to eliminating the illiteracy crisis currently facing the nation. Education, as a fundamental aspect of the foundation of contemporary American society, deserves consideration in the family, in the legislature, and in the courts.[39]

Another writer concludes an article regarding this issue by asking:

Isn't a child just as much denied the opportunity of an education when the educator performs his job inadequately? Isn't the child being deprived of the meaningful opportunity to learn? These questions must be answered in the affirmative. Denial of an education, whether it be through negligent testing, teaching, or placement, causes irreparable harm to the child ....

Clearly, "educational malpractice" actions sounding in negligence have been characterized as violative of

---

39. Kimberly A. Wilkins, *Educational Malpractice: A Cause of Action in Need of a Call for Action,* 22 No. 2 VALPARAISO UNIVERSITY LAW REVIEW 427, 460 (1988).

public policy, and have not been favored by the courts. Thus attorneys have become quite adept at framing the cause of action in such a way that the judicial stigma attached to negligence claims is avoided. Courts appear to be more receptive to actions based on intentional behavior, yet at this time no plaintiff has successfully pleaded an intentional theory. It appears that the future success of "educational malpractice" actions will depend upon the attorney's ability to fashion the cause of action in such a way that the court will not be required to review educational policy.

Plainly, it remains that public policy is the decisive factor. The plaintiff's interests must be balanced against competing public policy considerations and, thus far, Donald Snow [footnote omitted] is the sole plaintiff to have tipped the scales of justice.[40]

Di Liberto states:

Courts have consistently refused to recognize the tort of educational malpractice. Lack of a duty on the part of the educator and unrest about second-guessing the educator have been major reasons for refusal. However, we are faced with the cold, hard fact that students are graduating from high school, but cannot read their diplomas.

Many have an ethical, if not a legal duty to correct the problem. Students, parents, teachers, administrators, college professors, and legislators must combine their efforts to produce the end-product of quality education. Until they do, we will continue to graduate educationally-injured students with no judicial remedy.[41]

---

40. Theresa E. Loscalzo, *Liability for Malpractice in Education,* 14 No. 4 JOURNAL OF LAW AND EDUCATION 595, 607 (October 1985). *See also* Snow v. State of New York, 98 App. Div. 2d 442, 469 N.Y.S.2d 959 (1983).

41. Richard A. Di Liberto, Jr., *An Apple for the Teacher: Educational Malpractice Fails Judicial Test, But Core Problems Remain,* INSURANCE COUNSEL JOURNAL 215, 222 (April 1986).

Professor Foster concludes an article on educational malpractice by noting:

> In essence, therefore, the concern of the courts in educational malpractice actions would not be to ensure that educators guarantee that all students succeed, let alone achieve the same level of learning. This could never be attained given all the variables involved. Rather, the concern of the courts would be to ensure that students receive the benefit of an education from teachers and educational institutions who meet a minimum acceptable level of competency. After all, "[t]here is ... a critical difference between holding an educator directly accountable for his student's performance and holding him accountable for the quality of his influence in shaping that student's performance [footnote omitted].[42]

§ 16.3. Principles, Truisms and Statements.

The various arguments advanced by judges, justices, attorneys, educators, legislators, students, administrators, parents, commentators, and others have been compiled and analyzed, and the reader is in good position to determine the present status of educational malpractice. The future of educational malpractice largely will depend a great deal on the objectives and policies that will be pursued. One is reminded of the following statement by Lewis Carroll in *Alice in Wonderland:*

> "Would you tell me, please, which way I ought to go from here?"
> "That depends a good deal on where you want to go," said the Cat.

---

42. W.F. Foster, *Educational Malpractice: A Tort for the Untaught?,* 19:2 U.B.C. LAW REVIEW 161, 244 (1985). *See also* J. Elson, *A Common Law Remedy for the Educational Harms Caused by Incompetent or Careless Teaching* (1978) 73 NORTHWESTERN UNIVERSITY LAW REVIEW 641, 754.

"I don't much care where," said Alice.
"Then it doesn't matter which way you go," said the
Cat.[43]

The best time to prepare and set policy is before a wrong
is committed and before a claim is made. Preventive measures are preferable to corrective ones. It would appear
that any policy adopted to help direct judicial determination should be consistent and in conformity with the principles, truisms, and statements which have been drawn from
the previous discussions. These principles, truisms, and
statements are as follows:

1. Negligence does occur in the classroom just as it does
on the playgrounds, on highways, and in the operating
room.

2. Negligence has no place in the classroom. Teachers
should, and must, recognize that they are expected to foresee the consequences of their actions and their inactions.

3. Negligent acts or acts of omission can result in inadequate and/or inaccurate and/or improper education. Negligence by school districts cannot be allowed to continue. If a
student has been damaged because of unprofessional practice, justice demands that he or she be compensated (recom-
pensed).

4. An incompetent or negligent teacher can injure and
damage a student academically and cause "intellectual"
harm.

5. Teachers have been dismissed for incompetence by
school officials and the officials' actions have been supported by the courts.

6. A student suffers harm when a teacher knowingly or
negligently teaches him or her incorrect information,

---

43. ALLAN C. FILLEY, ROBERT J. HOUSE & STEVEN KERR, MANAGERIAL
PROCESS AND ORGANIZATIONAL BEHAVIOR (Glenville, IL: Scott, Foresman
and Company, 2d ed., 1976), p. 303, *citing* from ALICE IN WONDERLAND.

teaches in an incomprehensible manner, or does not teach at all.

7. Educators have a duty to teach; their teaching should and must be in a proper and meaningful way.

8. Teachers must carefully handle and instruct their classes; they must strive to become effective teachers of their subject matter.

9. It is not only important that teachers use good teaching methods in the classroom but it is also their duty.

10. Students vary in their capacity to learn as well as in their motivation to learn.

11. "Success in teaching is a function of the recipient as well as the communicator."[44]

12. Education is an evolving process. Education is an interactive process in which the child participates and is expected to indicate when he or she experiences difficulty.

13. Under the present status of the law, the student generally bears the "educational losses" caused by teachers' negligence.

14. Students, on occasion, are moved from grade to grade without learning to read and write. It is not uncommon today for a student enrolled in public school to move through the system without acquiring certain basic skills such as the ability to read and write.

15. When a student graduates from high school with a fourth grade reading ability and is unable to complete a simple job application, it would appear that an "injury" has occurred.

16. It is reasonable for society to expect that one who has attended public school for 12 years, evidenced by a standard high school diploma, is functionally literate.

17. Our legal system does not condone negligence; it is not in favor of sweeping negligence under the rug.

---

44. Harris, III, *supra* note 32, at 17.

18. No one can reasonably argue that an arbitrary action by a teacher or administrator denying a public education to a child should be unredressed by the courts.

19. The right to an education today means more than access to a classroom and more than a chair in a classroom.

20. No one should be above the law. School officials, school systems, and educators should not be above the law; they cannot be given the absolute right to do as they please.

21. Parents are entitled to know their children's true educational progress.

22. Public schools were not created, nor are they supported, for the benefit of teachers or administrators therein, but for the benefit of the pupils and the remitting benefit to their parents and the community at large.

23. School personnel should not be free from accountability.

24. Under our judicial system, if a person is wronged, he or she should have a legal remedy (legal redress for his or her injury).

25. Wrongdoers, rather than innocent victims, should bear the burden of losses occurred through negligence.

26. Refusal to recognize a cause of action for educational malpractice is incompatible with accepted tort principles.

27. It is the business of the law to remedy wrongs that deserve it.

28. Redress is a fundamental concern of human beings.

29. Students and/or parents may not just arbitrarily or irresponsibly attack the school system and its officials without accepting blame, where applicable, for their own shortcomings.

30. Teachers, generally, are not given a choice in the selection of their students.

31. Generally, students are not given a choice as to whether or not they must attend school due to our compul-

sory education system; furthermore, in many instances they have little voice in the selection of what school they will attend.

32. In many instances, students are assigned a particular teacher — the students are not given a choice.

33. Students do not shed their constitutional rights at the schoolhouse gate.

34. Teachers are professionals, and if not, they ought to be.

35. Public schools are creatures of law.

36. The hiring and retention of teachers is not a function of the students or their parents, but rather the responsibility of school officials.

37. Claimants, including students and/or parents, are entitled to have their grievances heard by an independent, fair, and impartial body.

38. There are presently no clear avenues of legal redress that are available to those injured (intellectually) when the schools do not meet their responsibilities.

39. Professional Practice Commissions, where available, are currently limited in their authority and scope to fully and adequately remedy such situations as "educational malpractice."

40. One of the main functions of the courts is to provide a forum to air, hear, and decide controversies or disputes.

41. We live in a litigious society.

42. Throughout our legal system courts have entered new areas of law.

43. The law of torts is not static.

44. Lawsuits are not uncommon or new in education; courts have many times entered the educational domain.

45. Courts have become an increasingly important vehicle for those who want to reinforce American education.

46. Justice cannot and should not be rationed.

47. It would appear that to educate implies a duty to educate with diligence and care. If it does not, it certainly should imply such a duty.

48. Public education in America is premised on a delicate balance of the interests of the child, the parents, and the state. Historically, the presumption has been that the state authorities exercise their powers reasonably and to the benefit of all parties. Courts regularly deferred to the discretion of school administrators, for parents (and children) had the alternative of private schooling. In *Brown,* the United States Supreme Court indicated that administrative discretion is not absolute, and there are constitutional guarantees that follow the child to school.[45]

49. Education and educators have held a high place in the minds of the people in America. (It has been said that "education, beyond all other devices of human origin, is the great equalizer of conditions of man — the balance wheel of the social machinery.")[46]

50. Education is very important to the preservation of our society. Society has to solve the problems associated with it properly, efficiently, calmly, logically, and above all, equitably.

51. It has been stated many times that today education is perhaps the most important function of state and local governments.

52. There is turbulence and dissatisfaction in the educational community. Public education, rightfully or wrongfully, has increasingly come under great scrutiny.

53. Many professionals, in various fields, have been held liable by courts for the negligent performance of their professional skills.

---

45. Patricia Wright Morrison, *The Right to Education: A Constitutional Analysis,* 44 UNIVERSITY OF CINCINNATI LAW REVIEW 796, 809 (1975).
46. 347 U.S. 483 (1954).

54. While the idea of suing a physician, an accountant, an attorney, and a psychiatrist is no longer novel, suing a school system for failing to educate a student properly is novel but may not be for long.

55. The axiom, "Ignorance of the law is no excuse," should hold as true for teachers as anyone else. Teachers must recognize the legal duties owed their students.

56. When conflict between educators, administrators, parents, students, and society as a whole surfaces concerning educational matters, it can be an asset toward the improvement of the educational process; however, when the said conflict cannot be properly managed or resolved by the parties involved, then an independent and impartial tribunal must step in and resolve it, otherwise resulting harm can ensue.

57. There have been many arguments advanced on both sides for recognizing and not recognizing "educational malpractice." The issue of whether to recognize a cause of action for "educational malpractice" has been decided by some courts. Thus far, however, a cause of action for "pure" educational malpractice has not been recognized.

58. Psychological damages, although often recognized in the absence of accompanying physical injury, are still treated cautiously by the courts.

59. Mental (as distinguished from physical) injuries are compensable in other areas. Mental injuries are as real as physical injuries.

60. A person who has been "intellectually" harmed has been damaged. It is as real as physical harm.

61. Teachers, school districts, and administrators can obtain malpractice insurance.

62. The impact on the educational profession, if educational malpractice were to be recognized, is not clear.

63. Future implications of student-teacher relationships, if educational malpractice were to be recognized, is not clear.

64. Implications for improvement of education as a whole, if educational malpractice were to be recognized, is not "crystal" clear.

65. There is little doubt that educational malpractice will continue as a subject for judicial consideration. A frustrated public continues to seek the ultimate solution to the problem of declining effectiveness of schools, and the courtroom provides an avenue for redress to dissatisfied parents and students.

66. Teachers are expected to help, to the best of their ability, each of their students to develop and maximize their "academic" skills.

67. A high school diploma should represent more than a certificate of attendance. It would appear that when 700,000 seniors graduate from high school who cannot read their diplomas there is some problem in our educational system.

68. The education provided to students should be "adequate" and "effective."

69. Students have certain responsibilities as learners in the learning process.

70. Since education is an ongoing process, generally "academic" damage will result if negligence persists for some time.

71. Failure to learn due to academic negligence is not a harm beyond the law's remedial capabilities. "The replacement of incompetent by competent teachers, the provision of, or payment for remedial instruction, and monetary compensation for diminished future income could 'make

whole,' in some instances, public school students who have suffered a loss of educational benefits."[47]

72. Because of the scale and complexity of the interests involved, courts will and should move cautiously in recognizing a cause of action for educational malpractice.

73. Laymen have to trust the professional's judgment when they place their affairs in the professional's hands. Consequently, parents, generally, do and must trust the teachers when they place their children in their classroom. The teachers, on the other hand, must work to earn that respect.

74. Education has been described by the United States Supreme Court as a "legitimate entitlement" and a "right which must be made available to all on equal terms" for the good of society as well as the "individual."[48]

75. When an educational problem surfaces, it is better that educators try to solve it themselves rather than have it aired in an arena of adversarial atmosphere; however, if the educators cannot solve it to the satisfaction of all the parties concerned, and the decision by the educators is, rightfully or wrongfully, perceived to be unjust, then an independent and impartial tribunal must step in to resolve it.

It is hoped that these principles, truisms and statements will serve as guidelines in arriving at a proper solution to the issue of educational malpractice.

---

47. *Educational Malpractice,* 124 UNIVERSITY OF PENNSYLVANIA LAW REVIEW 755, 803 (1976). Reprinted with permission of U. OF PA. L. REV.
48. Coultas, *supra* note 17.

Chapter 17

SUMMATION — NOT A CLOSING ARGUMENT

§ 17.0. Introduction.
§ 17.1. Summation.

> In the words of the ancient
> Romans: "Fiat justitia, ruat
> coelum" (Let justice be done,
> though the heavens fall).[1]

§ 17.0. Introduction.

The title to this chapter, "Summation — Not a Closing Argument," re-emphasizes that the purpose of writing this book is not to dictate or force anyone to take a particular position on educational malpractice, but rather, to inform the reader of the various issues involved in this area. To borrow a quote from Fred Friendly, "[O]ur purpose is not to make up anyone's mind but to open minds, and to make the agony of decision making so intense you can escape only by thinking."[2] A responsible scholar cannot place much emphasis on the conclusions of others, but rather, must carefully and painstakingly examine and analyze the facts, assumptions, and logic which led to those conclusions. The scholar must then determine whether or not the arguments advanced for supporting those conclusions are consistent with the facts. There are complex and sensitive issues in the area of educational malpractice that need to be carefully analyzed. However, the complexity of the issues

---

1. Hoffman v. Board of Education, 64 A.D.2d at 387, 410 N.Y.S.2d 99, at 111 (1978).

2. Fred W. Friendly, *Ethics in America* (Preview Packet). Produced by Columbia University Seminars on Media and Society (Englewood Cliffs, N.J.: Prentice-Hall, Inc. 1988); p. 9.

should not deter the proper decision-makers from calmly and professionally analyzing the problem and arriving at the best possible decision under the circumstances. It has been said:

> Good men belong in the heat of the battle, where issues are confused, where you're never sure you're right, where good and bad are inextricably fused with the partly good and partly bad, where often you can't do one worthy thing without endangering some other worthy thing.[3]

Equity and objectivity must be sought and maintained regardless of any change that may be needed and regardless of how hard it is opposed. In *The Prince,* Machiavelli states:

> There is nothing more difficult to carry out, nor more doubtful for success, nor more dangerous to handle, than to initiate a new order of things. For the reformer has enemies in all those who profit by the old order, and only lukewarm defenders in all those who would profit by the new order; this lukewarmness arising partly from fear of their adversaries, who have the laws in their favour, and partly from the incredulity of mankind, who do not truly believe in anything new until they have actual experience of it.[4]

People must be convinced by reason and not by force. In order to do that, there must be a clear understanding of the problems involved. This is a very troublesome and complex area. Reason sometimes may give way to emotion. The two must be distinguished.

---

3. J.W. GARDNER, NO EASY VICTORIES (New York: Harper and Row Publishers, 1968).

4. ALLAN C. FILLEY, ROBERT J. HOUSE & STEVEN KERR, MANAGERIAL PROCESS AND ORGANIZATIONAL BEHAVIOR (Glenville, IL: Scott, Foresman and Company, 2d ed., 1976), p. 70; *citing* from THE PRINCE.

§ 17.1. Summation.

Charles Smith begins his book on Products Liability as follows:

> Products Liability! *How do you react — apprehensive, enraged, calm, stunned, understanding, alarmed, disturbed, inept, frightened, dismayed, agitated, worried, harassed, terrified, confident, appalled, ignorant, knowledgeable, outraged, or ... ? [emphasis added].*[5]

Replace the words "Products Liability," in the above quote, with the words "Educational Malpractice!" *How do you react?* We live in a great nation — and some of us say, the greatest nation in the world. It is not great because of an accident, its greatness comes from its people — an informed populace; an informed populace just doesn't happen by chance, it is achieved through design — education plays a significant role in the design. So, it pains some of us, when we hear such topics as, "Illiteracy in America"; "A Nation at Risk"; "American Teenagers Come in Last in Assessment of Mathematics Skills"; "American Schools Are in Trouble"; "ProfScam"; "Schools Manipulate Athletes"; and "Education Report Rips U.S. Schools."

Some years ago, Dr. Leon Lessinger wrote:

> If one airplane in every four crashed between takeoff and landing, people would refuse to fly.
>
> If one automobile in every four went out of control and caused a fatal accident or permanent injury, Detroit would be closed down tomorrow. Our schools — which provide a more important product than airplanes or automobiles — somehow fail a youngster in four. And so far we have not succeeded in preventing

---

5. CHARLES O. SMITH, PRODUCTS LIABILITY: ARE YOU VULNERABLE? (Englewood Cliffs, NJ: Prentice-Hall, Inc., © 1981), p. ix. He used this phraseology, with the exception that he used the words "Product Liability" in the place of "Educational Malpractice."

the social and economic fatalities every school dropout represents.

For each child thus failed by his school, all of us pay a price in taxes and in social unrest, and the child himself is deprived of his chance to develop his potential.[6]

He further states, "In other spheres we do much better. In building rockets we engage in 'zero-defect' programs of quality assurance, for we know that if a single part fails, the rocket fails. Can we not find ways to do as well for our children?"[7] The validity of the criticism lodged against our educational system can be debated. Arguments abound on both sides of the issue. This book is not the place "to air" these arguments. Mention of the arguments has been made herein to serve as a backdrop for the issue at hand — educational malpractice, "academic negligence" or "intellectual harm." When speaking of these terms, one is reminded of U.S. Supreme Court Justice Stewart's famous statement about obscenity: "I can't define it, but I know when I see it."

There is no need to hypothesize about the filing of a lawsuit seeking damages for educational malpractice, for such suits have been filed. Arguments have been advanced in support of both positions. Courts have been drawn into this controversy and have indirectly taken sides by ruling on the suits. There are now a number of cases that represent the "present" law concerning educational malpractice. Thus far, a cause of action for "*pure*" educational malpractice has not been recognized. Whether one agrees or disagrees with the present law is not the main issue — the main issue is: what should the law be regarding educational malpractice. The law is not static. Wrong decisions

---

6. LEON M. LESSINGER, ACCOUNTABILITY IN EDUCATION: EVERY KID A WINNER (Palo Alto: Science Research Associates, Inc., 1970), p. 3.

7. *Id.* at 4-5.

can be corrected. It is obvious from the arguments advanced and reported herein, that there is certainly no unanimity in this extremely important area. A realistic and practical approach to this troublesome problem can lead to a better understanding of the delicate, complex, and intricate issues, which could ease tensions that may, or do, exist. Educators can no longer ignore these issues or wait to address them in a courtroom in an adversarial atmosphere. They must analyze them thoroughly and equitably — balancing all interests concerned. They must lead in this area — they should not be led, but led they will be, if nothing is done, because as long as academic negligence exists in the classroom there will be those who will turn to the courts for redress.

As long as there are students who graduate from high school that can hardly read or write, and as long as there are educators and administrators in the educational system that are viewed as less than "competent", rightfully or wrongfully, by those claiming that they have been injured, educational malpractice suits will continue. "If researchers and other members of the educational profession do nothing to improve the knowledge base in this area, such external forces as the legislatures and the courts, through statutes and judicial decisions, will eventually establish guidelines for educators, and all society will suffer the resulting inflexibility."[8] Those involved in the school system must keep abreast of trends if they want to avoid entanglements.

Would it not be much better if educators established their own rules — rules that reflect, and are consistent with, their educational philosophy — rather than have rules imposed upon them? It is much better to rule, or be

---

8. David G. Carter, Sr., "The Educator and the Liability Law of Professional Malpractice: A Historical Analysis." A paper presented for AERA Annual Convention, San Francisco, California (April 8-12, 1979), pp. 20-21.

ruled, by reason rather than by force. Educators tell their students to believe in truth and protest error. They encourage their students to pursue the search for truth — for the right answers. Could anything less be expected from the educators themselves? Sometimes, when the right answers are found it may require that adjustments be made in the current system. One must evaluate the situation at hand today, using the accessible means that are available today, and not the means that were available in the past. The new advances in education and the way they fit into the overall educational system must be carefully analyzed. It is important to determine how they effect the various publics — the students, the teachers, the administrators, the parents, the school system, the local community, and the public at large. Something that is new is not necessarily better. Dean Inge said:

> There are two kinds of fools. One says, "That is old, therefore it is good." The other says, "This is new, therefore it is better."[9]

Goldstein and Gee write:

> The legal power of various individuals and groups to control educational decision making is a central issue in the interference of law and education. Decision making by bodies charged with the administration of public education is one of the most significant areas of law in terms of its effects on the lives of individuals and groups in American society.[10]

Figures show that in the United States, in 1986, a total of 40,200,000 students attended public schools, of which

---

9. HERBERT G. HICKS & C. RAY GULLETT, ORGANIZATIONS: THEORY AND BEHAVIOR (New York: McGraw-Hill Book Company, 1975).

10. STEPHEN R. GOLDSTEIN & E. GORDON GEE, LAW AND PUBLIC EDUCATION (Indianapolis: The Bobbs-Merrill Company, Inc., 2d ed., 1980), p. 1.

3,300,000 were in kindergarten, 24,200,000 in elementary and secondary schools and 12,700,000 in high schools.[11] Moreover, in 1986, there were 2,243,000 elementary and secondary classroom teachers.[12] These figures point out the enormity of the school system and the tremendous number of relationships that may, and do, exist between students and teachers. Education is an interactive process. Consequently, it would not be unusual for errors to occur. If errors result from innocent misjudgments, that is one thing — perhaps they will be condoned. After all, to err is human. However, if errors occur due to a negligent act or a number of continuous negligent acts and a student is "intellectually" harmed, what then? If a student is injured academically through an intentional act or acts by the teacher, should that be swept under the rug and the student be denied redress? If the teacher's conduct is outrageous or a gross violation of his or her professional duty, resulting in an incontestable harm to the student, should that too be swept under the rug and should the student be denied redress? It would seem that reason, justice, and the law dictate otherwise. The concept of redress for an injured party goes back a few thousand years to at least the time of Hammurabi.[13]

It is a known fact that teaching is complex and complicated. What works well with one student may not with another. Courts "realize the imprudence of their reviewing teaching styles and diagnostic strategies for efficacy when even educators themselves are unsure. To meet the diverse

---

11. U.S. BUREAU OF THE CENSUS, STATISTICAL ABSTRACT OF THE UNITED STATES: 1989 (Washington, DC: 109th ed., 1989), p. 127.

12. DIGEST OF EDUCATION STATISTICS 1988 (National Center of Education Statistics), p. 67.

13. SMITH, *supra* note 5, at ix-x.

needs of their students, teachers need to be encouraged to innovate, to experiment, to create."[14]

Professor Epley continues his argument by noting:

> To threaten teachers with malpractice when their efforts fail, at least in the eyes of the plaintiff, would force them to seek harbor in sterile, regimented, but safe instructional techniques

> ....

> Nevertheless, judges cannot be expected to remain indifferent to the suffering caused by poor teaching or careless placement, or to ignore shallow and half-hearted attempts by the profession to prevent such malfeasance. The legal arguments supporting educational malpractice, particularly those grounded on justice for the individual, are sound, and advocacy to recognize educational malpractice as a legal solution for injured children will therefore continue.

> ....

> [E]ducation faces an imperative to take concrete steps to police itself. If educators are unwilling to take the internal steps necessary to eliminate shoddy practice, they risk the possibility that the courts, even with all the undesirable consequences attending such action, may do it for them. Worse, they will fail their moral obligation to provide an adequate education for each and every child.[15]

Professor Hazard notes, "[t]here can be little doubt that inadequate, inappropriate, or misfocused teaching causes educational injuries. To argue that educational injuries do not exist or cannot happen because educators' hearts are

---

14. B. Glen Epley, *Educational Malpractice: The Threat and Challenge,* 50 No. 1 THE EDUCATIONAL FORUM (Fall 1985), p. 63.

15. *Id.*

pure is potent nonsense."[16] Are there truly significant reasons to differentiate between educational malpractice and other forms of malpractice litigation which currently congest the courts? Could it be argued that a school system, under no conceivable set of facts, could be liable for the negligent or intentional infliction of emotional distress on a child? Negligence is negligence whether called negligence or malpractice. If that is the case, then could it be that some courts are troubled with the word "malpractice"? Could it be that some courts may very well recognize the fact that students have been damaged intellectually by someone in the school system but envision the difficult time the student may have in proving who did it? Perhaps an extension of existing theories such as *res ipsa loquitur* would alleviate the burden from the student to prove negligence and shift the burden to the school system to prove that no one in the school where the student was intellectually harmed was negligent. After all, it is reasonable for society to expect that one who has attended public school for 12 years, evidenced by a high school diploma, is literate. If it can be proven that the student is illiterate, shouldn't he or she be given an opportunity to have his or her grievance heard? Submitting a case to a jury for a determination of factual issues doesn't dictate its outcome.

Furthermore, the argument could be made, although perhaps weak, that once the student proves that he or she was academically injured while attending a certain school, he or she could proceed under the theory of products liabil-

---

16. William R. Hazard, *Educational Malpractice,* EDUCATION DIGEST (October 1982), p. 25.

ity,[17] strict liability,[18] or alternative liability[19] to prove his or her case. For the court to permit the student to proceed under any of these theories would require some stretching of their present applications. However, as previously stated, the law is not static. Elizabeth Dixon writes:

> Many people now are viewing education in the same sense as any other commodity that is purchased, meaning that, if the buyer is not satisfied with the product, he or she can return it for a complete refund. Since education is not a "returnable commodity," parents and lawyers believe the only recourse open to them is to sue in order to receive payment for damages suffered as a result of the failure of the product to work.[20]

It would appear that reason, justice, and the law demand a negative answer to the questions: Should school personnel be above the law? Should they be protected from their

---

17. SMITH, *supra* note 5, at 1. "*Products liability* is a legal term that arises whenever a product performs in such a manner that its integrity is challenged in a court of law. To put it somewhat differently, 'products liability' is a legal term describing action whereby a plaintiff (injured party) seeks to recover damages for *personal injury* or *property loss* from a defendant (producer and/or seller) when the plaintiff alleges that a defective product caused the injury or loss. The term 'products liability' also includes *commercial loss* by a customer or business operation due to alleged failure or inadequate performance of a product."

18. *Id.,* at 15. "Strict products liability, or strict liability in tort ... is the imposition of liability for damages on a person without requiring proof of negligence or fault. Defenses based on traditional warranty concepts have been eliminated. Privity is not required, nor is notice of injury. In addition, disclaimers are not valid."

19. Sindell v. Abbott Laboratories, 163 Cal. Rptr. 132, 607 P.2d 924 (1980). The court stated: "Plaintiff places primary reliance upon cases which hold that if a party cannot identify which of two or more defendants causes an injury, the burden of proof may shift to the defendants to show that they were not responsible for the harm. This principle is sometimes referred to as the 'alternative liability' theory."

20. Elizabeth Dixon, *In Climate of Educational Criticism, Threat of Malpractice Suits Looms,* 56 EDUCATIONAL HORIZONS 107 (Winter 1977-78).

negligent acts? Can society afford to give the educators complete freedom to do what they want? Should injured students be denied access to the courts? It would appear that reason, justice, and the law demand an affirmative answer to the questions: Should educators be held accountable for their actions or inactions which result in injuries to students? If a person is injured solely through the negligence or intentional conduct of another, should he or she be compensated for the resulting injuries?

While the idea of suing a physician, an accountant, an attorney, or a psychiatrist is no longer novel, suing a school system for failing to properly educate is somewhat novel, but may not be for long. Given the proper facts, a properly drafted complaint for educational malpractice, brought in a proper court and argued in a proper manner, may very well be sustained. Furthermore, given a litigious society and a climate of heavy criticism and dissatisfaction with public education, it should not come as a surprise that frustrated individuals who feel "academically" injured by the school system will continue to turn to the courts for redress. Perhaps the time has come for teachers, administrators, and other school personnel to be held accountable, as other professionals, for their actions and inactions in the performance of their job.

This book was written to report and inform — not to confuse or destruct. It was written to prevent and not to encourage litigation. An informed profession is a better profession. The teacher's presence is needed more in the classroom than in the courtroom. It is hoped that the book will help bridge any gaps and misunderstandings that may or do exist among students, school personnel and perhaps the courts. If the bridge between the students and educators is, in some instances, shaky, it can and should be made strong and steady. Both educators and students must try to understand the problems and concerns of each other. Cooperation and understanding is crucial. Students and teachers are and must be on the same side, and not on opposite sides. They must cooperate — not compete. They are not nor should they be adversaries. Since educators realize that negligence and incompetence have no place in the classroom and that to educate implies a duty to educate with diligence, regard and care, then it would appear only proper that they set up guidelines that are well thought out to protect against possible negligence or imcompetence. The hope is that all factors will be taken into consideration in arriving at a proper solution. If this can be accomplished, obviously, harmony will exist. As may be expected, however, the task of accomplishing this seems, at times, to be insurmountable. This, of course, should not be the case. They should not be insurmountable. They should be solvable. We must properly solve them. Education is too important to the preservation of our society. We have to solve the problems associated with it. They must be solved properly, efficiently, calmly and above all equitably. Anything short of that is not acceptable. The parents, the students, the teachers, the administrators and society through various groups and through their legislators need to join their efforts to produce the best education possible for our children. Time and effort expended to improve our educational system is well spent.

Educators must take the initiative and the time *now* to analyze any existing or potential problems, whether real or imagined, and try to solve them while they are able to do so under non-adversarial conditions — for if they don't, they may find their problems being solved under adversarial conditions in a court of law. Sad but true, other professions found that to be the case and can so testify. Educators should use this period of time to correct what is not right before the courts enter the arena. Suits sometimes tend to be epidemic. It may be much easier and much wiser for educators to work under the rules that they wrote, rather than the rules that someone else wrote for them. What the future holds in this area depends almost entirely upon how educators deal with this sensitive and troublesome matter. Neither the importance of their involvement, nor the importance of their work, can be overstated. Clark Mollenhoff describes that sentiment well in the following:

TEACHERS

You are the molders of their dreams.
The gods who build or crush their beliefs of right or wrong.
You are the spark that sets aflame the poet's hand or lights
    the flame in some great singer's song.
You are the gods of young — the very young.
You are their idols, by profession set apart.
You are the guardians of a million dreams.
Your every smile or frown can heal or pierce a heart.
Yours are one hundred lives — one thousand lives, yours is
    the pride of loving them, the sorrow too.
Your patient work, your touch, make you the gods of hope
    that fill their soul with dreams, and make those dreams
    come true.[21]

---

21. Clark R. Mollenhoff, *Teachers*. Pulitzer Prize winning investigative reporter, author and educator, Professor of Journalism, Washington & Lee University.

Appendix 1

Standards of Competency.

Teaching Profession, State of Nebraska

A. General.

The Standards listed in this section are held to be *generally accepted minimal standards within the teaching profession in Nebraska with respect to competent performance* and are therefore declared to be the criteria of competency adopted pursuant to the provisions of Section 79-1282, R.R.S.

1. The standards set forth herein shall apply to those who teach in classrooms and those who supervise and provide administrative services to those who teach in classrooms.

2. No finding of professional incompetency shall be made except where a preponderance of evidence exists of such incompetency.

B. Definitions.

As used herein the following words and terms have these meanings:

1. Administrative and Supervisory Personnel — Any certificated employee such as superintendent, assistant superintendent, principal, assistant principal, school nurse or other supervisory or administrative personnel who does not have as a primary duty the instruction of pupils in the public schools.

2. Available — That which can be used or obtained.

3. Communication Skills — The capacity, ability, or art of giving, or giving and receiving, through any of the senses, information, ideas, and attitudes.

4. *Competent — The ability or fitness to discharge the required duties as set forth in this chapter.*

5. Designated Task — The duty or assignment for which responsible at any given time.

6. *Diagnosis — Identification of needs, strengths and weaknesses through examination, observation and analysis.*

577

7. Educator — Any person engaged in the instructional program including those engaged in teaching, administering, and supervising and who are required to be certificated.

8. *Effective — Producing a definite, desired result.*

9. Management — Controlling, supervising and guiding the efforts of others.

10. Policy — Authorized written and dated expressions of public intent which have been communicated to the educator and which reflect the general principles guiding the efforts of the school system or school toward approved goals.

11. Preponderance of Evidence — A superiority of weight. Weight is not a question of mathematics, but depends on its effect in inducing belief.

12. Reasonable — Just; proper. Ordinary or usual. Fit and appropriate to the end in view.

13. Teacher — Any certificated employee who is regularly employed for the instruction of pupils in the public schools.

C. Administrative and Supervisory Requirements.

Competent Educators must possess the abilities and skills necessary to the designated task. Therefore,

1. Each educator shall:

(a) keep records for which he or she is responsible in accordance with law and policies of the school system.

(b) supervise others in accordance with law and policies of the school system.

(c) recognize the role and function of community agencies and groups as they relate to the school and to his or her position, including but not limited to health and social services, employment services, community teaching resources, cultural opportunities, educational advisory committees, and parent organizations.

2. Each teacher shall:

(a) utilize available instructional materials and equipment necessary to accomplish the designated task.

(b) adhere to and enforce written and dated administrative policy of the school which has been communicated to the teacher.

(c) use channels of communication when interacting with administrators, community agencies and groups in accordance with school policy.

3. Each administrator shall:

(a) use available instructional personnel, materials, and equipment necessary to accomplish the designated task.

(b) adhere to and enforce school law, state board regulation, and written and dated school board policy which has been communicated to the administrator.

(c) use channels of communication when interacting with teachers, community agencies and groups in accordance with school policy.

D. Analysis of Individual Needs and Individual Potential.

The competent educator shall utilize or promote the utilization of diagnostic techniques to analyze the needs and potential of individuals. These may include but need not necessarily be limited to:

1. *personal observation.*
2. *analysis of individual performance and achievement.*
3. specific performance testing.

E. Instructional Procedures.

Each competent educator shall seek accomplishment of the designated task through selection and utilization of appropriate instructional procedures. Therefore,

1. *Each educator shall:*

(a) create an atmosphere which fosters interest and enthusiasm for learning and teaching.

(b) *use procedures appropriate to accomplish the designated task.*

(c) encourage expressions of ideas, opinions and feelings.

2. *Each teacher shall:*

(a) *create interest through the use of materials and techniques appropriate to the varying abilities and background of students.*

(b) consider individual student interests and abilities when planning and implementing instruction.

579

3. *Each administrator shall:*

(a) *support the creation of interest by providing the materials, equipment and encouragement necessary for the teacher to accomplish the designated task.*

(b) make reasonable assignment of tasks and duties in light of individual abilities and specialties and available personnel resources.

F. Communication Skills.

In communicating with students and other educators, each competent educator, within the limits prescribed by his or her assignment and role, shall:

1. Utilize information and materials that are relevant to the designated task.

2. Use language and terminology which are relevant to the designated task.

3. Use language which reflects an understanding of the ability of the individual or group.

4. Assure that the designated task is understood.

5. Use feedback techniques which are relevant to the designated task.

6. Consider the entire context of the statements of others when making judgments about what others have said.

7. Encourage each individual to state his ideas clearly.

G. Management Techniques.

The competent educator shall:

1. Resolve discipline problems in accordance with law, school board policy, and administrative regulations and policies.

2. Maintain consistency in the application of policy and practice.

3. Use management techniques which are appropriate to the particular setting such as group work, seat work, lecture, discussion, individual projects and others.

4. Develop and maintain positive standards of conduct.

580

H. Competence in Specialization.

Each competent educator shall:

1. *Possess knowledge, within his area of specialization, consistent with his record of professional preparation.*

2. *Be aware of current developments in his field.*

3. *Possess knowledge of resources which may be utilized in improving instruction in his area of specialization.*

I. Evaluation of Learning and Goal Achievement.

A competent educator accepts responsibility commensurate with delegated authority to evaluate learning and goal achievement, and the competent educator shall:

1. Utilize several types of evaluation techniques.

2. *Provide frequent and prompt feedback concerning the success of learning and goal achievement efforts.*

3. *Analyze and interpret effectively the results of evaluation for judging instruction, the achievement of stated goals, or the need for further diagnosis.*

4. Utilize the results of evaluation for planning, counseling and program modification.

5. Explain methods and procedures of evaluation to those concerned.

J. Human and Interpersonal Relationships.

Competent educators should possess effective human and interpersonal relation skills and therefore:

1. Shall allow others who hold and express differing opinions or ideas to freely express such ideas.

2. Shall not knowingly misinterpret the statement of others.

3. Shall not show disrespect for or lack of acceptance of others.

4. Shall provide leadership and direction for others by appropriate example.

5. Shall offer constructive criticism when necessary.

6. Shall comply with reasonable requests and orders given by and with proper authority.

7. Shall not assign unreasonable tasks.

581

8. Shall demonstrate self-confidence and self-sufficiency in exercising authority.

K. Personal Requirements.

In assessing the mental or physical health of educators, no decision adverse to the educator shall be made except on the advice or testimony of personnel competent to make such judgment by reason of training, licensure and experience. However, certain behaviors are held to be probable cause to examine, and each competent educator within the scope of delegated authority shall:

1. Be able to engage in physical activity appropriate to the designated task except for temporary disability.

2. Be able to communicate so effectively as to accomplish the designated task.

3. Appropriately control his or her emotions.

4. Possess and demonstrate sufficient intellectual ability to perform designated tasks (emphasis added).

Appendix 2

Standards of Professional Competence for Utah Educators, (Revised 12/7/84),

Utah Professional Practices Advisory Commission

The standards listed in this section developed under the direction of the Utah Professional Practices Advisory Commission are held to be generally accepted standards within the teaching profession in Utah with respect to competent performance and are therefore declared to be the criteria of competency adopted pursuant to the provisions of Section 43-50-12(4); Utah Code Annotated, 1953 and the State Board of Education Policy on Professional Behavior and Performance.

1. The standards set forth herein shall apply to those who teach in classrooms and those who provide administrative and support services to those who teach in classrooms including district office staffs.

2. The standards are intended for use by the Utah Professional Practices Advisory Commission in a remediation review or formative evaluation for the improvement of a given educator's performance. Competent educators are expected to meet the standards and reflect a substantial number of the indicators listed under each standard.

3. Professional reviewers, designated by the Commission by virtue of the successful completion of special training under the auspices of the Commission, are available to review professional performance and form opinions of the quality of professional service rendered. They will assist educators being reviewed, and make recommendations for remediation.

4. *If a hearing is held where professional competence is at issue, involving the question of whether or not an educator should be allowed to continue in the profession, these standards may be used in a summative evaluation mode.*

DEFINITIONS:

Administrative and Supervisory Personnel — Any certificated employees such as superintendent, assistant superintendent, principal, assistant principal, or other supervisory or administrative personnel who do not have as a primary duty the instruction of pupils in the public schools and who are responsible for the evaluation of staff.

Commission — The Utah Professional Practices Advisory Commission.

Communicates — Gives and/or receives information, ideas, and attitudes through any of the senses.

Competence — *The ability or fitness to discharge the required duties as set forth in the following standards.*

Diagnose — *Identify the cause or nature of a condition through examination, observation, and analysis.*

Designated Task — The duty of assignment for which a person is responsible at any given time.

Educator — Any person who is certificated by the Utah State Board of Education to teach, supervise, or administer any aspect of public education.

Effective — Producing a definite, desired result.

Formative Evaluation — Judging educator performance for the purpose of improvement.

Indicators — Behaviors representative of a standard. In this document, indicators are numbered under each standard (1, 2, 3, etc.).

Policy — Authorized written and dated expressions of public intent which have been communicated in writing to the educator and which reflect the general principles guiding the efforts of the school system or school toward approved goals.

Professional Reviewer — An educator who has received training in the art and skill of reviewing the performance of a fellow educator in a similar professional area.

Reasonable — Just; proper; ordinary or usual; fit and appropriate to the end in view.

Remediation Review — A review of performance designed to assist an educator whose competence has been questioned to improve.

584

Summative Evaluation — Judging educator performance for the purpose of making management decisions, i.e., promotion, termination, etc.

Standards — Criteria upon which performance is evaluated. In this document standards are designated by capital letters (A, B, C, etc.).

I. CLASSROOM EDUCATOR STANDARDS AND INDICATORS: *The competent classroom educator.*

A. PLANS AND ORGANIZES INSTRUCTION.

1. Develops and/or uses learner objectives which are clear and sequenced.
2. *Diagnoses needs and potential of learners.*
3. Uses techniques and procedures that accomplish lesson and course goals described by school district policies and procedures.
4. *Adjusts levels of difficulty of content and materials as appropriate and provides for differences in learning styles.*
5. *Revises instruction as needed using evaluation and observation and prescribes appropriate learning activities.*

B. USES INFORMATION ABOUT PROGRESS AND NEEDS OF LEARNERS.

1. Uses information about learners from cumulative records.
2. Keeps records in accord with policies of Boards of Education.
3. Uses several types of evaluation and monitors learners' progress regularly.
4. *Identifies learners who require assistance of specialists.*
5. Uses information from co-workers and parents to assist learners.

C. USES INSTRUCTIONAL TECHNIQUES, METHODS, AND MEDIA RELATED TO OBJECTIVES.

1. *Uses available instructional materials necessary to accomplish task.*
2. Uses effective questioning techniques.

585

3. Uses homework as a review or practice of concepts introduced during classroom instruction.

4. Provides positive feedback by use of rewards, praise, and displays in a way that emphasizes the success of all learners.

5. Uses direct instruction technique when appropriate.

6. Communicates enthusiasm for teaching and learning.

7. Maintains a good pace of instruction, with a high level of interactive on-task activities such as discussion, review, and frequent feedback.

D. COMMUNICATES WITH LEARNERS.

1. Gives clear directions related to lesson content.

2. Clarifies directions when misunderstood.

3. Communicates with learners about their progress and needs.

4. Uses responses and questions from learners in teaching.

5. Provides feedback throughout lesson.

6. Uses acceptable written and oral expression.

E. DEMONSTRATES A VARIETY OF TEACHING METHODS.

1. Provides learning activities in logical sequence.

2. *Demonstrates ability to conduct lessons involving use of a variety of thinking skills.*

3. Demonstrates ability to work with individuals, small groups, and large groups.

4. Uses methods to get learners initially involved and provides for continued involvement.

F. ESTABLISHES CLASSROOM ROUTINES.

1. Provides an attractive, orderly environment.

2. Fosters reasonable, clearly understood expectations.

3. Develops positive standards of conduct.

4. Develops cooperation and group cohesiveness.

5. Begins and ends class on time.

6. Establishes a system for students to follow in handing in assignments, taking tests, and assuming other academic responsibilities.

586

7. Uses techniques which will engage the attention and promote consistent learning of students.

G. DEMONSTRATES UNDERSTANDING OF SUBJECT MATTER.

1. Helps learners recognize importance of topics.
2. *Demonstrates knowledge in subject areas.*
3. Demonstrates awareness of current developments in subject area.
4. *Possesses knowledge of resources to be used in instruction.*

H. HELPS LEARNERS DEVELOP POSITIVE SELF-CONCEPTS.

1. Demonstrates warmth and friendliness.
2. Demonstrates sensitivity to needs and feelings of learners.
3. Demonstrates patience, empathy, and understanding.
4. Provides feedback about learner's behavior.
5. Assigns reasonable tasks.

I. MAINTAINS EFFECTIVE CLASSROOM DISCIPLINE (MANAGEMENT).

1. Defines and maintains effective classroom behavior and encourages self-discipline.
2. Establishes appropriate discipline strategies.
3. Consistently manages disruptive behavior in accordance with school and district policy.
4. Manages behavior through contingencies, token economy, contracting, praise, etc.
5. Monitors students and follows through with consequences.
6. Uses proximity control (standing near disruptive learner).
7. *Restructures lesson when not working well.*
8. Removes distracting material (toys, food, etc.).
9. Provides for tension release.

J. MEETS PROFESSIONAL RESPONSIBILITIES AND DEVELOPMENT.

1. Works cooperatively with colleagues, administrators, and parents.
2. Follows policies of school and district.
3. Demonstrates self-confidence.
4. Demonstrates ethical behavior.
5. Performs assigned extra duties.
6. *Participates in professional growth activities.*
7. Shares and seeks materials and ideas.
8. *Maintains flow of information between school and home* (report cards, newsletters, parent-teacher meeting, etc.).

II. ADMINISTRATIVE AND SUPERVISORY EDUCATOR STANDARDS AND INDICATORS: The competent administrator/supervisor.

A. PLANS CURRICULUM.

1. Supervises planning of instructional and curricular programs.
2. Supervises program implementation.
3. Organizes programs with staff in harmony with financial resources available.
4. Interprets research data.
5. *Implements curriculum which reflects high expectations of learners and the learning process.*
6. Evaluates the educational program relative to goals.
7. Utilizes evaluative data to modify educational program.
8. Visits and evaluates classroom and other educational activities frequently.
9. Provides for an articulated scope and sequence.
10. *Defines student academic achievement consistent with district and school objectives.*
11. Develops long-range educational plans by involving parents, teachers, students, and central office personnel.
12. Encourages and supports feasible experimental educational projects in order to promote innovation and improvement in education.

588

B. ORGANIZES AND ADMINISTERS STAFF.

1. Comprehends and implements policy and goals consistent with district philosophy.

2. Provides district office with information to clarify position when complaints are issued.

3. Organizes and sequences procedures for establishing goals.

4. Supervises planning and scheduling in accordance with available facilities and equipment.

5. Recruits and selects competent staff.

6. *Evaluates the competence of staff regularly.*

7. Works harmoniously with staff.

8. Supervises and manages financial affairs relating to district and school funds.

9. Allocates available resources to staff equitably (supplies, money, etc.).

10. Communicates clearly and concisely.

C. ADMINISTERS THE BUDGET.

1. Maintains and operates the budget.

2. Allocates special supplies.

3. Makes capital improvements in accordance with district plans and projections.

4. Uses categorical funds only for the purposes designated.

D. ESTABLISHES SCHOOL ORGANIZATION AND CONTROL.

1. Works with staff to achieve regular attendance of students.

2. Establishes adequate control of the student body and provides necessary disciplinary rules with the help and cooperation of parents, teachers, and students.

3. Deals with the discipline problems of students.

4. Maintains school environment conducive to learning.

5. Supervises the management and operation of the plant, grounds, facilities, and the custodial staff.

6. Maintains a current inventory of equipment, furniture, and supplies of the school and establishes and checks on a plan for reasonable periodic inspection.

7. Maintains an effective program for energy conservation in the school.

8. Promptly and accurately submits all necessary forms and reports.

9. Provides for student security and safety.

10. Supervises school transportation requirements.

E. DIRECTS AND MOTIVATES.

1. Utilizes counseling techniques and directs guidance programs for students and staff.

2. Initiates procedures giving student participation in the development and implementation of student programs and activities.

3. Encourages and initiates studies that discover causes for difficulties and failures experienced by students.

4. Advocates for and communicates with students regarding various aspects of their school life.

5. Stimulates and encourages teachers, by example, to keep abreast of current educational developments.

6. Organizes and implements in-service training programs and summer workshops.

7. *Encourages teachers to practice innovative and creative educational methods and techniques and gives appropriate recognition.*

F. DISPLAYS LEADERSHIP AND MANAGEMENT QUALITIES.

1. Articulates and interprets district and school educational objectives.

2. Utilizes problem solving procedures.

3. Resolves conflict situations.

4. Generates a positive attitude about the school and the district.

5. Delegates tasks fairly.

6. Seeks input from staff and other sources to be well informed.

7. Involves staff in decisions and puts democratic principles into practice.

8. Keeps avenues of communication open by reflective listening.

9. Demonstrates self-confidence.

10. Seeks personal and professional self-renewal.

11. Takes appropriate action whenever educator and/or student welfare is at stake.

G. COORDINATES SCHOOL AND COMMUNITY NEEDS.

1. Serves as liaison between the school and Board of Education, district offices and community.

2. Fosters and maintains community support.

3. Maintains open communication with parents regarding their students.

4. Identifies and utilizes community agencies and resources which affect successful operation of the school education program.

5. Plans and establishes an effective public relations program [emphasis added].

Appendix 3

Criteria of Professional Practices and Criteria of Competent Performance,

Iowa Professional Teaching Practices Commission

Criteria of Competent Performance.

The criteria of competent performance, according to Chapter 4, "are held to be generally accepted minimal standards within the teaching profession in Iowa ... and therefore are declared to be the criteria of competency adopted pursuant" to the requirements of the Iowa Code. The standards are categorized as follows:

Administrative and Supervisory Requirements.

Each educator shall keep appropriate records, supervise students and personnel in accordance with law and school policies, and recognize the benefits and advantages of community agencies and groups (including, for example, cultural organizations, advisory groups and parents groups).

Each teacher shall use appropriate available instructional materials and equipment, adhere to and enforce the policies of the school district, and use available channels of communication in dealing with administrators, community agencies and groups, in accordance with school policy.

Each administrator shall use human and other resources appropriately in pursuit of the school district's goals; adhere to and enforce school law, state board regulations and school district policy; and use available channels of communication in dealing with teachers, community agencies and groups, in accordance with school policy.

Analysis of Individual Needs and Potential.

The competent educator shall use or promote the use of appropriate diagnostic techniques to analyze the needs and potential of individuals. Among the techniques to be considered are personal observation, analysis of individual performance and achievement, and specific performance testing.

Instructional Procedures.

Each competent educator shall create an atmosphere that encourages learning, use procedures appropriate to the designated task, and encourage expressions of ideas, opinions, and feelings.

Each competent teacher shall create interest through the use of appropriate materials and consider the individual interests and abilities of students.

Each competent administrator shall support the process of learning by providing appropriate and reasonable materials and equipment and by making reasonable assignments of tasks.

Communication Skills.

In communicating with various audiences, each competent educator will use information, materials and terminology relevant to the assigned task and appropriate to the audience and will recognize and consider the ideas of others.

Management Techniques.

The competent educator will resolve discipline problems in accordance with law and school policy, be consistent in the application of policy, use techniques of management appropriate to the setting, and maintain positive standards of student conduct.

Competence in Specialization.

The competent educator shall be informed in the area of specialization, be aware of current developments in the field, and be aware of resources available for improvement of instruction in the area of specialization.

Evaluation of Learning and Goal Achievement.

The competent educator shall use appropriate evaluation techniques, use the results of evaluations for planning and program

594

modification, and share the results of evaluation with affected parties.

Human and Interpersonal Relationships.

The competent educator shall encourage respect for diverse opinions, avoid misrepresentation of the statements of others, provide leadership by example, offer constructive criticism when necessary, comply with requests of proper authorities, avoid assignment of unreasonable tasks, and exercise discretion and judgment in the exercise of authority.

Assessment of Mental or Physical Health.

In assessing the mental or physical health of educators, no decision adverse to the educator shall be made by the IPTC except on the testimony of personnel competent to make just judgments. Each competent educator must, however, be able to engage in physical activity appropriate to the designated task, except when temporarily disabled by mental or physical conditions. Each competent educator must also be able to communicate effectively and to appropriately control emotions that may interfere with the learning process. Finally, each competent educator must possess and demonstrate sufficient intellectual ability to perform designated tasks [emphasis added].

Appendix 4

The Standards for Competent and Ethical Performance of Oregon Educators,

Chapter 584, Division 20 — Teacher
Standards and Practices Commission,
Oregon (March 1988).

Curriculum and Instruction.

585-20-015(1) The competent educator measures success by the progress of each student toward realization of personal potential as a worthy and effective citizen. The competent educator stimulates the spirit of inquiry, the acquisition of knowledge and understanding, and the thoughtful formulation of goals as they are appropriate for each individual.

(2) The competent teacher demonstrates:

(a) Use of state and district adopted curriculum and goals.

(b) Skill in setting instructional goals and objectives expressed as learning outcomes.

(c) Use of current subject matter appropriate to the individual needs of students.

(d) Use of students' growth and development patterns to adjust instruction to individual needs consistent with number of students and amount of time available.

(e) *Skill in selection and use of teaching techniques conducive to student learning.*

(3) The competent administrator demonstrates:

(a) Skill in assisting individual staff members to become more competent teachers by complying with state law, rules, and lawful and reasonable district policy and contracts.

(b) Knowledge of curriculum and instruction appropriate to assignment.

(c) *Skill in implementing instructional programs through adequate communication with staff.*

597

(d) *Skill in identifying and initiating any needed change which helps each student toward realization of personal learning potential* [citations omitted].

Supervision and Evaluation.

584-20-020(1) The competent educator is a student of human behavior and uses this knowledge to provide a climate that is conducive to learning and that respects the rights of all persons without discrimination. The competent educator assumes responsibility for the activities planned and conducted through the district's program, and assists colleagues to do the same. The competent educator gathers relevant information and uses it in the planning and evaluation of instructional activities.

(2) *The competent teacher demonstrates:*

(a) *Ways to assess progress of individual students.*

(b) Skill in the use of assessment data to assist individual student growth.

(c) *Procedures for evaluating curriculum and instructional goals and practices.*

(d) Skill in the supervision of students.

(3) *The competent administrator demonstrates:*

(a) Skill in the use of assessment data to provide effective instructional programs.

(b) Skill in the implementation of the district's student evaluation program.

(c) Skill in providing equal opportunity for all students and staff.

(d) *Skill in the use of employee techniques appropriate to the assignment and according to well established standards which insure due process for the staff being evaluated* [citations omitted].

. . . .

Grounds for Denial, Suspension, or Revocation of Certificate, or Other Disciplinary Action.

....

(2) *The Commission may initiate proceedings to suspend or revoke the certificate of an educator* under ORS 342.175 or deny a certificate to an applicant under ORS 342.143 who:

(a) Has been convicted of a crime not listed in section (1) of this rule, if the Commission finds that the nature of the act or acts constituting the crime for which the educator was convicted render the educator unfit to hold a certificate.

(b) Is charged with knowingly making any false statement in the application for a certificate.

(c) *Is charged with gross neglect of duty.*

(d) *Is charged with gross unfitness.*

(3) *Gross neglect of duty is any serious and material inattention to or breach of professional responsibilities. The following may be admissible as evidence of gross neglect of duty. Consideration may include but is not limited to:*

....

(e) *Substantial deviation from professional standards of competency set forth in OAR 584-20-010 through 584-20-030* [emphasis added].

Appendix 5

PETER W.
v.
SAN FRANCISCO UNIFIED SCHOOL DISTRICT

Court of Appeal, First District,
Division 4.
Aug. 6, 1976.
Hearing Denied Sept. 29, 1976.

Susanne Martinez, Peter B. Sandmann, San Francisco, for plaintiff and appellant.

Thomas M. O'Connor, City Atty., Burk E. Delventhal, Deputy City Atty., San Francisco, for defendants and respondents.

RATTIGAN, Associate Justice.

The novel — and troublesome — question on this appeal is whether a person who claims to have been inadequately educated, while a student in a public school system, may state a cause of action in tort against the public authorities who operate and administer the system. We hold that he may not.

The appeal reaches us upon plaintiff's first amended complaint (hereinafter the "complaint"), which purports to state seven causes of action. Respondents (San Francisco Unified School District, its superintendent of schools, its governing board, and the individual board members) appeared to it by filing general demurrers to all seven counts; we hereinafter refer to them as "defendants." The trial court sustained their demurrers with twenty days' leave to amend. When plaintiff failed to amend within that period, the court entered a judgment dismissing his action.

On plaintiff's appeal, which is from the judgment, the question is whether a cause of action is stated against defendants in any of the complaint's seven counts. (*Glaire v. La Lanne-Paris Health Spa, Inc.* (1974) 12 Cal.3d 915, 918, 117 Cal.Rptr. 541, 528 P.2d 357.) We must treat the demurrers as having provisionally admitted all material facts properly pleaded in it (*ibid.*), but not such allegations — which appear throughout it — as amount to

601

"'contentions, deductions or conclusions of fact or law.'" (*Venuto v. Owens-Corning Fiberglas Corp.* (1971) 22 Cal.App.3d 116, 122, 99 Cal.Rptr. 350, 354.) We limit our summary of its contents accordingly.

The First Cause of Action

The first count, which is the prototype of the others (each of which incorporates all of its allegations by reference), sounds in negligence. Its opening allegations may be summarized, and quoted in part, as follows:

Defendant district is "a unified school district ... existing under the laws of the State of California" and functioning under the direction of its governing board and superintendent of schools. Plaintiff is an 18-year-old male who was recently graduated from a high school operated by the district. He had theretofore been enrolled in its schools, and had attended them, for a period of twelve years. Allegations explicitly charging negligence next appear as follows:

"XI. Defendant school district, its agents and employees, negligently and carelessly failed to provide plaintiff with adequate instruction, guidance, counseling and/or supervision in basic academic skills such as reading and writing, although said school district had the authority, responsibility and ability ... [to do so] .... Defendant school district, its agents and employees, negligently failed to use reasonable care in the discharge of its duties to provide plaintiff with adequate instruction ... in basic academic skills[,] and failed to exercise that degree of professional skill required of an ordinary prudent educator under the same circumstances[,] as exemplified, but not limited to[,] the following acts:"

In five enumerated subsections which follow in the same paragraph ("XI."), plaintiff alleges that the school district and its agents and employees, "negligently and carelessly" in each instance, (1) failed to apprehend his reading disabilities, (2) assigned him to classes in which he could not read "the books and other materials," (3) allowed him "to pass and advance from a course or grade level" with knowledge that he had not achieved

602

either its completion or the skills "necessary for him to succeed or benefit from subsequent courses," (4) assigned him to classes in which the instructors were unqualified or which were not "geared" to his reading level, and (5) permitted him to graduate from high school although he was "unable to read above the eighth grade level, as required by Education Code section 8573, ... thereby depriving him of additional instruction in reading and other academic skills."

The first count continues with allegations of proximate cause and injury: "XII.... [A]s a direct and proximate result of the negligent acts and omissions by the defendant school district, its agents and employees, plaintiff graduated from high school with a reading ability of only the fifth grade [*sic*]. As a further proximate result ... [thereof] ..., plaintiff has suffered a loss of earning capacity by his limited ability to read and write and is unqualified for any employment other than ... labor which requires little or no ability to read or write...."

In the closing paragraphs of the first count, plaintiff alleges general damages based upon his "permanent disability and inability to gain meaningful employment"; special damages incurred as the cost of compensatory tutoring allegedly required by reason of the "negligence, acts and omissions of defendants"; that he had presented to the school district an appropriate and timely claim for such damages; and that the claim had been rejected in its entirety.

We proceed to assess the first count for the cause of action in negligence which it purports to plead; the others are separately treated below. In his own assessment of the count, plaintiff initially points out that the doctrine of governmental immunity from tort liability was abolished in *Muskopf v. Corning Hospital Dist.* (1961) 55 Cal.2d 211, 11 Cal.Rptr. 89, 359 P.2d 457; that *Muskopf* further established that governmental liability for negligence is the rule, and immunity the exception; that, as to the conduct pleaded in his first count, immunity from liability is not expressly granted by any provision of the 1963 Tort Claims Act which succeeded *Muskopf* (Gov.Code, § 810 et seq.); and that, in fact, one provision thereof makes defendant district vicariously liable for any tortious conduct of its employees which would give

603

rise to a cause of action against them personally. (Gov.Code, § 815.2, subd. (a).)[1]

The thrust of these observations is that defendants do not have statutory immunity from the negligence liability with which the first count would charge them. However, *Muskopf* holds that liability is the rule, and immunity the exception, only *"when there is negligence."* (*Muskopf v. Corning Hospital Dist., supra,* 55 Cal.2d 211 at p. 219, 11 Cal.Rptr. 89, 359 P.2d 457 [emphasis added].) The 1963 Tort Claims Act did not change this "basic teaching." (*Johnson v. State of California* (1968) 69 Cal.2d 782, 798, 73 Cal.Rptr. 240, 447 P.2d 352.) Since its enactment, all governmental liability in California has been dependent upon its provisions. (Gov.Code, § 815; *Susman v. City of Los Angeles* (1969) 269 Cal.App.2d 803, 808, 75 Cal.Rptr. 240.) This means that, to state a cause of action against a public entity, every fact material to the existence of its statutory liability must be pleaded with particularity. (*Susman v. City of Los Angeles, supra,* at p. 809, 75 Cal.Rptr. 240.)

A public entity may be held vicariously liable for the conduct of its employee, under Government Code section 815.2, subdivision (a) (see fn. 1, *ante*), only if it is established that the employee would be personally liable for the conduct upon some "acceptable theory of liability." (Van Alstyne, California Government Tort Liability (Cont.Ed. Bar 1964) § 5.33, p. 144.) Plaintiff's immunity points thus mean that he *may* state a cause of action for negligence. They do not mean that he *has* stated one, nor do they relieve him of the pleading requirements he must meet for this purpose.

According to the familiar California formula, the allegations requisite to a cause of action for negligence are (1) facts showing a duty of care in the defendant, (2) negligence constituting a breach of the duty, and (3) injury to the plaintiff as a proximate

---

1. "815.2. (a) A public entity is liable for injury proximately caused by an act or omission of an employee of the public entity within the scope of his employment if the act or omission would, apart from this section, have given rise to a cause of action against that employee or his personal representative."

result. (3 Witkin, California Procedure (2d ed. 1971) Pleading, § 450, p. 2103.) The present parties do not debate the adequacy of plaintiff's first count with respect to the elements of negligence, proximate cause, and injury; they focus exclusively upon the issue (which we find dispositive, as will appear) of whether it alleges facts sufficient to show that defendants owed him a "duty of care."

The facts which it shows in this respect — or not — appear in its allegations that he had been a student undergoing academic instruction in the public school system operated and administered by defendants. He argues that these facts alone show the requisite "duty of care" upon three judicially recognized theories, for which he cites authorities, pertaining to the public schools.

According to the first theory, "[a]ssumption of the function of instruction of students imposes the duty to exercise reasonable care in its discharge." (Summarizing this and the other two theories advanced by plaintiff, we quote the pertinent captions of his opening brief.) The decisions he cites for his first theory have no application here; in each, the question was whether a public employee's discharge of a function, the performance of which he had "assumed" in the exercise of his discretion, was reached by statutes which granted him immunity from tort liability for the results of his discretionary actions. (*Morgan v. County of Yuba* (1964) 230 Cal.App.2d 938, 940-943, 41 Cal.Rptr. 508; *Sava v. Fuller* (1967) 249 Cal.App.2d 281, 283-285, 57 Cal.Rptr. 312. See also *McCorkle v. City of Los Angeles* (1969) 70 Cal.2d 252, 258-262, 74 Cal.Rptr. 389, 449 P.2d 453.)

Plaintiff's second theory is that "[t]here is a special relationship between students and teachers which supports [the teachers'] duty to exercise reasonable care." He cites for this theory a wide-ranged array of decisions which enforced or addressed various "rights," "opportunities," or privileges of public school students (particularly in equal protection contexts), but none of which involved the question whether the school authorities owed them a "duty of care" in the process of their academic education. (See, e.g., *Lau v. Nichols* (1973) 414 U.S. 563, 564-568, 94 S.Ct. 786, 39 L.Ed.2d 1; *Ward v. Flood* (1874) 48 Cal. 36, 50-51; *Serrano v. Priest* (1971) 5 Cal.3d 584, 606-607, 96

Cal.Rptr. 601, 487 P.2d 1241; *Governing Board v. Metcalf* (1974) 36 Cal.App.3d 546, 550, 111 Cal.Rptr. 724.) The third theory is that the "[d]uty of teachers to exercise reasonable care in instruction and supervision of students is recognized in California." The decisions cited here are inapplicable because they establish only that public school authorities have a duty to exercise reasonable care for the *physical safety* of students under their supervision. (See, e.g., *Dailey v. Los Angeles Unified Sch. Dist.* (1970) 2 Cal.3d 741, 745-747, 87 Cal.Rptr. 376, 470 P.2d 360.)

For want of relevant authority in each instance, plaintiff's allegations of his enrollment and attendance at defendant's schools do not plead the requisite "duty of care," relative to his academic instruction, upon any of the three theories he invokes. Of course, no reasonable observer would be heard to say that these facts did not impose upon defendants a "duty of care" within any common meaning of the term; given the commanding importance of public education in society, we state a truism in remarking that the public authorities who are dutybound to educate are also bound to do it with "care." But the truism does not answer the present inquiry, in which "duty of care" is not a term of common parlance; it is instead a legalistic concept of "duty" which will sustain liability for negligence in its breach, and it must be analyzed in that light.

The concept reflects the longstanding language of decisions in which the existence of a "duty of care," in a defendant, has been repeatedly defined as a requisite element of his liability for negligence. (See, e.g., *Means v. Southern California Ry. Co.* (1904) 144 Cal. 473, 478, 77 P. 1001; *Dahms v. General Elevator Co.* (1932) 214 Cal. 733, 737, 7 P.2d 1013; *Richards v. Stanley* (1954) 43 Cal.2d 60, 63, 271 P.2d 23; *Raymond v. Paradise Unified School Dist.* (1963) 218 Cal.App.2d 1, 6, 31 Cal.Rptr. 847; 4 Witkin, Summary of California Law (8th ed. 1974) Torts, § 488, p. 2749.) The concept has not been treated as immutable; with respect to physical injury resulting from emotional "spectator" shock, for example it now incorporates a test — the foreseeability of the injury — which it had previously excluded. (*Dillon v. Legg* (1968) 68 Cal.2d 728, 730, 733-735, 69 Cal.Rptr. 72, 441 P.2d 912 [overruling *Amaya v. Home Ice, Fuel & Supply Co.* (1963) 59

Cal.2d 295, 310, 29 Cal.Rptr. 33, 379 P.2d 513 et seq.]. See *Mobaldi v. Board of Regents* (1976) 55 Cal.App.3d 573, 576, 579-581, 127 Cal.Rptr. 720; 4 Witkin, Summary, *op. cit.*, Torts, § 494, p. 2759.)

Despite such changes in the concept, several constants are apparent from its evolution. One is that the concept itself is still an essential factor in any assessment of liability for negligence. (See, e.g., *United States Liab. Ins. Co. v. Haidinger-Hayes, Inc.* (1970) 1 Cal.3d 586, 594, 83 Cal.Rptr. 418, 463 P.2d 770; *Valdez v. J. D. Diffenbaugh Co.* (1975) 51 Cal.App. 3d 494, 504, 124 Cal.Rptr. 467.) Another is that whether a defendant owes the requisite "duty of care," in a given factual situation, presents a question of law which is to be determined by the courts alone. (*Raymond v. Paradise Unified School Dist., supra,* 218 Cal.App.2d 1, at p. 8, 31 Cal.Rptr. 847; 4 Witkin, Summary, *op. cit. supra,* Torts, § 493, p. 2756.) A third, and the one most important in the present case, is that judicial recognition of such duty in the defendant, with the consequence of his liability in negligence for its breach, is initially to be dictated or precluded by considerations of public policy. From among an array of judicial statements to this effect, the following language by the *Raymond* court is particularly pertinent here:

"An affirmative declaration of duty [of care] simply amounts to a statement that two parties stand in such relationship that the law will impose on one a responsibility for the exercise of care toward the other. Inherent in this simple description are various and sometimes delicate *policy judgments.* The social utility of the activity out of which the injury arises, compared with the risks involved in its conduct; the kind of person with whom the actor is dealing; the workability of a rule of care, especially in terms of the parties' relative ability to adopt practical means of preventing injury; the relative ability of the parties to bear the financial burden of injury and the availability of means by which the loss may be shifted or spread; the body of statutes and judicial precedents which color the parties' relationship; the prophylactic effect of a rule of liability; in the case of a public agency defendant, the extent of its powers, the role imposed upon it by law and the limitations imposed upon it by budget; and finally, the moral

607

imperatives which judges share with their fellow citizens — such are the factors which play a role in the determination of duty. (Citations.) Occasions for judicial determination of a duty of care are infrequent, because in 'run of the mill' accident cases the existence of a duty may be — and usually is — safely assumed. Here the problem is squarely presented." (*Raymond v. Paradise Unified School Dist., supra,* 218 Cal. App.2d 1 at pp. 8-9, 31 Cal.Rptr. 847, at p. 851 [emphasis added].)

In *Rowland v. Christian* (1968) 69 Cal.2d 108, 70 Cal.Rptr. 97, 443 P.2d 561, the Supreme Court used similar terminology in defining various public policy considerations as exceptional factors which might alone warrant *non*liability for negligence. The court declared that the foundation of *all* negligence liability in this state was Civil Code section 1714,[2] paraphrased the section in terms of duty of care (as expressing the principle that "[a]ll persons are required to use ordinary care to prevent others being injured as the result of their conduct"), and stated that liability was to flow from this "fundamental principle" in all cases except where a departure from it was "*clearly supported by public policy.*" (*Id.,* at p. 112, 70 Cal.Rptr. 97, 443 P.2d 561, 564 [emphasis added].) The court then described the pertinent factors of public policy, and their role, as follows:

"A departure from this fundamental principle involves the balancing of a number of considerations; the major ones are the foreseeability of harm to the plaintiff, the degree of certainty that the plaintiff suffered injury, the closeness of the connection between the defendant's conduct and the injury suffered, the moral blame attached to the defendant's conduct, the policy of preventing future harm, the extent of the burden to the defendant and consequences to the community of imposing a duty to exercise care with resulting liability for breach, and the availability, cost, and prevalence of insurance for the risk involved. (Citations.)" (*Rowland v. Christian, supra,* 69 Cal.2d 108, at pp.

---

2. Section 1714 provides in pertinent part: "Every one is responsible, not only for the result of his willful acts, but also for an injury occasioned to another by his want of ordinary care or skill in the management of his property or person ...."

112-113, 70 Cal.Rptr. 97, at p. 100, 443 P.2d 561, at p. 564. See 4
Witkin, Summary, *op. cit. supra,* Torts, § 487, pp. 2748-2749.)

Such policy factors, and their controlling role in the determination whether a defendant owes a "duty of care" which will
underlie his liability for negligence in its breach, have been similarly defined in other decisions. (See, e.g., *Connor v. Great Western Sav. & Loan Assn.* (1968) 69 Cal.2d 850, 865, 73 Cal.Rptr.
369, 447 P.2d 609 and cases cited; *Valdez v. J. D. Diffenbaugh
Co., supra,* 51 Cal.App.3d 494, at p. 507, 124 Cal.Rptr. 467. See
also Prosser, Law of Torts (4th ed. 1971) pp. 21-23.) Some have
been classified as "administrative factors" which involve such
considerations as the possibility of "feigned claims," and the difficulty of proof, of a particular injury; others, as "socio-economic
and moral factors" involving the prospect of limitless liability for
the same injury. (See *Amaya v. Home Ice, Fuel & Supply Co.,
supra,* 59 Cal.2d 295, at pp. 310-315, 29 Cal.Rptr. 33, 379 P.2d
513 [applying the factors to negate "duty"]; compare *Dillon v.
Legg, supra,* 68 Cal.2d 728, at pp. 735-746, 69 Cal.Rptr. 72, 441
P.2d 912 [acknowledging the factors but disregarding them as
limitations upon liability].)

It has also been pointed out that the concept of "duty" may
actually focus upon the rights of the injured plaintiff rather than
upon the obligations of the defendant, but that the same public
policy considerations will control whether the one may state a
cause of action for negligence, against the other, in a given factual situation. In these respects, the Supreme Court has stated:

"The assertion that liability must nevertheless be denied because defendant bears no 'duty' to plaintiff 'begs the essential
question — whether the plaintiff's interests are entitled to legal
protection against the defendant's conduct.... It [duty] is a short-
hand statement of a conclusion, rather than an aid to analysis in
itself.... But it should be recognized that "duty" is not sacrosanct
in itself, but only an expression of *the sum total of those considerations of policy which lead the law to say that the particular
plaintiff is entitled to protection.'"* [3] (*Dillon v. Legg, supra,* 68

---

3. "Protection" of the plaintiff is the initial element in the Restatement formula defining the requisites of a cause of action for negligence.

609

Cal.2d 728, at p. 734, 69 Cal.Rptr. 72, at p. 76, 441 P.2d 912, at p. 916, quoting from Prosser, Law of Torts (3d ed. 1964) pp. 332-333 [emphasis added here]. See also Prosser, *op. cit.* (4th ed. 1971) pp. 325-326.)

On occasions when the Supreme Court has opened or sanctioned new areas of tort liability, it has noted that the wrongs and injuries involved were both comprehensible and assessable within the existing judicial framework. (See, e.g., *State Rubbish, etc., Assn. v. Siliznoff* (1952) 38 Cal.2d 330, 338, 240 P.2d 282; *Dillon v. Legg, supra,* 68 Cal.2d 728, at pp. 735-747, 69 Cal.Rptr. 72, 441 P.2d 912.) This is simply not true of wrongful conduct and injuries allegedly involved in educational malfeasance. Unlike the activity of the highway or the marketplace, classroom methodology affords no readily acceptable standards of care, or cause, or injury. The science of pedagogy itself is fraught with different and conflicting theories of how or what a child should be taught, and any layman might — and commonly does — have his own emphatic views on the subject. The "injury" claimed here is plaintiff's inability to read and write. Substantial professional authority attests that the achievement of literacy in the schools, or its failure, are influenced by a host of factors which affect the pupil subjectively, from outside the formal teaching process, and beyond the control of its ministers. They may be physical, neurological, emotional, cultural, environmental; they may be present but not perceived, recognized but not identified.[4]

We find in this situation no conceivable "workability of a rule of care" against which defendants' alleged conduct may be measured (*Raymond v. Paradise Unified School Dist., supra,* 218 Cal.App.2d 1, at p. 8, 31 Cal.Rptr. 847, at p. 851), no reasonable

---

The formula's essentials include negligence, causation, and injury (the "invasion of an interest" of the plaintiff) but, unlike the California formula, the first element is not a "duty of care" in the defendant: it is the condition that the "*interest invaded* is *protected.*" (Rest.2d Torts, § 281 [emphasis added].)

4. From among innumerable authorities to these effects, defendants cite Gague, The Conditions of Learning (Holt, Rinehart & Winston, 1965); Schubert and Torgerson, Improving The Reading Program (Wm. C. Brown Co., 1968); Flesch, Why Johnny Can't Read (Harper, 1965).

610

"degree of certainty that ... plaintiff suffered injury" within the meaning of the law of negligence (see fn. 3, *ante,* referring to Rest.2d, Torts, § 281), and no such perceptible "connection between the defendant's conduct and the injury suffered," as alleged, which would establish a causal link between them within the same meaning. (*Rowland v. Christian, supra,* 69 Cal.2d 108, at p. 113, 70 Cal.Rptr. 97, at p. 100, 443 P.2d 561, at p. 564.)

These recognized policy considerations alone negate an actionable "duty of care" in persons and agencies who administer the academic phases of the public educational process. Others, which are even more important in practical terms, command the same result. Few of our institutions, if any, have aroused the controversies, or incurred the public dissatisfaction, which have attended the operation of the public schools during the last few decades. Rightly or wrongly, but widely, they are charged with outright failure in the achievement of their educational objectives; according to some critics, they bear responsibility for many of the social and moral problems of our society at large. Their public plight in these respects is attested in the daily media, in bitter governing board elections, in wholesale rejections of school bond proposals, and in survey upon survey. To hold them to an actionable "duty of care," in the discharge of their academic functions, would expose them to the tort claims — real or imagined — of disaffected students and parents in countless numbers. They are already beset by social and financial problems which have gone to major litigation, but for which no permanent solution has yet appeared. (See, e.g., *Crawford v. Board of Education* (1976) 17 Cal.3d 280, 130 Cal.Rptr. 724, 551 P.2d 28; *Serrano v. Priest, supra,* 5 Cal.3d 584, 96 Cal.Rptr. 601, 487 P.2d 1241.) The ultimate consequences, in terms of public time and money, would burden them — and society — beyond calculation.

Upon consideration of the role imposed upon the public schools by law and the limitations imposed upon them by their publicly-supported budgets (*Raymond v. Paradise Unified School Dist., supra,* 218 Cal.App.2d 1, at p. 8, 31 Cal.Rptr. 847), and of the just-cited "consequences to the community of imposing [upon them] a duty to exercise care with resulting liability for breach" (*Rowland v. Christian, supra,* 69 Cal.2d 108, at p. 118, 70

Cal.Rptr. 97, at p. 100, 443 P.2d 561, at p. 564), we find no such "duty" in the first count of plaintiff's complaint. As this conclusion is dispositive, other problems presented by the pleading need not be discussed: it states no cause of action.

The Last Five Causes of Action

In each of his last five counts (the third through the seventh, inclusive), plaintiff repleads all the allegations of the first one. He further alleges, in each, that he had incurred "the damages alleged herein" "as a direct and proximate result" of a specified violation, by one or more of the defendants and as to him, of a respectively described "duty" (or "mandatory duty") allegedly imposed upon them by an express provision of law.[5] The theory of each count is that it states a cause of action for breach of a "mandatory duty" under Government Code section 815.6.[6]

---

5. The third count thus refers to the district's and the governing board's having violated their "mandatory duty," allegedly imposed upon them by Education Code section 10759 and Title V of the California Administrative Code, "of keeping the parents and natural guardians of minor school children advised as to their accurate educational progress and achievements." The fourth count alleges a violation, by the district, of its "duty of instructing plaintiff, and other students, in the basic skills of reading and writing" as imposed "under the Constitution and laws of the State of California." The fifth count refers to the district's having graduated plaintiff from high school as a violation of a "mandatory duty not to graduate students from high school without demonstration of proficiency in basic skills" as allegedly imposed by Education Code section 8573 et seq. The sixth count speaks to a violation, by the governing board, of its "mandatory duty" to inspect and evaluate the district's educational program pursuant to Education Code sections 1053 and 8002; the seventh, to the district's violation of its "mandatory duty," allegedly imposed by Education Code section 8505, "to design the course of instruction offered in the public schools to meet the needs of the pupils for which the course of study is prescribed."

6. "815.6. Where a public entity is under a mandatory duty imposed by an enactment that is designed to protect against the risk of a particular kind of injury, the public entity is liable for an injury of that kind proximately caused by its failure to discharge the duty unless the public entity establishes that it exercised reasonable diligence to discharge the duty."

If it be assumed that each of these counts effectively pleads the district's failure to have exercised "reasonable diligence to discharge the duty" respectively alleged, as mentioned in the statute (see fn. 6, *ante*), none states a cause of action. This is because the statute imposes liability for failure to discharge only such "mandatory duty" as is "imposed by an enactment that is designed to protect against the risk of a particular kind of injury." (See *ibid.*) The various "enactments" cited in these counts (see fn. 5, *ante*) are not so "designed." We have already seen that the failure of educational achievement may not be characterized as an "injury" within the meaning of tort law. It further appears that the several "enactments" have been conceived as provisions directed to the attainment of optimum educational results, but not as safeguards against "injury" of any kind: i.e., as administrative but not protective. Their violation accordingly imposes no liability under Government Code section 815.6.

The Second Cause Of Action

Plaintiff's second count requires separate treatment because the theory of liability invoked in it is materially different from those reflected in the others. After incorporating into it all the allegations of the first county, he further alleges as follows:

"Defendant school district, its agents and employees, falsely and fraudulently represented to plaintiff's mother and natural guardian that plaintiff was performing at or near grade level in basic academic skills such as reading and writing ...." The representations were false. The charged defendants knew that they were false, or had no basis for believing them to be true. "As a direct and proximate result of the intentional or negligent misrepresentation made ..., plaintiff suffered the damages set forth herein."

For the public policy reasons heretofore stated with respect to plaintiff's first count, we hold that this one states no cause of action for *negligence* in the form of the "misrepresentation" alleged. The possibility of its stating a cause of action for *intentional* misrepresentation, to which it expressly refers in the alternative, is assisted by judicial limitations placed upon the scope of the governmental immunity which is granted, as to liability for "misrepresentation," by Government Code section 818.8. (See *Johnson v. State of California, supra,* 69 Cal.2d 782, at pp. 799-800, 73 Cal.Rptr. 240, 447 P.2d 352; *Connelly v. State of California* (1970) 3 Cal.App.3d 744, 752, 84 Cal.Rptr. 257. See also Gov. Code, § 822.2.)

The second count nevertheless does not state a cause of action, for intentional misrepresentation, because it alleges no facts showing the requisite element of *reliance* upon the "misrepresentation" it asserts. (See 3 Witkin, Procedure, *op. cit. supra,* Pleading, §§ 573-574, pp. 2210-2212.) Plaintiff elected to stand upon it without exercising his leave to amend. The trial court's action, in sustaining defendants' general demurrer to it, is therefore to be regarded as conclusive for our purposes. (*O'Hara v. L.A. County Flood, etc., Dist.* (1941) 19 Cal.2d 61, 64, 119 P.2d 23; *Susman v. City of Los Angeles, supra,* 269 Cal.App.2d 803, at p. 822, 75 Cal.Rptr. 240.)

The judgment of dismissal is affirmed.

CALDECOTT, P. J., and CHRISTIAN, J., concur.

Appendix 6

DONOHUE

v.

COPIAGUE UNION FREE SCHOOL DISTRICT

Supreme Court, Special Term,
Suffolk County, Part I.
Aug. 31, 1977.

Siben & Siben, Bay Shore, for plaintiff.
Henry A. Weinstein, Garden City, for defendant.
PAUL J. BAISLEY, Justice.

Action by plaintiff, a former student against defendant school district, sounding in negligence and malpractice, and in breach of a statutory duty. Defendant moves to dismiss the complaint for failure to state facts sufficient to constitute a cause of action, and for failure to timely serve a notice of claim pursuant to Education Law § 3813 subd. 2 and General Municipal Law § 50 e. Plaintiff cross-moves for leave to serve a late notice of claim pursuant to G.M.L. § 50 e, subd. 5.

Addressing the motions in the order in which made, the first cause of action, in material part, alleges that plaintiff was a student in defendant's high school from September 1972 to June, 1976, when he was issued a graduation certificate; that defendant was under a duty to educate him and qualify him for a graduation certificate; that defendant failed to properly perform such duty, stating in particular the omissions complained of; that the failures to comply with accepted standards constituted educational malpractice; that plaintiff was not aware of his deficiencies in reading and in common branch subjects; that defendant issued a graduation certificate to plaintiff notwithstanding the foregoing; that plaintiff became aware of his condition in November, 1976; and that as a result of this violation of duty plaintiff was damaged to the sum of $5,000,000. The second cause of action alleges the constitutional duty under Article 11, § 1, of the New York State Constitution; that defendant agreed to and did maintain a statutory public school; that plaintiff was entitled to

615

receive a proper education as a third party beneficiary of the statutory duty; and that the breach thereof entitles him to damages in the sum of $5,000,000.

As stated, the first cause of action sounds in negligence and malpractice; the second in breach of a statutory duty. Taking the second cause of action first, the facts alleged fail to state a claim upon which relief can be granted. (*Steitz v. City of Beacon,* 295 N.Y. 51, 64 N.E.2d 704; *Moch v. Rensselaer Water Co.,* 247 N.Y. 160, 159 N.E. 896; cf. *Riss v. City of New York,* 22 N.Y.2d 579, 297 N.Y.S.2d 897, 240 N.E.2d 860). Turning to the first cause of action, a reading of the complaint reveals that it is parallel if not identical to the complaint in *Peter W. v. San Francisco Unified School District,* 60 Cal.App.3d 814, 131 Cal.Rptr. 854 (Court of Appeal, First Dist., August 6, 1976). While different statutes are concededly involved the Court finds the reasoning of the California intermediate appellate court persuasive. Concededly no statutory liability is here involved (*cf. Riss v. City of New York, supra*); based upon the cogent reasoning in the cited case, the Court finds no common-law duty in New York upon which the complaint at bar, alleging both negligence and malpractice, can be bottomed. Defendant's motion to dismiss for failure to state facts sufficient to constitute a cause of action is granted.

In view of the disposition of the first branch of defendant's motion, the second branch thereof, and the cross-motion, are both denied without prejudice.

The Court notes that this is apparently a case of first impression in New York, and that the commencement of this action has received substantial attention both in education circles and in the news media. This factor, combined with the recent adoption of 8 N.Y.C.R.R. § 3.45 by the Board of Regents (amended July 2, 1976 effective June 1, 1979), and the establishment by the Commissioner of basic competency tests pursuant to such provision, justifies the Court's suggesting that the grave policy questions posed by the issue at bar should be passed upon by Appellate Courts.

Appendix 7

DONOHUE
v.
COPIAGUE UNION FREE SCHOOL DISTRICT

Supreme Court, Appellate Division,
Second Department.

July 31, 1978.

Siben & Siben, Bay Shore (Bernard M. Rosen and Sidney R. Siben, Bay Shore, on the brief), for appellant.

Henry A. Weinstein, Garden City (Charles D. Maurer, Garden City, on the brief), for respondent.

Before DAMIANI, J. P., and SUOZZI, RABIN and HAWKINS, JJ.

DAMIANI, Justice Presiding.

The plaintiff appeals from an order which dismissed his complaint.

The issue before us is whether the courts of this State recognize a cause of action to recover for so-called "educational malpractice", or for breach of a statutory duty to educate. We hold that such causes of action are not recognized in this State.

The plaintiff was a student at a high school operated by the defendant school district. Although he received failing grades in several subjects and lacked basic reading and writing skills, he was permitted to graduate. Thereafter, he found it necessary to seek tutoring in order to acquire those basic skills which he had not obtained in high school.

The plaintiff then commenced this action to recover $5,000,000 in damages for the alleged deficiencies in his knowledge. The first cause of action asserted in the complaint sounds in negligence. It alleges that the defendant owed a duty of care to:

> teach the several and varied subjects to the plaintiff; ascertain his learning capacity and ability; and correctly and properly test him for such capacity in order to evaluate his ability to comprehend the subject matters of the various courses and

617

have sufficient understanding and comprehension of subject matters in said courses as to be able to achieve sufficient passing grades in said subject matters, and therefore, qualify for a Certificate of Graduation."

It further alleges that because the plaintiff, after graduation, was unable to read and write simple basic English and did not have an understanding of the other subjects covered in his high school courses, the defendant, its agents, servants and/or employees, breached their duty to him in that they:

"gave to the plaintiff passing grades and/or minimal or failing grades in various subjects; failed to evaluate the plaintiff's mental ability and capacity to comprehend the subjects being taught to him at said school; failed to take proper means and precautions that they reasonably should have taken under the circumstances; failed to interview, discuss, evaluate and/or psychologically test the plaintiff in order to ascertain his ability to comprehend and understand such subject matter; failed to provide adequate school facilities, teachers, administrators, psychologists, and other personnel trained to take the necessary steps in testing and evaluation processes insofar as the plaintiff is concerned in order to ascertain the learning capacity, intelligence and intellectual absorption on the part of the plaintiff; failed to hire proper personnel, experienced in the handling of such matters; failed to teach the plaintiff in such a manner so that he could reasonably understand what was necessary under the circumstances so that he could cope with the various subjects which they tried to make the plaintiff understand; failed to properly supervise the plaintiff; failed to advise his parents of the difficulty and necessity to call in psychiatric help; that the processes practiced were defective and not commensurate with a student attending a high school within the County of Suffolk; failed to adopt the accepted professional standards and methods to evaluate and cope with plaintiff's problems which constituted educational malpractice."

The second cause of action asserted in the complaint alleges that the plaintiff is the third-party beneficiary of a duty imposed

618

upon the defendant by section 1 of article XI of the New York State Constitution, which provides:

> "The legislature shall provide for the maintenance and support of a system of free common schools, wherein all the children of this state may be educated."

The plaintiff alleges that pursuant to this duty, the defendant undertook to operate a public school, but that it failed to educate him.

The defendant moved to dismiss the complaint, *inter alia,* pursuant to CPLR 3211 (subd. [a], par. 7) for failure to state a cause of action. Special Term granted the motion to dismiss, relying upon the California case of *Peter W. v. San Francisco Unified School Dist.,* 60 Cal.App.3d 814, 131 Cal.Rptr. 854. We affirm.

With respect to the first cause of action alleging negligence or so-called "educational malpractice", it is axiomatic that no recovery may be had unless (1) the defendant owed the plaintiff a cognizable duty of care, (2) the defendant failed to discharge that duty and (3) the plaintiff suffered damage as a proximate result of such failure (41 N.Y.Jur., Negligence, § 7). An action to recover for negligence does not lie unless there exists a duty on the part of the defendant and a corresponding right in the plaintiff (*Palsgraf v. Long Is. R.R. Co.,* 248 N.Y. 339, 341, 162 N.E. 99).

The question of whether, in any particular set of circumstances, one party owes a duty of care to another is entirely one of law to be determined by the courts (Prosser, Law of Torts [4th ed.], § 37, p. 206). Judicial recognition of the existence of a duty of care is dependent upon principles of sound public policy and involves the consideration of numerous relevant factors which include, *inter alia: moral* considerations arising from the view of society towards the relationship of the parties, the degree to which the courts should be involved in the regulation of that relationship and the social utility of the activity out of which the alleged injured arises; *preventative* considerations, which involve the ability of the defendant to adopt practical means of preventing injury, the possibility that reasonable men can agree as to the proper course to be followed to prevent injury, the degree of certainty that the alleged injuries were proximately caused by the defendant and the foreseeability of harm to the plaintiff; *economic* considerations, which include the ability of the defendant to respond in damages; and *administrative* considerations, which concern the ability of the courts to cope with a flood of new litigation, the probability of feigned claims and the difficulties inherent in proving the plaintiff's case (see Prosser, Law of Torts [4th ed.], § 4, pp. 16-23; *Raymond v. Paradise Unified School Dist. of Butte County,* 218 Cal.App.2d 1, 8, 9, 31 Cal.Rptr. 847; *Rowland v. Christian,* 69 Cal.2d 108, 70 Cal.Rptr. 97, 443 P.2d 561).

The issue of whether school districts are under a duty to exercise reasonable care in the instruction and supervision of students is one of first impression in the courts of this State. However, the First District Court of Appeal of the State of California has considered this precise issue and, in a comprehensive and well-reasoned opinion, has decisively held that no such duty exists (*Peter W. v. San Francisco School Dist.,* 60 Cal.App.3d 814, 131 Cal.Rptr. 854, *supra*). The plaintiff in *Peter W.* alleged that as a result of the negligence of the defendant school district he had graduated from high school with an ability to read at only the fifth grade level. While noting that it was a truism that educators are bound to discharge their functions with care, the court in *Peter W.* found no duty of care in the legal sense running from the defendant to the plaintiff. It noted that the wrongful conduct and injuries allegedly involved in educational malfeasance were neither comprehensible nor assessable within the existing judicial framework, stating (pp. 824-825, 131 Cal.Rptr. pp. 860-861):

"Unlike the activity of the highway or the marketplace, classroom methodology affords no readily acceptable standards of care, or cause, or injury. The science of pedagogy itself is fraught with different and conflicting theories of how or what a child should be taught, and any layman might — and commonly does — have his own emphatic views on the subject. The 'injury' claimed here is plaintiff's inability to read and write. Substantial professional authority attests that the achievement of literacy in the schools, or its failure, are influenced by

620

a host of factors which affect the pupil subjectively, from outside the formal teaching process, and beyond the control of its ministers. They may be physical, neurological, emotional, cultural, environmental; they may be present but not perceived, recognized but not identified.

"We find in this situation no conceivable 'workability of a rule of care' against which defendants' alleged conduct may be measured * * * no reasonable 'degree of certainty that * * * plaintiff suffered injury' within the meaning of the law of negligence * * * [referring to Rest.2d, Torts, § 281], and no such perceptible 'connection between the defendant's conduct and the injury suffered,' as alleged, which would establish a causal link between them within the same meaning.

"These recognized policy considerations alone negate an actionable 'duty of care' in persons and agencies who administer the academic phases of the public educational process. Others, which are even more important in practical terms, command the same result. Few of our institutions, if any, have aroused the controversies or incurred the public dissatisfaction, which have attended the operation of the public schools during the last few decades. Rightly or wrongly, but widely, they are charged with outright failure in the achievement of their educational objectives; according to some critics, they bear responsiblity for many of the social and moral problems of our society at large. Their public plight in these respects is attested in the daily media, in bitter governing board elections, in wholesale rejections of school bond proposals, and in survey upon survey. To hold them to an actionable 'duty of care,' in the discharge of their academic functions, would expose them to the tort claims — real or imagined — of disaffected students and parents in countless numbers. They are already beset by social and financial problems which have gone to major litigation, but for which no permanent solution has yet appeared * * The ultimate consequences, in terms of public time and money, would burden them — and society — beyond calculation." (See, also, the New York case of *Board of Educ., Levittown Union Free School Dist., Nassau County v. Nyquist,* Misc.2d, NYLJ, June 26, 1978, p. 14, col. 2.)

621

Upon our own examination and analysis of the relevant factors discussed above, which are involved in determining whether to judicially recognize the existence of a legal duty of care running from educators to students, we, like the court in *Peter W.,* hold that no such duty exists. Other jurisdictions have adopted this reasoning as well (see *Beaman v. Des Moines Area Community Coll.,* 5th Judicial Dist. of Iowa, March 23, 1977, Law No. CL 15 8532, Holliday, J.; *Garrett v. School Bd. of Broward Co.,* Circuit Ct., 17th Judicial Cir., Broward Co., Fla., Dec. 5, 1977, Case No. 77-8703). This determination does not mean that educators are not ethically and legally responsible for providing a meaningful public education for the youth of our State. Quite the contrary, all teachers and other officials of our schools bear an important public trust and may be held to answer for the failure to faithfully perform their duties. It does mean, however, that they may not be sued for damages by an individual student for an alleged failure to reach certain educational objectives.

The courts are an inappropriate forum to test the efficacy of educational programs and pedagogical methods. That judicial interference would be the inevitable result of the recognition of a legal duty of care is clear from the fact that in presenting their case, plaintiffs would, of necessity, call upon jurors to decide whether they should have been taught one subject instead of another, or whether one teaching method was more appropriate than another, or whether certain tests should have been administered or test results interpreted in one way rather than another, and so on, ad infinitum. It simply is not within the judicial function to evaluate conflicting theories of how best to educate. Even if it were possible to determine with exactitude the pedagogical course to follow with respect to particular individuals, yet another problem would arise. Public education involves an inherent stress between taking action to satisfy the educational needs of the individual student and the needs of the student body as a whole. It is not for the courts to determine how best to utilize scarce educational resources to achieve these sometimes conflicting objectives. Simply stated, the recognition of a cause of action sounding in negligence to recover for "educational malpractice" would impermissibly require the courts to oversee the administration of the State's public school system.

On a number of occasions, the Court of Appeals has explicitly stated that educational policies are solely the province of the duly constituted educational authorities of this State. Thus, in *Matter of Vetere v. Allen,* 15 N.Y.2d 259, 267, 258 N.Y.S.2d 77, 80, 206 N.E.2d 174, 176, the Court of Appeals upheld the power of the Commissioner of Education to direct local school boards to take steps to eliminate racial imbalance, noting:

"Disagreement with the sociological, psychological and educational assumptions relied on by the Commissioner cannot be evaluated by this court. Such arguments can only be heard in the Legislature which has endowed the Commissioner with an all but absolute power, or by the Board of Regents, who are elected by the Legislature and make public policy in the field of education."

In *James v. Board of Educ.,* 42 N.Y.2d 357, 397 N.Y.S.2d 934, 366 N.E.2d 1291, the issue was whether the courts have the power to enjoin, even temporarily, the administration of examinations to pupils based on contentions that the integrity of the examinations had been fatally compromised. In holding that defendant could not be enjoined from administering the examinations, the Court of Appeals reviewed the considerations governing review of educational policies, stating (pp. 367, 368, 397 N.Y.S.2d p. 941, 366 N.E.2d p. 1297):

"The courts had no role, and it is not argued that they should have, in selecting the form of examination to be administered. Statute requires the administration of a comprehensive examination and the examination purchased, if simon-pure, would surely be adequate for the purpose. It is not for the courts to say that considerations of educational policy, of the needfulness to make valid comparisons, of the need to prevent cheating, of the need to keep down costs, should have led the chancellor, and the board, to purchase a different form of examination.

623

* * * * * *

"Nor can this court evaluate the merits of petitioners' disagreement with the educational assumptions relied upon by the chancellor. (*Matter of Vetere v. Allen,* 15 N.Y.2d 259, 267, 258 N.Y.S.2d 77, 206 N.E.2d 174, *supra.*) Finally, the court is without power to decide whether the chancellor's answer to the difficulty, the administration of alternative examinations to students only in schools affected by irregularity, is sufficient to overcome any taint. 'While it is possible to question * * * the educational wisdom of this solution, it is not for the courts to do so. As long as the act was within the power of the city board [and, here, also the chancellor], which it was, the courts may not interfere. The courts may not under the guise of enforcing a vague educational public policy, suggested to it, assume the exercise of educational policy vested by constitution and statute in school administrative agencies. This is not to say that there may never be gross violations of defined public policy which the courts would be obliged to recognize and correct.' (*Matter of New York City School Bds. Assn. v. Board of Educ.,* 39 N.Y.2d 111, 121, 383 N.Y.S.2d 208, 347 N.E.2d 568, *supra.*) Under the circumstances presented, judicial intervention, of even a temporary nature, was unwarranted and in excess of authority.

* * * * * *

"In this case, petitioners raise 'questions of judgment, discretion, allocation of resources and priorities inappropriate for resolution in the judicial arena'. (*Matter of Abrams v. New York City Tr. Auth.,* 39 N.Y.2d 990, 992, 387 N.Y.S.2d 235, 355 N.E.2d 289.) The responsibility for resolving these questions is vested in a network of officials and boards, on both the local and State level. To permit this injunction to stand, and this proceeding to be continued, 'would in effect attempt displacement, or at least overview by the courts and plaintiffs in litigations, of the lawful acts of appointive and elective officials charged with the management of' the New York City

624

public school system (39 N.Y.2d at p. 992, 387 N.Y.S.2d 235, 355 N.E.2d 289). With these officials, the matter rests." (See, also, *Board of Educ. v. Areman,* 41 N.Y.2d 527, 394 N.Y.S.2d 143, 362 N.E.2d 943; *Matter of New York City School Bds. Assn. v. Board of Educ. of City School Dist. of City of N. Y.,* 39 N.Y.2d 111, 383 N.Y.S.2d 208, 347 N.E.2d 568.)

The plaintiff's second cause of action sounds in negligence and alleges the breach of a duty found in the State Constitution (art. XI, § 1) and enabling legislation (Education Law, art. 65). It is our opinion that these enactments merely require the creation of a system of free common schools. Their purpose is to confer the benefits of a free education upon what would otherwise be an uneducated public. They were not intended to protect against the "injury" of ignorance, for every individual is born lacking knowledge, education and experience. For this reason the failure of educational achievement cannot be characterized as an "injury" within the meaning of tort law (*Peter W. v. San Francisco Unified School Dist.,* 60 Cal.App.3d 814, 826, 131 Cal.Rptr. 854, *supra*). It is a well-established principle of torts that statutes which are not intended to protect against injury, but rather are designed to confer a benefit upon the general public, do not give rise to a cause of action by an individual to recover damages for their breach (*Steitz v. City of Beacon,* 295 N.Y. 51, 56, 64 N.E.2d 704, 706; *Moch Co. v. Rensselaer Water Co.,* 247 N.Y. 160, 166, 159 N.E. 896, 898; Restatement Torts 2d, § 288, subd. [c]).

The dissent seeks to sustain the second cause of action asserted in the plaintiff's complaint by concluding that the plaintiff has adequately alleged a substantive violation of former section 4404 of the Education Law. That section required, *inter alia,* that each pupil who continuously failed or who was listed as an "under-achiever" be evaluated to ascertain the physical, mental and social causes of the under-achievement and to further determine if the pupil might benefit from special educational programs. Although the plaintiff was a member of the class of pupils denominated as "under-achievers", the defendant's alleged failure to take the actions required thereby did not give rise to an action sounding in tort. For the reasons stated above, this statute was not intended to protect the plaintiff from injury, rather, it merely reflected a legislative direction that greater educational resources be allocated toward satisfying the learning needs of so-called "under-achievers". The grades on the plaintiff's periodic report cards gave notice both to his parents and himself that he had failed in two or more subjects, thus meeting the definition of an "under-achiever" provided in the regulations of the Commissioner of Education (8 NYCRR 203.1[2]). Having this knowledge, the plaintiff could properly have demanded the special testing and evaluation directed by the statute. Upon the defendant's failure to do so, the plaintiff's remedy would then have been an appeal to the State Commissioner of Education (see Education Law, § 310, subd. 7). As stated by the Court of Appeals in *James v. Board of Educ.,* 42 N.Y.2d 357, 366, 397 N.Y.S.2d 934, 941, 366 N.E.2d 1291, 1297, *supra):*

"The general legislative and constitutional system for the maintenance of public schools secures review by the board of education and, on the State level, by the Commissioner of Education. The purpose of these provisions 'is to make all matters pertaining to the general school system of the state within the authority and control of the department of education and to remove the same so far as practicable and possible from controversies in the courts.' (*Bullock v. Cooley,* 225 N.Y. 566, 576, 577, 122 N.E. 630; see, also, *People ex rel. Board of Educ. v. Finley,* 211 N.Y. 51, 57, 105 N.E. 109.) Indeed, at one time, the statute specifically forbade review of the commissioner's decision 'in any place or court whatever'. (Education Law, § 310, amd. by L.1976, ch. 857, § 1.) Although the determinations of the Commissioner of Education are now specifically subject to review, pursuant to CPLR article 78, in the same fashion as those of other administrative officers or bodies (see Governor's Memorandum of Approval, 2 McKinney's Session Laws of N.Y. [1976], p. 2450), the statutory alteration is of limited impact for, even under prior law, the courts possessed the authority to set aside the commissioner's decisions if arbitrary or illegal."

Finally, the plaintiff's complaint must be dismissed because of the practical impossibility of demonstrating that a breach of the alleged common law and statutory duties was the proximate cause of his failure to learn. The failure to learn does not bespeak a failure to teach. It is not alleged that the plaintiff's classmates, who were exposed to the identical classroom instruction, also failed to learn. From this it may reasonably be inferred that the plaintiff's illiteracy resulted from other causes. A school system cannot compel a particular student to study or to be interested in education. Here, the plaintiff is not totally illiterate and his academic record indicates satisfactory achievement in several subjects. In addition to innate intelligence, the extent to which a child learns is influenced by a host of social, emotional, economic and other factors which are not subject to control by a system of public education. In this context, it is virtually impossible to calculate to what extent, if any, the defendant's acts or omissions proximately caused the plaintiff's inability to read at his appropriate grade level.

Accordingly, we hold that the public policy of this State recognizes no cause of action for educational malpractice. We note that unlike the case of *Peter W., supra,* the complaint here contains no allegation of a cause of action for intentional and fraudulent misrepresentation. We, therefore, do not pass upon the viability of any such cause of action.

Order of the Supreme Court, Suffolk County, dated August 31, 1977, affirmed, without costs or disbursements.

RABIN and HAWKINS, JJ., concur.

SUOZZI, J., dissents and votes to reverse the order, deny the branch of defendant's motion which sought to dismiss the complaint for failure to state a cause of action and remand the action to Special Term to determine whether plaintiff complied with section 3813 of the Education Law, with an opinion.

SUOZZI, Justice (dissenting).

In my view, the complaint states a valid cause of action.

The first cause of action sounds in negligence and malpractice and alleges, *inter alia,* that the defendant school district was under a duty to educate the plaintiff and qualify him for a high school graduation certificate and the defendant failed to properly perform that duty.

As a second cause of action, plaintiff alleges the breach of a constitutional duty under section 1 of article XI of the State Constitution. This provision of the Constitution states:

"The legislature shall provide for the maintenance and support of a system of free common schools, wherein all the children of this state may be educated."

In dismissing the first cause of action, the Special Term and the majority rely on a decision of an appellate court in California which dismissed a very similar cause of action (*Peter W. v. San Francisco Unified School Dist.*, 60 Cal.App.3d 814, 131 Cal. Rptr. 854). An examination of the decision in *Peter W.* reveals that the cause of action was dismissed because of two distinct policy considerations (*Peter W.*, 60 Cal.App.3d 814, 824-825, 131 Cal.Rptr. 854, 861, *supra*):

1. "[T]hat the achievement of literacy in the schools, or its failure, are influenced by a host of factors which affect the pupil subjectively, from outside the formal teaching process, and beyond the control of its ministers. They may be physical, neurological, emotional, cultural, environmental; they may be present but not perceived, recognized but not identified."
2. "To hold [schools] * * * to an actionable 'duty of care,' in the discharge of their academic functions, would expose them to the tort claims — real or imagined — of disaffected students and parents in countless numbers * * * The ultimate consequences, in terms of public time and money, would burden them — and society — beyond calculation."

In dismissing the second cause of action for breach of a constitutional duty, the Special Term relied primarily on two New York Court of Appeals cases (*Steitz v. City of Beacon*, 295 N.Y. 51, 64 N.E.2d 704 and *Moch Co. v. Rensselaer Water Co.*, 247 N.Y. 160, 159 N.E. 896).

In *Moch*, the defendant, a waterworks company, contracted with a city to supply water for various needs, including service at fire hydrants. During the period that the contract was in force, a building caught fire, spread to plaintiff's warehouse and destroyed it. Plaintiff brought suit against the water company for failing to supply adequate water pressure and failing to stop the spread of fire before it reached plaintiff's warehouse.

In dismissing a cause of action for breach of a statutory duty (as well as for breach of contract and for common-law tort), the court stressed that the statutory duty was merely one to furnish water and that there was nothing in the statutory requirements to "enlarge the zone of liability where an inhabitant of the city suffers indirect or incidental damage through deficient pressure at the hydrants" (*Moch, supra,* p. 169, 159 N.E. p. 899).

In *Steitz, supra,* 295 N.Y. p. 54, 64 N.E.2d p. 705, plaintiff brought an action against the defendant city to recover for damage to property from fire, based on a City Charter which provided that the city "'may construct and operate a system of water-works'" and that "'it shall maintain fire, police, school and poor departments'." In dismissing the cause of action, the Court of Appeals stated (p. 55, 64 N.E.2d p. 706):

"Quite obviously these provisions were not in terms designed to protect the personal interest of any individual and clearly were designed to secure the benefits of well ordered municipal government enjoyed by all as members of the community. There was indeed a public duty to maintain a fire department, but that was all, and there was no suggestion that for any omission in keeping hydrants, valves or pipes in repair the people of the city could recover fire damages to their property. "An intention to impose upon the city the crushing burden of such an obligation should not be imputed to the Legislature in the absence of language clearly designed to have that effect."

Finally, Special Term noted that the commencement of this action had received substantial attention in educational circles and the news media and that this factor, coupled with the recent adoption of 8 NYCRR 3.45 by the Board of Regents, effective June 1, 1979, indicated that this case posed a grave policy question which should be passed upon by appellate courts. The regulation adopted by the Board of Regents states:

"3.45 Diplomas. No high school diploma shall be conferred which does not represent four years or their equivalent in grades above grade eight, and no such diploma shall be conferred upon a pupil who has not achieved a passing rating in each of the basic competency tests established by the commissioner."

Initially, it must be emphasized that the policy considerations enunciated in *Peter W., supra,* do not mandate a dismissal of the complaint. Whether the failure of the plaintiff to achieve a basic level of literacy was caused by the negligence of the school system, as the plaintiff alleges, or was the product of forces outside the teaching process, is really a question of proof to be resolved at a trial. The fear of a flood of litigation, perhaps much of it without merit, and the possible difficulty in framing an appropriate measure of damages, are similarly unpersuasive grounds for dismissing the instant cause of action. Fear of excessive litigation caused by the creation of a new zone of liability was effectively refuted by the abolition of sovereign immunity many years ago, and numerous environmental actions fill our courts where damages are difficult to assess. Under the circumstances, there is no reason to differentiate between educational malpractice on the one hand, and other forms of negligence and malpractice litigation which currently congest our courts.

Over and above these preliminary observations, there are additional reasons which dictate against dismissal of the complaint at this stage and which were not discussed by Special Term or by the majority.

The complaint herein is not drafted solely in terms of educational malpractice, i. e., the failure of the school system to successfully teach plaintiff at a certain level. The complaint also charges the following:

(1) That the plaintiff failed various subjects;
(2) That the defendant was aware of these failures; and
(3) That the defendant failed in its duty to ascertain the reason for these failures and to prescribe appropriate corrective measures, if necessary.

The language of the complaint is illustrative:

630

"[T]he defendant * * * gave * * failing grades in various subjects; failed to evaluate the plaintiff's mental ability and capacity to comprehend the subjects being taught to him at said school; failed to take proper means and precautions that they reasonably should have taken under the circumstances; failed to * * psychologically test the plaintiff in order to ascertain his ability to comprehend and understand such subject matter".

That the plaintiff was failing various subjects is readily demonstrable from his high school transcript, which is part of the record and which has numerous course failures (grades below 65, the listed passing grade) designated thereon, including two in English. Nor can the defendant claim that these failing grades did not violate any educational standard. It is true that the regulation of the Board of Regents establishing competency tests and passing grades thereon as a requirement for receipt of a diploma (8 NYCRR 3.45) will not be effective until June 1, 1979. However, it should be emphasized that at present, and during the plaintiff's four years at the defendant's high school, the State Commissioner had a regulation in effect which provided (8 NYCRR 103.2):

"103.2 High school diplomas. In order to secure a State diploma of any type the following requirements must be met:
"(a) The satisfactory completion of an approved four-year course of study in a registered four-year or six-year secondary school, including English, social studies including American history, health, physical education and such other special requirements as are required by statute and (regents regulations) established by the Commissioner of Education."

Anyone reading the plaintiff's high school transcript would be hard pressed to describe his work as a "satisfactory completion" of a course of study.

Having established that the plaintiff was failing numerous courses, which fact was known to school authorities, the crucial question to be resolved is whether the school had a duty under these circumstances to do more than merely promote this plaintiff in a perfunctory manner from one year to the next.

631

In this regard, former section 4404 of the Education Law, which was in effect at the time the plaintiff was attending defendant's high school, is crucial. Subdivision 4 of that statute provided, in pertinent part:

"The board of education of each school district shall cause suitable examinations to be made to ascertain the physical, mental and social causes of * * * 'under-achievement' of every pupil in a public school, not attending a special class, who has failed continuously in his studies or is listed as an 'under-achiever'. Such examinations shall be made in such manner and at such times as shall be established by the commissioner of education, to determine if such a child is incapable of benefiting through ordinary classroom instruction, and whether such child may be expected to profit from special educational facilities. The commissioner of education shall prescribe such reasonable rules and regulations as he may deem necessary to carry out the provisions of this paragraph."

Section 203.1 of the commissioner's regulations provides:

"Children who fail or under-achieve.

* * * * * *

"(2) A pupil who 'has failed continuously in his studies' within the meaning of subdivision 4 of section 4404 of the Education Law is one who has failed in two or more subjects of study for a year."

An examination of the plaintiff's transcript indicates that he came within the definition of a pupil who "failed continuously". Despite this fact, the complaint alleges that the defendant "failed to * * * psychologically test the plaintiff in order to ascertain his ability to comprehend and understand such subject matter", which was in direct contravention of the mandate of former section 4404 (subd. 4) of the Education Law.

The plaintiff has, therefore, shown the existence of a mandatory statutory duty flowing from the defendant to him personally and has alleged the breach thereof by the defendant. To dismiss

632

the complaint, as the majority proposes, without allowing the plaintiff his day in court, would merely serve to sanction misfeasance in the educational system.

In my view, the negligence alleged in the case at bar is not unlike that of a doctor who, although confronted with a patient with a cancerous condition, fails to pursue medically accepted procedures to (1) diagnose the specific condition and (2) treat the condition, and instead allows the patient to suffer the inevitable consequences of the disease. Such medical malpractice would never be tolerated. At the very least, a complaint alleging same would not be dismissed upon motion. In the case at bar, the plaintiff displayed, through his failing grades, a serious condition with respect to his ability to learn. Although mindful of this learning disability, the school authorities made no attempt, as they were required to do, by appropriate and educationally accepted testing procedures, to diagnose the nature and extent of his learning problem and thereafter to take or recommend remedial measures to deal with this problem. Instead, the plaintiff was just pushed through the educational system without any attempt made to help him. Under these circumstances, the cause of action at bar is no different from the analogous cause of action for medical malpractice and, like the latter, is sufficient to withstand a motion to dismiss.

Finally, it should be noted that even in *Peter W. v. San Francisco Unified School District,* 60 Cal.App.3d 814, 131 Cal.Rptr. 845, *supra,* the California appellate court recognized that a cause of action for intentional and fraudulent misrepresentation, if properly pleaded, could withstand a motion to dismiss. Accordingly, even though the majority has chosen to affirm the dismissal of the complaint, that affirmance should be without prejudice to replead a cause of action for intentional misrepresentation.

For the reasons heretofore set forth, I dissent and vote to deny that branch of the defendant's motion which sought to dismiss the complaint for failure to state a cause of action. It should be noted that the defendant also moved to dismiss the complaint based upon the plaintiff's failure to file a timely notice of claim pursuant to section 3813 of the Education Law. Since the Special Term dismissed the complaint for failure to state a cause of ac-

633

tion, it did not deal at all with the second branch of the defendant's motion, i. e., the plaintiff's failure to serve a timely notice of claim. Accordingly, I would remand to Special Term for determination of that issue.

Appendix 8

DONOHUE

v.

COPIAGUE UNION FREE SCHOOL DISTRICT

Court of Appeals of New York.

June 14, 1979.

Bernard M. Rosen and Sidney R. Siben, Bay Shore, appellant.

Henry A. Weinstein and Charles D. Maurer, Garden City, for respondent.

JASEN, Judge.

This appeal poses the question whether a complaint seeking monetary damages for "educational malpractice" states a cause of action cognizable in the courts.

Appellant entered Copiague Senior High School in September, 1972 and graduate in June 1976. The thrust of appellant's claim is that notwithstanding his receipt of a certificate of graduation he lacks even the rudimentary ability to comprehend written English on a level sufficient to enable him to complete applications for employment. His complaint attributes this deficiency to the failure of respondent to perform its duties and obligations to educate appellant. To be more specific, appellant alleges in his complaint that respondent through its employees "gave to [appellant] passing grades and/or minimal or failing grades in various subjects; failed to evaluate [appellant's] mental ability and capacity to comprehend the subjects being taught to him at said school; failed to take proper means and precautions that they reasonably should have taken under the circumstances; failed to interview, discuss, evaluate and/or psychologically test [appellant] in order to ascertain his ability to comprehend and understand such matter; failed to provide adequate school facilities, teachers, administrators, psychologists, and other personnel trained to take the necessary steps in testing and evaluation processes insofar as [appellant] is concerned in order to ascertain the learning capacity, intelligence and intellectual absorption on the part of [appellant]".

Based upon these acts of commission and omission, appellant frames two causes of action, the first of which sounds in "educational malpractice" and the second of which alleges the negligent breach of a constitutionally imposed duty to educate. To redress his injury, appellant seeks the sum of $5,000,000. Upon respondent's motion, Special Term dismissed appellant's complaint for failure to state a cause of action. (CPLR 3211, subd. [a], par. 7.) The Appellate Division affirmed, with one Justice dissenting. There should be an affirmance.

The second cause of action need not detain us long. The State Constitution (art. XI, § 1) commands that "[t]he legislature shall provide for the maintenance and support of a system of free common schools, wherein all the children of this state may be educated." Even a terse reading of this provision reveals that the constitution places the obligation of *maintaining and supporting* a system of public schools upon the *Legislature.* To be sure, this general directive was never intended to impose a duty flowing directly from a local school district to individual pupils to ensure that each pupil receives a minimum level of education, the breach of which duty would entitle a pupil to compensatory damages. (See *Steitz v. City of Beacon,* 295 N.Y. 51, 57, 64 N.E.2d 704, 707; *Moch Co. v. Rensselaer Water Co.,* 247 N.Y. 160, 169, 159 N.E. 896, 899.)

Appellant's first cause of action bears closer scrutiny. It may very well be that even within the strictures of a traditional negligence or malpractice action, a complaint sounding in "educational malpractice" may be formally pleaded. Thus, the imagination need not be overly taxed to envision allegations of a legal duty of care flowing from educators, if viewed as professionals, to their students. If doctors, lawyers, architects, engineers and other professionals are charged with a duty owing to the public whom they serve, it could be said that nothing in the law precludes similar treatment of professional educators. Nor would creation of a standard with which to judge an educator's performance of that duty necessarily pose an insurmountable obstacle. (See, generally, Elson, A Common Law Remedy for the Educa-

636

tional Harms Caused by Incompetent or Careless Teaching, 73 N.W.L.Rev. 641, 693-744). As for proximate causation, while this element might indeed be difficult, if not impossible, to prove in view of the many collateral factors involved in the learning process, it perhaps assumes too much to conclude that it could never be established. This would leave only the element of injury and who can in good faith deny that a student who upon graduation from high school cannot comprehend simple English — a deficiency allegedly attributable to the negligence of his educators — has not in some fashion been "injured".

The fact that a complaint alleging "educational malpractice" might on the pleadings state a cause of action within traditional notions of tort law does not, however, require that it be sustained. The heart of the matter is whether, assuming that such a cause of action may be stated, the courts should, as a matter of public policy, entertain such claims. We believe they should not.

Control and management of educational affairs is vested in the Board of Regents and the Commissioner of Education (N.Y. Const., art. V, § 4; art. XI, § 2; Education Law, §§ 207, 305; see *Matter of New York City School Bds. Assn. v. Board of Educ.*, 39 N.Y.2d 111, 116, 383 N.Y.S.2d 208, 211, 347 N.E.2d 568, 571; *Matter of Ocean Hill-Brownsville Governing Bd. v. Board of Educ.*, 23 N.Y.2d 483, 485, 297 N.Y.S.2d 568, 569, 245 N.E.2d 219, 220). We have only recently observed: "The general legislative and constitutional system for the maintenance of public schools secures review by the board of education and, on the State level, by the Commissioner of Education. The purpose of these provisions 'is to make all matters pertaining to the general school system of the state within the authority and control of the department of education and to remove the same so far as practicable and possible from controversies in the courts.' (*Bullock v. Cooley*, 225 N.Y. 566, 576-577, 122 N.E. 630, 633; see, also, *People ex rel. Board of Educ. v. Finley*, 211 N.Y. 51, 57, 105 N.E. 109, 110.)" (*James v. Board of Educ.*, 42 N.Y.2d 357, 366, 397 N.Y.S.2d 934, 941, 366 N.E.2d 1291, 1297).

In *James*, we refused to entertain an action to enjoin the administration to pupils in the New York City school system of comprehensive reading and mathematical exams the validity of

637

which had allegedly been compromised. Notwithstanding the existence of a statutory duty (Education Law, § 2590-j, subd. 5, par. [a]), on the part of the Chancellor of the City School District of the City of New York to administer comprehensive examinations annually, we held that the question whether these examinations had been compromised depriving them of their validity as a gauge of academic achievement rested in the professional judgment and discretion of the chancellor, the board of education and, ultimately that of the Commissioner of Education, rather than in the courts. (*James v. Board of Educ.*, 42 N.Y.2d, at p. 366, 397 N.Y.S.2d at p. 941, 366 N.E.2d at p. 1297, *supra;* see, also, *Matter of Bokhair v. Board of Educ.*, 43 N.Y.2d 855, 856, 403 N.Y.S.2d 216, 217, 374 N.E.2d 127, 128; *Matter of Vetere v. Allen*, 15 N.Y.2d 259, 267, 258 N.Y.S.2d 77, 80, 206 N.E.2d 174, 176, cert. den. 382 U.S. 825, 86 S.Ct. 60, 15 L.Ed.2d 71; *Bullock v. Cooley*, 225 N.Y. 566, 576-577, 122 N.E. 630, 633-634, *supra*; cf. *Jones v. Beame*, 45 N.Y.2d 402, 407, 408 N.Y.S.2d 449, 451, 380 N.E.2d 277, 279.)

This principle applies all the more to the case at hand. To entertain a cause of action for "educational malpractice" would require the courts not merely to make judgments as to the validity of broad educational policies — a course we have unalteringly eschewed in the past — but, more importantly, to sit in review of the day-to-day implementation of these policies. Recognition in the courts of this cause of action would constitute blatant interference with the responsibility for the administration of the public school system lodged by Constitution and statute in school administrative agencies. (*James v. Board of Educ.*, 42 N.Y.2d at p. 367, 397 N.Y.S.2d at p. 942, 366 N.E.2d at p. 1298, *supra*.) Of course, "[t]his is not to say that there may never be gross violations of defined public policy which the courts would be obliged to recognize and correct." (*Matter of New York City School Bds. Assn. v. Board of Educ.*, 39 N.Y.2d at p. 121, 383 N.Y.S.2d at p. 214, 347 N.E.2d at p. 574, *supra*.)

Finally, not to be overlooked in today's holding is the right of students presently enrolled in public schools, and their parents, to take advantage of the administrative processes provided by statute to enlist the aid of the Commissioner of Education in

638

ensuring that such students receive a proper education. The Education Law (§ 310, subd. 7) permits any person aggrieved by an "official act or decision of any officer, school authorities, or meetings concerning any other matter under this chapter, or any other act pertaining to common schools" to seek review of such act or decision by the commissioner.

Accordingly, the order of the Appellate Division should be affirmed, with costs.

WACHTLER, Judge (concurring).

I agree that complaints of "educational malpractice" are for school administrative agencies, rather than the courts, to resolve.

There is, however, another even more fundamental objection to entertaining plaintiff's cause of action alleging educational malpractice. It is a basic principle that the law does not provide a remedy for every injury (*Howard v. Lecher,* 42 N.Y.2d 109, 113, 397 N.Y.S.2d 363, 365, 366 N.E.2d 64, 66). As the majority notes, the decision of whether a new cause of action should be recognized at law is largely a question of policy. Critical to such a determination is whether the cause of action sought to be pleaded would be reasonably manageable within our legal system. The practical problems raised by a cause of action sounding in educational malpractice are so formidable that I would conclude that such a legal theory should not be cognizable in our courts. These problems clearly articulated at the Appellate Division, include the practical impossibility of proving that the alleged malpractice of the teacher proximately caused the learning deficiency of the plaintiff student. Factors such as the student's attitude, motivation, temperament, past experience and home environment may all play an essential and immeasureable role in learning. Indeed as the majority observes proximate cause might "be difficult, if not impossible, to prove".

I would, therefore, affirm the order of the Appellate Division on the ground that educational malpractice, as here pleaded, is not a cognizable cause of action.

COOKE, C. J., and JONES and FUCHSBERG, JJ., concur with JASEN, J.

WACHTLER, J., concurs in a separate opinion in which GABRIELLI, J., concurs.

Order affirmed.

Appendix 9

HOFFMAN
v.
BOARD OF EDUCATION OF THE CITY OF NEW YORK

Supreme Court, Appellate Division,
Second Department.
Nov. 6, 1978.

Allen G. Schwartz, Corp. Counsel, New York City (Bernard Burstein and L. Kevin Sheridan, New York City, of counsel), for appellant.

Pazer & Epstein, New York City (Perr Pazer and Helen B. Stoller, New York City of counsel), for respondent.

Before MARTUSCELLO, J. P., and DAMIANI, SHAPIRO, COHALAN and O'CONNOR, JJ.

SHAPIRO, Justice.

This is an appeal from a judgment of the Supreme Court, Queens County, which is in favor of the plaintiff, upon a jury verdict in the principal amount of $750,000. By the reasons hereafter stated, the judgment should be reversed and a new trial granted unless plaintiff stipulates to accept to produce the principal amount of the verdict $500,000.

Shortly after starting kindergarten in September, 1956, plaintiff was placed in a class for Children with Retarded Mental Development (CRMD) based upon a determination by defendant's certified psychologist that the child had an intelligent quotient (I.Q.) of 74. *Seventy-five was the cut-off point fixed by the defendant, so that if plaintiff had been given a rating of 75 he would not have been found to be retarded and would not have been sent to a class for mentally retarded children. He remained in classes for the retarded for 11 years,* until he was 17 years of age. At that age he was transferred to the Occupational Training Center for the retarded. He remained there for one year; at the start of the second year, in September, 1969, he was advised that he would not be continued there because an I.Q. test administered in May, 1969 showed that he was not retarded.

641

THE FACTS.

Plaintiff was born in April, 1951. He lived with his parents, an older sister and his paternal grandmother in Ridgewood, Queens. His father died when plaintiff was 13 months old. IIis mother became the breadwinner; she went to work as a bottle washer for Pfizer and Co., leaving the plaintiff in his grandmother's care during her working hours.

Before his father's death, plaintiff had started talking and walking. He retrogressed after his father's death; for a while he stopped both walking and talking. His speech was still not normal at the time of the trial.

In February, 1956, when plaintiff was 4 years and 10 months old, his mother took him to the National Hospital for Speech Disorders. The hospital's records noted that plaintiff was "a friendly child with little or no intelligible speech. Produces infantile equivalents for names of some objects—or will vocalize in imitations of inflection *** Appears to be retarded and should have psychological [sic]." It also noted: "Mongoloid eyes, otherwise no Mongoloid features". The stated "impression" was "borderline Mongolism". Plaintiff, in fact, was not a Mongoloid child. The notation of "Mongoloid eyes" apparently referred to the fact that the angles on each side of his eyes formed by the junction of the upper and lower lids was somewhat greater than is usual among occidental children. Also, he had unusually large ears, a characteristic he had inherited from his mother.[1]

One month later, on March 5, 1956, a nonverbal intelligence test known as the Merrill-Palmer Test was administered to plaintiff by a psychologist employed by the same hospital. *Plaintiff scored an I.Q. of 90, with a mental age of 4 years and 5*

---

1. As testified by Dr. Lawrence Kaplan, there is no such thing as "borderline Mongoloid". Down's syndrome (popularly known as Mongoloidism) is associated with a variable constellation of stigmata, caused by chromosomal abnormality; as stated in Stedman's Medical Dictionary (Fourth Lawyers' Edition, 1976, p. 1382), "no single physical sign is diagnostic and most stigmata are found in some normal persons"; one of these is *small* ears.

months, as against his actual age of 4 years and 11 months. This was within the range of normal intelligence. The "interpretation" included the note that "his range—particularly whenever form perception and problem-solving acuity are involved—indicates that he can work well into the average and even brighter range. Shows some over-dependent and restrictive characteristics, but eventually manages to adjust** Performance suggests organic dysfunction in speech expressive area, since he generally appears to understand well & respond as well as able to questions & directions." Pursuant to the follow-up recommendation, plaintiff's mother took plaintiff to the New York Speech Institute for weekly therapy for some period of time and, apparently, until after plaintiff's placement in his first CRMD class.

Plaintiff entered Kindergarten at his neighborhood school, P.S. 81, Queens, in September, 1956. Four months later, on January 9, 1957, Monroe Gottsegen, a certified clinical psychologist who started his employment with defendant about a week earlier, administered the primarily verbal Stanford-Binet Intelligence Test. At that time, Dr. Gottsegen had had his Master's degree for six years, during which period he had tested about 1,000 children. His report, dated January 23, 1957, included the following:

"Mongolian tendencies, severe speech defects, slow in response.
"RECOMMENDATION:

Eligible for placement in a CRMD class at P 77 Q in September 1957.

* * * * * *

"Danny impresses as a shy, cooperative youngster. <u>Mongoloid features are observable</u>.[2] There is a marked speech defect which makes Danny hesitant in speaking up. He obviously understands more than he is able to communicate. With care-

---

2. In this respect Dr. Gottsegen's report makes the same error that had been made in the earlier report of the National Hospital for Speech Disorders.

643

ful listening, it is frequently possible to understand what he is driving at.

"On the Stanford-Binet, L, he achieves a mental age of 4 3 and an I.Q. of 74, indicating borderline intelligence. The obtained I.Q. may be higher than it ought to be as the Examiner was confronted with the task of having to interpret what Danny was trying to say, Danny being given the benefit of the doubt when it seemed reasonable to do so.

"Danny is frequently bored in class and needs a specialized individualized teaching program. At this point, a continued, yet varied readiness program should be offered him. He is not yet able to do formal learning. He needs help with his speech problem in order that he be able to learn to make himself understood. *Also his intelligence should be re-evaluated within a two-year period so that a more accurate estimation of his abilities can be made.*" (Underscoring in original, except for emphasis of last sentence.)

Dr. Gottsegen testified as a witness for plaintiff pursuant to a subpoena. He stated that he recommended CRMD placement because an *I.Q. of 75 was the cut-off point pursuant to State law* and because of "the general incapacities that seemed to be there." In discussing his difficulty in understanding plaintiff's speech, he testified:

"It was like listening to a radio at a very low level, with a lot of static. *You think you know what is being said, but you can't be that sure, and I think that comes through here, that I really wasn't sure and that's why we wanted him retested within two years.* This was always Bureau procedure.[3] We were always concerned in the B.C.G. not to make mistakes with kids and we were careful to see to it if we had doubts about what we were doing, that *we recommend that he be retested and say it, and that's what happened here.*" (Emphasis supplied.)

When asked whether his notation "slow in response" was due to plaintiff's speech or to "slow mentality", he answered that it

---

3. This refers to the Bureau of Child Guidance (B.C.G.), where Dr. Gottsegen had been previously employed.

was very hard to determine this, that "[a]ll we could note was the slowness of the response and make a judgment" and that "very frequently the issue that creates the retardation may have some subtle organic component, which also affects speech and could affect hearing and balance and various other characteristics". He also testified that *"[i]t was assumed that there was retardation and there were also contributing factors. How much was a pure retardation and how much was the result of contributing factors couldn't be known, at least by me *** It was my feeling there was retardation, but I doubted some of the results and therefore I suggested a retesting."* (Emphasis supplied.)

Despite his borderline finding of retardation and that "he doubted some of the results", he made no request to interview plaintiff's mother, or to learn whether plaintiff had been receiving treatment for his speech condition. Indeed, no attempt was made to obtain his social history and the mother was never told that the diagnosis of retardation was based on her son's falling short of the cut-off score of 75 by only one point or that, upon her request, the school authorities, *by their own rules,* would be required to retest the child. If they had informed her of her right to have her son retested, they might well have learned that he had achieved an I.Q. rating of 90 on the nonverbal Miller-Palmer Test given only 10 months earlier at the National Hospital for Speech Disorders.

Plaintiff's mother was called to plaintiff's school after the administration of the I.Q. test in January, 1957. She then spoke to someone in the Principal's office. She testified:

"He told me they had a report from the Bureau of Child Guidance that my son was a Mongoloid child, and I asked him, I said, 'Well, what can I do?' and he says, 'Well, there are several things you can do. One, you can put him in an institution.' And I believe I asked him if that meant keeping him away from home and I told him I could never do that and then he says, 'The only thing, they could put him in special classes.' *** He said they didn't have special classes in 81. I said, well, I would agree to it as long as he could stay home and I believe I left after that. I really couldn't tell you. I do know I started to walk

645

and I walked and I walked home and I was crying, but it wasn't long after that that they transferred him to P.S. 11."

Because of plaintiff's CRMD placement, he was transferred to P.S. 11 on October 11, 1957 and remained there for two years. Thereafter he was transferred to P.S. 77 and then to P.S. 88; he remained in each school for two years; in September, 1963 he was transferred to P.S. 87, where he remained for one year; in September, 1964 he was transferred to P.S. 93, where he remained until the close of the 1967/1968 academic year. During all of this time, plaintiff resided at the same address. In September, 1968 he was transferred to the Queens Occupational Training Center (OTC). This is a manual and shop training school for retarded youths which provides no academic education. At the start of his second school year there (September, 1969) he was told that since it had been determined that he was not retarded he was not eligible to remain at the OTC.

In 1959 and 1960 (when plaintiff was respectively eight and nine years old) he received a "90 percentile" rating as to reading readiness. This placed him in the top 10% of persons who were ready to learn how to read. Nevertheless, his reading achievements (based on standardized achievement tests given twice a year) were extremely low. Thus, at the age of 9, his reading level was 1.7 (i. e., less than second year level); when he was 10, the level dropped to 1.6, and it remained at that level when he was 11. His achievement tests in mathematics were somewhat higher, but still well below what would be expected of a child in a regular class. When he was 13½ years old, his reading level was 1.7 and his mathematics level was 2.6. However, as the expert witnesses on both sides agreed, *achievement* tests are not definitive tests of *intelligence*.

Defendant's explanation for not having plaintiff's intelligence retested (until he was 18) may be summarized as follows:

Up to 1968 it was not its practice to retest CRMD children unless requested by the child's parent or teacher. As to the latter, the achievement tests showed such dismal results that plaintiff's teacher always assumed that his I.Q. was no better than originally indicated. However, they apparently gave no consideration

646

to the fact that his severe speech problem and the emotional fall-out therefrom might have masked a higher intelligence than that indicated by the achievement tests.

As to plaintiff's mother not having requested a retesting, it must be iterated that she had not been told of plaintiff's border-line I.Q. or that defendant's rules gave her the unqualified right to demand a retest. She testified that when she took plaintiff to his first CRMD class (in October, 1957), this was what happened:

"There were mothers there with their children and I asked if it was the special class and I was informed that it was. The children looked a little different, but I had no idea. Some of them wouldn't look up at you. They just kept their heads down. I remember one child his head—how shall I say it? He couldn't hold it straight. It just lulled around and his mother tried to help him. I inquired, 'My son is going to this class?' and I was told he was and I asked the teacher and she informed me that was a CRMD class and I said well, I didn't know what that meant and I was again informed that it was for retarded children, and I said, 'You mean to say my son is retarded?' and she said, 'He must be, otherwise he wouldn't be in this class.' Now, I did inquire, I said, 'Will he be getting speech?' She said 'Yes, he'll get everything that is needed here,' and I was very happy about that, and that's how it all started. He was in a retarded class and he stayed there."

On cross-examination of plaintiff's mother, defendant apparently attempted to show that she was to some degree responsible for the failure to have plaintiff retested. She admitted that she had never taken plaintiff to a psychiatrist or psychologist, but this was because she did not know "that there were doctors who treated children who had something wrong with their mind" and she had "never heard of psychiatrists *** It never dawned on me. I was a foreigner unfortunately."[4]

Finally, on May 12, 1969, *after he had been closeted with mentally retarded children for more than 12 years,* plaintiff was ad-

---

4. Her education had stopped at the junior high school level. She had come to the United States from Germany when she was three years old.

ministered an I.Q. test by Dr. William F. Garber of the Bureau of Child Guidance. At that time, plaintiff was one month past his 18th birthday and he was approaching the end of his first year at the Queens Occupational Training Center. Dr. Garber's report explains the reasons for administering that I.Q. test as follows:

"Danny is being re-evaluated as to intellectual status, following an interview with his mother, who came to the school very much disturbed because her son has been rejected by Social Security for continuance of payments after the age of 18, the S.S.A. feeling he was not sufficiently handicapped by his retarded status to pursue gainful employment. On January 9, 1957, the Bureau of Child Guidance found a Binet I.Q. of 74."

Plaintiff was administered a Wechsler Intelligence Scale for Adults (W.A.I.S.) test. He scord a verbal I.Q. of 85 and a performance I.Q. of 107 resulting in a full scale I.Q of 94.

The report of the test includes the following:

"He is a tall, well-built boy, alert looking and charming in manner, who is so incapacitated by a speech defect that communication is difficult for him. He relates very well, displays humor, and appears reality oriented.

"*On the W.A.I.S., he obtained a Verbal Scale I.Q. 85, Performance I.Q. 107, Full Scale I.Q. 94. This places hin the normal range.* However, his superior performance on tests of non-verbal intelligence, as well as the fact that his extremely poor academic background, severely depreciated his scores on some verbal tests, make it very likely that *his intellectual potential is at least Bright Normal.*

"*Projective tests and tracings of geometric designs confirm the impression of good intelligence and contraidicate organicity.* He is however extremely conpulsive, to a degree that sometimes reality testing suffers in his distribution of time for a task.

"*This boy has above average intellectual potential* and a good personality structure. Due to his being almost immobilized in the speech area, as well as considering his extremely defective academic background he would find it difficult, if not impossible, to function in a regular high school. Psychomotor coordination is good, however. Referral to [Division of Vocational Rehabilitation of the State Education Department] is suggested for specialized training and alleviation of the speech problem." (Emphasis supplied.)

Neither plaintiff nor his mother was advised of the test results at that time. Plaintiff remained at the Occupational Training Center until the end of the spring semester. He returned to the OTC on September 8, 1969. His mother testified as to the events of that day:

"Well, my son went to school as usual and then perhaps an hour, maybe an hour and a half later I get a phone call. My son is on the phone. He says, 'They threw me out of school,' and I yelled on the phone, 'What did you do wrong?' He says, 'I didn't do anything. They just said I don't belong here any more.' I said, 'Stay there, don't move, I'll be down.'
"Q. How did he sound?
"A. Very upset. I got in my car, drove down, and when I got there he was sitting on the stoop there. I said, 'C'mon inside.' He said, 'I can't go in there any more.' I said, 'Don't be silly, let's go.' I went inside to the principal's office, I believe it was. I spoke to Dr. Kurtzer and he told me from their tests they discovered he was not retarded and they could no longer keep him there because he doesn't qualify. So I wanted to know, 'What is he going to do now?'

* * * * * *

"Going home, all he kept saying, 'Where am I going to go now? I have no place to go.' That was his life. He got up in the morning. He got dressed, went to school and came home. That was his life. 'Where is he going to go now?'"

She then testified about plaintiff's activities in the following months:

"Well, when I was home—I was still working nights but when I was home he stayed in his room. He wouldn't come out. He'd

649

just close the door. We have a railroad apartment. So I would have to knock on the door to go through the other rooms. "Q. What did you see with relation to what he was doing? "A. He was just sitting in the corner, brooding, crying what was he going to do, he wasn't a little child, he was a grown man."

In December, 1969, at the behest of plaintiff's counsel, plaintiff was examined by Dr. Lawrence I. Kaplan, a neurologist and psychiatrist. At that time plaintiff had been out of the school system for three months. Dr. Kaplan found that plaintiff had a marked stutter, that his articulation was not clear and that he had difficulty in making himself understood. On neurological testing he found him to be normal in all respects and he ruled out any brain damage. Dr. Kaplan elicited that plaintiff had been having symptoms of "being upset, shaking, unable to eat properly, crying, feeling depressed, not sleeping well, walking the floor, had no friends". His opinion was that plaintiff was not mentally retarded, but that he had a "defective self-image and feelings of inadequacy". This was because plaintiff had been placed in a class of mentally retarded children and "this result[ed] in an alteration in his concept of himself, particularly because he is intelligent enough to appreciate the position in which he is placed". Dr. Kaplan added: "If *** [one] is treated as a mentally retarded patient, a person who cannot learn or cannot do something that normal children are doing, he assumes in the long run that that's the role that he should be playing in life and so this diminishes his incentive and diminishes the capacity to learn". He testified that plaintiff was still trainable and that he could be helped with special education and psycho-therapeutic support, but even that could not "correct all the damage of ten years or more of deprivation educationally and of characterization as a mentally retarded person". He continued that when one is told he is not retarded after 13 years of being considered otherwise, one cannot then simply go out and say, "Now I am not retarded. I am going to conquer the world or do something". Plaintiff's acceptance of his role as "retarded" was also understandable on the basis of his serious speech defect. Knowing that

650

he could not speak as well as other children, his self-image was already deflated, making it more likely that he would accept the conclusion that he was retarded.

Dr. Kaplan referred plaintiff to Dr. Lawrence Abt, a clinical psychologist who, in January, 1970, administered several tests including the Wechsler Adult Intelligence Scale. On the predominantly *verbal* part of that test he attained an I.Q. of 89; on the *performance* subtests he attained an I.Q. of 114. Combining the levels of these tests resulted in a full scale I.Q. of 100.[5] He explained that plaintiff's lower score on the verbal part of the test was largely influenced by his schooling. Dr. Abt concluded that plaintiff's learning potential had always been above average and that one of the reasons his intellectual development had been diminished was the assumption of the correctness of the school's diagnosis by his family and others, by reason of which they did not provide the stimulation that would otherwise have been given the child. The result was that, at the time Dr. Abt examined him, plaintiff felt that he was substantially without an education; that he did not know what he could do to earn a living; and that he did not know "where he fitted into the world, and even where he fitted into his family". All this was a competent producing cause of the condition of depression that he noted in plaintiff.

Plaintiff had no additional schooling up to the time of the trial. In August, 1970, when he was 19 years old, he was interviewed by the State Division of Vocational Rehabilitation. Its records show that he was "outgoing, cheerful and desirous of the company of his peers. He misses the Queens Training Center. However, medical examination indicates that *** [his] primary need is for speech training, since he is barely understandable. In addi-

---

5. Plaintiff was also administered a Bender-Gestalt Test which showed no brain damage; a human figure drawing test which showed a sophisticated artistic ability and also indicated at least average intelligence, and a sentence completion test which showed that plaintiff was "in a rather depressed state, that he had a very poor self-image or conception of himself, and that his attitude towards his future was not favorable".

tion to his handicap, his mother seems to have developed a deep need and a habit of doing all of *** [his] communication for him; they have a warm relationship."

The Division of Vocational Rehabilitation provided a speech therapy program for him in the National Hospital for Speech Disorders. He was provided 40 weekly sessions of therapy and he showed slow improvement. In July, 1972, when he was 21 years old, he was referred by his rehabilitation counselor to Dr. Bernard Stillerman, who noted that plaintiff was "very dependent on his mother who not only made the appointment for him but is his verbal contact, for the most part, with the world *** He described himself as being mildly anxious, nervous and tense when he is with people and I assume this was related to his ** speech. He is also moderately depressed because of the speech problem which precludes him from having friends. In fact, he is preoccupied with the thought that he can make friends but cannot keep them because of his speech."

Dr. Kaplan testified that when he saw plaintiff in 1975 (apparently in preparation for the trial) he had progressed in improving his speech, although he continued to have "persistent language problems, chiefly with some stammering and articulatory difficulties".

Plaintiff was trained by the Division of Vocational Rehabilitation to be a messenger and it obtained his first job for him. Thereafter he had 11 different messenger jobs. At the time of the trial he had a part-time job as a messenger, earning $50 per week for 20 hours of work. He testified that he did not like this work. A record of the division, dated June 20, 1973 (when plaintiff was 22 years old) states:

> Recent Psychological testing indicates that the client is capable of performance at a much higher level than was previously determined. The test material indicates that [the] client is capable of training in a skilled mechanical area. His motivation for doing better is extremely high *** He is unable at this time to relate to a specific vocational goal, and it is felt that a period of further evaluation would be appropriate prior to any lengthy training program.

652

At the age of 26 (as of the date of the trial) he had not made any advancement in his vocational life, nor any particular improvement in his social life.

AS TO DEFEDANT'S FAILURE TO FOLLOW THE RECOMMENDATION OF DR. GOTTSEGEN THAT PLAINTIFF'S "INTELLIGENCE SHOULD BE RE-EVALUATED WITHIN A TWO YEAR PERIOD SO THAT A MORE ACCURATE ESTIMATION OF HIS ABILITIES CAN BE MADE".

Defendant's principal argument for reversal is that Dr. Gottsegen's report of January 23, 1957 did *not* recommend that plaintiff be given another I.Q. test within two years, and that his testimony that it did was incredible *as a matter of law* and therefore could not act as a basis for the jury's verdict in favor of the plaintiff. Dr. Gottsegen testified that "we wanted him *retested* within two years" and that it was his "feeling there was retardation" but that he "doubted some of the results and *therefore I suggested a retesting*" (emphasis supplied). He also testified that he had followed the procedure of the Bureau of Child Guidance and "if we had doubts about what we were doing, that we recommend that he be *retested* and say it, and that's what happened here." *At no time was he cross-examined as to the propriety of his conclusion that that was what he had recommended.* Defendant argues, nevertheless, and Mr. Justice MARTUSCELLO agrees, that Dr. Gottsegen's testimony cannot be given factual acceptance because, in his report, he used the words "should be *re-evaluated"* and not "should be *retested".* However, in so arguing, defendant entirely omits to note that the direction was that his "intelligence should be re-evaluated".

It is defendant's position that the words "retest" and "re-evaluate" are words of art with different meanings. "Retest", argues defendant, means to administer a further I.Q. test, while "re-evaluate" means observation of the child and noting his achievements as a basis for determining whether a new I.Q. test should be administered.

Defendant maintains that the continuous observation of plaintiff by his succeeding teachers, each of whom noted the scores on the semi-annual achievement tests, amounted to "a *constant* re-evaluation, with Dr. Gottsegen's report not overriding their own observations." Defendant asserts that the record amply supported their judgments and, further, that if there was a difference of opinion as to this it was no more than an error of professional judgment not severe enough to constitute negligence.

Defendant's analysis flies in the face of the testimony of the expert witnesses on both sides to the effect that intelligence of children is determined in schools (and elsewhere) *only* by I.Q. testing, and that achievement tests and classroom evaluations do not determine the intelligence of a child.[6] Since Dr. Gottsegen's written recommendation was that plaintiff's *"intelligence* should be re-evaluated within a two year period", it could only mean that he was to be administered a new I.Q. test within that period. If it did not have that meaning, it meant nothing, since a CRMD child is alwalys being observed by his teacher for signs of improvement,[7] and achievement tests were being given semi-annually to *all* CRMD children. Actually, it would mean less than nothing for it would (absurdly) mean that (a) instead of the teachers observing him daily, they should do so only once in two years, and (b) instead of giving the required achievement tests twice a year, plaintiff (alone among all CRMDs) should be given such a test only once during the ensuing two years. Yet defendant argues, in effect, that such was the correct interpretation and that it is *incredible* to maintain otherwise.

If in fact Dr. Gottsegen's prescription was equivocal, or his recommendation that plaintiff's "intelligence should be re-evaluated" was puzzling or ambiguous, it was up to the school admin-

---

6. Thus, Dr. Donald Wiedis, a witness for defendant, who trained school psychologists for the Board of Education, testified that intelligence tests have nothing to do with what one has learned in the past and are not designed "to tap academic achievement." Also, Dr. Henry Lipton, who was employed by defendant as a manager of clinical psychology services for his school district, and who appeared as a witness for defendant, testified that although he did not know what Dr. Gottsegen's intent had been, the word "intelligence" would require an I.Q. evaluation (which, of course, could not be done without an I.Q. test).

7. Plaintiff's teachers testified that in a substantial number of cases they had recommended I.Q. retesting, on the basis of which some children were transferred to regular classes.

istration to find out what its own employee meant, for he was paid to give advice, not to intone as a Delphic oracle. In any event, an error due to his lack of clarity, if such there was, would be the responsibility of the Board of Education under the rule of *rcopondoat ouporior*.[8] Several of plaintiff's teachers were called by defendant and each stated that she must have noted Dr. Gottsegen's 1957 report that plaintiff's "intelligence should be re-evaluated" and that notwithstanding that direction no I.Q. tests were given to him at any time after 1957. Thus, plaintiff's teachers failed to follow the direction for a new *"intelligence"* analysis based solely on their observations that plaintiff was doing very poorly on his *"achievement"* tests. Certainly the very least that can be said is that the jury could properly have concluded that if Dr. Gottsegen's 1957 report was ambiguous, each teacher, and therefore the defendant as their employer, was negligent in failing to inquire as to its true meaning. Thus, the failure to follow Dr. Gottsegen's recommendation for an intelligence retesting to determine so vital a matter as whether plaintiff should be continued in a class for retarded children was an egregious error committed on a wholesale basis.

It may be contended that plaintiff's poor results on his achievement tests, his speech and his appearance, might have misled even well-intentioned and devoted teachers, but the obvious answer is that while it was within the professional judgment of each of plaintiff's teachers as to when to *recommend* retesting (based on their own observations or on plaintiff's achievement test scores), *it was not within their province or discretion to prevent Dr. Gottsegen's recommendation from being carried out, no matter* what they might have believed the result of such retesting would be.

---

8. We now know (albeit with hindsight) that Dr. Gottsegen, although he had "given the benefit of the doubt [on his I.Q. testing of plaintiff] when it seemed reasonable to do so", had not given *enough* benefit, since it is now unquestioned that plaintiff's true I.Q. was never as low as 74. That Dr. Gottsegen was doubtful of the accuracy of his conclusion is made manifest by his ordering of a new analysis of plaintiff's intelligence "within a two year period so that a more accurate estimation of his abilities can be made."

Of course plaintiff's teachers could not have had the foresight to know that when plaintiff would reach the age of 18 his intelligence would be found to be well within the normal range. The indisputable fact remains (and defendant now concedes) that plaintiff's intelligence was *always* normal since one's intelligence does not leap from less than three-quarters of average (74) to average (100). While this was masked by plaintiff's massive problems, it should have made no difference to his teachers. If they were right, no more would have been lost than the time and expense of having the school psychologist administer a follow-up test to a child who had been originally classified as having an I.Q. only one point below that required for placement in a regular class.

Fortunately, since 1968 no such error is likely to occur for both New York State and the New York City Board of Education now require frequent and periodic intelligence retesting of children in CRMD classes. Obviously the liability of defendant cannot be based on this later standard. However, for the years following 1957 (and prior to 1968) there were three ways in which a student's intelligence could be retested: the first was by recommendation of his teachers (as it was for all CRMD children); the second was by request of the child's parents (as it was for all CRMD children); the third (and this applies specifically to plaintiff) was where the school psychologist recommended that this should be done.

On the facts in this record, we need not reach the question of whether plaintiff's teachers, on their own, should have recommended I.Q. testing or whether plaintiff's mother was remiss in not requesting it (or, and more to the point, whether defendant was remiss in not advising plaintiff's mother that she had the right to make such a request, in which case it would be granted) since it is not necessary to go any further than to note that the school psychologist's recommendation was totally ignored. Only the test result showing an I Q. of 74 (and apparently the erroneous references to "Mongolian tendencies" and "Mongoloid features") was acted upon; the rest might as well have been written in sand. The consequences of defendant's failure to follow its own psychologist's recommendation were predictable. So little had to

656

be done to avoid the awesome and devastating effect of that on plaintiff's life, and that little was not done.

Citing *James v. Board of Educ. of City of N.Y.,* 42 N.Y.2d 357, 397 N.Y.S.2d 934, 366 N.E.2d 1291, defendant argues and Mr. Justice MARTUSCELLO opines that the issue of whether it had a duty to periodically retest plaintiff's I.Q. should not have been submitted to the jury. Defendant argues that the *James* case holds that a jury should not be permitted to evaluate the merits of a plaintiff's disagreement with the educational assumptions relied upon by the Board of Education "and that questions regarding the board's exercise of judgment and discretion, and its allocation of available resources, are inappropriate for resolution in the courts." That interpretation, apparently also adopted by Mr. Justice DAMIANI, is a misapplication of the *James* case. There the Court of Appeals denied enjoinder of a decision of the Board of Education to proceed with tests in reading and mathematics throughout the entire New York City school system. Plaintiffs there claimed that the integrity of the tests had been compromised by the accidental premature distribution of sample materials to certain schools. The court merely held that it was for the Board of Education, and not the judiciary, to decide whether to cancel the tests, because (p. 367, 397 N.Y.S.2d p. 942, 366 N.E.2d p. 1298) "[t]he court may not, under the guise of enforcing a vague educational public policy, suggested to it," assume the powers vested in school officials. It therefore declined to review what it considered were (p. 368, 397 N.Y.S.2d p. 942, 366 N.E.2d p. 1298) "questions of judgment, discretion, allocation of resources and priorities inappropriate for resolution in the judicial arena".

Defendant argues that the policy to retest only where requested by parents or where recommended by teachers also involved "judgment, discretion, allocation of resources and priorities". Defendant then posits that "[w]hat will not be done in a direct challenge *** should even more clearly not be done in the context of an individual's claim for civil damages."

Defendant's conclusion is a complete *non sequitur,* for the failure to retest plaintiff was not occasioned by a policy decision of the board as to "its allocation of available resources", but oc-

657

curred solely because of the negligence of its employees in failing to follow its own determination as to this specific child.

Defendant's affirmative act in placing plaintiff in a CRMD class initially (when it should have known that a mistake could have devastating consequences) created a relationship between itself and plaintiff out of which arose a duty to take reasonable steps to ascertain whether (at least, in a borderline case) that placement was proper (see *Schuster v. City of N.Y., 5 N.Y.2d 75,* 180 N.Y.S.2d 265, 154 N.E.2d 534; *Florence v. Goldberg,* 44 N.Y.2d 189, 404 N.Y.S.2d 5843, 375 N.E.2d 763). We need not here decide whether such duty would have required "intelligence" retesting (in view of plaintiff's poor showing on achievement tests) had not the direction for such retesting been placed in the very document which asserted that plaintiff was to be placed in a CRMD class. It ill-becomes the Board of Education to argue for the untouchability of its own policy and procedures when the gist of plaintiff's complaint is that the entity which did not follow them was the board itself.

New York State and its municipalities have long since surrendered immunity from suit. Just as well-established is the rule that damages for psychological and emotional injury are recoverable even absent physical injury or contact (*Ferrara v. Galluchio,* 5 N.Y.2d 16, 176 N.Y.S.2d 996, 152 N.E.2d 249; *Batalla v. State of New York,* 10 N.Y.2d 237, 219 N.Y.S.2d 34, 176 N.E.2d 729). Had plaintiff been improperly diagnosed or treated by medical or psychological personnel in a municipal hospital, the municipality would be liable for the ensuing injuries. There is no reason for any different rule here because the personnel were employed by a government entity other than a hospital. Negligence is negligence, even if defendant and Mr. Justice DAMIANI prefer semantically to call it educational malpractice. Thus, defendant's rhetoric constructs a chamber of horrors by asserting that affirmance in this case would create a new theory of liability known as "educational malpractice" and that before doing so we must consider public policy (*cf. Riss v. City of New York,* 22 N.Y.2d 579, 293 N.Y.S.2d 897, 240 N.E.2d 860; *Tobin v. Grossman,* 24 N.Y.2d 609, 301 N.Y.S.2d 554, 249 N.E.2d 419; *Howard v. Lecher,* 42 N.Y.2d 109, 397 N.Y.S.2d 363, 366 N.E.2d 64) and the effects of opening a vast new field which will further impoverish financially hard pressed municipalities. Defendant, in effect, suggests that to avoid such horrors, educational entities must be insulated from the legal responsibilities and obligations common to all other governmental entities no matter how seriously a particular student may have been injured and, ironically, even though such injuries were caused by their own affirmative acts in failing to follow their own rules.

I see no reason for such a trade-off, on alleged policy grounds, which would warrant a denial of fair dealing to one who is injured by exempting a governmental agency from its responsibility for its *affirmative* torts. Such a determination would simply amount to the imposition of private value judgments over the legitimate interests and legal rights of those tortiously injured. That does not mean that the parents of the Johnnies who cannot read may flock to the courts and automatically obtain redress. Nor does it mean that the parents of all the Janies whose delicate egos were upset because they did not get the gold stars they deserved will obtain redress. If the door to "educational torts" for nonfeasance is to be opened (see 29 Syracuse L.Rev. 147-152; *Pierce v. Board of Educ. of City of Chicago*, 44 Ill.App.3d 324, 3 Ill.Dec. 67, 358 N.E.2d 67; *Peter W. v. San Francisco Unified School Dist.*, 60 Cal.App.3d 814, 131 Cal. Rptr. 854; *cf. Donohue v. Copiague Union Free School Dist.*, 64 A.D.2d 29, 407 N.Y.S.2d 874), it will not be by this case which involves *misfeasance* in failing to follow the individualized and specific prescription of defendant's own certified psychologist, whose very decision it was in the first place, to place plaintiff in a class for retarded children, or in the initial making by him of an ambiguous report, if that be the fact.

As Professor David A. Diamond noted (29 Syracuse L.Rev. 103, 150, 151), when discussing this very case after the judgment at Trial Term, and contrasting it with the *Donohue* case, upon which Mr. Justice DAMIANI lays so much stress, "the thrust of the plaintiff's case is not so much a failure to take steps to detect and correct a weakness in a student, that is, a failure to provide a positive program for a student, but rather, affirmative acts of negligence which imposed additional and crippling burdens upon a student" and that "it does not seem unreasonable to hold a school board liable for the type of behavior exhibited in *Hoffman.*" I agree.

CONCLUSION.

Looking at the facts in this record in a light most favorable to the plaintiff, as we are required to do (see *Broderick v. Cauldwell-Wingate,* 301 N.Y. 182, 185, 93 N.E.2d 629, 630; *Faber v. City of N.Y.,* 213 N.Y. 411, 414, 107 N.E. 756, 757; *Matter of Foss,* 38 A.D.2d 638, 639, 327 N.Y.S.2d 235), a dismissal here as recommended by Mr. Justice MARTUSCELLO, would be "an intrusion on the jury's role as trier of the facts", and would constitute "an unwarranted finding of fact in a jury case" (see *Lane—The Real Estate Dept. Store v. Lawlet Corp.,* 28 N.Y.2d 36, 43, 319 N.Y.S.2d 836, 841, 268 N.E.2d 635, 639; *Pekar v. Tax,* 43 A.D.2d 957, 352 N.Y.S.2d 39). This is particularly true when it is recalled that the test of the credibility of witnesses is best left to those who heard the live testimony—the triers of the facts (*Kelly v. Watson Elevator Co.,* 309 N.Y. 49, 51, 127 N.E.2d 802, 803; *Amend v. Hurley,* 293 N.Y. 587, 594, 59 N.E.2d 416, 418). Thus Mr. Justice MARTUSCELLO, in discounting Dr. Gottsegen's "testimony as a matter of law" because in his opinion the doctor's "credibility has been strongly impaired", has disregarded the well-settled rule that "in any case in which it can be said that the evidence is such that it would not be utterly irrational for a jury to reach the result it has determined upon, and thus a valid question of fact does exist, the court may not conclude that the verdict is as a matter of law not supported by the evidence" (see *Cohen v. Hallmark Cards,* 45 N.Y.2d 493, 410 N.Y.S.2d 282, 382 N.E.2d 1145 [1978]).

Therefore, not only reason and justice, but the law as well, cry out for an affirmance of plaintiff's right to a recovery. Any other result would be a reproach to justice. In the words of the ancient Romans: *"Fiat justitia, ruat coelum"* (Let justice be done, though the heavens fall). However, the verdict should be reduced to $500,000.[9]

Judgment of the Supreme Court, Queens County entered November 3, 1976, reversed, on the law, and new trial granted with respect to the issue of damages only, with costs to abide the event, unless, within 20 days after entry of the order to be made hereon, plaintiff shall serve and file in the office of the clerk of the trial court, a written stipulation consenting to reduce the verdict in his favor to $500,000, and to the entry of an amended judgment accordingly, in which event the judgment, as so reduced and amended, is affirmed, without costs or disbursements.

COHALAN and O'CONNOR, JJ., concur.

MARTUSCELLO, J. P., and DAMIANI, J., dissent and vote to reverse the judgment and dismiss the complaint, with separate opinions.

MARTUSCELLO, Justice Presiding (dissenting).

We are faced with the determination of a delicate issue—whether the plaintiff was deprived of an adequate and suitable education for the 12-year period between 1957 and 1969, by reason of the defendant's alleged negligent evaluation of his intelligence and its failure to retest his I.Q. during those years.

After careful scrutiny of the testimony, I conclude that the initial placement of the plaintiff in the educational system was made in a proper manner and that retesting by giving another I.Q. test was not indicated during the period in question. The plaintiff has failed to establish the defendant's negligence on any of the alleged theories of liability. I would, accordingly, reverse the judgment, on the law, direct a verdict in favor of the defendant and dismiss the complaint, without costs or disbursements.

Although the majority opinion sets forth a detailed statement of the facts, for the purpose of my dissent, I deem it necessary to reiterate a large portion of those facts, and to include additional ones.

The plaintiff, Danny Hoffman, has had a severe speech impediment throughout most of his life. In February, 1956, when the

---

9. The dissenters have authorized me to say that if they were not voting to reverse and dismiss plaintiff's complaint, they would join in the reduction of the verdict.

plaintiff was nearly five years old, his mother took him to the National Hospital for Speech Disorders. Its records noted that he had little or no intelligible speech and that he appeared to be retarded.

On March 5, 1956 the plaintiff's intelligence was tested at that hospital at his mother's request. He was given a Merrill-Palmer (nonverbal) Intelligence Test, upon which he attained an I.Q. score of 90. This was well within the range of normal intelligence. It was found that he could work well into the average and even brighter range. Plaintiff was then placed in the New York Speech Institute for weekly therapy. Such treatment continued until he was enrolled in his first special education class.

Plaintiff commenced his formal education in September, 1956 at the age of five and one-half years. At the recommendation of his teacher, who observed "Mongoloid tendencies", severe speech defects and slow responses, Danny's I.Q. was individually tested. In January, 1957 Dr. Monroe C. Gottsegen, a psychologist from the Board of Education's Bureau of Child Guidance, administered a Stanford-Binet (verbal) I.Q. Test. In his report, dated January 23, 1957, Dr. Gottsegen concluded that the plaintif was eligible for placement in a class for children with retarded mental development (CRMD) and stated that:

"Danny impresses as [sic] a shy, cooperative youngster. Mongoloid features are observable. *There is a marked speech defect which makes Danny hesitant in speaking up.* He obviously understands more than he is able to communicate. With careful listening, it is frequently possible to understand what he is driving at.

"On the Stanford-Binet, L, he achieves a mental age of 4 3 and an *I.Q. of 74,* indicating borderline intelligence. The obtained I.Q. may be higher than it ought to be as the Examiner was confronted with the task of having to interpret what Danny was trying to say, *Danny being given the benefit of the doubt when it seemed reasonable to do so.*

"Danny is frequently bored in class and needs a specialized, individualized teaching program. At this point, a continued, yet varied readiness program should be offered him. He is not yet able to do formal learning. He needs help with his speech problem in order that he be able to learn to make himself understood. Also, his intelligence should be *re-evaluated within a two year period so that a more accurate estimation of his abilities can be made."* (Emphasis supplied.)

A CRMD class consists of a maximum of 18 students who have an I.Q. between 50 and 75. These children are considered to be capable of some degree of learning and are taught academic subjects such as reading and arithmetic in the earlier grades and additional subjects such as social studies and geography in the later grades.

Plaintiff attended CRMD classes in various schools for 11 years. During those years, he was taught, tested and observed by experienced teachers trained to work with retarded children. Danny's school records indicated that he was generally well behaved, pleasant, co-operative and well-liked by his teachers. However, academically he performed unsatisfactorily in reading, mathematical concepts and oral communications.

Danny's I.Q. had never been retested at any point during his placement in CRMD classes. During that period, it was the policy of the Board of Education *not* to retest a CRMD student unless such retesting was recommended by the student's teachers or requested by the parents. None of the plaintiff's teachers or his mother requested a retesting during this period. Nevertheless, the plaintiff was given standardized achievement tests semi-annually in reading and mathematics similar to those tests given to students in regular classes. The results of such tests were discouraging. The plaintiff's grades and his corresponding chronological age at the time, were as follows:

DATE	CHRONOLOGICAL AGE AT TIME OF TEST	READING GRADE	MATH GRADE
1961	10 yrs, 6 mos	1.6	1.7
1962	11 yrs, 6 mos	1.6	2.3
1963	12 yrs, 6 mos	1.6	2.2

663

DATE	CHRONOLOGICAL AGE AT TIME OF TEST	READING GRADE	MATH GRADE
1964	13 yrs, 5 mos	1.7	2.6
1965	14 yrs, 6 mos	1.9	3.7
1967	16 yrs	2.8	4.0

In September, 1968 the plaintiff was transferred to the Queens Occupational Training Center, a manual and shop training school for retarded youths. Thereafter, on May 12, 1969, at his mother's request, the plaintiff was administered an intelligence test known as the Wechsler Intelligence Scale for Adults by Dr. William F. Garber of the Bureau of Child Guidance. Danny, then 18 years of age, scored a verbal I.Q. of 85 and a performance I.Q. of 107, giving him a full scale I.Q. score of 94. The report of Dr. Garber recommended that the plaintiff return to regular classes. The doctor recorded the following *findings*:

"Danny is being reevaluated as to intellectual status, following an interview with his mother, who came to the school very much disturbed because her son has been rejected by Social Security for continuance of payments after the age of 18, the S.S.A. feeling he was not sufficiently handicapped by his retarded status to pursue gainful employment. On January 9, 1957, the Bureau of Child Guidance found a Binet I.Q. of 74. "He is a tall, well-built boy, alert looking and charming in manner, who is so incapacitated by a speech defect that communication is difficult for him. He relates very well, displays humor, and appears reality oriented.

* * * * * *

"This boy has above average intellectual potential and a good personality structure. Due to his being almost immobilized in the speech area, as well as considering his extremely defective academic background, he would find it difficult, if not impossible, to function in a regular high school. Psychomotor coordination is good however. Referral to [Division of Vocational

664

Rehabilitation of the State Education Department] is suggested for specialized training and alleviation of the speech problem."

Based upon Dr. Garber's findings and recommendation, Danny was terminated from the Occupational Training Center in September, 1969, at the commencement of his second year. The plaintiff was advised that he could not continue at the center because the results of the May, 1969 I.Q. test indicated that he was not sufficiently handicapped by his retarded status to preclude his obtaining gainful employment.

Thereafter, plaintiff commenced this action to recover damages for the injuries which resulted from his placement in CRMD classes. The complaint alleges two theories of liability: (1) the defendant was negligent in its original testing procedures and placement of the plaintiff, causing or permitting him to be placed in an educational environment for mental defectives and mentally retarded children and consequently depriving him of adequate speech therapy which would have improved his only real handicap, a speech impediment; and (2) the defendant was negligent in failing or refusing to follow adequate procedures for the recommended retesting of the plaintiff's I.Q.

The defendant took the position that the plaintiff's score of 74 on the Stanford-Binet I.Q. Test indicated that the plaintiff's placement in a CRMD class was proper. The defendant contends that the test was proper and administered by a competent and experienced psychologist. The defendant further alleges that it was the unanimous professional judgment of plaintiff's teachers, based upon their evaluation and the plaintiff's performance on his standardized achievement tests, that a retest of the plaintiff was not warranted. The board makes clear that it was its policy to retest only where recommended by the teachers or requested by the parents.

The two theories of liability as pleaded in the complaint were submitted to the jury. The jury returned a general verdict in favor of the plaintiff awarding him damages of $750,000. On this appeal the defendant challenges, *inter alia*, each theory of liability on the ground that the plaintiff failed to sustain his burden of

665

proving his claim as a matter of law and therefore neither theory of liability should have been submitted to the jury.

I find merit in the defendant's position. It is conceivable that a case of educational malpractice may be pleaded and established against a board of education for an act of misfeasance. However, the plaintiff in the instant case has failed to establish the negligence of the defendant by its breach of a duty owed to the plaintiff under either theory of liability. Therefore, the plaintiff's complaint should have been dismissed at the close of the entire case.

Taking each theory of liability in turn, it is apparent that the evidence does not support the plaintiff's position. In support of the first theory, the plaintiff attempted to establish, by a series of inferences, that Dr. Gottsegen's administration of the Stanford-Binet Verbal I.Q. Test in 1957 was improper.

The thrust of plaintiff's evidence on this issue was that on account of plaintiff's severe speech disability, Dr. Gottsegen should not have administered a Stanford-Binet Test, which relies heavily upon verbal responses. However plaintiff's own witness, Dr. Lawrence Abt, a clinical psychologist, testified that the Stanford-Binet Test was one of the tests that might have been used and declined to testify that Dr. Gottsegen's failure to administer a performance test had been a departure from good psychological practice. None of plaintiff's expert witnesses testified that Dr. Gottsegen had departed from good psychological practice by administering a Stanford-Binet Test. Defendant's witness, Dr. Henry Lipton, a clinical psychologist, testified that the Stanford-Binet Test would certainly have been the preferred test for a child six years old. In fact, other witnesses testified that the 1957 test record indicated that Dr. Gottsegen had taken plaintiff's speech disability into account and had compensated therefor in interpreting the results of the test. Although Dr. Abt stated that it would have been wise for Dr. Gottsegen to supplement the verbal I.Q. test with the nonverbal I.Q. test, we cannot infer from this that it was unwise not to supplement it. Nor can we infer that there was a deviation from accepted or standard psychological practice not to do so.

Moreover, we cannot utilize the 1956 intelligence test administered by the National Hospital for Speech Disorders and the 1969 intelligence test administered by Dr. Garber to draw a circumstantial inference that Dr. Gottsegen had negligently administered or interpreted the 1957 Stanford-Binet Test. Dr. Abt testified on direct examination that a child with an average intelligence might obtain an I.Q. score of 71 or less if he did not take the test seriously or if the test had been administered incorrectly, or if the test results had been incorrectly interpreted. Thus, the inference drawn by Dr. Abt was as consistent with the absence of liability as it was with liability. Where inferences are clearly equally consistent, the one with liability and the other with no cause of action, the plaintiff has not met the burden which the law has placed upon him (*Ford v. McAdoo*, 231 N.Y. 155, 162, 131 N.E. 874, 876).

Under the circumstances, I am of the opinion that, upon all of the evidence, plaintiff did not prove that Dr. Gottsegen had negligently administered or interpreted the Stanford-Binet Test. Accordingly, this issue should not have been submitted to the jury and the complaint should have been dismissed at the close of the entire case.

The plaintiff's second theory of liability is essentially built on Dr. Gottsegen's testimony at the trial that he recommended a retesting. He stated that:

"I was able to communicate with him, but I wasn't sure about what I was doing because the communication was coming out very muddy. It was like listening to a radio at a very low level, with a lot of static. You think you know what is being said, but you can't be that sure, and I think that comes through here, that I really wasn't sure and that's why we wanted him retested within two years. This was always Bureau procedure. We were always concerned in the B.C.G. not to make mistakes with kids and we were careful to see to it if we had doubts about what we were doing, that we recommend that he be retested and say it, and that's what happened here.

* * * * * *

"It was my feeling there was retardation, but I doubted some of the results and therefore I suggested a retesting."

667

In his opinion Mr. Justice SHAPIRO observes that:

> "Since Dr. Gottsegen's written recommendation was that
> plaintiff's 'intelligence should be re-evaluated within a two
> year period ' it could only mean that he was to be administered
> a new I.Q. test within that period. If it did not have that mean-
> ing, it meant nothing, since a CRMD child is always being
> observed by his teacher for signs of improvement, and achieve-
> ment tests were being given semiannually to all CRMD chil-
> dren."

However, after a study of Dr. Gottsegen's entire testimony,
and a comparison of its contents with the testimony of the plaintiff's teachers, I have to come to discount his testimony entirely.
First of all, Dr. Gottsegen's testimony at the trial that he recommended a "retesting" of the plaintiff, was totally inconsistent
with his written report, recorded 18 years earlier, that the plaintiff be "re-evaluated". Dr. Gottsegen's explanation at the trial,
that he intended or meant by the directive "re-evaluate" that the
plaintiff be in fact "retested", is not persuasive. The doctor communicated the word "re-evaluate". "Re-evaluate" is a term of art
that has a specific connotation. Therefore the defendant must be
judged in the context of its compliance with the recommendation
that was made and note with a recommendation that was possibly intended in retrospect.

It is very clear from the record that prior to 1968, retesting was
not the policy of the Board of Education unless such retesting
was requested by the student's teacher or parents. Dr.
Gottsegen's testimony that he believed that retesting was the
policy is irrelevant. His short association as an employee of the
Board of Education could well explain his unfamiliarity with the
board's policy. He was employed by the board for only the short
week before he administered the test to the plaintiff and he left
the Board's employ the following year, in September, 1958.

At the trial, Dr. Gottsegen could not recall the nature of
Danny's severe speech defect, which was markedly clear at the
time of the examination, as the doctor noted in his report. This is
a further indication of the witness' inability to recall the circumstances of the testing and examination. Not that Danny's iso-

668

lated case should have, as a matter of course, stood out in Dr. Gottsegen's mind, among the thousands of tests administered and evaluated by him during the 18 years that intervened between Danny's 1957 test and the trial.

The disparities between Dr. Gottsegen's written report and his in-court testimony, together with his limited association with the defendant, leads us to conclude that his credibility has been strongly impaired. I have therefore discounted his testimony as a matter of law.

With the removal of Dr. Gottsegen's testimony the plaintiff's case collapses. In its void the defendant developed a justification for its failure to retest the plaintiff's I.Q.

Miss Madeline Dalton was employed by the Board of Education for 35 years, first as a teacher of retarded children, later as a supervisor and, since 1968, as Director of the Bureau of Children with Retarded Mental Development. She explained that during the period in question there were generally 13,000 to 14,000 CRMD pupils in the system. Each year the I.Q. of approximately 500 of these pupils was formally retested. The remaining pupils were being re-evaluated each year as to their "functional level" to determine whether a retest of their I.Q. was warranted, on the basis of performance in class *and* on standardized achievement tests. Of the 500 retested each year about 125, or one-fourth, were returned to regular classes. Miss Dalton testified that in the plaintiff's case not one of his teachers ever recommended a retest of his I.Q. or considered it advisable that he be placed in a regular class. Nothing in Danny's record indicated to her that he could have functioned in a normal class.

The defendant's witnesses distinguished between the terms "retest" and "re-evaluated". Miss Dalton explained that while the plaintiff was in attendance in the CRMD classes, the term "re-evaluate" meant the administration of semi-annual achievement tests. A retesting would involve the administration of a new I.Q. test. If a CRMD student demonstrated, upon re-evaluation by his performance on the semi-annual achievement tests, that he was able to function beyond his expectancy level, he was then administered a new I.Q. test.

669

Dr. Donald Wiedis, a professor and licensed supervisor of school psychology, who trained school psychologists for the Board of Education, confirmed the distinction between "re-evaluate" and "retest". He explained that "re-evaluate" means merely "taking another look" at the child's record to discern whether there was a perceivable jump in scores on a series of achievement tests. The term did not necessarily imply a formal retest of the subject child's I.Q. The only conclusion that can be drawn from the defendant's evidence, is that the term "re-evaluate" was a term of art with a precise meaning. The plaintiff never rebutted this conclusion.

It has been established that the pre-1968 policy of the Board of Education was to re-evaluate CRMD students. This policy itself has not been challenged by the plaintiff at any time. Miss Dalton, who conceded that a policy of periodic retesting of a child's I.Q. would have been preferable to a policy of testing only upon a teacher's recommendation or parent's request, testified nevertheless that she did not regard the board policy to have been improper at that time.

I have examined the record for evidence establishing that the plaintiff had in fact *been* re-evaluated according to the then existing policy. I find that he was regularly re-evaluated. The plaintiff was given standard achievement tests in mathematics and reading for the years 1960 through 1967, inclusive. Dr. Lipton testified that although an achievement test is not the equivalent of an I.Q. test, he believed that such test demonstrates a child's academic performance. Where the child does not "stand out" from his classmates, based on these tests, then it is consistent with the decision that he has been appropriately placed.

I have examined the plaintiff's academic progress as indicated by his tests *and* his teachers' observations and find that there was no reasonable basis for any teacher to recommend that he be retested. The achievement tests showed such dismal results that it was reasonable for plaintiff's teachers to infer that his I.Q. was no better than had been originally indicated. In 1967 his achievement tests in reading and mathematics indicated that plaintiff read at a level below the third grade and that he had the mathematical understanding of a fourth grade level. Had he been an

670

average student in 1967, the plaintiff's reading and mathematics levels would have been at tenth or eleventh grade. Of all the achievement tests the plaintiff had been given since 1960, his 1967 scores were the highest he had ever obtained.

Mrs. Sally Stewart taught the plaintiff for two years, starting in 1964, in the subject areas of reading, arithmetic, social studies and speech. It was her opinion that the plaintiff was working to his full potential. In her judgment he could not have functioned in a regular class of eighth graders for which a normal child of his chronological age would have been suited. She rested her judgment not only on his scores on standardized achievement tests, but upon her daily observations of his work in class and his performance on daily and weekly tests.

Although she testified on cross-examination that she recommended that Danny's I.Q. be rechecked, she made this statement in the context of a generality. At this point there may have been confusion in her mind with regard to the post-1968 Board of Education policy of retesting CRMD students every two years. This would be consistent with her later testimony elicited on redirect examination by the Board of Education.

"Q Did Danny ever overcome anything in your class?
"A No, sir.
"Q Did you ever feel while Danny was in your class that he should be re-evaluated?
"A No, sir.
"Q In your opinion did he reach his level?
"A Yes, sir.

* * * * * *

"Q And did *** [Danny] at any time in your opinion warrant being retested for his IQ?
"A No, sir."

Mrs. Stewart testified that plaintiff's performance on achievement tests was consistent with a determination that he was retarded. Significantly, she testified that certain other students in the same class as plaintiff had improved their school work in the

671

CRMD class. Upon the basis of such improvement they had been placed in classes for children of average intelligence. This indicates that some students overcame the stigma of being labeled retarded.

Mrs. Vicari taught the plaintiff in Junior High School 93 between the years 1964 to 1967. She indicated that when a child in her class was working up to potential or had significantly improved during the year, she would request a further re-evaluation of his I.Q. However, she did not believe that the plaintiff could have functioned in a regular class.

Accordingly, the sole conclusion which could be drawn from the evidence at the trial was that plaintiff's intelligence was in fact, periodically "re-evaluated". This "re-evaluation" referred to the child's entire school record, which consisted of teachers' observations of him in class over several years and the results of standardized achievement tests.

The issue of whether the Board of Education had a duty to periodically retest plaintiff's I.Q. should not have been submitted to the jury. As I interpret the Court of Appeals' recent decision in *James v. Board of Educ. of City of N.Y.*, 42 N.Y.2d 357, 367, 397 N.Y.S.2d 934, 941, 366 N.E.2d 1291, 1297, a jury should not be permitted to evaluate the merits of a plaintiff's disagreement with the educational assumptions relied upon by a board of education. Questions regarding a board's exercise of judgment and discretion, and its allocation of available resources, are inappropriate for resolution in the courts (*id.,* p. 368, 397 N.Y.S.2d p. 942, 366 N.E.2d p. 1298). Under the guise of enforcing a vague educational public policy, a jury should not be permitted to assume the exercise of an educational policy that is vested by constitution and by statute in school administrative agencies (*id.,* p. 367, 397 N.Y.S.2d p. 941, 366 N.E.2d p. 1297).

On the evidence presented by the plaintiff, I cannot justify any recovery on his behalf. The record discloses no impropriety in Danny's initial placement in a CRMD class and the evidence, absent Dr. Gottsegen's incredible testimony, weighs conclusively in favor of the Board of Education's position that "retesting" was neither recommended nor appropriate in Danny's case. Accordingly, the judgment should be reversed and the complaint against the Board of Education dismissed.

DAMIANI, Justice (dissenting).

In my view the judgment in favor of the plaintiff in this case should be reversed and the complaint dismissed because it is the public policy of this State that no cause of action exists to recover for so-called educational malpractice (*Donohue v. Copiague Union Free School Dist.*, 64 A.D.2d 29, 407 N.Y.S.2d 874).

In the *Donohue* case, this court decided that the strong public policy of this State was to avoid judicial interference in educational matters and that the recognition of a cause of action sounding in negligence to recover for so-called "educational malpractice" would impermissibly require the courts to oversee and, with hindsight, to evaluate the professional judgment of those charged with the responsibility for the administration of public education. As was predicted in *Donohue,* this case has involved the courts in an evaluation of judgments and actions of educators. In addition, the jury here was required to decide, among other issues "whether certain tests should have been administered or test results interpreted in one way rather than another" (64 A.D.2d at p. 35, 407 N.Y.S.2d p. 879). The result was a trial transcript of some 2036 pages, wherein the parties explored every facet of the plaintiff's education. Questions as to the propriety of educational judgments and actions are inappropriate for resolution in the judicial arena (*James v. Board of Educ. of City of N.Y.,* 42 N.Y.2d 357, 397 N.Y.S.2d 934, 366 N.E.2d 1291).

The majority opinion contains a forceful denunciation of the "injury" allegedly done to plaintiff by the defendant, but overlooks what is readily apparent from its own statement of the facts, namely that plaintiff suffered from a severe speech disorder in early childhood before he ever attended one of the defendant's schools, that his other learning problems flowed from his inability to communicate effectively and that his speech was at least no worse when he completed his course of instruction than when it began. In *Donohue* (*supra,* p. 37, 407 N.Y.S.2d p. 880), this court held that "the failure of educational achievement cannot be characterized as an 'injury' within the meaning of tort law." The purpose of the public schools is to confer the benefit of

673

an education upon what would otherwise be an uneducated public. The failure to reach educational objectives with respect to a particular student does not result in an "injury" since the student commenced his education lacking knowledge, education, experience and, in this case, proper speech patterns. Hence, the failure to teach him how to speak properly has left him no worse off than when his schooling started.

The benefit of retrospection has enabled the plaintiff to convince a jury and the majority of this court that the defendant wrongfuly placed him in a class for the mentally retarded and that he was severely damaged thereby. However, the record is clear that during the time he was in a CRMD class no protest against that placement was ever lodged by plaintiff or his mother and that throughout his schooling the plaintiff received the best speech therapy program that the defendant offered to any pupil. He received instruction in social studies, mathematics, English and science and he is now able to read and write. Moreover, those of his teachers who were called to testify all gave their opinion that plaintiff would not have been able to function in a regular class. Thus, the total picture is not as dire as the one painted in the majority opinion. The defendant in this case may have failed to remedy plaintiff's speech problems, but it did not cause or aggravate them.

The majority seeks to distinguish the *Donohue* case upon the ground that it involved "nonfeasance" whereas this case involves "misfeasance". Quite apart from the fact that the complaints in both cases allege acts both of omission and commission, the main thrust of the plaintiff's case at bar was that the defendant failed to retest plaintiff within two years after his placement in a CRMD class as recommended by its own psychologist. This act of omission is one of nonfeasance, which is defined as the failure to perform an act which a person should perform (65 C.J.S. Negligence § 2[6], p. 470; Black's Law Dictionary [rev. 4th ed.], p. 1208; see Prosser, Torts [4th ed.], § 56). In *Donohue,* the gist of the plaintiff's cause of action was that although the defendant had given him instruction in reading, it had not done so properly or effectively and therefore he could not read upon graduation. This was an act of commission or misfeasance, which is defined

674

as the improper performance of a lawful act (Black's Law Dictionary, *supra,* p. 1151).

Even if the majority had assigned the alleged misfeasance and nonfeasance to the proper case, the distinction it seeks to draw is immaterial. Negligence exists when injury results from the violation of a legal duty that one owes to another, whether the act in violation be active or passive, of commission or omission, of misfeasance or nonfeasance (see 65 C.J.S. Negligence § 2[6], p. 471; *Indiana Harbor Belt R.R. Co. v. Jones,* 220 Ind. 139, 41 N.E.2d 361; *Taylor v. Northern States Power Co.,* 196 Minn. 22, 264 N.W. 139; *Hoeverman v. Feldman,* 220 Wis. 557, 265 N.W. 580; see, also, *Mazloum v. New York, New Haven & Hartford R.R.,* Sup., 115 N.Y.S.2d 238). The essential questions are whether a duty exists and whether it was breached, not whether the defendant's conduct in breaching the duty was active or passive. *Donohue* holds squarely that no such duty exists.

In my view, the result reached by the majority in this case arises from its implicit disagreement with the holding in *Donohue.* As above demonstrated, the grounds upon which the majority seeks to distinguish *Donohue* are legally unsound and, therefore, on established principles of *stare decisis* the judgment appealed from should be reversed and the complaint dismissed. The failure of the court to follow its own obviously controlling recent decision can lead only to uncertainty and a lack of stability in the law (see 1 Carmody-Wait 2d, N.Y.Prac., §§ 2:50 *et. seq.*).

Appendix 10

HOFFMAN
v.
BOARD OF EDUCATION OF THE CITY OF NEW YORK

Court of Appeals of New York.
Dec. 17, 1979.

Allen G. Schwartz, Corp. Counsel, New York City (Bernard Burstein and L. Kevin Sheridan, New York City, of counsel), for appellant.

Perry Prazer and Helen B. Stroller, New York City, for, respondent.

JASON, Judge.

The significant issue present on this appeal is whether considerations of public policy preclude recovery for an alleged failure to properly evaluate the intellectual capacity of a student.

The fact in this case may be briefly stated. Plaintiff Daniel Hoffman entered kindergarden in the New York City school system in September, 1956. Shortly thereafter, plaintiff was examined by Monroe Gottsegen, a certified clinical psychologist in the school system, who determined that plaintiff had an intelligence quotient (IQ) of 74 and recommended that he be placed in a class for Children with Retarded Mental Development (CRMD). Dr. Gottsegen was, however, not certain of his findings. The apparent reason for this uncertainty was that plaintiff suffered from a severe speech defect which had manifested itself long before plaintiff entered the school system. Plaintiff's inability to communicate verbally made it difficult to assess his mental ability by means of the primarily verbal Stanford-Binet Intelligence Test administered by Dr. Gottsegen. As a result, Dr. Gottsegen recommended that plaintiff's intelligence "be re-evaluated within a two-year period so that a more accurate estimation of his abilities can be made."

Pursuant to Dr. Gottsegen's recommendations, plaintiff was placed in a CRMD program. While enrolled in the program, plaintiff's academic progress was constantly monitored through the observation of his teachers and by the use of academic "achievement tests" given twice a year. Although in 1959 and 1960 plaintiff received a "90 percentile" rating as to "reading readiness", including that his potential for learning to read was higher than average, the results of his achievement tests consistently indicated that he possessed extremely limited reading and mathematical skills. As a result of plaintiff's poor performance on the standardized achievement tests, and, presumably, because his teacher's daily observations confirmed his lack of progress, plaintiff's intelligence was not retested on an examination designed specifically for that purpose.

In 1968, plaintiff was transferred to the Queens Occupational Training Center (OTC), a manual and shop training center for retarded youths. The following year plaintiff's mother requested, for the first time, that plaintiff's intelligence be retested. Plaintiff was administered the Wechsler Intelligence Scale for Adults (WAIS). The results of the test indicated that plaintiff had a "verbal" IQ of 85 and a "performance" IQ of 107 for a "full scale" IQ of 94. In other words, plaintiff's combined score on the WAIS test indicated that he was not retarded. Inasmuch as his course of study at the OTC was designed specifically for retarded youths, plaintiff was no longer qualified to be enrolled. As a result, plaintiff was allowed to complete the spring semester of 1969, but was not allowed to return in the fall.

Thereafter, plaintiff commenced this action against the Board of Education of the City of New York, alleging that the board was negligent in its original assessment of his intellectual ability and that the board negligently failed to retest him pursuant to Dr. Gottsegen's earlier recommendation. Plaintiff claimed that these negligent acts and omissions caused him to be misclassified and improperly enrolled in the CRMD program which allegedly resulted in severe injury to plaintiff's intellectual emotional well-being and reduced his ability to obtain employment. At trial, the jury awarded plaintiff damages in the amount of $750,000. The Appellate Division affirmed this judgment, two Justices dissenting, as to liability, but would have reversed this judgment and required plaintiff to retry the issue of damages had he not consented to a reduction in the amount of the verdict from

678

$750,000 to $500,000. The Appellate Division predicated its affirmance upon defendants' failure to administer a second intelligence test to plaintiff pursuant to Dr. Gottsegen's recommendation to "re-evaluate" plaintiff's intelligence within two years. The court characterized defendants' failure to retest plaintiff as an affirmative act of negligence, actionable under New York law. There should be a reversal.

At the outset, it should be stated that although plaintiff's complaint does not expressly so state, his cause of action sounds in "educational malpractice". Plaintiff's recitation of specific acts of negligence is, in essence, an attack upon the professional judgment of the board of education grounded upon the board's alleged failure to properly interpret and act upon Dr. Gottsegen's recommendations and its alleged failure to properly assess plaintiff's intellectual status thereafter. As we have recently stated in *Donohue v. Copiague Union Free School Dist.*, 47 N.Y.2d 440, 418 N.Y.S.2d 375, 391 N.E.2d 1352, such a cause of action, although quite possibly cognizable under traditional notions of tort law, should not, as a matter of public policy, be entertained by the courts of this State. (47 N.Y.2d at p. 444, 418 N.Y.S.2d at p. 378, 391 N.E.2d at p. 1354.)

In *Donohue,* this court noted that "[c]ontrol and management of educational affairs is vested in the Board of Regents and the Commissioner of Education (N.Y. Const., art. V, § 4; art. XI, § 2; Education Law, §§ 207, 305; see *Matter of New York City School Bds. Assn. v. Board of Educ.,* 39 N.Y.2d 111, 116, 383 N.Y.S.2d 208, 211, 347 N.E.2d at 568, 571; *Matter of Ocean Hill-Brownsville Governing Bd. v. Board of Educ.,* 23 N.Y.2d 483, 485, 297 N.Y.S.2d 568, 569, 245 N.E.2d 219, 220)." (47 N.Y.2d at p. 444, 418 N.Y.S.2d at p. 378, 391 N.E.2d at p. 1354.) In that case, the court was invited to undertake a review not only of broad educational policy, but of the day-to-day implementation of that policy as well. We declined, however, to accept that invitation and we see no reason to depart from that holding today. We had thought it well settled that the courts of this State may not substitute their judgment, or the judgment of a jury, for the professional judgment of educators and government officials actually engaged in the complex and often delicate process of educating the many thousands of children in our schools. (*Donohue v. Copiague Union Free School Dist.,* 47 N.Y.2d 440, 444, 418 N.Y.S.2d 375, 378, 391 N.E.2d 1352, 1354, *supra; James v. Board of Educ.,* 42 N.Y.2d 357, 366, 397 N.Y.S.2d 934, 941, 366 N.E.2d 1291, 1297.) Indeed, we have previously stated that the courts will intervene in the administration of the public school system only in the most exceptional circumstances involving "gross violations of defined public policy". (*Donohue v. Copiague Union Free School Dist.,* 47 N.Y.2d 440, 445, 418 N.Y.S.2d 375, 378, 391 N.E.2d 1352, 1354, *supra; Matter of New York City School Bds. Ass'n v. Board of Educ.,* 39 N.Y.2d 111, 121, 383 N.Y.S.2d 208, 214, 347 N.E.2d 568, 574, *supra.*) Clearly, no such circumstances are present here. Therefore, in our opinion, this court's decision in *Donohue* is dispositive of this appeal.

The court below distinguished *Donohue* upon the ground that the negligence alleged in that case was a failure to educate properly or nonfeasance, whereas, in that court's view, the present case involves an affirmative act of misfeasance. At the outset, we would note that both *Donohue* and the present case involved allegations of various negligent acts and omissions. Furthermore, even if we were to accept the distinction drawn by the court below, and argued by plaintiff on appeal, we would not reach a contrary result. The policy considerations which prompted our decision in *Donohue* apply with equal force to "education malpractice" actions based upon allegations of educational misfeasance and nonfeasance.

Our decision in *Donohue* was grounded upon the principle that courts ought not interfere with the professional judgment of those charged by the Constitution and by statute with the responsibility for the administration of the schools of this State. In the present case, the decision of the school officials and educators who classified plaintiff as retarded and continued his enrollment in CRMD classes was based upon the results of a recognized intelligence test administered by a qualified psychologist and the daily observation of plaintiff's teachers. In order to affirm a finding of liability in these circumstances, this court would be required to allow the finder of fact to substitute its judgment for the professional judgment of the board of education as to the type

680

of psychometric devices to be used and the frequency with which such tests are to be given. Such a decision would also allow a court or a jury to second-guess the determinations of each of plaintiff's teachers. To do so would open the door to an examination of the propriety of each of the procedures used in the education of every student in our school system. Clearly, each and every time a student fails to progress academically, it can be argued that he or she would have done better and received a greater benefit if another educational approach or diagnostic tool had been utilized. Similarly, whenever there was a failure to implement a recommendation made by any person is the school system with respect to the evaluation of a pupil or his or her educational program, it could be said, as here, that liability could be predicated on misfeasance. However, the court system is not the proper forum to test the validity of the educational decision to place a particular student in one of the many educational programs offered by the schools of this State. In our view, any dispute concerning the proper placement of a child in a particular educational program can best be resolved by seeking review of such professional educational judgment through the administrative processes provided by statute. (See Education Law, § 310, subd. 7.)

Accordingly, the order of the Appellate Division should be reversed and the complaint dismissed.

MEYER, Judge (dissenting).

I agree with Mr. Justice Irwin Shapiro, on the analysis spelled out in his well-reasoned decision at the Appellate Division (64 A.D.2d 369, 410 N.Y.S.2d 199), that this case involves not "educational malpractice" as the majority in this court suggests (49 N.Y.2d 121, pp. 125-126, 424 N.Y.S.2d 376, pp. 378-379, 400 N.E.2d 317 p. 319) but discernible affirmative negligence on the part of the board of education in failing to carry out the recommendation for re-evaluation within a period of two years which was an integral part of the procedure by which plaintiff was placed in a CRMD class, and thus readily identifiable as the proximate cause of plaintiff's damages. I, therefore dissent.

COOKE, C. J., and GABRIELLI and JONES, JJ., concur with JASEN, J.

681

MEYER, J., dissents and votes to affirm in a memorandum in which WACHTLER and FUCHSBERG, JJ., concur.

Order reversed, with costs, and complaint dismissed.

TABLE OF CASES

A

Anns v. Merton London Borough Council, 2 W.L.R. 1024 — § 13.1, nn. 49, 50

Asher v. Harrington, 318 F. Supp. 82 (1970) — § 8.1(B), nn. 8, 9, 10, 11, 12

Asher v. Harrington, 461 F.2d 890 (1972) — § 8.1(B), nn. 13, 14

Aubrey v. School District of Philadelphia, Pa. Commw., 437 A.2d 1306 (1981) — § 9.1(G), nn. 29, 30, 31

B

Battalla v. State, 10 N.Y.2d 237, 240, 219 N.Y.S.2d 34 (1961) — § 16.2, n. 14

Battalla v. State, 176 N.E.2d 729 (Court of Appeals of New York, 1969) — § 14.2, nn. 25, 26

Beaman v. Des Moines Area Community College, Law No. CL 15-8532, in the District Court of Iowa for Polk County (1978) — § 8.1(K), nn. 55, 56, 57

B.M. v. State, 649 P.2d 425 (Mont. 1982) — § 7.1(P), nn. 75, 76, 77, 78, 79, 80, 81

Board of Education v. Commission on Professional Competence, Mochson, Civ. No. 62857 Second Dist. Div. Two (Jan. 7, 1982), 127 Cal. App. 3d 522; 179 Cal. Rptr. 605 (1982) — § 13.1, nn. 42, 43, 44

Board of Education v. Rowley, 102 S. Ct. 3034 (1982) — § 7.1(O), nn. 71, 72, 73, 74

Brown v. Board of Education, 347 U.S. 483 (1954) — § 1.3, nn. 21, 22; § 10.1, n. 11; § 10.2, n. 41; § 16.3, n. 46

C

Camer v. Brouillet, Supreme Court No. 47394-3, in the Washington State Court of Appeals, Division 1 (1982) — § 5.1(F), n. 3

Cavello v. Sherburne-Earlville Central School District, 110 A.D.2d 253, 494 N.Y.S.2d 466 (1985) — § 9.1(F), nn. 27, 28

C. Goss v. Lopez, 419 U.S. 565 (1975) — § 10.1, n. 5

Clareen F. v. Western Placer Unified School District, Super. Ct. No. 53919, Ct. of App. Third Appellate Dist. (Calif., 1981) — § 7.1(H), nn. 31, 32, 33, 34, 35, 36, 37

G

H

I

J

K

L

686

M

Maas v. Corporation of Gonzaga University, 27 Wash. App. 397, 618 P.2d 106 (1980) — § 8.1(N), nn. 71, 72, 73, 74, 75

McCartney v. Hyman, 134 Pa. Super. 524, 530, 4 A.2d 581, 584 (1939) — § 2.2(E), n. 109

McNeil v. Board of Education, No. L 17297-74 Super. Ct. Law Div. (N.H., 1975) — § 7.1(A), nn. 2, 4, 5, 6

Millington v. Southeastern Elevator Co., 22 N.Y.2d 498 (1968) — § 11.2, n. 34; § 12.1

Moore v. Vanderloo, 386 N.W.2d 108 (Iowa 1986) — § 9.1(B), nn. 6, 7, 8, 9

Morris v. Jack McKay, No. 80-2-02559-6, Super. Ct., State of Washington for Yakima County (1982) — § 7.1(N), nn. 61, 62, 63, 64, 65, 69, 70

Morse v. Burnelle, United States District Court for the District of New Hampshire, Civil Action File No. C 85 608L. — § 6.3, nn. 41, 42, 43, 44, 45, 46, 47

Myers v. Medford Lakes Board of Education, Superior Court of New Jersey, Law Division, Burlington County, Docket No. L-56068-81 — § 5.1(E), nn. 30, 31, 32, 33

N

Nally v. Grace Community Church of the Valley, 157 Cal. App. 3d 912, 204 Cal. Rptr. 303 (Cal. Ct. App. 1984) — § 2.2(D), nn. 80, 83, 93, 94, 95, 96, 99

Neiderman v. Brodsky, 436 Pa. 195, 205, 401, 261 A.2d 84 (1970) — § 11.1, n. 14

P

Paladino v. Adelphi University, 89 A.D.2d 85, 454 N.Y.S.2d 868 (1982) — § 7.2(A), nn. 86, 87, 88, 89, 90, 91, 92,

Palsgraf v. Long Island R.R., 248 N.Y. 339, 342, 162 N.E. 99, 102 (1928) — § 13.1, n. 4

Passel v. Fort Worth Independent School District, 429 S.W.2d 917 (1968); 440 S.W.2d 61 (1969); 453 S.W.2d 888 (1970) — § 10.1, n. 10

Pavesich v. New England Life Ins. Co., 122 Ga. 190, 50 S.E. 68 (1905) — § 10.3, n. 62

Paynter v. New York University, 319 N.Y.S.2d 893, 894 (1971) — § 8.1(C), n. 19

690

Index

A

ACCOUNTABILITY IN EDUCATION, §16.1.

ACTIONS.
Increase in litigation, §1.1.
Suits in education, §1.2.

ARGUMENTS FOR AND AGAINST RECOGNIZING EDUCATIONAL MALPRACTICE.
Contrast of educational malpractice with malpractice in other professions, §10.2.
Duty of care.
Generally, §§13.0 to 13.6.
See DUTY OF CARE.
Financial burden argument, §§11.0, 11.2, 11.3.
Flood of litigation argument, §§11.0, 11.1, 11.3.
Generally, §§16.0, 16.2, 16.3.
Judicial intervention in the educational process, §§10.1, 12.0, 12.1.
Novel issue argument, §§10.0, 10.3, 10.4.
Proximate cause.
Generally, §§14.0 to 14.3.
See PROXIMATE CAUSE.

ASHER V. HARRINGTON, §8.1(B).

AUBREY V. SCHOOL DISTRICT OF PHILADELPHIA, §9.1(G).

B

BEAMAN V. DES MOINES AREA COMMUNITY COLLEGE, §8.1(K).

B.M. V. STATE, §7.1(P).

BOARD OF EDUCATION V. ROWLEY, §7.1(O).

691

C

CALIFORNIA, STATE OF.
California commission for teachers' preparation and licensing, §15.2(C).

CAMER V. BROUILLET, §5.1(F).

CAVELLO V. SHERBURNE-EARLVILLE CENT. SCHOOL, §9.1(F).

CLAREEN F. V. WESTERN PLACER UNIFIED SCHOOL DISTRICT, §7.1(H).

CLERGY MALPRACTICE, §2.2(D).

CLIMATE OF OPINION, §1.0.
Illiteracy in America, §1.4.
Importance of education, §1.3.

CONTRACTS.
Professional malpractice.
Theories for recovery.
Contract theory, §3.1(B).

D

DAMAGES.
Proximate cause.
Measuring damages, §14.2.
Who should pay damages, §14.3.

DEBRA P. V. TURLINGTON, §7.1(K).

DEFENSES.
Professional malpractice, §3.2.

DENSON V. OHIO BOARD OF EDUCATION, §5.1(G).

DE PIETRO V. ST. JOSEPH'S SCHOOL, §5.2(B).

DEROSA V. CITY OF NEW YORK, §7.1(Q).

DEVITO V. MCMURRAY, §8.1(E).

DISMISSAL OF TEACHERS, §15.1.

DIZICK V. UMPQUA COMMUNITY COLLEGE, §8.1(L).

DOE V. BOARD OF EDUCATION, §7.1(C).

693

"HYBRID" EDUCATIONAL MALPRACTICE CASES.
B.M. v. State, §7.1(P).
Board of education v. Rowley, §7.1(O).
Clareen F. v. Western Placer Unified School District, §7.1(H).
Debra P. v. Turlington, §7.1(K).
DeRosa v. City of New York, §7.1(Q).
Doe v. board of education, §7.1(C).
D.S.W. v. Fairbanks North Star Borough School District, §7.1(I).
Generally, §§6.01, 6.4, 7.0.
Goldberg v. Cronin, §7.1(E).
Hoffman v. City of New York, §6.1; Appx. 9, 10.
  See HOFFMAN V. CITY OF NEW YORK.
Jack M. v. School Board of Santa Rosa County, §7.1(L).
Lindsay v. Thomas, §7.1(G).
Loughran v. Flanders, §7.1(F).
McNeil v. board of education, §7.1(A).
Morris v. McKay, §7.1(N).
Morse v. Henniker school district, §6.3.
Paladino v. Adelphi University, §7.2(A).
Pierce v. board of education, §7.1(B).
Private schools, §7.2.
Smith v. Alameda County Social Services, §7.1(D).
Snow v. New York, §6.2.
Tobias v. New Jersey Department of Education, §7.1(J).
Tubell v. Dade County Public Schools, §7.1(M).
Village Community School v. Adler, §7.2(B).

I

IANNIELLO V. UNIVERSITY OF BRIDGEPORT, §8.1(I).

IOWA, STATE OF.
Criteria of professional practices and criteria of competent
  performance, Appx. 3.
Iowa professional teaching practices commission, §15.2(F).

IRWIN V. SCHOOL DIRECTORS, §5.1(D).

695

J

JACK M. V. SCHOOL BOARD OF SANTA ROSA COUNTY,
§7.1(L).

JACKSON V. DRAKE UNIVERSITY, §8.1(Y).

JOHN DOE I V. MAHARISHI MAHEASH YOGI, §8.1(O).

K

KANTOR V. SCHMIDT, §8.1(S).

L

LEGAL MALPRACTICE, §2.2(B).
Defined, §2.1.

LINDSAY V. THOMAS, §7.1(G).

LOUGHRAN V. FLANDERS, §7.1(F).

LOUISIANA PACIFIC V. STATE, §9.1(C).

LOUISIANA, STATE OF.
Louisiana teaching professional practices commission, §15.2(E).

LOWENTHOL V. VANDERBILT UNIVERSITY, §8.1(J).

LYON V. SALVE REGINA COLLEGE, §8.1(Q).

M

MAAS V. CORPORATION OF GONZAGA UNIVERSITY,
§8.1(N).

MANDAMUS.
Professional malpractice.
Theories for recovery, §3.1(D).

MCNEIL V. BOARD OF EDUCATION, §7.1(A).

MEDICAL MALPRACTICE, §2.2(A).
Defined, §2.1.

MISREPRESENTATION.
Professional malpractice.
Tort theories for recovery, §3.1(A)(3).

696

MONITORING OF EDUCATIONAL PROFESSION.
Dismissal of teachers, §15.1.
Generally, §15.0.
Teachers' professional practices commissions, §15.2.
    See TEACHERS' PROFESSIONAL PRACTICES COMMISSIONS.

MOORE V. VANDERLOO, §9.1(B).

MORRIS V. MCKAY, §7.1(N).

MORSE V. HENNIKER SCHOOL DISTRICT, §6.3.

MYERS V. MEDFORD LAKES BOARD OF EDUCATION,
    §5.1(E).

N

NEBRASKA, STATE OF.
Nebraska professional practices commission, §15.2(D).
Standards of competency, teaching profession, Appx. 1.

NEGLIGENCE.
Duty of care, §§13.0 to 13.6.
    See DUTY OF CARE.
Professional malpractice.
    Tort theories for recovery, §3.1(A)(1).
Proximate cause, §§14.0 to 14.3.
    See PROXIMATE CAUSE.

O

OREGON, STATE OF.
Standards for competent and ethical performance of Oregon
    educators, Appx. 4.

P

PALADINO V. ADELPHI UNIVERSITY, §7.2(A).

PAYNTER V. NEW YORK UNIVERSITY, §8.1(C).

PERETTI V. STATE OF MONTANA, §8.1(G).

PERIPHERAL EDUCATIONAL MALPRACTICE CASES.
Aubrey v. School District of Philadelphia, §9.1(G).

R

S

701